JUSTICE IN TRANSACTIONS

Justice in Transactions

A Theory of Contract Law

PETER BENSON

THE BELKNAP PRESS OF HARVARD UNIVERSITY PRESS
Cambridge, Massachusetts & London, England | 2019

Copyright © 2019 by the President and Fellows of Harvard College
All rights reserved
Printed in the United States of America

First printing

Library of Congress Cataloging-in-Publication Data
Names: Benson, Peter, 1953– author.
Title: Justice in transactions : a theory of contract law / Peter Benson.
Description: Cambridge, Massachusetts : The Belknap Press of Harvard University Press, 2019. | Includes bibliographical references and index.
Identifiers: LCCN 2019005908 | ISBN 9780674237599 (alk. paper)
Subjects: LCSH: Contracts.
Classification: LCC K840 .B464 2019 | DDC 346.002/201—dc23
LC record available at https://lccn.loc.gov/2019005908

For Marina

Contents

....

Preface	ix
Introduction	1

Part One: Principles

A. FORMATION	**35**
1. Consideration: Its Meaning, Role, and Consequences	40
2. Offer and Acceptance, the Objective Test, and Contractual Intent	101
3. Implication	122
B. FAIRNESS	**165**
4. The Paradigm of Contractual Fairness: The Principle of Unconscionability	167
5. Three Other Doctrines about Fair Terms	192
6. Fairness and Assent in Standard Form Contracts	215
C. ENFORCEMENT	**241**
7. Fundamental Ideas	243
8. Unity and Diversity in the Law of Contract Remedies	263
9. Expectation Damages and Contract Theory	298

Part Two: Theory

10.	Contract as a Transfer of Ownership	319
11.	A Moral Basis for Contract as Transfer	366
12.	The Stability of Contract as Transfer	395
	Notes	*479*
	Table of Cases	*587*
	Acknowledgments	*593*
	Index	*595*

Preface

....

Can the doctrines of contract law be accounted for in their own terms and on a basis that is morally acceptable from the standpoint of justice? In this book, I shall try to develop a theory of contract law that shows that this is possible. That this remains a real question, however, is noteworthy when we consider the present situation of modern contract law. Let me explain.

There is substantial scholarly agreement that the systems of contract law that now prevail not only in common law jurisdictions but also throughout most of the world share a similar doctrinal structure comprising the same kinds of basic and larger concepts, even though their particular legal formulations may sometimes differ from one jurisdiction to another. What is more, these legal systems all present contract law as a reasoned effort to work out and to give public recognition to general and intelligible principles in accordance with which parties can be held to enforceable rights and duties of performance just on the basis of their bilateral interaction consisting of mutual assents. This is the governing and publicly recognized contract law that we study, practice, and continue to develop. Now while it might seem that for certain so-called practical purposes it is enough simply to know and to use this law without seeing what holds it together or grounds its many doctrines and principles, it seems clear that unless one can make *some* sense of contract law in these terms, one cannot even begin to understand why it is the way it is or whether its apparently essential doctrines are really necessary or even consistent with each other. Indeed, since we can and must insist that contract law, like any form of coercive governance, be justified as reasonable and legitimate, we cannot avoid this further inquiry.

And if we may suppose further that the first task of a theory of contract law should be to provide a fully systematic and well-reasoned answer to these questions, this inquiry cannot stop short of developing such a theory. Now the striking thing is that far from resisting this approach, modern contract law, in virtue of its systematic and principled character, invites it. So what is the difficulty and why the need for a new theory?

Notwithstanding the many important scholarly efforts over the past decades, and in particular the impressive development of the economic analysis of contract law as well as influential attempts to ground contractual obligation on promissory morality, the difficulty with these predominant approaches is that they cannot explain even the most basic doctrines and premises of contract law in their own terms. The simple reason these theories cannot do so is that they take—or more exactly they *assume*—as central premises in their analysis what is irrelevant and indeed foreign to the actual legal point of view. For in specifying the kind of bilateral interaction requisite for contract formation, contract law does not take into account the interaction's individual, joint or systemic welfare effects; nor does it treat the parties' performance-related costs and benefits on a par, as an efficiency analysis requires. And in contrast with promissory accounts, the law sharply distinguishes between the features and prerequisites of the coercible contractual obligation to perform one's agreements and those of the moral duty to keep one's noncontractual promises, categorically excluding the latter. As a result, neither theoretical approach has the resources to provide a satisfactory account of contract principles as these are presented and elucidated from within the framework of contract law itself. Contemporary contract theorists, both economic and promissory, would do well to consider the words of Samuel Williston, the greatest contracts scholar, though himself not a theorist, of the last century: "A mild protest must be entered against a method of using . . . cases as if they would support equally any theory of the law which would involve the same result. Unless the ground on which the court rested the decisions can first be shown to be inadequate for their support, there is no necessity or, indeed, opportunity to seek for another basis. To do otherwise is to treat the rulings of the court 'as the utterings of Balaam's ass, absolutely true, but not presupposing any conscious intelligence in the creatures from whom they proceed.'"[1]

Williston's point is, I believe, deep and compelling. What I shall try to do in this book therefore is to develop a theoretical account for the common law of contract that, in contrast to the currently predominant approaches, is suited to answer the question of whether, in its own framework, contract law is both internally coherent and morally sound. This requires, first and foremost, that we begin with contract law itself. The challenge is to bring out the normative conception of contractual relation that seems to be reflected in its main doctrines and principles and, supposing that such a conception can be found, to explain the need for and the roles of the different doctrines in filling it out. For this purpose, a detailed examination of contract law is necessary and it takes up all of Part One. One of the widely recognized defects of current noneconomic theories is the restricted explanatory power of their favored moral principles. It is therefore important to confirm the more comprehensive reach of the theory proposed here. At the same time, I wish to emphasize that my purpose is not to provide a purely doctrinal summary of the law of contract. Rather, my central aim is to clarify the specific conception of contractual relation that animates it.

Through the detailed discussions in Part One of the main contract doctrines and principles—covering formation, fairness, and enforcement—I shall try to show that these reflect a conception of contract that is strictly juridical: neither economic nor the same as the moral duty to keep one's promises. Instead, they together articulate a conception of contract as a particular form of transactional acquisition between the parties: a transfer of ownership between the parties that is fully effectuated by and is complete at contract formation, prior to and independently of actual performance. In addition, I shall argue that both this conception and the doctrines of contract law are completely independent and distinct from considerations of distributive justice. Perhaps my most important contention here is that this organizing conception of contract as transfer is not introduced to or imposed upon contract law from the outside, on the basis of some favored moral, policy, or philosophical view. To the contrary, I hope to show in detail how it emerges wholly from an internal analysis of the main contract doctrines and principles themselves. The proposed conception of contract as transfer is needed to explain these doctrines in their own terms.

In Part Two, I take this analysis of contract doctrines to a more abstract level and seek to justify on theoretical grounds, continuous with the conception of contract worked out in the first part, why contract law viewed as a transfer of ownership between the parties is juridically coherent and morally acceptable, both in its own right and as part of a wider system of justice. I shall argue that this view of contract is fully consistent with pervasive ideas in private law (most importantly that of ownership) and that it is intrinsically reasonable, expressing a morally acceptable view of parties and their relation from the standpoint of liberal justice. Finally, I discuss the ways in which contract so conceived does not undermine, but is in fact harmonious with, other domains of moral and social life, in particular promissory morality, the functioning of markets, and the requirements of distributive justice. Of the alternative theoretical views, the proposed conception provides, I believe, the most appropriate moral basis for contract law consonant with its main doctrines, principles, and role in a liberal democratic society.

As I will later explain in more detail, my goal in developing this account of the nature and moral basis of contract is to work out for contract law what John Rawls in his later work referred to as a public basis of justification. Rawls's express aim was to develop such a justification for the background institutions of political and social justice, not for transactions that take place within this basic structure of society. At the same time, he emphasized that public justification, though essential for the moral (liberal) legitimacy of any exercise of coercive power in legal and political relations, is to be worked out afresh and specifically for the different kinds of subjects and relations that raise a question of justice. In attempting to do this for contract law, I hope to offer an account of justice in transactions that not only meets the essential needs of a theory of contract law but that also can suitably complement Rawls's own political conception of justice within a broader framework of liberal justice that includes both. In this way, I hope to show that what contract law publicly recognizes as legally valid and binding is, at its core, a work of reason worthy of acceptance and respect.

JUSTICE IN TRANSACTIONS

Courts' business is not the making of detailed contracts for parties; but courts' business is eminently the marking out of the limits of the permissible, and the reading of fair understanding. . . .

—KARL LLEWELLYN, *The Common Law Tradition: Deciding Appeals*

Introduction

....

In contemporary contract scholarship, two main theoretical approaches are predominant. The first, normative economic analysis of law, supposes that the purpose of contract law is to promote efficient transacting in the service of maximum joint or general welfare and evaluates the law from this standpoint. The second, promissory theory, takes contractual obligation to be a particular instance of the general moral duty to keep one's promises and assesses contract doctrines and principles on this basis.[1] Both approaches have been worked out systematically and in detail, and each purports to provide a comprehensive, yet competing, account of contract. Each starts from general principles and values that seem compelling and widely applicable even before we come to contract law. Moreover, seeing that contracts often consist of exchanges and standardly involve promises, it does not offhand seem unreasonable to explain contract law on one or the other of these two bases. If this is so, why attempt to develop an alternative theory of contract law that not only fundamentally differs from both approaches but that is also completely independent of them? For my aim in this book is to do precisely that. Let me briefly explain why I think that this is necessary.

I.1. What Should a Theory of Contract Law Do?

I believe that a first task of contract theory is, or at least should be, to see whether modern contract law—as specified by its main doctrines, principles, and values—can be accounted for in its own terms on a basis that is morally acceptable from the standpoint of a liberal conception of justice. For contractual obligation is always coercively enforceable obligation, and this, if it is to be legitimate, ought to be justified as a matter of justice and shown to be consistent with the freedom and equality of the parties. But what must be emphasized is that the subject requiring justification is the actual law of contract that regulates their interactions. Contract law is complex, comprising a variety of different and sometimes divergent doctrines and rules. At the same time, we also standardly assume—as does the law—that these doctrines belong to one subject and that they specify different aspects of a unified understanding that can apply in principle to contractual relations in general. Through a detailed analysis of the full range of contract principles, a theory of contract should therefore see whether it can bring out a specific moral conception that underpins and indeed animates both the whole and the parts of contract law: it should attempt to present a normative conception of the basic contractual relation. The crucial point is that ideally this conception of contract should be drawn from a concrete analysis of contract law itself and, in turn, the law's main doctrines should be explicable in light of this conception. This is what contract theory should aim to do.

There is a further point that underscores the need for and the challenge facing this theoretical undertaking. On its face, contract law itself presents a number of apparent internal conflicts or at least tensions within it. Prominent among them is that between the meaning and scope of liberty of contract and the role of norms of contractual fairness. If we provisionally suppose that the value of liberty of contract is embodied in the principles of contract formation, whereas doctrines such as unconscionability impose constraints of fairness, the question naturally arises of whether these doctrines can fit together in one unified conception of contract. The answer is by no means clear. In connection with common law systems of contract, it is standardly said that there need be only sufficient and not adequate consideration to satisfy contract formation and that, on this basis, parties' rights and duties are to be completely and definitively established. Yet the principle of unconscionability and other norms of fairness clearly scrutinize adequacy of consideration or the fairness of terms and can invalidate agreements on this ground. To account for this tension, it might seem natural to explain these norms of fairness as an external "policy" imposition on the operation of the internal contractual analysis. However, both sets of principles are integral aspects of contract law, the legitimacy of which would seem to rest therefore on its properly integrating and ordering the claims of both. We need to see, then, whether implicit in these and other contract doctrines, there is an underlying normative conception that can explain such apparently conflicting principles and values as in fact mutually supportive and structured aspects of a unified whole. Moreover, if this conception of contract is to be morally acceptable in a modern democratic legal culture, it would also be important to show that the conception expresses a suitable notion of liberal justice.

My aim in this book is to try to show that contract law is indeed amenable to this kind of justification. Contract law, I will argue, can be reasonably understood as specifying a distinct normative conception that not only is drawn from its principles and doctrines but also constitutes their organizing idea, underpinning and explaining the whole of contract law as well as its various parts. As I will shortly discuss in more detail, an account of this kind would provide what John Rawls called a public basis of justification—only in this case the justification would be one that is specifically worked out for contract law, in contrast with Rawls's own public political justification that he developed for the background institutional framework within which individuals transact with one another. Now, in my view, the principal reason why an alternative to the predominant economic and promissory theories of contract is needed is precisely because these theories do not—and arguably cannot—provide such a justification for contract law. This is because they seek to account for contract law on the basis of norms, values, and criteria that are not only disconnected from but also at odds with the fundamental normative ideas implicit in its doctrines and principles. Although my primary aim is to develop the requisite justification rather than to criticize the views of others, I think it is worth clarifying how the prevailing economic and promissory theories may be wanting in this respect. I shall do this as part of the detailed discussions of contract doctrines in subsequent chapters. For the purposes of this introduction and by way of illustration, I briefly note the following basic divergence between these theories and the law.

According to both economic and promissory theories, parties are obligated because this is what they want in light of their chosen purposes, whether the aim is their well-being via the mutual satisfaction of expressed preferences or the conveying of moral assurances via deliberate promising. Contracts are enforced because this furthers parties' subjective preferences (hence their well-being) or their intentional choices. Both approaches are ultimately modeled on the idea that contractual obligation is subjectively self-imposed and intended in a robust sense. This fundamentally diverges from the legal point of view. Even though the interaction requisite for contract formation must be voluntary and must involve the parties' mutual assents, this does not mean that the parties need have deliberately acted for the purpose of undertaking contractual legal obligations or of producing such legal effects. To the contrary, the fact that parties want or seek to subject themselves to some sort of contractual obligation is, we will see, neither necessary nor sufficient to establish it. It is truer to say that, in legal contemplation, parties have contractual rights and duties not because they want or intend them but because they have interacted in a certain definite way on the basis of which the law imputes these rights and duties as their interaction's appropriate juridical meaning and effect. In doing so, the law adopts an objective test that only takes into account how a party's words or acts reasonably appear to the other party in the context of their interaction. Thus, in and of itself, what a party consciously thinks he or she is doing or intends to do is ordinarily per se irrelevant. If we still wish to characterize contract law as "power-conferring" or contractual obligation as "self-imposed," its sense must be carefully specified so as to be consistent with this legal point of view.

Now any serious divergence between contract theory and contract law is particularly troubling with respect to modern contract law. Across the different systems of modern law, the point has now been reached when the entire analysis of contract—from formation to remedies—is embodied in generally settled basic principles and doctrines that can govern any and every contractually enforceable agreement. Moreover, framed as principle and doctrine, the legal analysis of contract law presents itself as based on and as accessible to reason, explicitly drawing its justification from requirements of justice. It is difficult to believe that systems of contract law that have arrived at general and intelligible principles on the basis of sustained collective analysis and reasoning over centuries and across jurisdictions do not contain within themselves, even if latently, normative ideas and reasons that can be suitably explored and perhaps explained in their own terms. If theory is out of sync with the law and has not brought out and made sense of the reason in the law, then perhaps the fault lies with theory, not the law. We must see if we can do better.

What kind of theoretical conception might be suitable to illuminate the internal rationality of contract law in its own terms? Here we may obtain guidance from an unexpected source. Lon L. Fuller and William F. Perdue Jr.'s "The Reliance Interest in Contract Damages" is widely considered in the common law world as the single most influential piece of writing in modern contract scholarship, one that arguably also inaugurated contemporary contract theory which has continued unabated ever since.[2] At least in part, this is because in their article Fuller and Perdue challenge the legal analysis of contract at its very core, disputing the law's understanding of the basis of contractual obligation and of its central remedy for breach. This core legal understanding, they conclude, cannot be validated in its own terms. But precisely for this reason, a critical examination of their objection may also point to the kind of conception of contract that could, if defensible, vindicate the legal point of view after all. I now hope to show that this is indeed the case.

I.2. Toward the Idea of Contract as a Transfer of Ownership

For modern contract law, it has long been settled and indeed axiomatic that, in remedying breach of contract, the aim of the law is and should be to give the innocent party, whether in specie or by damages, what the breaching party owes her by way of the promised performance. The law views this as a ruling principle and as a just principle, the purpose of which is to give compensation for injury. Now against this, and indeed on the very first page of their article, Fuller and Perdue object that in awarding such expectation or performance damages, the law gives the plaintiff "something he never had," with the consequence that "[t]his seems on the face of things a queer kind of 'compensation.'"[3] If correct, this challenges the cogency of contract doctrine at its core. Notice that their objection to the compensatory character of expectation remedies rests on whether the plaintiff has something at formation that she loses as a result of breach. Why so? It is important to consider this more closely.

To begin, in arguing that expectation remedies do not qualify as compensatory, Fuller and Perdue clearly assess them in light of the general notion of compensatory justice that is standardly supposed in private law. This idea of compensation entails, first, that some asset belongs to the plaintiff by exclusive right as against the defendant and, second, that the defendant does or omits to do something that injures the plaintiff's entitlement in it, thereby causing her loss. Compensation corrects the injury by compelling the defendant to provide the plaintiff with the equivalent of the loss, thereby restoring the plaintiff, so far as is feasible and reasonable in the post-wrong circumstances, to the position that she would have been in had the defendant respected her entitlement in the required way. By doing this, compensation corrects the defendant's injustice against the plaintiff.

In keeping with this general idea of compensation, it seems, then, that for expectation damages to be straightforwardly and directly compensatory, the value of performance awarded by such damages must measure the loss of an asset that the plaintiff has rightfully as against the defendant already at formation, and thus prior to breach, with breach representing the defendant's wrongful interference with that presently existing legal interest. Further, this asset must be one that the plaintiff acquired in this way through their agreement and therefore on the basis of their mutual assents alone. In other words, for expectation damages to qualify as compensatory, we must suppose that contract formation, constituted just by the parties' mutual promises, gives the plaintiff, as against the defendant, a present protected interest with respect to the promised performance.

But this is exactly what Fuller and Perdue deny. They suppose that, at most, promises can create in the promisee an expectation or hope of receiving something in the future if and when the promisor performs. Until then, the promisee "has" nothing that presently "belongs" to her to the exclusion of the promisor.[4] And while the promisee's expectations—we may also say her trust—may be disappointed if the promisor does not perform, breach is not viewed as working an injury to or a subtraction from something that is her own. To the contrary, by breaching, the promisor merely refuses to benefit her or to engage positively in a cooperative arrangement with her. In this connection, Fuller and Perdue cite with apparent approval Pierre de Tourtoulon's statement that "the principle that promise or consent creates obligation is foreign to the idea of justice."[5] Consequently, by awarding damages that equal the value of the promised performance, the law does not act restoratively "to heal a disturbed status quo" but instead brings into being a new situation, thereby passing, the authors note, "from the realm of corrective justice to that of distributive justice."[6]

Fuller and Perdue correctly point out that if, as they argue, the core principle of contractual enforcement cannot be justified in the case of the purely executory contract, this raises "the more general question, why should a promise which has not been relied on ever be enforced at all, whether by a decree of specific performance or by an award of damages?"[7] Indeed, their challenge, if valid, has very far-reaching implications for the analysis and theory of contract law. In addition to bringing into question the very coherence of the law's premise concerning the compensatory character of expectation remedies, two further related consequences seem to follow.

First, if Fuller and Perdue are right, contract liability does not fit within the parameters of the basic framework of private law responsibility, which may be summed up in the common law formulation that there is liability only for misfeasance and not for nonfeasance.[8] Briefly stated, misfeasance is any act or omission by one that impairs, damages, or otherwise affects something that comes under another's exclusive rights vis-à-vis the first, whether the other's right is with respect to her body or assets, corporeal and incorporeal. By contrast, nonfeasance is any act or omission that, even if it negatively affects another's interests or well-being, does not do so as a result of affecting or injuring something that rightfully belongs to her to the exclusion of the first party. It is not enough that the loss results from interference with his mere liberty (as opposed to exclusive right) to have or use the damaged thing.[9] Where loss sounds in nonfeasance, it is not ordinarily actionable or recoverable in private law but constitutes mere *damnum sine injuria*. Putting Fuller and Perdue's point in terms of this distinction between misfeasance and nonfeasance, their objection implies therefore that the most basic form of contract remedy anomalously makes the defendant liable for nonfeasance. Breach can only represent a failure to confer a future benefit, not the doing of a present injury. As Tourtoulon says, breach cannot qualify as an injustice.

There is a second and equally fundamental consequence—already alluded to above—that would follow from the Fuller and Perdue objection, if correct. Because, on their view, contract law's own understanding of its basic doctrines—in particular the compensatory character of expectation remedies—is incoherent at its core, the legal point of view cannot serve, even provisionally, as the starting point for deeper theoretical reflection that aims to explain and justify it. This, it should be emphasized, is a *necessary* consequence of their critique. In other words, the law cannot be understood and justified in its own terms and within its own framework. Instead, as the authors' own efforts to explain the rationale for expectation remedies illustrate, theory must begin with external policies, values, and purposes that are derived apart from, but then applied directly to, the law.

How might one answer Fuller and Perdue's argument? In my view, there is only one way that, if sound, could be decisive. If expectation damages and specific performance are to qualify as compensatory in the way assumed by contract law, it must be possible to understand contract formation as itself effectuating between the parties a kind of *transactional acquisition* that vests in them exclusive entitlements with respect to what they have promised one another. And since the acquisition of each party is from the other, it is constituted by a transfer between them. This acquisition must be juridically complete and effective just on the basis of their mutual assents alone, prior to and independent from actual performance and irrespective of whether either party detrimentally relies on the other's promise. If contract formation can be so conceived, breach of contract can now plausibly be viewed as an injury to the rights already vested at formation. Breach becomes the equivalent of attempting to "take back" or "withhold" what, as a matter of rights, one has *already* given over to the other. It interferes with the other's ability to take or receive in fact what, in accordance with the terms of the agreement, is rightfully already hers. By aiming to put the promisee in the position that she should have been in had the promisor not breached, the law can now be understood as correcting a loss that the promisee has suffered with respect to rights. Adopting the words of Fuller and Perdue, the law acts defensively, healing a disturbed status quo.

Both in everyday experience and in law, we are familiar with the possibility of transferring ownership in something from one person to another. It can be as a gift or as part of an exchange. A first person, owner of a book, hands it over to a second with the words "this is now yours." Assume that the second takes it. From a very early age, we understand that this interaction simultaneously divests the first of ownership and vests it with the second. With this transfer complete, the first must not act inconsistently with it: he cannot effectively cancel his decision or take back the book—at least not without the second's approval.

Now clearly, when applied to the parties' mutual promises or assents at the moment of agreement, this view immediately raises a number of basic questions. For example, how can such transactional acquisition or transfer be complete and effective before a party physically possesses or enjoys—or even has an immediate right to such physical possession or enjoyment of—what she has supposedly acquired? How can such acquisition be effectuated by the parties' assents alone? What exactly is the object transferred, if it is not the physical thing or service itself? And supposing that this involves a transfer of ownership in some sense, how can this be only as between the parties when ownership is standardly thought of as being "against the world"? Certainly, these and other questions must be fully addressed. I will try to do so in the chapters that follow. But for now, my contention is simply that the Fuller and Perdue challenge can be answered and its theoretical consequences avoided if—and only if—something like this view of contract formation as transfer is plausible. Moreover, if this view is correct, there is now at least the possibility that contract law can be explained in its own terms. For this reason, I shall take this conception of contract formation as a provisional working hypothesis and ask whether it is indeed latent in the main contract doctrines and principles, when these are taken severally and as a whole. The first and most important step in my argument will be to show, via a detailed discussion of these doctrines and principles, that this is indeed the case.

One thing seems clear: if we are to develop a theoretical response to the Fuller-Perdue challenge, it must be distinct from the prevailing economic and promissory approaches. This is because neither approach has the resources to do so. For economic theories, Fuller and Perdue's puzzlement over the compensatory character of expectation remedies is not even a question to which they seek an answer. The idea of compensation as standardly understood in private law is simply irrelevant in an economic analysis.[10] Economic theories merely take Fuller and Perdue's conclusion concerning the necessity of policy explanation as their assumed starting point and framework, seeking to refine and develop this approach and raising it to new levels of complexity and sophistication.

The difficulty faced by theories based on the moral duty to keep one's promises is different. These theories presuppose that the same normative analysis of party interaction that applies to the moral duty of promise-keeping also holds for contract. Yet the two seem prima facie different. The first is plausibly accounted for by one party, the promisor, soliciting and obtaining the promisee's trust in the former's capacity and will to live up conscientiously to his word. But this is perfectly consistent with the promisee *not* having as against the promisor any rightful control with respect to the promised performance. Indeed, this relation of respect on the one side and trust on the other is most clear where the relation is one of utter dependency by the promisee on the promisor's inner moral probity and conscientiousness in following through. The idea of exclusive rightful control—let alone any notion of exclusive ownership—vested in the promisee by the promise itself need not play any role in this moral transaction. Thus this analysis cannot possibly explain the compensatory nature of expectation remedies or even the moral necessity of any coercive response to the promisor's failure to live up to his moral duty.[11] Not only can it not answer the Fuller and Perdue challenge—which assumes precisely this very kind of promissory analysis—but even more importantly, it cannot hope to explain these axiomatic principles of contract law as they are authoritatively presented and understood by the law.

This last difficulty is confirmed by the following basic feature of the law. The moral duty to keep one's promise applies to all seriously intended promises without distinction. But one of the first and most important things that we learn in the study of the common law of contract is that not all promises are contractually enforceable in the sense of being protected by expectation remedies—irrespective of whether they are binding as a matter of everyday morality. Since at least the late sixteenth century, even the most seriously intended promise will count only as a so-called gratuitous promise that is contractually irrelevant and unenforceable unless made for consideration. A promise-for-consideration, we will see, involves a kind of promissory relation that is qualitatively and irreducibly different from that of a gratuitous promise, even though the latter may be fully binding as a matter of morals.

It is worth noting here that this distinction between kinds of promissory relations is not parochial to the common law of contract. In responding to the same kind of theoretical challenge as that posed by Fuller and Perdue—only several centuries earlier—the great natural law writers in the continental civilian tradition, including Hugo Grotius and Samuel Pufendorf, explicitly and categorically distinguished between promises that are fully binding morally but that do not vest in the promisee a coercively enforceable right to performance and those that can be viewed as intrinsically intended to confer such a right and do so.[12] The first kind of promise, which these writers called "imperfect," gives rise to a noncoercible duty to perform that, like the obligation to rescue, reflects a moral requirement to benefit others. The second kind, called a "perfect" promise, transfers to the promisee a right to performance, analogously, they said, to the alienation of property or services. According to these writers, it is only this second kind of promise that can ground contractual obligation and that, by the law of nature, is enforceable as a matter of justice between the parties.

One way of viewing my proposed conception of contract as transfer is that it represents the kind of promissory relation that the natural law writers called perfect. At the same time, I want to emphasize again that it will be through a detailed examination of the main doctrines and principles of the common law of contract that I shall draw out and develop this conception of transfer. For this purpose, I will try not to rely on frameworks or schemes of thought—philosophical or otherwise—that have not been shown to be part of these doctrines. The conception of contract as transfer is intended to be what is implicit in and suggested by contract doctrines and principles when we try to make sense of them in their own terms. Moreover, by working through the full justification of this conception, I hope to bring out its significance as an understanding of contractual relations that is morally acceptable in modern democratic societies. In this regard, I shall argue that the proposed conception of contractual transfer is governed by a definite idea of justice—justice in transactions—that is distinct and independent from norms of distributive justice. Though nondistributive in character, justice in transactions is a genuinely liberal conception of justice that not only expresses in itself an appropriate view of parties as free and equal persons but also can fit within a larger framework that includes robust principles of distributive justice as well as other values that are thought essential in a liberal society. For these reasons, I believe that this conception of contract provides the most appropriate moral basis for contract law in a modern liberal democracy.

Earlier I stated that my aim in developing this theory is to provide a public basis of justification for contract law that anchors the account of contractual obligation in a conception of reasonableness specifically framed for transactional relations. The ideas of public justification and the reasonable will be familiar to readers who know Rawls's work. However, the meaning and role of these ideas in my account are specific to contract law and so differ in certain respects from how they figure in Rawls's own theory of political justice. Since these ideas of public justification and the reasonable are central to my theory of contract and distinguish it from the predominant economic and promissory approaches, I should now try to clarify in a preliminary way their specific meanings and roles in the proposed theory. After doing this, I will conclude with an overview of the argument as a whole.

I.3. The Ideas of Public Justification and the Reasonable for Transactions

Contemporary scholarship often assumes that theories of contract law must be either "normative" or "positive." If the former, the aim is to propose and implement as law some ideally justified set of rules or principles that need not build on or coincide with the actual content and point of view already embodied in contract doctrines; if the latter, the theory seeks to understand these doctrines and principles as seems best to make sense of them in light of contract law's apparent aims and premises but without necessarily showing that the content and aims are normatively or morally acceptable. In contrast to both approaches, we might wish to see whether the main contract doctrines and principles embody, even if only latently, certain normative ideas and values that can be worked up into a coherent conception that can be morally justified at least to those who participate in and are affected by contractual relations. This third possibility is the path taken by a public basis of justification.

In general, a public basis of justification is appropriate and needed when it is morally essential that individuals (and societies) find a shared normative basis and point of view from which to explain and to justify among themselves the terms governing their interactions with each other. While a shared basis of justification may not be needed to validate one's individual moral, religious, or philosophical outlooks, it is necessary to legitimate the exercise of coercive power by citizens over each other when all count as free and equal. This would be particularly so—as is the case with contract law—where interpersonal obligations are determined and coercively enforced even though the parties need not have deliberately intended to be so bound. Rawls worked out a public justification for principles of background political justice applicable to the main political, economic, and social institutions, not those for private transactions between individuals.[13] However, as Rawls himself emphasizes in connection with his own theory, we must not simply assume that the public justification developed for one subject, such as political relations, is also immediately or directly applicable to some other, such as contract law, given that these relations may differ intrinsically in terms of their respective natures and roles. Moral conceptions should reflect the particular kind of relation that they are intended to regulate.[14] Thus the elements of Rawls's account of political justice—including the original position analysis with its specific conceptions of primary goods, of freedom and equality, and so forth—should not be mechanically applied to contract law as part of a public justification for it.

To the contrary, a public justification for contract has to be specifically worked out anew for contract law, taking into account not only its distinctive norms and values as reflected in its main doctrines and principles but also its specific role as but one part of a complete system of justice. The challenges, considerations, and solutions involved in developing the justification for contract law will be particular to it. We have to see whether contract law's principles and doctrines as publicly and authoritatively presented implicitly embody a normative conception of contractual relation that is acceptable as such to everyone who participates in or can be affected by the system of contract law. These relations are ordinarily promissory and always involve coercible correlative rights and duties of performance as between the parties, enforceable by courts on the basis of the parties' interaction *ex post*. How can this exercise of coercive power with respect to equals vis-à-vis one another be shown to be legitimate and morally acceptable? This is the ultimate question for which a public basis of justification for contract law seeks an answer.

In keeping with this idea of public justification, the terms and reasoning of the justification must be open to view as well as common, available, and reasonably acceptable to parties generally.[15] The justification is thus public only inasmuch as it is something that *all* parties can reasonably and identically be expected to share. Accordingly, the basic terms of the justification cannot rest on empirical or conceptual arguments that are beyond educated common sense or are too complex and controversial. Moreover, the interpretation, assessment, and application of the relevant considerations must be within the competence of the particular institutions tasked with doing this. In the case of the common law of contract, the central institution is the court performing its adjudicative function. Much economic analysis, for example, fails to meet this criterion and therefore, for that reason alone, is not well suited to provide such justification.[16]

Nor can such public justification invoke moral, aesthetic, religious, or philosophical ideas about which transactors, as members of a liberal society, cannot reasonably be expected to agree. Modern systems of contract law in liberal societies take as given that parties can come to transactions with their own divergent and even conflicting beliefs, ends, and sets of values. They need not have or share any such ends in particular. Thus legal determinations of whether parties have entered a contract or of their enforceable rights or duties under it do not depend on their moral, religious, or philosophical outlooks and the like. To the contrary, prior to contract formation, parties are viewed for purposes of contract law as wholly independent and free vis-à-vis each other, at liberty to act as they wish. There are no prior general ends, whether economic or otherwise, that they must fulfill for their agreements to be contractually enforceable. All systems of modern contract law present and justify their governing principles, standards, and rules as aiming, primarily, to do justice between the parties and, additionally, to ensure various relevant systemic requisites (of market relations, public policy, and the like), without needing to invoke more general comprehensive (philosophical, religious, or moral) doctrines to explain or ground them. In this way, contract law is presented as a freestanding and intrinsically reasonable framework for governing transactions. A public justification of contract must take seriously this utterly basic feature of modern contract law and appropriately reflect it.

To start, it does this by drawing its ideas from legal doctrines publicly available to all, in the hope that implicit in this public legal culture are normative ideas and ideals, more or less intuitively understandable to general educated common sense, that can be worked up into a coherent and morally acceptable account of contract law. At the same time, a public basis of justification does not look for any allegedly self-evident principles as the whole foundation upon which to build this account.[17] Instead, it sees if and how the different contract doctrines and principles—as well as the ideas and values that they implicitly embody—are mutually supportive and fit together in one unified and intelligible whole. In sharp contrast, because the predominant contemporary theories assume their own already elaborated and independent values and criteria, whether economic or moral, which they then simply apply directly to contract law, they cannot provide a public justification for contract.

The theory of contract law that I shall try to develop differs from these approaches not only insofar as it aims to draw and develop its organizing ideas from normative notions implicit in the doctrines of contract law but also because it contends that those notions are best understood as expressing a specific conception of the *reasonable*—one that is framed for justice in transactions. This is an important point that requires discussion.

To begin, what does the reasonable mean? The reasonable is to be contrasted with the rational.[18] The rational applies to persons (natural and corporate) who, when taken each by himself or herself and from his or her own standpoint, are viewed as deliberating about and as seeking effectively to realize ends and interests of their own. The ends coming under the idea of the rational need not be selfish in any standard sense. But whatever the content of his or her chosen interests and ends, a person, qua rational, pursues them without necessarily according any independent validity to others' ends, which therefore do not give rise to moral claims that can subject the agent to moral constraints or obligations of any kind. By contrast, the reasonable specifies fair terms that appropriately apply to relations between persons who are each viewed as having equal and independent standing to press valid claims vis-à-vis each other. Reasonable persons propose and accept as principles only those that they think all can reasonably endorse in their capacity as mutually equal. They are also willing to limit the pursuit of their interests as required by fair principles, as long as they are assured that others will do the same. In these ways, the reasonable constrains the rational and can be specified in the form of binding obligations. It clearly embodies an idea of reciprocity.

Now just as I emphasized that a public basis of justification should not be taken as a general standpoint that is the same for all kinds of relations but rather as one that is specifically worked out to reflect the distinctive nature and role of a given kind of institution or relation, so here also we should not assume that there is one general conception of the reasonable that equally regulates all domains, whatever their differences. The reasonable in transactions may not be the same as the reasonable in political or other kinds of relations. In fact, I will argue that the contractual relation, as specified by the doctrines and principles of contract law, embodies its own distinct conceptions of the reasonable and the rational as well as of the relation between them, with the reasonable constituting contract law's central defining characteristic. In this respect also, the theory that I develop differs fundamentally from leading approaches. To see what is needed, consider the following alternatives, each of which, I suggest, is in different ways unequal to the task of elucidating the nature of the contractual relationship because it fails to articulate a conception of the reasonable that is appropriate and specific to it.

A first view purports to dispense altogether with the idea of the reasonable as an independent and distinct element in the analysis, instead basing the account on the rational alone. For instance, one might think that the measure and the purpose of contract enforcement are set by the well-being of the parties as manifested by their choice of terms if certain contracting conditions—presented as independent from notions of fairness and the reasonable—are satisfied. In particular, suppose that both parties are fully aware of all their contract's provisions as well as appreciate their implications and that these provisions reflect the parties' correct assessments of the expected value and costs of performance, taking into account all relevant factors and contingencies. A preference-oriented contract law that aims to further each party's well-being requires that their contract be enforced as is.[19] Enforcement of this complete contract is thus the mutually ideal benchmark against which to assess all principles or approaches. To the extent that a principle or theory can diverge from this benchmark, it necessarily undermines the individual well-being of both parties and so cannot be morally acceptable. For how can a principle that requires the diminution of the well-being of one or both parties—and that also diverges from their choices—be morally justified?[20] A principle of fairness must either be superfluous (insofar as it upholds the welfare-based analysis) or be rejected (to the extent that it diverges from that analysis). This conclusion seems disarmingly straightforward and even inescapable.

Even on its own terms, however, this analysis only works if we suppose that a party has a coherent and determinate set of preferences that he or she wants to fulfill. Thus, if a party changes his mind and now has a different set of preferences, the analysis must decide which of the two competing sets to enforce. But this is precisely the dilemma that potentially arises in all contractual situations. In every case of contract enforcement, a promisor may be coercively held to a certain set of terms and therefore to a certain expression of preferences even though he has changed his mind and wants something else. Assessed from the standpoint of the rational specified in terms of actual preferences, there would seem to be no ground for doing this.[21] It is simply a matter of one preference as against another, and, if anything, it is a party's later preference, which is after all current and existent as well as potentially the more fully informed, that should be treated as his actual preference. This is true even if the second preference is formed *ex post* at the time of performance and the first preference reflects *ex ante* an accurate assessment of the expected costs and value of that performance. (We assume that in adopting the second preference, the party can and does take into account the expected impact, including from others' reactions, that his change of mind may have on the realization of his own interests and well-being. Otherwise it cannot be rational.) It is important to recall here that within the parameters of the rational, the claims of the other party have no independent standing and so cannot constrain the first party's conduct or choices. Of course, if the parties go through with their agreement, we may infer that their preferences have been fulfilled. But that does not in any way show that they can also be obligated or constrained to go through with their agreement despite a change of mind.

Accordingly, a theory of contractual obligation cannot rest on the idea of the rational alone. It must incorporate some notion of the reasonable that can appropriately account for the parties being coercively held as a matter of obligation to their initial expressions of preference or indeed to any set of preferences despite a change of mind. If correct, the point that I have just made means that the fact that a given theory justifies an analysis that deviates from what is suggested by welfare economics (when based solely on the rational as defined above) cannot, for that reason alone, be assumed to undermine the kind of well-being that is relevant and operative in the framework of contract law. The benchmark of the ideal complete contract in the service of welfare enhancement need not be the relevant measure. It will all depend on the nature and implications of the particular conception of the reasonable as applied to the parties' contractual relation. Indeed, once a conception of the reasonable must be introduced, it becomes clear that when terms are enforced despite a change of mind, it cannot be because the first expression counts as a preference that, as such, should be given priority but must be on some other basis. The assent is enforced as part of a different normative analysis. To see what that might be and which factors might be relevant, we first need to specify a conception of the reasonable that can justify the very possibility of coercible contractual obligation.

But the question of which conception of the reasonable should be used is not straightforward. Since we may assume that contractual obligations arise from parties' voluntary decisions or assents and so are legal effects that are imputed consistently with and perhaps even as expressive of their autonomy, it might seem natural to assume that the appropriate conception of the reasonable presupposes that parties have acted with the intention of deliberately incurring such obligations. Under the aspect of the reasonable, contractual obligations should thus be conceived as self-imposed in this robust sense. At the same time, if this conception of the reasonable is framed for the direct relation between promisor and promisee, at first glance it would seem suitable to explain contract law.[22] According to a leading version of this view, the direct relation is constituted by the twin elements of trust and respect between the parties independently of both the conferral of material benefit and the incurring of detriment: by promising, the promisor intentionally solicits and normally obtains the promisee's trust in the promisor's moral capacity to follow through and perform, and having deliberately invited the promisee to make herself vulnerable in this way, the promisor cannot renege without abusing the promisee's trust and treating her with lack of respect.[23]

Now, clearly this analysis expresses an idea of the reasonable that can arguably underpin a moral duty to keep one's word. The question is whether it also suffices to explain a legally enforceable contractual obligation, particularly when the latter is understood in terms of a relation of strictly correlative coercible rights and duties, the breach of which is an injury to what in some sense belongs to the promisee already at formation. We cannot simply assume that a conception of the reasonable specified for the morality of promissory duty also holds for the quite different sort of direct relation contemplated by contractual obligation. As suggested earlier, these seem to involve two quite distinct and different normative frameworks. Whereas the reasonable governing promissory morality is expressed in terms of respect arising from the deliberate inducement of trust and dependency in the promisee, the reasonable in contract involves respect for the promisee's coercible right to performance that is under her control as against the promisor. Moreover, utterly basic and settled features of contractual obligation—the centrality of the objective test, contractual liability being strict, the objective and limited character of excusing doctrines governing mistake and changed circumstances, and so on—do not make sense within and would denature the moral framework of promissory duty. Similarly, in contrast to promissory duty, contractual obligations may be imposed by courts *ex post* just on the basis of parties' interactions even though they have not deliberately intended such legal effects. At the most fundamental level, intention-based explanations of contract face the following challenge: without supposing any legal formalities, what gives another, as promisee, standing to enforce my promise against me just on the basis of my having intended or wanted this when I no longer intend or want it? If the source is wholly in me, how can another externally and coercively constrain me not to intend or decide otherwise? Unless it can show this, any intention-based approach must fail as an account of contractual obligation.

The upshot of the preceding discussion is that we need to specify a conception of reasonableness and respect that is suitable for the distinctive nature and essential features of contractual relations as presented in the principles, standards, and values of contract law. What that conception is can therefore only emerge from a detailed and in-depth examination of the law. At this point, following the discussion of Fuller and Perdue, I would suggest as a kind of provisional working hypothesis that the reasonable in contract is expressed in terms of some kind of transactional acquisition—a transfer of ownership—as between the contracting parties that is effectuated in and through their mutual assents alone, complete at the moment of agreement. But we will have to see whether this is the case. For the purposes of this introduction, I shall now provide an overview of the argument as a whole.

I.4. Overview of the Argument

My aim in this book, I have said, is to develop a theory of contract law that is independent and complete in its own framework and that provides a moral basis for contract that is superior to the prevailing economic and promissory approaches when judged from the standpoint of a public basis of justification in a liberal democratic society. I shall present the public justification for contract in two main parts.

In Part One, which is called "Principles" and is the longer of the two, I examine the different doctrines and principles of contract law to determine whether, singly and together, they embody a definite and unifying conception of contract and, if so, what that conception is. At the start and prior to examining the actual doctrines and principles of contract law, we cannot say whether there is such a unifying conception of contractual relation or what it is. In the case of a public justification for contract law, the nature of the contractual relation cannot simply be assumed or postulated ab initio, even on the basis of carefully reasoned and systematic philosophical accounts. Rather, it must initially be a question to which the answer should emerge from a concrete and detailed analysis of the specific doctrines. This is not, however, a straightforward or superficial undertaking. On its surface, contract law presents different and sometimes conflicting judicial formulations and interpretations even of the same principle or doctrine. As well, one finds varied judicial efforts to state the larger underlying conceptions, including that of the contractual relation itself. For the purposes of developing a public justification, none of these formulations is taken as decisive or final. The challenge is to try to construct a unifying and reasonable conception of contract by drawing on, and suggesting plausible interpretations of, what seem to be the core and stable meanings of doctrines. We look to the most careful doctrinal formulations in conjunction with their central applications as providing provisional starting points for working up a public justification for contract law. On this basis, I argue for interpretations of these doctrines and principles that, I hope, can make sense of them in their own terms, show them to embody reasonable normative ideas, and explain how they work together as mutually supporting and interconnected aspects of contract law as a whole.

Through such analysis, I try to show that contract formation may properly be viewed as a form of transactional acquisition that is effectuated in and through the purely representational medium of the parties' mutual assents, prior to and independent of actual performance. Moreover, as such, it also satisfies requirements of fairness and reasonableness and establishes entitlements that are properly enforceable by performance remedies as a matter of compensation. Of course, whether this analysis is persuasive will depend on the accuracy and soundness of my presentation and interpretations of the law. I should emphasize from the start that the detailed treatment of contract doctrines is not intended as a textbook or treatise on contract law. The detailed discussion is needed, as I have said, to show that the proposed conception of contract as transfer is in fact implicit in the main doctrines of the law and that this conception can in turn explain these doctrines as mutually supportive aspects of a unified whole. For the purposes of my argument, my hope is that my doctrinal analysis is sufficiently plausible and accurate so that deficiencies, which undoubtedly do exist, do not call into question my central claim that contract can be understood and justified as a form of acquisition.

After working up to the account of contract as transactional acquisition in this way, I then argue in Part Two, called "Theory," that this conception can be elucidated and explained more fully by viewing it as involving a transfer of ownership between the parties. Indeed, this is how I believe contract is best understood as a morally defensible interpretation of the law. For the purpose of showing this, I consider whether this way of conceiving the contractual relation is consistent with more general ideas in private law—in particular the idea of ownership—and is morally acceptable from the standpoint of a liberal conception of justice. Here it will be especially important to uncover the conception of free and equal persons that may be presupposed by contract as transfer and by private law more generally. Now the fact that this conception of contract as transfer is, we will see, purely juridical in character as well as distinct from the morality of promising and from both economic and distributive considerations gives rise to the last issue that I address in Part Two, namely, the stability of this conception of contract. Given the character of the proposed conception of contract, is it in tension with or instead supportive of the very different domains of promissory morality, the market, and the requirements of distributive justice that, we may suppose, are also integral aspects of modern liberal society? If contract norms must be viewed as conflicting with the latter, this would surely bring into question contract's full moral acceptability.[24] This would mean failure for the attempted public justification of contract. A complete theory of contract should show that it is not only morally defensible in its own right but also fully congruent with these other domains—moral, economic, and political.

Let me now discuss each of these two main parts in a little more detail. Beginning with Part One, it comprises three main sections: formation, fairness, and enforcement—each of which itself consists of three chapters. I begin with formation rather than remedies because, from a legal point of view, the latter are understood as responses to violations of terms already fully established at formation, which the remedies therefore presuppose as normatively prior. Between formation and enforcement stand the requirements of contractual fairness. I present the three sections in an ordered sequence in which the later sections presuppose and build on those coming before. The key point, however, is that they are intended to be mutually supportive and fully integrated.

In the three chapters on formation, I examine not only the doctrines of consideration and offer and acceptance but also interpretation and implication. The first chapter begins by explaining in detail the core features, meaning, and implications of the requirement of consideration, arguing that this doctrine specifies what I call the "promise-for-consideration relation" as the necessary and sufficient framework for every nonformalized contractual relation enforceable by performance remedies. In my view, this promise-for-consideration relation is the basic contractual relation. The other doctrines and principles fill out and specify further its essential aspects and effects. In short, it is the common law's organizing principle for contract. This relation, we will see, is also the basis of different kinds of contract types. It unifies the analysis of contract law in a way that simultaneously explains its internal complexity and richness. Showing that general principles of contract do not exclude but, to the contrary, ground and animate more specific categories of contractual transactions is an important aim of my argument. Finally, in connection with this discussion of consideration, I offer an account of reliance-based obligation that shows it to be distinct from that based on consideration and try to explain the nature and limits of privity of contract in a way that is at the same time fully consistent with the possibility of contract having certain definite kinds of third-party effects.

The second chapter is concerned with the other main doctrine of contract formation, offer and acceptance. The latter's role, as I see it, is to specify the dynamic dimension of the creation of the promise-for-consideration relation. Although the objective test for formation and interpretation governs every aspect of contract analysis (including consideration), I focus on it at this point in the argument and try to explain what it requires and why it is the appropriate standpoint for determining the existence, meaning, and effects of contractual relations. The objective test, I suggest, provides the appropriate relational standpoint in light of which all issues of contract are to be determined and assessed. Also discussed is the question of whether, in addition to consideration and offer and acceptance, a positive intention to create legally enforceable relations is or should be a further requirement for formation. I argue not.

The third and final chapter in the formation section is about implication, or what may be called contract's implicit dimension. Here I consider the main kinds of implication—including implied terms and obligations, constructive conditions of exchange, excusing doctrines of impossibility and frustration, and finally the requirement of good faith. With respect to all these forms of implication, I try to show that, contrary to the predominant view in contemporary contract theory, enforceable agreements are not contractually incomplete, nor do they have "gaps" that have to be filled in by externally introduced default rules chosen on the basis of economic or other substantive policy considerations. Rather, the basic contractual relation construed in accordance with the objective test has all the internal resources needed to determine what can and should be implied. Showing this is crucial to my overall understanding of contract as self-sufficient and complete in its own terms as well as independent of economic or other policy considerations.

It is often assumed that the values of contractual freedom and fairness must be in conflict or at least in tension with each other. My object in the second section, which is concerned with contractual fairness, is to show that this need not be so. For this purpose, in Chapters 4 and 5, I set out, interpret, and explain the principal doctrines ordinarily associated with requirements of contractual fairness (including unconscionability, undue influence, the penalty doctrine, and the prohibition against so-called "shackling" contracts such as those in restraint of trade). Through this discussion, I try to clarify the respective meanings of liberty and fairness in contract law, arguing not only that there is no tension between them but that in fact both dimensions are essential to the full elucidation of the contractual relation. More specifically, unconscionability and related norms of fairness are compatible with and needed to fill out the basic promise-for-consideration relation. These are general norms internal to every contractual relation, and together with the principles of contract formation they express an idea of justice in transactions that is distinct and independent from distributive justice or substantive policy considerations. After discussing these matters, I conclude the section on fairness by addressing in Chapter 6 the important but vexing question of the role of fairness in standard form contracts.

The third and final section of Part One concerns contractual enforcement, including remedies for breach. Chapter 7 is preliminary, discussing fundamental ideas relating to contractual enforceability. Contract liability is commonly said to be strict, but what exactly does this mean and entail? There is still considerable controversy even in the recent theoretical literature over this issue. After trying to clarify it, I then discuss the nature of breach, including the possibility of anticipatory repudiation. A key theoretical question is this: even though breach of contract usually involves only an omission, can it still be properly explained as a civil wrong that injures the innocent party's exclusive rights, thus fitting within the general private law framework of liability for misfeasance only? At this point, I introduce the idea of compensatory justice and consider the kind of relation between right, wrong, and remedy that this presupposes. The duty to perform is juridical, coercible, and required as a matter of justice between the parties, with the different principles governing remedies working in tandem to ensure compensatory justice in response to breach.

It is important to bring out the unity in the diversity of remedial principles. This is the task of Chapter 8. The unifying idea is this: to the extent possible and reasonable in circumstances of breach, compensation from the defendant to the plaintiff should aim to place the latter in the position of having no less but also no more than the promised performance, including its full and fair value. For example, I argue that both specific performance and expectation (or performance) damages share the same end of ensuring, via different routes, that the plaintiff can obtain factual possession in post-breach circumstances of the very thing (unique or generic) as promised. Damages for consequential loss under the rule for remoteness ensure that the plaintiff obtains the equivalent of the beneficial use (e.g., profit) reasonably contemplated by the parties at the time of contracting. And so on in different ways for other principles, including mitigation, reliance damages, damages for intangible loss, and gain-based damages. Finally, in Chapter 9, I argue that this account is superior to leading alternative approaches that, in one form or another, view expectation damages as the enforcement of an implied contractual term and contractual obligation as being in reality an option to "perform" or "pay value." This discussion brings us back to the Fuller and Perdue challenge. I conclude this chapter and the whole section on enforcement by taking up this theme one last time, restating the intrinsic connection between the nature of the contractual relation and the availability of expectation damages as a basic mode of compensatory relief.

The upshot of Part One's detailed discussions of the main contract doctrines and principles is that they fit together and completely specify the different aspects of the following conception of contractual relation: contract formation is a mode of acquisition that, since it is effectuated as between the parties through their mutual promises alone, is a form of transactional and purely representational acquisition. Recalling the previously discussed distinction between the rational and the reasonable, this entire analysis, I hope to show, expresses the priority and centrality of the reasonable in contractual relations. Indeed, it rests on the idea of the reasonable alone. Now it is one thing to show, as I try to do in Part One, that this conception of contract as transactional acquisition is implicit in and can make interpretative sense of contract doctrines and principles. While this is a crucial first step in working out a public basis of justification for contract, we can still ask further whether this conception is consistent with more general ideas in private law as well as morally acceptable as part of an ideal of liberal justice. Addressing these further questions is the task of Part Two, which consists of three chapters.

In Chapter 10, the main question is whether the conception of contract as a form of transactional acquisition entails a *notion of ownership* that is consistent with the wider understanding of ownership in private law relations. In other words, can contract formation be coherently viewed as a way of transferring ownership as between the parties? Offhand, the conception of contract suggested by contract doctrines seems to suppose some idea of ownership. After all, via the doctrine of consideration, contract law views formation as constituted by each party moving something of value into the other's rightful exclusive control and treats it as an acquired entitlement that is secured against injury via remedies that ensure its contractually contemplated fair value. At the same time, it is "ownership" only as between the parties—not against others in general—and it exists as part of a transactional relation that consists only of their assents and so just in the medium of pure representation. Moreover, this ownership right would vest prior to and independent of performance and therefore potentially even before the owner has an immediate right to take or enjoy the promised thing or service. If this is ownership, it seems on its face to be of a very different kind from that supposed in the standard analysis of property, which most would take as the paradigm of private ownership.

Given these differences, to answer the question of whether contract formation can be coherently viewed as a transfer of ownership, I consider the core nature and presuppositions of property ownership, and how these relate to transactional acquisition in contract. Along with this inquiry, I also try to clarify the important but by no means self-evident distinction between in rem and in personam rights. In contrast to the standard view, I argue, first, that the in rem/in personam dichotomy refers, not to property versus contract or to two utterly separate kinds of rights relations, but rather to two distinct dimensions that, albeit in different ways, characterize each of both property and contractual relations, and second, that however paradoxical it might seem at first glance, these dimensions are expressed most completely in contract rather than in property. My central conclusion in this chapter is that the idea of ownership that seems to be ultimately presupposed throughout private law is brought out most fully and explicitly in precisely the purely represented transactional conception of acquisition that characterizes contract as a transfer of ownership.

In Chapter 11, I address the next question requisite to working out a public basis of justification for contract: is contract, when viewed as a transfer of ownership, morally acceptable in its own right from the standpoint of liberal justice? For this purpose, it is essential to show that contract, so understood and taken in its own terms, expresses a suitable liberal conception of parties as free and equal persons with the requisite moral powers and features. Here it is important to keep in mind that we are looking for a conception of persons that is proper to the kind of relation in which contracting parties are engaged. They are parties to free and fair transactions in which they figure solely as individual private owners who make claims against each other within the parameters of misfeasance. This specific normative conception of persons' moral powers as well as of their freedom and equality I characterize as juridical, as distinct from political, economic, or ethical. Now the central moral power of juridical persons is, I will argue, a reflective capacity, expressible in conduct, to assert one's sheer independence from one's desires, needs, circumstances, and so forth. While these latter factors may distinguish and situate us, they need not define us, at least not initially, insofar as we view ourselves and others as free and equal responsible agents. I further try to show that respect for others as persons with a capacity for ownership expresses respect for them as such juridical persons. This respect is owed to others as a matter of justice in transactions, which, being itself indifferent to need, interest, and the like, must be conceived as wholly nondistributive in character.

It follows from this last point that in contrast to, say, Rawls's theory of political distributive justice, which views free and equal persons as needing certain things (primary goods) in order to develop and exercise their moral powers as citizens, there is no such parallel in the view of individuals as free and equal juridical persons in justice in transactions. Granted that this is a very limited and unusual conception of the freedom and equality of persons, I nonetheless believe that it can be shown to have a certain intrinsic reasonableness or acceptability. I shall try to do this without relying on philosophical accounts but instead will present the essentials in a hopefully intuitive way, referring wherever possible to notions implicit in the public legal culture and the private law of a liberal society. Here as elsewhere in the book, my aim is to suggest a public justification, not a philosophy, of contract law.

Now it is precisely on account of its limited and specific nature that justice in transactions raises a set of questions—specific to it—that must be addressed under the heading of stability. The juridical conception of contract as a transfer of ownership is, I argue, nonpromissory, not specifically economic, and nondistributive. Yet contracts are constituted by promises, are standardly exchanges, and specify entitlements to things and services that may also engage the concerns of distributive justice. Moreover, individuals have moral duties and responsibilities as promisors and promisees; they have vital economic interests and needs that they satisfy through market exchanges; and they have legitimate and compelling claims that the overall distribution of goods, services, and money should be regulated by principles that are fair. For the juridical conception of contract to be stable in the right way, we may suppose that individuals must be able willingly to internalize and to support it as part of their final ends and not merely strategically. But we cannot reasonably expect this of them if the juridical conception (including its full justification) is at odds with promissory morality or in tension with the requirements of market activity, or finally is incompatible with appropriate principles of distributive justice. As noted earlier, I assume that this would bring into question, not these other normative domains, but the juridical conception of contract and thus arguably contract law itself. To complete the public basis of justification of contract, it seems essential, then, to explain why there need not be such tensions, let alone incompatibility.

Accordingly, in Chapter 12, which is the last and longest, I try to show how the principles governing these different spheres are mutually supportive. For this purpose, I need to lay out, even if summarily, plausible accounts of promissory morality, the market, and distributive justice within a liberal legal and political framework. My argument will be that because of the limited nature and implications of the juridical conception of contract—and as long as it stays within its own proper bounds—there can be full congruence between contract law and these other domains within a larger framework that is legally and politically liberal. This holds not only for the relation between contract and promissory morality but also for its relations with market activity and reasonable requirements of distributive justice.

Particularly in connection with the last two sets of relations, I argue for a certain ordered normative-conceptual sequence between these different subjects: we begin with the transactional juridical conception of contract and arrive at the more systemic and needs-referring domains of markets and background distributive justice. But in this sequence, the autonomy and the normatively basic character of the juridical conception are respected and preserved. This point is crucial to my argument and should be emphasized from the start. On the one hand, the upshot of Part One is that the whole ensemble of basic contract doctrines—from formation and fairness to remedies—may be properly understood solely and self-sufficiently in the bilateral and transactional terms of the juridical conception, without recourse to economic considerations. On the other hand, in this final chapter I try to show in some detail that contract law has the normative resources to take into account and to support the systemic interests of market participants without derogating from or displacing its own juridical conception of contract. In doing so, contract law assumes an institutional role that recognizes and meets fundamental formal interests, both bilateral and systemic, that contracting parties identically share as market transactors.

Moreover, even though contract law remains strictly nondistributive when assuming an institutional and systemic role, I explain how, in contrast with the libertarian view of acquisition and transfer, the proposed conception of contract as a transfer of ownership not only can make room for but also can fit with appropriate principles of distributive justice for the background political and social institutions. For either set of principles—those for transactions as well as for distributive justice—to be fully acceptable in a liberal conception of justice, it must be one side of a division of labor with the other, with both sets of principles working in tandem in a way that does not detract from but on the contrary upholds the distinctive natures, roles, and central values of each. Rawls argues that this division of labor is necessary, but because he expressly focuses only on principles for background distributive justice, he does not fully explain the basis of this important idea. I hope that my account of contract fits with this idea of such a division of labor and contributes something toward the effort to elucidate it.

I.5. Concluding Remarks about Scope

Since my aim in this book is to develop a public basis of justification for the principles and doctrines of the common law of contract, I should conclude with some brief remarks about the scope of the argument. There are two main points that I wish to make here.

The first is this: a public basis of justification, I have said, must draw on normative ideas implicit in some public legal or political culture at some level of generality. I draw on such ideas that are latent in the private law cultures of existing common law systems of contract. At the same time, even though it is worked out for the common law in a judicial setting, the path taken by the proposed public justification may be relevant in developing a similar theoretical approach for other modern systems of contract law—most obviously, those belonging to the civilian tradition. This is partly because what the theory purports to discern as implicit in common law doctrines is a unifying general conception of juridical contractual relation that, when made explicit, is intelligible in its own terms and may therefore animate other non–common law systems of contract. The potential pertinence of this conception is further suggested by the fact, mentioned earlier, that the systems of contract law now prevailing throughout most of the world share a similar doctrinal structure comprising the same kinds of basic and larger concepts, even though their particular legal formulations may sometimes differ from one jurisdiction to another. As well, it is worth recalling here that it was the great natural rights thinkers, all working within the civil law tradition, who advanced and explored the conception of contract as a transfer of ownership with unparalleled depth and rigor. Although I do not present their contributions as the explicit basis of my account, I believe that the latter has an affinity with their views. Finally, the considerations discussed in Part Two relating to the moral acceptability and the stability of this conception within a framework of liberal justice are clearly not parochial to the common law. My hope is that they can be relevant to the justification of any system of modern contract law that shares this ideal of justice.

Turning now to my second point, the proposed public justification for contract law views it as embodying a distinct conception of justice: justice in transactions. Now both the term and the idea of justice in transactions harken back to Aristotle's seminal originating account.[25] According to Aristotle, there are two qualitatively distinct categories of justice, each of which has its own characteristic conceptions of equality and fairness and regulates a particular kind of social relation: justice in distributions and justice in transactions. For its part, justice in transactions, which Aristotle refers to as corrective justice, orders two kinds of transactions, voluntary and nonvoluntary. My argument only purports to provide a theory for contract law, not for nonvoluntary transactions governed by tort law or other parts of private law. Despite this focus, I think that the proposed account of contract law engages some fundamental themes and outstanding questions arising from Aristotle's account and subsequent theorizing about justice in transactions as a whole.

First, the book tries to set out in detail—though always within the parameters of a public justification—what justice in voluntary transactions entails, including its central requirement of fairness, equivalence in exchange. This is not something that Aristotle clarifies, and in fact he treats equivalence in exchange, and so exchange itself, as a puzzle that cannot, he thinks, be understood within the frameworks of either corrective or distributive justice.[26] Yet, as subsequent thinkers (starting with Thomas Aquinas and John Duns Scotus) who developed Aristotle's analysis made clear, exchange, with equivalence as its requirement, is surely the central instance of voluntary transaction that comes under corrective justice. If we cannot explain why this is the case, it is not clear to me that we really understand corrective justice itself. Moreover, my account of contract attempts to fill a gap in contemporary discussions of corrective justice, which standardly deal mainly with tort law and other instances of nonvoluntary transactions. Once again, a full understanding of corrective justice would seem to require such an account.

Second, there is the still controverted and fundamental question of whether corrective justice specifies its own transactional conception of entitlement or instead is merely remedial, rectifying losses that result from violations of entitlements established on some other (perhaps distributive) basis. This also bears on the relationship between corrective and distributive justice. It would seem that only an account of justice in voluntary transactions can definitively show that the first possibility—corrective justice having its own proper conception of entitlements—is in fact the case. Indeed, in Part Two, I try to explain why the entitlement in contract, when viewed as a transfer of ownership, represents in the most complete and explicit way the very kind of entitlement that is strictly transactional and so necessarily presupposed, even implicitly, by every instance of justice in transactions, both voluntary and nonvoluntary. It represents, I argue, the paradigm of entitlement that is intrinsic to corrective justice. Through this analysis, I believe that the proposed theory of contract not only vindicates Aristotle's original insight that there are two mutually irreducible and individually self-sufficient categories of justice—corrective and distributive—but also clarifies the relation between them, suggesting how they fit together in a more complete conception of justice acceptable in a modern liberal democratic society.

PART ONE
PRINCIPLES

SECTION A

FORMATION

....

Introduction: With What Should an Account of Contract Formation Begin?

Any viable theory of modern contract law must explain it as an instance of private ordering rooted in the parties' voluntary mutual assents. Indeed, in one form or another, the view that contract is consensual and bilateral has guided common law thinking about contract law since the fourteenth century, if not before.[1] Now, standardly, the mutual assents that give rise to contractual obligations involve promises or communicated assurances of some kind. Promises, in contrast with vows, are necessarily interpersonal and in some sense bilateral. But how exactly? Our differences, particularly at a theoretical level, often stem from how we understand the two-sided character of the parties' promissory relation.

Here we may distinguish two quite different ways in which promissory relations might be viewed.[2] In the first, promising is viewed as an undertaking—a fixed and communicated expression of commitment—that is made *to* or *for* another and that is accepted as such.[3] From the promisor's side comes an act that is completed by the promisee treating it as something that she wants or at least does not reject. The promisee's acceptance consists merely in her reacting to the promise in this way. But she does not need to do or give anything in return to complete the promissory relation and thereby to bring the promisor under a duty to perform. In the second conception, by contrast, the bilateral character of the relation involves contributions by both sides that are equally active and reciprocal. A promise is made not only to or for but also *with* the promisee in the following sense: as part of the very terms of his promise, the promisor solicits the promisee's own act, that is, her own fixed expression of decision, to be given in return. In this second model, the promissory relation is complete and gives rise to an obligation only if and when the first promise is joined by the promisee's return act. And supposing that the promissory relation can be wholly promissory and so constituted only by promises, the relation would itself consist of mutual and completely reciprocal promises, each soliciting and being solicited by the other, each made and given in return for the other. Here the promissory transaction is the product of the parties' joined and coequal contributions, with each side's promise counting as a promise only as part of this completely bilateral relation.

This simple contrast, I will argue, holds the key to understanding not only the prerequisites for contract formation but also the whole of contract law. So far as contract formation—our present topic—is concerned, it suggests why the promissory relation required by the doctrine of consideration should be the starting point and organizing idea of an account of formation. Let me explain.

Suppose we begin the account of contract formation, not with the doctrine of consideration, but instead with the intuitive idea that promises have to be accepted. We start, in other words, by supposing that there have to be both an offer and an acceptance. The problem with this is that it is by no means clear why a purely gratuitous promise—a promise not supported by consideration—cannot be appropriately accepted. You promise me a horse, with delivery in two days, and I say, "Thanks, I accept." Why should this not count in contract law as an acceptance? After all, it comes from the promisee's side and closes the relation.[4] Without this acceptance—or at least an implicit or even presumed acceptance—a promissory relation would not be established and a duty to perform should not arise. Promises are not intended to be, and cannot be, imposed on others.

But if this were to count as an acceptance in law, it would immediately break the widely assumed connection between the requirement of offer and acceptance and that of consideration as the twin pillars of contract formation. Ever since the introduction of offer and acceptance as a distinct legal doctrine during the first part of the nineteenth century, contract law has always treated it as working in tandem with the much older doctrine of consideration.[5] An offer that does not state a promise-for-consideration is simply not an offer, confers no power of acceptance, and cannot be "accepted" to effectuate contract formation. The law views this relation between the doctrines as basic and indeed axiomatic. More than that, if gratuitous promises can be accepted as a matter of contract law, this would deny that the requirement of consideration is a necessary condition of contract formation, contrary to the historically long-settled view of this doctrine. Offer and acceptance would be the sole necessary condition of formation.[6]

The first model of promising supports this very result. To elaborate, a gratuitous promise is the paradigmatic instance of a promise made to but not with another in the sense required by the second conception of promising. A gratuitous promise invites the promisee to place her trust in the promisor's word and moral probity, giving rise to her expectation that the promisor will act in fulfillment of his promise. This communicated intention via promising is the positive act that is one side of the promissory relation. We can see, however, that to be complete and morally effective, this first act need not be supplemented or met by a second act of any kind coming from the promisee and reciprocally given in return. The promisee need not take up the promise in this way. Instead, in the central case of a gratuitous promise, the promisee takes up the promise—accepts it—simply by deciding to place her trust in the promisor's conscientiousness and by beginning to imagine her future state, choices, and interests in light of the expectation of his future performance. This of course presupposes that she subjectively views the promised performance positively as something that she wants—which, we may assume, is precisely what the promisor intends and hopes is or will be the case when he promises.[7] While the promisee's positive reaction may be communicated to the promisor, this may not be necessary in given circumstances. In fact, in the absence of some indication of disapproval or rejection, her acquiescence can ordinarily be presumed.

The key point is that this change in the promisee's state of mind and her voluntary dependence on the promisor's probity is the promisee's sole necessary contribution to their promissory relation.[8] It completes the promise to form a promissory relation. It is also a sufficient and reasonable basis for viewing the promisor as now under an obligation to respect the promisee by fulfilling his word. Notice that although the promisor may certainly want and hope for this acceptance as the intended reaction to his promise, it is not something that he requests or views as what she is to give or do in return for his promise.

In sum, according to the first model—promises as made to or for another—there is a way of viewing acceptance (as what is needed to complete the interpersonal promissory relation) that would make it possible for gratuitous promises to be seen as accepted by an expression of thanks. This, I have said, would contradict consideration as a necessary condition of formation and break the legally settled connection between the two doctrines. Can the second model of promissory relations—promises as made not only to or for but also with another—avoid this result?

To fit with this second model, acceptance cannot be simply a reaction to the promise, or a presumed state of mind, or, finally, the promisee placing her trust in the conscientiousness and moral probity of the promisor. Like the promise, acceptance would have to be fully a coequal and reciprocal act, one that is solicited by and done in return for the promisor. Since acceptance of a gratuitous promise does not meet this criterion, there cannot be an immediate conflict with consideration. So far so good. But is there a principle that would *require* this conception of acceptance and the kind of interpersonal promissory relation that it is part of, excluding the first kind of acceptance discussed above? If there is such a principle, then it would be with it that our theoretical account of contract formation should properly begin.

I would like to suggest that there is such a principle: the doctrine of consideration itself. Now on its face, the essential function of this oldest requirement of nonformal contract formation is to differentiate promises-for-consideration from gratuitous promises, with only the former but not the latter being contractually enforceable. As I will try to show in some detail, this amounts to distinguishing promissory relations that are two-sided in the way required by the second model from those that are not. Not only does the doctrine of consideration require a promissory relation of the second kind. In addition, the actual legal doctrine of offer and acceptance, we will see, fits perfectly with this framework of the promise-for-consideration relation. And once acceptance is viewed as part of this framework, there cannot be a contractually effective or even recognizable acceptance of gratuitous promises. In this way, we can now show that the two main doctrines of contract formation must necessarily function in tandem with each other as mutually supporting parts of a unified conception.

With these points in mind, it seems reasonable to begin an account of contract formation with the doctrine of consideration, taking the promise-for-consideration relation as the basic framework that other doctrines fill in and further specify. The aim of Chapter 1 will therefore be to try to make clear the essential features, role, and implications of consideration. My central contention will be that by distinguishing the promise-for-consideration relation from gratuitous promises and making the former a necessary condition of contractual enforceability, the doctrine of consideration specifies the basic nature of the contractual relation in the common law of contract—and this relation, we will see, unambiguously reflects the second model of promising. With the basic contractual relation laid out, I then discuss in Chapter 2 the role of the doctrine of offer and acceptance. In my view, this doctrine specifies the *dynamic* dimension of interaction necessary to establish a promise-for-consideration relation. In this way, I explain it as a companion doctrine that not only fits with consideration but also makes explicit an essential aspect of the basic contractual relation. Finally, a complete account of contract formation should also include an analysis of implication. After all, a contract is the sum of its express and implied terms (and conditions), and all these are fixed at contract formation. Accordingly, Chapter 3 concludes the section on contract formation with a discussion of the nature and the basis of implied terms, excusing conditions, and good faith as some central examples of the implied dimension of contracts.

Chapter 1

Consideration

Its Meaning, Role, and Consequences

In this first chapter, I present and explain the requirement of consideration not only as a necessary condition for contract formation but also as providing the basic and general framework for the contractual relation as such. Because much has been written about consideration—most of it critical and reformist—and also because of the doctrine's centrality in the theory of contract that I will develop here, I begin with a discussion of the relation between this doctrine and contract theory (Section 1.1). In this connection, I examine in some detail Lon Fuller's influential qualified defense of consideration. Next I set out the doctrine's main features and try to make clear the nature of the specific kind of relationship—what I call the "promise-for-consideration relation"—that it always and necessarily establishes (Section 1.2). Any viable theory of consideration must in my view try to explain and justify the following four settled legal facts regarding voluntary transactions: the enforceability of promises under seal, the validity of executed gifts, the enforceability of promises for consideration, and the nonenforceability of pure gratuitous promises (absent detrimental reliance). This is what I shall try to do (Section 1.3).

Following that, I specify and explain the much discussed relation between consideration and reliance, arguing that, even though they both involve promising, they represent two qualitatively distinct bases of liability (Section 1.4). Consideration, I contend, specifies a distinct kind of juridical relation that, in contrast to reliance, may be properly called contractual. Finally, I take up the important but theoretically neglected question of the possibility of third-party effects of contractual rights and duties even prior to performance and suggest how these effects are possible without being inconsistent with a robust conception of contractual privity (Section 1.5). Through this detailed discussion of consideration, I hope to take the first—and perhaps the most important—step in developing my ultimate theoretical contention that contractual relations can be reasonably elucidated as a form of transactional acquisition—a transfer of ownership between the parties—that is contractually specified and complete at contract formation.

1.1. Consideration versus Contract Theory

No doctrine of the common law of contract has been longer settled or more carefully developed than consideration.[1] The historical product of intense and highly conceptual legal argument built from the ground up, consideration's main features were already evident by the end of the sixteenth century when it was fixed as an essential requirement for an action in assumpsit. From that time on, if not earlier, consideration embodied an idea of reciprocity that, even prior to this, continuously animated the long history of contract law stretching back to fourteenth- and fifteenth-century English medieval law. At the level of practice, and for the first time in this history, consideration stated a general requirement governing all nonformalized agreements: without consideration, no promise (not under seal) was actionable in assumpsit. Moreover, from the start, this actionability consisted in the possible enforcement of the plaintiff's performance interest. Even though assumpsit originated as a species of the action of trespass on the case and therefore in a mold that structurally focused on the defendant's wrongdoing and the loss caused, the law filled this trespassory form with the substantive idea of liability for the plaintiff's lost expectations resulting from the defendant's nonperformance of his promise. Thus, from the late sixteenth and early seventeenth centuries, consideration stipulated a general and necessary prerequisite for a kind of liability that is still widely viewed as distinctively contractual. If there has ever been a basic contract doctrine that as a matter of self-conscious legal practice has presented itself as reflecting a unified conception of contract, consideration is it.[2]

Why, then, is consideration so difficult for contract theory? For difficult it is. Indeed, no basic contract doctrine has proved more intractable for theoretical justification than consideration.³ This holds true for all the main theoretical perspectives, however much they may otherwise differ among themselves. Even the most influential defenses have been found wanting. When theories do not simply dismiss consideration as an outdated and rigid formalism that obscures the real concerns and purposes of contract law, they attribute to it functions that it need not fulfill even in central instances of its proper application and that can as well or more effectively be accomplished by other legal devices (such as the seal) or on the basis of other reasons for liability (such as reliance). Insofar as it is still acknowledged as a prerequisite for enforceability, consideration is explained as a control device that excludes gratuitous promises for reasons that often promote neither autonomy nor welfare. Most commonly, it is viewed as a sufficient, but not as a necessary, condition for contractual liability—merely as one among several possible bases—and, even then, only as indirectly significant as evidencing the normatively important factors such as an intention to contract or the presence of socially valuable transactions. Perhaps the most devastating indictment, which I discuss below, is Charles Fried's claim that at its very core, the doctrine is built on two essential yet mutually contradictory propositions.[4] Against this intellectual background, it is not surprising that a leading private law scholar has concluded that "the law would be rendered more intelligible and clear if the need for consideration were abolished."[5]

I would like to suggest that the problem is not with consideration but rather with the current theories that defend or challenge it. The theories are not equipped to explain the doctrine because they invoke functions and purposes that do not belong to the specific sort of relation that consideration necessarily establishes between the parties. Inevitably, they introduce factors and distinctions that are irrelevant from, or inconsistent with, the legal point of view. Categorical differences that do matter, such as those between mutual promises and gratuitous promises, turn out to be unjustified on this basis. This is true of both defenders and critics of the doctrine. In contrast to contemporary contract theory, I shall maintain that the requirement of consideration constitutes the contractual relation as such; consideration itself establishes and represents a particular kind of relation between the parties, thereby specifying the inner mechanism and core that animates the whole of contract law.

To illustrate these unavoidably general points about current approaches to consideration and to prepare the ground for my proposed alternative view, I will now discuss what still remains the most influential defense of the doctrine, namely, Lon Fuller's "Consideration and Form."[6] In this article, Fuller provides a qualified defense of the traditional view that consideration stipulates a necessary condition for the contractual enforceability of promises. He accepts the nonenforceability of gratuitous promises as an essential part of the doctrine. Fuller's stated aim is to uncover consideration's underlying policies and, on this ground, to provide its rationale. Beginning with the general and formal principle of private autonomy—"the most pervasive and indispensable" of the basic conceptions of contract law—he argues that, in relation to this principle, certain additional formal and substantive criteria are needed to demarcate the domain of enforceable nonformalized agreements and that the requirement of consideration satisfies these desiderata.[7] This, in a nutshell, is his core argument. Let us look at it a little more closely.

According to Fuller, the principle of private autonomy refers to the fact that, in contrast with the other grounds of contract liability (viz., reliance and unjust enrichment), the law here treats private parties as having, within limits, a legal power to change their voluntary legal relations inter se.[8] Not only the seal but also the enforcement of mutual promises and executed gifts are all settled instances of the application of this principle. Indeed, if the law were to enforce unsealed gratuitous promises, this too would involve an exercise in private autonomy. We can see, then, that because the principle merely states, without justifying, the conclusion that the law accords parties rights-altering and lawmaking powers, it cannot decide the fundamental question of whether consideration should be a necessary requirement for contractual enforceability, thereby excluding gratuitous promises. Additional elements are needed to account for this. As I now discuss, Fuller argues that these further elements involve policies of both form and substance that are satisfied by the requirement of consideration.

First, when persons are accorded lawmaking powers, it is desirable that they act with and for the purpose of producing the attributed legal effects and therefore under conditions that ensure what Fuller describes as the "desiderata of form."[9] As is well known, he specifies these desiderata in terms of the evidentiary, cautionary, and channeling functions of legal formalities, taking the common law seal as the most familiar example in contract law. Fuller's crucial argument is that certain nonformalized voluntary transactions—and in particular those that satisfy consideration—have features or arise from situations that naturally accomplish these functions of form, dispensing with the need for investing these transactions with formalities such as the seal.[10] Fuller contends that this can be true of not only exchange transactions and especially half-executed exchanges—the "contractual archetype"—but also executed gifts.[11] However, this is not the case with mere promises to give.

This exclusion of gratuitous promises is reinforced by the substantive considerations that Fuller brings to bear on the question of enforceability. In deciding which transactions should be upheld on the basis of private autonomy, he argues that there should be a cost-benefit analysis of the social and economic importance of the different transactions, including the impact of their enforcement on individual and social well-being. For this purpose, Fuller takes notice of the fact that in a society with a modern market economy, the most familiar and important field of regulation by private autonomy is that of the exchange of goods and services.[12] However, it is also socially and economically important, Fuller notes, that there can be a domain for voluntary social intercourse in which statements of intention and even assurances may be given, altered, or withdrawn without incurring legal liability—making the application of the principle of autonomy with its enforcement mechanism generally inappropriate. Moreover, imposing such substantive costs and burdens on nonexchange relations is not justified given their limited wealth-creating role.[13] Consideration carves out a sphere for the appropriate operation of private autonomy by singling out exchange transactions (including those ancillary to an exchange) as enforceable to the exclusion of gratuitous promises, with the half-executed exchange representing the contractual archetype.

This overview of Fuller's argument will be familiar to many. Equally familiar is the fact that it is subject to important qualifications and exceptions. As a number of writers have shown, consideration does not consistently or always effectively satisfy Fuller's formal and substantive policies. With respect to form, for example, as Fuller himself acknowledges, nonformalized mutual promises do not go very far in meeting the desiderata he views as fundamental. As a result, Fuller challenges the legally settled proposition that "where the doing a thing will be a good consideration, a promise to do that thing will be so too"; and in according centrality to the half-completed exchange, he makes a distinction that has no basis in the actual law governing consideration.[14] But conversely, Fuller's assertion that gratuitous promises cannot naturally satisfy the desiderata of form in the needed way seems questionable.[15] If the concern is to distinguish tentative statements of intention from seriously intended unqualified promises, the law can ensure this with respect to nonbargain promises. As for the substantive considerations favoring exchange transactions, it is well settled that bilateral and unilateral contracts need not involve commercially or economically significant exchange relations. The legal definitions of benefit and detriment are not limited in this way. And clearly nominal consideration cannot be so construed. Beyond this, promises for past consideration, promises in return for preexisting duties, and illusory promises are all contractually void or at least problematic from a legal point of view, even though they directly involve bargaining or may be ancillary to bargaining in commercial settings. Finally, the fact that executed gifts are fully enforceable shows that at common law there is no substantive policy against gifts, challenging Fuller's argued-for primacy of exchanges. Not only can gratuitous promises be welfare-enhancing; in contrast to enforceable executed gifts, promises to give also entail the distinct and additional welfare advantage that parties can project their transactions into the future, thereby accommodating their needs and purposes even more effectively.[16]

While these familiar criticisms are important and cogent, they ordinarily remain anchored in Fuller's basic premise that the rationale for consideration must be sought, if anywhere, in the kind of formal and substantive policy analysis suggested by him. To strengthen this claim, they standardly fine-tune the policy analysis and argue that the defense should be limited to showing that consideration need only be a sufficient and not also a necessary condition of contractual enforceability.[17] The presence of consideration, they contend, provides only one possible basis for contractual enforceability, and even then, its role is indirect and approximate as an indicator, via an intention to bargain, of the sort of transaction that should be enforced on grounds of autonomy or welfare.

I take a different view. The reason, I think, that the above criticisms apply in the first place is that Fuller's approach does not reflect the basic relation that consideration requires and establishes between the parties. As I will discuss in more detail in the following section, the function of consideration is, first and foremost, to specify a genuinely and completely bilateral or two-sided relation between the parties, which arises through the united and equal actions of both: promises made not only to or for but also with another, symmetrically and reciprocally. But Fuller's conceptions of form and substance are, separately and jointly, inherently unsuited to make sense of such a bilateral relation. Let me briefly suggest why.

First, recall the analysis of form in Fuller's account, which takes legal formalities such as the seal as the ideal benchmark for understanding and evaluating the doctrine of consideration. In the case of a seal, we may reasonably say that the legal formality itself is the source of the promisor's obligation to perform.[18] Now the legally operative facts giving rise to the obligation here need not consist in any strictly bilateral or two-sided interaction between the parties: it is the promisor alone who must do certain things—sign, seal, and deliver the document containing the promisor's sole undertaking—and it is legally valid and effective without any act or counterpromise by the promisee. Delivery can be complete and effective without actual acceptance by the promisee. Further, if the promisee wishes to make in return a similarly effective promise, she must likewise put it separately under seal. There would be two legally separate transactions. Similarly, the three functions of legal formalities discussed by Fuller also reflect this unilateral character.[19] Thus the focus of each function is on the promisor alone: channeling her objectives, discouraging her impulsive behavior, and providing evidence of her acts. At no point need the desiderata of form simultaneously refer to any such concerns on the promisee's side.

In a more detailed discussion in his casebook, Fuller himself emphasizes this unilateral character of the seal.[20] He brings this out by noting that delivery of the document is ordinarily taken by the courts to involve "the promisor's act in handing the deed over rather than the promisee's act in receiving it."[21] However, in contrast, as Fuller himself again notes, a promise for consideration involves a nexus between promisor and promisee in which the promisee's promise or act is no less required than the promisor's.[22] Here, the source of the obligation is not an instrument or a merely unilateral act by the promisor. Rather, the obligation arises through a specific kind of nonformalized interaction between the parties. This interaction is not reducible to, but is genuinely distinct from, delivery (or other acts) in case of a sealed document.[23] But if this is correct, there is no reason to assume that the functions of one can be properly understood and explained through those of the other. To the contrary.

As for the aspect of substance, Fuller's emphasis on the centrality of exchange substitutes just one possible instance of the relation that consideration allows—economically important exchanges—for the bilateral relation itself—the quid pro quo—which, we will see, the doctrine always and necessarily requires and which can certainly include transactions that are not economically significant in the sense taken by him. By doing so, Fuller displaces the necessary for the contingent and obscures the basis of the latter in the former. As I will shortly discuss, the familiar fact that the doctrine of consideration does not require equivalence in exchange but, to the contrary, traditionally has even allowed, as Fuller himself notes, a nominal consideration means that the quid pro quo requirement is not synonymous with economic exchange. There is no basis in the doctrine to treat the social or economic importance of a given transaction as per se relevant.

Instead of starting with a conception like the principle of private autonomy, which simply refers to the legal effects that are attributed to certain voluntary acts, the search for consideration's rationale should begin with the specific kind of interaction that, in legal contemplation, constitutes the promise-for-consideration relation and that gives rise to contractual effects. It is this basic relation that must be identified and explained. As a first step in doing so, I will now set out the doctrine of consideration's main features as historically settled and generally accepted across common law jurisdictions.

1.2. The Main Features of Consideration

The doctrine of consideration holds that, standing alone, a promise not under seal is categorically insufficient to generate an expectation-based enforceable contractual obligation, no matter how seriously and unconditionally it is intended, however carefully and deliberately it is made, and despite the fact that it may be recorded in writing or memorialized in some other way. To be enforceable according to its terms, a promise must be made in return for a legally valid consideration, which can be either a reciprocal promise or a reciprocal act that is requested by the promisor and provided by the promisee in return as part of a single transaction. These exhaust the two possible categories of consideration: where the consideration is a counterpromise, a bilateral contract is formed at the moment the mutual promises are made; if the consideration is a reciprocal act, a unilateral contract is formed when the act is executed.[24] Moreover, consideration is not the same as the motive or reason for the promise; rather, it must move from the promisee; and it must be of some value in the eye of the law.[25] Understood in this way, consideration is unequivocally a necessary condition of contract formation and enforceability. All this is trite law. Let me now unpack and explore these propositions in order to try to make explicit the conception of relation that they reflect.

To start, the consideration must be either a promise or an act. Any statement of apparent intention that falls short of a crystallized promise cannot function as consideration. Otherwise there must be an actual act that is executed and is similarly irreducible to a statement of intention. Consideration must therefore consist in a finalized and complete exercise of choice in the form of a promise or an act. It should be noted here that by promising or doing something, a person necessarily represents or evidences that something is subject to his potential or actual control. I will return to this point shortly. Beyond this, what does it mean to say that the consideration must move from the promisee?

To move from the promisee, not only must the consideration not move from a third party, but, just as importantly, it must also not move from the promisor. More exactly, this entails that consideration must be *independent* in the following way from the promise for which it is given: it must be possible to construe the content of the consideration as something that could genuinely originate with the promisee, not the promisor. Consideration must be something that is not simply reducible to a mere aspect, condition, or effect of the first promise or its execution. In other words, the consideration has to be something that can reasonably be viewed as potentially on and coming from the promisee's side and therefore as not produced by the promisor. This can be so even though in the actual circumstances of a transaction, a consideration must in fact be executed only after the promise is performed or only when the promisee already has received the use of the thing promised by the promisor. Neither the temporal sequence nor the material relation between consideration and the promised performance is per se determinative in this respect.

Consider the following examples that do *not* satisfy this requirement of independence. Suppose that the substance of alleged consideration is the promisor's natural love and affection for the promisee or the promisee's own feelings of satisfaction with and gratitude for the promisor's promise.[26] These can certainly motivate or be reasons for the promise. But in either case, the law will view the alleged consideration as moving from the promisor, not the promisee, and so as no consideration at all. With respect to natural love and affection, it clearly does not originate with the promisee. In the example of promisee gratitude or satisfaction, although it is felt by the promisee and so, in a sense, is on her side, it consists merely in the promisee's reaction to the promise; it represents just the effect that the promise has on the promisee, and so it can only be viewed as coming after and as resulting from the promise. It could not possibly have originated with the promisee. The same analysis applies where the alleged consideration consists in a promise to open or in actually opening a promised gift, where opening the package is merely the way for the promisee to have and enjoy the gift.[27] Opening or promising to open the gift has no independent or distinct existence as notionally something originating with the promisee and as moved by the promisee in response to the promisor's side: it is merely an aspect of the execution of what is, in essence, a gratuitous promise.

By changing the above scenarios, we can see how the requirement of independence may be met. Thus, imagine a situation where the promisee is naturally or by habit ungrateful toward others despite the benevolence that they may show her. There is a factual basis to say that she has a certain disposition that she could otherwise choose to indulge, possibly even in the face of receiving the promisor's promise. This happens to be her way and condition and the promisor wants to change it. If in return for the promisor's promise and at the latter's request, she promises to express gratitude in her conduct, now the promise to be grateful (or the act of manifesting gratitude) represents the moving of something independent and distinct from the promisee's side. Or, in the example of the gift, if we now suppose that in return for the promise of the item, the promisee agrees to use it in some way that the promisor requests but that she, the promisee, need not have done, this is distinct and independent, moving from the promisee—even though the promisee can only do this after she has received the promised item.

The requirement that the consideration must move from the promisee and in particular the idea that it must be independent of the promisor means that there must be two active sides that together constitute the contractual relation. Its fundamental import is the negative condition that contract is not reducible to the act of only one party. This requirement is further specified by the next feature of the doctrine: the promisor must expressly or by necessary implication *request* the consideration in return for his promise and the promisee must move the consideration as something given *in response to* that request. We might say that this further requirement determines the way in which the promisee must move the consideration—not only from the promisee but also to the promisor.

With this further positive condition satisfied, the two sides now become mutually related. The consideration must be the reason for the promise and, vice versa, the promise must be the reason for the consideration. Thus promise and consideration must be mutually and reciprocally inducing: "It is not enough that the promise induces the detriment [i.e., the consideration] or that the detriment induces the promise, if the other half is wanting."[28] This feature of mutual inducement builds on and fills out the previously discussed requirements that the consideration be independent and move from the promisee. Unless the consideration moves from the promisee and is not reducible to being the promise's mere effect or aspect, it cannot be reasonably construed as the cause of or reason for the promise. Promise and consideration could not be viewed as mutually inducing. To establish this two-sidedness, it is not sufficient if the promisor wants or even requests something for his promise if this something does not come from the promisee's side as independent from that promise.

Whether this relation obtains between the promise and consideration is decided by looking at the terms of the agreement in accordance with the objective test for formation.[29] The consideration need not be the promisor's actual sufficient reason for promising or even just one of his actual reasons: "No matter what the actual motive may have been, by the express or implied terms of the supposed contract, the promise and the consideration must purport to be the motive each for the other, in whole or at least in part."[30] As long as it reasonably appears from the parties' words and actions inter se, interpreted in the setting of their interaction, that the promise has been made in return for the consideration and vice versa, this is sufficient.

These features of consideration specify a definite and limited conception of cause of or reason for the promise: whatever a promisor's purposes or motives may be, the only thing that counts as the cause of his promise is the receipt of the other party's consideration in return. This sets the fundamental framework for contractual analysis. The way in which consideration functions as the reason for the promise is as part of a strictly bilateral and reciprocal interaction between the parties. The reason is *intrinsically relational*. In the case of mutual promises, each side—each promise—is only as related to the other. Apart from this relation, neither has actual contractual meaning or existence. In other words, each side is contractually relevant and operative—and indeed is defined and specified—only insofar as it is inherently oriented to and for the other side. My promise figures as such only insofar as it is given for your promise, which at the same time is requested by and requests my promise. No other conception of reason is relevant. The parties' purposes and reasons for contracting, though important to them, are not contractually operative factors. They do not as such form part of the contractual analysis required by consideration. Consideration is not just a (any) reason that a court finds sufficient for enforcing the promise.

That each side is viewed as the cause of and reason for the other explains a puzzling, though often expressed, legal characterization of the promise-for-consideration relation. Although the promisor goes first and promises for a consideration requested to be given in return, this process, involving an apparent temporal sequence, is construed in legal contemplation as being "at one instant."[31] How should this be understood? It does not mean that the two sides are viewed as initiated in fact at the same time. Rather, it implies that the idea of temporal sequence is ultimately irrelevant. On what basis? If we may suppose that a cause is conceived as preceding its effect in time, the fact that promise and consideration are each identically the reason for the other means that each is simultaneously both cause and effect of the other. When, therefore, the law conceives the two sides to be at one instant, it is saying that, for the purpose of ascertaining the existence and meaning of contract formation, neither side—not even the initiating promise—can be conceived as happening in law without the other. Even though the promise is made before the consideration is promised or done in return, it must be possible to conceive of them as two irreducibly copresent and relationally defined sides of a single unified transaction. Any interaction that cannot be reasonably construed in these terms of simultaneity and copresence does not meet the requirement of consideration.[32]

Whereas the foregoing features of consideration delineate what we might think of as the form or structure of the relationship between the parties that the doctrine requires, the next feature has more to do with the sort of content or substance that consideration must have to fit with this form: to qualify as consideration, what is promised or done by the promisee must have value in the eye of the law and more particularly, in the traditional formulation, it must be either a legal benefit to the promisor or a legal detriment to the promisee. What do these notions of value, benefit, and detriment mean in this context?

As a first step, it should be emphasized that the definitions of value, benefit, and detriment must be worked out as part of a framework that reflects the prior requirements of independence and mutual inducement. For instance, benefit and detriment must refer to the content of a crystallized promise or act. Being the content of an expression of intention that falls short of either of these does not count as a legal benefit or detriment, even if the promisor requests it and it has market value. Benefit and detriment must also be something that moves from the promisee to the promisor in response to the promisor's request. Thus, forbearance by the promisee in reliance upon the promise, even if foreseeable, will not count as the detriment required by consideration unless requested by the promisor and done by the promisee in return for the promise. Stated otherwise, detriment and benefit are the material embodiment of, respectively, the consideration moving from the promisee and moving to the promisor. Understood in this way, detriment and benefit are correlatives and must therefore both obtain.

In addition to being specified consistently with these prior requirements, the conceptions of value, benefit, and detriment contribute a further dimension. They specify the substantive content of the promise or act that constitutes consideration: *what* is promised or done by the promisee. This must be something of value in the eye of the law in either of the following two ways:

the consideration can be analyzed as some interest or advantage that the promisee might otherwise have enjoyed or some burden that she might otherwise have avoided but that she, respectively, either gives up or assumes—this is consideration functioning as detriment; or the consideration is viewed as some interest or advantage that accrues to the promisor and that the promisor does not already enjoy—this is consideration as benefit.[33] In terms of substance, the detriment and benefit may consist in goods, services, incorporeal interests, the promisee's freedom of action, or more generally any interest or right in anything whatsoever that, in virtue of its particular qualities, can be wanted, used, or enjoyed by either party to the exclusion of the other. The key here is that the substance of the consideration must be something that, as the determinate concrete thing that it is, can be viewed as *usable or wanted* in the widest sense—including its use as a means for obtaining other things, as is the case with money. As long as the content promised or done meets this test, it does not matter what it is or whether it has a market value. Gaining or losing it need not make a party better or worse off financially or otherwise. Benefit and detriment do not refer to states of well-being but rather to having or not having something that can be wanted as just discussed.[34]

Now the fact that consideration must be a detriment to the promisee or a benefit to the promisor ensures that the content or substance of the promisee's consideration is, as such, irreducible to being merely an aspect, condition, or consequence of the first party's promise. For presumably the latter's promise, including its consequences, represents a benefit to the promisee and a detriment to the promisor—the exact contrary of what the doctrine requires. In this way, detriment and benefit fit with, and indeed fill out, the structural requirements that the consideration be independent of the promise and move from the promisee to the promisor, as explained above. They specify a content that fits with the consideration being something that is intrinsically linked with the promise as one side of an irreducibly and reciprocally two-sided relation between them, such that the promise is not complete unless joined with the consideration and vice versa. It requires a content that can fill in the basic form of *actus contra actum*.[35]

Several points of clarification are in order here. First, as with all other contractual elements, whether something is a legal detriment or benefit is assessed and determined on the basis of what reasonably appears from the parties' actual interaction. It is not decided in the abstract or imposed on the parties. Strictly speaking, there cannot be an "invented" consideration if by this is meant a consideration that does not reasonably appear through an analysis of the parties' interaction, where such interaction includes both express and implied aspects as well as underlying assumptions that reasonably may be imputed to the parties in the surrounding circumstances of their particular interaction.[36] "Nothing is consideration that is not [reasonably] regarded as such by both parties."[37] Further, the detriment or benefit must refer to something that it is physically and legally possible for the relevant party to do or to have, as the case may be. For example, if the promisee purports to give up a course of action that she could not possibly have chosen or that she was already under a legal duty not to do, it is not a legal detriment and no consideration. But as long as the promisee might physically and legally have chosen (because at liberty) to do it, a promise to refrain or actually to refrain from doing so would be sufficient.[38] Accordingly, even if the promisee could and would have in fact refrained in the same way without the other's promise, this need not disqualify her promising to do so or her actually doing so as consideration: it is still subject to her choice and therefore the other party's promise can function as a reason or inducement. Lastly, the interests that are supposed in specifying the requisite conception of benefit need not be self-regarding in contrast to altruistic. As long as the interests can reasonably appear to be interests *of* a party, that is sufficient. Even benefiting another is perfectly intelligible as something that I might want and so can count as an interest of my own.[39]

There is a final substantive feature of the doctrine of consideration. While the consideration must be a legal benefit or detriment and have value in the sense just discussed, its *comparative* value in relation to the promise for which it is undertaken or done is irrelevant in determining whether it is a sufficient consideration. Hence, early in the history of the doctrine, courts readily held that there could be so-called "nominal" considerations.[40] Logically, a nominal consideration is simply the smallest conceivable "something" without a determinate market price that, in virtue of its particular qualities, can be a benefit to the promisor or a detriment to the promisee.

But to be a genuine and not purely symbolic consideration, it must meet the general definition of benefit or detriment and in particular the requirement that the parties view the particular content of the consideration as something they need or want for their use and enjoyment in virtue of its particular qualities, not just as a means to produce an enforceable agreement. The law does not present a nominal consideration as a legal formality.[41] To the extent that in actual circumstances it becomes difficult for courts to distinguish between a substantive though nominal consideration and one that is purely symbolic, they are, rightly, less ready to accept the possibility of a nominal consideration, which they may instead reject as "sham" consideration.

It is important to clarify the reason why the doctrine of consideration is not concerned about the equivalence in values between the two sides. The doctrine's indifference to adequacy of consideration does not entail a rejection of adequacy or of equivalence for the purpose of ensuring contractual fairness.[42] Rather, the whole idea of any quantitative comparison between the two sides is simply foreign to the doctrine's specific role, which is to ensure that the promise and consideration have substantive contents that are qualitatively different from each other and therefore can constitute two distinct sides irreducible to a gratuitous promise. For this purpose, consideration's requirement of value refers to a conception of use value that centers on the fact that something is usable and can reasonably be wanted as a thing or service specified by its concrete qualities and features.

As I discuss more fully in Chapter 4, this is not the same as exchange value, which is comparative and purely quantitative in form and therefore presupposes that the items compared have been reduced to a single qualitative dimension—their common denominator—that makes possible a comparison in merely quantitative terms. Even in the sale of X for $100, the $100, as consideration, does not function as the price or exchange value for X but simply represents a distinct asset that happens to be $100, the use of which is as a general means of payment. For the purposes of consideration, the key is that the $100 is not the same kind of thing as X.[43] By contrast, a promise of $100 for $1, where both sides are just identical currency, is not a promise for consideration but an unenforceable gratuitous promise for $99.[44] It is true that the two sides are standardly said to be related as quid pro quo. By this is meant: something for something else. Quid pro quo refers to the mutual relation between the two qualitatively different sides or, in other words, to the relation between the two distinct things with their concretely distinct use values. It does not refer to exchange value or equivalence. The different contents of the promise and consideration must both count as having value in the eye of the law. But the way they do so is not as exchange value.

Given these features of consideration—and in particular the irrelevance of exchange value—the doctrine allows for transactions that range from full-blown exchanges involving substantive equivalence to what may be called "mixed" transactions in which the parties reasonably intend a gift or donative element.[45] The crucial point is that all of these can fully embody the two-sidedness required by the doctrine. There is one and the same analysis of an exchange transaction and of a transaction that does not seem to involve equivalence in any market or economic sense. Given the wide definition of legal detriment, which can include the promisee giving up something that need not be wanted by anyone except the promisor and even then need not confer a material benefit on the promisor, nonexchange transactions are on a par with exchanges. Thus consideration appears to single out a certain kind of bilateral relation rather than economic exchanges as such: it ensures just that there are two mutually related, qualitatively different sides each of which induces the other and cannot be analyzed except in relation with the other; each side calls for the identical and simultaneous participation of the other as the necessary condition of its own validity and efficacy. Indeed, it seems difficult to conceive of requirements that more evidently and naturally specify this kind of two-sided relation in the element of nonformal promises than those of consideration. If one wishes to designate the doctrine of consideration as a "bargain theory" of enforceability, as many writers do, then "bargain" should be taken only in the limited sense of referring to the doctrine's requirements of mutual inducement and quid pro quo. Anything more would distort the doctrine's fundamental nature.

This brings me to Charles Fried's contention in *Contract as Promise* that, at its very core, the doctrine of consideration is internally incoherent and self-contradictory.[46] By showing this, Fried aims to answer the apparent challenge posed by this requirement to his proposed promise principle. But in light of our discussion of the doctrine's main features, we are in a position to see that his argument misunderstands consideration and fails to demonstrate the alleged incoherence.

According to Fried, the matrix of this inconsistency is the conjunction of the following two propositions: first, enforceable promises are limited to those that are part of an exchange; but, second, the law is not at all concerned with the adequacy of consideration. Whereas, Fried writes, the second proposition appears to affirm the parties' freedom of contract by giving them the power to choose whichever terms they wish, the first is not neutral in this way but instead confines them to exchange transactions and so does not take self-determination as a sufficient ground of contractual obligation. Fried views consideration as an unjustified control device that undermines the very value it is supposed to regulate. Freedom of contract, he contends, requires the law to be neutral as between gratuitous promises and promises-for-consideration. In both instances, promisors want the very same thing, namely the satisfaction of realizing their purposes through promises, but nonrecognition of gratuitous promises interferes with their freedom to do so. By becoming fully freedom of promise, freedom of contract can be liberated from the arbitrary limit to exchanges only imposed by the doctrine of consideration.[47]

There is no such contradiction at the heart of the doctrine. It is not a matter of promises being limited to exchanges versus the freedom to decide one's promissory relations. The promise-for-consideration relation is not equivalent to an exchange, and the freedom to promise as one wishes is neither the ground nor the goal of the law of contractually enforceable promises. Rather, as we have seen, the doctrine requires that there be a reciprocal relation in which every element—including the objects or substances promised—unambiguously establishes a requisite two-sidedness. Thus, as long as the mutual promises are of (just) something of value for (just) something else of value, there are two sides at once irreducibly distinct and inherently interconnected. Establishing this two-sidedness is the doctrine's sole concern. Within this framework of bilaterality, parties can choose the contents of the promises as they wish: what and how much they promise are matters of indifference so long as the chosen contents can function within this two-sided framework.

By contrast, there is no such two-sidedness necessarily involved in a promisor satisfying his purposes through a promise or in a promisee placing her trust in the promisor's moral probity. It is not enough that the promise is made to or for another: it must also be made with the other's reciprocal act as a second but equally essential constituent element, without which the first does not count as the promise it is supposed to be. Contrary to Fried's contention, consideration teaches that the freedom of contract that parties have is not the freedom to promise per se but rather the freedom to make promises that can be part of this two-sided relation, leaving the decision as to what and how much each of the sides are to the parties' themselves. Consideration is not a control device that regulates (arbitrarily or not) some prior and more fundamental moral value or relation. Nor is its function to signal the seriousness of promissory intent or the giving of an assurance of performance—for then writing, which was rightly rejected as a form of or alternative to consideration—would also be sufficient.[48] The doctrine of consideration specifies and indeed directly constitutes a definite kind of relation that is qualitatively and unambiguously irreducible to that of a gratuitous promise, however seriously made or memorialized.

With this last point in mind, I would now like to take a further step in elucidating the special bilateral nature of the contractual relation that embodies this consideration requirement by comparing it directly with executed gifts. Whereas gratuitous promises are not enforceable, executed gifts are. We must try to show that our account of consideration is fully consistent with this settled contrast. The next section attempts to do this.

1.3. Consideration and Control

Our first question here is this: given the enforceability of executed gifts—and in the absence of any policy against gifts—how can the common law reasonably and consistently deny the enforceability of *promises* to give? Since this question is often presented—and reasonably so—as a challenge to consideration, we must see whether the preceding account of the doctrine is vulnerable to it. To this end, it may be helpful to start with a brief summary of the chief elements of a completed gift.

According to the traditional common law view, for there to be a (non-formal) transfer of property via gift, the donor must deliver the object of the gift with the intent to give the donee present ownership and the donee must accept the object as so given.⁴⁹ In the standard case, delivery consists in the donor completely surrendering physical possession and control of the thing by yielding it into the exclusive control of the donee or his agent.⁵⁰ Thus gift presupposes an externally manifested act with the requisite intent on the part of the donor that moves an object from the exclusive control of the donor into that of the donee. This transfer, however, can be complete and legally effective as a gift without the same active and knowing participation by the donee. Though the delivery requirement must involve an externally manifested act, it can be satisfied even though the donee is not aware that it has taken place, as long as the donor has done everything necessary to put the object out of her exclusive physical control and into the donee's exclusive domain, thereby enabling the donee, not the donor, unilaterally to exercise his will over it. In these circumstances of donee ignorance, acceptance will be presumed, subject to the donee's freedom to reject the gift (within a reasonable time) after becoming aware of it.⁵¹ While, in these circumstances, the donee need not do anything further to perfect the gift, possession cannot of course be forced upon him.

Why can't a donor's mere communicated intention to transfer present ownership by itself effectuate a gift? Why, in other words, is delivery deemed an essential constitutive element of a nonformalized completed gift?⁵² I suggest the following answer.

A gift transaction starts with the external fact that, as against the donee, the donor alone has present and rightful exclusive control over an object in virtue of her actual or possible *physical* possession of it. As long as this initial state of physical possession continues, the donor continues to act as owner and can rightfully exclude the donee. Ownership is transferred only if the donor unequivocally cancels her physical possession and control of the object by yielding it into the exclusive power or domain of the donee, such that the donee, but not the donor, can take physical possession of it at will. The problem, for which delivery provides a solution, is this: how can this canceling and transfer of ownership be *reasonably apparent* as between donor and donee, when possession is and remains physical and there is, we suppose, no prior agreement between them that could be reasonably viewed as effectuating a transfer by their assents alone? Without delivery, the donor's statement of decision, "I give you this," would not suffice. Her words may create moral expectations in the donee and justified disappointment if there is no follow-through, but whether or not the transfer of possession takes place is still up to her. According to this analysis, to be legally operative, the intent—or, better still, the decision—to give must be embodied in certain definite acts of the requisite kind: it is only an act involving a change in physical possession—that is, delivery—that can cancel *de praesenti* the donor's original exclusive control over the object and surrender it into the donee's.[53]

Now, in striking contrast with the operative act that constitutes a gift, contract formation can be wholly prior to and independent of physical delivery, which now figures as obligated performance. Whereas in gift, delivery (with the requisite intent and supposing presumed acceptance) is a constitutive element of the interaction that gives the donee a protected property interest vis-à-vis the donor, in contract, it is the agreement itself consisting of parties' mutual promises, and not performance, that produces the contractual effect of vesting in the promisee an entitlement to performance. For consideration to be a necessary condition of contractual enforceability, it must be the case that there have to be mutual promises, and not just a gratuitous promise, to produce this effect. In light of the discussion of executed gifts, what might make mutual promises, but not a gratuitous promise, necessary for this purpose, keeping in mind that both mutual and gratuitous promises share the same feature of being independent of physical delivery?

The clue to the answer lies in another important contrast, already alluded to, between executed gifts and contracts: unlike a gift, a contract is constituted by the fully two-sided, equally active, and reciprocal contributions of both parties. I will now argue that in any case of nonformal promising that is to be contractually effective prior to and independent of physical delivery, this two-sided structure is both necessary and sufficient to effectuate a transfer of control as between the parties and that this purely nonphysical transfer parallels, while being distinct from, the transfer of physical control via delivery that constitutes completed gifts. Another way of putting this is that such reciprocal two-sidedness is necessary if, as between the two parties, the first party is reasonably to be held to have given up and yielded rightful control over something into the exclusive control of the second, even though at the time the first retains factual or physical control over it. This also means that despite the fact that parties promise each other and thus commit to do something in the future, it must be possible to view their mutual assents unambiguously as neither future-oriented nor leaving anything to a promisor's future choice or doing.[54] Instead, mutual expressions count as present and complete acts that accomplish in the medium of representation and prior to performance a present transfer of rightful control as between the parties. On this view, both enforceable gifts and enforceable promises thus operate wholly *de praesenti*.

To elaborate—I have emphasized that the doctrine of consideration requires that there be two sides, each of which counts as distinct from yet intrinsically related to the other. No side is more basic or more significant than the other. Whatever can be said of one, can and must be said of the other. Now, because my promise is stipulated as made in return for your promise, and vice versa, neither even counts as a promise outside of this relation of promise for promise. I have placed my promise and whatever it contains beyond my control because I have specified it in terms of something that you must do from your side to make it a promise. And the same holds for your promise. Each side has engaged the participation of the other in the most complete way that is available to us independently of and prior to delivery. Because each of our promises is defined in and through its being related to and with the other, there cannot be any residual unilateral power in either party to exercise control over, or to make any further future decision with respect to, that promise. Abstracting from the basis for normatively significant future individual action, the transaction is properly construed as wholly in the present and complete as such.

This relation of act with act is further specified through the doctrine's substantive dimension. Thus, in the medium of our mutual promises, each side is represented as moving or giving over to the other something of value only insofar as the other does the same from his or her side. Each side's act of moving is itself the acceptance of what is moved to him or her by the other side. The acceptance is therefore represented as no less and no differently an act than the moving of the consideration. It is not reducible to a mere reaction to an already completed promissory act of the other, but is itself an act that completes the other side's act of moving the consideration and together with it forms their contractual relation. Since each side at the same time gives and takes something of value, both sides, when viewed as such, are absolutely identical and count as coequal active constituents of the two-sided relation. Even though this relation necessarily takes the form of an exchange, this is not, I have emphasized, in order to single out substantive exchange transactions. Rather, it is because in this way, and indeed only in this way, can the two sides unambiguously count as mutually related acts, not as two separate and complete unidirectional acts on each side followed by reactions of trust, gratitude, expectation, reliance, and the like on the other side. Finally, because the contents of the consideration must be something of value in the sense that it can be held, used, or enjoyed by a party to the exclusion of the other, the parties' acts of moving and accepting consideration represent each giving up exclusive control over something by yielding it to the other, who exercises present exclusive control over it. Thus, Jeffrey Gilbert, early eighteenth-century author of the unpublished work "On Contracts" and later Chief Baron of the Exchequer, perspicuously characterized contract as "the act of two or more persons concurring, the one in parting with, and the other in receiving some property right or benefit."[55] The contractual relation is this present transfer in the representational medium of the parties' mutual promises.

Given this characterization of the interaction as fully *de praesenti*, what role does the future orientation of promises play? In virtue of it, promising distinguishes the two moments of making and performing the promise, and with this distinction comes the possibility of viewing the parties' relation in terms that are wholly independent of and prior to physical possession, thereby grounding the contractually fundamental difference between the moments of enforceable agreement and delivery. There is a further role. On the one hand, because promises represent in law crystallized, unreserved decisions, they can reasonably be viewed as acts unambiguously distinct from mere exploratory expressions of intention or negotiations. On the other hand, by making a promise that something will be given or done, a first party can engage the other to respond to it and promise something in return, in this way enabling the parties themselves to bring about via their interaction the needed bilateral relation. This last point, we will see, is integral to the analysis of offer and acceptance.

The contrast with gratuitous promises seems clear. The only act that constitutes a gratuitous promise is that of the promisor. The promisee's contribution is, as discussed earlier, placing trust and forming expectations in response to that already complete act. Moreover, a relation of trust and respect is perfectly intelligible without supposing that the promisor, even in the medium of representation, has transferred to the promisee any sort of control over his decision to promise, his promise, or what he has promised. The promisor's decision to perform in the future is still solely within his own domain and power. That is why the promisor can be judged in moral terms in light of his constancy, conscientiousness, and probity of will alone. In all these respects, both an executed gift and contract formation differ from the gratuitous promise. Both executed gifts and mutual promises require that both sides contribute to effectuating a transfer of exclusive control with respect to something of value from one party to the other. They do so, however, in different ways.

Drawing together the different points just made, we may say that in the case of executed gifts, the two-sided nexus between the parties is accomplished first and foremost by delivery, which places the thing outside the donor's exclusive domain and into that of the donee. Upon delivery, the donee can be presumed to have accepted unless he indicates differently and the gift can be complete and irrevocable. It is sufficient if delivery has placed the thing under the donee's exclusive power to have and to use. The donee need not do anything specifically to exercise control over the thing as long as it is physically possible for him, but no longer possible for the donor, to do so. There is bilaterality here, but the donee's "act" of taking possession from the donor can amount to his simple acquiescence in the donor's putting the thing under his exclusive power and out of her own. This is both possible and sufficient precisely because the transfer is effectuated in the medium of physical possession and through a change in physical possession.

In the case of nonformal wholly promissory relations, to show that the promising constitutes a transfer of control rather than a relation of mere trust, it is essential that the promise be made for and with another promise (or act) so that both function as coequal constitutive acts that cannot operate or even be determined except reciprocally in relation with each other, and further that these mutually related promises embody in their purely represented nonphysical medium a transfer of things of value from out of the control of one side into that of the other through their united acts. In contrast to both an executed gift and a gratuitous promise, it must be possible to construe contract formation as itself constituted by a mutual relation between two such reciprocally active sides having this two-sided substantive content and so not reducible to a unidirectional promissory act followed by a reaction or response to it. This is precisely what the requirement of consideration necessarily and always assures.

Now it is a basic premise of contract law that the parties' rights, duties, and powers are conclusively established by their mutual promises at formation. In light of the above analysis, we may tentatively construe this as follows: on the one hand, at formation, mutual promises vest with each party rightful control over the consideration moved by the other in return for his or her own; on the other hand, by the terms of their promises, actual receipt, use, and enjoyment of the consideration is postponed until the time performance is due. Since contract formation is a moving (in the medium of representation) of something usable from the exclusive rightful control of one party to that of the other, it seems to involve a form of acquisition as between the parties. This may provisionally be characterized as contractual or "transactional" acquisition because it is specified by the contract terms, fully operative at contract formation, and binding as between the parties. On this view, contract formation is nothing other than such transactional acquisition, complete and final at the moment of agreement. Performance or delivery does not add to or in any way change the rightful acquisition that is definitively effectuated at formation as between the parties.

Within this framework, what is contractually acquired—the object of acquisition—is not another's promise or act as such, but rather the content or substance of the consideration taken as part of this relation between the parties and as contractually specified in the medium of representation consisting of their mutual promises. Here we must keep in mind that without this substantive content, there can be no benefit or detriment and so no consideration at all. Taken by themselves, the mutual promises (or alternatively the act-for-promise) are the medium and means in and through which the parties move this substance inter se, not the object that is moved and that constitutes the detriment or benefit. At the same time, neither are the substantive contents of the considerations ever taken by themselves, as if these, apart from the relation between the parties, can be the objects acquired. No, it is the considerations as part of the parties' mutual promises—the considerations *as* promised each for the other—that specify what each side acquires from the other at formation. If this is so, contract formation does seem on its face to involve a true transfer between the parties: what one party has and moves to the other is the very same thing—the substance of the consideration transactionally specified by the contract terms—that accrues to the latter. And similarly, the character of exclusive control on both sides is represented as the same: a purely rightful, nonphysical control by each that is valid and exclusive as between the two parties only.

How, it may be asked, is this view of contract formation as effectuating full and complete acquisition as between the parties consistent with the fact that, by a contract's terms, a promisee may not be entitled to take physical possession of the consideration until after formation? As just stated, the proposed approach sees contractual acquisition as being not only as between the parties but also as completely determined in and through their agreement. Accordingly, the rightful control over the promised consideration that is acquired at formation is fully specified by the contract's express and implied terms. Now clearly, without a right to have and enjoy physical or factual possession and use, this acquired control and the beneficial character of the consideration would be wholly illusory and without value. As part of the complete transactional determination of this acquired rightful control, the contract must therefore include a specification of the timing and modalities of the exercise of this right. The contract must specify either expressly or by necessary implication when and how the party acquiring control at formation can rightfully exercise it by taking possession or enjoying the promised consideration. The answer will vary from contract to contract. The agreed-upon moment for exercising physical possession and use can be anywhere on a timeline from contract formation itself (so there is no temporal gap between formation and performance) to a point after formation.[56]

Now standardly (but not always), a promisee is only able to obtain possession, use, or enjoyment in fact of the promised consideration by means of or through the promisor himself positively doing something that counts as delivery. The question is how should we understand such positive acts of delivery done by the promisor (supposing that they are not simply part of the actual consideration promised) if, as I stated above, performance or delivery does not add to or in any way change the rightful acquisition that is definitively effectuated at formation as between the parties? Provisionally, I would suggest the following analysis: strange as it may seem at first blush, the promisor's acts, even if factually positive, should be characterized from the standpoint of rights as part of or as facilitating the contractually determined manner in which *the promisee* is to exercise her right to take possession of the promised consideration. The whole juridical significance of the promisor's performance consists only in this. Thus, in effectuating delivery or performance, the promisor does not act independently in pursuit of his own purposes or confer upon the promisee something that is not already hers. This seems to be the only view of delivery that can be consistent with the idea that the parties' entitlements, including their right to take possession and to enjoy the promised considerations, can be completely and definitively established at formation.

If correct, this view of delivery and performance has a further implication that I should briefly mention here. From what has been said, a promisor's mere failure to deliver the promised consideration as contractually stipulated directly interferes with the promisee's right to obtain factual possession, use, or enjoyment of it. If so, although breach of contract may involve a sheer omission, it can nevertheless be viewed in juridical terms as a decision that injures the promisee's contractual entitlements. Though factually an omission, it can count juridically as misfeasance. This also means that even if the duty to perform is expressed in positive form—as we do in saying *pacta sunt servanda*—this should properly be viewed as based on a negative prohibition: do not injure or interfere with what comes under another's rights.

In this regard, it should also be noted that, on the proposed analysis, what a party acquires at formation is not the right to performance or the respect owed by the promisor. The latter are the normatively required *consequences* of the former. This is in keeping with the idea of liability for misfeasance, which, as understood here, constrains conduct only with regard to something that is already under another's rightful exclusive control. Thus in the case of contract also, the requirement of respect, though specified transactionally as part of formation, presupposes and refers to the promisee's transactional acquisition of the promised consideration as something that is represented as having already come under her exclusive rightful control vis-à-vis the promisor at formation. This is what a promisee acquires transactionally and therefore what the promisor respects by performing.

To conclude this discussion of the main features and character of the promise-for-consideration relation, I add some final remarks. On its face, the doctrine of consideration seems to challenge the basic premise of most promissory and intention-based theories of contract, which, as I noted in the Introduction, hold that contractual obligations are imposed on the basis of parties' deliberate undertakings to assume, by promising, those very obligations. According to this robust "power-conferring" view of contract, parties are subject to an obligation to perform because this is what they want and intend to effectuate.[57] However, to meet the requirement of consideration, the only thing that parties need to intend—or, more exactly, that they must reasonably appear to intend on the basis of their outward assents reasonably construed—is the promise-for-consideration itself and whatever this presupposes. Thus each must reasonably appear to promise something of value in return for a requested counterpromise by the other of something else of value. The only contractually relevant object of want is the other's consideration promised as part of this relation of quid pro quo. As the problematic status of a purely symbolic consideration illustrates, the fact that one or even both parties want or intend something for the purpose of producing a contractual effect is neither necessary nor sufficient for nonformal contract formation. Finally, if we keep in mind that all this is decided from the standpoint of the objective test, it is clear that what the promisor—or the promisee—actually wants or intends is not per se the operative factor.

On what reasonable and voluntary basis, then, are parties contractually held to promises supported by consideration, if it is not because this is what they intend by so promising? Briefly stated, the answer that seems to be emerging so far is that this is how the parties' interaction may be reasonably viewed from a juridical (contractual) standpoint.

To explain: First, because each side has chosen to do something that brings into play the other as a coequal participant with separate and independent interests, each has chosen to enter a relation with the other that is subject to interpersonal norms and standards. Both parties, as reasonable persons, must accept the fair and reasonable meaning of their interaction as a transaction between two. At the center, therefore, is the idea of the reasonable. Next, the law can coherently construe the fair and reasonable meaning of their interaction as involving a form of transactional rightful acquisition between the parties in the specific sense discussed. More specifically, the law views their interaction thus: through their voluntary mutual promises and prior to actual performance, the parties manifest to each other present fixed commitments signaling (and representing) the moving of something, which they treat as having use value, from the exclusive separate control of one into that of the other. All of these aspects are readily understandable by both parties and can be imputed to them as part of their reasonable intention without requiring that they must want or intend to produce contractual effects. As long as this construction of the parties' voluntary interaction is both juridically sound (being, for example, consistent with other principles of contract law and with private law more widely) as well as morally acceptable when judged from the standpoint of justice, each side can be reasonably and fairly held to it and to whatever it entails. That, at any rate, will be the argument that I develop. If correct, it would, I believe, also fully answer the Fuller and Perdue challenge.

From the preceding account, the promise-for-consideration relation seems to specify in the most basic and general terms conceivable a kind of promissory relation that can reasonably be construed as transactional acquisition. The relation is completely two-sided and reciprocal and consists of mutually related promises representing the transfer (movement) of something of value from the exclusive rightful control of one party into that of the other. Indeed, a doctrinally more natural or simpler way of specifying the requisite promissory relation seems difficult to imagine. I have tried to show that it is consistent with both the enforceability of gifts and the nonenforceability of promises to give. It is also worth noting that this promissory relation (with its categorical exclusion of gratuitous promises) seems to fit with the earlier discussed conception of perfect (as distinguished from imperfect) promises that the natural law writers thought to be the necessary basis of contract.[58] In the chapters that follow, I will try to explain how the other main contract doctrines and principles—including those of contractual fairness—fill out essential dimensions of this basic framework, in this way bringing out more fully and clearly the sense in which contract formation can be analyzed as transactional acquisition.

Before moving on to examine these other contract doctrines and principles, however, I wish to complete the account of consideration by addressing two much debated topics: reliance-based liability and the idea of privity. In the preceding discussion, I tried to elucidate a conception of consideration that takes it to be a necessary, and not just a sufficient, condition for nonformal contract formation. However, many see the availability of reliance-based liability for breach of promise as proof that consideration is at most but one possible ground of contractual enforcement. It is important, therefore, that I explain reliance in a way that not only makes sense of it as distinct in its own terms but that also shows why it does not challenge the role of consideration as a necessary condition of contractual liability. I have also characterized contract as transactional acquisition, being a form of acquisition that is between the two contracting parties. This would seem clearly to imply or to presuppose a notion of privity. And certainly some idea of privity, even if limited, is widely accepted in contract law. Yet, if we look to recent scholarly discussions, it is not sufficiently clear what privity means or whether any such idea can be rationally defended at all. In addition to the meaning and role of privity in contract law, there is also the difficult issue of explaining the fact that in a variety of situations, courts hold that contracts can seemingly have third-party effects. How can this be consistent with a plausible notion of privity? I turn now to these and related questions.

1.4. The Contrast with Reliance

It is settled law that there can be liability for breach of a promise that has induced detrimental reliance on the part of the promisee even though the reliance, because neither requested by the promisor nor incurred by the promisee as quid pro quo, cannot count as consideration.[59] Although there may still be some disagreement, particularly among legal scholars, as to certain aspects of the reliance analysis, all seem to agree on this one point that the reliance need not satisfy the requirements for consideration. This immediately raises the questions: what is the basis of liability here, and how does it relate to the consideration-based contractual liability discussed so far? Since both kinds of liability involve promises and refer to party intent, one answer is that reliance-based liability shows that underlying both is the more general idea of voluntary undertaking and that reliance and consideration simply represent different ways of establishing the requisite intent to contract or to consent to binding relations.[60] On this view, the fundamental category is a general idea of promissory liability, with reliance and consideration providing alternative factors that justify enforcement. The notion that there may be a qualitatively distinct and basic category "contractual relation" for which consideration is indispensable is rejected.[61] Additionally, because offhand it seems difficult to construe reliance that does not function as part of a relation involving request and quid pro quo as specifying anything like a form of acquisition or transfer between the parties, this view would also seem to challenge the centrality of the transactional conception in understanding contract—unless, of course, consideration and reliance establish two qualitatively different kinds of relations. In keeping with the approach taken so far, I should try therefore to outline a plausible conception of reliance-based liability that is found in leading decisions and endorsed by a number of scholars and determine whether it presupposes a kind of relation and a type of protected interest that are genuinely distinct from, but at the same time not conflicting with, the parallel features of the doctrine of consideration.

I start, then, with the question of what reliance on a promise must entail if it is to ground a distinct basis of liability that does not contradict the requirement of consideration. To avoid such inconsistency, reliance must involve something more than the mere fact that the promisee trusts in the promisor's word and expects or hopes for the latter's performance, even planning some profitable course of action that depends on the promisor following through. If reliance-based liability were to protect the promisee's interest in these expectations and plans, it would be enforcing gratuitous promises—in direct opposition to the requirement of consideration. For reliance-based liability to be both distinct from and consistent with consideration, the conception of reliance must incorporate something more. But what?

Looking to the law itself, there is in fact widespread consensus across common law jurisdictions and among most legal scholars that reliance must consist in the promisee doing or omitting to do something that changes her prereliance position to her detriment.[62] Examples of such change of position are where, in reliance on the promise, the promisee does not pursue some alternative beneficial opportunity that is actually available to her or where she makes an expenditure that she would not otherwise have done. For there to be change of position, it must also be the case that in fact the promisee could and would have gone the other way by availing herself of the opportunity or refraining from the expenditure, but for her reliance on the promisor. Finally, such change of position must involve the risk of loss to the promisee if the promisor reneges. This reliance loss does not consist, however, in the promisee not receiving what the other has promised her. She must suffer loss in the form of costs (not necessarily pecuniary) incurred as a result of her change of position—for example, the alternative opportunity that she gave up in reliance is now no longer available, or only at a greater cost; or the expenditure that she made in reliance cannot be fully recouped and will be wasted at least to some extent if the promisor reneges. If detrimental reliance is understood in this way, the promisee's loss is determined in light of her prereliance position, not per se the content or value of (or her expectation in) what she was promised.[63]

But the fact that a party relies in this way is still not enough to make the other liable for her loss. For what if her decision to rely is something that the other neither encouraged nor even reasonably expected? If, wholly at her own initiative, a party chooses to rely, it should also be at her own risk. Something more is required here to make the second party responsible for the consequences of what is prima facie the first party's own uncoerced, freely chosen act. Since we are trying to carve out a basis of liability in relation to promises that is distinct from and yet consistent with consideration, the needed additional factor cannot be that the second party must have requested her reliance as quid pro quo for his promise. What remains, then, to justify imposing responsibility for the promisee's decision to rely?

Once again drawing on the law, the second party must, in effect, have invited or induced her to rely, without going so far as to request the reliance as quid pro quo.[64] Whether a party has invited reliance is determined objectively by how his words and acts reasonably appear to the one who relies.[65] Where a party reasonably appears to have made a serious, unequivocal, and firm commitment or assurance—a clear instance would be where the party has evidently promised—this will ordinarily be a reasonable basis on which to infer the element of invitation. Conversely, a mere representation of present intention, absent an explicit invitation to rely, will usually not suffice. Although an unequivocal promise will normally invite reliance, the critical factor is not the existence of an express promise per se, but rather words and acts that provide a credible basis for the addressee to infer an invitation to rely.[66] And since, absent clear and express words, it cannot be presumed that such invitations are open-ended and contemplate just any form of reliance, the party relying must be able to show that her reliance was of a kind that was within the scope of what reasonably appears to have been intended by the other.

Where a promisee (or representee) changes position to her detriment on the basis and within the scope of the promisor's invitation to rely, her reliance is justified and reasonable as against the latter. Emphatically, the conception of justified reliance is transactional and holds simply as a matter of fairness and reasonableness between the parties in light of their interaction—in sharp contrast with, say, an economic analysis that views reliance as a possible welfare-enhancing rational "investment" choice to be weighed in the balance of costs and benefits. Having induced the other to rely, the defendant cannot now reasonably treat the decision or loss resulting from it as at the other's risk. In effect, the one relying can say to the defendant: it was because of your invitation that I relied; this is the consequence of your act, and you are responsible for loss that you could reasonably have avoided.[67]

In keeping with this transactional analysis, the promisee has as against the promisor a protected interest in the fair value of her *prereliance* baseline position. This holds as between the parties even though the promisee, precisely because she relied, never actually had and lost the benefit of this alternative situation. It is sufficient that she could and would have been in that position but for the other's invitation to rely. Having invited her reliance, the other party cannot reasonably deny that this prereliance position counts *between them* as her protected interest or that her reliance losses count as a subtraction from what she was entitled to have and enjoy intact. Its legal status as a valid and effective entitlement is specific to the reliance-inducing interaction between the parties.

It also follows from this that the promisor's wrong here consists not in per se breaching his promise but instead in failing to take reasonable steps to avoid worsening the promisee's condition with respect to her protected interest in her prereliance situation.[68] Such steps ordinarily require the promisor to take reasonable measures to enable the promisee to regain her prereliance position without loss. Thus, as long as the promisor warns the promisee of his change of mind in time to enable her "to neutralize the consequences of persuasion and reliance," the duty of care is discharged.[69] Moreover, where the promisee relies but sustains no loss because she ends up in a position that is no worse or even better compared with her prereliance situation, the failure to perform is not actionable at all. In contrast with an action for breach of contract, but like one for negligence, there is no wrong without material loss and consequently nominal damages are not, and should not be, available.

If we suppose that the nature of the wrong sets the goal and measure of the remedy, what measure of recovery might be inherently appropriate for reliance-based liability?[70] The fair value of the prereliance position should in principle set the upper limit of damages. Depending upon the particular facts—for example, where it may be difficult to ascertain the value of the plaintiff's loss with respect to her prereliance position or where that loss comprises nonpecuniary aspects—adequate compensation may require damages equal to the value of the promise or even in specie remedies. In such circumstances, the law may presume against the wrongdoer (subject, of course, to his proving otherwise) that the value of the prereliance benefit was not less than that of the promise itself. But this does not alter the fundamental objective and measure of the remedial response. Justice does not require that damages place the plaintiff in the position that she would have been in had the defendant performed as promised. Indeed, awarding expectation damages or recovery in specie where these are disproportionate to the cognizable reliance losses suffered by the plaintiff would be "wholly inequitable and unjust" to the promisor.[71] This again is in sharp contrast with how these remedies are standardly characterized in actions for breach of contractually enforceable promises for consideration.

Here, then, is a definite conception of reliance that can stand on its own—distinct and not conflicting with the requirement or rationale of consideration. Liability for reliance presupposes a different protected interest embedded in a different relation than the protected interest that vests solely through the promise-for-consideration relation. There is an important point here concerning the normative significance of promises in private law. In contract, a promise is just one side of a bilateral relation in such a way that the promise has obligatory force and thus counts as a contractual promise only when joined by the consideration moved from the promisee in return for it.[72] The consideration is not the effect of the promise but instead completes it and thereby constitutes it as a promise. By contrast, in its role as an element in an action for induced detrimental reliance, the promise is complete as a promise when made by the promisor. Promisee trust and reliance are the invited *consequences* of the promise. Both contractual liability and reliance-based liability involve promises. But they do so differently because promises are specified in terms of qualitatively different kinds of relation.[73]

How should reliance-based liability be classified? The natural category would seem to be as a form of negligence.[74] This is not only because the defendant's duty here is also one of freestanding reasonable care to avoid causing the plaintiff foreseeable loss resulting from his conduct, but even more importantly because, as with negligence but not contract, the plaintiff's protected interest is with respect to a position that she could and would have occupied *independently* of her interaction with the defendant. For this is presupposed by any action in tort. Like negligence, reliance-based liability does not give the plaintiff a new entitlement. It is not a mode of acquisition.

The one feature that seems to align reliance with contract is the fact that the relation of invited reliance and dependence is established through the parties' mutually voluntary—though not reciprocal—interaction. But what role does this voluntary interaction play? I have argued that it sets the factual and normative conditions necessary for the defendant to be in a position to affect something that counts as the plaintiff's protected interest and to be responsible for exercising reasonable care to avoid injuring that interest. More specifically, in light of their interaction, the defendant cannot reasonably deny that, as against him, the plaintiff has a protected interest in the prereliance baseline or that she is worse off compared to it, even though she never "had" it in fact, having turned it down for something else in reliance on his invitation. It ensures that the plaintiff's claim is one for misfeasance, not nonfeasance. But this does not make her protected interest one that is conferred by the defendant via their mutually voluntary interaction. The difference with contract remains basic. The promise-for-consideration relation remains a necessary basis of the kind of liability that takes the promised performance itself as the plaintiff's legally protected interest and that therefore justifies the giving of expectation remedies (whether damages or specific performance) that seek to put her in the same position as she would have been in had the defendant performed as promised. This kind of liability has invariably been called contractual, and I shall do the same.

I wish to emphasize a final point. As noted earlier, it is sometimes suggested that reliance and consideration are but different ways in which promisors can manifest an intention to be contractually bound.[75] And the use of a legal formality is understood as still another mode of doing so. This view supposes that underlying the different prerequisites for liability lies a single idea of contractual intention and that these are merely different ways in which the law discerns evidence of its existence. We can now see why the proposed analysis of reliance rejects this view. Each of these bases of liability, I have argued, entails a definite and distinct kind of legal relation and these relations are constituted by different sorts of interactions between the parties. The relation of invited reliance and that of promise-for-consideration are intrinsically different kinds of transactions. Moreover, intention—like duty or liability—is not something that exists in the air. On the contrary, it is anchored in and specified through the different kinds of juridically relevant interactions between the parties. The relations of invited detrimental reliance and that of promise-for-consideration embody definite requirements of the reasonable, albeit in different ways. It is on the basis of these different requirements of the reasonable that parties are fairly held to the different kinds of transactional obligations. In this way, there is no need to try to explain—what seems clearly impossible within a liberal view—how parties can be legitimately coercively obliged just in virtue of an intention to be such. In short, it is not only unnecessary but also misleading to take these relations as evidence of a unitary underlying intention to contract or to form legal relations. I conclude that the principle of reliance and the doctrine of consideration are genuinely separate and distinct. Reliance-based liability does not challenge the integrity or the role of consideration and should not be theorized as a substitute for it.[76]

1.5. Contract and Third-Party Effects

A difficult but important topic that has been neglected by contract theory is the analysis of third-party effects resulting from contracts. Granted, there is theoretical discussion of the question of third-party beneficiary claims and the meaning of contractual privity. However, that is just one part of the picture. There are also third-party effects that are often labeled "proprietary" because they are distinct from, even though dependent upon, the contracting parties' correlative performance rights and duties that hold only as between them. Examples include the assignment of contractual rights and the recognition of third-party obligations enforced under the rubric of the common law tort of inducement or via injunctions in equity. Whereas the analysis of privity and third-party beneficiary claims turns on the in personam foundation of contract, these proprietary effects raise the question of whether contracts might have an in rem dimension as well. Through discussion of these matters, I hope to clarify further the meaning and scope of my central contention that contract is a form of transactional acquisition. I begin with privity.

1.5.1. Third-Party Beneficiary Claims and the Meaning of Contractual Privity

Historically, the question of third-party beneficiary rights has been one of the most controverted in the common law of contract. However, the difficulty and contentiousness of this issue are not peculiar to the common law alone. It challenged the Roman and civil law systems as well.[77] The reason is as simple as it is utterly fundamental.

In both the common law and civil law systems, contract is conceived as an intrinsically bilateral relation constituted by the parties' mutually related acts of assent, which are viewed as a manifestation of party intent. On the one hand, it is in virtue of being participants in the formation of the contract that individuals are juridically related to each other. But what if the parties intend that a third person, who has not done anything to establish their relation, is to receive the benefit in fact of a party's performance? There seems to be a tension here between the prerequisites of contract formation, by which people acquire contractual rights and duties on the basis of their reciprocal acts, and the contracting parties' intention, which is to confer the benefit of performance on a third party who, we suppose, has not participated in any such interaction. This also engages the fundamental issue of the role of intention in generating contractual or other rights. So we ask: what rights, if any, can the third party have just in virtue of contract formation?

At this point in the history of contract law, the leading jurisdictions—both common law and civil law—answer this last question, whether on the basis of judge-made law, legislation, or codal provisions, in ways that, taken broadly, are quite similar. Thus contracts for the benefit of third persons are definitely valid and enforceable, and third parties have some kind of legal standing to demand enforcement of contract terms in at least a number of fairly well-defined situations. What is striking, however, is that, for the most part, these answers do not make sufficiently clear such very basic matters as the particular juridical nature of third-party claims or how these claims fit with general premises of contract law. No system, for example, treats third-party claims as exactly identical in force and effect with the contractual in personam claims of the contracting parties. Yet there is uncertainty and disagreement over the exact legal character of the former and how they relate to, depend upon, or differ from the latter. Moreover, while all modern legal systems do, and indeed must, presuppose some idea of privity of contract—for otherwise the very issue of third-party claims would not arise in the first place and there could be no difference at all between the claims of contracting parties and those of third parties—there remains considerable controversy over privity's meaning and role, not to speak of its rationale.

I want to focus on these neglected or controverted but clearly fundamental aspects of the issue.[78] Building on the preceding account of the doctrine of consideration, I would like to see whether within this framework there is place for an idea of contractual privity and, if so, what that idea is. In particular, I want to see how third-party claims must be understood if they are to be coherent with this idea and with the basic framework set by the promise-for-consideration relation. As part of this discussion, it will also be important to ascertain how the proposed analysis fits with at least the relatively more settled and basic aspects of the law on this topic.

As already noted, the key feature that third-party contracts share is that performance is reasonably intended to confer the benefit in fact of the promised performance on a third party rather than on the promisee. Now in English contract law, at least since the end of the seventeenth century, the historically dominant factor shaping the legal analysis of third-party contracts has been the requirement of consideration.[79]

On the one hand, in contrast to legal systems such as the Roman or the French, which make self-regarding interest on the part of the contracting parties a prerequisite of enforceability and which must therefore immediately view the third-party contract as problematic, the common law, with its early acceptance of detriment as valid consideration, had no such difficulty.[80] The fact that the promisee is not materially enriched by the consideration does not preclude an agreement from satisfying this requirement. Third-party contracts and self-interested mutually enriching exchanges have exactly the same validity and status as fully enforceable agreements.

On the other hand, this very doctrine of consideration that enabled third-party contracts to be valid and binding as between the contracting parties soon became the central obstacle to third-party claims.[81] As noted above, starting from the late seventeenth century, the law "was, on the whole, moving towards the doctrine that was to be then and thereafter taken as settled," namely that only one who, as promisee, has provided consideration can have contractual claims in her own right under the agreement.[82] Notice that this combines in one person the fact of being a promisee and that of providing consideration, and it is this person—and *only* this person—who can have a direct contractual right to the other party's performance.[83] These two parties are in privity of contract. This forms the backbone of the traditional doctrine of contractual privity. In supposing this, the law seems to take the parties as having rights and duties as a result of their participation in the process of moving rightful control over the considerations from one to the other at contract formation. There is thus an undivided unity between the constitutive acts and contractual effects at contract formation.[84] Contract rights and duties reflect a definite form of interaction between two parties.

Some commentators have argued that there is no reason why one person should not be able to make an effective promise to a second person (who is therefore a promisee) for a consideration received from a third.[85] Others contend that once there is a promise supported by consideration, the basic requirement for enforceability is met and the issue of who can enforce it is a distinct and separate matter: it may be the promisee or a third person depending on circumstances.[86] Both these suggestions are at odds with the meaning and role of consideration.

Unless promise and consideration are mutually joined as each given for the other, neither can count as anything more than a gratuitous promise or act. Moreover, the notion that the promise-for-consideration interaction does not eo ipso specify those with rights or duties with respect to the promised performances decouples contractual effects from the acts that constitute the relation itself. This obscures the important point that parties have contractual rights (and duties) in virtue of their mutual assents, and therefore not only as a result of what they do in relation to each other but also, I have suggested, as part of an interaction that can be construed as involving transactional acquisition as between them.

Contractual rights and duties, I have said, are the juridical reflex of this interaction. A gratuitous promise—no matter what its content—cannot have these effects precisely because it does not involve this interaction of *actus contra actum*. The fact that parties may expressly stipulate—and therefore presumably intend—that a third party shall receive the promised consideration only goes to the content of the performance that the promisor moves to the promisee as a matter of rights and thus *owes the promisee* from formation on. Unless it is embedded in the promise-for-consideration relation, intent is contractually irrelevant. And once embedded, intent accomplishes, neither more nor less, what the promise-for-consideration relation effectuates: the mutual movement of considerations as between the contracting parties. The same point applies to the contractual significance and effects of "acceptance" or "ratification" (without detrimental reliance) by a third party who, we are supposing, is not part of an interaction establishing the promise-for-consideration relation. Acceptance can be contractually relevant only as part of that relation. Indeed, since the third party who "accepts" is not even a promisee—the promise is not made to her—it is not even clear why it should be viewed as the acceptance of a gratuitous promise.[87] I will return shortly to the question of whether third-party acquiescence can have effects that would be consistent with this analysis of privity.

The rational meaning of privity can now be stated. The core idea is that only a promisee from whom consideration moves in the required way is owed, in her own right, by the promisor the latter's own promised performance. Privity expresses a definite direct relation involving correlative rights and duties between promisor and promisee. The idea that the plaintiff must have a claim that is in her own right owed to her by the defendant is presupposed throughout private law as an essential and foundational general premise of liability.[88] Privity of contract, I suggest, is a particular manifestation of this general requirement. Where liability is with respect to a transaction that is voluntary on both sides and is established by the parties' mutual assents (promises) prior to actual performance, this essential nexus between the parties is ensured by the promise-for-consideration relation. Indeed, my argument has been that this connection is unambiguously established and ensured in this way. I should add that it is because the law anchors contractual rights and duties in the promise-for-consideration relation and vests them with the very persons who through this interaction bring themselves into this relation that the transactional conception that I have proposed can be a plausible immanent understanding of contract formation.

When, in the leading case of *Tweddle v. Atkinson,* Justice Crompton famously states that "it would be a monstrous proposition to say that a person was a party to the contract for the purpose of suing upon it for his own advantage, and not a party to it for the purpose of being sued," this should be understood as follows: contractual rights and duties—being strictly correlative—are both established within this transactional framework of the promise-for-consideration relation, and whatever is predicated of one must be predicated of the other.[89] Together they constitute the in personam dimension of rights that are solely as between the parties. If, therefore, a third party can properly claim a direct right to performance, she must eo ipso also be potentially subject to owing a duty to perform. In other words, if a third party can validly assert a claim, she must be taken to be fully part of this in personam dimension with its duties as well as rights no differently than are the promisor and promisee—which makes clear the absurdity of her purported enforcement right. The core idea of contractual privity is thus that a third party is not part of this in personam dimension and even more fundamentally that there *can be* such an in personam dimension that constitutes (in the sense of both establishing and expressing) the contractual relation itself.

In my view, this conclusion determines the necessary character of any claims that a third party can acquire with respect to the promised performance.[90] Any such claims must be consistent with the fact that the right to performance— that is, rightful exclusive control with respect to performance—has already fully vested with the contractual promisee alone as part of her direct relation with the promisor. Consistently with this, a third party can acquire for herself a genuine right with respect to that promised performance only derivatively via a further transfer from the promisee (e.g., by an assignment) but never as part of the mutual assents of the two contracting parties that effectuate contract formation. It is in light of this fundamental point that, I suggest, we should understand the recognition of third-party beneficiary rights in, for example, American contract law and elsewhere. Although the conception of privity precludes recognizing direct contractual rights in third parties for the reason just discussed, it does not rule out the possibility, for which Melvin Eisenberg has carefully and comprehensively argued, that it may be reasonable at the remedial stage to give the third party a power (as distinguished from a genuine right claim) to enforce the performance as owed to the promisee, if, but only if, this is necessary to effectuate the promisee's performance interest as contractually intended.[91] Let me elaborate.

If we suppose that for there to be *injuria* in private law there must be an interference with another's rights and, more particularly, with his or her rightful holdings, contract breach is a legal injury and wrong to the promisee only, not the third party. It is crucial to recognize this difference in the legal significance of the breach's impact. Consistent with the misfeasance framework, the breach does not do any injustice per se to the third party. The fact that the latter does not receive the subject matter of the performance owed the promisee—whether an asset or service—is therefore nonactionable *damnum sine injuria*. Even though the third party qualifies as an intended beneficiary in the sense that her receipt in fact of this material benefit is an intended and integral part of the execution of the performance, this performance is still owed to and under the rightful control of the promisee only.[92] At the same time, insofar as it is the third party and not the promisee who is the intended recipient in fact of the consideration's material benefit, the promisor's contractual undertaking toward the promisee is best construed as a promise to provide the promisee with a *service* consisting of the conferral of this benefit in fact on the third party. However, supposing that, as part of this service, the promisee is not to receive directly or even indirectly a material benefit or asset, ordinary expectations damages may not be adequate, thereby justifying specific performance (or its monetized equivalent) as the appropriate remedial response in a suit by the promisee for breach of the contract.[93]

But even if specific performance can be an appropriate remedy for breach of these contracts, there remains a further problem. Neither the promisee nor her representative may have a pecuniary or other interest in pursuing a claim even where the promisee has already performed her side, not because she or her representative has decided to waive the right to the performance, but simply because it will expose them to costs and risks that may not be offset even in the case of a successful suit. It is striking that in earlier English decisions that empowered third-party enforcement, the typical situation was precisely such a half-executed agreement where the promisee had died or faced the risk of uncompensated losses if she sued to enforce it.[94] In short, there can be situations where the promisee's right will not be enforced despite the fact that she has not waived her rights, resulting in the promisor being unjustly enriched at the promisee's expense. These are situations that can render the consideration promised her illusory, with the consequence that the promisee has given something for nothing. The risk of this happening seems particularly acute where the third party is a donee-beneficiary and, though arguably less so, is still present where she is a creditor-beneficiary.[95] According the third-party beneficiary standing in these circumstances to enforce what is owed the promisee may be necessary to give remedial efficacy to the transaction.

These considerations, I would suggest, provide a limited and appropriate basis for recognizing a third party's standing to enforce the obligation owed the promisee. It must be emphasized that this rationale is remedial in that it does not suppose that the third party is accorded standing to sue in order to vindicate a direct contractual right of her own; to the contrary, it is the promisee alone who has such a right. The third party's "right" of enforcement is thus a legally recognized power that is absolutely subordinate to and framed by the promisee's direct right.[96] It cannot qualify, compromise, or limit that right. As such, the third party's standing to sue can only be accorded when the promisee clearly cannot or will not enforce it in circumstances or for reasons that cannot fairly be held to manifest the promisee's decision to abandon or waive her rights.[97] It does not clarify the nature of the third party's position to say that this power arises from formation onward. It arises if and when it is instrumentally necessary for the remedial efficacy of the transaction between promisor and promisee. And since the third party's claim embodies the substance of what the promisee could have obtained against the promisor via specific performance or its equivalent, it cannot, by definition, increase the burden on the promisor beyond that for which the latter is already responsible under the agreement.

That the third party's standing to sue, even in those systems that explicitly recognize it as a separate right from that of the promisee, cannot have the character of a genuine right directly owed her by the promisor is suggested by the settled view that, subject to certain limits discussed below, it can be varied or even extinguished by the contracting parties without the third party's consent. The fact that the one who allegedly owes a right can unilaterally change it is inconsistent with the immunity that clothes every independent right.

At the same time, in those jurisdictions that recognize third-party claims, the powers of the contracting parties to modify or extinguish terms that confer a benefit on the third party may be effective vis-à-vis the latter only if exercised before she has acted by accepting, assenting to, relying on, or suing on the contract provision. Does this undermine the contracting parties' autonomy as the direct rights holders? It depends on what is deemed to count as such third-party acts and how the limit on contracting parties' freedom is justified. Where the contracting parties have purported to exercise their power to rescind or modify their agreement, the third party's standing to sue or obtain redress with respect to the original terms cannot be in order to effectuate remedial efficacy for the promisee's performance right. As a matter of basic principle, the fact that a third party "accepts," "assents to," or sues on the agreement should limit the contracting parties' control over their terms only if, and insofar as, such acceptance or assent involves the third party's actual or presumed detrimental reliance (involving change of position) and if this limit is reasonably necessary to prevent her reliance from materializing in loss.[98] Whether reliance is justified should be determined by whether the third party could reasonably view herself as invited by the contracting parties to rely on the parties' contractual intention to confer the stated benefit even though contracting parties presumptively have the power to waive, modify, or extinguish the contractual provision. Clearly, this matter must be ascertained in the context of the different sorts and circumstances of these third-party beneficiary contracts. Note that, in light of this analysis, the third party still does not have a direct right to the benefit of the promised performance even where she has reasonably relied on receiving it and is given the intended benefit of the performance by way of redress.[99] Her only genuine right, corresponding to a duty owed directly to her, is not to be injured in her circumstances of reliance, with a claim to compensatory redress for reliance losses that she may sustain. Thus in no instance does her standing to sue or to obtain redress even for her own losses suppose a direct right to the performance.[100] The latter would not be an exception to the idea of privity or the doctrine of consideration but rather their abolition.[101]

1.5.2. Third-Party "Proprietary" Effects in Relation to Contracts

In the previous section, I presented what I take to be the rational core conception of privity that must animate contract law, specifying the kind of relation that it is. This relation consists of the original rights and duties of performance that necessarily arise between parties through their participation in the promise-for-consideration interaction: it represents the pure in personam relation of rights that characterizes every contract. It has the immediate negative consequence that whatever rights or obligations third parties may have cannot consist in such direct in personam original rights to and duties of performance. There is no privity of contract between them and the contracting parties.

At the same time, across common law jurisdictions, there are a variety of situations in which the law unquestionably recognizes that, in relation to contracts, third parties can have rights or may be subject to duties in their own right. On the one hand, we shall see, these rights and duties do not conflict with privity of contract because they are irreducibly distinct from the direct in personam contractual rights and duties between the contracting parties. On the other hand, such third-party rights and duties always arise in relation to, and thus presuppose even if notionally, a prior subsisting contractual relation between the original parties. Indeed, such third-party rights and duties can arise from the moment a contractual relation is formed and thus prior to and independent of its physical execution. These rights and duties are often characterized as "proprietary," if only because indeterminately anyone in general can stand in the requisite juridical relation to the subject matter of the contract while not being a party to it. In this section, I wish to discuss in a preliminary way certain instances of such third-party effects: the assignment of contractual rights, tortious interference with contractual rights, and what are sometimes called equitable (contractually based) servitudes on chattels. Later, in Chapter 10, I will draw out some further theoretical implications of this discussion for our understanding of the important distinction between in rem and in personam rights.

A natural place to begin is the assignment of contractual rights. First in equity and then in law, common law systems have come to recognize the validity of assignments of contractual rights.[102] Despite this, the analysis of assignment remains challenging, both at the doctrinal level and in terms of explaining its underlying normative conception.[103] In addition, the law of contractual assignments addresses many issues and sub-issues, often quite technical and complex in nature, that inevitably arise in this context. Acknowledging this real difficulty and complexity, I will nevertheless try to clarify the most basic underlying juridical and normative ideas that seem to be implicit in the settled doctrinal analysis. For this purpose, I shall take the simplest and central case of a promisee ("assignor") assigning to a third party ("assignee") her contractually enforceable right to the promisor's ("obligor's") performance. Let me begin with some settled and uncontroversial basic propositions.[104]

An assignment has been defined as "the immediate transfer [by way of sale or gift] of an existing proprietary right . . . from assignor to assignee," where this right is "[a]nything that in the eye of the law can be regarded as an existing subject of ownership, whether it be a chose in possession or a chose in action."[105] The assignment of a contract *always* involves the immediate transfer of a chose in action. I will shortly discuss the juridical nature of a chose in action. For now, what should be emphasized is that a chose in action must be a present and existing asset and that a contractually enforceable right to another's *future* performance counts in legal contemplation as such a *present* asset. Therefore, contractual rights can be assigned. At the same time, *only* rights, not duties, can be assigned: it is not legally possible to assign the burden of a contract, that is, the contractual obligation to perform. A party cannot unilaterally change, displace, or in any way transfer her duty and liability to someone else.[106] There is a further important point: not all contractual rights are always assignable. Thus, a particular contractual right may not be assignable because, in light of the nature and terms of the contract including the subject matter of the right, the contractual right is deemed "personal" in the sense that the particular identity of the promisee (potential assignor) is material to the contractual relationship with the obligor.[107] But, it should also be noted, the fact that a given contractual right cannot be assigned does *not* preclude it from qualifying as a present chose in action and therefore as an existing proprietary right. To the contrary, every still executory contract right counts as such whether or not it can be assigned.[108] In this way, a right's being a chose in action is its more fundamental and intrinsic characteristic, with transferability being a further possible, but not always applicable, feature.

Now an assignment makes the assignee the *owner* of the assigned chose in action, and it is as owner that the assignee takes legal action against the obligor with respect to the latter's nonperformance.[109] It is crucial to keep in mind that, in taking legal action, the assignee claims protection, not of a contractual right, but of a proprietary interest vis-à-vis the obligor. At the same time, not only does this proprietary interest presuppose the prior existence of a validly formed contract between obligor and assignor—otherwise there would be no right or chose in action to be transferred at all—but assignment necessarily presupposes the continuing and subsisting existence of the contractual relation between obligor and assignor, which always remains wholly distinct both from the noncontractual proprietary relation between assignee and obligor and from the relation between assignor and assignee. This, we will see, has important legal consequences. Thus the assignee only takes his interest subject to the claims under the contract that would have been good against the assignor. As well, the assignee's claims against the obligor may be affected by interactions between the original contracting parties.[110]

Greg Tolhurst, in his careful and thorough account of the modern law of contractual assignment, argues persuasively that the above propositions, and indeed the complex and intricate case law dealing with contractual assignment, can be best explained on a model of assignment as a transfer of rights.[111] For there to be a transfer from assignor to assignee, the assignor must give up something that originates with her, by vesting it in the assignee. What the assignee gains thereby, the assignor must lose. Once transferred, the thing no longer remains with the assignor. According to Tolhurst, the fundamental principle that governs this transfer relation between assignor and assignee, as with any transfer conception, is the *nemo dat* rule: no one can give what she does not have.[112] An essential premise of this rule as applied to contractual assignment is that what an assignor has acquired as promisee via contract formation must be what the assignor transfers to the assignee via assignment. Now this immediately raises the following simple but utterly fundamental question: how can there be this identity of subject matter in the required way if the transfer of the assignor's right as contractual promisee is not to place the assignee in contractual privity with the obligor?

By way of answer, Tolhurst distinguishes between the assignor's contractual in personam right to the obligor's performance and her *title in* or *ownership of* that right. The assignor's in personam right to performance as owed to her (and to her alone) by the obligor is the subject of what she owns and has title in, *and it is this title*, with the assignor's right to performance as its content, that the assignor transfers to the assignee via assignment.[113] I think that Tolhurst's distinction is illuminating and that the juridical ideas that it presupposes can be further elucidated. This is what I shall now try to do.

I begin with the characterization of the object of the transfer as a present chose in action. How should this be understood? Over the centuries, there have been many efforts to define and distinguish this category of legal object. Depending on the background stage of legal development, the characterizations have often differed.[114] Clearly, the fact that the thing is "in action" rather than "in possession" has been historically pivotal. Drawing on more recent judicial formulations, we may say that a promisee's contractually enforceable (in personam) right to the promisor's performance counts as a chose in action insofar as both the promisee and potentially others can deal with this right as a presently valuable incorporeal asset that is legally protected as such. What the promisee owns or has title to is her right as a chose in action. This involves looking at a contracting party's rights from a different angle.

I have emphasized thus far the inherently relational nature of consideration and of the entitlements acquired at contract formation. Contractual rights are specified transactionally as just one side of a relation, with the corresponding duties on the other side. Rights and duties express terms of mutual respect owed by one party with regard to the other's rightful control over some consideration that the first has promised and thereby moved to the second in return for the same moving in the opposite direction, from the second to the first. At the same time, contract formation presupposes that something has moved from one party to the other and has thereby vested with the other as a legally present, certain, and protected asset that the latter (not the first party) has a right to possess and use in accordance with the terms of their agreement. (I should add that in connection with this asset a party has not only contractual rights but also the contractually relevant immunities and powers. For the sake of simplicity and brevity, I refer only to the rights component.)[115] In this way, the movement constituting the promise-for-consideration relation crystallizes at formation (in the medium of representation) as some definite valuable incorporeal asset—something of value in the eye of the law—and this asset, with the right to have and enjoy it in accordance with the terms of the contract, is the promised consideration and the benefit of the bargain that vest with each party to whom it has been moved. Moreover, there can be nothing in its being such an asset that per se precludes the promisee from treating it as having value vis-à-vis others as well. A contrary conclusion would arbitrarily limit the consideration's represented value and benefit. A complete account of contractual entitlements must therefore include this aspect as well. This it does when the promisee's right to performance is viewed as a chose in action. In principle, then, any and every contractual right can be so characterized.

But the fact that every contractual right must be a chose in action does not entail that every such right must also be alienable by assignment. Although a contractual right may be the promisee's chose in action, it does not follow that she can deal with it in any and every way that she could, say, with chattels that she owns outright. Whereas the chose in action is constituted on the basis of *both* contracting parties' voluntary assents, assignment is done and is valid *without* the consent of the contracting party who is under the contractual duty to perform. Assignment results in the latter owing a new duty to the assignee with regard to the performance promised the assignor. The upshot of assignment is that the promised performance is now to be done for the benefit of and, as it is sometimes put, *to* the assignee, not the assignor. For example, supposing that the obligor has proper notice of the assignment, the obligor's promise to deliver a bale of goods to the assignor is now "discharged" by delivery to the assignee or his agent instead of to the assignor. The question is whether this represents a material change in the nature, incidents, or effects of the obligor's promise and performance duty. For if it does, not only would any such change be unfair to the obligor because it is imposed on him without his consent. It would also have no basis in the very transaction that must be presupposed as giving rise to the chose in action in the first place, thereby violating the *nemo dat* rule that governs the transfer by giving the assignee something different from what the assignor initially had.

It follows that even though every contractual right counts as a chose in action in the sense explained above, a particular contractual right may not be assignable if this would be inconsistent with the underlying contractual relation between the two contracting parties. Apart from statutory or public policy limitations, a particular contractual right, as noted above, may not be assignable given the "personal" nature of the contract including its express and implied terms, the kinds of responsibilities and roles the contracting parties are supposed to have in performing, the material surrounding circumstances, and so on—in other words, in light of the contract as a whole reasonably construed in accordance with the objective test. Also to be considered would be the impact of assignment on the assignor's own discharge of her performance duties and incidental powers that are still owed to the obligor even though she can no longer enforce the assigned performance right. If the right is deemed personal, this means that the chose as it would be in the hands of the assignee would not be the same in its core performance meaning as the chose in the hands of the assignor. Therefore it cannot be assigned. But even if a particular contractual right is deemed personal and so nonassignable in the circumstances, the right to performance would still be a chose in action—a valuable incorporeal asset—in the promisee's hands. As I will discuss shortly, its still being such entails that it can be protected against interference by others who are not in privity with the promisee.

Apart from this question of the assignability of a given contractual right, a contract right that is deemed to be assignable will nevertheless be qualified and legally vulnerable in the exact same way that the assignor's contract right against the obligor would have been had it not been assigned in the first place.[116] If, for example, the assignor's right is subject to being set aside for unconscionability or if post-assignment events would justify discharging the parties for frustration or impossibility, this would also determine what the assignee can claim against the obligor even after the latter has received notice of the assignment. The same would hold for good faith modifications of the obligor's duty that are agreed to by the assignor and obligor (e.g., changes that can fairly and equitably be demanded by the obligor if he is to complete performance).[117] All this in entailed by the governing *nemo dat* rule. It also goes to the fundamental point, noted earlier, that the contractual transaction between assignor and obligor is the original basis and remains the necessary continuing substratum of the assignor's chose in action. Thus, whatever this contractual relation entails with regard to the assignor's contractual right to performance as this would be reasonably construed and enforced apart from the fact of assignment is what determines the content of the assignee's own chose in action.[118] Inasmuch as assignment can be analyzed as a transfer of the very same incorporeal thing from assignor to assignee without changing the nature or scope of the contractual rights and duties, the obligor cannot reasonably object to the assignor's assertion and exercise of the ownership that is conceptually possible with respect to her right to performance.

At the same time, by alienating her own ownership in the contractual right to the assignee, the assignor can no longer exercise rightful control in her own behalf and for her own contractual interests with respect to the performance as promised her by the obligor. Supposing that the assignor has validly transferred to the assignee the whole bundle of the rights, immunities, and powers that make up her performance interest as a chose in action, the assignor ceases ipso facto to have any beneficial contract interest of her own in the subsisting contract. In legal contemplation, she no longer acts or makes choices for her own contractual interests and purposes. Insofar as the assignor does anything that can directly or indirectly affect the nature or effects of the promised performance, the only question is whether it is consistent with preserving the performance's fair value as fixed by the contract's meaning, terms, and conditions at the time implicitly or expressly specified by the assignment. Her actions must not derogate from what she has transferred to the assignee. It is the assignee alone who may now claim this fair value as his own and who can deal with the chose in action in light of his self-chosen interests and purposes. If, after the assignment, the assignor nevertheless accepts performance by the obligor inconsistently with the terms of the assignment, the assignor's wrong against the assignee consists in a violation of and interference with the assignee's exclusive ownership interest acquired by virtue of the assignment.

How should the *obligor's* duty with respect to the assignee's chose in action be characterized? I have emphasized that there is no privity of contract between these parties. Their relation is not a novation of the original contract between the obligor and assignor. While the assignee's ownership has for its content the assignor's right to performance, it is not the latter's in personam contractual right. It is a genuinely distinct relation between assignee and obligor obtaining in virtue of the assignee's ownership interest. In essence, the possibility of assignment shows that the consideration moved (in medium of representation) from one contracting party to another vests with the latter not only something of value for her but also something that she can deal with as having value for others. That the consideration can have such value for others is, I suggested above, a potentiality inherent in its very conception and is therefore an intrinsic and necessary feature of every contract.

This intrinsic potentiality and whatever it entails, every obligor (as promisor) must be taken to recognize. The obligor must therefore recognize that the very same chose can potentially end up in the hands of someone other than the promisee as a result of a valid transfer (which supposes that the right is not shown to be personal). In this respect, as against the obligor, the assignee can have a present ownership interest in the chose from the moment of the transfer from the assignor. At the same time, knowledge that such a transfer has *actually* taken place may certainly be relevant in determining whether the obligor has properly discharged his duty to the assignee.[119] For example, the obligor who performs to the assignor rather than to the assignee does so at his peril only after receiving notice. Note, however, that what is required is notice to the obligor, not the obligor's assent to the assignment. But once the obligor has such notice, he must discharge his contractually specified performance duty for and to the assignee, not the assignor.

I have suggested that assignment represents one way in which a contracting party can deal with her contractual right as a chose in action, that is, the crystallization of her contractually embedded in personam right to performance as a distinct incorporeal proprietary asset. The contractual right can count as a chose in action because the right to performance is, from contract formation on, something that has present value not only for the promisee but potentially for others as well. As owner of a chose in action, the promisee is owner of this value. I have emphasized that whether a given chose in action can be assigned is a distinct matter from the conceptually prior and fundamental point that the contract right counts as such a chose that is itself the object of ownership rights, powers, and immunities. Assignment is a way of exercising these ownership rights via voluntary transaction with others in general. If the proposed analysis is sound, we should expect the law to recognize this ownership interest in *nonvoluntary* transactions as well, protecting it against injury by others who have no contractual relation with the promisee but who can be held to have reasonable notice of her interest. This protection should be available whether or not the particular contract right is in fact assignable. I will now discuss two situations that, I believe, confirm that this is indeed so. The first is the tort of inducing breach of contract. The second is a line of decisions involving what American commentators and courts have called "equitable servitudes on chattels" or what their English counterparts refer to as the "principle in *De Mattos v. Gibson*."[120]

Originally recognized in 1853 in the famous English personal service case of *Lumley v. Gye*, the tort of inducing breach of contract has since become firmly established across all common law jurisdictions, applying to contracts in general.[121] Nevertheless, even now, there continues to be some disagreement over the precise nature of its required elements and of how it fits within the larger domain of liability in private law.[122] With this in mind, the following features of the tort should be noted.

First, the tort involves a genuine three-party setting: there must be a valid existing contractual obligation between two that is breached by one of them ("the breaching party") as a result of the "inducement" or "procurement" by a third person, the defendant tortfeasor, who is a stranger to their contract. Second, the wrong consists in the defendant injuring the innocent party's (the plaintiff's) performance right, but in such a way that does not suppose that the defendant himself has violated any contractual duty to perform owed directly to the plaintiff. There is no privity of contract between plaintiff and defendant. Third, traditionally the tort has required "malice" on the part of the defendant, but over time it has become—and continues to be—unclear what exactly malice means in this context. This must be determined. To frame the discussion, I wish to note two main concerns that go to the very basis of this liability. Whereas the first concern focuses on the breaching contracting party's own responsibility, the second has to do with that of the third-party defendant.

The first concern is this: given that the breaching party decides to breach for reasons that seem good to her, why should the defendant be liable for having influenced that decision, whether by providing opinions, information, or even opportunity for her to come to that decision?[123] Even if the defendant participates in the process of the promisor coming to this decision, it is still her decision, and it is a wrong only because she has violated her contractually owed duty of performance, irrespective of her reasons for doing so. If we say that the defendant is also a wrongdoer simply because he has participated in this way, we must be supposing that he is subject to the same duty or at least to a joint duty to perform. This, however, would be inconsistent with the fact that he is not in privity with the plaintiff.

The second concern is that the mere fact that the defendant third party, for example, offers alternative employment or other opportunities that the promisor takes up instead of performing as promised cannot per se be a violation of the plaintiff's rights. Otherwise this would be incompatible with the liberties involved in free and fair competition. One is not prohibited from accepting the services of another who has responded to one's general offer of employment on market terms, even if one happens to know that the other is already contractually engaged to perform for another.[124] Even though this may affect the contractual rights as between the plaintiff and the breaching party, why should this matter as between the plaintiff and a third party who does this?

Together, the above concerns point to a single challenge: to show that the defendant's conduct injures a protected interest that the plaintiff has relative to the defendant (as required by misfeasance)—one that is distinct from, even while it presupposes, the plaintiff's contractual performance right as against the breaching party (consistent with privity). To explain how this is possible, it would seem that the third feature of the tort, namely, the requirement of malice, must play a key role. But, as already noted, there is disagreement over what malice entails. Is there a way to understand the malice requirement that makes sense of the tort's main features without making it vulnerable to the concerns noted above?

I would like to suggest that the requirement of malice can be understood in relation to two different scenarios in which the tort of inducement applies. In both scenarios, of course, the plaintiff is deprived of her promised performance as a result of the other contracting party's breach, which itself has been procured or induced by the defendant. However, in one scenario the defendant tortfeasor receives the very performance that the breaching party owed the plaintiff, whereas in the second the defendant does not.[125] *Lumley v. Gye* is itself a case that involves the first scenario, and, in my view, it is the type of situation where the meaning of malice and the basis for tort liability seem clearest and most cogent. I will therefore focus first and primarily upon it.

In this first scenario, the defendant's malice is found, not in some morally wicked intent, but just in the fact that he interacts directly with the breaching party for the purpose of specifically seeking to procure and obtain for himself a performance that, as the defendant knows, is already contractually owed to the plaintiff and must therefore be transferred to himself via breach of that contract.[126] In virtue of these features of knowledge and specific procurement, this interaction cannot be reasonably viewed as the defendant merely accepting the services from one who has responded to a general offer of employment or some other transaction on market terms. These features also explain how the defendant's action interferes with a protected interest that is juridically distinct from the plaintiff's right to performance as against the breaching party. By reason of the defendant's conduct in knowingly procuring and obtaining for himself the very content of the plaintiff's performance right, the defendant cannot be heard to deny that, as between him and the plaintiff, the substance of the plaintiff's performance right is something of value: more exactly, the defendant can be held implicitly to have treated the plaintiff's contractual right as the valuable asset or chose in action that it is but that he nevertheless misappropriated at will, without the plaintiff's consent.[127] The defendant has wrongly interfered with the plaintiff's chose in action by having the breaching party perform to and for him. This is a distinct wrong from that of the breaching party's own violation of the plaintiff's in personam right to performance—a wrong that only a contracting party can do.[128]

It is worth noting that in these cases, courts standardly refer to the contractual right that the defendant misappropriates as a "quasi-proprietary" interest.[129] The label "quasi-property" signals the existence of a transactionally specified proprietary asset—a chose in action—the content of which may be a contractual right to performance or some other valuable activity.[130] Note also that anyone in general can bring himself or herself into this legal relation as defendant with the plaintiff. This fits with the idea that the plaintiff has a present ownership in performance that is clothed with an immunity against *indefinite* others, making her interest one that in this respect is in rem in scope and import.[131]

What about the second scenario in which the defendant induces breach but neither intends to receive nor in fact does receive the performance that he knows is owed to the plaintiff?[132] The sort of analysis needed to explain how the defendant commits a distinct wrong that injures the plaintiff's performance right as a valuable chose in action is not as straightforward here. While not free from difficulties, I would suggest that to find malice, the defendant must have procured the breach for the very purpose of depriving the plaintiff of the promised performance.[133] This intent to injure must be the *only* reasonable explanation for the existence and manner of the inducement. In so doing, the defendant may reasonably be held to have implicitly recognized and targeted the performance as the valuable asset—the chose in action—that it is. Where, by contrast, the defendant induces breach in the pursuit of his own independent legitimate interests, this would negative the existence of malice and there could be no liability even though he counseled breach with resulting loss to the plaintiff.[134] Note that here again, as in the previous scenario, malice need not consist in a morally wicked intent.

Once the tort is understood in this way, we see that the two main concerns noted above need not apply. The defendant's wrong is not in contributing to the withholding of the promised performance as such—this concerns only the in personam responsibility of the other contracting party—but in impairing the fair value of the plaintiff's title or ownership in that right to performance or, in other words, the value of her right as a chose in action. That the breaching promisor's decision is his own responsibility and voluntary decision in relation to his duty is irrelevant to the analysis of this separate wrong. The breach must take place if the defendant is to affect the plaintiff's chose in action. But the fact that the breach is the factual conduit of the defendant affecting the plaintiff's chose does not prevent his wrong from being distinct from and irreducible to the wrong of the other party's breach.[135] These involve two different sets of relations, each with its corresponding distinct protected interests. Moreover, the tortfeasor's wrong involves the knowing and specific misappropriation or destruction of the very thing that the plaintiff has already secured as a matter of rights in the most complete and final way short of having actual physical possession or use via actual performance. Therefore, a misappropriation or sheer destruction cannot be justified on the basis of any reasonable conception of background free and fair competition. There must come a point where competing parties can actually acquire and secure the subject matter of free competition, and here, as between plaintiff and third-party defendant, that point has surely been reached.

In sum, the tort of inducement singles out for liability a particular way of injuring the plaintiff's ownership rights, powers, or immunities with respect to her contract, and this cannot be done except via the promisor's decision to breach. Paralleling the obligor-assignee relation in the analysis of assignment, the defendant and the plaintiff are not joined in contractual privity and the plaintiff's protected interest vis-à-vis the defendant exists prior to and independently of the defendant's interference. This same basic pattern of analysis involving third-party injury to the plaintiff's title in her contractual performance as distinct from her in personam right against the other contracting party also seems to explain the more controversial but arguably still valid line of English and American decisions associated with the frequently discussed English case of *De Mattos v. Gibson*—a most interesting but puzzling case indeed.[136]

The facts in *De Mattos* are as follows. One Curry owned a ship and chartered it to De Mattos, the plaintiff, for carriage of the latter's coal from the Tyne to Suez. Subsequently, Curry mortgaged the ship to Gibson, the defendant, with notice of the charter. En route, the ship had to interrupt the voyage for repairs, but Curry not only was unable to finance the repairs but had already defaulted on his mortgage repayments to Gibson. In these circumstances, Gibson ordered and paid for the necessary repairs to make the vessel seaworthy, but instead of allowing it to continue on its voyage to Suez as required by the agreement between the plaintiff and Curry, the defendant ordered the ship to be returned to Newcastle, where he planned to exercise his right of sale under the mortgage. Even though Gibson's actions were a facially valid exercise of his legal powers as mortgagee of Curry's ship, the question was whether Gibson himself, despite being a stranger to the charter agreement between the plaintiff and Curry, should be restrained by an injunction from removing the vessel to Newcastle or otherwise interrupting the voyage to Suez. In the Court of Appeal (Chancery), Lord Justice Knight Bruce granted an interlocutory injunction against Gibson to this effect, stating the applicable principle in the following general terms:

> Reason and justice seem to prescribe that, at least as a general rule, where a man, by gift or purchase, acquired property from another, with knowledge of a previous contract, lawfully and for valuable consideration made by him with a third person, to use and employ the property for a particular purpose in a specified manner, the acquirer shall not, to the material damage of the third person, in opposition to the contract and inconsistently with it, use and employ the property in a manner not allowable to the giver or seller.[137]

More specifically, Lord Justice Knight Bruce held that having taken the mortgage with express notice of the existing charter-party, Gibson could not have any higher or better title than Curry, being as much bound as Curry for every purpose of liability (at least to an injunction) with respect to diverting the vessel from the agreed voyage or interrupting it.[138] Even accepting, as Lord Justice Knight Bruce did, that, as between plaintiff and Curry, the latter remained the full and complete owner of the vessel and that all that the plaintiff had as against him was just a contractual right to have a specified use of the ship, his Lordship asked: "But if that is so, why is a Court of Equity, therefore not to act? Why should it not prevent the commission or continuance of a breach of such contract, when its subject being valuable ... the original owner and possessor or a person claiming under him, with notice and standing in his own right, having the physical control of the chattel, is diverting it from the agreed object, that object being of importance to the other?"[139] Lord Justice Knight Bruce answered that this power to restrain the defendant Gibson from doing this did exist and ordered accordingly.

On appeal, Lord Chelmsford concluded that the injunction against Gibson should not be issued.[140] While the Lord Chancellor, it seems, did not dispute Knight Bruce's general principle stated above, he emphasized that the defendant's only obligation vis-à-vis De Mattos was *not* to do something with the vessel that *actively* interfered with Curry's contractual obligation to make the needed repairs and to complete the voyage to Suez. But where, as here, there was effectively no prospect of actual performance by Curry (who was nevertheless in breach of contract) and seeing that Gibson himself incurred uncompensated expenses to repair the vessel and to make it seaworthy (which he was under no obligation to do), "it would be most unjust to restrain Gibson from availing himself of any rights which his possession of the vessel and his title as mortgagee have enabled him to exercise."[141]

What is the juridical basis, if any, of the *De Mattos* principle? I would like to see whether we can make sense of it in basic intuitive terms that continue the kind of analysis developed in the prior discussions of assignment and tortious interference with contract. What must be explained is how the defendant, who was not in privity with the plaintiff but who had notice of the plaintiff's contract, might possibly wrong the plaintiff by injuring the latter's contractually based right to use the ship in which the defendant had rights as mortgagee and possessor. The following analysis draws on the judgments at both levels.[142]

In my view, a necessary basis of the defendant's action being a wrong is that the defendant directly injures the plaintiff's performance right as a present valuable chose in action. Even though not a party to the contract, the defendant has notice of the contract right and cannot fairly deny its being valuable, seeing that the plaintiff's right is to use the very ship that the defendant himself, as mortgagee and possessor, treats as usable and valuable. Because he exercises possessory control over the very thing that is specifically the subject matter of the plaintiff's contractual right, the defendant is in a position to interfere with the plaintiff's right, even though he does nothing to procure or even to cause the other contracting party's breach.[143] While a defendant is not under a positive duty toward the plaintiff to do anything with or to the property, he must not stand in the way of the owner discharging his contractual duty to perform.[144]

However, this cannot be the whole analysis. The existence of the contract does not preclude the owner from mortgaging the vessel and cannot make illusory the defendant's rights as mortgagee and possessor of the boat. The defendant still retains his powers and rights as mortgagee. This must be given due weight. Thus the defendant cannot wrong the plaintiff simply by taking measures reasonably necessary to preserve and protect the fair value of his own rights as mortgagee, even if as a consequence, this results in the plaintiff suffering material loss. Paralleling the analysis suggested earlier for assignment, this is a kind of vulnerability to which the plaintiff's right is inherently subject ab initio in virtue of its being a right with respect to a property that could be mortgaged without violating the terms of their contract.

In *De Mattos,* Curry, the original owner of the ship and in breach of the contract with the plaintiff, was unwilling and unable to do the repairs needed to enable the ship to continue its voyage as contractually required. In the face of Curry's complete default and even though under no obligation himself to do so, the defendant advanced his own money to make the necessary repairs and directed the vessel to a different port in order to exercise his power of sale as mortgagee. In this situation of enhanced present risk of loss created by the owner's default, the defendant's actions were a reasonable response to preserve the fair value of his rights as mortgagee. As Lord Chelmsford concluded, it would be most unjust to restrain the defendant from doing so. The fact that the plaintiff's chose was vulnerable to this kind of impairment was the consequence, not of any wrong by the defendant, but rather of the owner's failure to meet his responsibilities as mortgagor. It was a vulnerability inherent in the underlying condition of his right. On this analysis, a different result might have been reached if instead Curry had been fully willing and able to repair the vessel with his own funds within a reasonable time but was prevented from doing so by the defendant exercising his power of sale or sending the ship in a different direction.[145] This would not be within the risks of such inherent vulnerability and would count simply as an injury to the plaintiff's chose.

Gathering together the preceding discussion of these different instances of third-party "proprietary" effects recognized in both law and equity, there seems to be a single underlying pattern of analysis. The paradigmatic instance is assignment understood as a transfer from assignor to assignee of the former's title or property in her contractual right—in other words as a chose in action. As a direct result of this transfer, the assignor must not do anything that derogates from her transfer to the assignee. Moreover, as a further effect of the transfer and even though without the consent of the obligor, the latter comes under a new negative duty owed directly to the assignee not to diminish or to impair this very same chose, the ownership of which is now vested in the assignee. This relation between obligor and assignee is not one of privity of contract, and it is distinct from (although presupposing) the original and still subsisting contractual relation between obligor and assignor. I have emphasized that the object of the transfer and of the new relation of rights between obligor and assignee is the assignor's contractual right as a chose in action: not the contractual right as part of the in personam relation of contract formation between obligor and assignor (promisee) but this right now crystallized as a valuable asset with respect to which the latter has exclusive powers and immunities in relation to others in general. Every content of an existing contractual right can potentially function in this distinct role. The promisee alone may rightfully decide what to do with her title, including whether to alienate it via a voluntary transaction (such as by assignment); others in general must not interfere with, misappropriate, or injure it, as they do, for example, when an obligor does not perform to the assignee.

This same analysis seems to underpin the imposition of third-party effects in the different kinds of situations covered by the tort of inducement and the principle in *De Mattos*.[146] Third-party defendants must not interfere with the plaintiff's chose by inducing breach or otherwise standing in the way of contractual performance. We have seen that as part of this analysis, the third-party defendant must, at least implicitly, specifically recognize and treat the promisee's in personam performance interest as a valuable asset over which the promisee has present exclusive control—thereby orienting his action to the promisee's interest as the chose in action that it is. Note, however, that the promisee's protected interest is constituted as a chose in action on the basis of her contract with the other contracting party, prior to and independent from interaction with the third-party defendant and irrespective of his viewing it as such. The defendant must have notice, not to constitute the promisee's interest as a valid chose in action, but rather to ensure that he is not taken unfairly by surprise when his action is viewed as impacting her performance interest as such a chose.[147]

This way of viewing the nature and protection of the plaintiff's interest is fully consistent with, because genuinely distinct from, contractual privity. Although such a chose in action conceptually presupposes contract formation and therefore the existence of an in personam right, it does not represent an extension of this in personam dimension. Nor is the protection of this interest merely a further remedial response to a violation of in personam rights of the original contractual relation. If the only duty owed is that as between the contracting parties, remedying the violation of the duty by imposing liability on a third party (even if factually connected to the breach) would be directly in tension with the limits of privity and its organizing framework of rights-protection. There is no such tension if we view the third party's action as a distinct wrong that impairs the plaintiff's title or ownership interest in the performance right owed her by the promisor. A third party's obligation is one of noninterference with the promisor's performance duty that forms the content of the plaintiff's chose in action.

It is important to note that, in the various examples discussed, a crucial feature of the plaintiff's title vis-à-vis third parties is that this title is in a right to performance that vests with her at formation and prior to actual performance. The plaintiff need not yet physically possess or receive in fact the promised performance. The source of the plaintiff's ownership right seems to be the inherent potentiality of the contractual right to be an object of ownership powers and immunities as a chose in action in relation to (nonspecified) others. Because this ownership right is always a right with respect to the right to performance, it never figures as an immediate property right over the physical thing that will be received on delivery. It is not a right in rem in that sense. The subject matter of the contractual right is the consideration as promised by one party to the other. This is also the content of the right-holder's chose in action and therefore of what she owns without physical possession in and through contract formation alone. Prima facie, this seems to be consistent with viewing contract formation as a form of transactional acquisition.

There is a final point that I wish to mention. These instances of so-called proprietary effects of contractual obligation seem to challenge the received understanding of in personam and in rem claims. We should not simply assume, as it is standardly done, that these categories correspond to the difference between contract and property or even that they represent two utterly separate kinds of juridical relations. A contractual right, prior to and independently of delivery, can have, it seems, both kinds of juridical effects, even if the "in rem" effects in contract are framed and specified differently from how they are in the law of possession and property. As just mentioned, a key difference would seem to be that with contract, the in rem and in personam dimensions are specified transactionally. I will return to these and related questions in Chapter 10.

Chapter 2

Offer and Acceptance, the Objective Test, and Contractual Intent

In contracts casebooks and treatises, the treatment of offer and acceptance is typically, and quite appropriately, detailed, intricate, and fact-oriented. For the purposes of the following discussion, however, I want to consider only those aspects that are most fundamental from a theoretical standpoint. Now it is standardly supposed that to be contractually operative or even relevant, the requisite assents for offer and acceptance must also satisfy the requirements of consideration.[1] In this way, the core principles of contract formation are thought to work fully in tandem. Our first and most basic theoretical task should therefore be to explain the distinctive contribution of the doctrine of offer and acceptance as one part of contract law and to see how it and consideration fit together.

We have seen that the doctrine of consideration requires a completely two-sided promissory relation—the promise-for-consideration relation—in which each side reciprocally and mutually moves something of value to the other. But the doctrine presents this relation simply as a result, without specifying the process through which it is brought about. In this chapter, I will suggest that the distinct doctrinal contribution of offer and acceptance is precisely to fill this gap by determining the kind of dynamic *temporal process* of party interaction that is needed to produce and to enshrine the promise-for-consideration relation. As part of this explanation, I address several related questions of theoretical importance. Beginning with a brief overview of the main features of offer and acceptance, I will try to show how and why this principle is needed to supplement consideration and, through this, to explain the necessity and the underlying unity of its central features (Section 2.1). Throughout the discussions so far, I have referred to the objective test as the relevant standpoint for determining the existence and content of the contractual relation. Clearly, we must try to explain its meaning, role, and rationale. I shall do this here (Section 2.2). Finally, I present the conception of voluntariness that seems to underpin the doctrines of formation, and I assess whether, as some commentators and courts contend, a further distinct principle of intention to create legal relations is needed to supplement them (Section 2.3).

Throughout, my aim will be to clarify how the requirement of offer and acceptance, like that of consideration, specifies a definite kind of relation that is purely promissory but that at the same time, being fully and intrinsically bilateral, is distinct from the structure and normativity of the gratuitous promise. It is often said, for example, that acceptance is needed in addition to offer in order to ensure that promises are not imposed on us. This negative nonimposition rationale may be true enough but it applies equally to gratuitous promises and so does not fully capture the specific nature and role of offer and acceptance. The key, in my view, is to see offer and acceptance as the dynamic genesis of the promise-for-consideration relation and therefore as an interaction positively constituting a kind of promissory relation that is robustly bilateral, in the sense of being made not just for or to a promisee but also with her coequal active participation. By accepting, the promisee does not merely signal to the promisor to go ahead but contributes her own act that joins with that of the promisor.

2.1. The Elements, Role, and Unity of Offer and Acceptance

First I present a brief overview of the settled features of offer and acceptance. According to the doctrine of offer and acceptance, contract formation requires voluntary, external, and mutually related manifestations of assent by the parties to the very same terms.[2] Negatively put, the parties' inner thoughts, wishes, or actual intentions, even if they happen to be the same for both, are not in themselves operative factors in effectuating contract formation. Rather, to be contractually effectual or even relevant, party intent on either side must be presented as a decision that can be reasonably recognized as such by the other party in the context of their interaction. It is these externally manifested assents that, as such, are the basic units of contractual analysis. As always in contract law, the existence and content of the requisite manifestations of assent must be determined from the standpoint of the objective test.

Now, according to the prevailing legal view, an offer must state a promise, that is, an unreserved present commitment to do or to give something in the future, which is presented to the offeree as made for what the latter must promise or do in return: the offer stipulates *both* sides of a proposed transaction. It is assumed that at least in the usual course the offer is made before the acceptance, which therefore follows the offer and responds to it. Absent some preexisting legal relation between individuals, no one is obliged to make an offer to anyone in the first place. In the basic case, one's reason for declining to do so can be arbitrary.[3] But once an offer has been made, its immediate legal effect is to confer on the offeree a *power* of acceptance. By exercising this power, the offeree can bring a relation of contractual rights and duties into existence. Crucially, this power of acceptance does not itself give the offeree any rights. Therefore, by first principles, prior to the offeree's acceptance, an offeror may effectively retract his offer without incurring any contractual liability at all. This must be the case even though, by its terms, the offer is expressly stated to be nonretractable for a period of time.

To accept, the offeree must manifest assent to the same identical transaction as stated in the offer: viewed objectively, the parties' assents must be *ad idem*. While the offeror may be "master of the offer" in the sense that he can, without injustice, propose any terms he wishes—even terms that the offeror knows the offeree cannot possibly fulfill—neither party alone is master of the contract: for this, the mutually related manifestations of assent of both are jointly required. With these basic features in mind, I turn now to the first question of why the doctrine of offer and acceptance may be needed to supplement consideration and how it does so.

We now take for granted that both doctrines are essential to the analysis of contract formation. However, historically, offer and acceptance was expressly introduced as a distinct requirement of contract formation only in the nineteenth century and principally in response to the challenges posed by noninstantaneous contracts, such as those concluded via correspondence.[4] Prior to this, the analysis of formation was worked out wholly in terms of consideration.[5] The fact that for more than two centuries, English contract law was seemingly able to get along without a distinct doctrine of offer and acceptance sheds light on the latter's significance as well as its role in relation to consideration.

Starting therefore with the requirement of consideration, we have seen that it postulates a certain definite relation between the parties where each is equally and identically active in bringing it about—neither side can produce any contractual effects without the other. Thus each side is inherently incomplete on its own and is only completed through being related to the other. Because consideration makes salient this relation between the parties and nothing more, it suggests that contract formation not only comprises, but also is effectuated by, a definite kind of strictly reciprocal interaction between the parties. Parties are held to have contractual rights and duties in virtue of such interaction involving promises given by way of mutually related request and response. Implicitly, the doctrine of consideration therefore suggests a model of contract formation that supposes that the parties themselves via an interaction of this kind can bring about the requisite relation embodying consideration. If this is so, why the need for a further distinct doctrine of offer and acceptance at all?

The answer, I think, is that the requirement of consideration does not explicitly specify how the parties *produce* this relation. There must be an interaction taking place in time through which the parties themselves bring about the requisite linking up of each with the other in such a way that both can reasonably know that this is what they have intended and done. The dynamic temporal process that this presupposes needs to be specified and regulated as a matter of contract doctrine. But this is not something that the doctrine of consideration is geared to do. Instead, it presents this relation in fully crystallized form: from the standpoint of the requirement of consideration, unless and until a first promise is already joined with a requested second promise made in return, neither promise has *any* contractual significance or effect.[6] Unless there is a complete and already formed promise-for-consideration relation, there is nothing at all. Yet the doctrine supposes a first promise that requests and is followed by the consideration. Thus the genesis of the relation remains doctrinally opaque. As I will now elaborate, it is the special role and contribution of offer and acceptance to specify this.

Supposing, then, that the requirement of consideration is in place, the analysis of this dynamic process starts with the idea of one party proposing to a second party a promise-for-consideration transaction. The addressee must therefore be one from whom the first party directly requests a valuable consideration in return. Notice also that, to request consideration, the first side's proposal has to state the whole transaction: not only what he will do but what the other side is to do in return for it. Hence, as already discussed, there is the basic feature of an offer that it must state both sides of a complete transaction.[7]

The next and particularly crucial step from a dynamic point of view is to show how, beginning with the first side, it is possible for that side, through its act and decision, to link up with a second side that is necessary to complete it. The mediating element that allows for this mutual linkage is the *power of acceptance*: the second party must reasonably be able to view the first party's expression of assent as intending to place in her hands the possibility of deciding to promise in return according to the terms of the whole transaction. The articulation of this power is perhaps the most important contribution of the doctrine of offer and acceptance because it is precisely this element that the doctrine of consideration lacks.[8] Even though it is not a right, the power of acceptance is in and of itself legally real and significant. Vested with this power, the offeree is now placed in a position of being able to complete the offeror's side through the offeree's act alone, thereby bringing into existence a relation of contractual rights and duties between them. Correlative to the offeree's power is the offeror's liability that their legal relation may be changed without the offeror's further act or assent. Once an offer is deemed to confer a power of acceptance—even before the return consideration moves—the offeror must retract his offer prior to an acceptance if he wishes to prevent contract formation. Still, being a mere power of acceptance, the offeror *can* before acceptance permissibly withdraw his offer at will even if, by its express terms, it is presented as unretractable for a given period of time.

Earlier, I noted that the standard view of offer and acceptance assumes that ordinarily an offer states a *promise* by the offeror and is made *before* the acceptance, which therefore follows and responds to it. Drawing on the central point that an offer creates a power of acceptance, I want to try to explain why these features may be, not just statistically or empirically usual, but in fact necessary and intrinsic aspects of the analysis of offer and acceptance.

First, must an offer always include a promise to the offeree?[9] In answering this question, we suppose here, as throughout the whole discussion, that offer and acceptance must at least be consistent with the requirement of consideration. So, apart from the offer stating a promise, the only other thing that it can refer to is an act—and more exactly a not yet completed act or forbearance—such as in the following example: if and when I choose (without promising) to clean your garden, do you promise to pay me x?[10] Now if you "accept" by making the requested promise to pay, you have certainly promised me, but no consideration moves until I do the work. In other words, your promise, though given as an acceptance, is still purely gratuitous and so unenforceable. However, if by definition an actual acceptance produces an enforceable agreement, then your assent cannot be an acceptance and likewise my proposal cannot be an offer. In fact, for our interaction to produce an enforceable agreement, either it has to be construed in reverse as a unilateral contract where now the offer is your promise of payment in return for my act of cleaning your garden (which when executed constitutes acceptance) or, in the alternative, my offer must incorporate, even if implicitly, a promise to clean in return for your return promise to pay. In short, there cannot be an offer that does not promise something in return for the promise or the doing of something else.

By virtue of this necessity of the offer expressing the offeror's promise as part of a represented two-sided transaction, it can communicate to the offeree the offeror's present decision and commitment to do something (in the future) on the condition that the other party accepts. In this way, there can be a fixed and settled decision by one side that is nevertheless presented as intrinsically incomplete unless met in return and joined by the other side's reciprocal decision. The offer can be both fixed and incomplete once it is viewed as one side of a bilateral relation constituted by the two expressions of assent. The promise is not to be construed as just to or for another but also as made with the other's coequal reciprocal act.

But this immediately raises a further puzzle. An offer, stating a promise, imports a present commitment of some kind—for otherwise it cannot be without reservation and final—yet it produces no contractual obligation whatsoever prior to acceptance by the other party. In legal contemplation, an offer does not even establish an obligation subject to defeasance by a condition subsequent—for, as already noted, the offeror is free to cancel the promise at will prior to acceptance, even if he has stated it in this form or specified that the promise is to be unretractable for a given period. The puzzle here is that the offer must communicate the element of a present commitment that nonetheless, prior to acceptance, does not import any contractually binding commitment at all.

I believe that here again there is a problem only when the offer is viewed from the standpoint of individually self-imposed promissory morality and as a promise made to or for but not with another. The offeror's promise or expression of present commitment should be taken, not as a ground of moral obligation by itself, but instead as but one side of a bilateral transaction that is itself the cause of obligation. The promise as it functions in this relation between the parties, not the promise taken in abstraction, is the fundamental normative factor.

What about the assumption that at least ordinarily contract formation involves a first expression of assent (the offer) that precedes the second (the acceptance) in time, with the second being given after and in response to the first? The necessity of this temporal sequence has been questioned.[11] So rather than simply assume it to be the case, we ask: *must* contract formation be so viewed?

To answer this question, it is important to keep in mind that offer and acceptance should specify a process of interaction between the parties that can itself be the basis of their enforceable contractual relation. This at least must be presupposed if we are to make sense of the truism that contractual obligation is based on parties' voluntary mutual assents. Thus the parties must be able to link themselves together through their own assents alone; and further, since we are supposing that contracting parties can fairly be held responsible toward each other solely on the basis of their voluntary interaction, it must be reasonable to view the parties as having chosen to have so interacted. I want to suggest that to ensure that these conditions are met, the parties must express their assents on the model of proposal and response arrayed in a temporal sequence, with one going before the other. One party must come to a decision in a way that places the possibility of a second related decision in the hands of the other party. And this second party must in turn be able to know that she is responding to the decision of the first that so links them. In this way, each party can reasonably view his or her decision as inherently joined with and completed by the other's, thereby establishing a genuinely bilateral relation that arises from their joint participation without being under the control of either side alone. Despite the complications and varieties of technologically sophisticated modern contracting, this basic bilateral model must guide the analysis of the nonformal generation of all contractual relations.[12]

By way of counterexample, one might put forward, as Arthur Corbin does, a hypothetical scenario in which a third person, C, prepares in advance terms of a possible agreement and communicates the terms in complete form, separately however, to each of the parties, A and B, telling them that if they wish to contract they should stand in each other's presence and repeat at the same time: "We mutually agree in accordance with the terms given to us by C."[13] A and B do so, saying, we may assume, precisely the same thing at the same time. There is no temporal difference between their utterances. While speaking, neither hears or knows, let alone responds to, what the other is simultaneously saying. Further, C is not the agent of either party and we are to suppose that the whole source of any possible contractual obligation between A and B is exclusively their expressions of assent. According to Corbin, their assents would produce a contract, despite the absence of any temporally sequenced process of offer and acceptance. To assess the significance of this scenario as a counterexample, consider the differences between the analysis of formation in this nonsequenced situation and that in a sequenced offer and acceptance.

When the assents are temporally sequenced, a first party solicits the active decision of the second as part of what she decides and intends. In so doing, the first party puts his decision potentially beyond his unilateral control and under the control of both. His decision inherently involves relation with another. When the second participates as solicited by completing the first, both can fairly be held by each other to this relational standpoint and to whatever it reasonably entails. But unless there is some temporal gap between the first and second utterances and an interaction involving proposal and response, the parties merely act and speak side by side and not *to* and *with* each other. Neither party can reasonably know what the other is saying or has said. A third-party external observer may tell them what they have said or done after the fact, but this does not change the absence of interpersonal knowledge and linkage during the very process that is supposed to give rise to a contract. In this hypothetical scenario, it is not at all clear why one party should be able to constrain the other from changing his or her mind after their simultaneous utterances. What standing has this process given to a party to object to the other's change of mind and to hold the other to the contents of his or her own assent? There have merely been two unilateral assents, neither of which engages or brings in the other. There is no basis in their actions—which do not comprise an interaction—to hold either to the standpoint of a relation between them. Indeed, the parties' simultaneous separate statements "we mutually agree" are mere words: there is nothing in their speech acts that shows they are acting or have acted as a "we" together.

The common law rightly treats even identical but temporally nonsequenced assents as mere cross-offers that, unless complemented by a further act in response, conclude nothing.[14] It does not view them as *ad idem* in the required way for contract formation. Of course, if there were a legally binding formal rule by which cross-offers could have operative effect as a contract, that would be another matter—but then their contractual obligation would no longer arise from their nonformal assents alone. Additionally, this would introduce a formal element that has no parallel in the doctrine of consideration, preventing the two doctrines from working in tandem with each other.

Offer and acceptance, I conclude, must be temporally successive because it is only in this way that the parties *themselves* can together establish—and reasonably be held to know that they have established—a promise-for-consideration relation via the very interaction that is constituted by their assents. If this is correct, we may also expect the doctrinal analysis of offer and acceptance to show that this sequenced interaction culminates in the copresent two-sidedness of the promise-for-consideration relation. This is in fact what the leading nineteenth-century offer and acceptance decisions established. They proposed the jurisprudentially novel view that, once an offer is made, it continues in time (unless it has been effectively retracted or expires) up to and including the moment an acceptance is made.[15] From this, it follows that, in the words of Lord Eldon, "the acceptance *must be taken as simultaneous with* the offer, and *both together* as constituting such an agreement as this Court will execute."[16] This expresses the real juridical nature of the meaning and operation of the interaction at issue. In sum, the doctrine of offer and acceptance ensures that the very kind of two-sided relation required by consideration is generated by an interaction that itself embodies this relation in a temporally sequenced form. Offer and acceptance specifies the dynamic process in time of the kind of interaction that both establishes and is identical with the promise-for-consideration relation.

It is only because the interaction of offer and acceptance effectuates and embodies the promise-for-consideration relation that it ensures this bilateral structure of acts. As I noted earlier in the introduction to contract formation, without consideration, offer and acceptance are potentially reducible to, respectively, a promise and a manifestation of satisfaction with the promise. Absent the doctrine of consideration, an offer might be thought to be merely a promise that is conditional upon the promisee wanting it. While such "acceptance" might enable the promisor to confirm the point and purpose of his effort to benefit the promisee via a promise, it would not make the promisee identically and equally the coauthor of a joint (promissory) interaction with the promisor—contract formation itself—or of the normative consequences attaching to it.[17] The unity of consideration and the doctrine of offer and acceptance is the indispensable lynchpin of the common law of contract.

2.2. The Objective Test: Transactional in Meaning and Basis

The preceding analysis of offer and acceptance, paralleling that of consideration, clearly reflects a fundamental distinction between promising that involves the promisor's act alone and promising that is intrinsically bilateral and the joint act of two parties. The latter is possible only where the second party's contribution is genuinely self-originating and distinct from a similar decision of the first party, yet requested by the first and given by the second in response to it as part of a single transaction constituted by both. Throughout the discussion so far, I have taken the relevant interaction as consisting in the parties' mutual assents functioning as acts that are reasonably apparent as between the parties. The building blocks of contract formation are these assents just as construed in accordance with the objective test. Now, at least in common law systems of contract, this is not because the assents so viewed are taken to be evidence of, or a surrogate for, what the parties may have inwardly intended or thought. For then this construction of their assents would be defeasible by proof of a contrary actual intent, even though not communicated. But this is not the law. Rather, the law seems to view the *transactional* existence and meaning of the assents as their sole actual and complete juridical reality—what alone is relevant and operative in establishing mutual assent for the purposes of contract formation. If so, we must see whether this view can be justified within the framework of analysis developed so far. This will lead into a discussion of the meaning and basis of the objective test.

To begin, suppose to the contrary that what counts is a party's actual inner intention and that the first party has, with full intention and understanding, made an offer, thereby communicating his intent. If what matters is actual intention, this initial offer must be continuously affirmed at every moment, including therefore also the instant when the second party accepts. It is only in this way that a continuing actual inner intent can be confirmed. But then the second party's acceptance cannot be in response to the offer—for this presupposes at least some gap (however brief) between them during which the first party does not say or do anything more but leaves it up to the second to decide. If we insist that there must be a sequenced interaction with a temporal gap in order that the acceptance can be given in response to the offer and in this way ensure that the parties themselves can bring about contract formation by their own interaction, this would require that the offeror confirm *after* the purported acceptance that he *still* actually intends the offer. And for the same reason, there must also be a yet further confirmation by the offeree that she actually intends her acceptance as well. And so on ad infinitum. We can see then that, were this the case, no contract could be concluded on the basis of the parties' interaction alone.[18]

This outcome can be avoided only if we take the legally operative assent to be the externalized expression itself, which now becomes in its own right the basic unit of analysis and of interpretation. So viewed, the external manifestation (assuming that the offer by its terms has not expired) can be thought of as existing unless or until it is withdrawn from the world by the offeror's further externally manifest act. It is something fixed and definite to which the second party can respond. And if the offeree does in fact accept, offer and acceptance necessarily coexist at one instant. In legal contemplation, offer and acceptance now represent "the act [not] of one party, but of both."[19] This is the consensus *ad idem* required by the common law of contract.

The next step is to specify the standpoint from which the existence and content of such external manifestations are to be determined. In this way, we further clarify the conception of external manifestation that is requisite for formation. The common law, we have said, takes an "objective" view of party assent. It is time to specify what exactly this entails. For present purposes, I will contrast two alternative understandings, both of which can be styled as "objective" in approach.[20]

The first approach assesses the meaning of the parties' words and conduct from the standpoint of a hypothetical third party.[21] According to this "detached observer" approach, the aim of the law, as it is sometimes put, is to ascertain the inherent meaning of words or conduct. Thus, even if a court could find that the parties mutually understood and used words in a particular way, this would not prevail against the applicable standard meaning that would ordinarily be given to them.[22] The premise is that parties can be held to intend this view of their interaction, not because, as a prima facie background assumption, parties presume that each intends to communicate standard or usual meanings, but simply because general understandings are conclusively reasonable and therefore to be imposed, save perhaps where there is express evidence to the contrary.

What is striking and, I suggest, problematic about this detached observer approach is that while it rejects the relevance of undisclosed intention and purports to base contract formation on the parties' external manifestations of assent, it allows for an interpretation of their assents that need not be anchored in the particularities of the parties' interaction except where the parties have expressly indicated. (But then how is this to be interpreted?) And whether either of the parties actually contracted on this basis is viewed as irrelevant. But this seems prima facie in tension with the basic idea that it is the parties themselves, through their actual interaction, who effectuate contract formation in a way that they—and not some third party—can reasonably know and intend. The requisite external acts should also be viewed from a standpoint that is anchored in their actual, and therefore particular, interaction. What is reasonable must be determined *as between* the two parties. If a meaning is to be imputed to one or both parties, it must be on a basis that refers to how *they* used words or expressed themselves in conduct in their actual interaction. The assent that counts is that which is communicated and understood by and as between the parties. Objectivity should be relational and transactional.

In fact, the most widely accepted formulations of the objective test do exactly this: they hold that both the existence and the content of a party's manifestation of assent are decided by how that party's words or conduct appear to a reasonable person in the position of the other party, taking into account the surrounding circumstances and context of their transaction, including any facts or underlying assumptions that are known by or reasonably available to both.²³ This second approach, which seems to take the standpoint of a reasonable addressee, anchors the analysis of reasonableness in the particular interaction between the parties. Moreover, this second approach, once more in contrast with the first, requires that an addressee, claiming to hold the other to a certain meaning because it is reasonable even though it differs from what the other subjectively understood, must at least have herself actually entered the contract on the basis of this reasonable understanding.²⁴

These features of the second approach raise several interconnected questions. First, by holding the first party to the understanding of a reasonable person in the position of the second, does this not unilaterally impose the perspective of one side on the other in a manner that is therefore incompatible with the bilateral nature of contract? This requires that we clarify the meaning and role of reasonableness as part of the objective test. Second, in what sense is this test "objective," given that, as stated above, standard formulations of it seem to require that at least one of the parties can establish that she has *actually* contracted on the basis of the "reasonable" understanding? On this basis, commentators sometimes characterize the modern test as an amalgam of objective and subjective elements. Is this correct? And third, what does—or at least what should—this test say where both parties—possibly even by sheer happenstance—attach the same, but idiosyncratic, meaning to their manifestations of assent in the face of a clear and generally available different standard meaning? Does the objective test require that the parties be held to the standard meaning that they neither understood nor expected or, alternatively, should it conclude that there was no contract at all? If, to the contrary, it upholds the contract in accordance with the parties' idiosyncratic understandings, is the test still "objective"? Answering these questions will go some way toward helping to clarify the meaning and the basis of the objective test as well as my view of it as transactional.

First, then, does reference to the standpoint of a reasonable person in the position of the addressee unilaterally impose upon the addressor? I would suggest that it does not. Indeed, as I now briefly elaborate, it is an appropriate formulation both in itself and heuristically to express the requisite bilateral or transactional point of view. Here, we should keep in mind that consistent with the requirement of consideration, the offeror (who is the addressor in this instance) must be taken to intend that the offeree (the addressee) participates by completing the offeror's manifestation of assent and therefore also to intend that the addressee, as a distinct and separate person, makes her own decision with respect to the proposal. This is how the offeror's intent must appear to the offeree. It is therefore implicit in this intention that the offeror's manifestation of assent reach and be understood by the offeree so that the latter can respond to and can act upon it by providing her assent in return.[25] Reference to the addressee's understanding is thus part of the addressor's own contractually necessary and reasonably apparent intent. The addressor's legally operative assent must be a manifestation of assent *for* the addressee: how the addressor's words or conduct appear to the addressee must be constitutive of their contractual meaning and significance.

But to ensure that this standpoint does not one-sidedly impose the addressee's understanding on the addressor—this would be incompatible with the bilateral character of the intended relation—the perspective to which the addressee holds the addressor must be one that the addressee could reasonably expect the addressor to accept in light of the actual circumstances of their interaction. For example, the addressee's understanding must be presumptively based on facts that are reasonably available to *both* parties in their interaction.[26] In other words, the addressee's understanding must be based on facts or circumstances that are shared or public as between the contracting parties: their common ground as it were.[27] This common ground or mutual context ordinarily involves a background of knowledge that parties assume their addressees share and that does not need to be mentioned specifically.[28] Depending on the particulars of a given interaction, the context is ordinarily specified at different levels of generality and provides the meanings, assumptions, and surrounding circumstances, both factual and normative, that are necessary for the parties to occupy a shared standpoint regarding their outward expressions and to be *ad idem* about them.[29]

Viewed in this way, the addressee's understanding must be such as to ensure that, by definition, the addressor could reasonably expect the addressee to attach this very meaning to his manifestation of assent—something that the addressee in turn should reasonably expect of the addressor.[30] Because the objective test specifies a standpoint that refers simultaneously to both sides in their mutual relation, it represents the transactional meaning of the parties' manifestations of assent that are the source of agreement between them. Indeed, it would seem difficult to conceive of another test that would more suitably reflect the bilateral character of the promise-for-consideration relation.

Understood in these terms, reasonableness does not reflect the standpoint of a hypothetical or actual third person, including a court, imposed *ab extra;* such persons are not the parties and the aim of the law is to enforce the transactionally shared meaning of the parties themselves, not that of anyone else.[31] Similarly, the idea of reasonableness applies to what a party has actually said or done: it does not refer in the abstract to what one or both parties might have done or agreed to in the pursuit of certain goals or values not already explicitly or implicitly rooted in their interaction. It is important to emphasize that reasonableness does not express some substantive principle or value—moral, economic, or other—that orders the parties' mutual expectations and understandings in light of this goal or standard. Reasonableness has to do with an actual interaction between two particular parties and is therefore a term of relation—more exactly, one that is thoroughly and intrinsically transactional. In this way, it shows itself to be categorically different from the idea of the rational and is specific to the nature of the relation at issue.

What about the further qualification that not only is the relevant understanding that of a reasonable person in the position of the addressee but also that the addressee must herself have acted on that understanding to make it applicable: is this a "subjective" element in an otherwise "objective" test?[32] In my view, it is not. Rather, it simply ensures proper application of the objective test.

Traditional formulations of the test often begin by ascertaining how an external manifestation of assent would be understood by "a" reasonable person in the position of the addressee.[33] The additional qualification ensures that an addressee holding the other to this meaning actually attached it to the latter's expression of assent. This seems reasonable. If there is no source of contractual obligation apart from our interaction, how can I reasonably claim to *hold* you to a certain interpretation (even if "reasonable") of your words or conduct unless, as a basic prerequisite, I actually entered the contract with you on the basis of that understanding? Similarly, where a party contends that she should not be held to the other's prima facie reasonable understanding of her words or conduct, a court must be able to infer, not only that there is another equally reasonable understanding of them, but, in addition, that she in fact adopted it.[34] Otherwise, the existence of an alternative "reasonable" meaning is transactionally irrelevant.[35] For a standpoint to be truly subjective, intent must be interpreted from the subject's *own* internal standpoint.³⁶ But this is not what this qualification, requiring that a party in fact has acted on the basis of a reasonable understanding, entails.

Now what if both parties attach the same meanings to each other's manifestations of assent although those meanings are nonstandard and, in the extreme, even if the parties do not know that they actually share the same understanding? For example, suppose that the parties (for whatever reason) assume "horse" to refer to the horned animal standardly called "cow." However, neither actually knows for a fact what the other thinks. Each just implicitly assumes that the other, like himself or herself, means the animal "cow," given that he or she has never even considered the possibility of a different meaning. They conclude the sale of a "horse for $1,000." To hold them to the sale of a horse would be to impose a bargain upon them that they never intended or expected. With no apparent indications to the contrary, each party assumed that the other understood the expressions in the same way as he or she did—and each happened to be right.

As between them, this assumption about each other is transactional. Had they expressly established their own shared meaning of the subject matter, the case against imposing a standard meaning and for upholding their actual agreement would be obvious. But the same analysis should apply even where their congruence was not planned but merely implicit and accidental, as long as neither side gave the other reason to suspect that his or her meaning was not shared by the first. In sum, there are manifestations of assent that the parties have conveyed to each other in the form of proposal and response; and these embody terms that each party assumes, correctly, that the other understands in the same way.³⁷ They should be held to this shared meaning. Consistent with the objective test, the analysis is thoroughly bilateral and does not impose one side's undisclosed self-understanding on the other.³⁸

The fit between the objective test and the nature of the contractual relation as rooted in the parties' joint and mutually related acts is brought out even more clearly by considering whether the same would be true if this test were to be used in determining the meaning and the morality of a seriously intended gratuitous promise that most would take to be binding in ethics. In the latter case, judging the promisor's intent via his use of words viewed as external expressions objectively construed, and not at all in light of his actual understandings and aims, would certainly seem to be a gross and unilateral imposition on him, doing violence to the promisor's assessment of the nature and implications of his decision.[39] It would certainly go beyond what good faith expectations and trust on the promisee's part would ordinarily justify.[40] This conclusion is even more evident if we keep in mind that, as framed by the objective test, the contractual meaning must be decided or be determinable with reference to a single point in time—the moment of contract formation—a limit that is certainly neither expected nor required when assessing either the meaning of a gratuitous promise or its obligational consequences.

2.3. Intent to Contract: A Distinct Requirement for Contract Formation?

It is sometimes suggested that in addition to offer and acceptance and the doctrine of consideration, there is, or at least should be, a third distinct requirement for contract formation, namely, an intention to create legal or contractual relations.[41] Indeed, some may see this as the fundamental principle underlying the whole of contract formation and view the requirements of consideration and of offer and acceptance as just one way, albeit pervasive, of evidencing it. To conclude this chapter, I wish to explain why, apart from the meaning and role of intention already presupposed by the doctrines of offer and acceptance and consideration, there is no need for a further positive principle of intention for contract formation. Not only would such a further principle be superfluous; it could also obscure the proper relevance of intention in contract law.[42]

Let me state at the outset what I think is the operative conception of intention. The only intent of the contracting parties that is necessary for formation is, in Williston's words, "an intent to say the words or do the acts which constitute their manifestations of assent."[43] What a party must actually intend—what must be the product of her purposive choice—are only her words or acts as consciously expressive conduct, not the manifestations of assent that the other party reasonably imputes to these.[44] Having acted in this way, a party may reasonably and fairly be held to what is objectively attributed to her as a contractually operative manifestation of assent. Where there has been no such actual choice in this minimal sense, there cannot be an offer or any other operative manifestation of assent and consequently there cannot be a contract, not even one that is voidable.[45] However, this requirement can be met even though a party does not understand or intend the contractual significance or consequences that the law attaches to her act.[46] Thus, it does not ensure that the resulting contractual obligation is a self-imposed voluntary obligation in the robust sense that a party's intention to undertake this obligation is taken as the reason for imposing it.

Is this view of intention contradicted by decisions that deny contract formation on the basis that one or both parties have made clear to each other (and have acted consistently with this expression) that they do *not* intend contractual relations, even though they may have agreed to terms that might otherwise seem to satisfy consideration? But how can one party rightly demand that contractual consequences be imposed on the other in the face of the latter's reasonably apparent communication of her refusal to enter such a contract? The answer is self-evident as long as contractual rights and obligations are deemed to arise from the parties' interaction—their relation of communicated choice by one with communicated choice of the other.

To show that there can or should be a distinct requirement of intention to enter legal relations, one must go further and argue that the existence of the kind of interaction required just by the doctrines of consideration and of offer and acceptance may not always generate contractual effects. An example standardly referred to in support of this possibility is judicial treatment of ongoing relations of friendship or family or other relations of solidarity where participants often make mutual promises that, at first blush, may seem to present the form and even the content required by the principles of formation. Yet, absent the parties' manifest shared intent to give these promises contractual effects, courts sometimes decline to enforce their mutual promises on the stated basis that there has been no intent to contract in these circumstances.[47] The fact that courts do not ordinarily refer to intent when enforcing ordinary commercial transactions need not mean, it is argued, that intent is not a general requirement because here, in contrast to such close relations, the requisite intent to contract can simply be presumed.[48]

However, this view of the cases rests on a basic assumption concerning the nature of consideration that is, I suggest, incorrect. It is not sufficient that there be consideration merely in form.[49] Viewing the parties' interaction as establishing a promise-for-consideration relation must be true to, and not denature, the real character of their relation. In particular, the real nature of their relation must support the inference that the parties reasonably intend considerations that move from the promisee's side to that of the promisor and that are requested by and given to the promisor as quid pro quo in return for her promise. This real relation is only possible where parties at least implicitly *treat* each other as mutually separate and independent individuals, each with his or her own separate interests, assets, rights, and opportunities under his or her initial exclusive control. What belongs to one eo ipso does not belong to the other. It is only on this premise that the idea of a party *moving* consideration from its side to the other makes sense. Where their real interaction can be so construed, the parties may reasonably be taken to treat the elements of consideration as consideration.[50] Even if this interaction is embedded in a concrete context, it is essential that the parties can fairly be taken to have treated each other as linked in and through this kind of interaction and not simply on the basis of shared substantive ends that they endeavor to realize by assuming distinct tasks and contributions via their promises. Unless this interaction represents the real basis of their interconnection at the moment of mutual promises, the doctrine of consideration has no traction.

Where, by contrast, on the particular facts, the parties make promises as part of an ongoing relation of solidarity and trust, they may, but usually do not, view their interaction in this way. Here, words and conduct that might superficially seem to fit the pattern of both consideration and offer and acceptance may not really do so. The idea that their back-and-forth expressions of commitment and promising represent two separate sides effectuating a transfer from the individual and exclusive control of one into that of the other would be foreign to, and indeed would conflict with, their mutual understanding of their relation at the time of their promises.[51] They do not treat their promises as in exchange for—as the price of—the other. Given "the nature of the agreed promises," the parties do not reasonably view each other as intending to engage in the kind of interaction that embodies the promise-for-consideration relation: "neither party contemplate[s] such a result."[52] Rather, they take their promises—even if reciprocal—as the way they show affection, responsibility, and care for each other as friends, family members and the like. To attach legal contractual effects to their promises—keeping in mind that this would entail the whole panoply of coercively enforceable and objective contract principles and remedies—would be no less an injustice than enforcing as contracts those promises that the parties themselves clearly and explicitly state should not have legal effect. Just as parties can expressly exclude the attribution of contractual effects, their actual relation, as one of ongoing close solidarity, may *implicitly* negative such consequences as well if it is inconsistent with the kind of underlying interpersonal relation supposed by consideration.[53] Whether this is the case is determined in each instance as a matter of fact construed transactionally in accordance with the objective test.[54]

It is important to keep in mind the proper task of intention in the law of contract. Unless we are to suppose that every promise should be treated as legally, that is, coercively, enforceable in accordance with the settled principles and practices of contract law, the conception of intention must unambiguously differentiate promises that can be so construed and enforced from those that cannot. Moreover, reference to this intent must be reasonable and justified even where—the prevailing situation—the parties, apart from stating their promises, have been silent as to their intentions. Finally, this conception of contractual intention must be manifested in relation to some kind of interaction between the parties since contractual rights and obligations can arise through their voluntary mutual assents alone. But the moral construction fairly to be placed upon a gratuitous promise and the moral obligations legitimately arising therefrom—even as accepted by the most honest promisor in good faith—are different in kind from what the law attaches to a contractually enforceable promise. For the purposes of legal and moral theory, it is essential that the varieties of normatively significant relations with their differing obligations be recognized and not elided. If we bear these points in mind, the sense and significance of the doctrine of consideration, the requirement of offer and acceptance, and the specific meaning and role of intention within this framework can be appreciated.[55]

On the view that I am suggesting, then, intention in contract law refers to the purposive dimension of acts requisite for contractual formation and not to some distinct further requirement in the air.[56] This forms the indispensable necessary voluntary basis for contract formation without which an agreement must be contractually void ab initio.[57] Once contractual intention is understood in this way, we may clarify the sense in which it may be said that the basis of contractual obligation is in the parties' voluntary assents. It does not mean that the reason for a coercible contractual obligation toward another is that the parties intend or will it as such. No one is or can be contractually bound simply because he or she subjectively wants or intends to be. Obligation entails constraint, but if the source is simply one's intention or will, why should an earlier (no longer existing) expression of intent or will have priority over a later (existing) expression? Moreover, how could this ever give standing to *another* to impose such constraint? Whatever the parties think or say, it is the law, not the parties, that fixes the requisite conditions of contract formation and assesses their interaction in this light. By interacting in a way that satisfies offer and acceptance and that embodies the promise-for-consideration relation, the parties voluntarily link themselves together in a kind of relation to which the law can attach a reasonable and fair transactional meaning that includes contractual meaning and incidents. It is only to this extent and in this sense that parties bring themselves under a relation of contractual rights and duties. In both tort and contract, the attachment of legal meaning and incidents is done by law in relation to definite kinds of purposive interaction.[58] But in contrast to tort, the relevant purposive interaction in contract consists in both parties' mutually related voluntary manifestations of choice satisfying offer and acceptance and embodying the promise-for-consideration relation.

Chapter 3

Implication

In this chapter, I discuss the nature and the basis of implication in contract law. It makes sense to consider this topic in conjunction with the chapters on formation because the procedure of implication applies with reference to contract formation and implied terms govern the parties' contractual relation from formation on. They are no less enforceable than terms expressly agreed to. A contract, it may be rightly said, is the sum of its express and implied terms. At the same time, there is the following basic difference between them. Standing alone, a certain minimum of express terms is not only necessary but also sufficient to satisfy the requirements of contract formation. They constitute a prima facie enforceable agreement. If further terms are to be implied, these spell out and specify further the full contractual meaning and import of these enforceable express terms. Implication does this by determining whether further conditions, rights, obligations, powers, or limits should also be part of the contract as adding to, conditioning, or qualifying its express terms. So understood, implication may further be contrasted with interpretation in a more restricted sense, which merely fixes the meaning of a contract's express terms.[1] Still, both interpretation and implication share the same aim of determining what the parties must do or forbear to do in order to comply with their contract, and they both do this in accordance with the objective test. In my view, there is but one goal: to ascertain as fully as possible the reasonable normative meaning of the parties' interaction as a promise-for-consideration transaction. Because implication in particular has been the subject of much intense theoretical discussion and because the prevailing view of implication, which I refer to as the "default rule paradigm," is directly incompatible with the kind of transactional approach that I have proposed, it is important to devote a separate chapter to this topic and to present in some detail how I think the main instances of implication should be understood.

To this end, I first discuss the premises and ramifications of the prevailing default rule paradigm and argue that it cannot be part of a public basis of justification. Instead, a transactional analysis is needed (Section 3.1). Next I explain in greater detail what this transactional approach to implication involves and how it fits with the principles of formation, drawing on the historically most important categories of contractual implication, namely, the development of implied constructive conditions of exchange and implied obligations (Section 3.2). To bring out more completely the nature and scope of the proposed transactional approach, I then consider the theoretically challenging excusing doctrines of impossibility and frustration (Section 3.3) as well as the still controverted implied covenant of good faith in performance (Section 3.4). My central claim in this chapter is that, in sharp contrast with the prevailing default rule paradigm, which views contracts as lacking the intrinsic normative resources to determine the contractual relevance of matters that have not been expressly addressed by the parties, these main instances of contractual implication evidence a coherent and practicable transactional approach that sees contracts as complete and self-regulating when they are understood in terms of their particular promise-for-consideration relations reasonably construed. There are no gaps to be filled on a basis that is external to this purely transactional analysis.

3.1. From the Default Rule Paradigm to a Transactional Analysis of Implication

Contractual liability lies for the unexcused failure to do what one has promised at contract formation in return for the other party's counterpromise or act. For there to be a contract at all, there must be this promise-for-consideration relation that meets the requirements of contract formation, including definiteness and certainty. The terms that are minimally required to constitute this relation may be called "primary" or "independent" insofar as they comprise the fundamental elements—the most basic building blocks—of the promise-for-consideration and are freestanding, being neither inferred from nor adjectival to other more basic terms.[2] The content of primary terms is decided by parties' contingent choices. Thus they are ordinarily express terms, or at least provide a sufficient substratum of express terms to enable a court to find and to fill out this essential relation.[3] As stated above, the existence of such express primary terms is not only a necessary but also a sufficient basis for prima facie contractual enforceability (subject to requirements of fairness and the like). As well, they are the indispensable voluntary ground of contractual obligation, which, it must always be emphasized, is coercively enforceable, whether by an award of damages or by an order of specific performance or injunction.

At the same time, since at least the late eighteenth century, courts have introduced a whole range of implied terms that, beyond the minimum of essential primary terms needed to satisfy the requirements of formation, fill out, qualify, and further determine the performances owed as between the parties. These "secondary" or "dependent" terms and conditions specify much, if not most, of the parties' contractual rights and duties and include so-called constructive conditions of exchange, implied obligations in fact and in law, implied warranties, doctrines that excuse or relieve performance such as mistake in assumptions, impossibility, or frustration, and so forth. In contrast to primary terms, these secondary or dependent terms and conditions need not be expressly provided for or actually assented to by the parties. Nevertheless, contract law views them, once determined, as integral to the parties' enforceable agreement and as fully equal in obligational weight to the primary express terms. While standardly parties may be able to displace or to contract around terms that would otherwise be implied, it is perfectly consistent with the judicial procedure of implication that parties are held to these terms even where they could not realistically have done so because they did not know about or never turned their minds to this possibility (as, for example, in a case of first impression). The fact that implied terms can be imposed in this way is a point of the first importance for both a proper understanding and a satisfactory theoretical account of implication.

There is more than one puzzle here. On the one hand, without express terms that meet the threshold requirements of contract formation, there is simply no performance owing and nothing to enforce and so no fixed point or basis for implying anything at all. As already noted, express assents provide both a necessary and a sufficient basis for determining the parties' rights and duties, and it is fundamental to contract law that all contractual rights and duties are exhaustively fixed at contract formation. Thus mutual assents at formation must in some sense contain the whole of their contractual rights and duties. But on the other hand, the parties ordinarily will not have specifically or explicitly addressed, let alone determined, the matters coming under implication. On their face, mutual assents do not cover matters that can nevertheless add to, qualify, or limit the express terms. How then can a contract, with its mutual rights and duties, be fully and completely established at contract formation on the sole basis of the parties' assents? And by what procedure, in the face of the parties' silence, can terms be implied and coercively enforced consistently with the voluntary nature of contract? This raises a question going to the very legitimacy of implication. The acuteness of this question is only reinforced by the fact, mentioned above, that the law may hold parties to such implied terms even where it is clear that, in particular circumstances, they did not know that they could have contracted around them. If implication is to be justified, this must be done, if at all, on a basis that does not depend upon the parties intentionally declining to take a contractually available escape route.[4]

Now almost without exception, contemporary contract theories, whether autonomy-based or economic, share the following view: contracts are not complete at formation and implication necessarily depends upon a procedure that does not derive from the parties' actual voluntary interaction.[5] Implication, they assume without further question, cannot be anchored in the actual contract concluded by the parties. Instead, according to this predominant approach, courts must first construct a preferred set of rules that forward values or goals that are valid independently of the legal contractual analysis of formation and then use these rules to provide the content needed for implied terms. Whether, and if so how, terms are to be implied depends on what furthers the underlying values and goals. Finally, this view accepts that, as required by freedom of contract, parties may ordinarily contract expressly around such terms. This model of implication is the default rule paradigm. I will now discuss these points a little more fully.

The default rule paradigm takes as its ideal benchmark the completely expressed transaction that explicitly and specifically provides for every matter that might be contractually relevant to the fulfillment of parties' individual and joint purposes. Whether on the basis of respect for individual autonomy or in furtherance of joint preference satisfaction and welfare, this is the only kind of contract—one that comprises express stipulations—that unproblematically can and ought to be enforced as is.[6] It represents an ideal of freely chosen as well as optimal transaction. Compared with this ideal benchmark, all transactions are, however, unavoidably incomplete because parties may have reasons for choosing or preferring not to provide for everything in this way; and, in any case, they normally face informational and transactional obstacles to achieving this even if they should want to do so.[7] Since, according to this model, the benchmark is the completely expressed contract, an incomplete transaction is necessarily one with gaps. These gaps cannot be filled by reference to the one and only thing that, according to this approach, represents the parties' actual choices or revealed preferences—the express terms. Hence the conclusion: once the parties have not expressly provided for a specific matter that may nevertheless be relevant to adjudicating claims, the normative force of their agreement is spent. If terms are to be implied, it must be on some basis other than their mutual assents.

However, for a party-based theory of contract—as both autonomy and most economic approaches purport to be—implied terms, if so understood, must be inherently problematic and always second-best. After all, the standard of the ideally complete contract refers to what the parties themselves choose or prefer, not what others might impute to them. Consistent with this approach, it would therefore be quite plausible to hold that in the case of an incomplete contract, the law should simply enforce the express terms as is, without supplementation or qualification. The express terms that satisfy the requirements of contract formation can stand on their own and may be interpreted widely enough or at a sufficiently high level of abstraction to decide most, if not all, situations or issues that have not been specifically addressed, without the need to introduce implied terms or conditions.[8] Actual performance is often physically possible, and, even if not, there is always the alternative route of a damages payment.[9] The risk of having to perform in almost any set of circumstances can be taken to have been assumed by the parties simply by their agreeing to express terms. This is widely supposed to be the older view found in such cases as *Paradine v. Jane,* and whatever its deficiencies, it is not simply incoherent or absurd.[10]

Nevertheless, most contemporary theories, like the law itself, do not take this route. And for seemingly good reason. Rejecting the general possibility of implication and always holding parties to their express terms seems to go counter to a reasonable appreciation of parties' expectations and shared understandings. We cannot suppose that express terms always and everywhere represent exhaustively the parties' whole agreement as they reasonably intended it. To the contrary, it is more reasonable to presume that parties always choose their terms against an unexpressed background of assumptions and views relating to the impact that unaddressed factors and circumstances may have on their performance interests and expectations. Parties cannot reasonably be taken always to have assumed the risks of all or any of these outcomes. Unless the agreement is to be set aside as being incomplete despite the existence of terms that satisfy the requirements of formation, the possibility of implication must at least be considered, given the shortfall of the express terms in fully and specifically addressing the nature and circumstances of actual performance.[11]

But what should be implied and on what basis? Because prevailing theories suppose that absent express terms the parties' agreement does not provide or require any answer in particular, neither the decision to imply nor the possible contents implied can draw on what the parties have *actually* chosen or expressed a preference for. These theories can only view implication as gap-filling with terms and conditions that the parties—or, more exactly, that representative parties—would *hypothetically* have chosen or desired if they had considered the matter or not faced transactional obstacles. Via implication, the law is at liberty—and should aim—to improve upon the actual contract by importing terms that representative parties might have chosen for themselves. And for this purpose there seems to be no reason for a court not to use the occasion to imply terms that further values, such as loss-sharing, joint welfare maximization, or distributive justice, that in its opinion may be pertinent or conducive to the promotion of contractual arrangements in general.[12] Finally, because these theories privilege actual choice as expressive of party autonomy or preferences, they reserve to parties the power to contract around implied terms: implied terms are justified and implemented only as *ex ante* default rules.

This default rule paradigm has spawned a veritable industry of models of hypothetical bargains and terms that, under the rubric of normative theory, have become ever more sophisticated and complex and at the same time increasingly remote from the actual operation of contract law as well as from the actual interactions between parties, which remain after all the sine qua non of the court's authority to adjudicate in the first place.[13] Indeed, more recent discussions in the law-and-economics literature have cast serious doubt about whether courts, given the evident limits of their institutional competence, can effectively implement these models or should even aim at improving upon parties' incomplete contracts. Proposed gap-filling default rules and standards, it is argued, will often be either unnecessary or inefficient and will simply impose further transaction costs on parties who will want to contract away from them notwithstanding. The default rule project should perhaps accept a much more modest role.[14]

These concerns are certainly legitimate in their own right. But I come back to an even more basic difficulty.[15] The only reason that parties can legitimately be brought under and held to these imputed standards and rules is that they are already contractually related via their express terms. This is the indispensable moral and legal condition of the parties being subject to coercively enforceable duties and rights in the first place. But given its premise of contractual incompleteness, the hypothetical bargain procedure of determining these defaults is and must view itself as independent of this actual transactional matrix. The disconnect with the parties' actual interaction is especially evident when the hypothetical bargain takes as its representative persons those belonging to a majority of transactors with notice of those terms. The representative persons of the hypothetical bargain need not correspond to the parties before the court. The terms that issue from this hypothetical procedure count therefore as new and original elements, and the procedure represents an alternative and separate method of the creation de novo of purportedly enforceable contractual norms. Moreover, the proviso providing parties with the power to contract around implied terms may be virtually meaningless so far as the actual parties before the court are concerned where, as is perfectly possible, the implied term is announced for the first time yet is fully binding upon them even without prior notice. The fact that *other* and *future* parties, perhaps having notice of the term, can contract around it is irrelevant to the reasonableness of imposing it upon the parties at hand. We may ask with John Dawson, "[F]rom what source does any court derive the power to impose on [the parties] a new contract without the free assent of both?"[16]

Can there be an alternative, perhaps autonomy or rights-based, account of implication that, in contrast with the prevailing default rule paradigm, does not view contracts as normatively incomplete or implication as gap-filling and so may possibly avoid posing this issue of legitimacy? For that is what the transactional approach that I am trying to develop would seem to require.

In an important and highly influential article, however, Richard Craswell argues in effect that such an alternative account is impossible.[17] He contends that for all autonomy theories, including transfer theories such as the one presented here, the normative incompleteness of agreements and the disconnect between the procedure of implication and contractual interaction are not by chance but rather necessitated by their basic theoretical premises. Policy-based default rules are a necessity even for these noninstrumental theories. Before going further, I should assess the strength of this argument.

According to Craswell, the incompleteness of these theories stems from the fact that they are wholly content-neutral and therefore unavoidably formal in the following sense. It is true that they view individuals as under a moral and legal duty to perform what they have promised or assented to. But this underlying principle of obligation does not specify or shape the content promised or consented to: it simply holds that one ought to perform *whatever* one has promised or consented to (assuming it is not prohibited by law or policy).[18] Consequently, the principle cannot offer *any* guidance *at all* as to which terms, if any, should be implied where the parties themselves have not expressly so promised or otherwise provided for. To do the work of implication, Craswell argues, autonomy theories *must* therefore refer to other, mainly instrumentalist, nonpromissory grounds—whether involving welfare analysis, considerations of distributive justice, or perfectionist ideals— that are not content-neutral in this way. At most, autonomy theories may be able to insist that terms implied on these other substantive grounds should be defaults that the parties can contractually waive or modify if they so desire. If correct, Craswell's argument rules out the possibility of a view of implication that can be a genuine and independent alternative to the default paradigm approach.

Now, here as elsewhere, it is important for a contention about contract law and theory to draw, at least provisionally, on features and conceptions that are part of and that are supposed by contract law itself. Otherwise, why should contract law view the argument as at all relevant to *its* concerns and soundness? This point also applies to the matter of its being content-neutral. In what way, if any, is contract law content-neutral?

Starting with the basic promise-for-consideration relation, we may say that contract law is content-neutral as follows: it does not stipulate what or how much either side of the relation must be as long as it conveys just something of value in the eye of the law. Even more, whatever the particular quality, quantity, and specifications of the substantive content promised, the law deems it to be not only a necessary but also a sufficient and complete consideration, which as such need not be improved or added to in light of the parties' purposes and preferences. Whether the parties might have chosen different or additional, better or more fully worked-out terms to achieve their goals is thus of no concern to contract law once there is just something of value for something else. Within these parameters, the choice of particular content is completely contingent and stands as is. And the same holds for the costs and benefits of parties negotiating improved or more detailed express terms that better meet their interests.

Although such considerations may certainly be pertinent to parties deliberating about and pursuing their purposes and interests in transactions with others, this does not therefore make them relevant as a matter of contract law. All these considerations fall under the rational and are relevant from that standpoint.[19] But precisely because of this content-neutrality of contract law and the purely contingent and fixed nature of these choices and considerations, the latter cannot be the basis for enhancing their transactions or for making them more cost-effective and efficient via the imposition of new implied terms or conditions that are not already part of their actual agreements. If this whole dimension of the rational in contract law cannot ground implication, it would seem then that, if implication is to be justified at all, it must be as an incident of the reasonable. But what sort of conception of the reasonable?

Instead of turning immediately to some extratransactional source such as distributive justice or welfare analysis, it would seem more appropriate to see first whether the basic promise-for-consideration framework itself can provide the needed guidance. After all, this framework sets the essential requirements for the attribution of coercive contractual effects to the parties' interaction. Should this not also be pertinent to the implied dimension of this interaction, no less than to its express dimension? To ignore this possibility and decline to explore it would be sheer theoretical dogmatism. In the sections that follow, I will try to show that the promise-for-consideration framework does in fact govern the procedure of implication. Far from being formal in the way Craswell contends, this relation has the normative resources to guide the when, what, and how of implication.

More specifically, we will see that implied terms and conditions are needed to ensure that the promisee receives the full and fair value of the contractually contemplated benefit of performance and correlatively that the burden of actual performance on the promisor is no more than the contractually contemplated detriment. What the parties owe each other and correlatively are owed by each other should be *fully* specified, in terms of what this includes as well as excludes, as the contract intended. As expressing the fair and reasonable in transactions, full value refers not only to the beneficial value that a party is intended to have in the actual circumstances of performance but also to the contractually intended proportion of the risks of benefits and burdens between the two sides. Thus implication spells out, not something more or other of value that parties might rationally want in light of their particular purposes (let alone some presupposed hypothetically shared purpose), but rather what is reasonably required to make sense and to secure the full and fair value of the terms actually agreed to.

If so, the procedure of implication can yield implied terms and conditions to which the parties can reasonably be held, even though they do not expressly choose them and are not even cognizant of them when transacting. Because implied terms are worked out as part of the reasonable, parties are not expected to provide them. Further, the fact that there are terms that must be implied need not mean that the agreement is incomplete in any contractually relevant sense. The absence of express terms in relation to these matters is thus not per se a deficiency or an incompleteness—any more than the fact that it is the law, and not the parties, that provides the required framework of transactional relation for contract formation in the first place. On the view that I am proposing, a contract would be incomplete only if it turns out that this reasonable transactional framework, though fully worked through, cannot settle issues that arise in transactions and that must be addressed if the parties' rights and obligations are to be adequately specified. But if this framework can do so, there is no need or point of entry for supplementary principles or norms.

My argument is, then, that contract law supposes a division of labor between, on the one hand, a definite reasonable framework—the promise-for-consideration relation—that is required and ascertained by law and, on the other hand, the parties' substantive choices of what they want to give and receive via transacting. It is up to the parties to choose their preferred contents but not the character of the kind of relation that determines the contractual juridical characterization and effects of their choice. This same relational framework determines not only whether something counts as an operative express contractual term in the first place but also the appropriateness of implying terms and conditions for a particular transaction: all terms, both express and implied, have their existence and meaning only as aspects of this promise-for-consideration relationship construed in accordance with the objective test. It provides a unified standpoint for contract formation, interpretation, and implication.

My central contention, to repeat, will be that this transactional dimension, expressing the reasonable, but not the parties' contingent choices of particular contents, expressing the rational, is the animating idea and basis of contractual implication. It is also this relational framework, as an expression of the reasonable, that justifies coercively enforceable contractual rights and duties. Hence, if implied terms to which the parties have not expressly assented are to be legitimately enforceable against them as a matter of legal compulsion, it seems reasonable to follow through this analysis and to ensure that the justification for implying given terms or conditions is anchored in requirements internal to this same framework. In this way, parties can be bound only by what they have done; and what they have done is, and must be, the basis of any further implication or inference that has these juridical consequences. Implication that satisfies this standard need not raise a question of legitimacy which, we saw, seems unavoidable for the default rule paradigm.

Against the background of these introductory remarks, I shall now present a transactional analysis of implication that, I believe, is superior to the predominant default rule paradigm in the way that it both makes sense of the main recognized categories of implication in their own terms and also reflects the fundamental normative nature of contractual rights and obligations. In doing this, my aim is to work out an account that can be part of a public basis of justification for contract law.

3.2. A Transactional Analysis of Implication in Overview

The implication of terms presupposes and applies to an existing valid contract with sufficiently clear and certain primary terms that satisfy the requirements of offer and acceptance and consideration.[20] In principle at least, it is therefore always open to a court to decide to enforce the contract as is, subject to reasonable interpretation. The agreement can thus definitely function as a complete contract.[21]

At the same time, precisely because a question of implication only arises where a court has before it what is prima facie an enforceable agreement, the court cannot avoid determining the meaning and scope of the contract with respect to matters that the parties have not expressly addressed but that can nevertheless affect the expected performances owed.[22] In particular, there may be factors and circumstances both at formation and after that can change the expected benefits and burdens associated with performance or even its core character. Implication determines what, if any, is their *ex ante* contractual significance. Notwithstanding the prevailing theoretical assumption that the parties' agreement does not contain the normative resources to answer whether, and if so which, terms should be implied, the law itself, we will see, presents an analysis of implication that demonstrates that it can indeed do so. Where a court concludes that terms or conditions should be implied, it draws on a particular contract's transactional meaning objectively construed and on that basis finds that the parties cannot reasonably be held to the express terms unless these are taken in conjunction with or qualified by the implied terms or conditions. Contract law does this via the legal construction of presumed intent with its companion idea of transactional necessity. Elucidating this analysis and showing how it is worked out in main instances of implication are essential to my aim of developing a public basis of justification for contract. I begin with the idea of presumed intent as developed in leading decisions.

The notion of presumed intent takes the parties' transaction itself as the first subject of contractual interpretation and implication. In answering the question of whether a court should imply terms and if so which, in Cardozo's words, "the genesis and aim of the transaction may rightly guide our choice."[23] The irreducibly basic unit of analysis is just this actual transaction, which must be understood from both sides at once. Presumed intention does not represent what either party, or even both parties jointly, would (probably or hypothetically) have intended if they had expressly addressed the significance of the event or circumstance that affects performance. Nor is presumed intent a second-best stand-in for or approximation of the parties' unknown subjective consents or a device for the imposition of extracontractual norms and values on a matter with respect to which party silence signifies sheer absence of agreement.[24] Rather, presumed intent refers to what the parties to a given contract *must* reasonably have intended because *necessary* to avoid a failure of consideration in the wider sense of an event or circumstance at or after formation that would render the contract futile, devoid of the fair value and benefit that it contemplated, or plainly absurd.[25] To illustrate and to flesh out further this understanding of presumed intent, consider one of its earliest articulations as enunciated by Lord Mansfield in the great case of *Kingston v. Preston* (1773).[26]

In *Kingston*, Lord Mansfield single-handedly overturned long-standing precedents, which held that, absent express agreement to the contrary, a party must go forward with her performance even in the face of the other's nonperformance. The second party's nonperformance does not excuse the first from having to perform. Her only relief is to recover damages against the other in a separate action for breach. But of course, there is no guarantee that she will succeed. In technical terms, these precedents held that unless parties expressly state that their covenants are mutually dependent (requiring the performance of one or each party to be a condition of the other's performance), the parties should always to be taken as intending their obligations to be mutually independent (requiring performance by each irrespective of the other's nonperformance).

Against this, Lord Mansfield insisted that the mere fact that parties might, but have not, expressly stipulated that their performances are to be mutually dependent does not automatically decide their contractually effective intent. According to Lord Mansfield, except where an agreement by its express terms clearly presents the obligations as mutually independent or dependent, it must remain an open question as to how the contract should be construed. And this, he emphasized, is to be decided on the basis of the "intent of the transaction," which is to be "collected from the evident sense and meaning of the parties," taking into account the express terms, the "object [or purpose] of the transaction," and the "essence [or nature] of the agreement."[27] Lord Mansfield's "intent of the transaction" is an early iteration of "presumed intent," and as reflected in Lord Mansfield's phrase, it is a thoroughly transactional intent. In the wake of this decision, it quickly became the law that it is only if the contract as a whole, reasonably construed, shows that a party assumed the nonreciprocal risk of having to perform despite the other's nonperformance that she will not be relieved from performance.

It is hard for us to comprehend how courts prior to *Kingston* could have taken any other view of the matter. To hold that a party has presumptively agreed to perform in the face of the other's complete refusal to do his part seems to us plainly unjust. Nevertheless, the older position was not wholly without logic or reason.[28] It took seriously the juridical fact that mutual promises, by themselves, are a sufficient basis for enforceability—with the legal consequence that each party is individually and separately bound to perform and is liable for nonperformance, sufficiently armed by having the power to bring a separate counteraction if the other party breaches. This view clearly treats the parties on a basis of equality, and by leaving it open to the parties to stipulate express terms conditioning their performances on each other, it also respects their freedom. The insufficiency of this view lies in the fact that, while it holds that promise and counterpromise must be mutually related at formation, it does not view the facts and circumstances of *actual* performance—including the risks associated with the order of performance—as even potentially relevant to ascertaining *ex ante* contractual intent at formation. How the parties' promised performances are mutually connected or otherwise realized at the time of performance is, contractually, a matter of indifference.

This is precisely what *Kingston* changed in one fell swoop. By expanding the scope of the parties' contractual intent in a way that integrates the incidents and circumstances of the actual performances—and in particular the temporal relation between them—the decision makes clear that in a bilateral contract "not only are the promises consideration for one another but . . . the parties [ordinarily] contemplate that the performances promised also shall be exchanged one for the other."[29] This view of the *ex ante* contractual relevance of the nature, modalities, and circumstances of actual performance in ascertaining the meaning and parameters of contractual intent is rooted in the promise-for-consideration relation. After all, the whole point of a transaction, without which it is difficult even to conceive of consideration as importing any value or benefit and detriment, is that each party should obtain the other's *actual* performance in return for her own within the parameters of the terms, circumstances, and risks contractually contemplated at formation. The circumstance or risk addressed in *Kingston* is that a party might be required to perform a "nugatory act" not for the other's performance or in fact for anything at all—not even as a prerequisite to bringing a claim that in the end might, however, turn out to be worthless.[30] In other words, a party might be compelled unilaterally to risk the loss of her assets, to say nothing of the time, money, and vexation of a legal action, in the face of the other's wrong. This could introduce a new and serious risk of prejudice not intrinsic to, and in fact inconsistent with, the benefit that was promised and contemplated under their contract: a great injustice to parties.[31]

On the particular facts in *Kingston,* this risk was clearly at odds with the intent of the transaction. The defendant had covenanted to transfer his business to the plaintiff on credit and the plaintiff had covenanted in return to give the defendant "good and sufficient security" for the deferred payment. To allow the plaintiff to enforce the transfer despite his failure to provide the required security and thus to force the defendant to trust to the plaintiff's uncertain personal financial circumstances would clearly undermine "the intent of the transaction" and "the very essence of the agreement." But even where there is no such security provision, a contractually assumed risk to give something for nothing should not be *presumed* of any party; to the contrary, there must be a reasonable and clear factual basis for finding such an intention—and this would be exceptional.[32] That is also why, in the absence of express terms, courts since *Kingston* take concurrent performances as their presumptive baseline—as the presumed intention of the parties—departing from it only where both parties should clearly know that temporally successive performances are called for by the nature of their transaction.[33]

Given the usual assumptions of contemporary contract theory, it is important to underline here that *Kingston* and its progeny view implication as necessary and geared to doing justice between parties as participants in executory bilateral contracts. This normative basis is presented as self-sufficient and complete in its own terms. The injustice, to repeat, lies in the risk of compelling a party to perform for nothing in return or at least for something vitally different from the performance owed her by the other party and thus, as the older cases put it, requiring performance despite, and in the face of, a total failure of consideration.

In this regard, it is noteworthy that Williston insists not only that the whole basis of the doctrine of dependent covenants, including the presumption of dependency, is simply about fairness as between the parties—what he calls the "inherent justice of the situation"—but also that at the center of this analysis is the principle of failure of consideration.[34] For Williston, the issue is not one of directly or indirectly discerning party intent, whether actual or even hypothetical. Rather, the court imputes an intent that is *reasonable in the circumstances of the parties' transaction;* and as for the basis of its doing so, the "only justification for such an [intention] is the fairness of dependency, as compared with independency, of promises in bilateral contracts, and this being so it is better to drop any talk about intention of the parties when they express none and rest doctrines of implied dependency solely on their fairness—a quite sufficient basis."[35]

Now once implication is justified as a matter of justice, it becomes clear, as Williston also notes, that injustice might equally result if in every case parties are presumed to intend mutually dependent performances such that *any* breach, however trivial, should excuse the innocent party's further performance. It is not surprising, then, that just four years after *Kingston*, Lord Mansfield in *Boone v. Eyre* (1777) further refined the analysis of implied conditions to prevent this injustice.[36] In that case, he held that where nonperformance goes only to a limited aspect or part but not to the whole (the root or foundation) of the consideration and the loss can be adequately compensated for by damages, the innocent party should not be excused from performing her side but instead must perform and be confined to an action for damages.[37] Underpinning the judgment is the idea that the defendant should not suffer forfeiture of the expected consideration for a trivial and adequately compensable breach.[38] Williston sees in this and similar decisions proof that courts can readily apply and mold the principle of failure of consideration to protect a party without subjecting the other to the risk of unjust forfeiture.[39] There are few if any judgments that better confirm or illustrate this point or that are more worthy of discussion in connection with the topic of implication than Cardozo's celebrated decision in *Jacob & Youngs v. Kent.*[40]

Briefly stated, in *Kent,* the defendant, owner of a country residence built by the plaintiff, refused to pay the plaintiff the balance owing under their contract when, after he had moved in, he discovered that, in breach of contract, the plaintiff had mistakenly installed the wrong brand of pipe, though the pipe actually installed was indistinguishable from the one stipulated in the contract in all other respects, including its appearance, quality, market value, and longevity. To correct the mistake, the plaintiff would have had to demolish at great expense substantial parts of a building that otherwise fully conformed to the contractual requirements. A central issue was whether in these circumstances the builder's breach should excuse the defendant from paying the balance under the contract, in effect treating the defendant's performance as dependent on that of the plaintiff. Giving the majority judgment, Cardozo answered no.

The judgment's most important and fundamental premise is: "Intention not otherwise revealed may be presumed to hold in contemplation the reasonable and probable. If something else is in view, it must not be left to implication."[41] With respect to the circumstances of this case, "the law will be slow to impute the purpose [of making every term a condition of recovery], in the silence of the parties, where the significance of the default is grievously out of proportion to the oppression of the forfeiture."[42] To determine whether there would be such disproportion, the court must first and foremost consider the significance of the breach: how serious is the breach in nature and extent when compared with what the owner is entitled to receive under the contract? The closer a breach approaches the point of depriving the innocent party of substantially the whole benefit of the consideration reasonably contemplated by their contract, the more clearly reasonable and fair will be the inference that the innocent party should be excused from further performance—this despite part performance by the breaching party and even supposing that the innocent party can sue for damages. The innocent party should not be compelled to accept a performance that is qualitatively different or inferior compared to what is reasonably contemplated under their contract.[43] This is so a fortiori if damages would not provide certain and adequate compensation, for in such a case the party will not obtain the performance or its market equivalent.

At the same time, if the innocent party has received substantially the whole benefit of the promised consideration and the breach affects her contractual interest only in an incidental or trivial way, the harshness of forfeiture resulting from excusing her own performance becomes salient: the more oppressive the forfeiture, the less inclined will the court be to impute to parties the presumed intent to treat the innocent party's performance as dependent on the other's substantially complete performance. Since these factors can vary from case to case, so will the determination of presumed intent.[44] The question of presumed intent regarding the independence or dependence of the parties' undertakings must be answered therefore, neither in the abstract nor on the basis of policy considerations independently of the character of the particular transaction at issue, but only relative to their actual transaction reasonably construed as a whole.

As for the particular transaction here, the contract was not for the sale of a simply described, standardized, mass-produced "common chattel" that can and must conform to its description and be merchantable and that, if defective, may be readily returned to the seller.[45] It was for the construction of a highly complex, intricate, and custom-crafted country mansion involving many details, not all of which would be important or even of interest to the owner. Moreover, the construction would be one of the builder's limited number of such projects annually, and unlike a mass-produced common chattel, the structure, when built, would be inseparable from the owner's land and so nonreturnable to the builder for disposal to someone else. Given the high probability of some defective performance of even a "venial" kind and the serious impact of forfeiture, treating the performance of any and every term or detail of the builder's obligation—"literal fulfillment"—as a per se precondition of the owner's duty to pay the balance should not be readily imputed to the parties in these circumstances. Only clear and apt words requiring this consequence should suffice. Here the majority found that the breach was trivial and did not cause the owner any loss, whether financial or intangible. In substance, the owner received the performance that he had been promised. By contrast, forfeiture of the balance owing would be grave for the builder. The parties could not reasonably be presumed to have intended this consequence for such a breach. Accordingly, fairness and reasonableness between the parties required that the owner be confined to claiming damages for the breach.[46]

It seems clear that Lord Mansfield's "intent of the transaction" and Cardozo's idea of presumed intent are one and the same thing. Both refer to an objectively construed intent that can be reasonably imputed to parties as participants in the bilateral and reciprocal promise-for-consideration relation. The analysis is transactional through and through. The implication of so-called constructive conditions of exchange molds and applies the principle of failure of consideration in a way that is fair to both parties: it ensures that the innocent party receives substantially the whole benefit of the promised performance without having to bear new risks not already reasonably assumed by her at formation, while at the same time it protects the breaching party from serious forfeiture when not necessary to effectuate such a performance interest. This whole analysis is possible only because consideration has the substantive dimension of being something of value in the eye of the law. Finally, Cardozo's explicit assertion, near the end of his judgment, of the priority of justice relative to other considerations, such as the possible *ex ante* certainty provided by "bright-line" rules, combines with his framing the standard in such a way that it operates to mark off only manifestly unjust results while giving due weight to the contractual expectations of both sides without subjecting either to unfair surprise.[47] Thus, even though the analysis is framed to specify the transactionally reasonable terms that are properly implicit in the parties' particular interaction rather than to shape their future conduct, including the more costly kinds of opportunistic behavior, this approach identifies and assesses the relevant factors in such a way that marks the bounds of legitimate claims and denies opportunistic conduct its intended effects.[48]

To complete this discussion of presumed intent and the transactional character of implication, I turn now to what is surely the leading and the most influential judicial statement of the basis of implication in general—Lord Justice Bowen's judgment in *The Moorcock* (1889).

The opinion begins with the clear and general statement that every implied warranty or obligation is "founded on the presumed intention of the parties, and upon reason."[49] In the face of the parties' silence as to the contractual significance of a particular circumstance or aspect of actual performance, it remains open to the court "to raise such inferences as are reasonable from the very nature of the transaction."[50] Such implications are drawn "with the object of giving to the transaction such efficacy as both parties *must have intended* that at all events it should have" and "preventing such failure of consideration as cannot have been within the contemplation of either side."[51] In doing so, the law's aim is "not to impose on one side all the perils of the transaction, or to emancipate one side from all the chances of failure, but to make each party promise in law as much, at all events, as it must have been in the contemplation of both parties that he should have been responsible for in respect of those perils or chances."[52] As has been underlined in all subsequent decisions, this test is one of transactional necessity: the law implies nothing other than what is necessary to spell out and to uphold the reasonable meaning of the actual, particular interaction between the parties at contract formation. In other words, *The Moorcock* opinion enshrines the kind of transactional analysis that we have seen at work in the previously discussed leading decisions.

Here the particular facts were that the plaintiff, owner of the vessel *Moorcock,* was contractually entitled for a fee to use the defendants' wharf and cranes to discharge and load its cargo. This could only be accomplished while mooring his ship alongside the defendants' jetty at low tide. But doing so exposed the ship to risk of serious damage if the riverbed mud happened to be unsafe. Both parties reasonably knew that this was a risk that only the defendants, not the plaintiff, could ascertain—in fact it was something that the defendants would easily know in the ordinary course of their business. The vessel sustained serious damage by settling on a ridge of hard ground under the mud, the defendants having taken no steps to check for danger or even to warn the plaintiff that they had not done so.

In these circumstances, Bowen held that, as part of their contractual obligations, the defendants owed the plaintiff a duty of reasonable care to notify the plaintiff either about the dangerous soil conditions or at least their failure to inspect. That the parties must be presumed to have intended this obligation followed from the fact that otherwise the plaintiff would be "simply buying an opportunity of danger" that would result in a total failure of consideration.[53] Implying an obligation here was necessary to protect the fair value of the promised consideration, in this way giving the transaction efficacy. To be reasonable between the parties, however, the implied obligation must be kept within the bounds of reason and fairness, taking into account the nature of the transaction. It must not impose "a trust further than the nature of the thing puts it in their power to perform."[54] Given the defendants' limited control over the site and the nature of their principal role in providing the wharf and cranes, it would be unreasonable to infer an obligation to guarantee the safety of the ground. A more restricted responsibility, one requiring only a duty of reasonable care to inspect or at least to warn that no inspection had been done, is what could be inferred as necessary to make the transaction efficacious. Thus what obligation, if any, should be implied depends upon the features and circumstances of the particular transaction at issue.[55]

It is time to gather together some of the main points in this overview of a transactional approach to implication. From Lord Mansfield's "intent of the transaction" to Lord Justice Bowen's "presumed intent of parties," there is but a single pattern of transactional analysis that specifies the meaning of a given promise-for-consideration relation for both its express and its implied terms, and it is on this basis that parties can fairly be held to them. Parties are reasonably presumed to intend the meaning that is necessary to avoid a total failure of consideration at the time of performance, which would render the promised performances futile, without value or benefit, or just manifestly absurd. This conception of transactional necessity does not refer to what is necessary to enable the parties to perform their express obligations—this often remains physically possible—but rather to what is necessary to ensure that the actual performance done is what their agreement, reasonably construed as a whole, must have contemplated. The aim is not to improve the contract the parties have made for themselves, even if such improvement might further the parties' joint welfare, social well-being, and so forth.[56] Thus "necessary" conveys that "it is not enough for a court to consider that the implied term expresses what it would have been reasonable for the parties to agree to [but rather] it must be satisfied that it is what the contract actually means."[57] The different kinds of implication aim to specify the transactionally necessary incidents, conditions, implications, and limits of a particular contract and, we have seen, govern not only the question of whether a term or condition should be implied but also its content and requirements, whether, for instance, the contractual obligation involves a warranty of result or is limited to the party exercising reasonable care.

That implication invokes this standard of transactional necessity cannot be explained on the basis that it advances the parties' rational pursuit of their contingent interests or even their joint welfare, as the default rule paradigm supposes. As discussed earlier, the content-neutrality of the requirement of consideration entails that the particular contents of the promise-for-consideration relation are simply whatever the parties happen to choose. The idea of necessity has no application to the contingent particular contents of the parties' mutual promises or to their consequences for party welfare.[58] The same applies to the fact that subjective and external conditions, including transaction costs, may impede parties making better or more complete provisions. In adopting the standard of necessity, the law stands in tension with the paradigm of hypothetical bargaining and all that it entails.

But the fact that the prerequisites for contract formation may incorporate a dimension of content-neutrality does not mean that they are also value-neutral. To the contrary, they express the very important moral value of the reasonable. And it is this normative value of the reasonable, as embodied in transactional requirements of fair and reasonable terms of voluntary interaction, that is the ground of necessity. Drawing on Cardozo's statement in *Kent,* we say: "Intention not otherwise revealed may be presumed to hold in contemplation the reasonable."[59] On this identity between presumed intent and the reasonable rests the whole law of implication. Implication has to do with what a party can reasonably be held to presume of the other in the framework of their particular transaction. Thus one party cannot reasonably impute to the other the presumed intention to provide a valuable consideration for nothing or worse in return or to take on an open-ended, indeterminate obligation to perform in any circumstance of risk for a limited consideration in return. Such one-sided effects cannot reasonably be presumed. This conclusion, being one of justice between the parties and wholly anchored in the nature of their transaction, is one of transactional justice.

Finally, we also see that just because parties might have but do not expressly provide for a contingency or circumstance in their contract does not necessarily mean that, reasonably viewed, they should be held to have assumed the risk of performing even in the face of it. This basic point—without which all instances of implication must instantly fall to the ground—is also consistent with the orientation of the law of implication being toward the reasonable rather than the rational. The reasonable, and all that it entails, does not represent what the parties prefer or choose in the pursuit of their individual or even joint interests. Rather, as I have tried to emphasize, it sets the appropriate relational framework and parameters for their so choosing. Unless the parties choose something, there is nothing to which this framework can apply. This must come from them. And, in this respect, no one else, including a court, has standing to make their contract. But while the parties themselves decide what they want to give and obtain through their transaction, they do not choose the relational legal requirements, both structural and substantive, which must be satisfied for their choices to have contractual effect or even contractual relevance. Nor do they choose the fact that, whatever they may actually intend, the contractually operative meaning of their intentions is whatever counts as a reasonable construal of their interaction in accordance with the objective test for formation. (Logically, parties cannot displace this test by agreement because whatever they attempt must satisfy its standard to be contractually effective.) As already discussed, this necessary relational framework, which expresses the reasonable, is provided by the law, not the parties.

Thus, the silence of the parties does not per se preclude a court from implying reasonable terms in the exercise of its inherent authority to interpret, construe, and enforce their assents as a contract. Given the role of the reasonable, courts may take the parties to have made their choices, even if tacitly, on the basis that the law will specify and enforce this framework. In a sense, the parties may objectively be viewed as having placed themselves under the protection of the reasonable, trusting in the law's articulation and upholding of it.[60] For the same reason, the fact that at the time of contracting, the parties may not have known that (or which) terms or conditions would reasonably be implied and so could not realistically have contracted around them does not give rise to an issue of legitimacy. The implication of terms and conditions specifies the reasonable and fair meaning of what the particular parties have actually (and not hypothetically) done. As transacting parties who through their interaction can reasonably be held to have drawn themselves together in a promise-for-consideration relation, neither can justly complain against the other when terms are implied on this basis. There are no grounds to claim unfair surprise. Certainly, parties can often preempt implied terms by stipulating their own express terms to regulate the matters that might otherwise come within the purview of implication. But the reasonableness of implication and its fairness toward parties as autonomous persons do not directly depend on this as a real precondition.

With this overview of a transactional approach to implication by way of background, I now wish to consider two important but theoretically still controversial sets of principles: the first, of impossibility and frustration and, the second, of good faith in performance.[61] I hope to show that they not only reflect the proposed analysis but also enable us to see its nature and reach even more clearly.

3.3. Impossibility and Frustration

The relatively modern doctrines of impossibility and frustration overturned an older approach, usually associated with the leading case of *Paradine v. Jane* (1647).[62] *Paradine* held that by promising something without express qualification or limitation, a party is eo ipso bound to perform "notwithstanding any accident by inevitable necessity" or other circumstance however unforeseeable, because he might have provided against it in his contract but did not.[63] The law does not protect parties from their own express agreements. Against this view, the doctrines of impossibility and frustration assert that the scope of the parties' rights and obligations is a matter of construction to be determined not only in accordance with the contract's express terms, but also on the basis of its implicit dimension. Thus even facially general and unqualified terms of wide application can be limited on an implicit basis. And if the terms are found to be so limited, they are construed as ab initio never being meant to apply in the excluded circumstances. All this must be ascertained from the standpoint of the objective test. According to Lord Macmillan, "[T]he doctrine of frustration . . . is a principle so inherently just as inevitably to find a place in any civilized system of law."[64] If so, can the principle, as presented in the leading cases, be accounted for within the transactional framework that I have proposed to explain the other instances of implication? Toward this end, a first task should be to understand how this implicit dimension should be specified and made the basis of such limitation. Here we must address the following basic tension.

Every contractually enforceable promise to perform must reasonably contemplate that the promisor is to follow through even in some circumstances that turn out to be unexpectedly onerous and that may not have been specifically contemplated by the parties at contract formation.[65] That there can be a range of such circumstances is a general fact knowledge of which may be imputed to the parties as reasonable persons when they agree to performance terms that are expressly of wide application. With respect to the particularities of these circumstances that may affect the costs and benefits of performance, the parties can be consciously ignorant. This is because, when deciding to contract and agreeing to terms, parties may reasonably be viewed as implicitly allocating and pricing specifically unknown risks as part of a package of a more broadly framed risk.[66] In this way and as part of their very obligations, parties undertake to perform in a variety of circumstances without the need to particularize those circumstances in advance. If this were not possible, it is not at all clear how parties could credibly commit to perform, because performance must always take place in necessarily unknown future circumstances.

At the same time, even before the modern doctrine of impossibility was settled, the common law had already recognized that general performance terms can and should be treated as not applicable in certain kinds of circumstances despite the absence of express terms to this effect.[67] For example, where a contract contemplated performance to be done exclusively by the promisor in her unique personal capacity, nonperformance resulting from her death, illness, or involuntary incapacity was excused even though express terms covering these risks might have been included but were not. As long as the events were not within the promisor's control, and absent an express provision or background understanding specifically warranting performance even in these particular circumstances, the obligation, though on its face general and binding, was held *not* enforceable in these situations despite the contract's silence about them and their relevance to the parties' obligations.

Our question is: on what basis can the law (then or now) reasonably carve out such implicit limits on the duty to perform, supposing as a baseline the prima facie assumption of risk of performance, even in unknown and specifically unforeseen circumstances, that is inherent in every contractual undertaking? Through a consideration of *Taylor v. Caldwell* (1863) that first enunciated the modern doctrine of impossibility, and then of *Krell v. Henry* (1903) that did the same for frustration, I think an answer can be found—one, we will see, that is fully consistent with the law's transactional approach in other instances of implication.[68]

In *Taylor*, the plaintiffs contracted with the defendants, owners of the famous Surrey Gardens and Music Hall, to rent the hall during four specified dates for the purpose of presenting a series of concerts as well as day and night fêtes. Just prior to the scheduled date for the first concert, the hall unexpectedly burned to the ground (through neither party's fault), with the result that the concerts had to be canceled. The plaintiffs brought an action for their losses, mainly reliance losses, incurred as a result of the cancellation. In deciding for the defendants, Justice Blackburn (as he then was) formulated and explained the modern doctrine of impossibility by generalizing and making explicit what he took to be the logic underpinning the older exceptions: a transactional logic, we will now see, referring to the nature of the particular contract in question and to presumed intention reasonably to be imputed to the parties.

The judgment begins with the acknowledgment that "there seems to be no doubt that where there is a positive contract to do a thing . . . the contractor must perform it or pay damages for not doing it, although in consequence of unforeseen accidents the performance of his contract has become unexpectedly burdensome or even impossible."[69] This initial premise is the already discussed baseline assumption of risk of performance that is inherent in every contractual undertaking. Any limit or condition that is to be implied under the impossibility analysis must be consistent with this premise even while it qualifies it. Now, given this baseline assumption of risk, a promise to perform presumptively implies that, in the absence of express provision to the contrary, the costs and means of performing due to changes in markets or trade conditions as well as in the planned uses and purposes to which received performances are put are factors that prima facie come under respectively the promisor's or the promisee's individual concern and responsibility and, even if adverse or unexpected, do not engage *both* parties.[70]

To establish impossibility, there must be something that qualifies or limits the scope of this presumptive general baseline of assumed risks. But how? Referring to the familiar examples of common law exceptions to the absolute enforcement of general terms, Blackburn formulates the following generalization:

> [W]here, from the nature of the contract, it appears that the parties *must* from the beginning have known that it could not be fulfilled unless when the time for the fulfilment of the contract arrived some particular specified thing continued to exist, so that, when entering into the contract, they *must* have contemplated such continuing existence as the foundation of what was to be done; there, in the absence of any express or implied warranty that the thing shall exist, the contract is not to be construed as a positive contract, but as subject to an implied condition that the parties shall be excused in case, before breach, performance becomes impossible from the perishing of the thing without default of the contractor.[71]

Although, in contrast to the early cases, the music hall in *Taylor* was not itself the consideration (as it would have been in a sale), its specific existence could still be reasonably viewed as foundational to the parties' transaction.

The express terms set out in particular detail what each party was to supply for these events and the manner in which they should be carried out, all to ensure that the specific (and specifically chosen) music hall and gardens would be in a state suitable and fit for the planned activities. Nothing was said during negotiations or in the agreement itself about the present or future physical existence of the defendants' facilities. The parties' silence in this regard merely strengthens the inference that the very terms of the contract, viewed in conjunction with the evident purpose of the transaction, clearly assumed that the defendants' concert hall would be physically intact to be used as a venue. This was an agreement to rent an existing named hall. The continuing existence of that specific hall was thus something that the parties reasonably, though tacitly, took as basic and necessary for performance without which the other terms would be useless and inapplicable and would presumably have been different. Here, therefore, the complete destruction of the hall by fire, found to be wholly beyond the defendants' control and vigilance, changed the very basis of performance so that holding the defendants liable for breach in these circumstances would be to impose an obligation upon them radically different in kind from what they must reasonably have contemplated at contract formation.[72] The defendants could reasonably say: "*Non haec in foedera veni.* It was not this that I promised to do."[73] This alone was the decisive and sufficient reason for relief.

Whether the defendants had or could have insured their hall or were in a better position to absorb the loss are factors about which the judgment makes no reference at all. In light of the court's analysis, there would be no need for the court to do so because these factors were irrelevant. Note that here the contract was deemed unenforceable by reason of impossibility in the sense that the *contractually contemplated* performance was impossible, even if it might have been physically possible for the defendants to rebuild the concert hall albeit at huge expense within a period to allow the plaintiffs' show to be put on. Such physical possibility—even if real—would not provide the performance contemplated by the parties, which, as already stated, rested on the assumed continuing existence of the concert hall as it stood at the time of contract formation. It would not be a performance of a kind within the parameters of risk that the defendants reasonably assumed. Performance was thus impossible because it could not be done as contractually intended.[74]

This possibility of a fundamental and qualitative divergence between the contractually contemplated performance and the actually feasible performance can be materially significant to the parties in two different ways. For the one who is to perform, it may mean that performance is unexpectedly more onerous and costly or at the extreme no longer physically possible; for the other party, it may mean that his purposes and plans associated with receipt of the contemplated performance cannot be fulfilled. These material consequences of a divergence can be serious and substantial. Moreover, as in cases of mistake in fundamental assumptions, the divergence can unexpectedly enrich one party at the expense of the other. But, in themselves, these consequences, even if onerous and unexpected, do not per se determine the existence of impossibility or frustration or make the enrichment unjustified. The cause lies rather in the qualitative and fundamental difference between the reasonably contemplated and the actually possible performances—what one leading judgment calls a difference "in the significance of the obligation."[75]

The foregoing analysis is consistent with the understanding of transactional necessity and presumed intent that we saw at work in the other instances of implication. Given the assumption of risk inherent in every contractual undertaking, the fact that one or even both parties may have assumed or expected that certain conditions would (or would not) exist when performance is due is not enough.[76] It is essential that both can reasonably be held to the implicit but affirmative assumption that the obligation to perform applies *only* if certain specific kinds of conditions or circumstances exist when performance is due.[77] Only this imports the necessity that the analysis clearly requires. In this way, the contract itself must transactionally, though implicitly, carve out these conditions and circumstances as necessary factors for performance not falling within the baseline presumption of risks that the parties are deemed to assume simply by promising to perform. There is no clearer or more succinct formulation of this view than Cardozo's judgment in *Canadian Industrial Alcohol Co., Ltd. v. Dunbar Molasses Co.*[78] There he writes: "The inquiry is merely this, whether the continuance of a special group of circumstances appears from the terms of the contract, interpreted in the setting of the occasion, to have been a tacit or implied presupposition in the minds of the contracting parties, conditioning their belief in a continued obligation."[79] What must be shown is that a special group of circumstances is "one of the presuppositions immanent in [the] bargain."[80]

In circumstances giving rise to impossibility, an event occurs that affects the way in which a promisor must perform, thereby changing the reasonably contemplated nature of the detriment that the promisor has undertaken at contract formation and thus potentially derogating from the parties' reasonably contemplated promise-for-consideration relation itself. Circumstances can also affect the reasonably expected nature of the benefit that the promisee was to receive by way of that promised performance. Here also actual performance may diverge from the contractually expected performance and so does not preserve the parties' promise-for-consideration as reasonably contemplated at contract formation. This second scenario brings into play the doctrine of frustration. Thus both impossibility and frustration can be viewed as protecting against a failure of consideration in the wide sense explained earlier. And the same transactional analysis that underpins impossibility also informs frustration. To see this, we turn to the landmark English decision of *Krell v. Henry*.[81]

In *Krell*, the unexpected cancellation of the king's coronation and attendant celebrations due to his illness wholly defeated the defendant's purpose in renting the plaintiff's apartment rooms on the days scheduled for the coronation processions. There was no express reference in the written terms to these processions or to any other purpose for which the room was taken. However, the plaintiff had exhibited on his premises an announcement to the effect that windows to view the processions were to be let, and he was only willing to rent out the rooms for the days, and not the nights, of the scheduled dates. Finally, the fee charged for these specific times was suitably enhanced. When the processions were canceled, the defendant refused to pay the outstanding rent and pleaded excuse on the basis of an implied condition.

Against this, the plaintiff argued that the fact that the defendant may have had as his principal or even sole purpose the viewing of the processions did not make it the basis of their contract or a reason to set the contract aside in the actual circumstances.[82] A party's reason or purpose for transacting and wanting the promised consideration is his concern alone. Moreover, as mentioned above, nothing in the express terms of their agreement referred specifically to this purpose or made performance conditional on the happening of the processions. As the plaintiff noted, it was surely within the range of foreseeable possibilities that, for any number of reasons, the coronation processions might not take place as announced.[83] Pitched at a certain level of generality, the risk of cancellation was arguably foreseeable and something that was amenable to being allocated by their contract. Finally, it was clearly possible for the parties to comply with the express terms—the plaintiff could and did make the rooms available as contractually specified and the defendant could have taken and paid for them. In light of the foregoing, the court, the plaintiff argued, should not excuse performance by reason of frustration of the defendant's undoubted purpose. It was the defendant's problem, not the plaintiff's.

Taking up and extending the analysis in *Taylor*, Lord Justice Vaughan Williams answered that, based upon the express terms (including the restricted times and days of the rental, the enhanced rate charged) and the surrounding circumstances of the contract reasonably known to both parties at formation (including the advertisement of the rooms as particularly suited for viewing the processions), the court could infer that the parties reasonably viewed the happening of the processions as going to the very root and foundation of their agreement—this was their presumed intention—with the consequence that the cancellation radically changed the character of the reasonably contemplated performance. The defendant could rightly say: this is not what I was promised. In effect, reasonably construed, the substance of the contract was a license to use the room during certain hours on certain days stamped with the purpose of viewing the coronation processions. It was thus not simply the defendant's own purpose; it was also and more importantly the presupposed aim of the transaction itself which both parties could reasonably be held to have intended.

This would not mean, however, that the defendant should be relieved if just anything beyond the parties' control had interfered with the possibility of viewing the processions.[84] According to Lord Justice Vaughan Williams, it must be an event that was not contemplated by the parties as part of their assumed risks. We may suppose, for example, that if some third party unexpectedly happened to impair the view while the procession was passing by the suite, this would not suffice to frustrate the contract. But here, paralleling the complete and calamitous destruction of the music hall in *Taylor*, there was the outright cancellation of the processions that had been publicly and officially fixed well in advance. Precisely because the transaction, reasonably construed as a whole, was shaped on the implicit affirmative assumption that there would be a procession to be viewed on those days—an assumption so basic that the parties would and did take it for granted without needing to state it explicitly—outright cancellation was something that was not reasonably contemplated by the parties as within either of their risks.[85]

It is important to comment, even if briefly, on the role of foreseeability in this analysis. Like virtually any event that might give rise to impossibility or frustration, cancellation or postponement of the coronation as a result of a variety of causes might have been reasonably foreseen by the parties at some level of generality and probability.[86] But the judgment does not present or frame the issue in this way. Instead, we have seen, the inquiry is whether the contract must reasonably be construed as having contemplated the happening of an event as its necessary foundation—in other words, whether the contract as a whole can only be made sense of on the affirmative assumption that the procession will not be canceled outright on the scheduled date.[87] Having found that this was the case, the judgment notes that it "seems difficult to say . . . that either party must be taken to have anticipated, and ought to have guarded against, the event which prevented the performance of the contract."[88] In other words, if the contract must be so construed, the parties' presumed intention in effect makes *irrelevant* the question of whether, in the abstract, they might have been able to foresee the possibility of cancellation at some level of generality and probability and hence whether they could have allocated this risk in their contract.[89] Thus even if the risk of cancellation had been foreseeable to the parties in *Krell*, this would not necessarily have changed the court's analysis of the substance and foundation of their contract—supposing that the contract terms, subject matter, and surrounding circumstances remained otherwise the same. The only requirement is that the event that destroys the foundation of the contract must be beyond the control of the parties, as distinct from being unforeseeable.

The criterion is therefore not whether parties can reasonably foresee an event but how their contract, reasonably construed in light of its terms and surrounding circumstances, treats it. If the contract does not carve out the risk of the particular event happening from the general assumption of risk that is inherent in agreeing to these terms, the contract necessarily contemplates the risk of this event and prevents frustration. The same is true where the contract evidently recognizes and is shaped by the risk of the particular event happening.[90] Foreseeability, especially of the particular kind of risk at issue, can be a relevant factor, not per se, but as part of this transactional analysis.[91] Thus, everything being equal, the more an event is specifically foreseeable by the party seeking relief, the more this reinforces the conclusion that the risk was not carved out of the presumptive general baseline of risk assumption or, alternatively, that the risk was incorporated into and allocated by the contract terms (particularly price), precluding frustration or impossibility.[92] But it should still be emphasized that on the proposed analysis, foreseeability, even when specific and probable, does not per se preclude a finding of frustration or impossibility.[93] Nonforeseeability is not a threshold requirement that must be satisfied or even considered prior to or independent of the transactional analysis of the contract's foundation and basis.

There is an evident continuity between the analysis of impossibility and frustration and the approach taken in the previously discussed instances of implication. In each, the proper legal determination is decided on the basis of the reasonable construction of the actual, particular contract itself, not some extracontractual principle of fairness or independently postulated criteria relevant to enhancing the efficiency of these kinds of transactions. The contractual determination of the meaning and the scope of the obligation are not exhausted by the express terms viewed by themselves and in abstraction from the whole transaction itself. What these terms mean is determined on the basis of the reasonable interpretation and construction of the promise-for-consideration relation as a whole. Although the express mutual promises at formation may have satisfied the requirements of consideration, thereby making their agreement prima facie enforceable, the circumstances at the time of performance can undercut the significance and basis of the parties' contemplated performances with the result that the promise-for-consideration relation cannot be effectuated as reasonably intended via actual performance. In the face of this risk of failure of consideration, the parties cannot be reasonably presumed to have intended enforcement of the express terms unqualified by these circumstances.

From beginning to end, this analysis expresses a pure transactional necessity that can stand on its own, that is complete within its own framework, and (as evidenced by the judgments in the leading cases) that is institutionally workable for courts in their adjudicative function. It does not add to, substitute for, extend, or improve upon the parties' actual choices. Rather, it articulates a dimension of the reasonable—what *both* parties can reasonably be held to by way of their claims and obligations inter se—that is essential to and implicit in their actual agreement as construed from the very same standpoint, the objective test, that decides whether there is a contract in the first place. It is never per se enough that one of the parties has contracted on the basis of an assumption of fact that turns out to be wrong. While this assumption may be crucial to that party's pursuit of his or her purposes (under the aspect of the rational), it does not itself provide a basis for holding the other party to that same assumption (as part of the reasonable). For that, what must be shown is that this assumption goes to the foundation of the contract itself.

In deciding what is reasonable between the parties and therefore what, if anything, should be implied, the fact that they have not explicitly addressed a given risk is not per se determinative. In fact, I have tried to show that, as elaborated in the leading decisions, this analysis does not admit any normative contractual gaps or lacunae (save the *ex facie* and not necessarily determining absence of express terms addressing the contingency at issue). With respect to impossibility and frustration, this absence of normative gaps is ensured by the two-step analysis that, we have seen, animates the cases: first, inherent in every contractual undertaking is the baseline assumption of the risk of performance even in unknown and unknowable circumstances; second, this baseline can only be qualified or limited if the contract itself, reasonably construed, affirmatively carves out the existence or continuance of a special group of circumstances as the tacit presupposition of the contractually contemplated obligation to perform, without which the agreement does not make sense or deliver reasonably intended value. Therefore, unless a particular contract can reasonably be shown to have limited or qualified the baseline assumption of risk in this way, it will be enforceable in the actual circumstances of performance, despite the fact that introducing other terms or limits serving one or more favored instrumental goals might make the transaction "better" or "more complete." Within this analytical framework, there are no gaps and so no point of entry or need for the introduction of extratransactional principles or values. Note finally that while the implementation of this transactional analysis to specific contracts certainly need not automatically yield a single right answer in any given situation, its qualitative considerations governed by the standard of necessity objectively construed do actually guide the inquiry and can lead to transactionally reasonable answers. This is quite sufficient for the purpose of specifying what the parties may reasonably be held to and what they can reasonably be expected to accept as fair and reasonable terms of their interaction.[94]

This transactional approach, which, I have tried to show, is not only intelligible and complete in its own terms but also actually at work in the case law, stands in sharp contrast with the economic analysis. Whereas the question for the law in deciding impossibility or frustration is in what circumstances after formation does the intention of a particular contract, reasonably construed as a whole, clearly exclude enforceability, the question for economics is "who should bear the loss resulting from an event that has rendered performance by one party uneconomical?"[95] A performance becomes uneconomical when its costs would be greater than its benefits. On this economic approach, therefore, in principle *any* resulting net cost sustained by either party (what about third parties?) must be taken into account and all situations of net cost potentially bring into play the economic goal of efficiently allocating the risk of this cost so as to maximize the parties' joint surplus. There is no basis—as the law does—for viewing situations giving rise to excuse as setting limits to the enforceability of contractual rights and duties. True, economic analysis may hold that where contract terms have expressly allocated the risk of loss, there is no reason for further inquiry on the assumption that this allocation is efficient. But consistent with the default paradigm, this analysis denies or more standardly simply ignores the possibility that the contract's implied dimension can provide answers even in the absence of such express terms.[96]

For the purposes of developing a public justification for contract, the crucial difference between this economic analysis and the transactional approach is not that the factors taken into account by the former are always irrelevant to the latter. It is rather that in the economic analysis, all the various factors in its inquiry—including the range of economically relevant interests, resulting costs and benefits, relative ability to bear losses via insurance, foreseeability of loss, and so on—are specified and evaluated from a standpoint that is independent and apart from the actual contractual framework: the qualitative and determinate performances reasonably owed as part of the promise-for-consideration relation, which is the indispensable voluntary basis of the parties having any contractual rights and duties at all and of the court having the authority to adjudicate their dispute in the first place. Everything turns on this difference.[97]

3.4. Good Faith in Performance

Speaking for US contract law, section 205 of *Restatement (Second) of Contracts,* announces that "[e]very contract imposes upon each party a duty of good faith and fair dealing in its performance and its enforcement."[98] The provision reflects the now prevailing definition of good faith as an implied covenant that comprises the two elements of "honesty in fact" and "the observance of reasonable standards of fair dealing."[99] Though it is true that not every common law jurisdiction has endorsed good faith as a distinct doctrine generally applicable to all contracts, the clear tendency is for them to do so.[100] Even where they have not, they arguably accomplish what good faith requires via other principles, doctrines, and forms of analysis. To complete this chapter, I would like briefly to consider whether good faith in performance has a distinct and essential role as part of the implied dimension of contract law and whether it can be satisfactorily explained within the proposed transactional framework without having to be supplemented by other theories and values.[101] For this purpose, I shall draw on the analysis in certain leading cases, particularly American, and on scholarly accounts of good faith. While the range of examples discussed is not comprehensive, my hope is that the main instances are covered sufficiently to bring out the nature and role of good faith in performance and to confirm the applicability of the transactional analysis to it.

There is wide agreement that the good faith requirement does not add new unbargained-for primary terms to a contract.[102] Thus it can never be bad faith performance for parties not to do something that, reasonably construed, they did not promise. This holds whether or not unbargained-for terms or performances would make the parties' transaction more desirable, efficient, or even more welfare-enhancing.[103] Nor does it convert parties into each other's fiduciary, requiring each to subordinate his or her separate interests in order to further those of the other.[104] Expressed in terms of rights, good faith does not require parties to forgo, compromise, or qualify their rights as established and reasonably construed at contract formation, keeping in mind that here as elsewhere in contract law the existence and the meaning of express terms are ascertained by construing the contract as a whole at contract formation, including its full context and background or underlying assumptions, factual as well as normative.[105] Emphatically, good faith is not "a stand-alone duty . . . that is independent from the terms expressed in a contract or from the objectives that emerge from those provisions."[106] Stated broadly and in positive terms, good faith in performance applies to, and within the parameters of, the particular promise-for-consideration relation entered into by the parties, and its task is to ensure that the expressly agreed-upon performances are construed and carried out in a way that the parties must reasonably have contemplated at contract formation. Paraphrasing the traditional formulation, good faith consists in an implied covenant that neither party will do anything, under cover of express terms or in their absence, that will have the effect of altering or destroying the other party's contractually contemplated right to receive the benefits and fruits of their bargain.[107] In short, parties must not act in a way that "eviscerates or defeats the objectives of the agreement that they have entered into."[108]

So understood, the requirement of good faith would seem comprehensive enough to encompass virtually any instance of implication, importing an open and general framework norm of reasonableness available to develop legal responses to a wide range of issues, and requiring parties to act with due regard for the contractually intended performance interests of each other.[109] It would ensure that the implicit but nevertheless contractually fully effective dimensions of *pacta sunt servanda* are filled out.[110] If good faith is viewed in this way, Lord Mansfield was surely correct when he characterized it as "the governing principle [that] is applicable to all contracts and dealings [and is] adapted to such facts as vary the nature of the contract."[111] Nor is it surprising that commentators take good faith as expressing "the unspecified inner logic of contract," "the essence of contract," and "contract's core value."[112] Good faith in performance seems to express at the highest level of abstraction the transactional conception of implication. Without denying this view of good faith as a general norm of reasonableness and fairness, the question is whether there is in addition a more specific conception of this requirement that, though regulative of every contract, is concerned with a distinct set of issues that any reasonable system of contract law must address. That this may be the case is suggested by the existence of an extensive and long established line of decisions, English as well as American, that seem to be concerned with a more delimited domain of implication and which American courts in particular associate with good faith in performance.

For example, consider the so-called "duty of cooperation" cases where the promisee does or omits to do something that unreasonably interferes with, or makes more difficult, the promisor's execution of his obligations, with the result that by the express terms of their contract, the promisor should be denied the benefit of the promisee's counterperformance.[113] Both English and American decisions view such conduct as in violation of an implied covenant that is imported into every contract.[114] For example, there is the basic case where A agrees to purchase B's goods with payment to be made upon delivery and receipt of the goods but, without justification, A refuses to accept the goods when B tenders them.[115] If the refusal stands, B cannot sue for the price. Or, as in the classic English House of Lords decision in *Mackay v. Dick*, A agrees to purchase B's machinery on condition that it satisfies certain performance requirements when operating in circumstances that require A to make her land available and suitable for testing the machinery, but A does not do this, so that the condition cannot be fulfilled.[116] Or finally, there is the well-known American decision of *Patterson v. Meyerhofer*, where the parties agree that the plaintiff vendor will sell the defendant purchaser land that the vendor does not yet own but that, as the purchaser fully knows, the vendor expects to buy at an auction and then convey to the purchaser.[117] The purchaser attends the auction and persistently outbids the vendor who is otherwise ready, willing, and able to buy the property, resulting in the purchaser obtaining the land at a lower price than the contract price and in the vendor losing his benefit of the bargain.

In these scenarios, what might specifically make the promisee's conduct bad faith in performance? Her conduct is not in violation of the contract's express terms and could represent in principle a simple exercise of liberty in pursuit of her own, perfectly permissible, interests and purposes. Thus the promisee might have legitimate reasons to reject the goods, to refuse to make her land available to the promisor, or even to participate in the auction. Acting in these ways need not be per se and necessarily bad faith even if (or just because) it causes loss to the promisor.[118] This can simply amount to *damnum sine injuria*. Good faith, it is true, is standardly formulated as an imperative against doing anything that will have the effect of destroying or seriously injuring the right of the other party to receive the fruits of the contract. This may be a necessary condition of the court discerning grounds for implication, as we saw in the other main instances. But as both the cases and commentators point out, this formulation must be approached with some care.[119] For whether or not the other party's *right* is affected is a normative question to be decided by the terms and underlying presuppositions of the contract itself. To establish bad faith, what the promisor must show is that the particular way in which the promisee has exercised her judgment and pursued her interests is not within—and indeed is excluded by—the reasonable, though implicit, meaning and purposes of their contract.[120] This analysis is internal to the particular contract at issue and is purely transactional.

Thus, in the first example, unless the promisee's rejection of the goods is justified because of, for instance, an unexcused deficiency in the promisor's performance, the law reasonably can view the promisee's conduct as simply aimed at manipulating a contractual condition contrary to its transactional purpose in order to deprive the promisor of her benefit under the bargain. The promisee's power to reject goods is for the protection of her interest in performance and against the risk of forfeiture in case of the promisor's breach, not to bar the promisor from performing and thereby to cause her to forfeit the price. Given the absence of any justification for the promisee's conduct that would be consistent with the reasonable expectations of the parties, the promisee's conduct can only be for the purpose of depriving the promisor of her benefit of the bargain and must therefore be bad faith performance.[121] And the same kind of transactional analysis applies mutatis mutandis to the other examples.[122]

Whereas the above bad faith scenarios focus on the promisee's conduct, the following examples involve the promisor's. For instance, A, the owner of a shopping mall, gives B the exclusive right to lease part of his premises for a supermarket, with the rent being calculated as a percentage of B's gross receipts.[123] B then leases from D other premises for a second supermarket but at a lower rent percentage and takes various measures (such as advertising, adjusting the quality and quantity of produce in stock, etc.) that divert customers away from A's premises to D's, resulting in lower rent owing to A. In a second example, in return for a fee, a promisor gives the promisee the nonexclusive use of his pier to unload goods at weekly intervals but then allows other companies to do the same in a way that results in the promisee facing unexpectedly long waiting times and incurring substantial additional expenses.[124]

As with the previous examples, here again the promisor's conduct may simply represent the pursuit of interests, purposes, and activities that the promisor would ordinarily undertake in the course of his business and with his own assets. It standardly involves the promisor's judgment as how best to conduct (e.g., expand, upgrade, or reorganize) his affairs in more efficient and more profitable ways.[125] It cannot be automatically presumed that the promisor has contracted away these options and interests when all that he has agreed to are express terms that do not specifically restrict their pursuit.[126] To presume this would be possibly to impose a serious and contractually uncompensated loss on the promisor and make him akin to the other's fiduciary—something that the law emphatically does not do. At the same time, where the promisor's action impacts seriously enough on the promisee's own performance-related interests, the court must determine whether the action, even if not in breach of an express term, can be justified on the basis of the promisor's own contractual or extracontractual interests pursued in the ordinary course of business or for bona fide commercial purposes. If not, and if instead the action is undertaken in a manner or for a purpose that conflicts with what the contract reasonably contemplates, it will likely be viewed as being for the sole purpose of depriving the promisee of the benefits of the bargain, making it bad faith performance.[127] There can be no a priori answer apart from a careful analysis of the particular contract as a whole.[128]

Thus far, the distinctive role of good faith seems to be to ensure that what a party does or decides, though not facially regulated by express terms, may reasonably be viewed as in furtherance of that party's legitimate interests (whether contractual or extracontractual) and not just a way for it to affect the other party's justified expectations of performance, to the latter's detriment. Good faith does not allow the exercise of judgment or discretion and the pursuit of interest to go against the contract's implicit dimension.[129] This role is brought out with particular clarity by the third and last set of examples that I will discuss, namely, where the contract itself *expressly* confers on one of the parties a power, involving judgment and discretion, to determine by itself matters that can affect the performance interests of both.

In these cases, the stipulated power may be expressly qualified or completely unfettered. An example of the first is a "requirements" contract where a purchaser promises to buy a certain quantity of goods at a fixed price, say, "as needed by the purchaser's business" or "provided the purchaser can use them satisfactorily in its business."[130] Alternatively, the party may be empowered to determine the matter simply and unqualifiedly "at her sole discretion and decision."[131] It is here—especially where the discretion is expressly unfettered—that the special contribution of the good faith requirement is most fully evident.[132] In these cases, "the object of our inquiry is whether it was reasonably understood by the parties to this contract that there were at least certain purposes for which the expressly conferred power ... could not be employed."[133]

Where the contract expressly stipulates definite considerations or criteria for the exercise of this discretion, these must be reasonably taken into account by the party—but, and this is crucial, the contract also intends that it shall be *her* own assessment of the existence, relevance, weight, and so forth of the various factors (including her own interests) that is validly determinative: "[T]he decision remains that of the decision-maker."[134] In this respect, the standard is honesty in fact, not reasonableness in the sense of conformity with an objective, third-party determination. The latter would be inconsistent with the contract's intention, which is to confer discretion and to ground the decision in the party's own judgment. At the same time, apart from express criteria, it is reasonable to presume that the nondeciding party has agreed to lodge this power in the other on the assumption that, at the very least, the latter will not exercise it in a way or for a purpose that is manifestly contrary to "the scope, purpose, and terms of the parties' contract [itself]," thereby changing the nature of the performance or "render[ing] valueless the right conferred by the contract."[135] Thus, in a requirements contract, the contract would ordinarily presuppose that the amounts ordered should reflect the "usual fluctuations incident to the character of manufacturing carried on by [the purchaser]."[136] Discretion is exercised in good faith when it is in response to factors that are genuinely incidental to the foreseeable working and development of a party's business resources or that constitute the presupposed framework within which she foreseeably must carry on her business. But when the reasons for and purposes of a decision cannot be explained within these implicit parameters and the decision impairs the benefit received by the other party from the first's performance, it may go beyond "the limit of the liberty allowed by the contract" and transgress the good faith requirement of honesty in fact.[137]

What about an unqualified express power to decide some matter at a party's "sole discretion"? At one extreme, there may be certain kinds of powers—such as the decision to require payment of a demand note or the power to reject consumer goods that are not to one's sheer subjective satisfaction—where a party's reason for exercising it would be generally and reasonably understood to be wholly irrelevant.[138] Consequently, to that extent at least, it cannot be exercised in bad faith. Indeed, it is conceivable that parties could agree to "complete" express terms that, when construed in accordance with the objective test, vested in one of them a power of unilateral decision "for absolutely *any* reason whatever, no matter how unreasonable or even fraudulent in any and every circumstance."[139] And, as long as this provision, if properly construed as unfettered, would not cancel some minimum residue of promised consideration moving from that party so as not to make her promise illusory, it could in theory "supersede" what might otherwise be presumed as a matter of reasonable implication. In such a case, the contract's express terms would show that the nondeciding party has knowingly assumed the risk of the other party's decision on whatever basis and with whatever consequences that this might have for their expected benefits under their contract.

But such intention and assumption of risk would have to be affirmatively and specifically established, not presumed of anyone even where a stipulated power is explicitly framed unconditionally and expansively. No one is reasonably presumed to intend to place the fate of his or her performance interests at the arbitrary and unlimited discretion of another.[140] In the absence of specific and express terms that compellingly establish acceptance of another's unfettered discretion, the one who exercises discretion must reasonably appear not to have acted on a basis inconsistent with at least certain justifying implicit criteria assumed by the parties.[141] Where, for example, a party's decision in its "sole discretion" involves the retroactive reduction of a main compensatory element of the bargain—"a large part of the quid pro quo that induced party's assent"—and the decision can be explained only on the basis of the party's purpose of not having to pay the other that compensation, there would be bad faith in performance.[142]

We may say, then, that the good faith standard comprises a subjective element in the form of honesty in fact as well as an objective dimension of reasonableness.[143] But note that, for the purposes of this standard, honesty is aligned with the contract's transactional criteria and has no independent significance apart from this. Thus an honest belief that what one is doing is "in good faith" is not sufficient to insulate against bad faith if the grounds or purposes of the decision are in conflict with those contractually envisaged. On the other hand, bad faith does not require or necessarily reflect a culpable mental state.[144] As long as the party's decision does not reasonably appear to be for a purpose that defeats the objectives and assumptions in the contract, there can be good faith in performance, whatever the party's real motives and reasons may be. The good faith requirement does not make a party's motives or reasons for contractual compliance or noncompliance per se relevant. It does not require parties to be morally good persons who conscientiously aim at respecting the contract. The requirement of good faith in performance is juridical, not ethical.

What about the often-stated mandatory nature of the good faith requirement? Parties are said to be unable to disclaim by agreement their obligations of good faith and reasonableness but can determine the standards by which such obligations are to be measured, so long as the standards are not manifestly unreasonable.[145] At the same time, the prevailing view, we have seen, is that good faith with its requirements of honesty in fact and reasonableness in conduct does not create a separate duty of fairness or reasonableness but instead mandates a certain interpretative stance toward every contract that is in keeping with its character as a doctrine of implication.[146]

Accordingly, I would suggest that good faith can be mandatory, not in the sense of imposing nonwaivable requirements of substantive contractual fairness, but in the way that the objective test is itself nonwaivable. Notions of commercial fairness, the avoidance of one-sidedness, and the protection of the benefits and fruits expected under a transaction are thus relevant but only insofar as they can be incorporated as baseline standards and considerations that specify presumed intent within the inescapable interpretative transactional framework of implication. Within this framework, parties have the inherent legal power to agree to express terms that settle the very matters which otherwise would be determined in accordance with these interpretative baselines. But the parties can do so only if they succeed in manifesting their joint intent in a way that satisfies the objective test of formation and interpretation and therefore only if their express terms unambiguously and reasonably convey an intent that the meaning of these terms should prevail over what would otherwise be found on the basis of presumed intent. The greater the difference between the two meanings, the more difficult it will be to show this; and where the court can find another equally or more plausible view that does not derogate as much from the baseline presumed intent, the court will choose it.[147] Here, as elsewhere, "[i]ntention not otherwise revealed may be presumed to hold in contemplation the reasonable.... If something else is in view, it must not be left to implication."[148] In this way, the objective test, expressing the idea of the reasonable, remains nonwaivable and regulative throughout and the analysis remains faithful to the transactional standpoint.[149]

Ultimately, the only thing inherently mandatory in the law of contract is the promise-for-consideration relation itself and whatever it necessarily comprises or entails. The requirement of good faith is further—perhaps the most definitive—evidence of the internal normative resources of this relation. The contribution of good faith is distinct, first, from the role of the implication of obligations (whether of reasonable care or guaranteed result), which is to require or prohibit certain acts necessary to ensure the transaction's fair value and efficacy and, second, from the role of excusing conditions, which is to specify the contractually contemplated limits of the scope and application of the obligation to perform. Good faith in performance applies where a contract has not fully and expressly settled how or for what purposes a party should perform any term or exercise liberties, powers, and judgment under the contract, but where these factors can substantially impact the other party's performance interests. Good faith requires that the party not do so in a way or for a reason that conflicts with the contractually contemplated expectations of performance to the other party's detriment. But in requiring this, it does not add to, improve upon, or make fairer the actual contract between the parties. In conjunction with the other main instances of implication, good faith seeks to ensure that a contract is enforced in accordance with its full and fair normative meaning as a promise-for-consideration relation by filling out its implicit dimension in a way that upholds the reasonable in transactions.

SECTION B

FAIRNESS

....

In a variety of situations, modern systems of contract law, both common law and civil law, give relief for unfairness under the rubric of principles such as unconscionability, lesion, or disproportionate advantage-taking.[1] The determination of a contract's fairness standardly involves an assessment of the fairness of its terms, and on this basis a court may either partially or wholly set aside an unfair agreement or alternatively reform it, even though it otherwise fully satisfies the requirements of contract formation. Historically, in common law jurisdictions, the power to set aside or to limit the effects of unfair transactions was developed and implemented with great sophistication, scope, and depth by equity. In more recent times, the explicit development of common law conceptions of unconscionability as a general principle applicable to all contracts is one of the signal accomplishments of modern contract law, representing a renaissance in the doctrinal treatment of contractual fairness.[2] In European civil law traditions, the doctrinal and theoretical treatment of contractual fairness began as early as the thirteenth century and has continued unabated ever since with the recent enshrinement of a general provision in the nonbinding but still landmark "Lando Principles" of European contract law.[3]

It is therefore striking that many if not most scholars view doctrines of contractual fairness as exceptions to, or even as in tension with, the values and principles that underpin the normative basis of contractual obligation.[4] An important question for contemporary contract theory is whether doctrines such as unconscionability represent definite (not vague or indeterminate) principles that suitably express a conception of contractual fairness that is fully compatible with the principles of contract formation and with the values of liberty and voluntariness that the latter embody. At stake is the central issue of how the relation between freedom and equality in contract law should be understood. My principal contention is that the claims of both may be appropriately interpreted and coherently integrated in the transactional conception of contract that I am proposing. I will try to show that there are a variety of recognized doctrines of fairness that, far from being based on considerations of policy, distributive justice and the like, are fully intrinsic to contract law and that fit within and further specify the transactional conception of contract informing the principles of contract formation. Within this transactional framework, formation and fairness doctrines function together as distinct but nevertheless equally essential and mutually supportive dimensions of the contractual relation. The doctrines of contractual fairness express a conception of justice that is specific to transactions. They represent a further indispensable step in fully working out a notion of the reasonable that is immanent in the promise-for-consideration relation.

To show this, I begin in Chapter 4 with an examination of unconscionability which I take to be the paradigm of contractual fairness and suggest how it should be understood and justified in its own right as well as in relation to the doctrine of consideration. Chapter 5 considers three settled areas of the law—undue influence, restraint of trade (and other kinds of overall imbalance), and the penalty doctrine—that specify important aspects of contractual fairness. My aim will be to clarify their respective contributions to ensuring contractual fairness in the overarching transactional analysis of contractual obligation. Finally, in Chapter 6, I draw together the proposed understandings of fairness and formation by providing what I hope is a comprehensive approach to the difficult problems of fairness and assent in standard form contracting—an approach that at once reflects the reasoning in the leading cases and is consistent with general principles of contract law.

Chapter 4

The Paradigm of Contractual Fairness

The Principle of Unconscionability

In this chapter, I discuss what I take to be the paradigm of contractual fairness: the doctrine of unconscionability. I begin by presenting the currently dominant theoretical approach to unconscionability that, following a suggestion of Arthur Leff, views it as consisting of two different and indeed two separate species of unfairness—procedural and substantive—and I argue that this account is wholly inadequate to explain the actual requirements and operation of unconscionability, both in practice and as a matter of contract theory.[1] Far from representing two different kinds of unconscionability, "procedural" and "substantive" concerns are inseparable and integrated dimensions of a single conception of unconscionability. Any finding of unconscionability necessarily requires both aspects. With this more adequate understanding of unconscionability on hand, I then take up the question of the relation between it and consideration and suggest that, contrary to the usual assumptions, there is no tension between them. In fact, unconscionability not only presupposes the promise-for-consideration relation but also determines it more completely. The doctrine of unconscionability builds on and is continuous with the requirement of consideration. Both express distinct but essential dimensions of the reasonable in contract law. To see this, it will be essential to keep in mind that, like unconscionability itself, the principles governing contract formation are not merely procedural but instead specify a definite kind of relation that has both formal and substantive dimensions. And while the prerequisites of consideration may be in certain respects content-neutral, they are not value-neutral. Finally, I argue that this principle of contractual fairness is wholly transactional and nondistributive in character. It expresses an idea of justice that is specifically framed for transactions and that is immanent in transactions.

4.1. Unconscionability and Contract Theory: The Procedural versus Substantive Dichotomy

Most theoretical discussions of the doctrines of contractual fairness view them as qualifying, limiting, or even negating the grounds of enforceability established by the principles of contract formation. These grounds are taken to be merely procedural and content-neutral and, as such, to be the whole and the exclusive basis of contractual enforceability. According to this prevailing view, so long as parties are legally competent, they bind themselves through their mutually manifested assents in accordance with whichever terms they may have chosen. It is true that where a party's assent results from the other's misrepresentation, deception, or wrongful threat, the latter may not be able to insist on performance, whatever the terms may be. In such circumstances, the traditional defenses of misrepresentation, fraud, and duress come into play. However, because these defenses apply irrespective of the content of the terms, they do not challenge, but to the contrary are consistent with, the assumed purely procedural and content-neutral character of contract formation. They do not concern the fairness *of the contractual terms themselves*. Yet the reason why the topic of contractual fairness is theoretically so important is, we will now see, precisely that there are settled general doctrines of contract law that present the reasonableness or justice of the terms themselves as pertinent to the determination of contractual enforceability.[2] Certainly, in a variety of situations, courts in all developed systems of contract law apply principles that set aside agreements for unfairness even where there has been no duress, mistake, fraud, or misrepresentation. Historically, equity was particularly active and developed in this regard. This judicial work has been neither exceptional nor marginal. To the contrary.

The way most contemporary theories—both autonomy-based and economic—manage this apparent tension between their conception of the content-neutral and purely procedural character of principles of contract formation, including the traditional defenses of duress, mistake, and so forth, on the one hand, and concerns of contractual fairness, on the other hand, is to introduce the distinction between procedure and substance into the analysis of contractual fairness itself. Following a suggestion first made by Arthur Leff, they presuppose that there are two genuinely distinct and separate forms of unfairness—thus two different kinds or categories of unconscionability—and that one of them, procedural unconscionability, is particularly suited to fit with the basic tenets of contract law. In this way, it is thought, at least some notion of contractual fairness is preserved.

For example, promissory and other autonomy-based theories standardly allow for the possibility of nonenforcement for procedural unconscionability on grounds that are closely analogous to those underpinning the traditional defenses of incompetence, duress, fraud, and misrepresentation.[3] So understood, unconscionability is justified, not on a distinct basis of its own, but only to the extent that it is in the service of these other doctrines and their underlying values. Even then, unconscionability is and must be a blunt tool that can merely approximate the operation of these defenses.[4] As for the second kind of unconscionability, substantive unconscionability, most assume that it is inherently problematic because it must rest, they suppose, on considerations of distributive injustice that cannot fairly be deemed the responsibility of any given individual. To strike down such agreements is implicitly, but arbitrarily, to shift the underlying collective and social responsibility for these circumstances onto a given individual.[5] Moreover, nonenforcement can often exacerbate the economic circumstances of the very persons whose position seems disadvantaged from the standpoint of distributive justice and who are supposed to be the beneficiaries of such principles of fairness.

Exceptionally, when advantage-taking violates some other serious moral duty, the resulting agreement may be liable to be set aside. But such grounds are extrinsic to the voluntary basis of contract. This is how Charles Fried, for example, explains what is surely a central and undisputed instance of unconscionable agreement: salvage contracts at a grossly excessive rate.[6] According to Fried, given the exceptional and restricted circumstances of salvage, nonenforcement of grossly disproportionate agreements does not ordinarily run afoul of the concern about arbitrarily displacing collective responsibility for distributive injustices.[7] So, to this extent, nonenforcement is not precluded. But what is the positive reason for setting aside these arrangements? They should be unenforceable, Fried suggests, because the salvor is already under a duty of humanity to assist the ship in distress and should not be allowed to reap an "unjust profit" for doing what it, the salvor, is bound to do anyway.[8] However, even on Fried's terms, the basis for characterizing the profit as unjust and for consequently setting aside the agreement is problematic because it rests on the salvor being under a duty that is not ordinarily enforceable and that is external to the promissory basis of contractual obligation.[9]

Economic theories present a basically similar analysis, though framed in terms of welfare considerations.[10] Thus a central concern of economic theories is that, except where there have been clear flaws in the bargaining process that can trigger the traditional procedural defenses, it may be too costly or institutionally too difficult for courts to determine whether contract terms—and in particular price terms—are disciplined by competitive market forces or result from some kind of wider market failure. Focusing on the particular bargaining process between parties before a court will not readily be sufficient to decide these matters one way or another. And like autonomy theories, economic analysis underlines the undesirable economic consequences of striking down, which may actually worsen the welfare of the very groups that are the apparent concern of the unconscionability doctrine. Even in those cases where courts can readily identify market failure, such as the situational monopoly scenarios of salvage, economic theories question the basis for deciding against enforcement.[11] A contract, they suppose, should be enforced as long as it is welfare-enhancing for both parties compared to the baseline of no contract at all. However, in the absence of true duress, misrepresentation, or fraud—which generally result in contracts failing to satisfy this criterion—a transaction can be welfare-enhancing for both parties even in situations where the terms would certainly be deemed unconscionable, such as in cases of grossly one-sided salvage agreements. Consequently, even in these clearly settled instances of unconscionability, an economic analysis provides no definitive positive reason for nonenforcement.

Despite their differences, these theoretical approaches share the same feature of failing to provide an account of the very possibility and the significance of terms being contractually unfair. But a theory that hopes to develop a public basis of justification for contract must try to do this since contract doctrine treats this as a reason for nonenforcement in a range of well-established instances.[12]

Consider, for instance, the already mentioned and noncontroversial category of salvage agreements. On the one hand, these agreements can be perfectly valid and enforceable even though they arise in circumstances of situational monopoly where the party needing salvage is in a condition of urgency and necessity with no practical access to markets or to viable alternative courses of action. The endangered ship must accept the salvor's terms or go under. It may do so with eyes wide open and without being affected by mistake or misrepresentation. These circumstances do not prevent contract formation. And because the salvor has not created the situation of danger or compelled the other party to contract, it need not be guilty of wrongdoing or at legal fault. On the other hand, to be enforceable, the price charged for the salvage must be reasonable and fair, reflecting the salvor's risks and costs, its skill and investment in rescue equipment, and including a reasonable premium that takes into account the value of the ship and cargo saved. To the extent that the agreed-upon price deviates grossly from this standard, it is not enforceable and the excess, constituting an unjust enrichment, can be recovered from the salvor. But even where an agreement is deemed unconscionable, the salvor's only misconduct may be—by implication—that, acting in its own self-interest, it has charged a (higher) price term made possible by the circumstances of salvage.

Thus, though not void ab initio and potentially fully valid and enforceable, a salvage agreement may sometimes be deemed unenforceable as unconscionable because the transaction is unfair; and the transaction is unfair because the contractual price is excessive in circumstances where the party who has paid more does not have effective recourse to a reasonable price. The question is: under which species of unconscionability—procedural or substantive— does such an agreement come? Since an unconscionable salvage agreement may certainly satisfy the requirements of contract formation and there need not be any mistake, misrepresentation, fraud, or duress within the usual meanings of these defenses, there can be consent on the side of the party needing salvage and an absence of legally cognizable wrongdoing by the salvor. So there seems to be nothing to impugn the process of contracting as such. In fact, the sine qua non for unconscionability here is the excessive price and hence a "substantive" aspect of the contract. But still, it must be emphasized, the substantive aspect is not "in the air." It is not a separate consideration all on its own. A finding of unconscionability cannot rest simply and solely on the fact that the price is excessive. It also seems crucial that the disadvantaged party lacks recourse to a reasonable rate and assents to the excessive price in these circumstances. In this sense, there must also be a "procedural" aspect. Thus, if we instead suppose that the endangered party might reasonably have obtained the service at a reasonable price but chose, with full awareness of this alternative, to accept the higher rate, the basis for unconscionability would be weakened, if not absent. So neither does the unconscionability of the salvage agreement stem simply from its result. The unconscionability of the agreement, it seems, cannot be explained in terms of either procedure or substance alone. Both process and terms appear to be essential factors in this determination and these factors are specified one in relation to the other as jointly necessary dimensions of a single analysis.[13]

Generalizing these points, there is another route to this same conclusion.[14] If we start with the seemingly plausible idea that procedural defects can by themselves trigger unconscionability, what sort of deficiencies might have this consequence if, as we must suppose, the deficiencies fall short of, or at least are distinct from, the traditional procedural defenses such as incapacity, duress, misrepresentation, fraud, and so forth? Let's grant that one or both parties may be subject in some degree to cognitive limits, poor judgment, ignorance, and pressing needs, financial or otherwise. But what makes these factors relevant to a contractual analysis even if they impact on the contractual process and outcome? Ordinarily, their presence does not per se prevent contract formation or affect contractual analysis, including the application of excusing doctrines such as mistake, impossibility, or frustration. We might think that the further element needed is that one of the parties has pursued his or her individual self-interest at the expense of the other. But all contracts presuppose this possibility, and so we still need a criterion to single out when "at the other's expense" is unfairly so. In the salvage scenario, the only thing that remains to make deficiencies contractually relevant so far as enforceability is concerned, despite there being offer and acceptance and consideration, are the *disproportionate terms* of the contract in the form of an excessive price. To affect the question of contractual enforcement, a party's ignorance or necessity must bear on his or her acceptance of the disproportionate terms: the party does not properly understand that the terms are disproportionate, is ignorant of going market prices or is unable to access a market price.

We can also reach this required combination of process and substantive terms by starting with the latter. Thus, even a large disproportion between the terms may be insulated from unconscionability if it results from the disadvantaged party's assumption of risk or donative intent.[15] (By donative intent, I do not mean an altruistic intent—this would confuse consideration with motive—but simply the manifest intent to give something in return for something else of lesser exchange value.) The term outcome, taken by itself, cannot be determinative. The explanation for the outcome must therefore include some factor that negatives such assumption of risk or donative intent: the presence of ignorance or necessity supplies the needed factor. In short, neither procedural deficiencies nor disproportionate terms count as defects except if both are specified with respect to the other in this way. To produce unconscionability, procedural factors must be, in Mindy Chen-Wishart's apt phrase, "substantively inspired and substantively oriented."[16]

It is time to propose, even if provisionally, a conception of unconscionability that has been judicially presented, interpreted, and applied and further that appropriately combines the procedural and substantive as twin dimensions of a unified analysis of the fairness of contractual terms. Though not free of all ambiguities, Lord Denning's influential formulation of a general conception of contractual unfairness in *Lloyds Bank v. Bundy* remains in my view the clearest and most complete modern judicial statement to guide thinking about unconscionability. I shall therefore quote from it in some detail:

> No bargain will be upset which is the result of the ordinary play of forces.... Yet... there are cases in our books in which courts will set aside a contract or a transfer of property when the parties have not met on equal terms... [such] that as a matter of common fairness, it is not right that the strong should be allowed to push the weak to the wall.... Gathering all [these cases] together,... there runs a single thread. They rest on "inequality of bargaining power." By virtue of it, English law gives relief to one who, without independent advice, enters into a contract upon terms which are very unfair or transfers property for a consider-

ation which is grossly inadequate, when his bargaining power is grievously impaired by reason of his own needs or desires, or his own ignorance or infirmity, coupled with undue influence or pressures brought to bear on him by or for the benefit of the other. [By] "undue" I do not mean to suggest that the principle depends on proof of any wrongdoing. The one who stipulates for an unfair advantage may be moved solely by self-interest, unconscious of the distress he is bringing to the other. I have also avoided any reference to the will of one being "dominated" or "overcome" by the other. One who is in extreme need may knowingly consent to a most improvident bargain, solely to relieve the straits in which he finds himself. Again . . . [not] every transaction is saved by independent advice. But the absence of it may be fatal. With these explanations, I hope this principle will be found to reconcile the cases.[17]

Consistent with Lord Denning's general conception of contractual fairness, the principle of unconscionability, which I take to be the paradigm of contractual fairness, can be stated as follows.[18] It holds that parties who reasonably appear to be intending an exchange transaction are presumed, as between them, to intend to transact for equal value and that a serious disproportion in value between the promised performances, as measured against a competitive market price or some other appropriately reasonable standard, calls for an explanation. To be enforceable, the disparity in values must, in effect, be found to have been positively intended by the party who receives less. But this intent cannot be reasonably inferred where that party accepts the unequal terms as a result of impaired bargaining power, including the party's failure to understand or ignorance that the terms are grossly unequal, pressing need or necessity that prevents the party from accessing more equal terms, and the like.[19] Pertinent, though not necessarily decisive, in this inquiry will be whether the party obtained appropriate independent legal advice before agreeing. My central claim in this chapter is that, understood in this way, unconscionability represents a definite and coherent nondistributive or purely transactional conception of fairness that is intrinsic to contract. Far from conflicting with the principles of contract formation, it fits with and develops them. The first and perhaps the most challenging step in showing this is to clarify the relation between the doctrines of consideration and unconscionability. I turn now to this question.

4.2. From Consideration to Unconscionability

We saw in the discussion of consideration that it does not suppose or concern itself with equivalence in values or even with the entire question of comparative values between the promise and consideration. As long as just *some*thing of value is done or promised in return for something *else* of value, that is sufficient. A disproportion in values cannot, by itself, prevent contract formation. Because consideration is indifferent to the adequacy of consideration, whereas this is precisely the concern of unconscionability, the question immediately raised is whether these two doctrines can stand together.

According to the nineteenth-century will theorists, the answer must be no.[20] They took the doctrine of consideration's indifference to adequacy as meaning that, as long as consideration has been requested, a party should reasonably be presumed to have accepted it as a suitable equivalent to what he or she has given up and that the party should be held to it. Supposing a noncoerced agreement to the mutually requested considerations, there is, they thought, necessarily present whatever fair exchange may be required by contract law, no matter how disproportionate the actual values exchanged.

That this view, which is still echoed in contemporary theories that restrict unconscionability to a purely procedural conception, is questionable is suggested by the historical point that the doctrine of consideration's indifference to adequacy was rarely, if ever, expressly used to justify enforcement of a clearly unfair agreement. Rather, when courts invoked this absence of the need for market equivalence, it was usually to show that despite first appearances of being gratuitous, a transaction was in fact bilateral in the required way and so enforceable on that basis.[21] More telling is that consideration's indifference toward adequacy was never an obstacle to courts of equity refusing certain remedies and setting aside agreements for gross inadequacy of consideration—even while these same courts fully accepted and indeed insisted on the requirement of consideration for nonformal promises.[22] To understand how this was possible and why the view of nineteenth-century will theory is mistaken, we must recall the core features and role of consideration.

We saw that in virtue of its structural requirement that consideration must be requested as quid pro quo by one party from the other who in turn must provide it in response, the law ensures that every contract must have the form of mutual relatedness and reciprocity. Through its substantive requirement that the consideration be something of value in the eye of the law, the doctrine assures that there are two qualitatively different substantive contents that can be construed as wanted or usable, as subject to a party's exclusive control and as something that can be moved from the exclusive control of one into the exclusive control of the other. What the doctrine of consideration requires, then, is that each side moves to the other something that can reasonably count as a substantive use value, which is qualitatively different from the other use value moved in return. The nineteenth-century will theorists made the mistake of not seeing that the sort of value involved in establishing a sufficient consideration is just use value. As a consequence, they also did not see that, in ascertaining whether the contents of the parties' mutual promises meet this criterion of conveying two distinct substantive use values, any comparison between them in terms of equivalence or, in other words, as exchange values is simply and totally irrelevant.

My fundamental contention shall be that whereas the doctrine of consideration views the content of the required quid pro quo as use values, the aim of unconscionability is to regulate this content under the aspect of equivalence and as embodying exchange value. These doctrines thus have different roles and concerns. At the same time, there is a division of labor between them within the framework of the basic promise-for-consideration relation. They work in tandem and specify essential and indeed mutually supporting aspects of that relation. Whereas the requirement of consideration prepares the ground for the normative elements of unconscionability, the latter builds on the former, filling out and completing what it begins. This dynamic has its source in the following tensions at the core of the doctrine of consideration.

First, although the substantive dimension required by consideration specifies a content that is unambiguously two-sided, this content does not itself express *in its substantive aspect* the structural fact of mutual relatedness or quid pro quo which is nevertheless a defining feature of the promise-for-consideration relation. Substantively, there are simply two qualitatively different things, each having different use values and each being something that can be wanted in itself without reference to the other. The fact that each side is something of value does not establish any relation between them. Hence there is a gap between the inherently relational character of the promise-for-consideration relation, on the one hand, and its substantive dimension comprising qualitatively different and separate use values, on the other. Further, we saw that the parties' mutual assents, when they satisfy offer and acceptance at contract formation, are absolutely identical and copresent: they are *ad idem*, willing the very same terms at the same time without any factor or feature that distinguishes one side from the other. As participants in contract formation, the parties are abstractly identical and thus equal. But this also is not mirrored in the substantive contents of the considerations that must be qualitatively different and unequal.

If there is a conception of value in which these substantive contents figure as in and of themselves mutually related and abstractly identical, this would make for a complete congruence between the form and content of the basic contractual relation. And, necessarily, this conception of value, being wholly transactional, would indeed exhaust the idea of value pertinent to the contractual relation. Now there is such a conception of value—as already intimated, it is exchange value as distinguished from use value.[23]

We have seen that use value concerns an assessment of something's usability in light of the thing's particular physical and other concrete qualities and the ways it can serve possible needs and purposes. The fact that the thing belongs to anyone, let alone to someone else, need not change the assessment. Exchange value is fundamentally different. Here, the value of a thing is conceived *in relation to* that of another thing, where both things are objects of exclusive ownership and their owners voluntarily dispose of one thing for the other.[24] Exchange value always presupposes two qualitatively different usable things, but abstracts from these qualitative aspects and treats the objects as commensurable in purely quantitative terms: so much of x equals so much of y.[25] This is different from my wanting something that you have more than what I have (a judgment that makes it rational for me to transact with you). A comparative assessment of this sort refers merely to which of two things I prefer and so does not go beyond use value. By contrast, exchange value involves the mutual relatedness of relational judgments of worth by *both* sides. This is because exchange value consists in a thing's worth as expressed in relation to something else via a transaction formed by both owners reciprocally disposing of their things as between themselves. Each side's judgment of her thing's worth and her decision to dispose of it implicitly makes reference to the reciprocal judgment of the other.

Thus exchange value is necessarily transactional, whereas use value is not. Indeed, a thing's exchange value need not be expressed only in relation to one other thing, but can be systemically expressed in purely quantitative terms that show its worth in relation to indefinitely many other things, all exchangeable with each other. Its exchange value can be expressed as market price. But whether something may be viewed as usable by me, and therefore as a legal benefit, is a matter that can be determined without taking its price into account. Moreover, the thing may still be deemed useful whether I have paid more or less for it than the price that would ordinarily be charged on the market. The two aspects are distinct.

There is a further important contrast between use value and exchange value: whereas the first, as already suggested, comes under the rational, the second engages the reasonable.[26] To elaborate, the decision to choose something instead of something else, which underpins the assessment of use value, engages a party's deliberation about her preferences and rational advantage. If she wants x (which the other party has) instead of y (which she has), she may decide to transact: this is her decision alone and she has no basis for complaint as long as she receives x in place of y. By contrast, a judgment in terms of price has to do with exchange value and a relational judgment as between the two sides. Whereas the first judgment underpins the individual decision to contract and provides grounds for thinking that the party will be better off as a result, the second judgment, I shall argue, determines whether the transaction is *fair* to both. The price judgment, being relational and coming under the idea of the reasonable, is something that a properly constituted third party, such as a court, can appropriately assess.

Given that the conception of value in the doctrine of consideration is limited to use value, its aim cannot be to ensure the reasonableness of exchange value and price as between contracting parties. By not distinguishing between use and exchange value, the nineteenth-century will theorists not only mistook consideration's indifference to adequacy as entailing that all noncoerced exchanges necessarily satisfy equivalence—thereby making the whole matter of equivalence irrelevant—but also, and for the same reason, they failed to recognize in the existing law of contract notions of value and principles of fairness that are relevant in deciding this further and distinct question. For, understood in the way suggested in the previous section, unconscionability seems prima facie to be just such a principle. It treats exchange value as normatively salient and seeks to regulate the quid pro quo against a benchmark of contractually contemplated equivalence, requiring a gross disproportion in the values exchanged to be transactionally justified. Its role seems therefore clearly distinct from that of consideration.

Now, it is one thing to point out the difference between the two doctrines. It is equally important to see whether and, if so, how they might fit together. Indeed, it would seem difficult to have a clear idea of the specific role of either doctrine unless we understand how they fit together. This is what I now wish to examine. In keeping with the idea of a public basis of justification, determining this question of fit should, however, be done within a particular framework: one that takes the principles of formation as given and fully satisfied *first*. This order reflects the fact that a failure to satisfy the requirements of consideration or of offer and acceptance precludes contract formation in the first place and makes the parties' agreement void ab initio. Absent this first step, there simply cannot be a contractual relation and the question of unconscionability has no traction. At the same time, this does not mean that fairness cannot also be a prerequisite of enforceability. The challenge, then, is to explain how a distinct contractual concern about equivalence in exchange value as embodied in a doctrine such as unconscionability might fit with, and in effect build on, the requirement of consideration, all within the framework of the promise-for-consideration relation. We begin, therefore, once again with the requirement of consideration and see how a principle such as unconscionability might seamlessly emerge from and complement it.

Starting, then, with the doctrine of consideration, we have seen that it ensures that there is a genuinely two-sided relation constituted by two qualitatively different objects, each of which is something that can be reasonably viewed as usable by the party to whom the consideration moves at contract formation, thereby transferring exclusive rightful control from promisee to promisor. In virtue of being two-sided, the promise-for-consideration relation is irreducible to a merely gratuitous promissory relation. But, as I have already noted, whereas the doctrine of consideration stipulates as necessary the relational form of quid pro quo, its substantive requirement of legal value, as use value, is *not* relational. For this, the content of the quid pro quo must be viewed in terms of exchange value.

Now although the doctrine cannot itself provide this further step, it prepares the way for it. By requiring that the content of each side's consideration be qualitatively different from that of the other, while counting as something that can be wanted by the other side, consideration sets up a relation that can be further specified in terms of the form of exchange value, which by its very nature obtains only between two or more qualitatively different usable objects. Further, the relational structure that consideration requires can reasonably be understood as involving a transfer of rightful exclusive control from each party to the other, thereby ensuring the very kind of relation requisite for exchange value. Finally, precisely because the doctrine is indifferent to comparative value, consideration is *permissive* with respect to the sorts of value relations that may obtain between the two sides of the promise-for-consideration relation: in effect, permissible terms can be on a continuum ranging from truly equal values at one end to what substantively represents an enrichment by one party of the other at the other end. Consideration for one's promise does not make the relation an exchange of equivalents but rather ensures that it is a two-sided promissory relation that, in this purely promissory medium, may be substantively either an exchange of equivalents or a gift or some coherent combination of both elements. In other words, the relation sets up the *possibility*—always within its promissory framework—of an intrinsic contractual distinction between exchange and gift and of assessing contracts in these terms. As long as it stays within this promise-for-consideration framework, a distinct doctrine that views the quid pro quo in terms of exchange value need not undermine or displace but rather can complement and complete consideration's own contribution to the construction of the contractual relation.

The principle of unconscionability would seem to satisfy these desiderata. It is limited to judging the fairness of terms against the benchmark of equivalence and holds that an unexplained gross disproportion in the values exchanged is subject to being not enforced at the request of the disadvantaged party. More specifically, the principle presupposes that parties should reasonably take each other as intending an exchange for equal value and that this presumed intention goes to the very root and foundation of their agreement. Therefore, where the terms involve a gross disproportion in value, the basis of the agreement fails unless it is clear that the disadvantaged party has intended the difference as a gift or alternatively has assumed the risk of this loss. Unconscionability construes the quid pro quo in terms of exchange value by insisting on the difference between gift and exchange in promise-for-consideration relations.

This presumption of an intention to exchange for equal value is not based on a statistical or an economic truth but rather is imputed as what is fair and reasonable as between transacting parties. But why? Here I give a preliminary answer that bears on the relation between unconscionability and consideration. The more complete and deeper analysis of the relation between equivalence and the equality of contracting parties is pursued in Chapter 11.

As participants in the promise-for-consideration relation, parties objectively view each other as promisors and promisees—as movers and receivers—of something that has value in legal contemplation. Because each of the parties contributes from his or her side exactly in the same way as the other, the interacting parties may be viewed in this respect in identical terms and as equals. Moreover, in this relation and vis-à-vis each other, they count as mutually separate and independent persons, each with something usable that is initially under his or her exclusive rightful control and that the party uses by giving it up in order to obtain the consideration provided in return. This use of one's thing as a means to obtaining another's is the thing's purchasing power.[27] Now, purchasing power, when generalized in relation to many other things, becomes a quantifiable potentiality that transcends any one transaction and yet at the same time can only be realized in and through particular transactions. And, supposing the existence of market relations, this generalized purchasing power is potentially measured as the thing's price. Thus, unless there is reasonable basis for saying that as an exchange transactor independent from and equal to the other, one party would accept a loss that no one else need incur—and a loss that simply enriches the other party—he or she must be presumed to have an interest in, and to be transacting on the basis of, obtaining the going market price for the object or service that he or she transfers to the other.

But in general, no one is presumed to want to give away one's own for nothing or to intend the enrichment of another who is separate and independent and with whom one has no preexisting moral or juridical ties apart from contract. If we are not to impute to parties an indifference as to whether they lose the purchasing power or value of what is theirs, each must be presumed to assent to giving up his or her thing's purchasing power in return for something else with purchasing power, and given their status as independent and equal, each party must fairly be presumed to consent on terms that give him or her the quantitatively same purchasing power in return.[28] In this situation of equality, there would be no basis to presume that parties would accept anything less.[29] As between themselves viewed as separate and equal persons with mutually exclusive protected interests, neither party can be presumed to intend to enrich the other at his or her own expense. They cannot reasonably expect this of each other.

At the same time, parties are not obliged to transact for equal value but can instead intend to confer what is objectively a gift on the other or alternatively to take upon himself or herself the risk of obtaining less than equal value in return. Each can dispose of his or her thing as that person wishes—if this is the party's manifested intent, reasonably construed. As long as the party who receives less than equal value is promised just something of value, there is the two-sided relation required by consideration for contractual enforceability.

I wish to emphasize that even in a situation of proved donative intent or assumed risk of unequal value, the presumed intent to transact for equal value remains regulative as a fair and reasonable benchmark. A large disproportion in values is not simply upheld as valid without further inquiry. The disproportion must be explained by showing positively the existence of donative intent or assumption of risk. And for this, it must be reasonable in light of the particular circumstances of the parties' interaction to infer that the intending party has in effect waived the opportunity to obtain equal value: the party must intend the unequal transaction against a background of knowing and having access to the going market price. Clearly, where the party's decision stems from ignorance or necessity, it will be difficult to draw this inference. Unless the law requires that the existence of donative intent or acceptance of risk is positively and clearly established in this way, each and every disproportion would automatically amount to a gift or intended loss. This would not only be inconsistent with the presumed intent that should be imputed to the parties as equal and separate transactors, but it would also immediately and completely oust the doctrine of unconscionability.[30] In short, we see here how the principle of unconscionability, expressing the reasonable in contract, both frames and makes appropriate room for parties' choosing their terms and in this way exercising their powers as rational persons.

We can now state the relation between consideration and unconscionability. The doctrine of consideration fixes the first step by specifying the requirement of a two-sided promissory transaction that may be construed as a mutual and two-way transfer of rightful exclusive control with respect to some usable things or services. Because consideration is indifferent to comparative value, it establishes two-sided promissory transactions that can substantively be anything from an exchange for equal value to what is in effect a (still two-sided) gift transaction that approaches the giving of something for nothing. Building on this, the principle of unconscionability takes the second step of reasonably differentiating between, and ensuring the transactional integrity of, the two basic categories of two-sided transfer, namely, exchange and gift. The law can make this qualitative distinction between gift and exchange because it does not automatically view a transaction for unequal values as an exchange for equivalents and it can ensure the integrity of these two categories by not automatically presuming that every enrichment is intended as a gift. In this way, the transaction terms, reasonably construed, must express either an intent to exchange or one to give, or some intelligible mixture of the two. This is the meaning of legally operative intention in contractual relations. An agreement that does not express such intention is not a fair transaction enforceable against the disadvantaged party, despite the fact that it may satisfy consideration.

Thus we arrive at the following division of labor between consideration and unconscionability: whereas consideration establishes genuinely two-sided promissory transfers that may but need not involve equal value, unconscionability ensures that the contents of these transfers count substantively as genuine exchanges, gifts, or some combination thereof. Together, consideration and unconscionability establish, respectively, the possibility and the actuality of two-sided promissory exchange and gift transfers. Neither doctrine conflicts with the other: consideration does not address the issue of equivalence and so does not rule out its contractual relevance; for its part, unconscionability does not require that all transactions be equal exchanges and so allows for consideration being everything from a peppercorn to something of equal value. Finally, if we think of the principles of formation as specifying the meaning of freedom of contract and of unconscionability as embodying fairness and equality in contract, we can now see how these fundamental yet seemingly divergent values can in fact be coherently ordered in one unified account of contract.

4.3. The Transactional and Nondistributive Character of Unconscionability

I noted earlier that contemporary contract theories often assume that unconscionability reflects a collective judgment externally imposed on contracting parties and that if it is to be justified at all, it can only be on the basis of distributive justice. According to this view, unconscionability analysis is not internal to the determination of contractual obligation or to the meaning of the contractual relation. Taking up certain elements and features of the doctrine that might be thought to suggest this view, I would like now briefly to explain why this is not the case.

To begin, does the fact that contract law—in both common law (including equity) and civil law systems—widely uses competitive market price as the measure of value hold contracting parties to a standard external to their particular relationship? In fact, the use of market price has a long history. It is well documented that even the medieval jurists and philosophers took the "just price" that regulated fair exchange to be the price, or the range of prices, set by competitive markets. According to these writers, prices can vary from place to place and from day to day, depending upon the costs of production, scarcity and need.[31] Granting that the market price functions as an economic mechanism for the efficient allocation of the different factors of production and consumption, what features might make it an appropriate standard of equivalence from a (contractual) juridical point of view?

Briefly stated, the crucial feature, which was already explicitly recognized by the earliest writers even with their more rudimentary analysis of markets, is that a competitive market price is ordinarily fair to all transactors. It is fair, first, because of its tendency over time to be actually or at least actuarially the same for all and, second, because being by definition given to and unaffected by the specific purposes, needs, situation, or conduct of any given individual, it represents a "common estimation or judgment" of value that abstracts from the particularities of market participants while being realized through their indefinitely many bilateral transactions.[32] Being inherently relational, the same for all and not decided by anyone in particular, it embodies the very same kind of abstractly equal relational standpoint that contractual equality requires and that parties, as equal persons, may reasonably be presumed to accept when contracting with each other. Far from being a collective judgment foreign to and imposed upon transactions, it is one that can count as shared, impersonal, and ordinary and that therefore provides contract law with a metric by which to judge terms of exchange as reasonable as between the parties. It is a standard that is independent of which side of a transaction a party happens to be on. In all these ways, it fits exactly with what we have seen the objective test requires. In addition to performing allocative and distributive functions, prices can provide this purely juridical and transactional measure of equality.[33]

Thus, wherever the subject matter of a contract can be priced in this way, this will be the presumed standard of equivalence to which parties can reasonably be held by each other. At the same time, it should be emphasized that this does not preclude parties from jointly establishing their own measure of equivalence, from treating two differently priced items as equivalent, or, as stated above, from simply deciding donatively to forgo equal value. No less with the determination of value than with the meanings of words, the objective test allows for parties jointly to fix their own, even idiosyncratic, measures and estimations. But that they have done so is not to be presumed: it must be specifically inferred from what the parties have (contractually) said and done against the backdrop of an applicable and reasonably available market price. Finally, if there is no measure to assess the values of things apart from their immediate relation—a case of pure barter—then, by definition, the exchange terms must be equivalent and fair as between the parties under the unconscionability doctrine.

Should a price that deviates from the competitive market price be upheld if the difference reflects either the special value placed by the seller on her item or alternatively the special benefit to the buyer in obtaining it? The principle of equivalence in exchange is dispositive here as well.

If we suppose that the item can be shown to have special significance to the seller such that, in giving it up, she will sustain a loss that is not fully compensated by the going market price for such items in general, it is consistent with contractual fairness that she receive more than market price to offset this loss. No one is obliged or reasonably expected to accept uncompensated losses as part of transactional fairness. To the contrary, where a transaction entails particular losses or risks of loss for a party that are peculiar to their transaction, fairness imports that the price or terms be adjusted to reflect this. This highlights the importance of assessing the particular circumstances and incidents of individual transactions when determining whether the standard of equivalence has been met.[34] This means that consistent with transactional fairness, the terms obtained by a financially disadvantaged party who poses a credit risk may be harsher than those available to one who is wealthier. At the same time, however, it must be emphasized that this holds true only insofar as the terms are needed to compensate for such risk of loss. Thus the fact that one party may greatly need the other's item or may derive special benefits from having it is not a basis, consistent with fairness, for charging more. The first party's gain does not impose any loss or risk of loss on the second. The particular advantage to the first party is due not to the second but rather to the former's own circumstances or condition. If the second party charges more on this basis, it is tantamount to her selling what is not hers.[35]

Still, it may be objected that by postulating market price equivalence as a regulative baseline, the principle interferes with the liberty of a party (as owner) unilaterally to set her price, which, if accepted by the other, should be enforced as is.[36] Since a vendor, say, is under no prior obligation to others to sell her item at all, she can decide not only whether to do so but also the terms upon which she will consent to part with it. It is up to others whether or not they wish to purchase it on those terms. In reply, this objection establishes at most that the seller cannot be obliged to sell at the market price or, for that matter, at any price at all. However, the issue here is not this but whether the seller can reasonably hold the other party, the buyer, to a price that seriously deviates from going market rates and that can only be explained on the basis of that other party's ignorance or necessity. The fact that the seller owns the item and is the only one who can consent to part with it (this is the seller's immunity as owner) does not, by itself, determine the reasonableness of terms that can be binding upon the other (this involves the seller's contractual rights against the buyer). Those terms must be consistent with the equality of the parties and their reasonable expectations as participants in a contractual transaction.

Now when determining whether a contract should be set aside for unfair terms, courts—starting with those of equity—ordinarily require that there be a *gross* inadequacy of consideration: there must be a disproportion of such a large magnitude that makes it striking, clear, and, as it was often said, such as would shock the conscience of the court.[37] Why this high threshold if the underlying principle is simply (any) quantitative nonequivalence?[38] The brief answer is that in this way the disproportion will be both reasonably evident to the gaining party and readily ascertainable by a court acting within the parameters of its institutional competence. Let me elaborate.

That the disproportion should be such as to be reasonably manifest to the gaining party is in keeping with the objective test and is fair toward this party. A disproportion exists for the purposes of contract law just insofar as it is reasonably cognizable as between the parties and therefore in accordance with this standard. We must keep in mind that in the scenarios of possible unconscionability, the essential requirements of contract formation—consideration and offer and acceptance—have been fully satisfied. To this extent, then, both parties may therefore reasonably conclude that they have brought about a two-sided, voluntary transaction. There is a basis for a reasonable expectation to which the law attaches prima facie enforceability. To set this aside in a way that properly acknowledges it, there must be clear and evident facts that put the advantaged party on notice that they have transacted on terms that manifestly conflict with the other party's presumed intent to receive equivalence. Only in this way does the law avoid unfairly surprising the gaining party.

It must also be possible for a court readily and predictably to ascertain the existence of such disproportion.[39] This requires the court to determine the relevant market and the going market prices as the background standard against which to ascertain the existence of a disproportion and so forth. Direct assessment of a given market may sometimes be difficult or impossible—for example in a situation of market failure or in the complete absence of any market. Here a court must be able to construct a credible competitive price, even if very roughly, via extrapolation and inference from comparative factual assessments.[40] Yet, as rightly emphasized by economic approaches to unconscionability, a court whose focus is on the particular transaction before it may face serious informational limits in determining these matters, which standardly involve systemic considerations, even where a competitive market exists.[41] Such difficulties are endemic and exacerbated because, in reality, markets are not fixed and stable states but, to the contrary, are dynamic processes that need not be in a condition of equilibrium. It may be unclear what the competitive state of the market is, and, at best, a court may only be able to ascertain a range of possible prices. But unless a court can make these determinations and establish that particular terms are indeed outside the parameters of the ordinary, judicial intervention on grounds of unconscionability is without a basis in fairness, quite apart from other considerations. In addition to preventing unfair surprise to the parties, a threshold requiring striking and evident disproportion gives courts more confidence that they are setting aside a genuine deviation from market prices and not simply interfering with "the ordinary interplay of forces" by which markets move toward competitive prices in equilibrium.[42]

Does the doctrine of unconscionability—and the conception of contractual fairness that it embodies—authorize setting aside otherwise enforceable agreements because of a party's moral wrongdoing or in order to protect certain categories of transactors, such as the economically or cognitively disadvantaged, the commercially inexperienced or the emotionally vulnerable, or finally to correct disparities in bargaining strength as such? If so, this would seem to conflict with the transactional nature of contract law as I have explained it thus far and more specifically with its particular conception of party equality, the objective test, and the fact that contractual liability is widely viewed as strict. But this is not the case.

Properly understood, unconscionability does not require wrongdoing or even independently unconscientious conduct on the part of the enriched party.[43] Nor need there be bad faith in a subjective sense. Certainly, unconscionability does not depend upon fraud, duress, or misrepresentation by the gaining party. Even the earlier cases that analyzed transactional unfairness in terms of fraud meant by this, not actual dishonest or deceitful conduct, but a contract that is unequal and *therefore* unjust in an extreme degree. As Lord Denning correctly stated, "The one who stipulates for an unfair advantage may be moved solely by self-interest, unconscious of the distress he is bringing to the other."[44] There is unconscionability, then, if enforcement of the transaction would unfairly enrich a party at the other's expense and the unfairness consists simply in a gross inadequacy of consideration that, given a party's value ignorance or inability to access equal value, cannot reasonably be explained on the basis of donative intent or assumption of risk. Unconscionable conduct, it has been rightly said, can consist merely in the "passive acceptance of a benefit in unconscionable circumstances."[45] Whatever moral "fault" or "unconscientious conduct" is necessary need only consist in this.

The contrary view, which would stipulate a separate and additional requirement of some form of morally culpable or reprehensible conduct, must explain why this is necessary if there are unfair terms of the kind just discussed and how it can be relevant if the terms are in fact fair.[46] Overreaching, high-pressure tactics or gross indifference toward the other party's necessitous circumstances, price ignorance, or emotional frailties may be morally reprehensible. But assume that, as it happens, the terms actually agreed upon are not disproportionate but in fact balanced, proportional, and exactly what each party might reasonably have expected and intended if there were no such infirmities: the fact that a party may have acted in these ways will not, and cannot, be a basis on which to impugn the fairness or indeed the validity of an otherwise enforceable contract. These factors, which can of course include such conduct, are irrelevant unless they result in terms that, because they are seriously imbalanced or disproportionate, require an explanation; and the relevance of such factors can be at most that they provide evidentiary support for the inference that the disadvantaged party did not intend this disproportion donatively or as part of her assumed risks of loss.

For the same reason, unconscionability does not seek to correct disparities in bargaining power as such or to single out per se particular categories of individuals for heightened protection.[47] It cannot be emphasized too much that it is not on the basis of parties' particular attributes or circumstances but because of an unexplained gross inadequacy of consideration that terms are deemed unfair and set aside. Inexperience, infirmity, ignorance, emotional vulnerability, and so forth are relevant only if, and insofar as, they result in unequal terms and preclude an inference of donative intent or assumption of risk. Unconscionability is a judgment about transactions, not parties, and it depends wholly on whether the contract terms are unfair in this way. Thus, even though experienced commercial and business transactors may usually be held to have assumed the risk of loss, this need not always be the case, and it will ordinarily be so only within certain parameters.[48] Everything depends on the particular terms and circumstances of the particular transaction.

It seems clear, then, that understood in this way, the principle of unconscionability is nondistributive in character. A "ship in distress agreeing to salvage for an exhorbitant price" does not constitute a meaningful class of persons from the standpoint of social distributive justice. Yet it is arguably the clearest and the least controversial occasion for the application of unconscionability. Need, which in some form must be taken into account by any credible conception of distributive justice, is not per se a normatively relevant factor. Unconscionability's exclusive focus on given transactions viewed separately and not as part of the more comprehensive social system makes it unsuitable as a principle of distributive justice. At the highest, unconscionability ensures that one who *already* has rightful exclusive control over something of value and agrees to transfer it is presumed to intend equal value in return. Unexplained gross departures from equivalence result, via rescission, in a return to the status quo ante or, more rarely, in the judicial enforcement of a reformed and now equal exchange. Such a principle does not aim to rectify economic or social inequalities by transferring resources from one group to another in accordance with a norm—any norm—of distributive justice. It does not aim to regulate starting positions and is consistent with the most extreme inequality of resources. Its effects are distributively neutral or arbitrary. As noted above, transacting with persons with more limited or uncertain resources may expose those who do so to heightened risks of loss, and it is fully consistent with unconscionability that the latter parties insist on terms that compensate them appropriately for undertaking these risks. Hence the terms that the economically vulnerable can expect under this principle may only reflect and reproduce their disadvantageous positions in the distribution of wealth.

Unconscionability represents a conception of fairness in transactions or commutative justice, not justice in distributions.[49] It treats parties as equal by recognizing and protecting in each the power to receive something of equal value from the other in return for what he or she gives. Parties can be held only to terms that are consistent with this possibility. At the same time, parties are not obliged to transact for equal value and can freely decide not to do so. But this is something that must be reasonably apparent in their interaction and cannot be simply presumed as their intent. Within these parameters, unconscionability can function as a supreme regulative principle that is internal to the transactional elucidation of contractual obligation. It is transactional not only because it builds on and completes the bilateral structure of the basic promise-for-consideration relation but also because it is fully consistent with this relation being interpreted as a transfer of purely rightful control as between the parties.

Chapter 5

Three Other Doctrines about Fair Terms

Undue Influence, Restraint of Trade, and the Penalty Doctrine

Having discussed the principle of unconscionability, which I view as the paradigm of contractual fairness, I now want to turn to three other prominent and settled doctrines that, I shall argue, also regulate the fairness and reasonableness of contract terms: undue influence, restraint of trade, and penalties. What requirements of contractual fairness does each of these embody and how do their specific norms relate to the proposed account of unconscionability and the transactional conception of contract? For there are important differences among them. My aim in this chapter is to bring out the richness as well as the unity of these norms of contractual fairness. I will now consider each of the doctrines in turn.

5.1. Undue Influence

Historically, English equity distinguished between two different categories of undue influence.[1] The first, referred to as "actual undue influence," requires proving, directly or by inference, the existence of actual instances of pressure that induce the complainant to transact. While the sorts of pressures that amount to actual undue influence can certainly fall short of duress and, unlike duress, they generally operate in the context of a relation of trust and confidence, they can readily be conceptualized as relationally inappropriate or illegitimate pressure analogous to duress in arm's-length dealings.

By contrast, no such ready analogy is plausible with respect to the second category, called "presumed undue influence." Here, apart from certain specially protected relationships, a complainant must establish, first, that there is a relation of so-called influence and confidence between the parties and, second, that the resulting transaction between the parties (whether contract, conveyance, or gift) is manifestly disadvantageous to the complainant in a way that appears inexplicable except as resulting from the defendant having exercised his influence inappropriately at the complainant's expense. Such a transaction, as it is now put, is one calling for an explanation.[2] The transaction, which to all appearances can only have been procured by undue influence, will not be enforced and the defendant will not be permitted to retain his benefits unless he can show that the complainant's consent to the transaction was based on a fully informed understanding of the nature and effects of the transaction, enabling the complainant to decide independently from such influence. To show this, the defendant may have to establish that the complainant obtained independent legal advice of an appropriate kind. I wish to focus the following brief discussion on this doctrine of presumed undue influence. It represents a requirement of fairness in transactions that is distinct from, and yet that at the same time invites comparison with, the doctrine of unconscionability.[3]

For the purpose of establishing presumed undue influence, there must first of all be a relation of influence. What does this consist in? Briefly stated, it is a relation where a complainant places trust and confidence in the defendant whom the complainant expects to exercise influence (whether through guidance, management or other forms of control) in ways that can affect the complainant's decisions to transact with him, thereby impacting her assets and other interests, material or intangible. This relation of confidence and influence can arise in different ways, but it almost invariably involves the defendant being granted and taking some measure of control over the complainant's affairs or assets via a voluntary arrangement between the parties. The requisite relation does not necessarily suppose closeness or intimacy. Nor does the latter automatically involve the former. And while a relation of influence may develop as a consequence of the complainant's physical or mental frailty, it certainly need not arise in this way. For example, in the leading case of *Allcard v. Skinner*, the complainant, a young novice nun, entered a convent, taking vows of poverty and obedience and giving all her worldly possessions to the defendant, Mother Superior, to whom she owed by the convent's rules—which she willingly accepted—the most absolute and exclusive submission. The court expressly found that she did not enter this relation because of infirmity or incapacity.[4] Whatever the source and circumstances giving rise to the relation, we must not presume that a relation of influence is per se problematic or inappropriate, let alone irrational. To the contrary, such trust and influence may be freely and rationally wanted by both parties. It can certainly be in the fully deliberated and self-chosen interests of the complainant, as was the case in *Allcard*.

It is the exercise of undue influence in such a relation that is the problem. The doctrine, it must be stressed, does not protect per se against the results of enthusiasm, friendship, excessive generosity, improvidence, or prodigality, even if the consequences for the complainant are severe and sorely regretted. Unless a transaction results from the defendant's exercise of *undue* influence in his relation with the complainant, the doctrine simply does not apply. What, then, makes for the exercise of influence being undue?

There is undue influence when the party placing confidence in the other enters a transaction with him on terms or with consequences that are clearly inconsistent with that party's proper interests, purposes, or well-being in such a way that cannot be explained except on the basis of the other party's failure to show due regard for or to protect the complainant's interests.[5] The transaction is not otherwise readily explicable by the relationship between the parties. Where the transaction is an exchange, an unfair price may be the factor calling for explanation. However, it need not be limited to this. To the contrary, the impugned transaction may often be donative where the whole issue of unequal exchange is irrelevant. The gift may be too large or otherwise inappropriate given the nature of their relationship, the complainant's circumstances, and so forth. The prejudice to the complainant's assets, material independence or ability to further her interests and ends would "have been obvious as such to any independent and reasonable person who considered the transaction at the time with knowledge of all the relevant facts."[6] At the same time, it should be emphasized that the better view—consistent with Lord Denning's own generalization in *Lloyds Bank* v. *Bundy*—is that undue influence does not require that there be any wrongdoing, fraud, misrepresentation, or bad faith on the defendant's part. The defendant may have been acting selflessly and honestly throughout, unaware of any undue pressure being brought on the complainant.[7] From the standpoint of equity, the defendant's conscience is fettered simply by his failure to ensure the complainant's proper protection in this relation of influence and confidence, precluding the defendant from treating the complainant's consent to the transaction as the expression of her free choice to which she may fairly and reasonably be held.[8] This procedural dimension must be present and combined with the substantively problematic aspect or outcome of the transaction to satisfy the prerequisites of presumed undue influence.[9]

How does this analysis of presumed undue influence fit with the conception of transactional fairness that, I have suggested, is embodied in unconscionability? The latter, we saw, is a general principle applicable to any contract and so does not presuppose a relation of influence. Its role is to preserve transactional fairness by requiring that apparently grossly disproportionate values be given a satisfactory explanation in light of the parties' relation. The disproportion must be shown to be positively intended by the losing party (whether in the form of donative intent or assumption of risk) in circumstances where he or she understands the nature of the terms and has reasonable access to generally available more equal terms. In this way, the doctrine of unconscionability blends procedural and substantive requirements.

The doctrine of presumed undue influence further specifies this integrated substantive and procedural analysis of contractual fairness by protecting against transactional unfairness in the enriched and more particularized context of relations of trust and influence. As just discussed, within this enhanced context of a relation of dependence and control, the undue influence doctrine holds that a defendant ought to take the complainant as intending a transaction that not only, if an exchange, is for an equal return but also that, whether exchange or gift, is reasonable and appropriate in light of the complainant's particular needs, purposes, and welfare. In a relation of influence, there will be ordinarily less room for the defendant to impute to the complainant any assumption of risk of loss and, in addition to the requirement of showing clear donative intention, the defendant will have to establish that the complainant was in a position to exercise separate and independent judgment about whether to give at all and in what manner. As John Dawson suggests, the defendant must not divert a gift, supposing it is appropriate at all, from its usual and natural course in light of the donor's total particular circumstances, including her character, habits, and the particularities of the relation between donor and donee.[10] In this way, the law safeguards a party's donative powers and carries through the task of ensuring the transactional integrity of contractual relations.

Requiring the defendant to take into account the complainant's purposes and interests does not, however, impose upon him a positive duty to assist or preserve, which would be inconsistent with the limits of liability for misfeasance. It means, rather, that a defendant in a position of control and influence can reasonably and fairly hold the complainant to the transaction and can retain the resulting benefit only if he does not exercise influence at the latter's expense. At the same time, terms that prima facie appear harsh may, on examination, be explicable as reasonable as between the parties, given the defendant's own legitimate interests.[11] And to repeat, despite a prima facie inference of undue influence, if the complainant is shown to have acted on the basis of independent judgment, the fact that the contract terms are disadvantageous will not be per se fatal to enforcement because in these circumstances the complainant will be viewed as having in fact accepted the risk of this prejudice. We see, then, that in both the unconscionability and undue influence doctrines, the procedural and substantive aspects are indissolubly integrated.

In sum, as a doctrine of contractual fairness, undue influence upholds the transactional equality of the parties in a relation of trust and confidence. Relations of confidence or dependence are the natural soil for gifts and other transactions that do not result from ordinary competitive forces and bring into play a range of considerations that are absent or irrelevant in arm's-length dealings. The doctrine of undue influence regulates these relations to ensure the more complete integrity of exchange and gift transactions. What counts as an unfair price, donative intent, or an assumption of risk is now worked out within the framework of the particular relation between the parties and the normative expectations that are reasonable and appropriate to it. The richer, more particularized analysis in undue influence develops a fuller, more complete scrutiny of the different dimensions of the two basic forms of contractual promissory transfers—exchange and gift—as these are brought into play by the factors of trust and control. In this way, the doctrine also confirms our previous conclusion that, within the basic framework of the promise-for-consideration relation, contract law supposes a distinction in material terms between gift and exchange and requires that enforceable contracts be genuinely one or the other or some combination of these. The doctrine of undue influence supplements unconscionability in a manner fully consistent with the latter's transactional character.

5.2. *Campbell Soup Co. v. Wentz*, Contracts in Restraint of Trade, and Shackling

The Uniform Commercial Code explicitly singles out the famous case of *Campbell Soup Co. v. Wentz* to illustrate its stated rationale of unconscionability as being "the prevention of oppression and unfair surprise . . . and not the disturbance of allocation of risks because of superior bargaining power."[12] In his last detailed examination of unconscionability, Dawson also singled out this decision, writing that it is "*the* case that it is compulsory to cite in *any* discussion of unconscionability."[13] But whereas the code does not elaborate how *Campbell Soup* reflects the principle of unconscionability, Dawson suggests that it exemplifies what German contract law condemns as *Knebelung* or "shackling."[14] According to Dawson, shackling occurs if the total effect of all the contract provisions taken together is to interfere seriously with or even to destroy a party's powers to use his or her assets or productive energies and pursue economic opportunities with third parties where these contract terms and effects are not reasonably necessary to protect the legitimate contractual interests of the other party.[15] Here the unfairness is not so much the extraction of an unjustified gain via a gross disproportion in values exchanged as the subjection of one party to contractually specified constraints and often discretionary powers for the sole benefit of the other, contrary to good morals and the views of fair and right-thinking persons.[16] As Dawson notes, seemingly minor elements can tip the scales against enforcement if they clearly point to the imposition of a constraint that is not justified when all other things balance out.[17] I think that Dawson was correct and that the facts and decision in *Campbell Soup* are referable to this "shackling" paradigm. What exactly is the conception of contractual fairness at stake here and how does it relate to the principle of unconscionability as presented in Chapter 4? To answer these questions, we first turn to *Campbell Soup*.

Briefly stated, the facts in that case were that the parties agreed to an exclusive selling arrangement, set out on a printed form provided by the plaintiff

Campbell Soup, that obliged defendant farmers to sell to the plaintiff their entire crop of Chantenay carrots at a fixed price per ton. Although one of the clauses excused the parties from performing in certain circumstances beyond their control, the contract specifically prohibited the farmers, without Campbell Soup's consent, from selling carrots that the plaintiff might be excused from accepting—this despite the fact that such carrots were and would remain the farmers' property. Additionally, there was a liquidated damages clause for any breach by the defendants but nothing similar for breach by the plaintiff. When market prices rose sharply, the defendants, in breach of contract, refused to deliver their carrots and began to sell them to others at the going market rate. Because the carrots were of a kind unavailable on the market, damages would be inadequate, and the court stated that, in principle, specific relief should be available to the plaintiff. But in declining to order specific performance, the court held that the agreement as a whole—"the sum total of its provisions"—was too one-sided and drove too hard a bargain for a court of conscience to enforce. The tipping point for the court seems to have been the provision giving Campbell the sole power to decide whether carrots that it was excused from accepting would be resold or left to rot—the court calling it "carrying a good joke too far."[18] This was so even though the clause did not come into play in the actual circumstances because Campbell was fully willing and able to accept delivery of all the defendants' carrots.

What should be emphasized is that the court did not express any concerns about the fairness of the price term or about any procedural irregularities or unfairness. From what the court briefly indicated, it may not have viewed the change in market price as grounds for excuse under either the contract provision or the doctrine of impossibility.[19] Not only did the arrangement for exclusive sale provide evident economic benefits to both parties, but, it should be noted, most of the provisions were appropriately mutual and balanced. The court did not regard these as problematic or unconscionable. It is as if, apart from the provision restricting the sale of unaccepted carrots and the clause stipulating liquidated damages one-sidedly for defendants' breaches only, the burdens imposed on each side were sufficiently reciprocal and mutual, canceling each other out.

As already noted, these two provisions, and particularly the first, tipped the scales the other way. The no-sale provision gave Campbell Soup unilateral power to sterilize the use and value of carrots that belonged to the defendants and that Campbell Soup was not obliged to purchase. This would amount to a unilateral power over an asset that, by the very terms of the contract, might not be the subject matter of the contract. Although the court did not discuss it, it is difficult to see how this unilateral power over the defendants' extra-contractual property was reasonably needed to protect or to ensure Campbell's legitimate interests in relation to their contract—and clearly the prejudice to the defendant farmers could be serious.[20] The court failed even to mention the point that the provision did not apply in the particular circumstances of the breach and it implicitly rejected any notion that the clause could be saved by implying an obligation on the part of Campbell Soup to exercise the provision in good faith. Instead, though the court acknowledged that the provisions were separable, it declined to help a party "who has offered and succeeded in getting an agreement as tough as this one is" by severing the offending clauses and enforcing what remained.[21] Clearly, the court refused specific performance because it viewed the contract as a whole to be, we might say, rotten at its core.

Indeed, in seemingly similar circumstances, courts not only have declined to order specific performance but have also refused to enforce contracts altogether. A clear instance is the nineteenth-century English case of *Young v. Timmins*.[22] In this case, a manufacturer in Birmingham agreed during the remainder of his life to keep his factory open, ready, and able to fill the defendants' orders as the latter might (but need not) choose to make and also not to do such work for anyone else, except within the vicinity of London, without the defendants' express and specific permission on each occasion.[23] The contract entitled the defendants alone to exit the agreement with three months' notice and authorized them, at their unfettered choice, to employ others instead of the manufacturer, during which time the latter would not be released from working exclusively for them and so might be given no work and receive no remuneration for considerable periods. The court held that, taken together, the contract placed the manufacturer "completely at the mercy" of the defendants and imposed a regime that foreseeably compelled him to operate even at a loss, thereby threatening his livelihood and severely impacting—indeed possibly sterilizing—his productive energies without a right to exit.[24]

What is both interesting and noteworthy is that the court in *Young* declared the contract unenforceable on the ground of being void because in partial restraint of trade, and in the leading House of Lords decision of *Esso*

Petroleum Co. v. Harper's Garage (Stourport) Ltd., Young is referred to with approval as illustrating the underlying rationale of this doctrine.[25] Could it be that the old and well-established doctrine of restraint of trade sheds light on the kind of unfairness of the contract terms in *Campbell Soup?*

A contract that is found to be in undue restraint of trade is void at common law as a matter of public policy.[26] Historically, this doctrine, originating in the Elizabethan period if not before, initially took a negative stance based on public policy against all contracts deemed to be in restraint of trade. All such contracts were simply illegal and unenforceable. The current doctrine began with the landmark case of *Mitchel v. Reynolds* (1711).[27] *Mitchel* effected a fundamental and far-reaching conceptual transformation of the issue by focusing on the fairness and reasonableness of the contract terms and by exempting fair and reasonable contracts from the previously undifferentiated exclusion. After *Mitchel,* it became essential to specify, first, what sorts of agreements come within the purview of the doctrine at all and, second, what are the criteria of fairness and reasonableness that decide whether or not such agreements will be upheld.[28] As settled for more than a century, the present legal position is that a contract in restraint of trade is void unless shown to be reasonable as between the parties and in relation to the public.

The first question, then, is what brings a contract within the scope of the restraint of trade doctrine and thereupon subject to the positive requirement to establish its reasonableness. To begin, the mere fact that a contract obliges a party to do or to provide something *exclusively* for the other party for a given duration and thus precludes her, *pro tanto,* from doing this very thing for others, thereby possibly restricting the alternative use of her skills, productive energies, property, and so forth, does *not* per se bring the agreement within the purview of the doctrine. Similarly, a simple contract of sale of something unique has always been specifically enforceable despite the obvious limits that both the obligation and the enforcement necessarily place on the promisor's actions. Notice, however, that with all these contracts, the limit is strictly unavoidable if the party's powers are to be absorbed and used via her performance owed the other.[29] The restriction, we might say, directs or channels rather than interferes with or sterilizes the party's productive or other powers.[30]

To bring an agreement within the doctrine's purview, a restriction must go beyond or be distinct from the mere absorption of the party's powers essential to fulfilling her primary performance for which a quid pro quo has been promised or given in return. Examples include an obligation not to compete after a party leaves the other's employ (and so prima facie is no longer in a contractual relation with the other) or, as in *Young*, an obligation of exclusive dealing that allows a party unilaterally to refuse the other's performance while prohibiting the latter from dealing elsewhere. Although generalization is hazardous, one might suggest that in these and similar cases, the contract may prima facie be viewed in substance as placing constraints directly on a party's ability to control and use her *productive powers qua capital resource* for other purposes and relations, distinct from the particular performances that she has committed to. Parties can, for a valuable consideration, part with a specific limited exercise of their liberty or sell their business with its goodwill—this does not even come within the doctrine.[31] However, it is a different matter if the terms *ex ante* limit their ability (as a general power and potentiality) to engage in business, productive activities, or market relations with others.[32] In addition to the negative interest that parties have in protecting their individual exclusive control over their powers, they have a positive interest in being able to maintain their personal and material independence and to do this by participating in economic activity.[33] These interests are protected as a matter of the policy of the law.[34] That the doctrine has to do with protecting one's powers to trade, to produce, and to maintain one's independence and, further, that unless justified, restraints impacting these powers are deemed void (as opposed to voidable) are the two core manifestations of this policy.[35]

As noted above, constraints of this kind are deemed in restraint of trade and are void unless shown to be reasonable, first, as between the parties and, second, in relation to the public. Invariably this determination turns on satisfying the first prong of reasonableness as between the parties.[36] What does this first prong entail? In a nutshell, the party benefiting from the prima facie restraint has the onus of showing that it is reasonably and proportionally necessary—"no more than adequate"—to protect either the performance owed him (including its fair value) or more usually his proprietary or capital interest and investment that enables him to transact with the other party—and thereby to benefit both of them—in the first place.[37] An example of the first sort of protection (viz., of the performance owed him) would be a constraint needed to ensure reasonable security in the face of evident risks of nonperformance posed by the second party. Instances of the second kind are most frequent in the leading cases: these can involve noncompete and other provisions imposed on a former employee to protect trade secrets and customer lists; or restraints placed on the seller of a business to ensure she does not derogate from the full value of the goodwill of that business that has been paid for in good faith; or, finally, constraints on individual garage outlets and other such facilities for the purpose of enabling producers to maintain stable, effective, and profitable systems of gas distribution to thousands of outlets via individual exclusive selling agreements.[38]

In other words, it is for the party for whose benefit the restraint is imposed to show that the restraint is contractually justified as necessary—but no more than necessary—to protect his transactionally legitimate interests and nothing else.[39] Protecting the benefited party's legitimate interests is transactionally essential to prevent the contract from becoming a source of loss for that party through the other party impairing or appropriating a benefit or interest that was not reasonably intended to be part of what was contractually owed her but, to the contrary, was supposed to continue to belong to the first party and indeed enabled this party to transact (e.g., employ, enter an exclusive dealing agreement) with the other for the benefit of both. The contract terms as a whole, including the price paid by the restrained party, are presumed to reflect this limit. Stated in other terms, to be reasonable as between the parties, the restriction on the other party's powers and freedom must be strictly ancillary to—that is, transactionally necessary to ensure—balanced and fair terms such that it cannot be set aside "without injury to a fair contractor."[40] The restraint of trade doctrine ensures that a transaction does not enable the other party to misappropriate or undermine what is not reasonably contemplated as going to her as part of their fair exchange.

A restraint that "is larger than the necessary protection of the party . . . can only be oppressive, and, if oppressive, it is, in the eye of the law, unreasonable."[41] Like "shackling" in German law, the characterization as "oppressive" in the common law cases, though not strictly a term of art, is a widely used and long-standing label of condemnation aimed at certain particular kinds of unfairness that go beyond the issue of inadequacy of consideration in a narrow sense.

For unjustified restraints do seem to effectuate a kind of contractually imposed servitude. At the very basis of every nonservile contractual relation is the assumption that parties retain control over their powers, productive or otherwise, as constitutive of their personal and material independence even while they carve out for transfer to each other circumscribed uses and crystallized products of those powers.[42] Hence free and fair transactions presuppose a baseline distinction between the inalienable powers that parties retain and the particular performances that they transfer as between themselves.[43] Delineating and preserving this baseline distinction is the special task of a transactionally oriented conception of policy in contract law such as we see here. The specific contribution of the modern restraint of trade doctrine is to assess terms of restraint to ensure that an exchange is not a means for a party simply to limit the other's inalienable freedom to engage in productive and market activities.[44] It is the possibility of such oppression that brings this policy-based judicial scrutiny into play.[45] It is also because an unjustified restraint arbitrarily shackles a party's independent powers which must remain altogether beyond the other's reach that even a scintilla of transactionally unjustified imposition is oppressive. For the same reason, the very idea of a good faith implementation of such restraints must be out of the question. Good faith can only apply to the exercise or enforcement of powers and rights that can be legitimately part of the parties' transaction.

Explained in this way, the restraint of trade doctrine protects against a different kind of contractual unfairness than unconscionability.[46] Its concern is not with the question of equal value between the two sides of an exchange relation. Because the doctrine protects against unilateral imposition on parties' inalienable powers as distinct from ensuring the fairness of the terms on which they dispose of their alienable things and services, there is no role here for assumption of risk or donative intent—in contrast to the analysis of unconscionability. Nor should impairment of bargaining power be a relevant consideration in deciding whether a contract is one that is in restraint of trade or the question of its reasonableness.[47]

At the same time, as part of an integrated transactional approach, the restraint of trade doctrine can plausibly be viewed as supplementing and supporting the principle of unconscionability by ensuring that the fairness and equivalence of an exchange is decided only with respect to the parties' legitimate contractual interests, while insulating their contractually excluded assets and interests from the unilateral control of the other party. As with the doctrine of unconscionability, the unfairness here is completely distinct and independent from the traditional procedural defects of misrepresentation, duress, or fraud. It concerns the terms of the contract and does not depend on fault or wrongdoing by either party. Very importantly, the pertinent notions of interest and burden are transactionally objective and are specified as part of the reasonable. Thus the fact that a contract in restraint of trade may, in some way, be mutually beneficial and in the rational interests of even both parties does not satisfy the requirement that it be reasonable between the parties.[48] It is a matter of ascertaining the qualitative natures of the interest restrained and the interest protected by the restraint and of ensuring that they are of the right kinds and that the protection is both necessary and proportioned.

Note that this analysis is squarely in terms of transactional necessity that does not require the direct balancing of two competing abstract principles or policies, such as the enforcement of voluntary and free agreements versus the liberty of citizens to pursue a livelihood, economic opportunities, and so forth.[49] Apart from the evident difficulties in properly specifying each of these abstract criteria, the idea of balancing them would require recourse to and implementation of some overall value such as welfare maximization. Not only is this institutionally unworkable for a court but there is nothing in the nature of the promise-for-consideration relation that supports reference to, let alone the use of, any such overriding substantive goals. This cannot be part of a public basis of justification.

Returning to the *Campbell Soup* decision with which we began, we can now see how just the single contract clause that vested the plaintiff with the unilateral power to dispose of or sterilize the defendants' own nontransferred property might be deemed oppressive, even though, taken by themselves, the other contract provisions may together have been balanced and reasonable.[50] As already noted, the decision does not indicate any attempt on the plaintiff's part to show that—and it is difficult to imagine how—this provision was needed to protect its legitimate interests arising from their contract. Although the provision did not apply in the circumstances of the actual breach, it was, from formation on, per se oppressive (assuming that it was not justified). Given their exclusive sale arrangement, it represented a substantial and serious potential sterilization of the only nontransferred property that was contractually relevant. Moreover, it was tied to the other clauses as an integrated provision in a total arrangement, as also evidenced by the liquidated damages clause, which applied to any breach by the defendants, including breach of this particular term as well. Having framed the terms as a whole to give itself this control, Campbell Soup could not fairly expect the court to view the challenged provision as unimportant to or severable from the other provisions.[51] In light of the teaching of the restraint of trade doctrine, a court of conscience might well be justified in refusing specific performance of the whole agreement as a "shackling" contract.

5.3. The Penalty Doctrine

Originating in sixteenth- and seventeenth-century equity and taking its modern shape as part of the common law by the first decades of the twentieth century with leading decisions such as *Dunlop Pneumatic Tyre Co. v. New Garage and Motor Co.*, the basic elements of the law governing agreed damages are now relatively well settled across common law jurisdictions.[52] Where a contract includes an express provision purporting to fix damages in case of a breach by one or both parties, courts decide whether it should be deemed either a penalty, which (like a term in restraint of trade) is void, or a valid liquidated damages clause, which is enforceable. A court does so on the stated basis that the latter, but not the former, can be construed as a genuine preestimate of the loss likely to be sustained by a party as a result of breach. Being such, it can in principle be upheld as a contractually binding term. Yet the underlying rationale for this settled distinction has proved elusive.

Like the restraint of trade doctrine, the penalty doctrine is standardly taken to be based on policy.[53] Supposing this to be correct, we still need to clarify here also in what way this is so and whether or not the conception of policy that it involves is part of, not imposed on, a transactional analysis. There are other challenges. Although both the restraint of trade and penalty doctrines assess the enforceability of expressly agreed-upon contractual terms that otherwise meet the criteria of contract formation, the penalty doctrine seems to be concerned, not with the parties' specification of primary rights and duties, but rather with their explicit intent to determine directly and definitively—to fix and settle—the quantum of damages. But doing this is a function generally viewed as coming under the exclusive authority of the law to exercise.[54] This internal tension goes further. If, as one court more recently put it, "it is now evident that the power to strike down a penalty clause . . . is designed for the sole purpose of providing relief against oppression for the party having to pay the stipulated sum," yet this power, the court noted, is also "a blatant interference with freedom of contract."[55] Clearly, the penalty doctrine is concerned in some sense with the fairness of contractual terms.[56] But if so, how does it relate to the conception of fairness reflected in the unconscionability principle, and does it conflict with the consensual basis of formation? The need to articulate a coherent basis for the doctrine recently impelled the English House of Lords in *Cavendish Square Holding BV v. Talal El Makdessi* and *ParkingEye Ltd. v. Beavis* to provide what is arguably the most important discussion by any common law court since *Dunlop*.[57] Drawing on the pattern of analysis in these and other leading cases, I will now try to identify the doctrine's rationale and to elucidate its relation to the proposed transactional conception of fairness.

As already noted, the assessment of a stipulated damages clause goes to the character of a provision expressly agreed to at formation. Thus, as with any other such contract term, the characterization of an agreed damages clause is decided as a matter of interpretation and construction with reference to the time of formation and in accordance with the objective test.[58] Williston was therefore correct, in my view, when he wrote that "whether a sum is liquidated damages or a penalty ... is not a question of the law of damages [but of] the legal validity of a stipulation in a contract ... the real problem is whether the bargain of the parties is enforceable or not."[59] Now because agreed damages clauses are expressly stipulated by parties in their otherwise enforceable agreements, it is not surprising that, particularly in the nineteenth and early twentieth centuries, courts not infrequently presented their task of characterizing these provisions as simply one of construing the parties' intentions and enforcing them.[60] How should this reference to intention be taken?

The relevant sense of intention cannot be "expressed intention," because, as Williston noted, every stipulation for a damages sum would be enforceable—which would patently contradict the division of such stipulations into enforceable and void.[61] It is also clear that how the parties actually understand or designate their clause is not conclusive.[62] As the courts have uniformly emphasized, what must be determined is whether a sum agreed upon by the parties is in its real nature a penalty or liquidated damages. In determining a stipulation's real nature, the inquiry is whether or not the parties may reasonably be presumed to have intended the stipulated sum as compensation for breach.[63] Intention in any other sense is irrelevant. But what does this presumed intention refer to? And how can it be presumed with respect to a matter—compensation—that represents the law's coercive response to the wrong of breach? This is the penalty doctrine puzzle. I suggest the following answer.

To constitute a presumed intent as to compensation, first of all the provision must stipulate a sum that, reasonably construed, is intended to be payable upon breach and is not, therefore, in truth an alternative performance, in which case the clause would not even come within the purview of the penalty doctrine.[64] In addition, it must be reasonable to construe the agreement as intending the stipulated sum to be commensurate with the losses that the parties, at formation, could reasonably expect to result from breach, taking into account not only what could be reasonably contemplated without the agreed damages clause but also what should now be contemplated with the notice provided by the clause. Because the objective test applies here as elsewhere and the relevant standpoint is contract formation, the stipulated sum must be for contractually actionable types of losses that both parties reasonably would have contemplated when they entered the contract.[65] Thus the reasonableness of the sum is not decided per se by its proportionality with the losses that actually result. Actual loss may be relevant but only insofar as it affords "valuable evidence as to what could reasonably be expected to be the loss at the time the contract was made."[66]

At the same time, it is crucial that this analysis of presumed intent not be understood as conferring on parties the joint power to determine directly and conclusively the compensation owing for breach. To the contrary, as already emphasized, the determination of what, if any, compensation is owing—or how the contract is to be enforced on breach—represents *the law's* decision as to the appropriate coercive response to a party's breach as a civil wrong. Indeed, the notion that parties can directly will this would be self-contradictory in conception. This is therefore not something that the parties can be viewed in law as fixing by their presumed intent.

Instead, as I will now discuss in more detail, parties by their agreed damages provision can only *indirectly* contribute to the law's determination of damages. This is done by the law assessing whether the damages provision may reasonably be construed as fixing at contract formation the fair and full value of the performance(s) owing. Very importantly, this full value can include a party's indirect and not readily measured performance interests that, in the absence of the damages provision, might not have been enforceable by reason of remoteness or uncertainty. Assuming that the law's aim in giving damages for breach is to protect a party's performance interest, such fixing of value by the parties can certainly be relevant in the determination of damages even though it is the law, not the agreement, that decides what counts as and what is needed for just compensation. In fact, if the damages provision can be reasonably so construed, it must also be presumed to be so tied in with the other terms and provisions of the contract—especially the price term—that not to take the agreed amount as fixing value, and hence as settling the quantum of damages, would undermine the internal balance of the agreement, thereby unfairly surprising the plaintiff and unexpectedly enriching the defendant.[67]

If these conditions are satisfied, the law, we may say, adopts the expressly agreed sum as a fair and reasonable measure of damages. The law does this, to repeat, because it views the sum (if upheld) as reasonably fixing the full and fair value of the plaintiff's performance interest. In this way, the penalty doctrine also ensures that the stipulated sum represents the fair value of a party's rights or obligations *already established* as part of the promise-for-consideration exchange, not a means of adding, via the route of an agreed damages clause, new obligations or rights that are not already part of that quid pro quo.

According to this view, which English law presents most clearly, the unfairness that the law attributes to a penalty clause rests at bottom on there being a manifest and unexplained incommensurability between the stipulated sum and the fair value of the parties' contractually enforceable performance interests. The core inquiry becomes: viewed at contract formation and in accordance with the objective test, what is the nature and extent of the non-breaching party's interest in the performance of the relevant obligation and is the quantum of the agreed damages sum reasonably commensurate with that interest?[68] To illustrate and fill out this analysis, consider two different paradigms of transactions that are at opposite ends of a continuum of possible instances and for each of which the appropriate application of the penalty doctrine is clear and settled.

At one end, there is "one of the most ancient instances" where the breach consists merely in not paying a fixed sum of money and the expected loss sustained is, and can only be, for that amount.[69] Here the innocent party's legitimate performance interest, as reasonably known to both parties, is fully specified with reference to the receipt of a fixed and certain definite sum. There cannot be any stipulated damages amount that is commensurate with this except for the very same quantum. Without the need to refer to any other factors—procedural or otherwise—any discrepancy between the two disqualifies the provision and makes the agreed sum in the words of Lord Dunedin "extravagant and unconscionable in amount."[70] Its unreasonableness consists in this difference alone. Very importantly, the fact that the innocent party may wish to secure and reinforce the probability of the other's performance by stipulating a higher amount cannot justify the discrepancy. Even if the higher amount serves *both* parties' *ex ante* rational interests by providing such additional assurance of performance, this does not make it count as a legitimate or reasonable performance interest for the purpose of assessing damages. It cannot be such because this would conflict with the nonwaivable policy of the law that requires damages to be compensatory in character and nothing else.[71]

If, however, the stipulated damages equal the proper sum, a court can, and fairly should, enforce the provision as a valid liquidated damages clause and give damages on its basis. The clause is not only reasonable as between the parties (because the amount is not incommensurate or disproportionate) but also rational in the sense of being for their mutual and joint benefit.[72] Agreeing to an amount that fixes damages *ex ante* makes "good business sense."[73] Through the law's adoption of this sum for the purposes of determining damages, the parties can know what will be the financial consequences of a breach, dispel any possible uncertainty as to their expectations, and manifest to each other their intents to minimize the costs and uncertainties of judicial determination of loss.[74] This will, presumptively, be reflected in the other terms, particularly price. Not only can a court adopt the agreed sum as providing a reasonable measure of loss and damages on this basis; it should do so if it is not to enrich one party at the other's expense, contrary to the reasonable expectations of both. These general considerations supporting judicial enforcement of damages clauses, though always relevant in principle, are admittedly not strongly engaged in these sorts of situations where loss is direct and either known in advance or readily determined by a court. But they become increasingly weighty as scenarios move toward the other end of the continuum.

At this other end are paradigmatic scenarios in which a party's contractual interests are such that the reasonably contemplated injury involves losses that are indirect, cumulative, intangible, idiosyncratic, or uncertain. Here, the point applies with special force that "the more difficult it is likely to be to prove and assess the loss . . . the greater the advantages to both parties of fixing an easily ascertainable sum."[75] Examples include losses from breach of noncompete covenants, contracts for oil exploration, agreements in relation to marketing or trade associations, undertakings affecting goodwill, or contracts with public and governmental entities.[76] All the leading English decisions, from *Clydebank* and *Dunlop* to *Philips* and *Cavendish Square,* as well as foundational American decisions such as *Jaquith,* involve losses of this kind.

Thus in *Dunlop,* three of the four law lords emphasized that the plaintiff's main contractual interest was in the stability and preservation of its price maintenance scheme among its distributors, even though the direct and immediate monetary loss sustained by the plaintiff as a result of any one dealer selling at a lower price might be next to nothing. To hold that the stipulated damages sum of £5 for the sale of a tire at below the listed prices is penal because manifestly in excess of the plaintiff's reasonably apprehended direct financial losses would be to misconstrue the actual transactional situation and to compare the wrong things. Reference to the plaintiff's wider contractual interests explains what would otherwise appear to be manifest disproportion in the same way that, as we saw, it could justify a contract's reasonableness under the restraint of trade doctrine. Rightly, the court held that "on the evidence it would appear . . . impossible to say that that interest was incommensurate with the sum agreed to be paid," so that the agreement "contains nothing unreasonable, unconscionable, or extravagant."[77]

Fixing damages in advance in scenarios where the occurrence of indirect losses is plainly foreseeable allows parties to ensure recovery of losses, including intangible losses, that might otherwise count as too remote because they are special or extraordinary. In particular, the quantum of damages that may be upheld as valid compensation can be different from what a court, applying the remoteness test in *Hadley v. Baxendale,* might otherwise have concluded in the absence of the clause.[78] At the same time, this assessment of damages is consistent with the rationale of *Hadley* insofar as the express stipulation of the sum can be reasonably viewed, in effect, as an effort by the parties to "provid[e] for the breach of contract by special terms as to the damages."[79] The insertion of a provision stipulating a higher level for damages can put the defendant on notice of losses that might otherwise be deemed non-ordinary and too remote, without the need to communicate to the defendant what the special circumstances are; and such provisions should be enforceable as long as the amount can be explained in this way.[80] Enabling parties to so provide in advance is "[an] advantage [of which] it would be very unjust to deprive them."[81]

Moreover, it is precisely in these sorts of scenarios involving wider contractual interests and indirect losses that the value of the performance can be affected by extrinsic vicissitudes and risks, which may make it difficult for parties to know and to evaluate its worth when they contract.[82] By stipulating damages in advance, the parties can therefore specify and make jointly clear to each other its full and fair value as between themselves. The same is true where the subject matter is specialized or unique and parties wish to fix its value in advance.[83] In all such circumstances, the agreed sum will be ordinarily bound into the consideration: the price charged evidently depends upon the set sum. Courts rightly hesitate to set aside these sums as penalties, given that this can result in a party being unexpectedly enriched at the other's expense. Even where the range of anticipated losses is broad, courts will not "be astute to descry a 'penalty clause.'"[84] Unless the sum is shown to be clearly extravagant in relation to the range of losses reasonably to be anticipated, the provision should and will be enforceable as a valid liquidated damages clause.[85]

This brings me to the following two questions. First, what is the relation between the penalty doctrine's specific kind of protection against unfairness and unconscionability's regulative ideal of equivalence in exchange? Second, is the penalty doctrine consistent with the consensual basis of contractual obligations?

As to the first question, both unconscionability and the penalty doctrine express the idea of reasonable constraints based on a conception of commensurability or proportionality that applies to contractual terms. They are both doctrines of contractual fairness as between the parties, the elements of which are not reducible to the procedural defenses of misrepresentation, duress, fraud, or incapacity. As we saw with unconscionability, the party seeking enforcement of a damages clause need not have acted wrongly, certainly not in law and perhaps not even in morals: after all, she may only be trying to increase and secure the probability of performance.[86] But whereas unconscionability focuses on the commensurability between the two sides of the promise-for-consideration relation, the penalty doctrine looks to the commensurability between the stipulated sum and what can reasonably count as the legally cognizable fair value of the innocent party's performance interest as affected by breach. In this way, the penalty doctrine ensures that only an agreed damages term that stays within the limits of the promise-for-consideration relation and does not circumvent it is enforceable.

It is with respect to this determination of contractual interests and expected loss, particularly where breach foreseeably can result in uncertain, indirect, or intangible losses, that considerations of bargaining power and risk allocation can play a role. Indeed, the very fact that parties have included an express damages provision suggests that they have assumed some level of risk as to the fair value of their interests and their expected compensation upon breach. At the same time, the fact that the fair value of a party's interests may be opaque to herself or to the other party should appropriately be taken into account. Where, however, both parties are sophisticated and experienced businesspeople who are independently advised, the damages clause will more readily be deemed reasonable even if the stipulated sum is greater than the actual losses or if the provision applies to a range of possible breaches, which can involve losses of differing amounts.[87] (A fortiori where the parties know well their own and each other's contractual interests.) But as the contracting circumstances begin seriously to diverge from this baseline, the reasonableness of the provision becomes more vulnerable to challenge and to being subject to being set aside either as a penalty (if the stipulated sum is disproportionately high) or as a kind of forfeiture or unfair limitation (if the sum is too low).

It must be emphasized that here, as with unconscionability, the fact that one of the parties may be comparatively less knowledgeable, experienced, or able in dealing with the subject matter, market aspects, extrinsic factors, and so forth is not relevant in and of itself and does not per se make the term oppressive. The basis is not in parties' cognitive or other limits as such.[88] It is an unexplained disproportion between the stipulated sum and reasonable protection (i.e., the fair value) of the innocent party's legitimate interests in performance that is decisive. While, as an empirical causal fact, limits in cognition may account for the inclusion of a provision that is unreasonably disproportionate, we must keep clear the crucial point that such cognitive limits are contractually pertinent, not in themselves, but only insofar as they bear on this essential substantive dimension.[89]

Beyond this, if the penalty doctrine is understood as I have suggested, it need not be viewed as conflicting with freedom of contract. The key point is that, properly understood, contractual freedom is the freedom to bring into existence by voluntary interaction contractually enforceable relations and, as part of this, parties can only hold each other to terms that are reasonable as between them. Therefore, the mere fact that parties expressly agree on terms cannot, by itself, be determinative. First, their assents must satisfy a promise-for-consideration relation and, as part of what this relation entails, the expressly agreed-upon terms must also be consistent with each side obtaining the fair value that their contract must reasonably have intended they should have. Now, like the requirements for formation, the distinction between contractual terms (both express and implied) and remedies for breaches of those terms is both basic and mandatory. It is not surprising therefore that this distinction is presented as the policy of the law. (Indeed one might say that the requirements of consideration and of offer and acceptance, being mandatory and nonwaivable, also represent the policy of the law.) Remedies are the law's coercive response to civil wrongs. Through such remedies, contract law seeks to ensure that parties receive the fair value of what each has rightfully acquired at contract formation, in this way following through the transactional analysis under the aspect of compensatory justice.[90]

Supposing, then, that parties have not been trifling and reasonably appear to have transacted for value, there must be at least some residue of contractual obligation and therefore some minimum of remedies for breach that cannot be cancelled by their contractual terms. This limits what can count as contractually enforceable assumptions of risk with respect to agreed damages. Within these parameters and for the purpose of determining the appropriate remedy, the law may adopt what it construes as the parties' efforts via agreed damages clauses to fix and make certain *ex ante* this fair value. The requirement that the stipulated sums be reasonable as between the parties ensures that they in fact reflect and represent just such efforts. This is not the case where, without transactional explanation, a stipulated sum clearly exceeds the fair value of a party's performance interest—or, what is the same thing, exceeds the expected losses resulting from interference with that interest—as contemplated at contract formation. Upon analysis, a provision deemed to be in the nature of a penalty attempts, under the guise of a term regarding damages, to add to the other's obligation without, however, giving something in return as part of the parties' already established promise-for-consideration exchange. In effect, it seeks to obligate the defendant to his or her prejudice without a contractually legitimate basis. To bind another person in this way is unreasonable and oppressive because it simply subordinates him or her. Thus, there is no need to view the penalty doctrine as paternalistic in motivation, any more than with the other doctrines of contractual fairness. Freedom of contract does not, and cannot, include the freedom to bind others to a penalty.[91]

Chapter 6

Fairness and Assent in Standard Form Contracts

Some fifty years ago, Karl Llewellyn wrote that he knew of few private law problems that remotely rivaled the economic and legal importance of standard form contracts and none, he said, that were more baffling to lawyers.¹ Though the pervasive and predominant role of standardized contracts is a relatively recent phenomenon, it is now commonplace for scholars to point out that the vast majority of commercial and consumer transactions involve standardized terms and that standardization is particularly adapted to the requirements of a modern market economy.² I want to focus on the single question of the place of these contracts within the framework of general principles of basic contract law. More specifically, do standardized contracts give rise to issues of assent and fairness that are amenable to analysis and resolution within this framework, or, to the contrary, do they challenge it?

So far as contemporary contract theory goes, one answer, reflected in the characterization of such agreements as "contracts of adhesion," is decidedly the latter.³ In particular, because of their one-sided "take-it-or-leave-it" quality, standard form consumer contracts, it is argued, break with the traditional premises and incidents of free contracting and should therefore be treated as prima facie unenforceable. Critics allege the illusory character of mutual assent, the rights-deleting effects of standard terms, and the systemically corrosive impact that mass proliferation of these contracts has on regulation by the rule of law and fair access to legal redress.⁴ Contracts of adhesion are, and should be treated as, a different category of transaction altogether. Yet it is a basic fact that modern legal systems do not view these contracts as per se unenforceable, unconscionable, or against public policy. And, as I will discuss, leading common law decisions apply general principles and norms of contract law to analyze assent and fairness in standard form contracts no less than for bargained-out agreements.

More commonly, however, contemporary theories, especially economic, see standard form contracts as in fact particularly well suited to modern mass markets and not at all necessarily inimical to efficiency concerns. Like the standardization of commodities, standardization of contract terms can be generally welfare-enhancing. According to this approach, if there is to be legal scrutiny, the focus should not be on the bilateral relation between the parties.[5] Rather, it should be, if at all, on systemic variables such as the operation of actual, often imperfect, markets; the many different economic roles—both visible and hidden—of standard terms; the economic impact of enforcing or striking out standard terms; and so forth.[6] At the same time, this literature emphasizes that such inquiries are often subject to serious theoretical and factual complexities in determining the relevance and existence of these factors against a background of incomplete information about the conditions and behavior of actual markets.[7] As a result, courts are subject to serious limits regarding what they can effectively do to assess and to enhance the efficiency of these contracts. Even if the economic criteria are valid in their own framework, they are not of the sort that can be readily and transparently implemented by courts in discharging their adjudicative function through the giving of public reasons.

It is true that standard form contracting, particularly in the consumer and small business context, can give rise to problematic legal, economic, and social effects that need to be addressed at a systemic level and often via legislative or administrative mechanisms.[8] Nevertheless, there are important issues of assent and fairness in form contracting that courts have effectively identified and addressed within the framework of general contract principles. My central claim in this chapter is that courts have done this in a way that reflects a purely bilateral transactional conception expressing the idea of the reasonable. When evaluated from the standpoint of advancing efficiency, the leading judicial decisions often appear to focus on the wrong factors or seem to be under- or overinclusive.[9] Understood in terms of the proposed transactional analysis of assent and fairness, this, I will try to show, is no longer the case. I should add that far from being original, my argument draws on and tries to bring out the full force of the approach that was most brilliantly argued by Llewellyn himself and subsequently enshrined in the *Restatement (Second) of Contracts,* section 211.[10]

6.1. What Is the Problem with Standard Form Contracts?

To begin, I should identify, even provisionally, some basic features that characterize standard form contracts as a distinct type of transaction.[11] In doing so, we must keep in mind that, as already mentioned, modern legal systems do not view these contracts as per se unenforceable, unconscionable, or against public policy. To the contrary, they recognize that these contracts can and generally do perform important positive legal, economic, and organizational functions.[12] The selected features should be compatible with this positive assessment and not necessarily indicate pathology.

First, standard form terms are presented on preprinted forms (or their electronic equivalent) that have not been individually negotiated by parties as part of the process leading to contract formation. They are prepared and largely finalized prior to the interaction between the particular contracting parties.[13] If the form is presented by just one of the parties without input from or participation by the other, the first party may be called a "form-giver," the second a "form-taker."[14] In consumer contracts, only one side, the business, is typically the form-giver. By contrast, in transactions between businesses, each side can present to the other its own form and thus be simultaneously a form-giver and form-taker.

Second, on their face, the printed forms purport to be integrated contractual instruments containing terms that are contractually (legally) significant.[15] We suppose that they differ in this respect from other printings that may, for example, reasonably appear to be intended to serve merely as vouchers or records.

Third, the standard terms are ordinarily intended for use in indeterminately many transactions with indeterminately many other parties. They have this *general* orientation.[16] Parties have reason to believe that particular standard form agreements are widely and regularly used as contractual instruments to embody contractually intended nondickered terms of the same kind. This, we will see, gives rise to the possibility that prima facie parties can reasonably be held to have given contractually effectual assent to the agreement as a whole or, in Llewellyn's phrase, "en bloc," including therefore to terms that they may not have discussed, deliberated about, or even read.[17] Moreover, because of the general orientation of the form, parties may reasonably assume that (indefinitely many) others are and will be assenting likewise and on the same footing. Parties are viewed not in their particularities but as members of a large, undifferentiated line or mass of users. Consequently, the agreement is interpreted, whenever reasonable, as treating all form-takers presumptively the same way without regard to the actual particular knowledge or understanding that they in fact may have: the standard terms are to be taken as generally applicable and depersonalized norms that are intended to govern an indefinitely large number of transactions past, present, and future.

Fourth, and finally, standard form contracts aspire to be *more complete* agreements in the sense that ordinarily they explicitly incorporate two kinds or categories of express terms. This completeness does not necessarily entail that forms must therefore include many pages of printed clauses and conditions, although they often do. There must simply be express terms of two kinds. Let me elaborate.

As a general matter, contract terms can be divided into two categories. A first kind of term includes what parties promise to give or do, credit terms, ancillary promises and conditions that specify the modes of delivery, and so on. These form the core terms that standardly constitute the promise-for-consideration. In the legal literature, these terms are referred to as "dickered," "central," "core," or "primary." Following Llewellyn, I will refer to these as dickered because, even if they do not result from active negotiation, they ordinarily will be the focus of the form-taker's attention and deliberation as well as possible discussion with the other party.[18] In Russell Korobkin's apt characterization, such terms are "salient" inasmuch as they are specifically evaluated, compared, and implicitly priced by parties when deciding whether or not to transact.[19] While to some minimum extent such terms must be express, they may also be implied in accordance with the general principles of contract interpretation and construction, taking into account trade usages, past performances, and so forth. In the absence of material express or implied terms of this first kind, the agreement may be deemed incomplete for the purposes of contract formation.

But in addition, standard form contracts also ordinarily include a second kind of express terms—call them nondickered or secondary—that typically aim to settle those matters that might otherwise be determined by the law on the basis of contractual implication, as discussed in Chapter 3: for example, implied warranties, limitations on recoverable losses, excusing conditions, and so on. Legally implied terms, we saw, are ancillary to the primary terms because they specify, fill in, qualify, or limit the contractual significance and consequences of those terms. These are matters that parties need not expressly determine to satisfy the requirements of contract formation. At the same time, parties are not precluded from doing so, in this way aspiring to greater completeness and particularization of the contents and parameters of their respective rights and duties. Now at least in many if not most consumer transactions, these secondary terms, even though explicit and even if printed in the same way and with the same visibility as the first kind, are ordinarily not salient for form-takers in the sense referred to above. This is a fundamental difference between the two kinds of terms.

Here is where standard form contracting makes its entry. Because standardized contracts incorporate both kinds of terms, the express terms are typically more complete and complex. This drive toward greater completeness reflects the very impetus for standardizing contract terms in the first place and enables standard form contracts to contribute positively to the working of a modern economy. What is needed and potentially beneficial to both sides are terms that are appropriately specific to a particular kind of transaction and at the same time stable and certain across individual transactions of the same sort. Even though the law provides general legal prescriptions where the parties have not, these terms may not successfully reflect the particular needs, risks, circumstances, and conditions of specific trades, undertakings, and business. Nor, *ex ante,* are the legal determinations and applications of the implied background principles, being in the form of general standards subject to interpretation, always straightforward and certain. By fashioning and using standard form agreements, parties try to achieve this.[20] Where only one of the parties knows and cares about the particular requirements, risks, and conditions of a given trade or service, it is only to be expected that it will be that party who takes the initiative and works out the standard terms. Making the terms subject to negotiation in any individual transaction would defeat the whole point of this effort.

While there may be other factors—for example, those pertaining to the internal hierarchies and efficient workings of businesses—that also explain these initiatives, the foregoing is sufficient to show that there is nothing inherently unreasonable in one party drafting standard terms in advance and offering them on a take-it-or-leave-it basis to others.[21] Note that this rationale can apply whether or not a business is operating in a competitive market situation. In accordance with this tendency, the range of transaction decisions that must be taken by form-takers, particularly consumers, may be reduced to what is minimally necessary. Form-takers will almost always want and need to decide such matters as what and how much to purchase at stated prices, credit terms, dates and methods of delivery, basic warranties, and so on—but not necessarily much more. As for terms governing other matters, there will ordinarily be a functional basis for form-taking parties simply to assume or consciously to ignore the existence of such terms without deliberating about or even discussing them in deciding whether to contract.[22] As virtually all courts and commentators have recognized, this stance can be in the interest of *both* sides in saving time and expense, in simplifying and limiting the range of issues to be considered, and so on. This is reinforced by the evident and often great difficulty facing the nondrafting party if he or she wishes to assess, let alone negotiate, such matters.

The upshot of these preliminary observations is that it would be irrational for the law mechanically to deny the legitimacy of such efforts and to withhold enforcement per se. What, then, can be problematic or unfair—whether procedurally or substantively—about such transactions?

Consider first the form-taker's assent. We shall assume the paradigmatic case of the consumer standard form transaction where the form is presented to the consumer on a take-it-or-leave-it basis, where the consumer does not know or appreciate the specific content or import of its standard (nondickered) terms, and finally where the alternative standard terms, if available from other businesses, are not materially different. This contracting scenario might seem to lack meaningful choice and to make a mockery of the moral basis of contract in genuine mutual assent. If so, many if not most consumer transactions should be deemed presumptively unenforceable. But this, it should be repeated, is not the law. From the standpoint of general principles, these facts alone do not in themselves impugn a standard form contract's validity or enforceability. I will explain.

In connection with general requirements of offer and acceptance, the fact that the form is presented "unilaterally" on a take-it-or-leave-it basis does not prevent it from conferring a power of acceptance on the offeree that, when exercised, clinches the bargain on those terms.[23] It is sufficient if there are mutual assents constituting offer and acceptance that agree on the same terms, whether or not this results from actual bargaining or negotiating. An offeree can be held to have assented to an offer despite the fact that he or she does not know or appreciate the significance of particular terms that it in fact contains, as long as the offeree reasonably should be aware that it may contain such terms in addition to those that are up-front or dickered.[24] If the offeree manifests acceptance without reading or understanding those terms, that is his or her choice and decision. The generally known features of the standard form contract enable the form-giver reasonably to view the offeree as assenting to the agreement as a whole.[25] It is not surprising therefore that the older cases regularly held parties, in the absence of fraud or misrepresentation, to have assented to printed terms whether or not they had read them.[26] And of course, the fact that one or both parties may not understand or even know at all the law of implied warranties or other instances of implication, let alone the ordinary remedies for breach, does not per se prevent their mutual assents from being fully effective in satisfying contract formation.

To confirm that this contracting scenario cannot be per se procedurally problematic, one merely has to ask whether a consumer would have legitimate grounds for complaint if the unread terms are perfectly reasonable and usual: the answer must surely be no. Llewellyn was not alone when he correctly emphasized that, on the basis of his or her assent en bloc to the whole transaction, a form-taker can reasonably also be held to standard terms that are fair and balanced even though unread by and unknown to the party.[27]

But what if a form contract does contain terms that are bizarre, unexpected, or irrelevant to the matter at hand and the net effect of the terms is to add substantially to the form-taker's performance obligations or to subtract seriously from his or her rights? In the presupposed circumstances of standard form contracting, can the form-giver reasonably take the other to have intended to assent to these terms as well? It is important to emphasize that what the form-giver would have to be able to impute here to the form-taker would be the latter's presumed, that is, implicit, assent to materially unusual and prejudicial terms. And the only basis for this inference could be that, by agreeing to the whole transaction en bloc, the consumer has eo ipso assumed the risk of any and every term that it might contain, however unusual, irrelevant, and onerous that term might be. As I now discuss, the same features of standard form contracting that justify an inference of assent en bloc also suggest that the answer must be no.

Consistently with the positive role and justification of standardized agreements, form-givers do not expect or even want form-takers to read and appreciate all the standard terms, and both sides can be taken to know that it would not advance the mutually beneficial purposes of such transacting if they did so.[28] Consequently, and in accordance with the objective test applied to this transacting scenario in general, form-takers can reasonably view the offer of standard form terms as inviting their assent on this basis. But at the same time, in viewing form-givers as so inviting them (and indefinitely many others) to accept the offer on this basis, form-takers can also assume that they can reasonably place confidence and trust in the other party that the unread standardized terms are not irrelevant or seriously unreasonable in light of what they and others similarly situated are expected to know in this context. The form-giver's invitation must therefore include what is in effect a tacit representation that, in the absence of clear and effective notice to the contrary, there are no unknown terms that are beyond what would reasonably and fairly be expected in the circumstances.[29] This analysis, which is in accordance with the objective standpoint, is already recognized in the leading nineteenth-century English ticket case, *Parker v. South Eastern Railway Co.* In this case, while emphatically upholding the reasonableness and justice of presumed blanket assent where there has been sufficient notice that a writing contains contractually relevant terms, Lord Justice Bramwell concurrently implies a qualifying proviso in the following way:

> The truth is, people are content to take these things on trust. They know that there is a form which is always used—they are satisfied it is not unreasonable, because people do not usually put unreasonable terms into their contracts. If they did, then dealing would soon be stopped.... The very fact of not looking at the paper shews that this confidence exists. It

is asked: What if there was some unreasonable condition, as for instance to forfeit 1000 *l.* if the goods were not removed in forty-eight hours? Would the depositor be bound? I might content myself by asking: Would he be, if he were told "our conditions are on this ticket," and he did not read them. In my judgment, he would not be bound in either case. I think there is an implied understanding that there is no condition unreasonable to the knowledge of the party tendering the document and not insisting on its being read—no condition not relevant to the matter in hand.[30]

Given the characteristic assumptions and circumstances of form contracting, there must be imputed to the parties an implied understanding to this effect. Llewellyn, for one, saw this clearly when he wrote that "accompanying that basic deal [assent to the discussed or "dickered" terms and to the type of transaction as a whole] ... [is] ... another, which, if not on any fiduciary basis, at least involves a plain expression of confidence, asked and accepted, with a corresponding limit on the powers granted."[31] And it is also expressly adopted by the Second Restatement.[32] The form-giver cannot reasonably take the form-taker to have accepted or submitted to terms except on this basis. Terms that do not meet this criterion would not be reasonably and fairly expected by the form-taker, subjecting him or her to unfair surprise.[33] By assenting to the form, he or she cannot by that fact alone be reasonably presumed to have intended them.

In sum, far from representing a pathology, the characteristic features of standard form contracting give rise to a presumed expectation on the part of the indeterminately many form-takers toward the form-giver as to the reasonableness of terms that they are not expected to read or understand. The form-giver can be held to know that they have accepted the whole form en bloc on this condition—which, when fulfilled, ensures that these transactions can be not only in the rational interests of both sides but also reasonable as between them. Accordingly, if there is a problem with standard form contracts, it seems to be because of the presence of unreasonable terms that unfairly surprise the form-taker. This brings us to the obviously crucial issue of specifying what might constitute unreasonable or unfair standardized terms. We are looking for instances of unfairness that are particularly linked to these sorts of contracts. In the next two sections, I outline what these may be.

6.2. The Sources of Unfairness Peculiar to Standardized Terms

To begin, it may be helpful to have in mind a clear and settled example where courts have not enforced standardized terms because of their unreasonableness in this particular contractual context. My illustration is the leading Canadian case of *Tilden Rent-A-Car Co. v. Clendenning*.[34]

The facts were as follows. Upon arriving at the Vancouver airport, the defendant, Clendenning, rented a car from the plaintiff company as he had done on many prior occasions. Before signing the printed document provided by the company, he elected to pay an additional premium to obtain a "collision damage waiver." In the past, he had been told by the defendants' clerk that the waiver would provide full nondeductible coverage unless an accident resulted from the driver being so intoxicated that he was unable to control his car. But on this occasion nothing was said, and, as was apparent to the clerk, the defendant signed the contract without reading it. On the front of the printed document was clause 15, "Collision Damage Waiver by Customers," which the defendant initialed and which stated:

> "In consideration of the payment of $2.00 per day customers [sic] liability for damage to rented vehicle including windshield is limited to NIL. But notwithstanding payment of said fee, customer shall be fully liable for all collision damage if vehicle is used, operated or driven in violation of any of the provisions of this rental agreement or off highways serviced by federal, provincial, or municipal governments."[35]

The defendant also signed under clause 16, which read, "I, the undersigned have read and received a copy of above and reverse side of this contract."[36] On the back of the contract, in small type and so faint as to be hardly legible, were a series of conditions that entailed that a driver would be completely responsible for all damage if it occurred, for example, while he or she exceeded the speed limit by even one mile per hour, was parked in a no-parking area, or was driving in a shopping plaza or after consuming even a single glass of wine. While trying to avoid a collision with another car, the defendant had an accident. Although he had consumed some alcohol, he was not intoxicated, was able to control the vehicle, and had not violated the criminal law. The plaintiff company sued for the resulting damage.

Rejecting the so-called "rule in *L'Estrange v. F. Graucob Ltd.*" that, in the absence of fraud or actual misrepresentation, one who signs a document containing contractual terms must automatically be held to have specifically assented to all its terms whether read or not, Chief Justice Charles Dubin stated that Tilden must have reasonable grounds to view the defendant's signature to the transaction as a whole as conveying his assent to the particular standard terms at issue; but this could not be presumed where, as here, the standard clauses were seriously inconsistent with the evident meaning and scope of the express waiver of liability.[37] While the defendant reasonably should expect—and in fact did expect—that the exclusion of liability would not be absolute or without any conditions, the extent of the standard terms went beyond anything that could reasonably be anticipated. The plaintiff would have to suppose that in return for the additional premium paid, the defendant reasonably understood that he was not purchasing complete coverage but, to the contrary, was assuming full responsibility for all losses, whether or not caused by his neglect, that might result from operating the vehicle in an almost open-ended variety of ordinarily innocuous and practically unavoidable ways and circumstances! (But, then, why would Tilden reasonably think that the defendant or anyone else would pay for that?)

Such "stringent and onerous" exempting conditions, the Court held, could not be relied upon by the plaintiff where the only ground for inferring acquiescence was the defendant's signature. There must be something more to make this inference. For example, Tilden must bring home to its clients both the content and the subtracting implications of the onerous standardized terms in such a way that Tilden could reasonably view individuals as having specifically agreed to these clauses so understood.[38] And the more serious and far-reaching the tension between the up-front and standardized provisions, the more explicit, specific, and salient such notice must be.[39] But in the particular circumstances of this transaction, where speed and informality were attractive features of the service provided by Tilden, such notice was neither given nor expected. In these circumstances, a client "is entitled to assume that the form contains nothing unreasonable or oppressive."[40] The exempting conditions must therefore be deleted. Quoting Lord Denning, Dubin stated, "We do not allow printed forms to be made a trap for the unwary."[41]

In *Tilden,* the court refused to enforce the provision on the ground that the defendant cannot reasonably be presumed to have assented to terms that eviscerate the reasonably apparent meaning and scope of up-front express primary terms (the collision damages waiver) that shape his understanding of what he has contracted for. What is striking is that the court's determination of the unfairness of the terms depends on an analysis of the reasonable meaning of the transaction in relation to itself, without reference to any external considerations whatsoever. The analysis does not rest upon any inquiry into aggregate market structure, competitive conduct, and so forth. In fact, there need not be a finding of inequality of bargaining power between the parties. The unfairness arises through a kind of contradiction *within* the transaction between a salient express term that seems reasonably to say one thing and impugned provisions that say in effect the opposite. What the contract gives with one hand (the express damages waiver) it takes away with the other (via the impugned provisions). But where, on a reasonable interpretation of the contract as a whole, the first term is more foundational in shaping the parties' reasonable expectations, this cannot be reasonable. In an objective sense, the second term takes the party unfairly by surprise.

This ground for setting aside certain standard form clauses is perfectly general in that it can apply to any contract that displays this internal tension, irrespective of the identity of the parties. Thus, in addition to applying to consumer transactions, it can be pertinent to contracts between businesses. For example, the analysis applies to a number of the cases referred to in the Uniform Commercial Code, section 2-302, the results of which, the comment states, illustrate the underlying basis of unconscionability.[42] These include situations where a manufacturer or seller relies upon a standard term to defend against liability for a product that completely fails to meet the express description of the item sold.[43] The same analysis as is found in *Tilden* also applies here so long as the description, whether oral or in writing, may reasonably be viewed as having decisively influenced the basis of the other party's decision to transact. The standard clause, albeit printed, will not be permitted to defeat it.[44]

We may tentatively generalize thus far. The law distinguishes between up-front salient primary terms and those that are secondary and nonsalient; and it views the latter as normatively subordinate to and as regulated by the reasonable meaning of the former, when construed prima facie on their own and apart from the secondary. This view supposes that there is an internal transactional standpoint that regulates the contractual significance of different terms in light of how they have shaped the form-taker's reasonable understanding of what he or she has contracted for.[45] More specifically, form-takers are given notice of certain terms with the (at least) implicit understanding and expectation that these are the only ones which they need to know, deliberate about, or understand: the contracting process presents these terms as salient, and, accordingly, form-givers must reasonably take form-takers as transacting on this basis. These up-front terms are the contract's primary terms, and they constitute, in Llewellyn's words, "the dominant and only real expression of agreement."[46] Because these terms are presented first and by themselves, their reasonable meaning is fixed without considering the other terms that the form-taker is not expected to read or internalize. And the reasonable meaning, thus ascertained, is the baseline that regulates the contractual significance and role of the other, nonsalient terms.[47] Therefore, the law supposes that while the latter may supplement or clarify the reasonable meaning and import of the up-front primary terms, they must not unreasonably undercut or oppose it. Only if they do not, can a form-giver fairly and reasonably infer that the form-taker's assent en bloc also and specifically includes such nonsalient standard terms.

This transactional approach contrasts with widely assumed premises of contemporary contract theories that, by their terms, severely limit the relevance of considerations of fairness and reasonableness in relation to these contracts. As we saw in the discussion of implication, contemporary contract theories standardly view contracts as no more than the sum of their express terms, and they justify the implication of terms on the basis that contracts so viewed are fundamentally incomplete and can only be supplemented on grounds of policy that are external to the reasonable meaning of the actual contract between the parties. Indeed, these theories do not at all rely on the objective test with its regulative determination of a contract's reasonable transactional meaning. The contract itself provides no internal meaning or measure in light of which terms can be understood or assessed as primary and fundamental as opposed to incidental and secondary. A standard term that severely subtracts from what the law would otherwise imply by way of warranty or a term that drastically limits the damages that would otherwise be actionable for breach is simply what the contract has given.[48] There is no standpoint internal to the transaction that allows the law to evaluate the contractual propriety and reasonableness of such terms or to characterize them as departures or derogations from what the contract must have contemplated.[49] Therefore there cannot be an intratransactional clash between contract terms. On this view, an apparently nonsalient express term unread and not considered cannot unfairly surprise the buyer or be incompatible with the fundamental basis of the agreement. By agreeing to a transaction en bloc, a party presumptively agrees therefore to each and every term specifically.[50] For, to repeat, a contract is identical with all the terms, including the printed clauses at issue, which are viewed as being on a par with all the rest. Whether parties deliberate over certain terms and not others or the fact that some terms are salient while others are not may or may not be significant depending on the economic or other external criteria that the theorist brings to bear on the analysis of the transaction. But that is all.

To summarize so far. The law seems to view form-takers as unfairly surprised by the inclusion of standard terms that manifestly and without fair justification change, defeat, eviscerate, or contradict the baseline reasonable meaning and significance of the up-front primary terms. This conception of unfair surprise is purely transactional and objective. If a term has this effect, then, in Ellinghaus's words, it "aspires . . . to be more than itself, to modify the 'iron essence' of the . . . contract of which it is a part and which, in fact, is its raison d'être," and "to the extent to which it thus seeks to transcend itself, the court is entitled . . . to strike it down or to limit its application."[51]

Llewellyn himself distinguished three basic instances of such intratransactional contradiction and unfairness in standard form contracting: where the nonsalient standard terms conflict with the reasonable meaning of the contract's salient express terms, or with the implied terms and conditions entailed thereby, or finally with what he called the "iron core" of the contract's transaction-type.[52] Having already considered the first category of conflict in the discussion of *Tilden,* I want now to examine briefly the second and third kinds. My aim will be to clarify and explain the underlying pattern of analysis that seems to be embodied in leading cases rather than to address more particular issues that may rightly preoccupy scholarship and legal practice in a given jurisdiction, such as, for example, the enforceability of mandatory arbitration provisions or of exclusions of class actions in current contract law.[53] At the same time, I hope that the following discussion assists in thinking about how questions of assent and fairness raised by such provisions may be approached.

6.3. Standard Terms versus Implied Terms and Transaction-Types

To illustrate the second kind of intratransactional tension—that between nonsalient standard terms and the *implied* dimension of the up-front primary terms—I will discuss what is arguably one of the most important decisions about contractual fairness in any common law jurisdiction, namely *Henningsen v. Bloomfield Motors Inc.*[54] Certainly, the impugned provision and surrounding circumstances in *Henningsen* were extreme and have since been superseded by more reasonable trade practices and regulation in the automobile industry. But far from being dated or simplistic, the decision's analysis is still highly relevant.

The facts in *Henningsen* are well known. The Henningsens brought an action for damages against the manufacturer Chrysler and a local dealer that had sold and delivered a Plymouth automobile to Mr. Henningsen in early May 1955. Just ten days and some 468 miles later, while Mrs. Henningsen was driving the car at a moderate speed on a paved highway, the steering mechanism suddenly failed, the steering wheel spun in her hands, and the car veered, crashing into a brick wall and causing Mrs. Henningsen personal injuries as well as leaving the car a total wreck.

Defending against the plaintiffs' action based on an implied warranty of merchantability, the manufacturer and dealer relied on provisions in the standard printed form contract signed by Mr. Henningsen. Two paragraphs in fine print, which Mr. Henningsen had not read and which had not specifically been brought to his attention, stated that the form constituted the entire agreement and that the buyer has read and agreed to the printed matter on the back of the form. The latter, headed "Conditions," disclaimed any and all express or implied warranties except for the following: if a part or parts of the car were found to be defective in workmanship within ninety days from sale and were sent back by the purchaser at his own expense to the manufacturer's plant with transportation charges prepaid, and, further, if after examining the part, the manufacturer concluded "to its satisfaction" that the part was defective, then it would make good that part at its factory. The provision made this the sole and entire remedy for breach of warranty. Because the car was totally wrecked, it was of course impossible to determine whether the accident resulted from defective workmanship. The express warranty was not even applicable. Writing the opinion for a unanimous decision of the Supreme Court of New Jersey, Justice Francis found the express warranty void for reasons of public policy and affirmed the lower court's ruling in favor of the plaintiffs' claim for damages, including compensation for personal injury and for breach of the implied warranties of merchantability.

Whether approvingly or critically, most commentators focus on the court's discussion of the background circumstances of the transaction and specifically the preponderant market power of the defendant Chrysler, the unavailability of better alternative terms in an automobile industry dominated by the "Big Three" (Chrysler, Ford, and GM), the powerlessness of the plaintiffs as ordinary consumers, the lack of notice to the plaintiffs, and so on.[55] It is true that the decision includes discussion of procedural and structural market factors, summed up in its citation of the passage from Friedrich Kessler that the consumer's "contractual intention is but a subjection more or less voluntary to terms dictated by the stronger party, terms whose consequences are often understood in a vague way, if at all."[56] But this does not state the whole or even, in my view, the principal basis of the court's decision. For the judgment clearly turns on a transactional analysis of the injustice of the standard terms.[57] We see this in the following crucial passage:

> [W]arranties originated in the law to safeguard the buyer and not to limit the liability of the seller or manufacturer. It seems obvious in this instance that the motive was to avoid the warranty obligations which are normally incidental to such sales. The language gave little and withdrew much. In return for the delusive remedy of replacement of defective parts at the factory, the buyer is said to have accepted the exclusion of the maker's liability for personal injuries arising from the breach of the warranty, and to have agreed to the elimination of any other express or implied warranty. An instinctively felt sense of justice cries out against such a sharp bargain.[58]

The court's core concern here is with the printed express warranty's virtually complete evisceration of the kinds of contractual rights and remedies that the plaintiff would have had under the warranty terms ordinarily implied by law: rights and remedies, we should emphasize, that are implied by law because they are necessary to ensure the fair value of the performance owed her.[59] It is difficult, the court states, to imagine a greater burden on the consumer or a less satisfactory remedy—so much so that the court deems illusory the express warranty's promise of "security." The court frames the test of fairness in terms of a direct intratransactional comparison between what the purchaser receives from the express warranty and what she gives up by way of baseline implied warranties with their panoply of remedies. Here the disproportion is quantitatively and qualitatively extreme.

It is important to underline that, in this mass consumer contract and as with the analysis in *Tilden,* this intratransactional comparison does not per se require the court to ascertain market conditions, unequal bargaining power, or a particular consumer's ignorance.[60] Of equal interest is the fact that the court views its analysis as consistent with, and as a development of, the previously discussed line of cases that refuse to enforce disclaimers of liability or warranty that eviscerate the fair meaning of the express terms or undermine the main basis and purpose of the transaction.[61] These cases include contracts between (often experienced) businesspeople. The hapless consumer is not always the victim of the deletions of such important rights. Finally, in none of the cases discussed by the court, nor in *Henningsen* itself, does the defendant present evidence of a reasonable commercial purpose or interest that might justify or explain such fundamental subtractions from rights and remedies. There is nothing to suggest that the disclaimer in *Henningsen* is needed to tailor general norms to the particular demands and circumstances of the defendant's business. Had evidence to this effect been presented, the outcome might certainly have been different.[62]

Why, then, does the court consider and discuss in some detail the procedural deficiencies and market features referred to above? I suggest that it is not because these deficiencies are per se problematic and justify striking out the impugned provisions. That might be an important concern to be directly addressed by regulative agencies or other such institutions that are set up to assess and regulate market concentrations and other systemic circumstances. Rather, the court refers to these procedural and market considerations because this shows that the contract cannot reasonably be viewed as a bargained-out allocation of the risks that are regulated by warranties. The absence of negotiation responds to the objection, noted by the court, that, whether or not the terms are prima facie unreasonable, the plaintiffs are bound in virtue of "the general principle that, in the absence of fraud, one who does not choose to read a contract before signing it, cannot later relieve himself of its burdens."[63] The issue is whether, simply by signing a document that clearly is contractual, the plaintiffs, beyond manifesting assent to it en bloc, should reasonably be taken to have accepted the risk of this deletion of their contractual rights and remedies. In this regard, the surrounding circumstances do matter. Given the nature and surrounding circumstances of the parties' standard form contracting, the court here, as in *Tilden*, answers no: there is no such automatic assumption of such risk in these circumstances.

In cases like *Henningsen*, the law seems to compare the value of the contract with its nonsalient printed provision (here the express warranty) against the fair value the contract would have with the rights and remedies that would ordinarily be provided by law.[64] Where there is a manifest and gross disproportion between the two that cannot be explained by particular risks or requirements borne by the form-giver, party assent is not presumed to the specific provision and the contract may be set aside or enforced without it. This analysis is consistent with the transactional approach not only seen in *Tilden* but also underpinning the whole law of implication.

To elaborate, form-takers reasonably assent on the condition that the contract as a whole preserves the fair value of express terms that are presented up-front and therefore as alone salient and primary. In *Henningsen*, that salient and up-front express term is the car itself to which the implied warranty of merchantability automatically and necessarily attaches as a matter of contract law. Keeping in mind that terms are legally implied because they are transactionally necessary for the reasonable meaning and fair value of the primary terms, the law views implied legal norms as regulative in the sense that it is relative to them that the courts assess the significance and reasonableness of nonsalient terms that stipulate something different and that impact on the presumed fair value of the primary terms. In this way, the law treats nonsalient terms as the form-giver's effort to specify and fix the implied dimension of the up-front primary terms and scrutinizes them if they manifestly and seriously undermine the baseline of fair value that legal implication ensures for those primary terms.

Form-takers are thus presumed to assent to the contract as a whole on the assumption the nonsalient terms do not eviscerate this baseline of fair value and form-givers are reasonably held to know this and to invite their assent on this basis. Where, then, nonsalient express terms appear not to preserve but instead substantially to subtract from this substratum of fair value, this calls for explanation. For example, there may be particular performance-related risks or requirements that affect the form-taker but are not properly addressed and factored in by the ordinarily implied terms and conditions.[65] The important thing is that the discrepancy must be explained on a basis that can be reasonably claimed by the form-giver as part of what he or she is owed by way of transactional fairness and reasonableness in their contract. Nonsalient express terms that cannot be so explained objectively take the form-taker by unfair surprise. Such terms may be said to perpetrate a transactional fraud on the form-taker inasmuch as, though part of the transaction, they empty the particular performances promised in the up-front primary terms of their presumed fair value. But parties cannot be presumed to intend that a real price be exchanged for a pseudo-obligation.[66]

If we suppose that, in this context of mass consumer contracts, form-takers are not expected to read or ponder the nonsalient express terms, reasonableness in standard form contracting can ordinarily be satisfied if the standard terms themselves *embed* a fair and reasonable allocation of risks: one that preserves the substratum of fair value that is basic to their promise-for-consideration relation and that does not effectuate an uncompensated shifting of risk onto the form-taker. Transactional equivalence in this sense must be preserved and parties must know the kind of performance they are receiving and at what price. One way of ensuring this would be for the contract clearly to provide the option of different performances involving different levels of protection and benefit at appropriately different corresponding prices.[67] Leff acutely formulates the law's problem in connection with standard form contracting as how "to discourage dickering and overreaching simultaneously."[68] Embedding terms that preserve fair value provides a form-giver with reasonable grounds to infer in a nonbargaining situation that the form-taker not only has assented to the transaction en bloc but also has unambiguously accepted such nonsalient, unread standard terms that replace his or her legally implied rights and remedies. The possibility of intracontractual conflict between express and implied terms and its consequence of transactionally unfair surprise are averted. Moreover, in keeping with the general or public orientation of standard form transacting, there is no need to look to the actual circumstances of the consumer to assess whether he or she has specifically assented to a given term or risk.

In the absence of embedding appropriate terms, a form-giver may have to give specific express notice of standard terms and their consequences if they are in tension with what would otherwise be implied by law.[69] However, this solution must always remain exceptional in the characteristic circumstances of mass consumer contracts if their efficiencies and advantages as well as general orientation are to be preserved. Furthermore, to meet the requirements of reasonableness, notice would have to be of a particularly robust kind. Thus, notice of, say, an express warranty that subtracts from what the law otherwise provides would have to transform radically the way the transaction *as a whole* presents to the form-taker and shapes the latter's understanding of what he or she has contracted for: instead of the transaction being presented on the basis that its up-front terms are primary and alone salient, its defining and dominant feature would have to be the express warranty itself, with the up-front terms now appearing as wholly subordinated to it. Only by presenting the express warranty—and *not* the up-front primary terms—as the "dominant and only real expression of agreement" would notice have the effect of completely dissolving the underlying objective tension between the express warranty, on the one hand, and the legally implied reasonable meaning and fair value of the expected performance, on the other hand. To achieve this without any residual ambiguity, there would also ordinarily have to be a suitable adjustment in the price term. The lack of motivation for notice of this kind in the usual circumstances of mass contracting is obvious.

This brings me to the third and final category of intratransactional tension mentioned earlier—that between the nondickered standard terms and the contract's "transaction-type." In his discussion of assent to standard forms, Llewellyn notes that there is assent, not only to the "few dickered terms," but also to the "broad type of the transaction."[70] And in his brief mention of past judicial efforts to ensure contractual fairness, Llewellyn also refers to the important equitable tradition, instanced by the Chancery's battle against contracting away the equity of redemption, of viewing loans as a transaction-type that has an iron essence which neither form nor formula can reach.[71] Does such judicial concern about preserving the internal integrity of transaction-types as a matter of fairness fit with the approach discussed so far? I think so. The basic idea can be explained as follows.

Starting from the most general and abstract "iron essence" (to use Llewellyn's phrase) of a contract as a promise-for-consideration relation, contract law, as we saw in the discussion of unconscionability, further divides this relation into the substantive subcategories of exchange (requiring equivalence) and gift (requiring donative intent or assumption of risk). Moreover, the nature of the contractual performance interest transferred at formation can be anything on a continuum from the merely temporary use, benefit, or security of the promised consideration to its full and complete ownership as stipulated by the contract terms. Finally, through the pressure of commercial and other needs over time or via judicial and statutory declarations, these more abstract categories are concretized and specified at different levels of particularity with diverse social, commercial, and legal meanings, including distinctive contractual incidents and effects, which individuals learn and may reasonably be presumed to know through participation in social and commercial interaction.

Hence there emerges and continues to develop over time a range of different transaction-types, all variants of the basic promise-for-consideration relation and each with its own organizing features and particular incidents.[72] Thus parties may be presumed to understand, to intend, and to have patterned expectations related to the given type of transaction into which they have entered, and the law takes this into consideration when assessing the reasonableness of the actual contract terms.[73]

For example, there is the basic difference between a contract of loan and a contract of sale, each with its distinct and defining qualitative features and incidents.[74] They involve different allocations of risk. While transactions need not always be purely one type rather than another, but in fact may combine the incidents of different types, this must be done in a way that is internally coherent and fair to the parties. It must not take them unfairly by surprise. Historically, equity struck down fetters on the right of redemption in the case of loans because the transfer of title to the mortgagee was neither intrinsic to a loan (in contrast to a sale) nor necessary to compensate him for losses resulting from breach of the loan.[75] Such fetters were also viewed as attempts to "convert" a loan into a conditional sale, with the form of a loan being in effect a misleading and injurious disguise, once again threatening a party with transactional unfair surprise.⁷⁶ The fetter was not enforced as being repugnant to the apparent character and dominant purpose of the transaction-type—as denaturing the transaction.⁷⁷ This doctrine was, of course, applied to individualized written agreements—and so well before the advent of the modern mass standard form contracts. The analysis is therefore general in scope of application. But on account of their internal complexity and drive toward completeness, standard form contracts can easily and acutely create this same difficulty and so are definitely subject to this correcting doctrine.

Take, for example, a bailment that transfers complete control and possession of an object from bailor to bailee. A bailment imports as legal incidents of this relation certain definite core rights and obligations—for instance, a bailee has the legal burden of explaining damage to or the disappearance of the bailed object—and this burden cannot be canceled without destroying the particular transaction-type that it is. Thus a bailee cannot avoid the legal consequences of failing to give any explanation at all by relying on a printed clause that exempts from all liability for loss or damage "however caused," even where the bailor has reasonable notice of the exemption.⁷⁸ To allow this would "make meaningless the purpose" of the whole transaction as a bailment.⁷⁹ For the same reason, no automatic assumption of risk on the bailor's part should be implied. As I will now suggest, this same sort of conflict between standard terms and transaction-type may also be at issue in another famous American unconscionability case, *Williams v. Walker-Thomas Furniture Co.*⁸⁰

In *Williams,* a retail furniture store, Walker-Thomas, had sold to Williams at her home a number of household items (including sheets, curtains, chairs, beds, mattresses, and a washing machine) over a five-year period, for which payment was to be made in installments. The terms of each purchase were contained in a printed contract form, which Williams signed but did not read and which was not explained to her. It set out the value of the item bought and purported to lease the item to her for a stipulated monthly rent payment. It also stated that title would be transferred to the purchaser only when the total of the monthly payments equaled the stated value of the item. In the event of a default in the payment of any monthly installment, the store could repossess the item. The printed form agreement contained a further provision—which the court characterized as obscure—stipulating that any payments made would be spread "pro rata" over all other outstanding accounts, resulting in keeping "a balance due on every item purchased until the balance due on all items, whenever purchased, was liquidated."[81]

The effect of this "cross-collateralization" provision was that none of the items previously purchased could be paid off fully in the order of purchase or be immune from summary repossession under replevin statutes and protected as statutorily exempt property as long as there were any existing or new purchases not yet fully paid for. The seller retained title in all such not yet completely paid-off items and could repossess them through summary process if there was a default of even one credit payment on any outstanding item.[82] Williams purchased a stereo set of stated value of $500 but defaulted on a monthly installment. At the time, she owed $160 from previous purchases. To put the situation in perspective, she had paid $1,400 of the total $1,800 worth of purchases (including the stereo) made over the past five years. But the store sought repossession of all the items previously purchased and still in her possession.

Circuit Judge J. Skelly Wright for the United States Court of Appeals held that the doctrine of unconscionability was a possible legal basis for refusing to enforce the clause and remanded the case to the trial court for further proceedings on this issue. The court famously characterized unconscionability as involving an absence of meaningful choice by one of the parties together with contract terms that are too unfair or unreasonably favorable to the other. The decision noted that "in determining reasonableness or fairness, the primary concern must be with the terms of the contract considered in light of the circumstances existing when the contract was made."[83] Ordinarily, one who signs an agreement without full knowledge of its terms may be taken to have assumed the risk of even a one-sided contract. Citing Llewellyn's discussion of boilerplate agreements, the decision stated that where, however, a party signs a nonnegotiable and commercially unreasonable contract with little or no knowledge of its terms, a court cannot presume specific assent to those terms and "should consider whether the terms of the contract are so unfair that enforcement should be withheld."[84] As for the criterion of unfairness, the court emphasized that the test is not simple or to be mechanically applied and that the terms must be so extreme as to appear unconscionable when considered "in the light of the general commercial background and the commercial needs of the particular trade or case."[85] Given the limited scope of the court's decision, there was, however, no discussion of whether or why the security provision in the *Williams* contract was commercially unreasonable or unfair as between the parties.

There are clearly a number of aspects of this transaction that might qualify as contractually unfair and in bad faith.[86] I want to suggest that one way in which the unread and nonsalient provision may be unfair is that it conflicts with the reasonable meaning of the salient primary terms and transaction-type of the individual purchases by the defendant. As with prior purchases, the contract for the stereo set appears to be the sale of a discrete item for a certain price on credit terms. Each separate item is purchased under its own separate contract of sale of this kind. Until the price is paid, title remains with the seller. But, by the same token, if and when the price is fully paid, title ordinarily vests with the purchaser. Now whether the defendant decides to purchase an item at all is a matter for her to decide in light of her needs and priorities. Similarly, the ordinary understanding of a credit provision would be that the purchaser-debtor has the power to pay off the outstanding amount according to the schedule and possibly at an accelerated rate.[87] Since having full title in certain items rather than others can obviously be important to a consumer, she can be presumed to want to be able to do this with respect to a given sale on its own.

A security provision applying merely to the individual item sold and reasonably related to the seller's transactional interests and risks with respect to that item could be consistent with this ordinary understanding and the reasonably expected measure of control and decision in the purchaser.[88] This was not so with the cross-collateralization provision. Not only that, but its impact was clearly arbitrary with respect to the defendant's own preferences and priorities as a consumer: foreseeably, she might have almost paid off—and was planning to pay off completely—a much needed item but, having then purchased a "luxury" item and defaulting on a single payment, she would be forced to forfeit all her past payments and sacrifice the important item to pay off the less needed luxury purchase.[89] The contractual conversion of what reasonably appeared to the purchaser as a conditional sale into a continuing, interlocking security for other transactions was foreseeably oppressive to the purchaser in the way that, we saw, a penalty clause could be. The market value of used items might not come close to their continuing utility or replacement costs for the purchaser.[90] If these items were repossessed and sold, the loss to the purchaser would be disproportionately greater than the limited value recouped by the store. This would be especially so where, as in *Williams*, the purchaser bought numerous items in the past, almost paid them off completely, and then defaulted early on with respect to a recently purchased high-priced item. Given a judicial concern to ensure the integrity of apparent transaction-types because of the reasonable expectations generated thereby, a cross-collateralization provision in the consumer contracting circumstances of *Williams* could be transactionally unreasonable, once again threatening buyers with unfair surprise.[91]

6.4. Concluding Remarks

According to the 1950 version of the present Uniform Commercial Code, section 2-302, "The basic test [for unconscionability] is whether in the light of the general commercial background and commercial needs of the particular trade or case the clauses involved are so one-sided as not to be expected to be included in the agreement. The princip[le] is one of prevention of unfair surprise." The upshot of my discussion of standard form contracts is that unfair surprise results when standardized terms are in conflict with the fair and reasonable import of a transaction's express terms, its otherwise implied terms, or its core type. This form of contractual unfairness is particularly, though not exclusively, associated with standardized contracting. "Unfair surprise" is thus neither in the air nor a matter of subjective reaction to subjectively anticipated terms but rather is firmly anchored in the objective test and a purely internal transactional standpoint that links assent and fairness. Here we see clearly that presumed intent—the aspect of assent—coincides with the articulation of reasonableness—the aspect of fairness—thereby vindicating Cardozo's great generalization that "intention not otherwise revealed may be presumed to hold in contemplation the reasonable and probable."[92]

In the circumstances of their interaction as form-giver and form-taker, the first cannot reasonably view the second as having intended and accepted terms that would eviscerate the reasonable meaning and fair value of the contract's up-front primary terms. Even though the source of impairment may arise through an internal conflict between a standard term and the reasonable meaning and fair value of the salient terms, the ultimate situation is one where a party may have given substantial value in return for something either not contemplated or of practically no value—in other words, a total failure of consideration "reducing the contract to a mere declaration of intent."[93]

Here again, we see the elementary premise at work that parties to an exchange are presumed reasonably to intend and to expect in return some basic substratum of equivalence and fair value as ordinarily measured and generally available. And note that, like the conception of unconscionability discussed earlier, this analysis does not presuppose a dichotomy between "procedural unconscionability" and "substantive unconscionability." Circumstances of transacting such as take-it-or-leave-it with little "meaningful choice" can be relevant insofar as they provide grounds for inferring a relation of confidence asked and accepted and for negating an assumption of risk by the form-taker with respect to a massive subtraction from his or her baseline expected performance interest.[94] Such circumstances do not, however, represent a distinct procedural form of unfairness but are merely an element in the analysis of unfair terms. Llewellyn was both correct and insightful when he remarked eighty years ago that, in the face of parties' attempts to give nothing or ludicrously little for a real price, courts "have grown restive under non-equivalence."[95]

SECTION C

ENCORCEMENT

ENFORCEMENT

In this third and final section dealing with the main principles of contract law, I discuss basic issues relating to contract enforcement and remedies with the aim of showing how the relevant principles and doctrines fit within the transactional conception that I have developed so far.

In Chapter 7, I discuss certain fundamental organizing ideas that are widely recognized in the case law as basic to the analysis of contractual liability. Although contract liability is standardly said to be strict, it is by no means self-evident what this means or why contract liability should be so viewed. To begin, I therefore try to explain its sense and how, properly understood, it sheds important light on the nature of contractual liability, the relation between contract and tort, and the meaning of breach. I also address the central question of how the wrong of breach, which ordinarily consists merely in an omission and a failure to perform, can still represent an injury to the plaintiff's rights, amounting to misfeasance. As part of this discussion, I try to explain why anticipatory repudiation should count as a breach even though, by the express terms, performance is not yet due. Finally, I present the important idea of compensatory justice that underpins the law's coercive response, via remedies, to breach. Here the challenge is to show how compensatory justice is required by and completes the transactional analysis presented so far.

The more detailed discussion of different contract remedies takes up Chapter 8, the longest in this section on enforcement. All contract remedies specify and respond to the loss that results from the injury that breach represents and seek, as far as possible, to cancel that loss, thereby affirming the plaintiff's performance entitlement in the face of the defendant's wrong. There is, I argue, but one fundamental protected interest, namely, the performance interest, that all contract remedies seek to uphold. I try to show how settled legal principles and doctrines determining matters such as the choice between expectation damages and specific performance, liability for consequential loss, the availability of reliance damages, and the requirement of mitigation all fit within this unified framework. I also emphasize that this framework is purely transactional and complete in its own terms, without requiring other nontransactional values or goals.

In Chapter 9, which completes both this section on enforcement and my account of the main principles of contract law, I turn briefly to the treatment of expectation damages in certain leading contract theories. My focus will be on those theories that directly challenge the very possibility of a complete and independent transactional approach, such as the one I am proposing, as well as the conception of compensatory justice that this presupposes. I argue that they do not provide a viable alternative, at least not if we are seeking a public basis of justification for contract law. I finish by coming back to the fundamental claim in Part One that contract can, and indeed must, be viewed as a form of transactional acquisition if we are to make sense of basic contract doctrines within their own framework. Not only are the main features of the doctrines of formation and fairness consistent with the contractual relation being plausibly so construed, but the compensatory character of the expectation remedies *requires* that it be understood as such. I then briefly indicate what additional steps need to be taken to justify fully this view. This sets the stage for Part Two, in which I make those further arguments.

Chapter 7

Fundamental Ideas

In this chapter, I present and elucidate some fundamental ideas that underlie the law's approach to contract remedies. I focus on three main questions. First, in what sense is, as is widely thought, contract liability strict, and how does its being so situate contract law vis-à-vis tort law? Second, in light of contractual liability's being strict, what is the juridical meaning of breach of contract as a civil wrong within the parameters of misfeasance? Third, when it is said that remedies for breach aim at compensating the innocent party for her loss, what is the conception of compensatory justice that this presupposes, and how do these remedies, as legal coercive responses to wrong, relate to the plaintiff's entitlement? Answering these questions is preliminary to Chapter 8's more detailed consideration of the different remedies to which the law has recourse in securing contractual rights.

7.1. How Is Contractual Liability Strict?

A widely accepted generalization about the common law of contract is that contractual liability is strict.[1] However, what this means or implies is not exactly clear. Commentators suggest, for example, that contractual liability's being strict distinguishes it from "fault-based" liability for tort; that it entails the rejection of reasonable care, foreseeability, and other "moral" elements that are nonetheless recognized elsewhere in the analysis of contractual obligation; or finally that it favors "bright-line" rules over less determinate "standards."[2] In addition, its being strict seems to imply that contractual liability is not thoroughly rooted in pervasive notions of responsibility and choice, despite the fact that contractual obligation is supposed to be based wholly on the parties' mutual assents. After all, contract, not tort, is the paradigm of voluntary interaction. Why contract liability should be characterized as strict does seem to present a puzzle for contract theory.[3] My first task, then, is to try to clarify the meaning of contract liability being strict and to see whether it is fully consistent with contract's voluntary basis as well as with the role of fault in tort law. In keeping with my aim of working out a public basis of justification for contract, I shall do this by drawing on analysis that is at least implicit and latent in settled legal doctrines and principles. To begin, it may be helpful to make clear what strict liability in this context of contract law does not entail.

First, the conception of contractual liability being strict should not be compared with fault understood as involving *moral* culpability. This is because "fault," whether in tort law or in contract law, is a *juridical* conception that is specified in terms of the objective test of reasonableness. Therefore, the juridical conception of fault need not at all coincide with notions of moral fault that may be relevant in assessing individual character or action and that, in contrast to assessments in both contract and tort, ordinarily take into account factors such as subjective intentions, efforts, honest (mis)understandings, personal circumstances, and so forth. Thus, the fact that a defendant tries his or her best and conscientiously intends to take care is irrelevant so far as tort liability for negligence is concerned. This distinction between the juridical and the moral with respect to fault is particularly important in the case of contract law because contracts are constituted by promises, and this might lead one to assume that norms of moral blameworthiness applicable to the immorality of promise-breaking might also be relevant in the analysis of contractual liability. But in legal contemplation, a breach is a civil wrong that is normatively independent from and so not directly affected by whether a defendant fulfils or falls below the requirements of morality in either intention or conduct.

There is a second important point. Jurists distinguish the level or, as it is sometimes put, the "intensity" of obligation that a given agreement enshrines, whether by its express terms or as a matter of judicial implication.[4] Thus the primary obligation to perform may require only reasonable care or, more onerously, a guarantee of result or outcome. For example, in both common law and civil law systems, service contracts, in contrast to contracts of sale, ordinarily impose only an (implied) obligation to exercise reasonable care in contrast to a guarantee of result.[5] Common law courts deem the latter, more onerous level or intensity of obligation as inconsistent with the particular nature of and risks associated with the promised performances in service transactions. By contrast, both legal traditions view the obligation to pay money or to deliver sold generic goods as involving strict requirements of result, such that a failure to do either, even because of factors beyond the promisor's control, may be unexcused and so in breach.[6] At common law, this can be a matter of implied obligation. Here again, the higher level or intensity of obligation is ordinarily justified on the basis of the particular nature of the kind of performance and its background circumstances and risks.[7] The crucial point for present purposes is that the characterization of contractual liability as strict applies equally to transactions with *either* level of obligation.[8] Thus, accepting the generalization of contract liability being strict does not dictate the intensity of obligation and therefore how pervasive elements of reasonable care are or should be in contract law.[9] Liability would still be strict even if the most frequent level of obligation turned out to be that of reasonable care.

With these preliminary caveats in mind, what, in positive terms, might be the meaning of strict liability in contract? The Second Restatement seems to suggest that it lies in the idea of *pacta sunt servanda:* contracts are to be kept.[10] On this view, wrong in contract consists simply and solely in any unexcused departure from the performance owed by one party to the other as determined by the contractual terms and conditions, both express and implied. In other words, the *whole* of a party's duty is contained in and specified by the *performance owed*. Where nonperformance is excusable by reason of impossibility, frustration, or mistake, then, of course, there is no breach, no wrong, and no violation of the other party's right to the performance. But, as I tried to show earlier, such excusing conditions are also established on the basis of an internal and transactional construction of the contract itself. They represent a contract's self-limiting determination of the circumstances in which performance is not owed.

From a legal point of view, there is thus no contractually relevant consideration that is extrinsic to the promised performance. Consequently, there cannot be reference to any freestanding standards of reasonableness, due care, best efforts, guarantee of outcome, and so on. As discussed above, depending on the nature and circumstances of the transaction, the standard of the performance obligation may be to use reasonable care or to produce a definite result. But these are just ways of specifying the content of the particular performance that is owed. Whatever the content of the obligation, the promisor *must perform this or incur liability*. Irrespective of his motives, efforts, subjective understandings, and external circumstances, whether foreseeable or not, the risk of unexcused nonperformance is wholly on the promisor.[11] This obligation is correlative to the promisee's right, and both fully vest at contract formation without the need to show detrimental reliance of any sort on the part of the promisee. If unexcused, a mere omission to perform is per se an injury or wrong and is the basis for at least nominal damages, irrespective of resulting loss. The meaning of contractual liability being strict must somehow lie in the fact that unexcused nonperformance can be in and of itself an actionable wrong.

Now, in general, the main moral concern that people have about strict liability is that defendants should not be held liable for outcomes which they could not have reasonably avoided or which they did not choose to undertake with the requisite intent and knowledge. But this is not the case with breach and contractual liability when understood as I have suggested above. If we provisionally suppose that parties can owe each other something as a performance on the basis of their mutual assents at formation, the fact that contract liability is strict in the sense just indicated neither contradicts the voluntary basis of contract nor imposes consequences on parties that they did not choose or could not reasonably have avoided. In particular, contractually enforceable terms, both express and implied, are established by the parties' mutual assents as construed in light of the objective test, and it is these terms that specify the performances owed. I have argued that, from a moral point of view, parties can appropriately be held to these terms as the contents of their own chosen acts because, in this contractual context, choice is properly assessed from a relational and transactional standpoint. Furthermore, as I will discuss in further detail, breach consists in the defendant choosing to withhold the promised performance that he has already moved to the plaintiff at formation, and it is only the resulting loss for which the defendant can reasonably be taken to have assumed responsibility at formation that is actionable. This is true of the basic expectation measure of recovery as well as recovery of consequential loss under the principle in *Hadley v. Baxendale*.

If, as I am suggesting, contractual liability's being strict seems to lie in the actionability of mere nonperformance (measured against the contract terms) as a per se injury, the kinds of losses that are contractually relevant, and so potentially actionable, are nothing other than the different ways in which this injury can materialize. Of course, I must show in detail that this is reflected in the main remedial principles. But if so, we may say that contractual liability seems to embody a unified conception of obligation and liability rooted in this idea of breach being a per se injury that deprives the plaintiff of the promised performance that the defendant has vested with her, as a matter of rights, at contract formation.

This analysis distinguishes contract liability from liability in negligence even where the standard or intensity of obligation (e.g., a doctor's obligation to use reasonable care and skill in performing surgery) happens to be the same in both kinds of transactions. In contract, an obligation to use reasonable care is owed *as a performance* that *must* take place as specified at formation— so that the mere omission to go forward with and complete the surgery with the contractually required level of skill would be per se a wrong.[12] This is not so in negligence. There the plaintiff, strictly speaking, does not have a right to the defendant's reasonable care as such. Instead, her right is that she should not suffer damage to her body or property as a result of conduct that the defendant should reasonably have avoided. Her protected baseline is her condition *prior* to interaction with the defendant. Whether the defendant's omission to perform the surgery at all or his doing so without reasonable care is actionable negligence depends on whether it unreasonably puts the plaintiff in a worse position when viewed as against this baseline. This is the same baseline that, I suggested, is supposed by the analysis of detrimental reliance.

Most discussions of the issue of contractual strict liability do not go further than a comparison between contract and negligence. But this does not exhaust the relevance of the relation between contract and tort. What is generally overlooked is the striking parallel between the analysis of contractual liability and that of the intentional torts, such as conversion and trespass.[13] This is surprising because, like breach of contract, the latter have always been characterized as strict liability wrongs that import per se injury without the necessity of showing physical, financial, or other loss. Moreover, as with breach of contract but unlike negligence, nominal damages are available. I would like now to examine this parallel more closely.

The tort of conversion has been called "the principal means whereby English law protects the ownership of goods" and, for centuries, it has been taken to be strict.[14] The wrong in conversion consists in an assertion of direct exclusive control over the plaintiff's goods that eo ipso interferes with the plaintiff's exclusive possessory right even though the "doer may not know of or intend to challenge the property or possession of the true owner."[15] The defendant, in Lord Mansfield's words, "acts at his peril and is answerable for any mistake."[16] There can be conversion even though the defendant acts with the genuine and reasonable belief that the goods are his—indeed, even if both parties reasonably but mistakenly think at the time of the conversion that the goods belong to the defendant. As long as the defendant manifests an intent to control or use the particular thing to the exclusion of others, there is the requisite voluntary basis for the wrong in conversion.

This interference with the plaintiff's possessory right is the per se *injuria* of the wrong in conversion and, being such, is actionable for nominal damages irrespective of whether there is material loss. Still, this per se injury can materialize in two different kinds of actionable loss. First, there is the basic loss of possession itself.[17] The standard remedy for conversion is that the defendant must pay the plaintiff the full value of the item at the time and place of the conversion.[18] By bringing an action, the plaintiff is viewed, in legal contemplation, as compelling the defendant to purchase the chattel at a forced sale, with title transferring to the defendant upon satisfaction of the judgment.[19] There is no question here of having to establish or even of taking into account the foreseeability of this basic loss, whether or not it could have reasonably been avoided, and so forth. Given the nature of the loss—the interference with the plaintiff's possessory right by the defendant's immediate exercise of direct physical control over the thing—it makes no sense to ask, and there is no need to ask, whether the loss is foreseeable. The requirement of voluntariness is satisfied simply by the fact of this voluntary exercise of control over what is in law the plaintiff's thing.

However, this does not mean that reasonable foreseeability has no role at all to play in the analysis of liability for conversion. It does—for example, with respect to lost profit that may have resulted from the plaintiff being deprived of the use of the converted item. Such loss is an instance of a second category of actionable loss that is standardly referred to as "consequential" loss. Reasonable foreseeability applies to this kind of loss on the basis that the same "requirements which are considered fair in other cases of consequential loss flowing from wrongful acts should . . . also be applied [to conversion]."[20]

Offhand, such consequential loss is different from the basic loss of possession because it is not immediately contained in the defendant's wrongful exercise of direct control but depends on the various contingent uses and purposes to which the plaintiff is putting or is planning to put her item. Here a requirement of foreseeability seems to make sense and to be required if the resulting impact on the plaintiff's uses is to be imputed to the defendant's initial choice to exercise control over the chattel. It must be emphasized, however, that this foreseeability requirement does not conflict with, but to the contrary presupposes, the starting point of per se injury to the plaintiff's possessory right: the question is whether, given this wrongful deprivation of or interference with possession, some foreseeable use by the plaintiff has been frustrated or impaired, resulting in further loss. Such consequential loss can therefore be actionable even though it results from a conversion due to reasonable mistake or from the fact that the return of the item is impossible due to circumstances beyond the defendant's control.

Unlike negligence, then, conversion is a per se injury that necessarily gives rise to nominal damages. The foundation of its being such—and hence, I would suggest, the basis for its being a strict liability wrong—is precisely that the wrong consists in an assertion of exclusive control directly over another's property or possession inconsistent with the latter's exclusive right. The defendant exercises choice in doing this. And, we saw, as long as the defendant intends the act of asserting such control over the object (even if he mistakenly assumes that it is his), it counts as a voluntary exercise of his choice. This exercise of control is per se an injury because it necessarily and intrinsically entails interference with the plaintiff's possessory right whether or not this causes her financial or other loss.

By contrast, in negligence the defendant does not exercise control directly over anything that belongs exclusively to the plaintiff. In fact, in the paradigmatic situation, the defendant is using something of his own (e.g., *his* body or object) or at least something that is *not* the plaintiff's, and so does not eo ipso oust or interfere with the plaintiff's rightful possession of her thing. Instead, the wrong consists in the fact that the defendant's choice as to how he uses an object consequentially impacts on the plaintiff's person or property, impairing its use or value as a result. As discussed above in connection with conversion, such consequential impact is distinct from the defendant's use of that object. If the impact is to be imputable to the defendant's choice, it should be something that the defendant reasonably could and ought to have avoided. Not only must the impact be foreseeable, but, further, since the plaintiff's own uses can be contingently of any kind or degree and are beyond the defendant's immediate determination and control, these also must be foreseeably affected if the resulting loss is to be imputable to the defendant's use of something that does not itself belong to the plaintiff. Liability for negligence cannot be for a per se injury or give rise to nominal damages but, being *entirely* for such contingent consequential losses that do not result from an interference with possession, should simply be governed by reasonable foreseeability.[21] And so it is.

Both conversion and contract seem to share certain features of liability. In both, the wrong consists in a per se injury that gives rise to nominal damages and, further, that can materialize as an inherent basic loss (pertaining to the loss of possession in conversion or the loss of performance in contract) as well as foreseeable consequential loss that results from this basic loss.[22] It is the fact of per se injury in both breach of contract and conversion that seems to make both kinds of liability strict and distinguishes them from negligence. We also see confirmed here that the meaning of strict liability in both contract and intentional tort does not preclude the incorporation of standards of reasonable care or of reasonable foreseeability where necessary and appropriate. Strict liability seems to turn, not on the presence or absence of such standards, but rather on the nature of the wrong and the kind of protected (rightful) interest that is invaded.

7.2. The Nature of Breach

I have suggested that it is because conversion is an exercise of exclusive control over something that belongs to another that it is per se the doing of an injury to the owner, irrespective of whether it causes her financial or other loss. Being an assertion of possession over something belonging to another, it must be eo ipso an interference with the other's possessory or proprietary interest in it. I would like to take the parallel between contract and the intentional torts a step further. The fact that the wrong in conversion involves an assertion of exclusive control inconsistent with the plaintiff's own possessory rights has its analogue in how breach of contract and ultimately contract formation are properly understood.

Analogously to the wrong of conversion, unexcused nonperformance, even though it may consist in a sheer omission, entails the defendant exercising factual control over that to which the plaintiff, not the defendant, is entitled in accordance with the contractual terms. In the case of contract, the defendant does this by withholding the promised performance from the plaintiff. From a contractual point of view, failure to perform is thus conceptualized as an interference with the plaintiff's exclusive right to an asset—the substance of the consideration—that has already been moved to her at formation in the promissory medium of representation. It is true that the plaintiff's contractual entitlement at formation is not ordinarily an immediate right to possess an existing physical asset, such as is supposed and protected by conversion. In contract, the asset is the promised consideration, and the plaintiff's right to have immediate possession of it is specified by the contract terms, taking effect at the contractually stipulated time for performance. Still, on the proposed view, the plaintiff's contractual entitlement involves her having rightfully an asset as against the defendant in such a way that is valid and complete prior to and independent of the defendant's breach. This rightful holding vests with the plaintiff through the parties' interaction, consisting of their mutual assents at contract formation. It forms the basis of her contractually determined right to immediate possession and must be presupposed if breach is to be intelligible as a per se wrongful deprivation and injury. In this way, the fact that contractual liability is strict seems fully intelligible if we suppose that contract formation can plausibly be viewed as a form of transactional acquisition and transfer of rightful control as between the parties.

Given this analysis and paralleling conversion, the wrongfulness of breach need not involve anything more than the defendant simply having in fact what the plaintiff should have in right by virtue of her better transactional title as between them. It is the contract itself reasonably construed, not the parties' beliefs, however sincere and conscientious, that decides whether this is the case. To breach, the defendant need not do anything other than merely to withhold the promised asset in a way that is contractually excluded. The existence of an intent to injure or any other punishable conduct is not necessary for there to be the wrong of breach. A defendant's motives or reasons (good, bad, or indifferent) for not performing do not per se enter into the analysis of whether he has breached. If "willfulness" is to be a contractually relevant qualifier with respect to breach, it must consist in something more than breaching for a selfish or even an opportunistic reason.[23]

It is tempting to think of breach as a failure to do a positive act—that of delivery—which confers a fresh benefit de jure on the promisee as against the promisor. But on the view that I am developing and as I suggested earlier, delivery does not add anything, as a matter of rights, to what the promisee has acquired at contract formation.[24] To the contrary, what the promisee acquires at formation already includes the necessity of delivery as an incident of the rightful control over the consideration that has been moved to her. The consideration as moved at formation is not mere puff and words: it is the interpersonal juridical representation of something of value being moved from the exclusive control of one side into that of the other. To be genuine and complete, this representation must include (even implicitly) the time, place, and manner of the promisee having this consideration as a factual reality. The promisee enjoys this via the promisor's delivery. Thus, delivery should be construed in juridical terms as part of the purely factual modality and mechanism that enables the promisee to exercise her contractually specified right to have and enjoy the consideration. By delivering, the promisor simply acts in a way that does not prevent or interfere with the promisee's exercise of her contractual right to have or enjoy the promised consideration in accordance with contractual terms. By failing to deliver, the promisor must necessarily be viewed vis-à-vis the promisee as wrongfully exercising factual control over the promised subject matter against the promisee's right to have or enjoy it. Delivery has no independent or further contractual (normative) significance as between the parties. The fact that delivery may—although it need not—entail positive acts by the promisor does not change this normative analysis.

Thus far, breach of contract has been equated with unexcused nonperformance that is contractually specified as due at a time for performance. But can a contract be breached *before* this moment? Or must we say that, prior to it, parties have no contractual obligations inter se and are therefore completely at liberty to do as they will?

Announced some 150 years ago, the common law doctrine of anticipatory repudiation holds that, even before performance is due, a party may (but need not) treat as an actionable breach of contract an unambiguous representation by the other party that he will not or cannot perform his contractual obligation.[25] Underlying this doctrine is the premise that "where there is a contract to do an act on a future day, there is a relation constituted between the parties in the meantime by the contract, and . . . they impliedly promise that in the meantime neither will do any thing to the prejudice of the other inconsistent with that relation."[26] This clearly supposes that a party can suffer a contractually relevant prejudice prior to and apart from nonperformance at the date when performance is expressly due. Can we make sense of this? To help out, consider the following explanation from the leading case of *Frost v. Knight*:

> [Prior to the time of performance] . . . the promisee . . . has a right to have the contract kept open as a subsisting and effective contract. Its unimpaired and unimpeached efficacy may be essential to his interests. His right acquired under it may be dealt with by him in various ways for his benefit and advantage. Of all such advantage the repudiation of the contract by the other party . . . must of course deprive him. It is therefore quite right to hold that such an announcement amounts to a violation of the contract in omnibus, and that upon it the promisee, if so minded, may at once treat it as a breach of the entire contract, and bring his action accordingly.[27]

I suggest that this explanation can be elucidated as follows. Without an initial manifestation of assent that can reasonably be taken as firm and unequivocal, there cannot be a promise that represents the moving of something of value from one party to the other and that therefore meets the requirements of contract formation. The whole existence of all contractual benefit and detriment is in the medium of representation constituted by the parties' promises. The implied continuation of this commitment is essential to upholding the consideration's fair value as representing an asset that is under the promisee's rightful control from formation on, consistently with the contractual terms. For example, unless expressly or implicitly excluded by their contract, the promisee must be able to deal with her right as a chose in action assignable to third parties.

For this to be the case, it must be possible for the promisee to view and present to others the promised consideration as something that will with certainty take place in fact as promised.[28] This certainty and present value are immediately negated by a promisor's deliberate renunciation or its equivalent.[29] Instantly, the promisor's anticipatory repudiation impairs the exchange value that the promisee might have obtained for her right to performance even prior to performance; and further, it would impose a new and unbargained-for risk of loss on the promisee if, to obtain the full benefit of the bargain and in the expectation of actual performance, she were to decide to perform her side (essential reliance) or to pursue her own interests, financial or otherwise (incidental reliance). In return for what she gives up, she would receive, not actual performance, but an effectively illusory promise plus the chance to win a lawsuit. Anticipatory repudiation interferes with the promisee's ability to deal with and beneficially to rely upon the performance right vested in her from formation on, in this way causing her a prejudice that is inconsistent with their contractual relation. As a matter of implication, the parties may reasonably be presumed not to intend this consequence as an incident of their agreement.

To counteract this prejudice fully and thereby to preserve the fair value of the promisor's initial representation of commitment, the new and unbargained-for risks that anticipatory repudiation unilaterally imposes should be borne by the promisor, not the promisee. The promisee must be freed and insulated from the promisor's power so to impair and frustrate the promisee's legitimate contractual prospects and expectations. This is accomplished by the promisee being at liberty not only to treat her own performance as excused but also to view the contract as "at an end," with the anticipatory repudiation counting as an actionable breach.[30] The same reason for permitting the promisee to be excused from performing her side also supports her power to treat the repudiation as an immediate actionable breach: she cannot be obliged to continue to be a party to a relation that is incompatible with essential implications going to the foundation of their agreement and without which there will be a total failure of consideration.[31]

Thus, as is true of other aspects of contractual analysis, the determination of breach is also transactionally based. What the anticipatory repudiation doctrine shows is that nonperformance at the time expressly or impliedly specified for performance does not exhaust the possible ways in which contractual rights may be violated. As we saw with implication, what happens after formation can be within the scope of the contract's meaning and regulation as established at formation.

7.3. Compensatory Justice

Contract remedies are the law's coercive response to the civil wrong of breach, and there is no idea more fundamental to or more settled in the whole law of contract remedies than that the aim of the law in providing such remedies is to compensate for loss caused, not to punish the wrongdoer. Understood in terms of this basic contrast, this axiomatic compensatory character of contract remedies must be as true of specific performance as it is of damages.[32] Compensation, nothing less but also nothing more, is required as a matter of justice.

The requirement of compensatory justice is a general idea that applies to the different kinds of liability in private law.[33] It presupposes that the defendant has injured the plaintiff's rights in some asset that rightfully belongs to her exclusively—is under her own rightful exclusive control—as against the defendant, and it views remedies as the law's effort to respond to this transactional wrong by restoring, so far as possible, the plaintiff to the position that she would have occupied with respect to this asset had the defendant not wronged her.[34] Liability is thus for violating a negative prohibition against interference and injury, not a positive duty to preserve, assist, or enhance. In other words, the idea of compensatory justice presupposes a framework that embodies the organizing principle of liability for misfeasance only.[35] A principal and distinctive task of compensatory justice is both to specify and to measure, against the baseline of the plaintiff's pre-wrong rightful control over her asset, the loss or damage suffered by her and to fashion the appropriate remedial response that rectifies it.[36] Since the wrong is transactionally imposed by the defendant on the plaintiff as a loss, a remedy that purports to cancel it is also transactionally effectuated through a coerced transfer of the amount of this loss from defendant to plaintiff.

On the one hand, because the remedy is paradigmatically a coercive *response* to a wrongful loss, the remedial restoration and the position in which the plaintiff would have continued to have rightful control without the defendant's infringement are and must be conceptually and normatively distinct: the remedy can at most ensure that the plaintiff is put in a position that is *equivalent* to the one in which she would have been with respect to her asset had the defendant not wronged her. On the other hand, this equivalence presupposes an implicit identity between the two positions, and what the remedy secures must be, as far as possible in the post-wrong circumstances, the same as that which the plaintiff would have had with respect to her asset absent the wrong.[37] This is the way in which compensatory justice vindicates the plaintiff's rights and how the compensation principle in private law should be understood. I will elaborate and fill in these more general points about the conception of compensatory justice by discussing how it specifically applies in the case of contract.

In contractual no less than in other kinds of private law liability, unless the plaintiff "has" something that is rightfully hers as against the defendant, there is no basis for the compensation principle to apply. In the case of contract, this entitlement is with respect to the transactionally specified promised consideration. Viewed as compensatory in character, contract remedies are not independent or freestanding legal determinations but, to the contrary, are ancillary to and protective of this baseline entitlement.[38] Remedies must therefore take as their starting premise what this entitlement is at contract formation—in other words, what has been promised as part of the parties' promise-for-consideration relation: some definite asset (whether property or service), fully specified by the contract's express and implied terms, that has present value in the eye of the law and that, as such and via their mutual promises, is moved to the plaintiff from and to the exclusion of the defendant.[39] This constitutes the "performance" with respect to which the plaintiff has a baseline entitlement against the defendant: she has in right the whole value of this performance as a legally certain asset at formation before and independently of actual performance in fact. Moreover, without the plaintiff's assent, the defendant can do nothing to change the legal existence and status of this asset or its value. The compensation principle presupposes this immunity in the plaintiff vis-à-vis any unilateral decision or action by the defendant with respect to the plaintiff's performance entitlement.

It should therefore be emphasized that even though breach injures the plaintiff's right, this does not, and can never, change the right or transfer it to the defendant. To the contrary, breach is always just a wrong that is devoid of any normative (contractual) validity whatsoever: its sole juridical meaning is that it is something incompatible with the plaintiff's right. Being such, it can and, from a legal point of view, must be canceled by a forced compensatory transfer. This simultaneously brings out its normative nullity and vindicates the primacy and immunity of the plaintiff's right. As I will discuss in Chapter 8, all the different remedies for breach respect and incorporate this same presupposition of the primacy and immunity of the plaintiff's entitlement.

I have suggested that it is because the plaintiff's contractually protected performance interest consists in her having at formation and therefore prior to performance exclusive rightful control over something as against the defendant that breach can be conceptualized as an injury rather than a mere failure to confer a future benefit. Breach, I have said, is a wrongful withholding in fact of what belongs in rights to the plaintiff. On this basis, breach of contract can count as misfeasance, that is, as the violation of a negative prohibition against acts or omissions that are inconsistent with the plaintiff's right to exclude.

But as noted above, the principle of compensation takes the further step—and this is its essential contribution—of specifying and measuring the way this injury materializes as a determinate loss or damage and also of constructing a remedial response that is normatively equivalent to it. In the case of breach, the basic loss is the materialization of the defendant's wrong of withholding performance. The plaintiff is entitled via suitable remedies to be put, so far as is possible in post-breach circumstances, in the position of having this performance. As I discuss in Chapter 8, the various remedies specify the different ways in which this single imperative is accomplished. Supposing, for example, that in the post-breach circumstances the cost of obtaining what the innocent party was promised now exceeds the contract price, this difference between the prices "is, therefore, the true measure of [the] loss from the breach, for it is that which it will cost him to put himself in the same position as if the contract had been fulfilled."[40] Each contract and its accompanying breach must be examined in its particulars to determine the specific ways in which the violation of rights (i.e., the injury) may have materialized as loss and the proper measures of that loss.

It should be pointed out that, on the view that I am proposing, injury and loss (or damage) are distinct, though interconnected, concepts in the analysis of contractual liability.[41] Breach is an injury to the plaintiff's right, but as an injury, although it is incompatible with the plaintiff's right, it does not change or subtract from that right (for this would be inconsistent with the right's immunity). Not only does breach "not entail a loss of the bargained-for contractual rights," but, to the contrary, the latter "remain . . . the necessary legal basis for a remedy."[42] However, because this injury withholds in fact the actual performance to which the plaintiff is entitled, it deprives the plaintiff of something that should be available for her to possess and use as contemplated by the contract, and it is this deprivation, with its resulting kinds of interference, that comprises the loss that is the materialization of the injury. Loss does represent a real subtraction from what the plaintiff should have obtained (the position in which she should have been) with respect to the promised actual performance. So understood, every injury may be said to import a loss but, depending on the particular circumstances, this loss need not entail a determinable quantum, whether in the form of increased costs, lost value, or the like. For example, if the going market price at breach is less than or equal to the contract price and supposing no other actionable loss has been incurred, there is injury and loss but no determinate loss. Awarding nominal damages is the way the law recognizes this possibility.[43]

Compensatory justice requires that the breaching party transfers to the innocent party what is necessary to place the latter in the position equivalent to the rightful position contemplated by their contract. The fact that this transfer is coercively imposed and required in response to and therefore (in the standard case) temporally after the breach means that it should not be viewed as affording the defendant a further opportunity to fulfill his original duty, as a different form of it, or finally as the next best thing.[44] In sharp contrast to the primary obligation to perform, it does not involve any duty resting on the defendant's voluntary assent or assumption of responsibility: it represents the *liability* that the defendant incurs upon breach.[45] At the same time, within this framework of unavoidable temporal sequencing, the compensation principle requires in all cases that the innocent party obtains as nearly as possible the very same subject matter and terms of her bargain or, where this is not available, at least its value. Otherwise, by breaching, a wrongdoer would be permitted to change the object of the plaintiff's entitlement without her consent; but this would be inconsistent with her immunity as against the defendant and make her baseline entitlement in performance illusory. As mentioned earlier, this requirement of an identity between thing lost and thing coercively transferred is the distinguishing and essential feature of compensation and makes the remedy restorative. As I will explain in Chapter 8, it is true of both damages awards and in specie remedies. Insofar as the defendant does not restore the whole of the loss, there is a violation of the remedial equivalence required by compensatory justice.

To conclude this chapter on the fundamental ideas presupposed by the law of contract remedies, it may be helpful to highlight briefly how the approach that I have presented departs in a number of ways from the assumptions that are a staple of much contemporary contract theory.[46] This will also allow me to recap the main points and bring out more fully some of their implications.

First, within its own framework, compensatory justice imports a kind of moral necessity that is transactionally specific and complete as between plaintiff and defendant. It is neither concerned with nor aims to influence other transactions, whether between these two parties or those involving other parties. Nor does it take into account any factors that are extrinsic to their immediate actual relation.[47] Compensatory justice requires that a particular transactional injury be redressed by a remedy that is its transactionally equivalent negation. As I will explain more fully in Chapter 11, its moral or, more exactly, its juridical necessity lies in this: that once the plaintiff is viewed as having rightful control over some asset as against the defendant, any appearance of interpersonal validity attaching to the defendant's violation of this control *must* be annulled if the rightfulness of the plaintiff's holding is to be vindicated as valid and effectual vis-à-vis the defendant's act. The required transfer does not erase the wrong but rather explicitly brings out and confirms its normative invalidity. This simply preserves the normative significance of the plaintiff rightfully having something as her own to the exclusion of the defendant.

To vindicate this, however, not only must there be as far as possible an implicit identity between the thing lost and the thing coercively transferred, but it is equally necessary that this coerced transfer be from defendant to plaintiff. Thus any "decoupling" of what the defendant transfers from what the plaintiff receives means that compensatory justice has not been done.[48] And it is the very effectuation of this transfer that, insofar as it embodies equivalence, is by itself the complete and self-sufficient actualization of compensatory justice. Because the normative work of compensation is complete when the wrong is appropriately annulled, it is not necessary to investigate the incentive effects of various possible legal responses on the many different aspects of similar transactions in order to establish and justify the remedy. As specified and applied in its own framework, compensation for breach can—and, by its own requirements, must—be self-sufficient without any such further inquiry.

Second, the compensation principle is not an "indifference principle" that seeks to make up for a loss of well-being or preference-satisfaction resulting from breach.[49] In themselves, such considerations of subjective satisfaction, happiness, or welfare are remedially irrelevant. Loss is not conceived in terms of the impact of breach on these aspects of the parties. Rather, the compensation principle, I have suggested, specifies loss in the objective and publicly ascertainable terms of the plaintiff being deprived of exclusive control in fact of an asset, namely, of the promised performance, and more particularly, as I will elaborate in Chapter 8, of its possession, use, or disposal. The principle remedies this loss objectively and publicly by requiring the transfer of something from the defendant to the plaintiff that restores her, as far as possible in post-breach circumstances, to the position of having this asset as contractually contemplated. It is this contractually contemplated exclusive control over a particular thing or service and not a state of well-being or preference-satisfaction that is restored. This is the aim of compensation. The fact that this may have the effect of enhancing the plaintiff's well-being does not therefore make party welfare its goal. The only way a party's well-being can be remedially relevant is where a given contract specifically contemplates it as part of the promised performance. For example, nonperformance of a service (e.g., a medical operation, an insurance payout, or a vacation package) may leave the plaintiff in a worse physical or emotional condition than she would have been in had the defendant performed as promised.[50] Assuming that the contract reasonably contemplates the plaintiff enjoying a certain positive physical or emotional condition as an aspect or consequence of receiving the promised performance, her pain, disappointment, or loss of enjoyment becomes relevant in specifying her contractual loss and in determining the appropriate remedy—not because, to repeat, the plaintiff is worse off in these respects per se, but only insofar as the contrary of these conditions is part of what she was supposed to have or to enjoy by the agreement.[51]

Third, the proposed account excludes all classifications of remedies that are incompatible with the plaintiff having an indefeasible immunity with respect to her contractual entitlement vis-à-vis the defendant. Thus there cannot be any remedies for breach that must be understood as according the defendant a liberty to impose unilaterally on the plaintiff any terms or any transaction that would, without her consent, alter or impair the full and complete integrity of her entitlement. This would particularly exclude the validation of unconsented-to changes that are justified on the basis of extratransactional considerations, such as economic efficiency. To this extent, then, the proposed idea of compensatory justice is incompatible with the well-known distinction between property and liability rules, originally proposed by Calabresi and Melamed and now widely adopted by economic theories, that, under the rubric of "liability rules," mandates cost-justified defendant-imposed involuntary transfers from the plaintiff for a price decided by a third party (the court) and that standardly explains damages awards in this light.[52] In connection with this third point, the plaintiff's immunity entails that, from formation on, her baseline performance interest is contractually (normatively) fixed and certain. While a party may not in fact perform as required by the contract, the plaintiff is deemed as a matter of rights to have this performance and whatever it comprises, unqualified by the possibility or probability of breach. This means that at no point in determining compensation is the probability of performance a pertinent factor. Therefore, contra theories of "overreliance," the mere fact that a plaintiff's reliance may not be cost-justified when compared to the value of performance as discounted by the probability of breach must be and is irrelevant in the assessment of damages.[53]

Fourth, and finally, the proposed conception of compensation categorically distinguishes between formation and remedies and thus precludes any theory that blurs or fails properly to recognize this difference. Remedies represent a second and distinct step that is completely ancillary and subordinate to and that aims to vindicate the plaintiff's performance interest as exhaustively specified at contract formation and as injured by breach. As already noted, by complying with what the remedy (whether damages or in specie) requires, a defendant does not fulfill his contractual duty (which ex hypothesi has been violated) or replace it with a substitute performance, but simply complies with what compensatory justice (embodied in a court award or order against him) coercively imposes as part of his liability toward the plaintiff for breach (wrong). It also follows from this conception of compensatory justice that remedies cannot be viewed as implied contractual terms (which necessarily belong to contract formation)—as in theories that conceive contract rights as a bundle that, if complete, would include terms as to remedies.[54]

Freedom of contract, it is sometimes suggested, entails that parties should be able to choose the kind of remedy or measure of recovery that they wish and that the law should respect and indeed follow the parties' decisions without imposing mandatory rules or requirements.[55] We have seen that even though parties do have the power to limit or even to exclude some remedies, they can do so only within parameters set by law that take as fixed the framework of compensatory justice and that assess their agreement in terms of a conception of presumed intention that fits with this framework. Thus, all such limitations and exclusions must leave some minimum of remedy that adequately vindicates the plaintiff's contractually-specified entitlement, without which it is illusory to view their transaction as a contract. As I will discuss in detail in Chapter 8, it is the law alone that spells out and applies the kinds of available remedies, the meaning of contractually relevant loss, and the criteria of remedial adequacy. More fundamentally, it bears repetition that all legal remedies for breach are forms of coercive redress that aim to secure the plaintiff in her contractual rights as against the defendant. What the remedy intrinsically is must reflect the character of the right and must assert its primacy vis-à-vis the wrong. This is a central premise of compensatory justice. This intrinsic relation between remedy and right is a matter of normative necessity and is normatively self-sufficient. Expressing the reasonable in contractual relations, this framework is not the contingent product of the parties' individual or joint decisions.

Chapter 8

Unity and Diversity in the Law of Contract Remedies

In this chapter, I examine the main principles governing remedies for breach of contract and I try to show in some detail how they fit together within the framework of compensatory justice, consistently with the idea that contractual liability is strict in the sense discussed in Chapter 7. In particular, I shall consider, first, the distinct functions of and relation between expectation damages and specific performance, next the rule governing remoteness for consequential loss, then the nature and role of reliance damages, and finally the mitigation requirement. My overall aim is to bring out the unity in these diverse principles and to show how they individually and jointly fill out the requirements of compensatory justice in the face of breach of contract.

In prior discussion, I argued that a baseline protected interest in performance is a conception of entitlement that fits with, and indeed that can be intrinsic to, the transactional analysis of the promise-for-consideration relation, whereas this is not true of the protected interest in reliance. Moreover, it is because breach represents a per se injury to this entitlement that contractual liability has the general character of being strict. Presupposing these points about the contractual character of the performance interest, I shall now try to deepen and develop them through this discussion of different remedies. So far as the principles of contract remedies are concerned, my contention is that it is the contractual performance interest that gives them unity and meaning. As such, the performance interest is both remedially basic and regulative. I wish to emphasize that my claim for its being such is neither "deductive" nor "a priori." Rather, as I hope to bring out clearly, it is a matter of showing that, as with the doctrines of formation and fairness, the different aspects of contract remedies can be reasonably understood in this way and that, so understood, they fit together and are mutually supportive. This is the sort of explanation that a public basis of justification of contract law calls for.

In pursuing this path, I am consciously departing from the three-interest framework presented by Fuller and Perdue and subsequently adopted by the Second Restatement in its general introduction to contract remedies.[1] Fuller and Perdue sought to challenge and to replace the notion that there is a single protected interest—the expectation interest—that is contractually basic and unifying in favor of a nonunified pluralism consisting of the expectation, reliance, and restitution interests, with the consequence that contractual enforcement—or more precisely "the binding effect of a promise"—should now be understood as "a matter of degree" arrayed along a continuum from expectation at the highest through reliance and thence to restitution at the other end.[2] There is the obvious initial question as to why the reliance and restitution interests, which take as their protected baseline the position the plaintiff would have been in had the parties not contracted, should count as contractually protected interests at all. But more fundamentally, it is by no means clear that the three interests—including the expectation interest—function in the Fuller and Perdue account even as protected interests in the sense presupposed by the idea of compensation. Let me briefly explain.

Fuller and Perdue introduce the three interests, not as in any way implicit in or presupposed by the principles of contract formation nor as normatively prior to the remedies that protect them, but rather as associated with potential purposes that the authors postulate as possible ways of enforcing (not contracts as such but) promises in general.[3] On their view, the law might have the purpose of preventing a defaulting promisor from gaining at the expense of the promisee, or of undoing the promisee's reliance on a promise, or of giving the promisee the value of what she was promised. There is no apparent necessity to choosing these rather than other purposes. Corresponding to each of these purposes, promisees have a "protected interest" in being put in the position effectuated by that purpose. Thus, these interests are not conceived as *reasons* for the law to effectuate compensatory justice—this despite the fact that Fuller and Perdue assume that the remedial protection of both reliance and restitutionary interests is compensatory.[4] The interests do not count as genuine and normatively prior entitlements within such a compensatory framework, but instead simply restate, under the label of interests, the different goals that the law may pursue in dealing with broken promises. In themselves, the interests play no distinct let alone prior justificatory or even conceptual role.[5] At the same time, because Fuller and Perdue simply *assume* this view of remedial interests and the instrumental approach that motivates it, it need not stand in the way of our undertaking a fresh assessment of the idea that contract remedies are genuinely compensatory and that in being such they reflect but one basic contractual interest in performance. This is what I shall try to do.

The common law, like other developed systems of contract law, determines which of a number of possible remedial responses are needed to do justice between the parties in the particular circumstances of a breach. Indeed, Farnsworth suggests that the whole system of remedies may be explained in terms of seven critical choices that have to do with, among other issues, damages versus in specie remedies, expectation damages versus reliance damages, a principle of remoteness, and a requirement of mitigation.[6] This multiplicity of remedial concerns might seem to doom any thought of their fundamental unity. To the contrary, I wish to argue that this multiplicity of remedial aspects is necessary. The remedies chosen are needed to ensure as fully as possible the complete and fair compensatory protection of the performance interest. Conceiving them in this way enables one to see their underlying unity. Finally, I should note that the following account assumes that remedies are fully operating as intended and thus seeks to explain them as part of ideal theory. With these introductory points in mind, I now take up each of the more specific issues in detail.

8.1. Expectation Damages versus Specific Performance

All contemporary systems of contract law provide remedies in specie as well as award damages, and they also must determine the circumstances in which one or the other of the two should be available to plaintiffs.[7] This is the first, and perhaps the most basic, choice of remedies to be considered.[8] In common law jurisdictions, the most important determining criterion remains the adequacy of the remedy judged in light of the fundamental purpose of doing full compensatory justice between the parties. Inadequacy of damages is a necessary, though not a sufficient, condition of the availability of specific performance.[9]

According to the adequacy criterion, then, where an award of money can fully and completely compensate the plaintiff for impairment of her contractual interest in performance, the damage remedy is adequate and specific performance is ordinarily refused. Clearly, if the plaintiff's sole loss is pecuniary and the amount of such loss can be determined with the requisite degree of certainty, money damages will be adequate by way of compensation. Beyond this, expectation damages (measured by the difference between contract price and market price at the time of breach) are adequate if, but only if, they would enable the plaintiff readily and reasonably to obtain from some source other than the defendant (such as from the market) the promised subject matter that was reasonably contemplated under their agreement.[10] Damages that are able to compensate the plaintiff for the cost of doing this will be deemed adequate, and supposing there are no other losses, specific performance will be refused.[11] Where, however, the subject matter, reasonably viewed, is either inherently or circumstantially unique in the sense of not being readily available on the market or from some other source, damages will not be adequate because, in these circumstances, they would not enable the plaintiff to obtain—and so cannot represent the cost of obtaining—the actual subject matter of the promised performance.[12] This is the paradigmatic situation where specific performance is needed to ensure compensatory justice between the parties. Given the centrality of the criterion of remedial adequacy, the first and most fundamental questions are: what is the promised performance and which remedy ensures that the plaintiff receives this and not something else? These questions provide a unified framework of analysis that guides not only the choice between expectation damages and specific performance but also a range of other remedial issues, some of which are more controverted.[13]

Now what is striking and important about the law's recourse to this criterion of adequacy is that it would seem to presuppose that there is a single standard of ensuring compensatory justice that governs both damages and in specie remedies. Otherwise, how can the adequacy of one be directly relevant to the availability of the other in the way that the law supposes?[14] For if, to the contrary, the standards of these remedies were genuinely different, it would make little sense to hold that the availability of one should be limited by whether the other can be effectuated in accordance with its own distinct purposes and justification. Nor can damages and specific performance be differentiated on the basis that whereas the latter aims at securing the 'actual performance' owed, the former tries to place the plaintiff in merely 'the same financial position' that she would have been in had the defendant performed as promised. This distinction is inconsistent with the nature of a party's baseline protected interest that, as required by the doctrine of consideration, must be with respect to a qualitatively determinate performance which need not be equated with a purely financial asset or with value as such. Further, since the law could in theory assign a pecuniary value to virtually any item or service, whether unique or not, if the aim of damages were indeed merely to ensure that parties are not made financially worse off by nonperformance, there would be few if any situations where damages would be deemed inadequate and specific performance appropriate.[15] Indeed, the very idea of a given performance being deemed unique would have no application.

When judged in terms of adequacy, the purpose of expectation damages, like that of specific performance, must therefore be taken to be the same. And this is in fact how the law views the matter.[16] What is more, traditional formulations of this shared end specify it in terms of the ideal and hypothetical effectuation of specific performance itself. As stated by Lord Redesdale in the often-quoted English case of *Harnett v. Yielding* (1805):

> Unquestionably the original foundation of these decrees was simply this, that damages at law would not give the party the compensation to which he was entitled: that is, would not put him in a situation as beneficial to him as if the agreement were specifically performed. On this ground, the court in a variety of cases, has refused to interfere, where, from the nature of the case, the damages must necessarily be commensurate to the injury sustained.[17]

What is often referred to as a "liberalized" conception of adequacy that now arguably prevails in contemporary contract law seems to embody this view and may be stated as follows: a plaintiff should be confined to monetary damages instead of specific performance only where damages would put the plaintiff in the same position in all material respects as she would have been if she obtained performance in specie of the contractual obligations in question.[18] Thus, where damages are fully adequate, they achieve the very same complete justice that would be accomplished by an in specie remedy. Both seek to secure, as far as possible in post-breach circumstances, the very performance, specified qualitatively and quantitatively, to which the plaintiff has a right in accordance with the contractual terms. The damages award and order of specific performance are merely two different routes to this same end. What more specifically can be said of this shared end?

I would suggest the following: both remedies aim to put the plaintiff in the position of having *actual possession* of the subject matter of the contractually contemplated performance in post-breach circumstances. In the case of specific performance, the plaintiff obtains the very thing promised, including its value and the possibility of using it, through the defendant's compliance with the court's decree. For its part, an award of money damages represents the reasonable costs that the plaintiff would have to incur in order to obtain the very thing promised (only now generic rather than unique) through her own action and at the contractually stipulated price from someone other than the defendant.[19] Specific performance and expectation damages give the plaintiff what is necessary within the contract terms to obtain possession of the promised subject matter and thereby access its use and value. This is the sole immediate and necessary consequence as well as goal of both remedies. I shall refer to this contractually protected performance interest as a party's "performance interest in possession."

Breach, I have argued, always and necessarily interferes with this protected interest in performance because, by withholding the promised performance, it per se interferes with the promisee's right to possess and receive it, whether or not this interference results in financial or other loss. A violation of this right—or in other words injury—necessarily imports a loss of possession. Hence nominal damages are available for breach, paralleling their availability for trespass and conversion, which, we saw, interfere with a person's immediate right to possession. Note finally that, in keeping with the nature of compensatory justice, the contractually protected performance interest in possession tracks what the plaintiff was promised: the promised consideration coming from the defendant, which, I have emphasized, refers to some determinate subject matter (whether unique or generic) that has been specified transactionally and so objectively as between the parties, not something else that is deemed equivalent in value to it or equally productive of satisfaction and well-being.[20] Of course, by receiving this subject matter, a party may also experience the latter effects. But these contingent by-products of the remedy do not define its aim or adequacy and are, in themselves, contractually, and so remedially, irrelevant. Here, as elsewhere in private law, the ideal operation of remedies seeks to reflect the precise nature of the protected interest. Anything less would unilaterally change the content of the baseline entitlement as specified by consideration and would therefore violate the plaintiff's immunity in relation to the defendant. And, as I emphasized earlier, it is precisely this conceptual continuity between baseline entitlement and remedial object that makes both damages and specific performance compensatory in character.

Drawing on the terminology of G. H. Treitel, I shall refer to this shared goal of both remedies as the "enforced performance" of the contractual terms, always keeping in mind that the remedies can only effectuate this goal as far as is possible in post-breach circumstances.[21] Treitel makes clear that "enforced performance" is an analytical category, not a term of art of the positive law, and so comprises damages that, for example, compensate for cover or cost of performance and completion. I want to include under this category damages that give the plaintiff the means to obtain the promised subject matter from someone other than the defendant. Because in common law jurisdictions an award of damages is nominally viewed as a means of obtaining a substitute for the promised performance, it is not typically considered as a process of enforced performance. Only specific performance is said to "enforce the obligation." But, as Treitel notes, this characterization is a legacy of the historical-jurisdictional division between equity and law. Moreover, courts standardly take both kinds of remedies as based on the "simple principle . . . that the party [has] a legal right to the performance of the contract."[22] What is needed is a rational analysis that elucidates the fundamental nature of remedies understood in light of their actual legal operation and the protected interests that they aim to secure. The foregoing explanation of both expectation damages and specific performance as instances of the enforcement of the performance interest in possession is proposed as such an analysis.

I have already suggested that if both expectation damages and specific performance share the same goal of protecting the plaintiff's performance interest in possession, anything that is not part of the promised performance—in other words, anything that is not part of the promised consideration reasonably and fully construed—is per se irrelevant to the remedial analysis. One such factor, often referred to in economic theories of so-called efficient breach, is the *promisor's* benefits from nonperformance, whether in the form of savings or profits. Even though this factor may certainly be pertinent from an economic point of view, it is per se not relevant in determining whether damages are adequate or specific performance is justified. Efficiency theories ignore the legally basic criterion of adequacy—a term of difference that requires a qualitative assessment of damages and specific performance in light of their shared goal—and instead conceive of all remedies as existing on a single continuum of quantitatively heavier or lighter sanctions. Differences in economic approach among such theories do not affect this basic point. Thus, against efficient breach theory, there is also an efficient performance hypothesis that argues that it is consistent with efficiency to allocate the promisor's benefits from nonperformance to the promisee and, what is more, that doing this is in keeping with the ordinary conception of contractual obligation.[23] But this view is not more consonant than efficient breach theory with the law's conception of contractually protected interests. Even if we assume specific performance as a prima facie baseline, this does not entail that the promisee has a claim per se to the promisor's benefits from nonperformance. From a legal point of view, the fact that specific performance may deprive the promisor of these benefits is simply the consequence of the remedy, not directly part of its inherent aim or rationale.

Further, the proposed analysis provides no support for the view that expectation damages should be intrinsically taken as the "default" remedy, with specific performance counting as merely "exceptional." The fact that damages may be adequate in the majority of situations simply reflects the statistical frequency of contracts that have as their promised subject matter something generic, which can therefore be obtained on the market or from someone other than the defendant. From the standpoint of the doctrine of consideration, whether the content is generic or unique is a purely contingent matter that does not affect its status as something of use value and hence as sufficient for contract formation. And the same goes for the law of remedies, which reflects and secures the promised consideration. Recall here the basic point that the content of consideration is some qualitatively determinate and usable item or service. This is true even when the consideration is money. The latter's determinacy is that it counts as a universal means of obtaining other things; and if it is one side of the promise-for-consideration relation, the other side must be something other than money. The subject matters of the mutual assents cannot both be exchange value.

But, at the opposite extreme, if specific performance and damages serve the same end, why not always choose specific performance over damages as the presumptive general remedy since, except in the unusual circumstances where specific performance cannot properly be implemented or is precluded on the basis of public policy, it will always and fully protect the plaintiff's performance interest?[24] Indeed, this approach seems to be the official position in civil law.[25]

The answer lies in the fact that these remedies are justified only insofar as they are necessary to do compensatory justice between the parties and therefore embody, in Cardozo's phrase, "the needs of equal justice."[26] Within the parameters of compensatory justice, neither party can affect or make an impact on the other's freedom of action or assets via contract remedies except insofar as this is strictly *necessary* to protect his or her rightful performance interest. Thus if, in given circumstances, a remedy can fully protect the plaintiff's performance interest while impacting less on the defendant's otherwise pursuable interests than would another remedy, the first *must* be chosen over the second; relative to the first, the second remedy imposes a further loss on the defendant that cannot be justified as a matter of just compensation. But this is standardly the situation if specific performance is chosen even where damages are adequate. Far from being a just remedial response, specific performance would be an unjust imposition in these circumstances.[27] (Is this conclusion challenged by the fact that damages merely cover ex post the plaintiff's costs of obtaining her promised performance and therefore also suppose that she must take action for this purpose? I address this question in section 8.4 on mitigation.) Note, once again, that this conclusion does not depend upon a direct comparison between the costs and benefits of each remedy to the parties in their circumstances, choosing the remedy that is more cost efficient in light of their various interests. While exceptionally there are decisions that seem to take this approach, the traditional and still prevailing common law view—certainly in Anglo-Commonwealth contract law—is otherwise.[28]

To summarize so far: the choice of remedy requires that the content and scope of the plaintiff's performance interest be carefully determined.

Whether damages or specific performance is given depends on what is necessary to protect fully this entitlement when considered in its own right and by itself, without giving equal weight to or even taking into account the defendant's own interests. It is of the first importance to emphasize that throughout this remedial inquiry, the law respects the plaintiff's baseline immunity and therefore rejects any supposed power in the defendant to change the content of the former's entitlement as established at formation. Where damages would not be adequate, the fact that specific performance may impose upon the defendant "the sacrifice of large prospective profits," even if unanticipated, will not ordinarily stand in the way of the remedy "if the just rights of the other party cannot otherwise be fully and adequately maintained."[29] As already noted, this embedded normative priority and immunity of the plaintiff's entitlement are directly incompatible with any justificatory basis framed, for example, in terms of efficient breach. Moreover, as noted earlier, the self-sufficiency and completeness of the transactional remedial analysis in its own framework of compensatory justice make irrelevant, from this standpoint, any consideration of the possible incentives or disincentives that a just remedy happens to produce.

Still, it may be pointed out that, even where damages are not adequate, courts may properly decide against ordering specific performance if the burden of performance on the defendant would be wholly out of proportion to the benefit of that performance for the plaintiff. Doesn't this judicial discretion to decline specific performance in cases of so-called hardship imply that, in the end, the choice of remedy depends upon the court comparing the impact of the alternative remedies on the divergent interests of the parties, giving these interests equal standing if not equal weight? To see whether this is indeed the case, we must clarify, even if briefly, what amounts to hardship or gross disproportion, the sorts of situations where these considerations are typically invoked as a reason for refusing specific performance, and how the analysis of hardship fits within the whole inquiry as to what remedy is appropriate.

Very briefly stated, hardship must be something more and different than merely the foreseeable cost of performing, whether in terms of foregone opportunities or necessary expenditures and preparations.[30] Indeed, even where this cost turns out to be unexpectedly higher as a result of changed circumstances at the time of performance, this will ordinarily not suffice. In general, for there to be hardship, specific performance must affect the defendant's interests in such a way that he would have to bear a completely different kind of burden from that which was reasonably expected (even though it may fall short of excusing performance on the basis of impossibility or frustration).[31] At the same time, it is crucial that the impact on the plaintiff of not receiving specific performance but only damages does not impair the *core* of her performance interest, including contractually contemplated consequential benefits. The impact on the plaintiff's performance interest must be very limited and readily quantifiable in financial terms of lost value.[32] If not, a court will not consider the burden on the defendant as a reason for declining specific performance. The important point here is that, both in law and in theory, there is no question of choosing damages instead of specific performance on a balance of convenience that gives equal weight to the defendant's costs of all kinds. Specific performance must be such as to impose exceptional and unexpected hardship amounting to oppression, where it is not necessary to protect the plaintiff's core interest in performance when the latter is assessed by itself and in its own right.[33]

A court that exercises its discretion by declining to order specific performance for reasons of hardship may still award damages.[34] If, in such circumstances, we suppose that damages would not be adequate in the sense of covering the costs of the innocent party purchasing on the market the thing promised her, these damages can only represent, and aim to give the plaintiff, the *value* of her performance interest. And where that performance interest is not itself pecuniary in nature, the determination of damages can only be an estimate and conjecture based on presumed and actual factors that are reasonably pertinent. I shall call such damages "compensation for lost performance value," as distinct from damages intended as enforced performance.

This second category of compensation for lost performance value may be explained as follows. We saw that expectation damages (when adequate) and specific performance presuppose that the plaintiff is able to obtain possession in fact of the particular subject matter promised by the defendant. But if, ex hypothesi, this particular object is not, or no longer, obtainable, what is to be done? We suppose the existence of a fully enforceable contract, breach and loss. It would be patently absurd and destructive of any notion of rights to hold that in such a case no damages at all should be awarded. However, instead of aiming to give the plaintiff the means of obtaining the particular qualitative thing promised, damages are now given to represent the thing's character as value. As consideration, the promised subject matter must be something of value, usable, and potentially a means of exchange for something else that also shares these features. By obtaining possession, the plaintiff also necessarily obtains the subject matter's value. Even though the substantive performance cannot be obtained via market damages or specific performance, its value remains untouched and must be accessible to the plaintiff to ensure that the performance—the promised consideration—and her immunity with respect to that performance are not rendered illusory by the defendant's breach. Though always second-best to remedies that contemplate the plaintiff obtaining possession of the promised thing itself, damages for lost performance value can and must be awarded when they are the only way of vindicating her contractual right.[35]

Given this justification, it is clear, and it bears emphasizing, that in determining the damages that can reasonably count as an equivalent of the value of the plaintiff's loss, the law remains oriented toward, and regulated by, the goal of protecting the plaintiff's baseline entitlement in performance. What the plaintiff has been promised is not per se value in the abstract but some determinate asset or service that itself has value. The aim of damages is therefore to fix a quantum for *this* lost value. Irrespective of the measure chosen—whether based on estimate and conjecture or even the defendant's gain—compensation for lost performance value always seeks to restore the plaintiff's loss, not per se what the defendant has gained or saved.[36] To repeat, the crucial difference between what I have called "enforced performance" damages and "lost performance value" damages is that the latter are given not with respect to obtaining (actual possession of) the very subject matter promised to the plaintiff—which, ex hypothesi, is factually or legally precluded—but in substitution for this and as a way of expressing its value.

8.2. Recovery of Consequential Loss: The Principle in *Hadley v. Baxendale*

A standard view of the principle in *Hadley*—and for that matter of mitigation as well—is that it serves to limit the compensatory impulse that would otherwise fully obtain if the protection of the performance interest were given complete force and effect.[37] This shows, it is thought, that the law of remedies does not fully and unqualifiedly pursue compensation and that, even in ideal theory, plaintiffs are undercompensated by the law of damages. I think that this standard view is mistaken and that the conclusion regarding undercompensation is unwarranted. To the contrary, I will argue that, as with specific performance and expectation damages, the choice of the principle in *Hadley* is integral to compensatory justice and helps to specify more fully at the remedial stage the determinate content of a party's protected performance interest. My basic claim is that all of the remedial principles are expressed fully and without abbreviation and together work in tandem to achieve complete compensatory justice between the parties. Turning now to the principle in *Hadley*, our first question is: when an issue of remoteness arises in contract law, what exactly are the kinds of losses at stake and how is the plaintiff's performance interest engaged?

In the earlier discussion of liability for breach of contract and for conversion, I distinguished between direct or basic loss and consequential loss, noting that a necessary condition for the latter sort of liability is a requirement of reasonable foreseeability. Whereas basic loss refers to the materialization of interference with a plaintiff's possessory right or, contractually, with her right to receive and possess the subject matter (item or service) as promised, consequential loss refers to those losses that result from interference with the plaintiff's planned *use* of the asset or the promised performance. Indeed, interference with contractually contemplated use is the central kind of loss at issue in the leading remoteness cases.

For example, in the well-known facts of *Hadley* itself, the plaintiffs contracted with the defendant common carriers to transport their broken shaft from their milling factory to a third-party manufacturer for the purpose of providing the latter with a model for replacement. Until the shaft was replaced in this way, the mill would be stopped, with resulting loss of profit. Here the plaintiffs' planned use of the defendants' promised performance, namely, the service of timely delivery of the broken shaft, was ultimately to obtain a new shaft, enabling their factory to resume production and thereby generate revenue. The defendants' late delivery of the shaft, in breach of contract, delayed the restart of manufacturing, causing the plaintiffs lost profit.

In addition to these more usual commercial uses, breach may also interfere with performance uses that involve a psychic or emotional dimension (such as with a vacation package or an insurance policy), thereby giving rise to consequential losses of an intangible nature.[38] The loss tracks the contractually expected use of the service as intrinsically involving a purpose of enjoyment. Note that the element of enjoyment is made possible by, but is conceptually (and legally) distinct from, obtaining the service itself (which comes under the plaintiff's performance interest in possession, and the loss of which is measured by the cost of obtaining a similar service in post-breach circumstances). Finally, there can be consequential loss where a plaintiff's intended use of a promised service or item involves her other assets in a way that exposes them to risks of damage if the defendant does not perform as promised.[39] If the assets are damaged as a result of breach of contract, these losses may also represent consequential damage because they are related to the plaintiff's performance interest in use.

Now in all these cases, if the defendant performs as required, the plaintiff will be able in fact to use what she was promised in whatever way she wishes. It might seem, therefore, that the performance interest should properly be construed with reference to this possibility—the protection of any and all of the plaintiff's planned uses—and thus that there should be liability for any and all consequential losses resulting from their frustration by breach. This, it would seem to follow, is what full protection of the plaintiff's performance interest requires. *Any* limit on recovery—in other words, any distinction between actionable and nonactionable consequential loss—must therefore represent undercompensation.[40] And if we view the performance interest as the protected interest that underpins contract remedies, any such limit would have to be justified on a policy basis that is external to the purely transactional character of contract formation and compensatory justice.

But this view supposes that compensatory justice requires that the defendant be contractually responsible for losses that result from interference with the plaintiff's unilateral and very possibly unknown and reasonably unknowable purposes, assets, opportunities, and circumstances. How can this be consistent with treating the parties as equals and therefore even be part of compensatory justice? Indeed, going a step further, because liability for consequential loss has to do with the breach's impact on the plaintiff's *independently* chosen purposes and uses, it seems to protect something that is not self-evidently part of what the defendant has promised by way of performance or of what he has moved to the plaintiff as consideration. One might say, with Robert Pothier, that consequential loss, "although it was occasioned by the non-performance of [the] obligation," is "foreign to the obligation" because it does not "relate to the thing that was the object of contract ... [and does not result] *propter rem ipsam non habitam* [on account of my not having the thing itself]."[41] By this logic, liability for *any* consequential loss becomes immediately problematic.

Both of these opposing conclusions—that all or no consequential loss is actionable—conflict with the approach taken by the common law and civil law. For in both systems, there can be liability for consequential loss but, at the same time, only where, in addition to the loss being caused in fact by the breach, certain further normative criteria are met. What, then, is the analysis of liability in *Hadley* and subsequent decisions? As I will now try to explain, all these decisions present the basis of liability for consequential loss as both *intrinsic* to the protection of the performance interest and *transactionally specified*—hence limited—as part of a purely internal contractual analysis. In doing so, their analysis meets fully the requirements of equal compensatory justice by vindicating what the contract itself must reasonably contemplate with respect to a party's planned uses and purposes and so what counts in the first place, normatively and as between the parties, as a contractually relevant use or purpose.

To begin, what is striking but often not sufficiently noticed about *Hadley* is that in setting out the limits of actionable consequential loss, the judgment's central proposition states a principle of *inclusion* that recognizes that there can be recovery of consequential loss. Despite the fact that consequential loss seems to be only contingently related to the defendant's performance and goes beyond the direct and immediate interference with the plaintiff's performance interest in possession, the court famously holds that in certain cases such loss may "fairly and reasonably be considered [as] arising naturally, i.e., according to the usual course of things, from such breach of contract itself."[42] Clearly, the court presupposes here that the plaintiff's performance interest involves not merely the possibility of possessing or receiving the performance (Pothier's "having the thing itself") but also the possibility of using it in some way or other. Parties are reasonably presumed mutually to intend that the consideration given and received imports an interest in use.

By recognizing the performance interest in use, the analysis of liability at the remedial stage reflects and carries through the prerequisites of formation and therefore the characterization of what the plaintiff thereby acquires. For, as the discussion on consideration in Chapter 1 tried to make clear, it is basic to this requirement that what is promised must be something that is amenable to being used or enjoyed by the plaintiff. The fact that the consideration must be usable makes contractually relevant—and thus necessarily, although implicitly, contemplated—at least some particular purposes and uses to which the plaintiff may put the promised performance. Unless this dimension of usability is explicitly recognized at the remedial stage, damages do not fulfill the idea of compensatory justice but instead render consideration illusory and without fair value, emptying it of the notion of benefit. For this reason, Treitel is correct in suggesting that every contract gives rise to two quite different kinds of expectation: "that of receiving the promised performance and that of putting it to some particular use."[43]

Accordingly, a contract implicitly contemplates or, in Adam Kramer's helpful phrase, is "oriented toward" a party having a performance interest not only in the possession but also in the use of the promised subject matter.[44] It follows from this that in promising consideration and therefore at contract formation, a promisor eo ipso implicitly but necessarily assumes at least *some* contractually defined responsibility for the promisee's interest in using and dealing with what has been promised. Even though and indeed precisely because it is coercive, the law's remedial response to breach must presuppose the parties' voluntarily assumed responsibilities, in this way preserving the voluntary basis of contractual obligation.[45] But note that this assumption of responsibility is imputed to the defendant—he is *held* to it—as a reasonable and fair incident of his contractual engagement with the plaintiff, not because he subjectively intends or desires to assume it. Moreover, what a party is held to have assumed responsibility for is the fulfillment of these aspects of the other's contractual interest in performance, not compensation for losses that result from failing to do so.[46] Framing it in this way ensures that the party's obligation arising at contract formation is not conflated with the law's coercive response at the remedial stage to a violation of it.

At the same time, and in keeping with the transactional character of the process and elements of contract formation, the scope of this assumption of responsibility must be determined by the parties' contract itself—by what can be "fairly and reasonably contemplated by both the parties when they made [their] contract" and not by either party or any factor considered on its own and apart from their bilateral relation.[47] Thus the fact that a party may have planned a particular use for the performance owed her does not, as such, make that use contractually relevant. To count as a use that comes within the contractually recognized interest in performance, it must be shown to be reasonably and mutually contemplated by the parties' mutual assents at contract formation. As Williston aptly puts it, a person "is charged with the apparent value of the performance that he promised, not with what ultimately proves to be its value."[48] The metes and bounds of the responsibility assumed are transactionally determined. The whole analysis begins from and is anchored in this standpoint. It is therefore fundamentally mistaken to take a consequential loss as contractually relevant simply because, as a matter of fact, it would not have been suffered had the defendant fully performed. This is not the starting point in the analysis of liability.[49] Hence also the incorrectness of viewing the requirement that the use be contemplated at formation as limiting what should ideally count as a contractually relevant interest, thereby constraining the full operation and scope of compensatory justice. To the contrary, the requirement specifies and indeed constitutes what is part of the performance interest in use. Apart from this, there is no contractually relevant use.

In *Hadley*, Baron Alderson lays down the rule that where the loss is of a kind or type that flows "naturally" from the breach, that is, as he puts it, in the usual course of things and in the great multitude of cases under ordinary circumstances, the defendant should reasonably and fairly be held to have contemplated the loss and on this basis be liable in damages for it. In the absence of express terms to the contrary, contemplation of consequential loss deemed to be "general" or "ordinary" is thus imputed to the defendant for the purposes of contractual responsibility. Expressed in the terms of the approach that I have proposed, "ordinary" and "general" consequential loss represents the kind of loss that *must* be recognized if the plaintiff is to have *any* protected performance interest in use at all. Now if, as is invariably supposed in the case law, the analysis of liability turns on a distinction between general or ordinary and particular or special types of loss, the question that immediately arises is how to decide whether a given loss is of one type rather than the other. The difficulty we face here is that, even though Baron Alderson clearly views the kind of loss in this case as neither ordinary nor general, the judgment does not actually explain why.

To elaborate, the court in *Hadley* asks: where the defendants reasonably know at contract formation only that the article to be carried is the broken shaft of a mill and that the plaintiffs are the mill owners, do these circumstances reasonably show, in the great multitude of cases, that the profits of the mill must be stopped by an unreasonable delay in the delivery of the broken shaft by the defendants to a third person? But to answer this, the court proceeds with the following further questions. What, the court queries, if the plaintiffs have another shaft to use and they only wish to send back the broken one to the engineer who made it? Or if the mill machinery is in some other respects malfunctioning and so unable to operate in any event? These are just some of the possible hypothetical scenarios that would be consistent with the known circumstances, and yet, if they obtained, the delay in delivery would in itself have no effect on the mill's profits. Given these points and for the purpose of fixing liability, the court then characterizes the kind of loss that did occur and that the defendants must have contemplated at formation as one arising from the following *very specific* facts: "that the shaft was actually sent back to serve as a model for a new one, and that the want of a new one was the only cause of stoppage of the mill, and that the loss of profits really arose from not sending down the new shaft in proper time, and that this arose from the delay in delivering the broken one to serve as a model."[50] With the consequences of breach described in this way, the court finds that "it is obvious that, in the great multitude of cases of millers sending off broken shafts to third persons by a carrier under ordinary circumstances, such consequences would not, in all probability, have occurred."[51] Thus, Baron Alderson concludes, the lost profits "cannot reasonably be considered such a consequence of the breach of contract as could fairly and reasonably be contemplated by both parties when they made this contract."[52] Hence no recovery.

I have quoted the words of the judgment in detail to highlight that the apparent ease with which the court reaches its conclusion depends wholly on its adoption of a very specific factual description of the circumstances and nature of the loss. To see this, suppose that instead the court were to describe the loss in less specific, more general terms such as "a merely financial loss (of some kind) arising from nondelivery or late delivery of an article used in the plaintiffs' manufacturing process or business."[53] Should not the defendants, in the circumstances known to them, have reasonably contemplated this consequence so described as ordinary and general? At the very least, they arguably should have.

The problem is that the whole analysis of whether a loss is deemed ordinary (i.e., in the "usual course of things" or occurring in the "great multitude of cases") and therefore should reasonably be contemplated necessarily rests on a description of the relevant loss at some level of specificity.[54] However, the court in *Hadley* does not explain why the more specific description that it adopts is appropriate despite the fact that both the specific and the general descriptions would factually be equally correct. There must be, in Lord Hoffmann's phrase, "other unexpressed factors operating beneath the surface."[55] Since the appropriateness of a description at a given level of specificity cannot be decided on purely factual grounds, the basis of the choice must be normative: "whether the loss for which compensation is sought is of a 'kind' or 'type' for which the contract-breaker ought fairly to be taken to have accepted responsibility."[56]

This normative basis, I want to suggest, is decidedly transactional: it specifies what, in light of the terms, surrounding circumstances and the kind of transaction they entered into, the parties mutually could reasonably expect and would reasonably suppose at contract formation with respect to the plaintiff's (protected) performance interest in use.[57] In this way, liability for consequential loss, like every other aspect of contract law, is anchored in the reasonable, if implicit, meaning of the parties' express terms—"neither cutting them down so that [the plaintiff] obtains less than he was reasonably entitled to expect, nor extending them so as to impose on the [defendant] a liability greater than he could reasonably have thought he was undertaking."[58] Crucial factors in this transactional analysis include not only the contract's express terms (particularly the price charged) and the reasonably imputable knowledge available at formation to both parties but also the nature of the transaction at issue. This last point concerning transaction-types requires elaboration.

More specifically, at one end of a continuum, there are cases where the contract is almost completely nonindividualized and the defendant provides a service at the same low price to an indefinite number of customers, each with potentially widely different financial or other interests at stake: for example, the common carrier in *Hadley* who, I shall assume, cannot decline customers or individualize the terms to reflect different risks but who must charge the same rate to all on a basis that is independent of the value or importance of the contents transported.[59] At the other end are cases where the contract is the sale of an item manufactured, delivered, and installed by the defendant who is well aware (perhaps through past dealings) of the plaintiff's particular circumstances and intended uses of the item and where the defendant's obligations standardly would include the range of implied warranties concerning fitness for use, and so forth.[60] These differences between the two kinds of transactions shape the determination of what counts as ordinary or general, and therefore reasonably contemplated and recoverable, consequential loss. Let me explain.

In the first kind of transaction with its characteristically wide and indefinite range of potential consequential losses resulting from delayed or defective performance, the consequential loss is not ordinarily recoverable. Why not? For such loss to count as ordinary and therefore to be reasonably contemplated at contract formation, its factual characterization has to be pitched at a fairly high level of generality, leaving out the particular details of the manner in which the loss was caused. Once details are included, it is no longer possible to view the more specified loss as being a kind that would happen in the ordinary course of events and the great majority of cases. But if we move to the more general description, this automatically makes the defendant responsible for an open-ended and indeterminate range of financial (or other) losses that neither party can quantify at the time of contracting and against which the defendant cannot insure.[61] It would be unreasonable to presume—in the absence of clearly manifested intent—that the defendant has accepted such unbounded responsibility. This is even more evidently so where the defendant receives a price that, as both parties reasonably know, does not reflect the specific qualitative and quantitative risks involved in any particular transaction and is in fact the same low rate charged to all of the indefinitely many customers, with their widely varying interests and purposes. This purely transactional analysis reflects the reasonable notion that "anyone asked to assume a large and unpredictable risk will require some premium in exchange."[62]

Without the need to refer to extratransactional grounds of policy, we may conclude that in this situation there cannot be a presumed intent to assume responsibility for such an open-ended risk. With a more general characterization of the loss ruled out, the consequential loss should be viewed as arising in "special circumstances." But, for such loss to be recoverable, there must be appropriate notice. These more specific circumstances must have been brought home to the defendant in such a way that the parties "might have specially provided for the breach of contract by special terms ... and of this advantage it would be very unjust to deprive them."[63]

What about the second kind of transaction-type, where, however, the contract is individualized in the sense that the defendant knows, or reasonably should know, the particular types of uses and purposes to which the plaintiff intends to put the performance and may reasonably be presumed to have provided contract terms in light of that knowledge? Here, the consequences of breach for which the defendant may reasonably be held to have assumed responsibility can fairly be described as including this range of uses without worrying about the exact particulars insofar as this need not expose him to indeterminate liability. For example, in the famous case of *Victoria Laundry v. Newman Industries,* the defendant vendors were found liable for the plaintiffs' lost profits resulting from late delivery of a boiler, which the defendants had sold them with clear knowledge that the plaintiffs needed the boiler for immediate use in their dyeing and laundering business, although the defendants did not know the precise role it would play in that business. In striking contrast with the analysis in *Hadley,* the court here referred to the loss simply and in general terms as loss of business resulting from late delivery of an item intended for business use and viewed such loss characterized in general terms as ordinary, not special.[64] A more specific description detailing the boiler's role, though factually correct, was not needed or even relevant in characterizing the kind of loss for which the defendants ought fairly to be taken to have accepted responsibility. Given the kind of highly individualized contract in this case, an imputed assumption of responsibility framed with reference to loss more generally described would not unfairly expose the defendants to indeterminate liability.[65]

Legal scholarship often presents the analysis of liability in *Hadley* as based simply on reasonable foreseeability taken as an independent and distinct element that is specified in terms of degrees of probability.[66] This, however, is not the case. The question of foreseeability is always "foreseeability of what?" and this "what" necessarily involves a description that can be pitched at different levels of specificity or generality. Unless we specify it, the application of foreseeability—including the requisite degree of probability—is indeterminate. Thus foreseeability must also presuppose some prior determination of the appropriate description, and this can only be decided on normative, not purely factual, grounds. Even if it is a necessary prerequisite for liability, foreseeability is also embedded in the kind of normative transactional analysis proposed here and is strictly subordinate to the following ultimate question: in light of a transactional interpretation of the contract as a whole in its surrounding circumstances, is the loss for which compensation is being sought of a kind for which the defendant ought fairly and reasonably be held to have assumed responsibility?[67]

Clearly, foreseeability is relevant in the sense that, once the level of specificity for the type of loss is settled, an assumption of responsibility will not be imputed by way of implication for an unforeseeable consequence. Still, because foreseeability is relevant and specified only as part of the transactional analysis of assumption of responsibility, it may be displaced by other factors that shape the reasonable construction of the parties' presumed intent. For instance, particular background commercial practices and shared understandings that reasonably would be assumed by both parties may in fact preclude an implication of responsibility for a given type of loss despite its occurrence being perfectly foreseeable at formation, even when described in relatively specific terms.[68]

Moreover, because the concept of foreseeability has no juridical meaning or application except as embedded in such transactional analysis, the fact that, in the abstract, foreseeability may be relevant to the analysis of contractual liability for consequential loss and also to liability for negligence does not make its operation the same in both.[69] The difference is not merely the obvious one that in contract "reasonable contemplation" is at the time of formation (not breach), whereas in tort "reasonable foreseeability" is at the moment of the wrong. This difference reflects the more fundamental fact that, in contrast to tort, contract is a *mutually voluntary* transaction that establishes the parties' remedially protected interests at formation.

In the circumstances of their voluntary transaction, each contracting party may reasonably assume in the absence of evidence to the contrary that the other's interests in use and the sorts of risks that nonperformance may impose on those interests are those that would be generally shared and incurred by similarly situated contracting parties. Presuming such a baseline of ordinary and usual kinds of uses and making a distinction between ordinary and special losses for a given performance is fair and reasonable as between the parties. A party wishing to protect himself or herself against a risk that in the absence of notice must reasonably appear to the other as unusual or special (i.e., not occurring in the great multitude of cases) can direct the other's attention to it before the contract is made and thus make it salient as between the parties for the purposes of establishing their mutual expectations and responsibilities. Insofar as contracting parties can alert each other to and allocate risks of even the most unusual and unexpected kinds of loss, the scope of contractual liability is potentially as wide as the parties make apparent to each other. Not so in tort interactions, which, being nonvoluntary, give no such opportunity for the injured person to protect himself or herself in this way, and in which the contractually relevant distinction between ordinary and special must therefore have a different sense and application, if any.[70] Here a wrongdoer cannot reasonably complain if he must take the plaintiff as he finds her and is held liable for unusual, even though at some level foreseeable, losses.

Like all contract principles, the rule in *Hadley* also supposes performance to be a moral fact, fixed and certain, because it is required as a matter of rights between the parties. The plaintiff can rightfully treat the other's performance as forthcoming. The difficulty is that the particular use to which she intends to put it—the manner in which she chooses to rely on it—may or may not be reasonably apparent to the defendant in the circumstances of their interaction. The question of reasonableness is, which, if any, of these uses must the defendant take into account as part of his obligation to respect the plaintiff's performance interest, and the contribution of *Hadley* is that it provides a coherent answer to this question.

Thus the test in *Hadley* need not, and should not, be explained as a (rather blunt and indirect) instrument to distinguish efficient from inefficient reliance and for disallowing the latter.[71] As noted earlier, the economic analysis of efficient reliance turns on the expected costs and benefits of reliance investments and thus on the expected probability of actual performance. But the legal analysis of remoteness does not give standing to this probability (because in legal contemplation it represents the probability of a wrong). More generally, as I noted in connection with the various instances of implication, there is no need to justify the imposition of liability under *Hadley* as a majoritarian or penalty default rule in the service of welfare maximization or efficiency goals. While application of the rule in *Hadley* may certainly produce incentive effects, these are merely its by-product and are not part of its justification or rationale as presented in the case law elucidated here. Viewed in its own framework, the principle in *Hadley* embodies a purely transactional analysis that aims at compensatory justice in ensuring the full and fair restoration of the plaintiff's performance interest, consistent with requirements of reasonableness and equality as between the parties.

By setting out a general principle that anchors contractually recoverable loss in an analysis of what parties must reasonably have contemplated at contract formation and as part of their fairly imputed assumption of responsibility, *Hadley* remains true to the basic character of contract as a mutually voluntary transaction and may rightly be viewed as providing a unified general standpoint for the determination of all remedial claims in contract law.[72] To conclude this discussion of consequential loss, I want very briefly to suggest how we might draw on the preceding analysis to help frame a plausible approach to the controverted question of whether damages for breach of contract can ever appropriately be measured by the defendant's gain.

In connection with this issue, it is particularly important to keep in mind the conceptual distinction between injury and loss as discussed earlier. Thus the fact that, say, a contract term expressly prohibits certain actions by the defendant does not as such imply that his doing those actions in breach and more particularly any resulting gain are to be viewed as directly belonging to the plaintiff or as directly constituting the plaintiff's loss. Rather, the actions represent simply an injury to the plaintiff's contract right, with the next step being the determination of what, if any, loss the plaintiff may have sustained thereby.[73] And in determining loss, because it must fundamentally relate to the plaintiff's (and not the defendant's) interest in possessing or using the promised performance including its value, the defendant's gain should prima facie be irrelevant.[74] How, then, might a defendant's profits from breach become appropriate as a measure of loss?

If, by the express or implied terms of the contract, certain profit-generating activity engaged in by the defendant is supposed to be exercised for the benefit and gain of the plaintiff, here the loss would arguably directly consist in the gain wrongly appropriated by the defendant. But apart from this limiting (and legally straightforward) case in which gain-measured damages would give the plaintiff the very performance owed her and thus represent what I have termed enforced performance damages, the other way in which the defendant's gain can be an appropriate measure of loss is if it qualifies as the reasonable measure of the *value* of the injury, or in other words as an appropriate measure of damages for lost performance value. The latter, we have seen, becomes relevant where actual loss cannot be directly or definitely assessed or the performance is not obtainable by an adequate remedy (whether via expectation damages or specific performance) but where it can be reasonably presumed that the breach has substantially affected the plaintiff's contractually contemplated interests. This can certainly be the case where breach would give rise to consequential loss that is irreversible, intangible and indirect. In these circumstances, if the plaintiff's right is to be vindicated at all and the promised consideration not rendered illusory, gain-measured damages, if readily determinable and reasonably certain, may be appropriate and indeed necessary. The reasonableness and fairness of choosing the defendant's gain as the measure of lost value can be particularly evident where the plaintiff has a legitimate performance interest, reflected in the contract's express and implied terms reasonably construed, in preventing the defendant's profit-making activity made possible via his breach.[75] Lost performance value measured by the defendant's gain can qualify as compensatory in character. As I now discuss, a somewhat similar analysis can also explain the appropriateness of reliance-measured damages in certain circumstances of breach.[76]

8.3. Reliance as a Measure of Contract Damages

The question of the relation between reliance and contract law, which has loomed large since at least Fuller and Perdue's discussion, comprises two different issues that should not be conflated. Reliance may be relevant either as a distinctive substantive basis of liability or as a measure of damages for breach of contract. I have already discussed the first issue in Chapter 1 in connection with the contrast between reliance and consideration. Whereas reliance-based liability presupposes neither contract formation nor, therefore, even a breach of contract, reliance as a *measure* of contract damages supposes both. The questions here are: given the proposed primacy of the performance interest, how should we understand damages for breach of contract measured by a plaintiff's reliance losses, and, more particularly, can such reliance damages, properly understood, ever qualify, limit, or displace the full protection of the performance interest via expectation damages or specific performance?

To begin, what does reliance on a contractually enforceable promise entail? To fix ideas, I draw on Fuller and Perdue's distinction between "essential" and "incidental" reliance.[77] Essential reliance refers to what the plaintiff must do (whether directly or by way of preparation) in order to be entitled to the defendant's promised performance. For example, the plaintiff may have to incur the costs of producing a highly specialized customized product sold to the defendant. "Incidental" reliance, by contrast, refers to all other acts (or forbearances) by the plaintiff done in the expectation of receiving the defendant's promised performance. For instance, the plaintiff may upgrade his own facilities to receive and to use profitably the item promised by the defendant. Now if the defendant breaches and the plaintiff does not receive the promised performance, these expenditures and arrangements may be wasted or lost, causing the plaintiff financial or other prejudice. In arguing that the law does and should compensate for such losses, Fuller and Perdue also stress that in doing so, the law should never put the plaintiff in a better position than he would have been in had the defendant fully performed as promised. This suggestion that actionable reliance losses should be so limited squarely raises the question of the relation between a reliance measure of recovery and the performance interest, which I now address.

As just defined, the plaintiff does acts and incurs costs of essential and incidental reliance for the purpose, and in the expectation, of obtaining the defendant's performance and its benefits. Such acts and costs of reliance are not, however, per se a detriment or a loss to the plaintiff. He sustains loss only if and to the extent that his reliance efforts are wasted as a result of not receiving the promised performance. If, therefore, breach can be adequately compensated by expectation damages or by specific performance so that the plaintiff is able in post-breach circumstances to obtain the actual performance promised and its full beneficial use, to that extent his reliance is not wasted and there are no specifically reliance losses.

But suppose now that there is some residual performance loss that is not so remedied by expectation damages or specific performance (e.g., consequential loss) and further that the value of this loss cannot be directly and readily measured with the required certainty in the post-breach circumstances: what compensatory redress can the law provide? Here, the reliance costs wasted as a result of breach (assuming that these costs could be reasonably contemplated at contract formation) might seem to offer an alternative credible measure of the (estimated) value of this residual performance loss.[78] In other words, wasted reliance costs might provide a suitable substitute measure of damages for the purpose of measuring lost performance value.

But this suggestion immediately raises the following problem. The reliance costs must be shown to have been wasted *because* of the breach, if they are to be actionable and used as a measure of recovery. Yet how can the plaintiff show this where, in the circumstances of breach, we cannot tell what would have been the value of full performance? Perhaps the reliance costs would have been wasted anyway even on full performance because the contract was a bad bargain for the plaintiff.

Courts resolve this difficulty by presuming against the defendant that, in the absence of evidence to the contrary, the reliance costs would have been at least offset or justified by the reasonably expected benefits of full performance.[79] This "break-even" presumption is, however, rebuttable. Insofar as the defendant can show that the value of full performance would have fallen short of the costs of reliance or that the plaintiff would not in any event have obtained the benefit that he expected from the use of the defendant's performance, the reliance loss is not wasted by reason of the breach and so does not constitute a loss resulting from breach.[80] What might justify the court's rebuttable presumption? We need not say that it is because statistically or as a matter of fact most contracts are profitable or because, as is certainly correct, it would not be rational for the plaintiff knowingly to enter a losing bargain. Rather, the presumption is made because this is fair and reasonable as against the defendant, seeing that it is the defendant's breach that is responsible for making it impossible to establish the value of the lost benefits, and therefore the defendant should not be able to rely on this impossibility to escape liability.[81] As between the parties and in the absence of facts to the contrary, the burden of this evidentiary difficulty should fairly be borne by the defendant, not the plaintiff.[82]

Well-known judgments across the major common law jurisdictions reflect this analysis of the role of reliance damages as a measure of recovery for breach of contract.[83] What must be emphasized is that in view of this analysis, far from being an independent and alternative remedial response, the reliance measure of recovery is simply a way of securing the fair value of the plaintiff's performance interest in circumstances where expectation damages would not be fully adequate and there is no direct measure of the loss. Even though wasted reliance is reimbursed, this is done only to the extent that it presumptively evidences what the plaintiff has been deprived of by the breach, namely, the benefit of the defendant's promised performance.

Strictly speaking, therefore, the aim of the law in giving such damages is not to redress or undo a wasted expenditure as such. Nor can it ever be a matter of *confining* the plaintiff to reliance damages. In the circumstances where the direct assessment of the lost value of performance is not possible because it would be wholly conjectural and uncertain, reliance damages may be the only relatively certain measure of the plaintiff's performance interest loss that is available. Clearly, where a direct and certain measure of the performance interest is available or even more, where expectation damages are adequate because they reflect what is necessary to enable the plaintiff to obtain his promised performance including its beneficial use, he should not be restricted to reliance damages. Like all remedies that presuppose and enforce contractual claims, the reliance measure of damages is therefore a mode of upholding via compensation the plaintiff's right to the promised performance.[84] In contrast to the law's goal in protecting reliance as a substantive basis of liability, here the aim in resorting to reliance losses as a measure of recovery is not per se to reinstate the plaintiff in his prereliance position.[85]

My chief conclusion is that reliance damages reimburse wasted expenditures as a measure for the value of presumptively lost but unascertainable benefits of the bargain. Being a species of what I refer to as lost performance value compensation rather than enforced performance, reliance damages should not limit, displace, or replace expectation damages where these are adequate and enable the plaintiff to obtain, so far as possible in post-breach circumstances, the actual promised performance.

There is a further point. Once reliance damages are understood in this way, we can see that actual reliance is not even an essential ingredient in the analysis of recovery. There can be, for example, unascertainable consequential loss that is fairly measured by expenditures that were made before the parties contracted.[86] As long as the defendant reasonably should have contemplated at formation that these costs could be incurred *before* the parties contracted, that they were reasonably related to the plaintiff's foreseeable (prospective) use of the defendant's promised performance, and that they would be wasted if the defendant breached, the costs can be used to quantify the value of the loss of the bargain's presumed but unascertainable benefits—supposing, as discussed, that the court can fairly assume against the defendant that the plaintiff would have broken even. In cases where essential or incidental reliance is referred to, such reliance serves to establish the requisite connection between (wasted) expenditures and the plaintiff's interest in obtaining or using the defendant's performance. It is sufficient to establish the connection with the plaintiff's performance interest. But, as just indicated, reliance is not always necessary for this purpose. For this reason, calling them reliance damages is not particularly conducive to clarity of thought.[87]

8.4. Mitigation and the Performance Interest

Like remoteness and the reliance measure of damages, mitigation also raises the issue of whether it limits or subtracts from the principle of full compensation for the performance interest and, if so, on what justified basis. Indeed, it is widely assumed that the principle of mitigation is in tension with the law's commitment to protection of the expectation interest and its conception of contractual liability as strict.[88] The mitigation doctrine has different components and involves interesting and sometimes difficult questions of application in certain factual scenarios. There are many details. My focus here, however, shall be on its core meaning and its relation to the performance interest, as well as its role within the remedial scheme of the common law of contract. These matters are the most fundamental and need clarification to complete the theoretical account of remedies presented thus far. For this purpose, I shall discuss the central tenet of the mitigation principle, familiarly referred to as the "duty to mitigate," which holds that a promisee cannot recover damages for losses caused by breach that she could reasonably have avoided.[89]

Chief Judge Cardozo, in his concurring opinion in *McClelland v. Climax Hosiery Mills,* presents the meaning and role of the mitigation principle as follows:

> The statement is made not infrequently in treatise and decision that a servant wrongfully discharged is "under a duty" to the master to reduce the damages if he can.... What is meant by the supposed duty is merely this: That if he unreasonably reject he will not be heard to say that the loss of wages from then on shall be deemed the jural consequence of the earlier discharge. He has broken the chain of causation, and the loss resulting to him thereafter is suffered through his own act. It is not damage that has been caused by the wrongful act of the employer.[90]

The core idea here is that, after the breach and beyond whatever loss this immediately and necessarily entails, any further loss that the plaintiff can reasonably avoid is not, to use Cardozo's term, the jural consequence of that breach and therefore does not come within the defendant's contractual responsibility. To the contrary, because it is deemed in legal contemplation to be the result of the plaintiff's own choice and not that of the defendant, the loss is at the plaintiff's risk and cannot be recovered. Is this a cogent rationale for the mitigation requirement?

The first and most basic question is: what justifies the law's view that the promisee's failure to mitigate breaks the chain of jural consequences of the breach, though, as a factual matter, even avoidable losses would not have occurred but for that breach? The analysis of causation supposed here clearly has a normative dimension and is not simply factual. It is a matter of assigning responsibility as between the parties for certain events. Now the only positive normative link between the parties is their contract. It makes sense, then, to look to this as the source and framework for determining responsibility.

Consistently with the proposed conception of contractual liability as strict, the fundamental idea here must be that the metes and bounds of the promisor's responsibility are set by the reasonable meaning and the fair value of the performance owed. Now such performance is always determinate as to when it becomes binding and when it is discharged. Prior to contract formation, the parties are mutually independent in the sense that they owe each other no contractual obligations and are at liberty to act as they wish from a contractual point of view. As against the other, what a party does is simply his or her own choice and is wholly at his or her own risk. Next, as a result of their mutual assents satisfying the requirements of formation, they become bound up with each other—and so become mutually related—according to the agreed-upon terms. As part of this relation, each can expect and deal with the other's performance as a normatively fixed and certain contractual reality. But this normative nexus ends with full performance, and performance is to take place at a certain time. Thereafter, the parties resume their precontractual stance of mutual independence where whatever each one does is at his or her own risk once more and has no bearing on the other from the standpoint of contractual responsibilities.

We have seen that the fundamental aim of remedies for breach is, post-breach, to put the promisee as far as possible in the same position that she would have been in had she received the performance owed, giving the promisee both possession and use of what was promised as specified by the contractual terms and, in this way, vindicating the promisee's performance interest in the face of the promisor's wrong. If so, then notionally and normatively, the remedial response should reflect the temporal determinacy of the contractual performance interest itself: the remedy should aim, as far as is practically possible, to secure the promisee's performance interest when performance is due, not after this point. We should therefore expect the remedial analysis to incorporate both the moment of promisor responsibility *and* the end of that responsibility, when the parties once more resume their mutual independence. My suggestion is that the way the common law accomplishes this twofold task is via the principle of mitigation.

To explain, the doctrine of mitigation is a part of the law's *remedial* response to the defendant's breach. It starts from the fact of breach and holds the defendant responsible for the loss that crystallizes at the time of breach, which, we assume, is also the time when performance is due and the defendant's obligation would have been discharged. Prima facie, recoverable loss and therefore also compensation owing are determined at this point. If the subject matter of the promised performance is readily available on the market, damages represent the means to enable the plaintiff, immediately upon breach, to go into the market and to obtain the promised performance. In the absence of any other loss, these damages are deemed in law to secure at the remedial stage the performance owing to the plaintiff and hence fully and definitively to redress the defendant's breach of obligation. Where the subject matter or any aspect of lost performance is not available in this way, the performance is restored by an in specie remedy or, failing this, an award of value. All these responses are remedial representations of the plaintiff's performance interest at the time performance is due, which, being owed by the defendant and being his responsibility, is vindicated by a transfer from him to the plaintiff.

The mitigation principle says, in effect, that the plaintiff can claim against the defendant only those losses that are tied to or that result from the plaintiff taking reasonable measures (e.g., going into the market, arranging her affairs, or seeking specific performance) to protect her performance interest as crystallized in these remedial representations, taking the moment of breach as the notional starting point for evaluation. Whatever the plaintiff loses in doing this counts as unavoidable loss—the jural effects of the defendant's own act, not the plaintiff's. These losses should be viewed as resulting from the plaintiff's continuing contractual dependence on the defendant, given that the plaintiff is simply doing what she can in the circumstances of breach to obtain possession of the promised consideration. The law says to the defendant: the plaintiff is not to be damnified as a result of taking these measures; this is what you promised the plaintiff and for which therefore you are remedially responsible if she suffers loss thereby. The law does not view the plaintiff as acting independently and at her own risk but as incurring losses that arise from the fact of being dependent on the defendant for the execution of his obligation. Where, however, the plaintiff's losses do not result from taking such measures, they are jurally the consequence of the plaintiff's own act, not the defendant's: whatever she now does is as independent of their relation and whatever losses she incurs are at her own risk, avoidable and nonrecoverable as against the defendant.

In assessing whether the plaintiff's conduct is within these parameters, the principle of mitigation views it in the context of (often) uncertain circumstances obtaining at the time of breach and done in light of the plaintiff's reasonable assessment at that time as to what she has been promised, what she can expect by way of benefit of the performance, and whether the subject matter of the performance is in fact readily available on the market. She is held to this transactional remedial standard and not to what a court or anyone else might view in hindsight as reasonable or required. Moreover, various practicalities—including the time or access to resources needed to take reasonable steps—must also be given due weight.[91] Thus, unless, when judged from the plaintiff's reasonable standpoint in the circumstances of breach, the market available performance is substantially identical to the promised performance—with any difference being readily and accurately reducible to money terms—neither the mitigation principle nor good faith requires the plaintiff to seek what is, in effect, a different performance from that promised, in derogation from her performance right and immunity. In these circumstances, reasonableness may be satisfied if she seeks specific performance on a timely basis (unless this would be in vain because the subject matter is clearly no longer available to the defendant) even if in the end the court declines to order specific performance and awards damages.

On the proposed view, mitigation makes explicit at the remedial stage the parameters of what is necessary to secure the plaintiff's protected interest in performance—nothing less but also nothing more. Its function is not to diminish the extent of the defendant's liability, but rather to crystallize the time and measure of injury, excluding losses that cannot reasonably be construed as part of or as unavoidably consequential upon that injury. However, we still have to address the following question that has most troubled commentators: adding insult to injury, why should the innocent party have to do *anything*—even notionally—to secure her promised performance in the face of the defendant's breach?[92] Since it is the defendant's duty to perform, the burden of securing it should only and always be on him, not on the plaintiff who has the right to the performance. Mitigation, it is objected, compels the innocent party to confer a gratuitous benefit on the breaching party by having to take measures that limit or reduce the extent of the latter's liability. Some writers suggest that nonpromissory principles of cooperation and altruism can be invoked to answer this objection.[93] Others refer to general conceptions of fairness or efficiency.[94] In my view, the way to a better answer lies in keeping in mind that mitigation is an aspect of compensatory redress for contractual breach, not part of promissory morality.[95]

In the case of the morality of promising, it can certainly be true that a promisor must continue to take seriously the fact that he has promised, even after he has failed to perform in the promised way or at the promised time. In fulfillment of his moral duty to the promisee, he must still conscientiously try to put the promisee in the promised position.[96] This is part of the execution of his continuing *original* obligation to perform. For this purpose, an offer of compensation might or might not be appropriate. But, if so, it would have to count as an appropriate, even if "second-best," way of directly fulfilling his promissory duty. And any expectation that the promisee should herself do something would also be assessed on this basis.

The analysis of compensation for breach of contract is categorically different. Damages or specific performance belong to the remedial stage of contract law and reflect the requirements of compensatory justice. Taken from the defendant and transferred to the plaintiff, damages are not the defendant's execution of his obligation, but the law's *coercive response to its breach*. Putting the plaintiff in the position of performance is the law's act, *not* the promisor's. Juridically, it does not represent the promisor's fulfillment of his contractual obligation to perform. The requirement of mitigation must be assessed as part of this coercive response and the idea of compensatory justice, including the principle that damages can be adequate (so that specific performance should be withheld) where the promised performance is readily available on the market.

Viewed in this light, the mitigation requirement seems normatively justified. In awarding damages for and in response to breach, a court of law (not the promisor) aims so far as possible to put the plaintiff in the position of having the promised performance despite the breach that has occurred. It does this by covering the reasonably unavoidable costs that the plaintiff would have to incur in order to purchase the subject matter of the performance from a third party. If the court could act instantly in response to breach and provide the plaintiff with damages on the spot, the plaintiff would be able to use the money taken from the defendant to obtain performance without loss. (We suppose that any losses resulting during the reasonable time needed for the plaintiff to obtain performance would be covered by the damages given.) But the practical institutional reality is that courts cannot respond to a breach until sometime later, both when awarding damages and in ordering specific performance. In this situation, the mitigation requirement *notionally* deems the plaintiff to have acted as soon as reasonably possible to obtain her promised performance on the market. But it also seeks to ensure that the plaintiff is not prejudiced by the fact that she may in effect first have to use her own funds for this purpose. If we assume (as part of ideal theory) that she can be fully compensated for any loss incurred as a result of using her own funds, measuring damages at a later point cannot be justified as a matter of compensatory justice for breach. To the contrary, it represents an unreasonable imposition on the defendant that does not advance the plaintiff's reasonable interest in having the promised performance as close as possible to the time and manner of performance.

Finally, what about the moral objection that this account still countenances, wrongly, the innocent plaintiff notionally having to act? We can see why this objection fails if we keep in mind that whether it is the defendant or the plaintiff who acts after breach, neither act fulfills a primary duty to perform but is simply part of the legally determined means of effectuating compensatory justice as part of the law's remedial coercive response to breach. The objection that it is intrinsically wrong to expect the plaintiff (rather than the defendant) to act at all thus reduces to the proposition that it must always be the defendant, never the plaintiff, who obtains (and provides the plaintiff with) a substitute performance. In other words, specific performance should be the *sole* legal remedy for breach. But on the assumption that damages would be adequate, placing the burden always on the defendant would be not only unreasonable toward the defendant but also not even more protective of the plaintiff's own rational interest in having the promised performance as soon as possible. In these circumstances, a plaintiff could not have a legitimate good faith contractual interest in insisting on specific performance.[97]

To conclude: mitigation expresses a requirement of reasonableness that is neither freestanding nor based on an affirmative duty to benefit others. Instead, it is wholly embedded in, and justified as part of, the remedial analysis of the protection of the performance interest against injury in accordance with the ideas of strict (contractual) liability and compensatory justice. The mitigation requirement ensures that this protection of the performance interest reflects the limited obligation that contractual responsibility entails. One may plausibly say that just as the doctrines of frustration and impossibility draw the inherent transactional limit of the scope of a contractual obligation, so mitigation sets the intrinsic transactional limit of the remedial enforcement of that obligation.

Chapter 9

Expectation Damages and Contract Theory

To conclude this section on enforcement and by way of transition to Part Two in which I take the proposed contractual analysis to a more theoretical level, I wish to consider a set of theoretical accounts of contract that, if sound, demonstrate the necessity of an approach to contract remedies and ultimately to the whole of contract law that is incompatible with what I have argued for here. At different points, I have referred to and discussed various aspects of these views. But since they challenge the proposed transactional account at a fundamental level and in one way or another are reflected in much of contemporary contract theory, it is important to assess them together and in greater depth. This is what I shall now try to do. To begin, I briefly recap some main points in the prior discussion of enforcement.

I have tried to show through a detailed examination of the main doctrines and principles of the law of remedies that the organizing aim of remedies, whether in specie or damages, is to vindicate a party's performance interest in a manner required by compensatory justice. Unexcused nonperformance of contractual terms represents a wrongful injury to the plaintiff's baseline entitlement and immunity in having and using the promised performance as contractually contemplated. This performance interest is established by and at contract formation, and it is normatively as well as conceptually first in the analysis of remedies. Under the idea of compensatory justice, remedies are, it must always be emphasized, the law's coercive response to the civil wrong of breach. The law does this by ascertaining the loss that represents the materialization of the injury to the plaintiff's right to receive full and complete performance and by effectuating, so far as possible in the post-breach situation, full and complete restoration of that loss via a coerced transfer in specie or of money from defendant to plaintiff. Such loss need not be pecuniary in nature. Moreover, while damages are clearly monetary, performance damages that count as adequate are given, not because the law converts the plaintiff's promised performance into value and views (monetized) value as what the plaintiff should receive by way of compensatory justice, but instead because such damages represent the cost and the means of the plaintiff obtaining the subject matter of the performance from third parties, thereby seeking to ensure that the plaintiff has possession and use (including value) of that performance in accordance with his or her baseline entitlement. It is only where there is a genuine loss that neither damages nor specific performance can repair and restore in this way that, at the remedial stage and for remedial purposes, the law tries to assign a value to the loss, which is compensated by what I have called lost performance value damages. In this way, contractual rights-formation and remedial response to wrongful injury are sequenced distinct steps in a unified transactional analysis. The unity of this analysis rests upon the premise that the performance interest specifies a distinct and definite kind of juridical relation between parties and that the remedies for breach are modes of redressing different but interconnected aspects of the materialization of wrongful injury to that interest under the idea of compensatory justice.

The lynchpin of this transactional analysis is the possibility of explaining the performance interest as a distinct juridical reality presupposed by and thus conceptually prior to remedies for breach. This view has been criticized as "hark[ing] back to a pre-modern, pre-realist, pre-Calabresi-and-Melamed approach to remedies."[1] It seems clear that the intellectual starting point of this criticism is Fuller and Perdue's challenge to and rejection of the performance interest as the central and unifying basis of the analysis of remedies.[2] In the last chapter, I noted that while Fuller and Perdue famously identify three different "interests" that, they say, the law aims to protect in giving contract damages, they do not introduce or explain these interests as conceptually or normatively first in the remedial analysis, but present them as mere crystallizations of different possible remedial purposes that courts may pursue in enforcing promises.[3] This is part and parcel of the purposive approach that they simply presuppose from the start as the appropriate form of analysis. The need for a remedy does not reflect a requirement to protect a given interest but rather is simply part of the realization of a set of given remedial purposes.

With this attenuation of the role and significance of the protected interest, the question that naturally arises is, why these three purposes and these three only?[4] Fuller himself saw the contribution of the article as lying in an "analysis which breaks down the Contract-No-Contract dichotomy, and substitutes an ascending scale of enforceability."[5] The question is why, on this view, should legal or theoretical analysis be concerned with identifying discrete (and, even more, just three) protected interests? One might think that the central aim of theory should henceforth be to identify the full range of possible purposes that contract remedies might aim to achieve. That the article does not fully embrace this as its theoretical agenda may be because it is still, even if implicitly and to a degree, wedded to the primacy of protected interests. This seems to be reflected in Fuller and Perdue's well-known but brief discussion of the different claims to judicial intervention that the three interests present as a matter of justice.

According to Fuller and Perdue, the most pressing claim in justice is for protection of the restitution interest, followed by protection of the reliance interest and finally by that of the expectation interest at the bottom. Taking the purpose of justice in private law to be the maintenance of an equilibrium of goods among members of society, they note that unjust enrichment, involving not only a loss to the plaintiff but also a gain to the defendant, results in a discrepancy of two units, whereas injury to the reliance interest (as a result of the plaintiff's change of position) involves just a loss to the plaintiff and so a discrepancy of only one unit.[6] Therefore, they argue, the claim to protection of the restitution interest is twice as strong as that of the reliance interest. As for the expectation interest, Fuller and Perdue emphasize that here the promisee's claim relates merely to "satisfaction for his disappointment in not getting what was promised him."[7] This does not represent a loss at all in departure from the baseline equilibrium of goods. In contrast to the restitution and reliance interests, there is no injury—at least not in the same sense—to the expectancy. Here, therefore, the aim of the law in directly protecting the expectation interest cannot be restorative. It "passes from the realm of corrective justice to that of distributive justice," and "[w]ith the transition, the justification for legal relief loses its self-evident quality."[8]

It seems clear that Fuller and Perdue treat judicial relief as reflecting compensatory justice only to the extent that a breach results in the holdings of one or both parties being greater or less than their initial baseline share of goods, where, crucially, this baseline share is set prior to and independent of the parties' contractual interaction. With respect to the restitution and reliance interests, they assume that one party, through his or her breach of promise, has caused the other a loss relative to this baseline. The protection of these interests restores the parties to what each held as his or her own under the baseline equilibrium. By contrast, in the case of the expectation interest, no such loss has been caused because the "expectancy is created by the promise," and thus, as just noted, it does not belong to the plaintiff as part of his or her baseline holdings.[9] Nonperformance does not, therefore, per se deprive the plaintiff of something that is his or her own from the standpoint of justice, and so relief cannot be construed as "giving back" but must instead be understood as "bring[ing] into being a new situation."[10] Only where the law acts restoratively does the justification for legal relief have a self-evident quality. Because damages for loss expectancies do not do this, Fuller and Perdue conclude that the rationale must be sought, if at all, in an amalgam of social, economic, and contractual policies that they call "juristic."

What this means is that protection of the one and only interest that is generated by contract—and which for this reason would be entitled to be designated as distinctively and inherently contractual—cannot be characterized as compensatory in nature or as coming under corrective justice. There is no such thing as a specifically *contractual* baseline for the purposes of compensatory justice. The very thing that might distinguish a protected interest as "contractual"—that is, its being "created" by the parties' mutual assents—now makes the interest enforceable only if there are good and sufficient extratransactional values that support this conclusion. It no longer makes sense or seems necessary to think in terms of a specifically contractual protected interest. The analysis of remedies need not turn on a supposed "contractual" nature of the relation or of the obligation, so long as there is promise and breach of promise. Indeed, inasmuch as expectation remedies for breach can no longer be explained in terms of compensation, they are now to be characterized as quasi-criminal sanctions or penalties for breach of promise that differ merely quantitatively in their impact on the breaching party.[11] Just as with the normative differences between contractual and promissory transactions, this rationale erases the difference between punishment and compensation.

It is important to highlight the point that Fuller and Perdue assimilate the analysis of contracts to that of promises in general and, indeed even more widely, to expectancies created by words or conduct.[12] It is on this basis that they contend that liability for detrimental reliance losses, even though independent of contract formation, belongs to the same normative domain as contractual liability for expectation losses: in both cases, liability is imposed "because a promise was made and broken."[13] Further, the bilateral relation of mutual promises—the fact that it is irreducibly two-sided in a way that the gratuitous promise is not—has no intrinsic significance as a distinct kind of normative relation. The normative difference between promises made to or for others and those made with others is not per se significant as a matter of justice between the parties. Its significance lies wholly in the fact that, if and when promising takes the form of economic exchange and bargain, it serves vital economic and social purposes and is a transaction where, because reliance is very likely to occur but often difficult to prove, reliance may be "conclusively presumed" to have taken place.[14] According to Fuller and Perdue, the legal understanding and assessment of such diverse relations as a gratuitous promise, a representation inviting detrimental reliance, and a promise-for-consideration should be based primarily on *instrumental* considerations, not on any supposed nature of the kind of obligation, relation, or liability they may each entail.[15] The idea of an immanent transactional analysis that specifies normatively different categories of promissory relations and transaction-types cannot frame this account. There are simply no qualitative differences.

Before proposing their particular policy-based rationale for protecting the expectation interest, Fuller and Perdue briefly consider an alternative view—"the much discussed 'will theory' of contract law"—which holds that by awarding expectation damages or by ordering specific performance, the law is merely implementing a private rule or law already established by the parties in their contract.[16] Against this view, they note that even if a contract represents a kind of private law, it is one that need not—and usually does not—say anything at all about what should be done when it is infringed. Thus, they conclude, there would be "no necessary contradiction between the will theory and a rule which limited damages to the reliance interest. Under such a rule the penalty for violating the norm established by the contract would simply consist in being compelled to compensate the other party for detrimental reliance."[17] But Fuller and Perdue do not develop this point or draw out its implications for promissory theories.

This further step is taken by Richard Craswell.[18] Deepening and generalizing Fuller and Perdue's point about the will theory and their critique of expectation damages, Craswell argues that, without exception and even within their own framework, promise-based and entitlement theories cannot justify the invariable primacy of the expectation interest—or of discrete interests in general—in contract damages. He does this by applying his more general argument about the failure of autonomy-based approaches to explain the implied dimension of agreements to the specific issue of remedies.

As I discussed earlier in Chapter 3, Craswell's general claim is that promissory and entitlement transfer theories are empty and indeterminate with respect to any matter that the parties have not expressly addressed in their contract.[19] He does not dispute that general principles such as "promises should be kept and enforced" or "entitlements contractually transferred at formation should be respected" can account for the binding force of the parties' mutual assents. Rather, the problem, according to Craswell, is that because these principles are content-neutral in the sense that they leave it to the parties to choose the terms of their mutual promises or entitlement transfers (within the parameters of legality, public policy, etc.), they do not guide the law at all in deciding whether or how it should fill in content when the parties have not expressly done so themselves. Now a crucial premise in Craswell's more specific argument about remedies is that he views enforceable contracts as comprising a bundle of rights, powers, liberties, and immunities, with the remedy being just "one of the many parameters that defines the total package of rights that each party has promised [or transferred]."[20] A remedial provision is thus simply another possible term, express or implied, that, as such, specifies more exactly what parties have promised or the entitlement that they have transferred. A promise to sell a horse for $100 can without contradiction explicitly and also implicitly promise reliance or expectation (or other) damages in the event of breach. Unless the parties have made this choice of remedy explicitly, promissory and entitlement theories tell us virtually nothing as to what the appropriate remedy should be. For this purpose, we must therefore resort to substantive principles and values such as economic efficiency, distributive justice, and so on, which, according to Craswell, do provide the necessary guidance as to content, subject always to parties expressly agreeing otherwise. But, on this basis, the invariable primacy of expectation remedies can no longer be presumed. It all depends on which further substantive principles or values are brought to bear and the factors that these single out as relevant.

I have noted that a key premise in Craswell's argument is that remedies for breach simply represent a kind of express or, more usually, implied term that is binding from contract formation on. At the same time, Craswell (no less than Fuller and Perdue before him) fully acknowledges that despite his normative recommendations, the law persists in recognizing the centrality of the performance interest and seeks to protect it as a matter of compensatory justice via damages or specific performance.[21] Showing that a policy-based analysis could indeed justify this primacy of the performance interest and its protection via expectation remedies *as an implied term* of contracts in general would therefore take Craswell's argument a step further. The starting point of this analysis would be policy and the conclusion would be a default rule of expectation damages, which would function as an implied term not only instrumentally justified by reason of that policy but also capable of being affirmed consistently with party autonomy. In this way and in contrast with the limited explanatory power of standard promissory and entitlement transfer theories (at least according to Craswell), the value of autonomy could be upheld without sacrificing the possibility of a fully specified and complete contractual obligation.

Daniel Markovits and Alan Schwartz have elaborated a promissory conception of contract—which they call the "dual performance hypothesis"— that aims to do precisely this.[22] Their primary goal is to justify what they see as the common law's preference for expectation damages over specific performance (and disgorgement) in the face of recent theories that would replace this liability rule with a property rule as the presumptive default rule for contract remedies.[23] I will focus on some main points of their argument that are particularly pertinent to the comparison with my own account of contract enforcement.[24] And because the authors provide the most nuanced and carefully reasoned justification of the idea—itself widely invoked in contemporary contract theory—that contracts generally involve an option to "perform or pay," I will consider these points in some detail.[25]

Starting from the premises that individuals contract in order to realize gains and also that they commonly divide gains through the pricing mechanism, the theory supposes that moderately well-informed parties understand and appreciate that they can produce a surplus not only through performing (or "trading" as the authors call it) but also in circumstances where it is cost inefficient to perform ("nontrading"). Parties have reason to plan so that the maximum surplus is achieved across both states in ways that enable each of them to gain in whichever circumstance obtains. Supposing that the defendant (seller) can gain from trading with third persons and that these gains are greater than the costs of nontrading to the plaintiff, not trading with the plaintiff holds out the potential for a surplus that can be shared by both parties. The question is how the two basic remedies of expectation damages and specific performance (or disgorgement) divide this surplus between the parties and which, of the two, maximizes their joint and individual gains.

If the contract is enforced by a liability rule of expectation damages, the defendant must pay the plaintiff's costs but can keep the additional surplus. If, by contrast, the plaintiff's entitlement is protected by a property rule, such as specific performance, the plaintiff is in the position of exacting a bribe from the defendant for waiving the remedy. On this basis, the plaintiff has a reason to prefer the property rule. But this is not the whole story. As Markovits and Schwartz point out, the fact that under the liability rule the defendant does not have to transfer to the plaintiff more than his costs—it does not include the bribe—means that the defendant's own costs are lower under the damages remedy and that in competitive market conditions, similarly situated sellers will be compelled to reduce their prices to reflect this saving. Through this price reduction, plaintiffs receive a further nontrading gain, which, according to the authors, makes the outcomes of liability and property rule enforcement equally advantageous to them. But there is a still further step in this analysis. Once transaction and other costs are taken into account, plaintiff indifference to the outcomes of the two remedies changes. Markovits and Schwartz suggest that, for a number of reasons, including the fact that, unlike buyers' *ex ante* gains under liability rules, property rule gains require costly and uncertain *ex post* negotiation, the net benefit of a regime of expectation damages should be greater than one of specific performance or disgorgement in the usual commercial circumstances. Given these transaction cost savings, rational transactors will therefore prefer a contract that ex ante affords the defendant the option of either trading or transferring value under a liability rule of expectation damages.

Supposing that this conclusion is justified as a matter of rational modeling and economic analysis, the dual performance hypothesis then holds that, as an interpretative legal matter, contracts should be construed as generally embodying this preference *as an implied-in-fact term.* The option is taken as an intrinsic and general normative feature of the parties' contractual relation in the usual commercial circumstances. Thus a party who does not trade but instead transfers the appropriate value to the other party in fact performs his contractual obligation and commits no wrong—no less than if he had performed the trade prong of the option. The ordinary contractual promise made at arm's length—the bargain—is a promise of genuine (albeit implied) alternative performances.[26] According to the dual performance hypothesis, the parties can reasonably be viewed as actually intending this option and agreeing to it. The sign of such intention and agreement is the price term which, the authors argue, memorializes the transfer prong of the option. When courts award expectation damages for breach, this should therefore be interpreted as follows: the defendant has done neither of the two alternative performances of trading or transferring and the award of expectation damages is not substitutionary relief but rather *direct* enforcement of the actually intended and obligatory transfer prong of the dual performance contract. In this respect, both expectation damages and specific performance (when given) are direct enforcement remedies—the first of the transfer, the second of the trade prong. The dual performance hypothesis holds that conceptually there is but one kind of remedy: direct or specific performance of a party's dual performance contractual obligation.

I would like to examine more closely how the theory justifies the interpretative claim that the parties' rational preference for an option contract should also reasonably be viewed as an implied-in-fact term of an enforceable contractual agreement. For the purposes of working out a theory that can provide a public basis of justification for contract law, this, in my view, is by far the central issue. Here it is important to emphasize that the economic analysis that supports the conclusion about party rational preference is not the same kind of reasoning that is needed to justify the second conclusion which holds this to be an implied-in-law term of their contract. To support the latter, we must find a basis that is anchored in an analysis of the contractual relation viewed as a mutually voluntary transaction giving rise to genuine legal obligations between the parties: an interpretative account, as the authors rightly hold, that is suitable to make normative sense of the conception of respectful relation that is latent in the law.[27] Otherwise, the dual performance hypothesis would provide no more than an economic approach to the issue. Now as a background legal fact, it is certainly true that contract law recognizes and enforces *express* stipulations of genuine alternative performances. And parties can also plan for and agree to terms that regulate what should happen if circumstances arise that make trade more difficult and costly or less valuable. But where a contract is silent, why *imply* the proposed dual performance option of trade or transfer?

Markovits and Schwartz seem to answer as follows. Insofar as the contract price is lower than it would be if the obligation were subject to a property rule, we may view the price as evidencing ("memorializing") the plaintiff's actual intent to agree to the option of trade or transfer and to waive recourse to the property remedy; and having so agreed, the plaintiff is precluded from later changing her mind and converting the dual performance obligation to trade or transfer into one to trade only.[28] Thus the parties have manifested an intention to obligate themselves either to trade or to transfer.[29] Indeed, the parties should be taken to have made dual performance contracts unless there is evidence to the contrary.[30] The authors conclude by characterizing the price term as an implied-in-fact liquidated damages clause, which "fixes transfers by reference to the named price (and its associated promisee surplus)."[31]

Is this analysis consistent with the conception of contractual relation embodied in the main doctrines of contract law and more particularly in the principles governing remedies? There are many points that could be addressed here, but I will focus on what seems to me the most crucial, namely, the argument regarding implication. Taking as given the authors' analysis of what transacting parties rationally prefer and in the absence of express contract terms that enshrine this preference, should the parties therefore *reasonably be held* to intend it as a matter of interpersonal coercible contractual obligation? In my view, the answer must be no, for to do so would not only be unsupported by legal doctrine but would also conflict with its most basic presuppositions. I will briefly explain.

Markovits and Schwartz emphasize, correctly in my view, that contract law allows parties to "cabin their obligations as narrowly as they wish and thus to remain, in spite of their contracts, at arm's length in respect of all matters that their agreements do not cover."[32] Consistent with the law's animating commitment to respecting the voluntary basis of contract, parties are held to—but *only* to—the agreed-upon and mutually intended contract terms, including whatever these terms must reasonably entail.[33] Recalling first principles, the essential terms—the "primary" terms—of any contract consist of the promise-for-consideration relation. These are the narrowest and most basic constituents of an enforceable contract. The authors, we have seen, support the option conception of contractual obligation as an implied set of alternative performance terms. The question is whether this can be justified within the basic framework of the promise-for-consideration relation as understood by the law.

In the discussion of consideration, we saw that it merely requires that something of legal value be promised or given in return for something else of value: at its core, the consideration requirement is necessarily indifferent as to what in particular that something is. This feature corresponds with Craswell's characterization of content-neutrality. The content that specifies the "something of value" is whatever the parties happen to choose and to agree upon. In this respect, the filling-in of content is contingent. But precisely because of this, the law has no principle or basis for determining this primary content where the parties themselves have not done so. Parties must either expressly stipulate all the primary terms needed to satisfy the consideration relation; or if certain required primary terms (e.g., the price) have not been expressly fixed, they must be inferred (e.g., "a reasonable price") as clearly supposed by the actual express terms reasonably construed and as determinable with certainty.[34] Otherwise, the parties have not done enough to establish clear and certain primary terms and, despite their expressions of assent, there will not be a contract.

Now alternative performances of any kind, though perfectly consistent with the requirements of formation, represent just one possible set of *primary* terms *contingently* chosen by the parties.[35] There is, to my knowledge, no generally accepted decision that views them otherwise. Thus the law has to determine in a given transaction whether the required express or inferred required primary terms show that the promisor wanted or requested *each* of the two performances as genuine considerations for his own promise. If the promise of a monetary sum (which is supposed to function as the transfer prong in the dual performance view) is to count as an alternative performance along with the promise of some concrete thing or service, that sum must therefore be wanted as consideration in its own right as an alternative to the other thing or service—and not as ancillary to it, as mere security for it or as a consequence of not transferring it.[36] In all cases, the fundamental point is that whether a monetary sum counts as an alternative performance must be positively shown and established, not merely presumed as an ancillary implied aspect of the exchange. It is a truism of life and of law that in commercial or other kinds of relations parties can—and indeed ordinarily do—request and want something precisely because of its concrete substantive features. With the promise of substantive x for y money, there need not be anything more that needs to be filled out and so no general reason within the framework of consideration to view the first promise as being presumptively the promise of this substantive *x or money* for y money.

There is nothing, then, in the basic analysis of the promise-for-consideration relation that supports a *general* presumption of intended dual performances in contractual (even commercial) relations. As for further factors that might support such a general presumption, we have seen that the dual performance hypothesis refers to the contract price in a liability rule contract and specifically to the fact that it may as a general matter be lower because of the defendant's cost saving in not having to purchase from the plaintiff a waiver (i.e., nonpursuit) of the latter's power to obtain the remedy of specific performance. For the purposes of this discussion we must suppose that, in the particular circumstances of their transaction, the parties have not expressly or clearly treated the price as reflecting this waiver. The question is whether the price in such contracts in general must nevertheless reasonably be taken as a matter of construction to reflect a subtraction from the price of a property rule contract and a waiver of this kind when the contract's actual terms are interpreted in light of generally supposed and applicable transactional norms, shared understandings, surrounding circumstances, and so forth.

The clear, and in my view, the decisive difficulty here is that as a matter of contractual, that is, legal, construction and interpretation, the reference point from which the price can be construed as "lower"—namely, recourse to specific performance that is then waived—does not exist. Parties do not have a *general* right or power to obtain specific performance. As discussed earlier, whether specific performance is available and ordered is decided by courts on the basis of considerations of adequacy of damages and policy applied to the particular transaction at issue. Therefore, as a matter of contractual interpretation and implication, specific performance cannot figure as a preexisting baseline or opportunity that can be presumed in general to have been contractually priced or waived as the dual performance theory requires. This is particularly the case in circumstances where damages would be adequate—precisely in commercial market transactions. Nor can there be a presumed background understanding that the market price impounds this waiver. This would only be true if there was an actual, publicly understood power to stipulate for specific performance in general or at least to obtain it—but neither exists. So there is contractually no reason to presume in general (and particularly in commercial transactions) the existence of a lower price or a waiver and therefore no such reason to hold even informed parties generally to have intended the price to be so construed, absent transactionally specific express or necessarily inferable terms to that effect.[37]

This objection, which in my view is decisive, is reinforced by other related points, each of which makes the basis for general implication of a presumed intent to trade or transfer implausible. I mention briefly only the following further difficulties.

First, there is an ambiguity with respect to the particular content to be implied as the transfer prong of the dual performance contract. Markovits and Schwartz seem to formulate the transfer prong as the promised transfer of a sum equal to the gain that the promisee would have made had the goods or services (under the trade prong) actually been delivered.[38] This would seem to include the beneficial use that the promisee would have made of the goods or services had she received them. Indeed, it would have to include such gains to ensure symmetry on the plaintiff promisee's side given the inclusion of opportunity costs on the side of the defendant promisor. It is thus this sum that must be transferred if the requirement of mutual gains is to be satisfied. The problem is that is no guarantee that this sum will equal the amount that would be legally actionable under *Hadley*. It is one thing if parties expressly stipulate a sum as an agreed damages provision. Depending on the particulars of the transaction when reasonably construed, we have seen that the provision may be upheld as a valid liquidated damages clause even though the stipulated sum diverges from actual actionable loss. But here the question is whether this sum should be added to existing terms as a judicially *implied* term. Even assuming for the sake of argument that the law could in principle imply a term of this kind, it could not be for that sum insofar as the latter would differ from what the law would recognize as an actionable loss. Within its own framework, the law cannot imply any term that would be inconsistent with basic contract doctrines.[39]

There is a further inconsistency I should note.[40] The transfer prong would be the promise of money as an alternative performance. But according to general contract principles, promises of money cannot be excused by reason of impossibility. Therefore, because every ordinary contract would include the transfer option, no ordinary contract could come within the excusing doctrines—a consequence clearly inconsistent with settled legal doctrine and decisions.[41] To avoid this difficulty, the parties might be presumed to intend an implied transfer prong consisting of a formula for value rather than a definite sum. But this would mean that the parties must be held to have intended a quantum unknowable at formation and determined by legal principles that the parties themselves need not have known, applied to circumstances of breach that the parties could not know when they contracted. It is difficult to see how such an empty term could ever be necessary to make sense of the express and certain terms to which the parties agreed—besides the fact that pointing to, without specifying, what the law will decide would be superfluous in any case.[42]

There is a final point that concerns what is perhaps the most basic premise of the dual performance hypothesis in particular and of economic approaches to contract law in general, namely, that parties contract in order to realize and indeed to maximize gains in both trade and nontrade scenarios. Now this may be clearly true as a matter of fact, particularly in certain kinds of transactions. But unless in a particular contract this can be taken as part of the aim and genesis of the transaction itself when it is reasonably construed—in other words, as going to the transaction's underlying specific though tacit assumptions conditioning its interpretation and enforcement—it is not *contractually* relevant.

Parties have their different and common purposes when transacting, but the only contractually relevant "purpose" that a party must have is to obtain the other's qualitatively different consideration (and whatever this necessarily entails) in return for his or her own. "Gain" has no contractual meaning apart from what is part of this substantive relation. Unless the dual performance hypothesis includes only elements that specify this relation and construes them as they are in that relation, it orients us in the wrong direction, at least if the stated aim is, as the authors say it is, to develop a coherent and comprehensive reconstruction of the immanent structure of contract doctrines. What is certainly excluded both from a legal point of view and also by the authors' own characterization of the nature of contractual obligation is holding the parties to an extratransactional general substantive purpose in light of which courts, via implication, supplement the agreed-upon terms in order to make the contract better or more desirable.[43] Not only does this not meet the requirement of transactional necessity, but imposing any such general goal on the parties is incompatible with the limits of a liberal conception of the contract relation and the sorts of purposes and values that parties may reasonably be deemed to share.[44] It cannot be part of a liberal public basis of justification of contract.

To summarize: Markovits and Schwartz build on Craswell's basic contention that contract remedies can and should be treated no differently than ordinary contract terms as potentially part of a contract's implied dimension. On this view, remedies can properly be understood as just one more possible stick in the bundle of rights that comprises promised performances. This premise is pervasively supposed by contemporary theorizing about contract law, particularly from an economic standpoint. Unlike most theories, the dual performance hypothesis does not simply assume this view but tries to show, by nuanced argument, that on this basis it can explain the primacy of expectation damages consistently with the legal point of view and the immanent normativity of the contractual relation.

However, the objections that I have raised would seem to cast serious doubt on whether the authors' contentions have been made out. Even supposing the economic argument for the rationality of parties' preferring a dual performance contract to be compelling in its terms, the transition from the economic analysis to the claim that this intention should also be reasonably imputed to them as autonomous participants in the rights-respecting character of the contractual relation is by no means clear. Indeed, as I have tried to show, it seems to conflict directly with the actual law at its most basic level. For present purposes, it is enough to say that it does not provide an alternative explanation of the role of expectation damages that is superior as an interpretative theory to the transactional approach with its idea of compensatory justice.

Beyond this, there is an intrinsic instability in the dual performance theory's attempt to combine the economic and the legal contractual analysis in one unified conception that applies directly to contract law and principles. Whereas the economic analysis relies on an argument framed in terms of the rational and preference-satisfaction and is independent of notions of ownership, rights owed as between the two parties, compensatory justice, and the like, the juridical contractual analysis rests on what is reasonable as between the parties and incorporates those very notions as intrinsic and indispensable to it.[45] Each of these standpoints is relatively autonomous and distinct in its own terms. Starting with the rational, the dual performance theory fails to show that what may be rational for parties to want is also something to which they can be reasonably held for the purpose of determining the implied dimension of contracts. What needs to be explained is how these two notions of the rational and the reasonable might be suitably specified and fitted together as required parts of a unified account of contract law. I shall try to do this in chapter 12 where I argue that this is possible only if we begin with and accord priority to the reasonable in transactions.

The simple idea, so fundamental to the legal point of view, that contract remedies are not implied terms but rather the law's coercive response to the civil wrong of breach as required by compensatory justice, still stands. And a theory that tries to understand this idea in its own terms without recourse to economic or other instrumental analysis is still possible. An account of implication and more generally of contract law that ignores or elides this legally categorical difference between terms and remedies cannot purport to explain contract law within its own framework or to provide a public basis of justification. But supposing this difference between terms and remedies, we then come back to Craswell's critique of the inherent indeterminacy of promissory and entitlement theories (of which the proposed transactional conception is one) to fill in the implied dimension of contracts. We saw that according to Craswell, contract law does not have the internal normative resources to specify the implied terms that are to be vindicated by remedies and so cannot guide thinking about the appropriate kind or level of remedy. Even granting the distinction between implied terms and remedies, contract law cannot be explained within a purely noninstrumental framework.

The answer to this objection is as follows.[46] Craswell's critique has traction if, but only if, the fundamental principle of contractual obligation is purely formal and applicable to whatever happens to be the parties' choices, without in any way determining or framing what can count as a contractually relevant or effective choice in the first place. This is how Craswell interprets the promise or transfer principles that say "whatever has been promised or whatever entitlement has been transferred should be enforced simply because it has been promised or transferred." But contract law itself presents a very different kind of principle or framework of obligation. It is not at all purely formal or applied in this way. To the contrary, it mandates requirements of structure and substance that specify the kinds of choices or assents that can be contractually operative and that also guide the procedure of implication so that parties' rights and obligations can be completely determined at contract formation. This framework of obligation is the basic promise-for-consideration relation, and in the detailed discussions under the rubric of contract formation I tried to show how this is in fact the case. The principle of transfer, as I have explained it so far, is completely immanent in and constitutive of these framing and regulative principles. And while parties can certainly choose the particular contents of their mutual assents—hence the "content-neutrality" of the doctrines of formation—these chosen contents must fit into and satisfy the structural and substantive requirements of the promise-for-consideration relation or else suffer the consequence of being contractually irrelevant and without effect.

This brings us back to the Fuller and Perdue challenge with which this chapter began. It is one thing to argue against Craswell and others that remedies are not implied terms at all and that contract formation seems to have the normative resources to determine completely the contractual salience of any matters that may possibly affect parties' mutual rights and duties. The Fuller and Perdue challenge goes deeper and questions whether, even if normatively determinative, contract formation can be construed in a way that justifies the centrality of the performance interest as the appropriate object of enforcement. Their answer is that as a promissory relation, contract formation cannot be so viewed. At the same time, the manner in which they frame their challenge suggests the very sort of analysis that, if plausible, might explain expectation remedies as compensatory justice: contract formation must figure as a way in which parties can acquire from each other something that can count as their own to the exclusion of the other, with the consequence that breach involves a party "tak[ing] from another what belongs to him."[47]

In the detailed examination of the main doctrines and principles of contract law from formation and fairness to remedies, I have tried to show that latent in these is a conception of contract that is amenable to this interpretation. Not only do the doctrines of formation suggest this view, but, if it is to make sense in its own terms, the axiomatic legal principle that expectation damages are compensatory requires it.

Now strikingly, in their survey of possible justifications for the protection of the expectation interest, Fuller and Perdue consider just this possibility of viewing contract as a species of acquisition. In a credit economy, they argue, "expectations of future values become, for purposes of trade, present value," and with this elimination of the difference between present and promised goods, it is "inevitable that the expectancy created by an enforceable promise should be regarded as a kind of property, and breach of the promise as an injury to that property . . . [that] works an 'actual' diminution of the promisee's assets—'actual' in the sense that it would be so appraised according to modes of thought which enter into the very fiber of our economic system."[48] However, they reject this analysis as a sufficient basis for explaining contract law. This is because they see this view of contract as reflecting economic conditions, which, they argue, are themselves the product of law and so cannot explain it. A distinct normative basis must be found. But this normative basis, Fuller and Perdue assume, must refer to the promissory nature of contracts (in contrast with property), and, we have seen, they also assume that promises can only create moral expectations, not transfer entitlements of any kind. Consistently with these premises, they do not even consider the possibility of a noninstrumental and transactional juristic justification of this view of contractual rights.

Fuller and Perdue are right to point to the difference between contractual entitlements and property rights. Contractual entitlements with respect to promised considerations are produced and exist solely in the purely *representational* medium or element of the parties' mutual promises. This is not the case with property rights in things effectuated by acts of first possession, executed gifts or immediate exchanges. But we need not assume that economic conditions are the direct basis of contract's specific nature, that the normativity of promising is only of one kind, or that the evident difference between contract and property precludes any meaningful parallel between them.

Instead, we should consider whether the promise-for-consideration relation, which is distinct in being completely bilateral—promising not only to or for the promisee but also robustly with the promisee's coequal active participation—and which can plausibly be construed as involving reciprocal acquisition between the parties at formation, may also be properly elucidated as a *transfer of ownership* of some kind within its own juridical framework. Showing this would provide a complete answer to Fuller and Perdue. As part of working out a public basis of justification, it is important to see whether contract can be so explained consistently with underlying notions of ownership that are presupposed in other parts of private law. Going a step further and deeper, such justification should also include an account of how this view of contract as a transfer of ownership might embody suitable normative ideas of freedom and equality requisite for a liberal conception of justice for transactions. Finally, because promises play a role not only in contract law but also in individual morality and economic (market) relations, and because the recognition of nondistributive, purely transactional entitlements might seem to be in tension with the requirements of liberal distributive justice, it is essential to try to explain how the proposed transactional conception of contract, including its full moral justification, can be congruent with these other domains of promissory morality, markets and distributive justice. Nothing less will fully answer the Fuller and Perdue challenge or show that the proposed transactional conception of contract is an independent and morally acceptable alternative, superior to the prevailing promissory and economic theories as a public basis of justification for contract law. In Part Two, I take up these next steps.

PART TWO
THEORY

Chapter 10

Contract as a Transfer of Ownership

In Part Two, I try to justify on a wider and deeper normative basis the transactional analysis of contract law doctrines and principles developed in Part One. This is the final step in my working out a public basis of justification for contract law. In this chapter, I consider whether contractual acquisition can reasonably be viewed as a form of ownership acquisition within a wider private law framework. Then, in Chapter 11, I suggest a reasonable moral basis for this conception of contract as a transfer of ownership. My aim is to develop a moral account that is true to the analysis of contract doctrines presented in Part One and that also is acceptable as a liberal conception of justice in transactions for the purposes of a public basis of justification. These first two chapters, Chapters 10 and 11, argue for the intrinsic reasonableness of the proposed conception of contract when taken by itself. By contrast, in Chapter 12, the last and longest chapter of this second part, I discuss how the proposed conception of contract connects up with three important noncontractual domains for which, nevertheless, the analysis of contractual entitlements is directly or indirectly important. At stake here are the relations between contract, on the one hand, and promissory morality, the market, and the requirements of liberal distributive justice, on the other hand. The topic of Chapter 12 is the stability of the proposed conception of contract and its congruence with these other domains when viewed from their standpoints.

Turning now to the present chapter, I shall argue here that the conception of contractual relation reflected in contract law can be understood as a form of acquisition involving ownership: a transfer of ownership as between the contracting parties. In fact, I will try to show that the kind of ownership that is specific to contract—and in general to any instance of transactional acquisition—represents, from a juridical point of view, the most complete and satisfactory expression of ownership. This will require comparing the ideas of ownership in property and contract as well as determining the meaning of, and the relation between, so-called in rem and in personam rights. It should be emphasized here that, in keeping with my overarching aim of providing a public basis of justification for contract, the idea of contract as a transfer of ownership is proposed as a theoretical elucidation of what is implicit in and suggested by the doctrines and principles of contract law. Thus what a contractual transfer of ownership entails—the specific meaning, elements, and incidents that I ascribe to it—is wholly anchored in and developed from the transactional analysis of the basic promise-for-consideration relation. It is this relation that guides our theoretical construction. In order to present the argument clearly and in an integrated way, it is important therefore to begin with this relation, recalling briefly some of the main conclusions already reached and drawing out their further theoretical significance and implications. Unavoidably, there will have to be some overlap between this and earlier discussions.

10.1. The Promise-for-Consideration Relation as Transfer

I start by reemphasizing the following basic point. In the central case of consideration—the bilateral contract comprised of mutual promises—contract formation is wholly constituted by an interaction consisting of representational acts. Every element and aspect of the contractual analysis belongs to and is specified as part of this representational medium of interaction and therefore independently of and prior to physical delivery or performance. The contractually binding terms, both express and implied, and thus all the parties' rights and obligations are fully and definitively established by this interaction at the single moment of contract formation. In this way, the parties' mutual promises may be said to function jointly as practical signs that effectuate what they signify.[1]

We have seen that to satisfy the consideration requirement, each party's promise must be specified in relation with the other's, making both sides intrinsically and identically relational. The promise-for-consideration relation is itself a transactional process consisting in each party reciprocally and identically moving a substantive content from its side to the other—all in and through the representational medium of mutual promises. Thus, necessarily, each party's promise represents the content as on his or her side, as actually or potentially under his or her exclusive control, and as moving into the recognized rightful exclusive control of the other side in return for the very same movement of a second content from that other party. Each side gives up only insofar as the other gains, and the substance that the first gives up is precisely what the second gains. In fact, given the mutually consensual character of this interaction, we may plausibly say that each side objectively recognizes the other's exercise of exclusive rightful control over what he or she either gives up or takes. This is the process that constitutes the promise-for-consideration relation in which cause—the reciprocal moving of considerations in return for each other—and effect—the vesting of each party's consideration with the other—are inseparable.

As part of the promise-for-consideration relation, each of the represented substantive contents—for there must always be two such qualitatively different contents—includes everything pertaining to its having legal value, that is, to its being something that in virtue of its concrete particular features can be individually and exclusively possessed, enjoyed, used, or disposed of as the parties agree. At the same time, the doctrine is content-neutral and does not investigate adequacy of consideration. There is therefore the following doctrinal division of labor between consideration and unconscionability: whereas, in requiring a relation of quid pro quo, consideration ensures the existence of an irreducibly two-sided promissory transaction that can, in substantive terms, be anything from what is in effect a gift to an exchange of equivalents, unconscionability tests these terms to see whether they can reasonably count as between the parties as genuine equivalents or, if not, whether the nonequivalence may be explained on the basis of donative intent or assumption of risk rather than on some transactionally unintended basis, such as the disadvantaged party's ignorance or necessity.[2] In this way, the doctrines of consideration and unconscionability complement each other, ensuring, respectively, first, the possibility and, second, the actuality of a genuinely two-sided contractual promissory relation being substantively intelligible as an exchange or gift contract or as some coherent combination of the two.

I have also argued that, consistent with the idea of compensatory justice, the thing that is given by way of remedy is and must be, so far as possible in post-breach circumstances, the same thing to which the plaintiff was entitled at contract formation. This is essential if the plaintiff's immunity vis-à-vis the defendant is to be upheld. Both expectation damages, when adequate, and specific performance ensure that the plaintiff has so far as possible the substance of the consideration as promised in accordance with the terms of their contract. This compensatory character of these remedies can be explained directly only on the supposition that at formation and as a matter of rights, the plaintiff acquires this substance (and all that it includes) from the defendant as specified by their promise-for-consideration relation. Contract formation must therefore count as a mode of transactional acquisition if, as the law holds, the expectation remedies are to qualify as compensatory in nature.

Such transactional acquisition may plausibly be characterized as a *transfer* as between the parties. For the idea of transfer brings out the point that in this unified two-sided process, there is no gap whatsoever between the giving and receiving of the very same thing: it is the double reciprocal process in which what each side obtains is something *as* given by and from the other. Based squarely on the analysis of the consideration relation, what each party acquires via transfer can only be the substance of the consideration, including its full value and its other incidents both express and implied, as moved from the other side in return for the first party's promised consideration. And since the parties' mutual promises not only embody the representation of this substantive element but also bring about this reciprocal acquisition, their promises may plausibly be interpreted as the *acts* that effectuate this transfer. Through these acts, the parties mutually recognize each other's capacity to hold, to give up, and to take rightful exclusive control of the promised considerations.

On this view, then, which takes the parties' promises as the mutually related acts that effectuate or cause the transfer, the *objects* of the transfer are *the substantive considerations as mutually promised*, not the promises or the substantive contents viewed independently from the other. From formation on, each side holds in the medium of representation a substantive something of value on terms of (and only insofar as it is specified as) quid pro quo for the other side: I hold something not by means of and as subject to my individual act alone but rather by means of and as presently subject to our jointly related acts. And it is *this* transactionally specified rightful control that must be respected by each party as a matter of duty. In this sense, we may say that both the acts that effectuate contractual transfer and the objects of that transfer refer to the same thing, though under the conceptually different aspects of cause and object.[3] As I will further explain and elaborate in due course, this understanding of transfer, which I am elucidating in connection with the promise-for-consideration relation, is characteristic of any form of transactional acquisition.

Theories that ground contractual obligation on some notion of autonomy often present contract's central underlying principle as the legal power of parties to effectuate a change in their mutual rights and duties. Recall Fuller's principle of private autonomy, which he viewed as the most pervasive and indispensable substantive basis of contractual obligation.[4] Clearly, the conception of contractual transfer proposed here is consistent with this view. However, the principle of private autonomy is purely formal and states the creation of legal effects merely as an outcome and fact without explaining the mechanism of their production. By contrast, far from being merely formal in this way, the idea of contractual transfer entails a definite relation constituted by the parties' mutually related acts intelligibly functioning as the efficient cause of contractual acquisition, and it is this acquisition that is the basis of their mutual rights and duties at formation.

Following this last point, it is important to note that the idea of transfer that I am presenting is different from the often-assumed view that sees it as consisting in the transfer of a right to performance, where this right is itself taken as the object transferred.[5] Because parties are said to "acquire" rights to performance at formation, the latter view may seem at first glance to be a natural interpretation of the transfer. However, as a general matter, what is acquired or transferred is not a right to x but always some substantive content that can be rightfully and exclusively held and transferred.[6] Given the definition of consideration, this substantive content can of course include legal rights—even the right to performance as a chose in action in the case of assignment. But it still figures as something substantive of value that can be moved from one party's exclusive rightful control into that of the other.

Beyond this general point, the right to performance is the normative *consequence,* not the object, of the promisee's base entitlement at formation.[7] The right and correlative duty of performance signify *the terms of respect* that arise as a result of the conceptually prior moment of acquisition at formation. This view of the right to performance as a normative consequence is the only one that is consistent with the framework of liability for misfeasance. For within this framework, it is always necessary to specify as a conceptually first step the present existence of something that is under a party's rightful exclusive control, with respect to which others can come under a prohibition against interference and injury. In the case of contract, it is the represented substance of the consideration as promised that is under the promisee's exclusive control; whereas the acts or omissions that constitute performance are simply what the promisor must do or not do so as not to injure or interfere with the promisee's rightful, contractually specified mode of exercising control over it (including her right to have physical possession of it in accordance with the contract terms).[8] Here again, it is important to keep in mind the categorical difference between this juridical contractual point of view and the morality of promising, which takes promises as having for their primary object the promisor's future conduct conscientiously fulfilling his word—this is what the promisee expects and hopes to receive.

To sum up so far. The process that constitutes the promise-for-consideration relation consists of the parties' joint and unified representational acts of reciprocally and simultaneously moving from each to the other substantive contents of value that they present as under one party's exclusive rightful control and as vesting in (moving to) that of the other. Thus, *what* each acquires from the other expresses or embodies their jointly related choices: something as given and as taken as between them. To be contractually relevant, any and every element or factor must be specified as part of this reciprocal movement. This must also be reflected in any conception of transfer that purports to fit with this relation. A contractual transfer should not be understood as vesting anything as it may be prior to or apart from the promise-for-consideration relation: the transfer is never of some preexisting right.[9] This does not properly model the purely transactional and representational contractual transfer at formation. Nor does it vest something that, properly viewed, is the normative consequence of the transfer.[10]

This brings me to the following challenge. I have tried to emphasize that this mutual moving of considerations should be understood as taking place in and through the representational medium of the parties' promises. This "ideal utterance" of the transfer is, in normative-juridical terms, the complete and exhaustive determination of the contractual relation.[11] It establishes what the parties reciprocally acquire from each other as well as their resulting transactional rights and obligations, both express and implied. The contractually relevant and effective interaction takes place in this realm of ideation prior to and independently of actual performance. Once contract is so viewed, it is, I believe, relatively clear and transparent how contract formation may be conceived as a mode of acquisition by way of transfer between the parties. But for this view to be plausible, it is not enough to argue, as I have done so far, that a transfer analysis seems, as a matter of interpretation, to fit with the doctrinal features of consideration. We must take the further step of seeing whether this analysis is consistent with deeper or at least more general ideas in private law. If contract formation is to be intelligibly and fully viewed as a way of acquiring something, it would seem natural to construe it in terms of ownership. We must see, therefore, whether the conception of contractual transfer presented so far can be reasonably characterized as a transfer of ownership. As part of a public basis of justification, we ask: does the purely representational and inherently transactional mode of contractual acquisition express a conception of ownership acquisition that is defensible in its own right and consistent with underlying basic notions of ownership in private law? Now if any part of private law indisputably invokes a notion of private ownership, it is surely the law of property. Accordingly, for the purpose of assessing whether contract also embodies a conception of ownership, a brief and limited theoretical comparison between property and contract should be illuminating. This is our next topic.

10.2. The Idea of Ownership in Private Law: From Property to Contract

What is ownership in private law? No idea is more basic to private law and yet few concepts are more elusive. As numerous writers have noted, "ownership" is not a term of art in the common law and has no clearly defined content.[12] We must nonetheless still try to suggest a provisional idea. Since our question is directed at private law, I shall suppose from the start that the sort of definition we are seeking must fit within the framework of liability for misfeasance. Ownership refers to the sort of connection between person and object that involves the claimant having a kind of rightful control over it to the exclusion of others that is sufficient to found a claim that their acts or omissions affecting the object can injure the claimant's right with respect to it. Further, the claimant has an immunity with respect to this connection such that nothing others do unilaterally and without his or her consent can make the thing their own. So understood, ownership would seem to encompass anything that can count as an object of the claimant's rightful exclusive control and with which he or she can be so connected vis-à-vis others.

Now this preliminary conception would seem to include not only ownership of external things but also ownership of one's own body. However, there are basic differences between these, universally recognized in modern law, that make questionable the appropriateness of taking the relation between oneself and one's body as involving the kind of ownership that refers to external things separable and distinct from one's bodily integrity. One crucial difference is that whereas ownership of external things must be acquired by certain requisite acts, the immunities and rights of bodily integrity are not acquired but rather innate—one need not do anything to be entitled to assert them.[13] Thus, whereas individuals come into the world as already "self-owned," things do not. To the contrary, they are available to and may be appropriated or transferred by anyone as possible objects of ownership.

The fact that ownership of things is mediated by acts of acquisition should not be assumed to be irrelevant to the conception of what ownership of things entails. Indeed, I will try to show that the definition of ownership of things is properly worked out through the elucidation of how things come to be owned. Ownership is expressed in and through the external acts that establish it. This identity is implicit in the proposition that one acquires things and becomes an owner only by presently exercising acts of ownership. It is only in and through these acts that ownership has juridical reality, and it is these acts alone, imputable to persons, that attract the requirements of respect coming under the right of ownership. We therefore fully understand and explain the normativity of ownership by understanding and explaining the normativity of the acts of acquisition.

If we start from the premise that external things are acquired on the basis of individual acts and that the resulting ownership can be private and individual, we may provisionally distinguish between two mutually exclusive basic categories of acquisition: first, an individual can acquire something that is presently unowned on the basis of his or her separate act alone; second, one can acquire something that is already owned by another in conjunction with the other's consent and decision. Following tradition, we may refer to the first kind of acquisition as "original" or "first" and the second as "derivative." Thus presented, this distinction is purely definitional and settles no important issues. As I now hope to show, however, by going into this distinction more deeply, we may clarify the relation between property and contract and show how both presuppose a conception of ownership as representational. The different ways in which property and contract do this are decisive for understanding their distinct natures.

I begin with the following point. If these two kinds of acquisition—original and derivative—are to be genuinely distinct, derivative acquisition must be irreducibly *transactional*. To see this, suppose that a present owner voluntarily abandons his or her thing, thereby making it unowned. If another then acts to acquire it, he or she does so with respect to a now ownerless thing that is unconnected to its previous owner. When the second party takes it, this is therefore simply an instance of original acquisition. To be derivative, then, the second party must acquire the thing, not in the condition of being unowned, but rather *as* something that is (still) owned by the first party. In other words, the second must acquire it from the first in such a way that the latter also participates as an owner in the acquisition. Assuming that ownership acquisition of things is in general effectuated by persons' acts, this second category of acquisition must therefore be effectuated in and through a definite interaction between the two parties in *which one appropriates the thing as something that is alienated by the other*. At no point can it become ownerless. This is a required condition if derivative acquisition is to be qualitatively irreducible to first acquisition and thus if there are to be two such distinct categories of acquisition at all. Derivative acquisition, in contrast to original acquisition, is always and inherently transactional acquisition.

To achieve clarity about the respective meanings and roles of ownership in property and in contract, it is essential, in my view, to keep in mind this difference between these two kinds of acquisition. Now under the rubric of property law, the sorts of acquisition that are standardly discussed in textbooks and treatises can be of both kinds; by contrast, if contract law is in fact a form of acquisition, then, being transactional, it seems that it can only be derivative. To clarify the possible meaning and role of ownership in contract and to assess whether it is consistent with underlying notions of property ownership, it makes sense to draw the contrast between contract and property as sharply as possible. For this reason, I will focus on the analysis of instances of property ownership that only come under the rubric of original acquisition and that do not presuppose at all the idea of a bilateral transfer. Instances of original acquisition in the common law of property include first possession, finding, and (possibly) adverse possession.[14] Though the occasions for original acquisition in current social and economic circumstances may be relatively rare, such acquisition may still occur in fact and logically, in order to avoid an infinite regress, transactional acquisition must itself presuppose its possibility.[15] I will therefore consider property ownership within the parameters of original acquisition first. For the purposes of the following discussion, we may take decisions such as the well-known case of *Pierson v. Post* as judicial statements of the governing principle.[16] I should also note that throughout the following discussion of both property and contract, my analysis concerns forms of acquisition as basic juridical categories specified in terms of their requisite acts, objects, and relations between persons, without reference to the use of legal formalities or other institutional devices.[17]

Recalling what was noted above, the distinctive character of original acquisition contrasts, first, with the right of bodily integrity and, second, with derivative acquisition. Unlike the right of bodily integrity, original acquisition is always of an object that is separable and distinct from the individual's body, including his or her physical and psychological powers and faculties. Given this immediate contrast, the central case of an object of original acquisition is something external that by its nature can exist spatially apart from one's body—a physical entity of some sort.[18] Being unowned, the object is available in this state to be appropriated by anyone in general. This means that services, that do not exist and are not available in this way but must arise through an individual exercising his or her mental and physical powers, cannot be an object of original acquisition by others, though they may function, we will see, as objects of contracts and other voluntary transfers. Moreover, as already noted, precisely because original acquisition involves an external object separate from everyone, such ownership is not innate but must be acquired by some sort of act. Whereas I have a right of bodily integrity simply in virtue of being alive here and now, I must *do* something to make an object that is distinct and separate from me so connected with me that it counts as mine and not someone else's. While I take it as given here that everyone has a capacity for ownership, this remains merely a potentiality unless and until someone does the requisite acts to acquire something. Only then is there actual ownership of anything at all and with this any rightful claims to something as against others.

But it is precisely with respect to this requirement of an act that original acquisition differs categorically from derivative acquisition. In keeping with the fundamental framework of liability for misfeasance in private law, others' consent is required only insofar as they *already* have something under their exclusive rightful control. This does not obtain in the circumstances preceding original acquisition, where the thing to be appropriated is not presently owned by anyone. Consequently, within the misfeasance framework, original acquisition by one without the consent of others must be permissible. Whereas derivative acquisition, being acquisition of something that is already owned, must always be effectuated with the owner's consent, original acquisition, being of something presently not owned, can be accomplished by the single person acting alone without the participation or actual consent of others.[19] One who does the requisite act with respect to a presently unowned object acquires it and becomes its owner. Relative to others who come after, he or she is first. Hence the principle of original acquisition is first possession. But note that the reason the first is the rightful owner is not because he or she is first but simply because that person has done the acts necessary to acquire the unowned thing, "for" as Hegel notes, "it is only by another's succeeding him that he becomes the first."[20]

What, more exactly, must one do to acquire something originally?[21] Traditionally formulated as being occupancy with possessory intent, the act must *presently and recognizably* subordinate an external object to one's individual and exclusive control, in such way that one is manifestly in a position to use it at will and to put it to one's own chosen purposes without the assistance of others (who are not acting as agents). Note that for the person's exercise of control to be deemed *exclusive*, nothing more is necessary than the fact that he or she purports to be deciding what to do with or to the thing for his or her own ends and uses: on this basis, others are eo ipso excluded from doing anything with or to it that limits, displaces, or supplants the claimant's choice and decision.[22] This general conception of occupancy can be further specified in terms of the three forms of taking possession, using, and disposing of things, all of which can be unilaterally effectuated by the appropriator without the participation of others. Moreover, in each of these, someone becomes and continues to be an owner by presently doing the acts of an owner.

First, there must be an initial act of taking factual possession of the external thing whereby one recognizably shows that one has subjected to one's own control an object that is separable and independent from oneself. This is the moment of initial appropriation. Since the object must be a separable physical object, taking possession ordinarily involves affecting or changing the object's physical features or condition in some way—for instance, by holding, forming, or marking it—that shows that it is no longer independent of everyone's control but is now under someone's exclusive control. Second, there is the moment of use. This is the act of using or using up the object in some way whereby one actualizes the subordination of the object to one's power and purposes. Third, one may dispose of the object by giving it up and thus, by a final exercise of one's choice, returning it to the condition of being unowned and once again available for original or first appropriation by others. It is only the one who is the owner and who is acting as owner who can alienate or dispose of it in this way.

These three aspects—taking possession, use, and alienation—all involve exercising present exclusive control over an external object and so are modes of exercising ownership. Moreover, because taking possession, use, and disposition form a complete circle of unilateral acts of exercising control with respect to an initially unowned object, they together exhaustively express the basic kinds of acts that pertain to original acquisition. Note finally that because these acts of control express an individual's unilateral decision of what to do with an object in accordance with his or her chosen ends, their juridical significance and effects do not depend on the particular content of these purposes at any given moment. This content-neutrality makes manifest a claimant's effective and present open-ended power to treat the object as he or she alone decides irrespective of the assent or accord of others.

Within these parameters of original acquisition, one cannot take possession of something that is not yet existent or is merely a kind of thing. It must be some individuated and spatially existing thing that is treated as a single separate entity—an individuated unit that can be physically held, formed, or marked.[23] Even though one usually holds or touches a thing only at a particular point and so takes direct physical possession piecemeal—for example, I directly grab or mark this piece of wood at one end—the thing that one manifestly and recognizably intends to take into possession for use is a whole determinate thing: this stick. And although the temporal duration of control can be variable, there is no such act as partial control or control of a partial interest in a thing that meets the threshold requirement for original acquisition. Control, whether it lasts for a moment or for a lifetime, must be complete and unlimited with respect to something or it is juridically nothing at all. Thus within the parameters of original acquisition, there cannot be an ownership spectrum consisting of greater and lesser ownership interests.[24] For there to be qualified, limited, conditional, or partial ownership interests, parties must do more than acquire something originally and unilaterally—as I will discuss, they must acquire it via contract or on some other transactional basis.

We need now to consider more closely the fundamental point, simply stated above, that the acts required for taking possession, use, and disposal establish and express ownership only insofar as they reasonably *manifest or signal to others* present subjection and control over an object. Others must be able to recognize that, here and now, I am exercising control over something and manifestly subjecting it to my effective power for my chosen purposes and ends.[25] Thus, it is not enough that I inwardly intend, need, or hope to do so. More than this, the requisite outward appearance of control is not merely required as the best or most reliable evidence of inward intent, taking the latter as the real underlying consideration. To the contrary, it is the control as reasonably apparent to others—and just this—that per se counts as the legally operative factor. This control must appear to others as present, not past. And within the framework of misfeasance, the control must be complete. To be at once already complete and yet present, what must therefore be signaled to others is a claimant's manifest *continuing* control.[26] More exactly, reflecting the already discussed contrast between original acquisition and the right of bodily integrity, what must be signaled and made externally manifest to others is present continuing control over something *as an external object*. These points require elaboration.

I have said above that, in order to establish original acquisition, the act of initially taking possession of something involves *physically or materially doing* something with or to the object—whether by grasping, forming, or marking it. We can now explain why this is juridically necessary. In the absence of any prior binding agreement with others as to formal requirements for appropriation, it is only in this way that one can *unambiguously show* others that one has subjected a separate physical thing—the only kind of thing that is available for first appropriation—to one's effective exclusive control. A thing of this sort must be physically affected in some way to manifest a person's external, not merely inward, act and decision with respect to it. However, this does not mean that, to have property in the thing, the claimant must *continue* to be in direct physical contact with (holding) it, once he or she has initially taken possession. While it is essential to signal clearly that one has present, hence continuing, possession of it, continuous *physical* holding is not necessary for this purpose.

Suppose that I am holding an apple and you pull it from me and proceed to eat it yourself. How have you wronged me?[27] By wresting the apple from my grasp, you may certainly have interfered with my bodily integrity and may be liable for whatever damage to me (my bodily integrity) that results from this. But then my claim is not with respect to the loss *of the apple*, and compensation need not (and should not) be measured by *its* value. A proprietary claim, in contrast to one of bodily integrity, must be with respect to the control and use of something *as an external object* (distinct from me), and it must be this control that you have injured by taking it from me. It is also this control that must be manifested unambiguously and unequivocally to others. However, to do this it is not necessary that a claimant always have direct physical possession of the object. It all depends on the facts—on whether the object itself has been marked, changed, or affected in such a way that, even though it is not being physically held at every moment, others can reasonably infer that it is still currently subject to someone's present control and use. Even though directly holding or affecting the object may be initially indispensable to establish the requisite control, this need not be required to signal the reasonably recognizable continuation of such control.[28] What counts, to repeat, is simply whether something is recognizably subject to someone's present control and use as an external object separable from the claimant's body. Breaking the normative necessity of direct physical holding and therefore of any factual necessity of the thing being an extension of my body brings out unambiguously the nature of acquisition, being the rightful holding of things as external separable objects.[29]

At the same time, unless others exercise control directly or indirectly over my thing in some way that is incompatible with my exclusive control, I do not suffer proprietary injury. Thus, insofar as the thing is not in my immediate physical grasp, the wrong or injury must physically touch or affect the thing itself. But it is important to be clear about the basis of the thing's role in this analysis. It does not stem from things being attributed intrinsic normative importance or from the fact that they are physical per se. To the contrary, the thing functions merely as an object of purposive action—more specifically of an exercise of control over it—and it is this purposive action as directed toward an object, not the thing taken by itself, that is normatively the subject of rights-protection. This remains true even where the injury to the claimant's property right is via damage to the object itself, physically unconnected to the claimant. In all circumstances, what is protected is a determinate action that represents or signals present exclusive control over an external object that is distinct from bodily integrity.

This raises the following question: supposing that original acquisition does not require continuous physical holding and that therefore physical holding is not per se necessary or significant in and of itself, is there a kind of acquisition that can dispense *entirely* with physical holding as a necessary condition of signaling the requisite present exclusive control over an external object, even at the initial point of taking possession? Can there be, in other words, a purely nonphysical mode of ownership acquisition? This would bring out most clearly that what is at stake even with original acquisition is the possibility of acquiring and possessing an object in a way that is distinct from bodily integrity.

In the case of original acquisition, I have suggested that the need for initial physical possession to signal this control to others can be explained by the fact that the object is something that is physically separable from everyone, presently unowned and available to anyone, and appropriated by an individual's unilateral action without the consent or participation of others. In one sense, marking an object is the way of taking possession that is most explicitly representational. However, even here there must be a physical alteration of the thing that touches it spatially and temporally at a particular point and that can therefore remain quite ambiguous in signaling continuing use of something as a determinate whole. This point applies even more clearly to the act of disposition in original acquisition: this act must signal the physical presence of the owner's will in the object but in such a way that at the same time breaks any physical connection between the owner and object. Hence, the inherent difficulty and ambiguity of alienation within the parameters of original acquisition.

But once—*if*—there can be a kind of acquisition that is constituted wholly by the *two-sided* participation of two parties with respect to objects that they *already* own—in other words, if there can be derivative or transactional acquisition—we should not assume that it, like original acquisition, must also depend on even an initial physical holding to signal the requisite control associated with private ownership. Indeed, I will now argue that it does not and that the fully enforceable executory contract is the most complete and satisfactory expression of such transactional acquisition, demonstrating this possibility of a wholly nonphysical process of appropriation that signals clearly and determinately what is being acquired. In effect, the parties' mutual assents in contract function as a kind of bilateral and purely representational marking, which, in contrast to the merely unilateral and indeterminate marking in original acquisition, expresses the content of acquisition in determinate or at least determinable terms. Now historically, recognition of the executory contract at common law was the culmination of a long development that began centuries earlier with a quite different paradigm of transactional acquisition, which I shall refer to as the immediately executed barter or exchange.[30] To arrive at the idea of contract as a transfer of ownership, I shall begin with an admittedly simplified version of this earlier model.

An immediate exchange does not entail any transactionally established distinction between agreement and delivery. Instead, a specific item is exchanged for another specific item or for currency, and any words prior to the actual exchange are strictly preliminary and without any obligational consequences, showing only that the parties have communicated a mutual interest in making the exchange. Indeed, according to the earliest law, prior to payment of the price or to delivery, the parties might withdraw without penalty—all the legal effects occurring only with the actual performance. Legal regulation with regard to such transactions was primarily concerned with the evidentiary issue of determining in the case of dispute whether an immediate sale or barter of particular items had in fact taken place. If it had, the direct legal consequence, coeval with it, was that each party would be vested with the property or possession of the item received in exchange from the other. The transferee's entitlement might in principle be good as against third parties, though, except where the market overt doctrine applied, it would be defeasible in the face of an original owner's prior and continuing proprietary claim.

Now for our purposes, a most remarkable point about this early model of the immediately executed exchange or barter is the fact, recognized by all early European legal systems when they permitted such transactions, that the parties' interaction can result in a transfer of ownership. What one side gives and loses is the same thing that the other appropriates and gains—and this "same thing" refers to and includes as its defining, regulative feature the very *same* ownership interest that the transferor has with respect to the item. If it is true that *nemo dat quod non habet,* it is also the case that, by immediate transfer, one *can* give to another the ownership interest that one has. An immediate exchange or barter is then a form of derivative acquisition that transfers ownership. It is important to underline its transactional character. The parties' mutually related acts constitute the transaction. Irrespective of the parties' purposes, these acts are the necessary and sufficient cause of the transfer of ownership. The transfer can be effective whether or not a party regrets his or her decision, whether or not the transfer enhances his or her welfare, and even if other terms would have been in the parties' interests. None of these factors is a condition of, or even relevant to, the validity of the transaction.

The fact that the transaction transfers ownership supposes that the parties can act with each other as owners of their things. As owner, each has rightful exclusive control over an item, and this includes the power to dispose of it so that it ceases to be his or hers and can become another's. This same capacity for ownership also entails the power to appropriate something in a way that does not violate the ownership of others. But clearly, by itself, the physical act of transfer is insufficient to change ownership. It is in and through a relation of reciprocal recognition and acceptance (express or implicit) by both that each side's act counts as an other-related giving over or taking of something ownable: you accept my item as something that is under my exclusive control and that I give to you in my capacity as owner; and you can do this only because I give it over to you as something that you can appropriate and have under your own exclusive control. Thus, I do not abandon my thing unilaterally, making it available to just (indefinitely) anyone else or to no one; rather, I alienate my thing to you qua something that I own, as reflected in the fact that it counts as alienation only insofar as you take it with my consent, thus recognizing my right over it as present owner. In this way, what each party acquires is specified and framed in and through their interaction. Something counts as mine or yours because it is treated as such through this united giving and taking. Moreover, you acquire the very same thing that I give up; and what you acquire is something as owned by me and so, necessarily, the very same protected ownership interest. Any difference between what is given up and what is acquired would introduce a gap that would be directly incompatible with the essential normative meaning and character of this relation of transfer. The two acts must be conceived as absolutely simultaneous and copresent, as intrinsically inseparable and reciprocal, and thus as two sides of a unified act or unity of wills.

In original acquisition, the operative acts are those of the single individual who unilaterally subjects something to his or her power and purposes. Because these acts are operative just insofar as they are recognizable by others who are thereby brought under an obligation not to injure, original acquisition certainly contemplates relation to others. But for this anticipated or potential relation to others, the acts would be without juridical significance. This essential nature of being for others is also operative in the requirement that occupancy be of something that is presently ownerless—that it must not be already owned by another. However, this requirement is merely negative and does not refer to an actual relation to others. To be rightful, occupancy must be consistent with others' rights and more specifically with their equal capacity to own. This reciprocity requirement is an implicit precondition that must be satisfied at the point of the claimant's action. But in original acquisition, this is not a positive and defining feature of the requisite act, which remains unilateral.

In the immediate exchange, by contrast, such recognition of and by others is embodied in the parties' interaction and is mutual. Ownership acquisition via immediate exchange is now grounded in a relation of *act with act* and is completely two-sided. It is important to underline that the constituent elements of this transactional analysis comprise and interconnect only factors pertaining to the exercise of ownership, indeed taking up into its own bilateral framework the elements already found in original acquisition: persons with a capacity for exclusive ownership and the ability to recognize this in others, acts of alienation and appropriation, alienable things subject to present exclusive control, and so on. We may say, then, with plausible justification that were persons as owners not permitted to engage in and to effectuate transfers of ownership in this way, this would represent an inherent limit upon the full realization of the exercise of their powers as owners. But even at this stage in the argument, it seems difficult to see how such a restriction could be anything else but arbitrary. The full and complete exercise of the powers of ownership entails the normative possibility and intelligibility of such transfer.

This characterization of immediate exchange is, I suggest, a necessary interpretation of the objective process of transfer that brings out the crucial factor of the mutual relation of will to will as the essential ground and medium of any transfer of ownership and therefore of any and every form of derivative acquisition. But the striking thing about immediate exchange or barter is that this factor, however fundamental, is not expressed on the face of these transactions. The juridically essential dimension of the relation of will to will is submerged, as it were, not in an immediate unilateral act of taking possession as in original acquisition but now in the immediate physical transfer of objects. The representational dimension is at most implicit in the operative bilateral acts. As a result, immediate exchange is, conceptually, not yet complete as a way of realizing this essential juridical basis of any transfer. This incompleteness is manifested as follows.[31]

Because it is impossible for the whole reciprocal transfer of physical possessions constituting an immediate exchange to take place literally in a single instant, the transfer must be a physical process that transpires over time, involving manifold steps that gradually execute empirically different particular aspects of the transfer. Paralleling the manner of taking possession in original acquisition, acquisition here must also be at any given instant piecemeal. And because the whole relation of will to will is coeval with this physical process, there is no point in the transaction at which complete present control of the whole object(s) transferred is established or exercised. The physical transfer begins, continues, and ends without any inner necessity or goal. Recall that any preexchange communications are here without obligational force in establishing a right to any performance by the other side. The parties may therefore change their minds as they proceed without wronging each other. The transaction just comes to an end when they decide to take no further steps. While the parties may want, expect, or even intend a completed present transfer, the form of an immediate exchange does not make this its explicit and necessary goal. Such expectations remain purely subjective and, strictly speaking, extratransactional. That the parties can mutually recognize each other as together transferring exclusive control as between themselves is a representation that is only implicit, and not fixed or established, in or by this transaction.

But if, as I have suggested, the direct relation of will to will constituting the parties' mutual recognition is indeed the true juridical ground and mechanism of this transfer of ownership, it should be possible for a form of transaction to make this explicit and visible on the face of its operative acts. The mute immediate exchange must declare its nature. The parties accomplish this by jointly positing this moment of mutual recognition as the sole and complete determining basis of their transaction. And with this, there is contract.

The crucial conceptual move from immediate exchange to contract is the explicit (and therefore doctrinal) positing of a normative-temporal difference between agreement and performance, with the whole of the juridical force and effect of the transaction being lodged in the moment of mutual assents alone: whatever the transaction is and does qua transaction is established in and by this agreement. This relation between assents, being explicitly representational, is now embodied in an element that is adequate to signal this, namely, via the use of words or their equivalent in symbolic conduct, and therefore in a mode that *is* what it signifies and represents. Because the second party expresses his assent in response to the already completed and fixed assent of the first party, which, in accordance with the objective test, he can reasonably deem to be continuing as long as it has not been manifestly retracted, there can now be in principle a determinate moment in time that marks the joinder of the two assents. Doctrinally, this is the instant of contract formation, which provides the sole and exclusive time reference for determining and interpreting the content, scope, and limits of contractual obligation.

Here, then, the transfer of exclusive control over a determinate object need not be piecemeal but can be explicitly complete and present. Independence from all physical aspects of possession and transfer is unqualified and unconditioned. Performance or delivery—the dimension of physical giving up and taking—is no longer necessary to establish the rightful relation. Whereas agreement embodies the complete crystallization of the relation of will to will, the juridical significance of performance, now a mere normative consequence, can be merely this: it shows that the parties have not acted inconsistently with the very transfer that they have jointly *already* effectuated in and through the medium of their mutual representations.

What this conceptual move from immediate exchange to contract also accomplishes is to specify, and thus to make clear, the actual character of the kind of ownership interest that is immanent, though not always explicitly operative, in all forms of derivative acquisition: a purely transactional ownership interest. Via the differentiation between contract formation and performance, contract incorporates all that an immediate exchange merely implicitly entails. It establishes the moment of the transfer of present exclusive control over a determinate object as a necessary, certain, and complete juridical fact, in this way resolving the indeterminacy and piecemeal character of immediate exchange and also that of original acquisition.

Thus, like immediate exchange, contract is also constituted by mutually related acts of alienation and appropriation, only here they are operative via the parties' mutual assents alone and therefore not only by but also as representations.[32] Conceptually, there can be just two basic categories of such mutually related acts: gift, where one party alienates and the other party appropriates, and exchange, where each party does both. These are the two most elementary kinds of transactional acquisition, including therefore contract. As a form of transactional acquisition, contractual relations must be either one or the other (or some intelligible combination of the two). These are, in other words, the two most basic transaction-types. Moreover, reflecting this distinction, there are two contrasting categories of transactional objects: something for nothing versus something for something else that is equivalent in value. Through this classification we see that the objects acquired transactionally are themselves specified transactionally. And this must be expressed solely in the medium of the parties' mutual assents or, in the case of the promise-for-consideration, in and through their mutual promises. Of course, how or how adequately this is worked out in any given legal system will depend upon its particular positive contract doctrines. In this connection, I have tried to show how, working in tandem, the doctrines of consideration and unconscionability ensure, respectively, the possibility and the integrity of what in substantive terms are two-sided promissory exchanges and gifts. My main point here, however, is that this classification of the two transaction-types of gift and exchange must be basic and intrinsic to any law of contract whenever contract formation is analyzed as a kind of transactional acquisition.

This leads to the following view of the object of contractual acquisition. Whereas the object in original acquisition, we saw, is some particular physical entity actually existing in space separately from our bodies, in contract formation, the object of original acquisition is reconfigured as a determinate content that is both inherently two-sided or transactional and valid independently of any physical holding whatsoever: a content that is therefore adequately and necessarily suited to the medium of representation as the real presupposed juridical basis of any and all ownership acquisition.[33] Thus, the objects of original and contractual acquisition are indeed qualitatively different and distinct but *only* in respect of the transformation and the expansion that result from the contractual reconstitution of the object in this transactional and purely nonphysical representation. This point is well illustrated by the regulative role of exchange value in the determination of contractual enforceability. For value is the indestructible and unchanging substance of the represented object of acquisition when this substance is fully relational and completely independent of any physical holding. It is the dimension of objects that makes them count not as the particular concrete physical entities that they happen to be but as what they are supposed to signify in relation to other things viewed in the same way.

The expansive nature of what the law views as consideration also fits with this transactional reconfiguration of the object in contract. This goes far beyond anything possible under original acquisition or even an immediate executed transfer. Stated abstractly, the substance of the consideration can be *anything determinate* that can be expressed or represented in words or their equivalent as a definite usable or wanted content promised by (and thereby moved from) one side to the other independently of temporal or spatial conditions. At the time of formation, the object may be generic in description, merely determinable, and even nonexistent or qualified by reference to future external conditions involving as yet unknown or unresolved events, and so on. The interest transferred may be stipulated as anything along the ownership spectrum from full-blown ownership to the most limited, partial, and specified interest in something. Now a service can be an object of contractual acquisition (and consideration), clearly fitting with its transactional character. For here the very subject matter—my doing something for you rather than giving something to you—cannot preexist the consensual relation between us, as if it were some sort of separate object available for anyone to pick up and appropriate. Prior to the transaction, what exists is merely my inherent and inalienable power to do this or that. This power becomes expressed as an alienable act or service only if specified as part of the very interaction by which I transfer it from under my rightful control into yours. Finally, as we saw in the discussion of assignment, the object of contract can even be a second-order title in the performance interest—the latter as an incorporeal right or chose in action.

My central contentions in this chapter are that, considered in terms of its juridical meaning and value, forms of ownership are conceptually unstable until ownership becomes transactional and further that the parties' agreement at formation contains what is essential for the full determination of the kinds of ownership relations that can obtain in private law. Certainly more needs to be said to justify these claims, and I will do so in the following sections. However, even at this point, I believe that we can see why an ownership interest, such as in original acquisition, that is not fully transactional is, *as ownership*, conceptually unstable and incomplete in its own terms. Although transactional acquisition, being derivative acquisition, logically presupposes the possibility of original acquisition, it is the former and not the latter that most completely and positively expresses the idea of ownership that is at work in both.

To recall: the problem with original acquisition is that its requisites acts, being necessarily physical and unilateral, do not in themselves express this other-related representation of nonphysical possession that is at the basis of any form of possession counting juridically as the ownership of external things at all. Because of this lack of fit between the meaning of ownership and the way it is established and expressed in original acquisition, the latter is inherently unstable as a form of ownership. Indeed, this must be the case for any form of ownership that is not predicated on an act that is intrinsically and reciprocally two-sided, consisting explicitly and necessarily in a direct relation between persons interacting as owners in and through an element or medium that is itself representational.

What is needed therefore is a union of acts consisting of the parties' mutually related representations signaling their reciprocal recognition as owners and constituting a single juridical event. But, I have tried to show, this is precisely how contract formation, consisting of mutual promises satisfying consideration and, more abstractly, the idea of contractual transactional acquisition, should be understood. In contract, parties do not acquire from each other anything that can be described apart from the very process of transfer that constitutes contract formation. According to the view that I am developing, every element and aspect of a contract—from formation to performance—reflects this transactional framework. At no point does contract confer a nontransactional ownership interest such as may be acquired via original acquisition.

Against this view, there naturally arise a number of challenges. For example, when contracts are performed, parties end up having actual possession or enjoyment of the things that they were promised by each other at contract formation. Doesn't this, coupled with the fact that the essence of contract is said to be merely an obligation to perform, suggest that contractual acquisition should be understood as a step toward the acquisition of a physical thing, taken as an object of property and freed from its transactional origin? Such a property interest, conceived like the object in original acquisition, would be a contract's real goal and completion. I will argue that this is not the case and that even the nature of the ownership interest that performance confers on a party is itself transactionally determined, irreducible to and distinct from that of original acquisition. Beyond this, how can the proposed view be sound if, as is standardly assumed, property claims are in rem, whereas contract rights are first and foremost in personam? Isn't this division incompatible with contract incorporating a genuine conception of ownership and inconsistent with my theoretical claim that contract completes property by containing in the most developed form what is essential in the determination of ownership in private law? I will have to provide an account of the in rem / in personam distinction that explains why this need not be so. In the next section, I address these and related matters.

10.3. The Property in Contract: In Rem and In Personam Dimensions

The traditional and still prevailing view of the in rem / in personam distinction may be summarized as follows.[34] First and most fundamentally, the distinction is taken to represent a categorical and juridically ultimate division between two different kinds of rights that are each embodied as different and separate kinds of legal relations. In particular, the different legal incidents and effects of property and contract reflect the fact that the first is essentially in rem, whereas the second is in personam. Thus, rights in rem are said to be with respect to things vis-à-vis others in general (i.e., "against the world"); by contrast, in personam rights are against other definite persons with respect to the fulfillment of their promises of future performance. Moreover, consistent with this difference, a claimant's exercise and enjoyment of his or her rights in rem do not require any positive act or intervention on the part of others but only their noninterference, whereas precisely the contrary is true of rights in personam. Finally, of the two kinds of rights, those in rem are deemed juridically the more real, substantial, and final. This is supposedly shown by the greater scope, subsistence, and reach of property rights compared with contract rights and by the fact that upon performance, contracting parties acquire rights in rem to what they were merely promised at formation. In this way, a right in personam seems to be a step toward the attainment of the more consequential and full-blown right in rem.

Departing from this standard view, Hohfeld famously argued that the difference between the two kinds of rights is not intrinsic or qualitative but only extrinsic and quantitative.[35] "Point for point," Hohfeld writes, they are "intrinsically of the same general nature," and whether a right refers to a thing or to a promise is not in and of itself important.[36] To the contrary, they have the same identical inherent character of always being rights against other persons with respect to a variety of different possible objects. Since both kinds of rights are defined as relations to persons rather than to objects, the fact that they may have different objects does not distinguish them. Rather, the only difference between them is extrinsic in the following sense. In the case of in rem rights, a given right that A may have against B with respect to some object x is but one of a very large number of fundamentally similar though separate rights that he or she has against C, D, E, F, and many others of an indefinite class with respect to the same object x. By contrast, A's right in personam against B has few if any such "companion" rights.[37] This difference is not exactly one of scope or compass.[38] Instead, it is the difference between whether a single relation of right and duty travels alone or as one along with many others. Accordingly, Hohfeld suggests that clarity would be better served by referring to the in personam right as "paucital" and the in rem right as "multital."[39]

I would like to propose a third view of the in rem / in personam distinction. Even though it shares certain elements with the other two approaches, this conception differs from both of them in basic respects. Stated negatively, my central theoretical claim is that the in rem / in personam distinction should not be understood either as conceptually ultimate or as referring to two utterly separate and freestanding kinds of relations. The various features associated with this distinction—such as whether a right is "general" and "against the world" or only against a definite person, whether it is with respect to a singular thing or another's performance—are variables that rest more fundamentally on the specific nature of a mode of acquisition. As I will try to explain, *both* original acquisition (property) and transactional acquisition (contract) have in rem and in personam *dimensions* (going to a right's scope, numerosity, and object). But they do so in qualitatively different ways. In the previous section, I argued that contractual acquisition incorporates the elements of original acquisition in a wholly transactional and nonphysical framework and that therefore all aspects of property acquisition reappear in contractual acquisition in this transactional form. This also holds for the meaning and role of the features associated with the in rem / in personam distinction. My aim, then, is to provide an account of these features that makes them intelligible through their genesis.[40] To show this, I begin, as in our previous discussion, with original acquisition.

10.3.1. The in Rem / in Personam Dimensions of Original Acquisition

We have seen that in every instance of private acquisition and in contrast with the innate right of bodily integrity, the operative cause of the entitlement is a definite act by the one who is deemed to have rightfully acquired. This act of acquisition must itself consist in an exercise of present exclusive control over some object: act and object are both distinguished but always inseparable. To become an owner, one must act as an owner. We have also seen that the crucial distinguishing feature of original as opposed to derivative (transactional) acquisition is not only that the thing to be acquired is ownerless but also that the cause of acquisition is the unilateral act of a single person alone, without any required direct participation of others. To make a thing her own, a claimant must do something to or with the thing that signals to others that someone is presently exercising unilateral effective control over it for her own chosen purposes. Everything about original acquisition reflects this defining feature of its source being in individual unilateral action. But, as noted in the previous section and as I now discuss more fully, precisely because of this defining feature there is at the core of original acquisition a basic tension, one that we will see is directly reflected both in the kind of rightful relations with others entailed by such acquisition and in the in rem / in personam distinction as applied to it.

The tension is this: On the one hand, it is the claimant's *independent act* of exercising effective control that, standing alone, is the *sole* cause of first acquisition, without the need for the actual participation or even possibly the presence of others. It is this independent act that must be recognized and respected by others. On the other hand, for the claimant's act to be juridically relevant and operative—for it to require respect on the part of others—it must be *recognizable by them* as such an exercise of present control. Yet, as just stated, at the very point of action that establishes and consolidates acquisition, these others are not actually or necessarily part of the relevant analysis. The standpoint of others is essential yet not presently actual or operative when the act is done. Consequently, original acquisition seems paradoxically to require that the claimant's act be both prior to and simultaneous with its recognition by others—in effect, to be both independent of and at the same time related to others. This core lack of integration affects at every point both the character and the limits of entitlements based on original acquisition and also, I will now suggest, the way in which the in rem / in personam distinction applies.

Thus, at the moment of action, though the claimant's act is juridically nothing unless recognizable by others as present exclusive control, this is only a *potentiality* referring to *anticipated* relations with others. The constituting act does not itself make reference to any definite others.[41] As such, the claimant's act, whether initially or even in its continuation, must therefore refer to *indeterminate others as potentially relevant*. This entails, further, that indeterminately anyone can potentially come under the legal effects of such acquisition, whether it be the disability corresponding to the claimant's immunity with respect to her rightful holding or the prohibition against injuring it. Now offhand, this seems to express a fundamentally in rem orientation of the rights based on first acquisition. But while this is an inherent incident of original acquisition that is regulative vis-à-vis others, it postulates not an *actual* but only a potential legal relation with the world en bloc or even with anyone in particular. Because this distinction between potential and actual legal relations is pivotal in my view as to the way in which original acquisition comprises an in personam as well as an in rem dimension, I should discuss it now in a little more detail.[42]

Consistent with the dynamics of original acquisition, we need only suppose that, at the point of the claimant's action, others exist somewhere and may subsequently be in a position to affect the claimant's thing. However, given their own independence and rights, this cannot be sufficient to bring them into an *actual* legal relation with the claimant. Simply being and existing somewhere—as opposed to being in a position to *do* something that can affect others—cannot possibly engage, let alone violate, another's private rights.[43] To hold otherwise would be to subordinate them to the claimant. Further, if we suppose that in private law *individuals* are the moral units of action and responsibility, it is they who owe, and whom in turn are owed, requirements of respect. Therefore, it is only if and when there is relative to the claimant some individual—some determinate other—who can affect the claimant's holding that there can be a relation of right and duty under first acquisition. Just as original acquisition requires that the claimant has the present power to exercise control over her object, so another must have the power to affect that control if the latter is to come under a primary duty of respect toward her. The merely potential and indeterminate "anyone else" at the point of action must become a determinate "someone" able to affect the thing if there is to be an actual legal relation of any kind with respect to that thing. At the same time, it should be underlined that whether there are in fact other such persons in the particular circumstances is a matter of chance: as noted throughout, there is nothing in the normative prerequisites or operation of the claimant's act of taking first possession that necessitates their presence, let alone a situation in which they can affect the claimant's holding.

If we may assume that a definition of in personam rights should at least make reference to a relation between two determinate persons, it would seem, offhand, that once the relation to others is not merely potential but also actual there is an in personam dimension to the entitlement in original acquisition. Indeed, taking individual persons as distinct and separate sources of claims and units of responsibility, this relation between claimant and other must itself be distinct and separate from any other such right-duty relations in which the claimant might be with others. Now, given that, as a matter of empirical fact, possibly many—indeed, at the limit, all—others can be in a position to affect the claimant's physical thing and thus be under the same abstract duty not to interfere with her holding, it might seem natural to view their duties as inherently joint, collective, or unified and the right as correlative to a duty imposed on persons "in general." However, this way of understanding the relation would be mistaken. The fact that it is intrinsic to this form of acquisition that many others may be similarly and even simultaneously under such a duty in virtue of their individual power to affect the claimant's thing means simply, as Hohfeld correctly emphasizes, that there may be numerous similar, though distinct and separate, such relations with respect to the same object.[44] This is how original acquisition is expressed in actual, not merely potential, relations with others. The claimant's entitlement with respect to her thing has juridical existence only in and through one or more distinct rightful relationships, each of which is as between two determinate parties.[45]

Taking this analysis a step further, we may say that to bring others into an actual (and not merely potential) legal relation with the claimant within the parameters of original acquisition, these others must be in a position not only to affect the claimant's thing but also to do so in circumstances in which they can reasonably recognize that she has brought it under her exclusive control. The creation of a relation of rights between the parties depends on this. This requirement of recognizability, I noted, also applies to the claimant herself, inasmuch as she can claim the thing only if, at the point of taking it into her possession, it reasonably appears to her to be ownerless. Indeed, given the general scope and the relativity of title under first acquisition, the determination of any one person's claims makes potentially and simultaneously relevant this same requirement of recognizability for any and all others in general. If parties are to be entitled to assert their viewpoints as reasonable and valid vis-à-vis others, there must be, at least as between a given claimant and another, a unified standpoint that establishes a fair basis on which it is reasonable to hold the claimant to what the other takes to be recognizable. It must be a unified reasonable standpoint that can directly apply to their interaction.

The problem, however, is this. Stemming from the basic tension within original acquisition noted above, there is no direct relation between parties to frame this needed unified standpoint: the relation that does exist is established, not jointly by and as between claimant and defendant, but rather by their two completely separate unilateral acts (of taking versus interfering with possession), and this does not provide a basis for constructing a single standpoint to which they can reasonably be held.

To elaborate, we have seen that the crucial feature of original acquisition is that the source of appropriation lies in unilateral action and not in a direct will-to-will relation between the parties. Thus, on the one hand, the claimant must do something that signals to indeterminately anyone in general and therefore apart from any particular contextual framework that she is exercising continuing present control over a thing. On the other hand, others can only recognize this from within their own inevitably particular contexts with their particular understandings, assumptions, and so forth.[46] This difficulty applies at all points in the analysis: to whether the thing appropriated is not already under someone else's control; to whether there has been an effective taking into possession; to whether there is an apparent user of a kind and degree that demonstrates continuing occupancy; and finally to whether there is unambiguous evidence of intended abandonment. A shared understanding on any of these matters must be contingent. Yet without this identical standpoint, there is nothing to ensure that the ownership right holds good even in a single case, let alone against everyone in general. A determination must therefore be made, and for this courts must try to find considerations that do not take parties unfairly by surprise but, it seems, cannot be justified on the basis of the logic of original acquisition alone.[47] Moreover, for the legal effects of a party's occupancy to be consistent with the equality of those subject to them, it seems essential that the latters' own capacity for ownership of things be reciprocally recognized by the claimant at the point of his or her action. Within the parameters of original acquisition, this requirement of equal recognition, as stated above, can at most be implicitly and negatively satisfied by the claimant only occupying something that is ownerless. This remains, however, at the level of potential, not actual, relations with others, and, even so, the absence of a shared standpoint is an obstacle to this as well. The unilaterality that characterizes original acquisition means that any relation between the parties cannot embody reciprocity.

To summarize so far, I have argued that it is the category of original acquisition, not the features associated with in rem, that is juridically basic and ultimate. The specific character of the relation of rights in original acquisition stems directly from the fact that here acquisition is fully and completely instituted by the claimant's act alone without the participation of others, even though, at the same time, the whole juridical meaning and effect of this act is and must be specified in relation to those others. On this basis, its in rem and in personam aspects are generated and conjoined. That rights based on original acquisition involve a relation to indeterminately many others "en bloc"—this is what is usually said to make a right in rem—is only true at the point of the claimant's unilateral and separate action and therefore as a matter of a merely potential relationship with such others. To give rise to an actual relation of rights, there must be a paired relation between the claimant and other determinate persons, each such relation being distinct and separate. These actual relations with determinate others—which can be called in personam—are, however, never directly between the parties but always mediated by the physical thing to which each side can have an individual, separate, and unilateral actual connection. This explains why property rights involve potentially and actually many separate but identical relations between claimant and determinate others. But precisely because of the feature of unilaterality and the resulting lack of a direct, unmediated relation between the parties, there is no interpersonal basis for constructing a unified standpoint which affirms their equal status as owners and to which both, let alone all, can be reasonably held. This inherent indeterminacy affects every aspect and element of the property analysis, including the direct protection of these rights in tort law.[48]

10.3.2. The in Personam / in Rem Dimensions of Transactional Acquisition (Contract)

Building on earlier discussions in Part One, I shall now argue that contract not only has an in personam dimension but also—and inherently—includes features that can be properly characterized as in rem. At the same time, in keeping with the qualitative differences between the two forms of acquisition, the in personam / in rem distinction appears differently in contract than in original acquisition.

All acquisition must be consistent with the (ownership) rights of others. In the case of original acquisition, this condition remains merely negative and potential (inasmuch as the thing must be ownerless and so something over which others have not yet exercised their ownership powers). By contrast, in contract, as a form of derivative or transactional acquisition, this requirement becomes positive and necessary because appropriation by one now takes place only with the other's consent and thus through both sides mutually recognizing each other's actual ownership. Unlike in original acquisition, where a relation between persons is not constitutive of the act of appropriation and exists, if at all, only via the middle term of the material condition of things, in contract the central factor is that here an actual (not just a potential) legal relation between two determinate persons is the absolutely necessary foundation of acquisition and is embodied in and through a direct and unmediated joining of wills.[49] Acts and objects of appropriation are now specified in and through this direct relation between the parties, which is constituted by their mutual and reciprocal recognition as owners in a way that is completely self-sufficient and without any need to be anchored in the physical materiality of things as the vehicle of representations. In contract, the "physical thing" enters as performance, which, in legal contemplation, neither adds to nor in any way changes the parties' normative relation inter se. The features that in original acquisition are unilateral, contingent, and physical are reconfigured in contract as transactional, necessary, and purely representational. Reflecting this transformation, contract has both in personam and in rem dimensions that, as I now discuss, are also differently specified.

First, there is the *immediate* relation formed by the parties' mutual assents alone. Although anyone can potentially be the first party's addressee and there can be many offerees (in principle all individuals but the offeror), a contractual relation at formation exists only with another determinate party. (If more than one offeree accepts, there will be as many contractually separate and distinct such relations.) By specifying the relation as one between act and act, contract carries through the premise that it is only in and through one's acts that one can acquire objects distinct from oneself. These assents necessarily embody in the medium of representation—and indeed *as* representation— each side's recognition of the other as having rightful exclusive control of a determinate object through the process of moving something of value from one to the other, reciprocally and jointly. In doing so, the assents themselves give existence to—by expressing—the purely rightful, nonphysical juridical meaning of holding and transfer, the possibility of which is presupposed by any form of ownership and acquisition of external things. Moreover, given that neither side acquires anything except in and through their reciprocally active relation between themselves, there is now the proper interpersonal basis in this unity to anchor and to spell out a determinate and complete reasonable meaning of their representations, to which *both* parties can simultaneously be fairly held inter se. As a matter of principle, the parties can and must be *ad idem* and all essential terms must be determined or be reasonably determinable within the parameters of the parties' agreement if they are to be contractually bound in the first place.

Now, if we suppose that, in keeping with the framework of liability for misfeasance, the kind of rights and duties at issue in private law in general are such as flow from and reflect the fact that individuals innately have or have acquired something to the exclusion of others and also that contractual acquisition in particular is strictly by one from the other and so as between them, contracting parties' rights and duties (as resulting requirements of respect) must also be specified solely as between them. When the basis of acquisition is the parties' interaction consisting of their mutual promises, the terms as promised must be owed only as between them: the promisee alone has the right to performance with the correlative duty being solely on the promisor. This, we saw earlier, is the core meaning of contractual privity, and it expresses the simple but utterly essential idea that the right-duty relation arises from an immediate and irreducible connection between the parties: a connection that is constituted through the process of their strictly mutual assents, which, in turn, are understood as reciprocally related acts of acquisition completed in the parties' shared representational medium.

Here, then, is clearly a dimension—indeed *the* dimension—of contract that may properly be characterized as in personam. It consists in a direct and immediate normative relation as between determinate persons: a form of acquisition constituted by the unity and mutuality of each side's objectively manifested reciprocal recognition of the other as owner. Though their linkage is solely in and through this relation of will with will that is wholly independent of the aspect of physical holding and physical transfer, it is not a relation devoid of determinate objects of acquisition. To the contrary, determinate objects, I have emphasized throughout, are essential elements in the representation, without which the parties' assents cannot satisfy the requirement of consideration or be recognized as acts of acquisition, as must be presupposed if expectation remedies are to count as compensatory. In contrast with frequently stated standard definitions, the contractual specification of in personam therefore makes essential reference to things but with the difference that these are now reconfigured in purely transactional and nonphysical terms.

I note further that despite what is sometimes said, contract's in personam character does not lie in a claimant's dependence on the other party to obtain or enjoy the promised performance.[50] To the extent that it exists, this dependence is merely factual, not normative. Indeed, the contractual relation at formation enshrines the basic normative independence of each party vis-à-vis the other insofar as each obtains rightful exclusive control against the other with respect to the substance of the consideration, always in the medium of representation and as transactionally specified. Performance does not perfect or in any way affect the promisee's entitlements. When the promisor performs, the law does not view him as acting for his own chosen purposes. The whole normative significance of performance amounts to this: it is the contractually stipulated necessary mode of the promisor not injuring the promisee's already complete entitlements.

In contrast with the indeterminacy and the potential defeasibility of rights based on physical possession because of others' conflicting prior or simultaneous claims, the in personam right in contract is not only determined or determinable but also independent and insulated from exogenous claims of third parties as well as from the consequences of being tied to the material condition of things. The basic entitlement at formation, including the right to be put into possession of the promised thing or its value, is fixed and crystallized as between the parties, and this in personam entitlement is protected under the aspect of immunity vis-à-vis any and all others.

Thus, if what parties promise may reasonably be construed as the sale of x for \$$y$, the fact that x may not already be in existence at formation, or that, as it turns out, the promisor may not even have title to x relative to some third party, or finally that he has already promised it to someone else need not affect the promisee's entitlement to receive x or its value. This is decided only by the reasonable interpretation of the terms of their interaction, and, as interpreted, the promissory representation of the sale of x eo ipso vests this rightful interest in the promisee as against the promisor, complete and immune from all other claims. Indeed, because parties can in principle allocate at formation any and all of the risks of performance, the promisee's entitlement can be practically absolute and unconditional as against the promisor, so that no events (not even the destruction of the promised object, however caused) or third-party claims can have any impact whatsoever on her performance right. To repeat, what the promisor transfers to the promisee as an entitlement in personam is decided by what, in the medium of representation, the promisor is taken to be promising, not by what the promisor has in fact or in title relative to third parties. Thus, as part of their in personam relation, the contract may confer on the promisee an entitlement as against the promisor that is greater than what the promisor himself may have with respect to this subject matter as against third parties.

In light of what has been discussed, this analysis of contract's in personam dimension and its companion conception of privity seems compatible with viewing contract formation as ownership acquisition. Most fundamentally, the fact that this acquisition is only as between those who reciprocally and jointly move considerations from one to the other should not be an objection, because this simply expresses the essential elements and core premises of acquisition in its most adequate and most fully realized terms and medium: as an actual direct legal relation between determinate persons mutually recognizing each other as presently exercising ownership powers of alienation and appropriation independently of physical holding or transfer. The contract terms are merely the determinate transactional expression or representation of these decisions. Moreover, as I tried to show in the discussion of remedies, the main heads of damages and specific performance protect a party's performance interest in having the possession, use, and value of the promised consideration. As with original acquisition, this interest is content-neutral and defined in terms of exclusive rightful control.

What about the fact that contract formation gives rise to an obligation to perform that is integral to the contractual relation? But this does not preclude contract formation from constituting a mode of ownership acquisition as between the parties. Indeed, not only transactional acquisition but also original acquisition incorporates—and must incorporate—both aspects of ownership and obligation.[51] This is because they both reflect the shared private law framework of liability for misfeasance that requires that something be brought under a party's rightful exclusive control vis-à-vis others (the moment of ownership acquisition) and holds that this gives rise to a duty on the part of others not to interfere with or to injure this base entitlement (the resulting obligation). In the case of contract, this base entitlement is established via formation. The promisee's right to possess or enjoy in fact the promised consideration is part and parcel of what she thereby acquires. As discussed earlier, in contract, unlike original acquisition, the content, mode, and timing of the exercise of this right are specified and fixed ab initio through the parties' mutual assents. It is this ownership right and all that it comprises as established at formation that the promisor is duty-bound to respect, and the right to performance is simply the correlative of this duty. A party does not own, but instead is owed, this performance. However, this duty, being the normative consequence of acquisition at formation, does not preclude (transactional) ownership itself from being an essential constituent of the in personam relation. The specific contribution of contract is that these always essential twin elements of ownership and obligation are both distinguished and linked as integrated aspects of a unified transactional analysis.

We have seen that the in rem dimension in original acquisition, which obtains at the point of taking possession, refers to a potential relation between claimant and indeterminate others who subsequently may be in a position to recognize the existence of the claimant's (continuing) present exclusive control and to affect this control by doing something to or with the thing. If, as I am suggesting, contractual acquisition incorporates all the basic elements of original acquisition in a mode that is thoroughly transactional and independent of physical holding or transfer, we might ask whether contract also has an in rem dimension of which this is true. In the discussion of third-party effects of contracts, I argued that a variety of doctrines having to do with third-party effects (including assignment, interference with contractual relations, and the *De Mattos* principle) seem to recognize what may be characterized as an in rem or "proprietary" dimension in contract.[52] A key feature of these third-party effects is that though these rights and obligations have to do with and indeed presuppose the performance owed as between the contracting parties, they constitute legal relations that are categorically distinct from it. Expanding on this earlier discussion, there seem to be two principal sets of such third-party relations that may be plausibly viewed as genuine in rem contractual dimensions. These two sets of in rem relations are intrinsic to any and every contract, analyzed without referring to the use of legal formalities or other institutional devices.

The first set of relations can obtain *at formation* and has as its object the content of the performance right functioning as a second-order valuable asset—as a chose in action—in both voluntary and involuntary relations with third parties. There is no reason why such title in performance cannot be characterized as an ownership interest.

Third parties, who can be indeterminately anyone, bring themselves into a legal relationship with the promisee's title via a mutually voluntary transaction (such as assignment) or an involuntary transaction (such as by tortious interference or under the *De Mattos* principle). This title in performance is clothed with the basic immunities of ownership and is protected by the kinds of trespassory rules that are appropriate for nonphysical objects of entitlement. As part of this analysis, the defendant must at least implicitly recognize and treat the promisee's interest in performance as a valuable asset over which the promisee has present exclusive control—thereby orienting his action to the promisee's interest as the chose in action that it is.[53] Recall that, consistently with the general nature of proprietary interests, the promisee's interest here is fully and determinately constituted as a chose in action *prior to and independent from* interaction with third parties and irrespectively of their viewing it as such. Notice to third parties is required simply to prevent unfair surprise in given circumstances. When combined with appropriate notice, the promisee's protected interest can produce effects that remain categorically distinct from the necessarily subsisting in personam rights, which it presupposes and builds upon. There is no reason to withhold from these effects or the promisee's protected interest the character of being in rem. Here the in rem dimension refers to a transactionally determined distinct juridical relation that is always actual, not merely potential, and that subsists only as between determinate persons with respect to a fully determinate protected interest that can be valid and effective independently of physical holding or transfer. In all these respects, it differs sharply from the parallel analysis of rights that characterize original acquisition. And with these distinctive features, both the in personam and in rem rights of contract fully and adequately embody the juridical idea of ownership relation in private law.

The second set of relations in contract that I would characterize as in rem obtains, not at contract formation, but *upon performance or delivery* when the promisee takes possession in fact of the promised consideration. Prior to delivery, the promisee's immunity is *only* as against those third parties who can affect or interfere with and have specific notice of her title in this promised performance. After delivery, it is trite law that the promisee can automatically have vis-à-vis third parties in general the very same proprietary right in the thing delivered that the promisor had at that moment.[54] The nature and scope of the promisee's proprietary right can be automatically the same as—no more but also no less than—the promisor's. Moreover, in contrast with third-party effects arising at formation, here, to be obliged toward the promisee, third parties need not know of the promisee's contractual title in the performance or even of the contract's existence. How should these third-party proprietary effects be understood and explained?

While the promisee may have a possessory claim against third parties just on the basis of her having taken or received, via delivery, physical possession of the thing prior to them, this would be by reason of the principle of first possession and so shaped by the relativity and indeterminacies of title in the analysis of original acquisition. It would not readily explain the promisee having *automatically* the same proprietary right against them as did the promisor.[55] This automatic effect, it seems, has to be explained on the basis of *some transfer* from the promisor to the promisee. But which transfer? For there seem to be two possibilities here: either the purely representational transfer consisting of the parties' mutual promises at formation or the actual physical transfer via delivery.

Suppose we take the source to be the physical transfer via delivery.[56] In order for delivery itself to effectuate this transfer of proprietary ownership in the promised thing (in the absence of legal formalities), the delivery would at least implicitly have to embody or represent the parties' present reciprocal intents to give up and take ownership. This is essential because, as a mere physical event, delivery cannot transfer ownership. We must also keep in mind that prior to delivery there is a contract and that, by its terms, this contract requires delivery. The argument must therefore suppose the existence of two transfers—contractual agreement and proprietary delivery—with the first "obligationally" requiring the second. But, according to the argument, it is the second (contractually required delivery) that would nevertheless have to express the *whole* intent to transfer in rem rights without depending for this purpose on the meaning and effects of the contract terms fixed at formation. This view leads to the following difficulty.

We are supposing that only one of the two transfers—either the moment of contract formation or that of physical delivery—can be the essential source of the intent requisite for the automatic passing of the promisor's proprietary interest to the promisee. Now if delivery is this essential basis, what would be the role of the first (merely contractual) agreement at formation? It could amount at most to the creation of a right and corresponding duty to do a *future* conveyance with the *future* proper intent to transfer ownership. What would this entail? In answering this question, it is important to bear in mind that, at the time of delivery, the parties would have to manifest the whole of their intent to transfer ownership. For this, their decisions to transfer at the time of delivery would have to express as between themselves their wholly unconstrained choices as owners, completely at liberty to deal with their things as owners and thus as they wish. But then how can we view their contract (prior to such delivery) as binding with respect to the delivery—at least to a delivery that is more than just a physical act—and as conferring this entitlement as a present asset? Indeed, in what way would it bind at all? In fact, it would seem to be perfectly consistent with this view of delivery that, at the moment of contracting, the promisee assumes the risk that the promisor may decide in the future *not* to convey his property interest as long as the promisor, exercising reasonable care, notifies the promisee of his change of mind on a timely basis or takes other measures that neutralize foreseeable detrimental consequences of the promisee's reliance. It is by no means clear why the compensatory remedy for breach of that agreement should not be reliance damages rather than expectation damages or specific performance.

In other words, taking delivery as the source of the requisite intent to transfer ownership empties the first purely contractual transfer of any specifically *contractual* power with respect to the very thing that it requires—delivery of the promised consideration. We no longer need this first purely contractual transfer consisting of the parties' mutual promises. The second, purely proprietary transfer can operate on its own independently of the first. Apart from its possible relevance for reliance-based liability, the moment establishing "contractually required delivery" is emptied of any juridical significance or effect.

The more coherent and internally stable view, I suggest, is that *already at formation*, the parties' mutual assents contain *the whole and complete intent* necessary for the promisor's proprietary interest in the thing to pass automatically to the promisee upon performance. Not only does this avoid the difficulties discussed above, but it takes seriously the fact that it is contract formation that alone and completely determines the content of the substance of the consideration, fixes it ab initio as a legally certain present asset in which a party also can have title as a chose in action, and makes normatively necessary its delivery in accordance with the contract's terms. In addition to generating the obligation to perform, their mutual assents at formation already contain the *iusta causa traditionis,* stamping factual delivery with the normative (juridical) meaning of being a transfer of the promisor's whole interest as promised to the promisee.[57] This reflects the fundamental points discussed earlier that, first, it must be possible to concentrate the full meaning and power of ownership in the juridical reality of purely nonphysical rightful possession and the transfer thereof and, second, that such possession and transfer are unqualifiedly established in and through the representational medium of the parties' mutual assents at contract formation.

Accordingly, whatever ownership interest the promisor has with respect to the promised consideration is the same as what is transferred to the promisee. The complete ownership interest on the promisor's side translates into, on the promisee's side, not only her in personam right to performance against the promisor but also her title in that right as a chose in action vis-à-vis third parties. The full nature of the transferor's ownership interest is equal to the combined in personam and in rem rights (powers, immunities) that vest with the transferee. Anything less would limit or subtract from the full value of the consideration and make it impossible for the promisor to alienate what he owns without altering or diminishing it even in part by this process. But in light of the argument that contractual acquisition can count as a distinct mode of ownership acquisition in private law precisely because it is transactional and effectuated in the element of representation alone, any such limit, subtraction, or qualification must be arbitrary. Thus at delivery the promisee's right against third parties can be automatically the very same as the promisor's. Ownership can be and is conserved through mutually related exercises of the powers of ownership. There is no need to postulate two distinct, let alone two separate, transfers to explain this automatic effect.[58] There is but one unified contractual transaction, which is the rights-establishing source of in personam as well as third-party effects.

What, then, does delivery contribute in this unified analysis—since we are supposing that the in rem right is consolidated upon delivery? In contrast to its function in establishing original acquisition, here taking possession via delivery does not perfect the rights-establishing power of the contract, which is whole and complete at contract formation. Instead, it only makes this power operative vis-a-vis third parties through the provision of appropriately public notice.[59] By changing the locus of rightful physical possession from promisor to promisee, delivery provides the kind of indeterminately *general* notice that is necessary to bind third parties who may not have specific notice of the contractual relation itself. Indeed, in the absence of legal formalities, registration, and the like—in other words, when, as here, the transaction is completely nonformal—physical possession would seem to be the sole or at least the most obvious mode of signaling such general notice.

I take it to be axiomatic that for acquisition and transfer to be rightful and to give rise to obligations imposable on others, the requisite acts must always be reasonably recognizable by them. With respect to nonformal transactions, obtaining possession in fact is a necessary condition of the contract having proprietary effects vis-à-vis third parties in the absence of the kind of specific transactional notice of title that is a requisite for tortious interference or other third-party effects arising from formation on. As a consequence, the proprietary interest that the promisee obtains upon delivery cannot be greater than what the promisor has at that point as against third parties.[60] At the same time, the reason why the promisee's proprietary interest can be and is automatically the same as the promisor's interest at that point is the contractual transfer of ownership as between the parties at contract formation. In this way, physical possession obtained via delivery represents the final expression of the transfer of ownership that is established completely and fully at formation. The role of possession in ensuring publicity is not independent of contract but, to the contrary, is fully integrated as part of the meaning and operation of transactional acquisition. This automatic passing of the promisor's proprietary interest shows definitively the juridical priority of what Kant called the "ideality" of purely rightful possession relative to physical holding and within this framework the dependence of the latter on the former, rather than conversely.[61] In contract, it is the representation, not the physical thing, that is the whole juridical reality and is regulative throughout.

To sum up. Each of both property and contract embodies in personam and in rem dimensions. But they do so in different ways. At the point of action, original acquisition immediately and necessarily establishes potential relations (in rem) with indeterminate others in general; and these relations contingently can, but need not, become actual (in personam) if and when determinate individuals happen to be in a position reasonably to recognize and to affect the possessor's thing. Whether or not there are such actual relations is a matter of happenstance, and the two sides of any given relation are not directly linked inter se—each being unilateral and one-sided—but rather are connected through the thing as their middle term.

By contrast, contract formation necessarily and immediately embodies an actual (in personam) relation between the parties and at a second level the many potential (in rem) relations with third parties that can arise with reference to the in personam performance interest, while remaining distinct from it. Each and every aspect or dimension of contract is integrated in this rights-generating direct nexus of transfer between the parties. From formation on, each contracting party has not only a transactionally constituted in personam right to performance but also a second-order title in (though distinct from) that right: her contractual right to performance figures as an asset of crystallized value—a chose in action—that she owns and that can be alienated to and be injured by third parties via their own separate relations with the contracting parties. From formation on, the contract also establishes the possibility of the automatic transfer at delivery of the promisor's interest as against third parties. There is but one unified contractual transaction, which is the rights-establishing source of all in personam as well as third-party effects.[62]

10.4. Concluding Remarks

In this chapter, I have tried to clarify what the idea of a transfer of ownership entails and why contract can reasonably be understood in these terms. This is the first step in developing the theoretical account of the transactional analysis of contract principles presented in Part One. In keeping with the aims and nature of a public basis of justification, this first step has been to argue that the legal understanding of the basic contractual relation consisting of the promise-for-consideration relation embodies a conception of ownership transfer and to articulate this conception more fully and explicitly. The idea of transfer is familiar both in law and in everyday experience and highlights central features of the contractual relation as well as of the kind of acquisition that the main contract doctrines seem reasonably to presuppose—for example, the requirement of strictly mutual and coequal participation by two sides, the unity of these two sides, and the fact that something moves from the exclusive rightful control of one side into that of the other as part of a reciprocal and identical movement of something else from the latter to the former. Misconceptions of what the proposed theoretical idea of transfer consists in can be avoided, I believe, if one keeps in mind the simple but central thought that the contractual transfer at formation is merely transactional acquisition transposed in the form and medium of representation, prior to and independent of delivery.

I have proposed this idea of transfer as a solution to the problem of the compensatory character of the performance remedies—a question that Fuller and Perdue made central for modern contract theory but that, despite the passage of more than eighty years, has yet to receive a fully satisfactory answer. The problem arises from the difference in time between the promise of something and its delivery via performance, given the juridical fact that the thing itself, including its value, as transactionally specified, is treated as the content of compensatory relief. The solution must show that there is one identical object at both points in time with the first moment, namely, contract formation, being normatively regulative.

The conception of formation as a form of transactional acquisition that has normative reality and effect as mutually related representations independent of and prior to actual performance provides, I believe, the necessary analysis. But for this purpose, it is not enough to show that the doctrines of formation can plausibly be conceptualized in terms of transfer or even that the compensatory nature of expectation remedies requires this. Although essential, this is merely an argument of fit and does not explain the conception of transfer itself in light of more basic and pervasive private law ideas. To answer Fuller and Perdue, and also to provide a satisfactory theoretical account of the kind that I am seeking, it is also essential to show that this conception is intrinsically acceptable from a more general juridical point of view. For this purpose, I have considered whether the conception of transfer implicit in the common law of contract expresses a plausible and coherent idea of private ownership, understood as a relation between persons in which individuals have rightful exclusive control over objects as distinct from their bodies. In other words, can contract be plausibly understood as a transfer of ownership?

In trying to show how this is possible, I have argued that what ownership in private law entails can be fully and properly understood only when analyzed in terms of possible modes of acquiring such rightful exclusive control. This is because, in contrast with the right of bodily integrity that is innate, ownership, so understood, necessarily involves *acts,* and these acts at one and the same time both effectuate and express ownership. One *becomes* an owner by presently and actually *exercising* the powers of ownership, and *being* an owner involves a continuous assertion in time that *establishes* ownership. What is recognized and protected as ownership are these acts themselves. At the most basic level, there can logically be only two such kinds of acquisition—original and transactional—and so the questions become: What specific notion of ownership is embodied in each? Do their respective notions express a common element? And if so, what is the exact relation between them?

The difference between these two forms of acquisition is both clear and qualitative, and since I treat property as an instance of original acquisition in contrast to contract, which exemplifies transactional acquisition, the comparison between them seriously tests the central contention that contract can also be analyzed in light of a shared idea of ownership. Not only do they share the same underlying idea of ownership. Perhaps paradoxically from the standpoint of the standardly assumed view, contract completes property by being a more developed and integrated expression of this underlying idea, and it does this precisely in virtue of the act of acquisition in contract being itself an inherently bilateral unity of acts constituting a transfer of ownership.[63] Contract's bilateral form of mutual recognition is not only a distinct way of effectuating ownership. It also represents what ownership *is* as an organizing normative idea in private law when its juridical meaning is fully and explicitly articulated.

A further serious challenge to the proposed understanding of contract is the contention that whereas property rights, being simply in rem, have to do with ownership, contract rights, being merely in personam, express only obligations: in the first, one *owns* something, whereas in the second, one *owes* it.[64] Against this view and continuing my basic argument that the ultimate determining factors are the forms of acquisition, I have tried to show that the standardly assumed features of in rem and in personam rights are generated through an analysis of the forms of acquisition and figure as distinct but interconnected dimensions of the two kinds of acquisition, each of which incorporates both aspects of ownership and obligation, even if in different ways. In both property and contract, ownership must be acquired and is presupposed as conceptually prior to obligation. This reflects the framework idea of liability for misfeasance. The fact that contract involves an in personam relation at its basis does not preclude understanding it in terms of private ownership. It must be emphasized that not only are the in rem and in personam rights in property and contract specified differently, but the way in which they are embodied in contract is also, I have argued, a more satisfactory expression of the analysis of rights in property. In contract, with its direct and unmediated relation between wills as the basis of everything, in personam and in rem rights, powers, and immunities are necessarily distinct but also fully integrated dimensions of one unified wholly transactional analysis. Clearly, then, the proposed theory of contractual transfer does not suppose that contract transfers the kind of in rem rights that characterize property acquisition. It does not view contract as a transfer of property understood in this sense.

As I have tried to present it, the proposed conception of contract as form of transactional acquisition does not depend on the fact that the mutual promises may be morally binding or on the notion that parties are contractually bound just because this is what they intend or want to effectuate. The proposed account does not view contractual duty as a form of self-imposed voluntary obligation in this robust sense. These divergences make it all the more acute that I address the following fundamental question: on what moral basis can parties reasonably be held by coercive law not only to the juridical effects of their transfer but also, and even more basically, to the very interpretation of their voluntary interaction as a form of transactional acquisition in the first place, with all that this entails? Here, by way of a compressed and provisional answer, I build on what I suggested in the earlier discussion of formation.[65]

First, in virtue of each party's individual and voluntary decision to engage the other in a way that makes the other's equal and active participation as essential as his or her own, each can reasonably be held to have submitted to a *relational* point of view, expressing the requirements of the reasonable. Furthermore, from this point of view and in light of the specific form and content of their voluntary interaction (satisfying the features of the promise-for-consideration relation), the law can reasonably and fairly construe their interaction as a form of transactional acquisition. This bilateral transactional conception, I have tried to show, can be justified as between the parties in more general juridical terms as a transfer of ownership. Having interacted in a way that can be so construed, neither party can reasonably object if the other asserts such a claim of ownership vis-à-vis the first and holds him or her bound by what this entails. This could only count as an unjustified imposition if viewed from a party's isolated standpoint that does not accept the relational view and what this implies juridically in terms of the reasonable. But the upshot of my discussion of the conceptions of ownership in original and transactional acquisition is that the moral possibility of viewing the meaning of their interaction as a transfer of ownership cannot be denied without directly rejecting the very basis of *any* ownership claim in private law.

If plausible, this approach suggests that viewing the parties' interaction as a transfer of ownership and holding them to be contractually bound under it can be consistent with the reasonable juridical meaning of their conduct. This is an important step in the argument, but it still takes certain crucial points and ideas as given without providing a deeper moral justification that shows them to be acceptable from the standpoint of a liberal conception of justice.

In particular, we have seen that the entire analysis of acquisition, both original and transactional, takes certain definite acts as, in and by themselves, the necessary and sufficient causes of private ownership acquisition. At the same time, within the framework of liability for misfeasance and in contrast to promissory morality or other standpoints, the parties' purposes and motives, the presence of regret, whether the results of acquisition further their substantive interests or well-being *ex post* or even *ex ante,* and so forth, are each and all in themselves normatively irrelevant to determining whether there has been original or transactional acquisition. Granted that acquisition requires acts, on what moral ground might it be justified to view the normative significance of their acts in this specific way and to hold that on this basis alone parties can be subject to coercible claims as between each other with respect to their acquisitions? It is by no means straightforward that this is intrinsically reasonable or legitimate from the standpoint of a liberal conception of justice that takes the freedom and equality of all citizens as its organizing ideal. Similar questions arise with respect to other key notions such as the moral basis of ownership itself in private law and the acceptability of viewing parties *solely* as owners or transactors in abstraction from all their other morally pertinent qualities and features. How does this view express their freedom and equality? Clarifying these and related matters is the essential next step to working out a satisfactory public basis of justification for modern contract law. In Chapter 11, I try to do this.

Chapter 11

A Moral Basis for Contract as Transfer

In this chapter, I work out in some detail a moral basis for contract when the latter is viewed as a transfer of ownership between parties. The proposed moral basis is not the only kind that might be plausible. However, I will suggest that it is one that is particularly well suited to be part of a public basis of justification for contract law in a modern liberal legal system.

The subject to be justified is the transactional conception of contract, which, I have tried to show, unifies the main doctrines and principles of contract law within their own framework. In keeping with this legal point of view as explained thus far, the proposed moral basis should not invoke or rely upon any substantive extratransactional purposes or values, whether economic, moral, or political. The law does not view the parties or their transactions as subject to any such ends. As participants in contract formation and in making contractual claims, individuals need not share anything except what is necessarily comprised in their promise-for-consideration relation. This should therefore be reflected in the moral justification.

Moreover, building on the argument that contract can reasonably be construed as a transfer of ownership, the proposed moral basis seeks to justify the moral salience of the parties being viewed solely as owners and of their transaction being constituted by their mutually related representational acts of ownership. I will argue that viewing the parties and their transaction in this way can be rooted in a certain conception of their freedom and equality and involves attributing to them moral powers that express their rational and reasonable autonomy. This immediately suggests a relation between the proposed moral basis and the kind of public justification proposed by John Rawls. Despite its being a public basis of justification in the general sense intended by Rawls, the justification developed here, we will see, differs in important respects from Rawls's political conception. While both express liberal conceptions of freedom and equality, they do so in distinct ways that reflect the different natures and intrinsic features of contractual transactions and political relations. This is in keeping with Rawls's fundamental insight that public justification is framed for specific kinds of relations between persons. If contractual and political relations are different—as Rawls himself insists they are—so will be their justifications.[1] What I propose is a public basis of justification that is specifically worked out for contract law.

11.1. A Juridical Conception of the Person

To begin and by way of review, I should restate exactly what it is that I am seeking to justify at a deeper level. The starting point is the transactional conception of contract. In prior chapters, I have argued that this conception animates and unifies the main principles and doctrines of contract law and also that it may be plausibly characterized more abstractly as involving a transfer of ownership between the parties at contract formation prior to and independent of performance. The transfer is effectuated by and exists in the medium of the parties' mutually related representations in complete abstraction from the aspects of physical holding or delivery. The only thing relevant in determining this transfer is whether the parties have done the necessary acts, irrespective of their purposes for contracting or the impact of the transaction on their needs and well-being.

Moreover, this conception of contract reflects private law's normative framework of liability for misfeasance only. As already discussed, according to this limited conception of responsibility, a party is subject to liability only insofar as he or she may reasonably be viewed as injuring or interfering with another's ownership or rightful exclusive possession of something.[2] Parties' purposes, needs, or well-being are not per se part of this conception of protected interests and are not accorded positive normative significance. Within this framework, claims do not arise from and are not affected by one's needs and purposes but must be based on what one owns or rightfully has to the exclusion of others. Liability for misfeasance is only for wrongs against others and more specifically for conduct that interferes with or otherwise injures their ownership interests. Thus, the requirements that come within misfeasance are always based on prohibitions, even when they are expressed in positive form. Even though breach ordinarily consists in a defendant's pure omission, its normative significance is not that it is a failure to confer a benefit but rather a wrongful injury that interferes with what the promisee has already rightfully acquired at contract formation. Despite its positive form, *pacta sunt servanda* should be understood in this light.

In taking the theoretical inquiry a step further, we should suppose all these points as provisionally established and see whether we can uncover a suitable moral underpinning that justifies their different aspects as well as their unity in the transactional conception. Our main question, then, is the moral acceptability of this conception of rights in contract and, more exactly, whether it is consonant with a liberal conception of justice in which individuals count as free and equal persons and are accorded respect as such.

This issue is far from straightforward. While this conception of contract upholds individuals as persons worthy of respect and as having a capacity for rights, it acknowledges them, we have seen, *only* as owners vested with exclusive rightful control against others and protected by merely negative imperatives prohibiting injury, with apparent total indifference to their needs, purposes, and well-being. And while it treats the parties' acts as the necessary and sufficient cause of contract formation, and in this way views the parties as autonomous sources of valid claims against others, the normative significance of their acts and claims is also strictly specified within the limited parameters of this conception of liability. Certainly, this cannot be the whole of what justice requires. Even so, does this conception of contract reflect certain, even if limited, normative values and ideas that can and should be part of a more complete liberal conception of justice? Since justice is owed to persons and views them as having a certain inherent moral status, we must see whether this account of contract embodies, even implicitly, its own morally acceptable conception of the person.

In particular, the following issues should be addressed: What inherent moral capacities or powers characterize persons when they are viewed solely as owners who have contractual rights and correlative duties sounding in misfeasance? How, if at all, are they free and equal in virtue of these powers and rights? Does the contractual relation, understood as a transfer of ownership between the parties in the medium of representation, appropriately express these moral powers and the parties' freedom and equality? Finally, if parties did not have an inherent power to make such ownership or contractual claims, what would be lost in the complete realization of our freedom and equality in relation to others?

In working out an appropriate conception of free and equal persons for contractual relations, I have already emphasized that it is intended to fit only with the particular kind of relation that is characteristic of contract. It is presented as a specific rather than as a general conception of the person: juridical and indeed contractual, as distinguished from political, familial, or economic.[3] As such, the juridical conception of the person should be consonant with the basic features of the understanding of rights in contract as part of the misfeasance framework. It should also be emphasized that, in keeping with the idea of a public justification, this juridical conception is not derived from or presented as part of any philosophical accounts or other comprehensive doctrines. Rather, it connects up with everyday moral experience. It suffices if we implicitly view ourselves and others in this way when we consider how we ought to act—on which reasonable principles—as responsible and accountable agents who can be subject to genuine legal obligations, even within the parameters of misfeasance. Via introspection, anyone should be able to recognize these powers in himself or herself except in extreme cases of disability amounting to legal insanity, automatism, and the like. Now I want to suggest that when persons are so viewed, they are attributed the following two moral powers: first, a moral capacity to assert their sheer independence from their needs, preferences, purposes, and even their circumstances; and, second, a moral capacity to recognize and to respect fair terms of interaction that treat everyone as independent in the specific sense supposed by the first moral power. Let me elaborate.

To recognize these two moral powers in ourselves, we simply reflect on what we are when we take ourselves as completely defined and situated individuals who nevertheless have an unbreakable consciousness of the possibility of choosing reasonable principles on a basis that is *not* determined by those features and circumstances. On the one hand, we immediately find in ourselves particular features, desires, needs, and purposes that seem to specify who and what we are or are doing at any given point in time. We find ourselves situated in different particular contexts, relations, and other external circumstances. This is simply how we happen to be. Yet, on the other hand, we also know that we can in reflection at least possibly (even if we do not consciously do so on every particular occasion at the moment of action) stand back and distinguish ourselves from as well as reject the force of any and all such desires, needs, characteristics, and circumstances as reasons for doing what we otherwise judge to be morally unacceptable. We do not think that the fact that we just happen to be this or that—the fact that we are a certain gender, have certain desires, or are bound to others by ties of friendship or commitment—is automatically and without critical evaluation a sufficient moral ground for justifying our actions. If we were inherently and inevitably tied to anything in particular, including even the desire to preserve ourselves, we could not view ourselves—or be viewed by others—as morally accountable choosing selves in the first place. Instead, we would figure as mere passive carriers of this or that feature, desire, need, or situation.[4] Thus, we recognize that we have the reflective power and capacity to take up a point of view in which we consider ourselves and others as units of responsibility not inevitably bound by but rather as *independent* from any and all of these factors as immediately given to us.[5]

This reflective capacity to distinguish and distance ourselves from what we happen to desire or need and from the situation in which we find ourselves represents our first basic moral power as accountable agents. It is essentially a *negative* moral power, because far from specifying our need for or dependency upon certain goods, it is restricted to the bare point that we can stand back from everything and so be in a position to choose whether to treat it as a reason or ground for action. In taking up this negative standpoint to everything given, individuals necessarily view themselves as persons conceived in abstraction from all such particular factors. In other words, they have themselves—and only themselves—so conceived for their object: a standpoint involving sheer self-relation.

Thus, as responsible agents, individuals have a higher-order interest in asserting and preserving this standpoint of sheer negative independence from everything immediately presented by their needs, desires, circumstances, and the like. Asserting and preserving this independence is their self-relating aim and end, and, as such, it may be thought to express an idea of the rational (in contrast with the reasonable), but with this important caveat: their end here is *just* this negative formal stance and does not refer to any substantive purpose or determinate conception of their good, let alone one that is self-interested. It represents the *mere potentiality* for actual choice, which must always be directed toward a determinate end. Finally, precisely because individuals can reflectively view themselves as independent from the very factors that, being particular, differentiate them from others and even from themselves across time, everyone necessarily counts as *identical* when taking up this point of view. All must be regarded as having this very same higher-order interest in asserting their independence from everything given.

In addition to this first moral power to assert our independence from everything given, we also suppose that we have a second moral power, which belongs to our capacity for reasonableness: an ability to recognize and accept the normative significance and implications of our independence, not only for ourselves but for others as well. Reasonable persons recognize and accept whatever requirements of respect are owed when everyone is viewed as having the same higher-order interest in asserting his or her independence. Hence, persons must not be subjected to acts or effects that are incompatible with their moral nature of being independent and that simply impose on them, treating them merely as a means to external ends. In virtue of their having the first moral power of viewing themselves as self-relating ends, persons are recognized as sacrosanct and never as merely usable—in other words, as having an inherent and untouchable dignity. It is part of their normative identity that they fully accept this requirement of respect and whatever it entails. In the next section, I try to explain what this requires and how it is violated.

In what sense are persons, who can reflectively view themselves and others as having these two moral powers, free and equal? Their freedom consists just in their independence and whatever this entails. First, individuals assert the right to view their persons and whatever embodies their personhood as independent from, and so not identified with, their particular purposes, desires, needs, or circumstances—their particular conceptions of their good and whatever happens to differentiate and situate them in relation to other things and persons. They assert a view of their own normative identity—and must recognize the same in others—that is irreducible to and independent of these factors. Thus, if, as I will shortly argue, the legal capacity for ownership directly reflects this view of their personhood, that capacity would not depend on individuals having or pursuing a particular set of purposes or be affected when they change their purposes over time. Similarly, neither the prerequisites for acquisition nor the powers incidental to this right would be determined on the basis of parties' needs, purposes, preferences, or the consequences for their well-being. In excluding these factors, the right would express only the parties' freedom as independence.

In addition, as free, such persons assert the right to be independent of the purposes and needs of others and to act without having to justify their conduct in light of these or any other substantive ends. As a result, they view themselves as having the capacity to make claims in relation to others that have a weight of their own, and so they regard themselves, in Rawls's phrase, as self-authenticating sources of valid claims.[6] The basis of the validity of claims is in the persons themselves who make them. A final way in which individuals are free is that, in virtue of their moral power to distance themselves in thought from their desires, needs, purposes, and so forth, they view themselves and are viewed by others as having the capacity to take responsibility for their ends and for conforming their actions to whatever respect for others' rights requires of them.[7]

In what sense are such persons equal? Because they assert their independence from (and nonidentity with) the very factors that differentiate them, there is, as noted above, nothing that inherently distinguishes them qua such persons. Their equality consists here simply in being identical. Accordingly, the whole range of factors that differentiate individuals must fall outside, and be irrelevant to, their status as equals. This would also apply to whatever expresses or intrinsic to their equal personhood. So once again, if, as I will suggest, the capacity for ownership can be understood as intrinsic to their personhood, the right of property would not aim at any notion of equality that treats these differentiating factors as per se normatively relevant. This, we will see, has far-reaching implications.

For example, it underpins the possibility of a purely nondistributive conception of justice in transactions. Thus settled principles such as first possession or the requirements of contract formation, which on their face are indifferent to distributive considerations, need not be viewed as morally deficient just for being so. How much and what individuals own may be per se a matter of indifference. It also follows that whatever one party asserts from this standpoint must be true of everyone else. And this is something that all who can so view themselves can be held to recognize in others. Therefore, the claims parties make in relation to each other must be absolutely the same. No one claims the right to place others under any obligation or constraint that others could not similarly do vis-à-vis him or her. Note that this equal status is inherent in individuals, not something that they must acquire through their actions. Most importantly, a person's equal standing does not depend on the fact that he or she has this or that purpose, and it does not require one to share another's ends or conception of their good. This follows from the fundamental point that the conception of the person as independent abstracts from all such factors.

Here, then, seems to be a specific normative conception of the person that precisely like the orientation of misfeasance, does not treat as morally salient in themselves the whole range of considerations having to do with particular purposes, needs, preferences, and so forth. Because of its character and this apparent fit with misfeasance, I will refer to this conception of the person as "juridical" and to the notion of autonomy that it expresses as "juridical autonomy." But what about the connection, if any, between this juridical conception of the person and the fact that misfeasance treats rightful exclusive control over something ("one's own") as a necessary basis for claims as well as restricts its imperative to the negative of prohibiting conduct that injures or interferes with such control? In other words, how do the legal relations involving individual and exclusive private ownership acquisition— including a transfer of ownership—express this view of individuals as free and equal juridical persons with their two moral powers as discussed above? And is there anything morally necessary in this form of recognition? Addressing these questions is the next step.

11.2. From the Juridical Conception of the Person to Ownership and Contract

My central contention here is that the role of private ownership is to express and to embody in the medium of action the kind of respect properly due persons with their higher-order interest in asserting their independence from everything given. In fact, I shall argue that it is only by infringing my right of ownership that others can possibly injure me when I assert myself as such a person. To show this, I start with the juridical conception of persons with their two moral powers and from this arrive at the proposed rationale and role of ownership.

As juridical persons with the first moral power noted above, our higher-order interest is in asserting our sheer independence from everything given. The question is, how must we show respect for persons who are so viewed? Stated otherwise, what does the reasonable require or constrain with regard to this interest?

The answer is not self-evidently obvious if we assume, as seems reasonable, that any applicable norm of respect would at least have to prohibit conduct that violates that interest, therefore presupposing that this interest can be infringed in the first place. For it is not immediately clear how this is possible. I have said that it would be wrong to impose external purposes on persons so viewed, this being incompatible with their self-relating moral nature. But how can persons who have the moral power of asserting their independence from everything given be *imposed* upon at all? Not by their own conduct in relation to themselves. No matter what I do in relation to myself and no matter what apparent restriction I set up for myself, I can simply dissipate it by consciously distancing myself from and thereby viewing it as *not* a restriction (hence as distinct from me). I need only assert my independence, which therefore remains untouched. What about others' conduct in relation to me? But here also, I can assert my independence and distance myself in thought from whatever they do to me—in chains I can still be free. It seems then that, taken by itself, my purely inward moral power for independence is beyond imposition or injury by anyone. But if this is so, how can there be an applicable requirement that constrains respect for it?

There would seem to be only one answer: it must be possible for me to express my inward power of independence externally in the here and now and *in this external existence* for me to be vulnerable to imposition and injury. It is true that, even with respect to any such external expression of myself, I can assert my independence and so cannot be bound to recognize it as a limit or constraint. I can also distance myself from any imposition on it by others. But that is the result of *my* assertion of independence in relation to something that expresses me. So far as *others* are concerned, however, this expression of myself remains external to them and they must treat it as something in which I am present and as something untouchable—unless or until I indicate to them otherwise. How *they* treat it has a moral significance that is distinct from the way that I view it solely in relation to myself. Here, respect is owed by persons with regard to something external to them, which they must take as expressing another's capacity for independence. This, I am suggesting, is the way respect for juridical personality is—and can *only* be—shown.[8]

To illustrate these rather abstract points, consider the right to bodily integrity. It seems obvious that I can exist as a responsible agent only insofar as I am alive in my body. Now my bodily existence is something definitely specific and external—something that is externally recognizable by others. It is true that I can reflectively withdraw into myself and in thought treat my body and my feelings as distinct from me, thereby asserting my inward independence from all this. That, however, is my decision. When others affect my body without my consent, they subject it to their decisions, not mine. Even if I choose to distance myself from what they have done, this does not dissipate the external fact that my body has been touched or affected by them in the pursuit of their unilateral purposes. This residual effect does not express or contain my self-relatedness.

Such unilateral imposition can be a matter of moral indifference only if we confine the existence of juridical personality to a subject's merely inward self-relatedness and deny the possibility of freedom having an external existence as well. Once, however, this possibility of freedom's external existence is accepted—and at this point in the argument I provisionally suppose this to be the case—the external existence of personality must be treated as untouchable, and therefore any unilateral imposition on another's body represents an injury to juridical personality itself. It is important to underline here that it is only this external existence that can be injured and that this can only be done by others. Because this requirement holds only in relation to others, it is fully consistent with the absolute and unfettered power of individuals to continue to assert, in relation to themselves, their independence from anything they do to themselves—including their own bodies.

With these preliminary points in mind, the next step is to explain why an imperative to respect juridical personhood should take the more specific form of a duty to recognize and to respect another's *right of ownership*.

Through this discussion, I hope to bring out more fully why we might view the possibility of juridical personality having external existence as morally compelling.[9]

The answer regarding the pertinence of ownership is found, once again, by following through the implications of persons having a higher-order interest in asserting their sheer independence from everything given. Now this standpoint implicitly entails the following basic normative contrast: persons as independent and self-relating separate units of responsibility versus whatever can properly be distinguished from them and therefore counts immediately as the contrary of personality, thus as what is *not* independent or inwardly self-relating—in other words something that counts as purely external, a "thing." As discussed above, consistently with their independence and self-relatedness, persons—and whatever expresses their personhood—cannot be unilaterally imposed upon or subjected to external purposes. They cannot be used merely as means. But this is not the case with things. By definition, they can be so used without infringing their normative character, when the relevant moral standpoint is that of freedom and more specifically the freedom of juridical personality.[10] In light of this contrast between nonusable persons and usable things, I wish to suggest—and will try to show—that when persons are recognized as subjects with a moral capacity to use things and at the same time are treated as themselves wholly beyond use, the moral significance of juridical personhood is expressed and respected externally in the here and now.

Now, offhand, this seems to fit exactly with what respect for private ownership entails. For the liberal conception of ownership supposes that certain acts—namely, those that consist in a person treating a thing, but only a thing, as usable and so as an object of external control—are to be respected by others. Respect here takes the shape of not interfering with or unilaterally imposing on this manifest exercise of control and use. By not interfering, others in effect recognize the act of exercising control as expressing the untouchable freedom of juridical personality. That ownership is individual, and exclusive—private—ownership fits with the fact that when persons assert their independence, they view themselves as separate selves. For it is this standpoint, if any, that must be expressed. Moreover, because ownership is always of some determinate object that can be used and therefore, being usable, must be contrasted with the sheer inward independence of personhood, both the object and the act of exercising control over it can count normatively as external and determinate expressions of the presence of personhood. Thus viewed, ownership would seem to be a basic and rudimentary way in which the immediate contrast between independent persons and usable things is expressed in the element of external relations, in this way exhibiting a person's freedom as something more than merely inward.

Emphatically, the whole normative significance of this external and determinate existence of juridical personality via ownership is entirely other-related. As owner, one is under no duty of respect with regard to one's own control over one's own thing. Thus individuals need not acquire anything in the first place or retain something once taken. All this is a matter of their arbitrary, unconstrained decision. An owner need not take his or her connection with the thing as in any way morally necessary, fixed, or untouchable. Only others must recognize his or her particular acts as morally salient and so view them as acts of ownership that must be respected. So far as others are concerned, the owner is present as person in his or her exercise of control; they must treat that connection as morally necessary and as beyond their unilateral reach or decision.

But at the same time, others are under such a duty only insofar as someone has already placed something under his or her present actual control, thereby recognizably superseding the pure inwardness of personality, which, we have seen, can never be affected or violated by others. Consistent with the organizing idea of liability for misfeasance, their duty of respect is therefore always based on a negative prohibition against interference with or injury to an actual, presently existing, exercise of control. It does not impose a positive duty on anyone to assist others to become or to remain owners, whether by ensuring that they have adequate means of doing so, that there are enough objects left for them to appropriate, and so forth.

There is a related point. We have supposed throughout, and it is axiomatic, that the requirement to respect ownership takes the form of correlative rights and duties between parties: one side has the right, the other the duty and the two sides refer not only to each other but also to the very same content (for example, a party's rightful holding of something).[11] The fundamental unit of analysis is always one person's duty of non-interference with respect to another's rightful control over something. Even where there is full reciprocity (as in an exchange) and each side has both a right and a duty, the analysis remains the same—only now there are *two* sets of correlative rights and duties, each of which is with respect to a *different* thing. At no point in this analysis does a party have *both* a right *and* a duty with respect to the *same* thing. Contrast this with, say, the parental relation, where a parent's right of supervision over her child is equally a duty to exercise such control for the child's well-being and proper development. The correlativity of rights and duties in private law is the way individuals necessarily relate when they respect each other as mutually exclusive private owners within the framework of misfeasance. One should not assume that it applies to other kinds of relations.[12]

The other-related and merely negative character of the requirement to respect ownership is consistent with, and may be viewed as reflecting, the further fundamental point that our inherent independence, and thus our freedom and equality as juridical persons, is complete whether or not we actually acquire or own anything. What makes us persons is simply the reflective power to assert our sheer independence from everything given, and for this we need not do anything in particular. But if and when we do something that manifests external control over an external thing, there is the moral basis for others to recognize in this the presence and act of juridical personhood. We may say, then, that all persons as independent and equal have an inherent and identical capacity for ownership, which, if exercised in the here and now, must be recognized and respected by others as an act of ownership and all that this entails.

According to the proposed normative analysis, when individuals are respected as owners on the basis of their exercise of control over things, this cannot be in virtue of their particularity. To the contrary, it rests on the moral possibility of viewing their acts as expressing nothing but their power to assert their independence from everything particular, including from their needs, particular interests, and circumstances. In respect of this power, all are the same. Thus, while it is a single individual who asserts control, it embodies nothing but what is universal and identical in all. Therefore, the requirement of respect cannot rest on the fact that ownership furthers individual needs, interests, or well-being, but rather expresses the equality of others as juridical persons. It is not as this particular individual with particular needs, purposes, and circumstances, but only as someone who counts abstractly and identically as a juridical person and so as representative of just anyone and everyone, that someone is respected as an owner. Recognition of another's ownership shows simply that juridical personhood as such, which is identical in everyone, is something that can and must be respected in the here and now.

Finally, we may ask: why is it morally important that freedom not remain merely inward but also be recognized in this external way? A first point is that there is nothing in the analysis of freedom as independence that precludes this possibility. Viewing a person's exercise of control over things as expressing this independence and as worthy of respect does not compromise his or her independence in any way when this view is from the standpoint of others and is binding on them within the parameters of a negative duty against interference. Beyond this, the following may be said. Were the role of freedom to be confined to the merely inward assertion of abstracting from the given, this would mean that freedom could neither be expressed in actual human conduct in the here and now nor be shown to be something untouchable and nonusable—in other words, something that must be respected as a matter of reasonableness. If so, the standpoint of freedom would inexplicably and indeed arbitrarily preclude the inward potentiality for action, as entailed by the inward stance of asserting independence, from being realized and expressed in action and choice. There could be no moral world that appropriately actualizes this conception of juridical freedom as independence. This transition from inward to external freedom must therefore be morally possible. And supposing that the right of individual ownership is how this inward freedom is expressed and respected in the external world, such ownership must also be morally possible. More exactly, it must be possible to require of persons that they recognize and respect each other's acts that appropriately exercise control over things as rightful acts of ownership. From the standpoint of freedom, ownership acquisition, though not obligatory, is protected by a permissive law of our freedom. Hence, the requirement to respect our capacity for ownership and the results of its proper exercise.

With these preliminary and general points about the relation between juridical personality and ownership in mind, I would like now to discuss more specifically how contract, as a form of transactional acquisition and as a transfer of ownership, reflects this same moral basis. To do so, I propose to elucidate contract as one step in a sequence comprising the right of bodily integrity, original acquisition, and finally contract, where each is considered as a way of embodying freedom as independence. Since the following builds on my earlier discussion of these rights in Chapter 10, some overlap between them is unavoidable.

We begin, then, with the right of bodily integrity (physical and psychological) as the sine qua non of any further mode of the external determinate existence of free and equal juridical persons. It is a fact that it is only as being alive in my body that I exist in the here and now. But because of my moral power to distance myself in thought from everything given, including even my life itself, my body counts as a protected interest only as against others. When freedom consists in the power to assert our sheer independence, only others can be constrained to treat me and my body as one and the same. Consistent with the nature of freedom as independence, this constraint imposes on them merely a negative prohibition against interference with my bodily integrity, without any requirement to assist, preserve, or benefit me. Anything more than such a negative duty owed by others would have to be based on something other than respect for my moral power to be independent from everything given, which, as emphasized already, involves independence from needs, satisfaction of substantive interests, and so on. The right of bodily integrity expresses only juridical personality and nothing else.

Now this right against others vests in individuals simply in virtue of their being alive without their having to do anything to establish it. Whatever we do, we are already and always present in our bodies. The notion that we might have to do something in order to have this right is self-stultifying; since I can only act qua alive in my body, the needed act could not produce rightful juridical effects imputable to me unless I already had this very right with respect to my body. Thus the right of bodily integrity is best characterized as "innate" rather than as "acquired." For the same reason, it is neither necessary nor helpful to construe it as a form of ownership because our bodies are not "things" that we bring within a protected sphere by subjecting them to our control and purposes. Rather, our bodies count simply and immediately as the very way in which we exist in time and space as distinct persons—our individuated identity in relation to everything else. Because the right of bodily integrity is innate and individuates me externally as an independent and separate person vis-à-vis others, it is conceptually the first way, and indeed is the necessary condition of any other way, in which I count as a self-authenticating source of valid claims.

Being innate, one's right in one's body must be respected by others even before one has exercised actual control. So what is protected is a person's mere capacity to exercise control—the pure potentiality of doing so. For if it is a question as to whether another has violated my right of bodily integrity, the injury is always with respect to some aspect (physical or psychological) of my bodily existence, even where I am touched or affected while I am in the process of doing something. The fact that my *action* may have been interfered with is not distinguished as a relevant moral consideration in its own right. At the same time, the reason why my body is untouchable is because it belongs to one who can choose. From this standpoint, the difference between body and act is merely that between, respectively, a power or potentiality and its realization. But it is in the very nature of a potential to be realized. If we accept—as we do—the right of bodily integrity, we cannot, without evident arbitrariness, refuse the transition to a form of rightful relation that makes *acts themselves* the basis of claims and the vehicle of expressing in the here and now our status as independent juridical persons. It must be possible for action itself to be an object of respect.

This further development can only be via ownership of things. If one's acts, as such, are to be accorded moral significance as the expression of juridical personhood, then, as I tried to explain above, these acts must consist in the exercise of exclusive individual control over things in relation to others. This is the only aspect that is morally relevant from this standpoint, which exhaustively divides the moral world into persons and usable things. The fundamental norm against treating my bodily existence as a thing clearly presupposes and enshrines this moral difference between persons and things. But this distinction between person and thing is even more explicitly and fully expressed in the right of ownership: for in ownership, as contrasted with the right of bodily integrity, not only the moral necessity of respecting persons but also the moral possibility of using things are simultaneously and jointly affirmed in one single principle. Ownership counts conceptually as a further and more complete development of the normative meaning implicit in the right of bodily integrity.

Earlier, I argued that to be genuinely irreducible to aspects of one's bodily integrity, the acts of ownership must establish exclusive control over things that can be represented as separable from one's body and protected as such.[13] There are, we saw, two modes of doing this: original or first acquisition and derivative (including contractual) acquisition. In order to make clear the distinctive way in which contract expresses the freedom and equality of juridical persons, we must first reconsider, even briefly, the basis and role of first possession or property.

As discussed earlier, acquisition by first possession is effectuated by a person's unilateral external act alone, representing to others the present and complete subjection of a separable physical thing to her control without the participation of anyone else. The normative meaning of this act is wholly other-related, holding potentially against indeterminate others in general. Rightful control vests with the first in occupancy, not others, who not only can no longer rightfully make the object their own without the possessor's consent (which is her immunity and their disability) but, further, are prohibited from doing anything to it that conflicts with the possessor's exclusive right of control (which is their duty). By treating the thing as not subject to their power and use, others recognize the possessor's act of control as beyond reach and as untouchable, and, by implication, they show respect to the presence of the person whose will the act embodies. Because it is the determinate existence of a person's will that is the object of respect, an actual and continuous physical connection with the thing cannot be morally necessary. What is necessary is simply that the will's presence via control be recognizable by others. We can now see that to require such continuous physical connection would contradict the capacity for independence that is definitive of juridical personality. Hence, first acquisition must reflect the juridical possibility of nonphysical possession.

Moreover, the right in original acquisition is and must be open-ended in the sense that the uses the owner can make of her thing are not specified in advance or in terms of any set of determinate purposes. What counts is simply whether use involves an exercise of present and effective control over something, and because there is nothing in the normative characterizations of either abstract juridical personhood or things that precludes things from being put to uses and purposes of any and every sort, no such limit can be inferred. Here, as elsewhere, the content and the scope of the right are wholly regulated by the fundamental contrast between person and thing—and thus the direct relation of control by person over thing—as this reasonably appears to others in general.

It is only if and when someone reasonably appears to have actually subordinated something to her power that there is a morally significant act that engages the imperative to respect juridical personhood and whatever this entails. There is no positive obligation to act in a way that enables or ensures that others have the opportunity to acquire. This limit reflects what respect for our moral nature as juridical persons requires. As I have tried to emphasize, persons do not need (and so have neither a duty nor even a right, as opposed to a mere power or capacity) to acquire anything in order to be mutually independent as understood within the framework of misfeasance. It is this power or capacity to appropriate that is inherent in juridical personality. What must be respected is just their capacity for ownership and whatever is established through its actual and effective exercise. As long as others do not prevent or interfere with the actual exercise of my capacity for ownership or impair the fruits of its exercise, my right of ownership is not not violated even though their own effective appropriation leaves little or even nothing for me to acquire. My capacity remains intact and untouched—it's just that there happens to be nothing upon which I can exercise it. At the same time, the fact that only a present, completed act of control establishes the right clearly shows that, within this framework, an individual's needs, preferences, wishes, or purposes do not, as such, give rise to any claims. Consistent with the framework of misfeasance and its basis in the moral powers of juridical persons, the possibility of individual original acquisition of something and the no-claims of others with respect to whatever is thus acquired are simply two sides of the same analysis. Both express the freedom and equality of juridical persons.

However, the full and complete operation of the principle of original acquisition in any given instance results in just one person acquiring something to the exclusion of others: it effectuates the merely nonreciprocated recognition by one side of the other's ownership powers and rights. Yet, given the identity between individuals as juridical persons, my assertion of a claim against others can only be valid if, at the same time and as part of the same principle, I also am reciprocally under a disability and duty with respect to their acquisitions. This must be intrinsic to the very basis of my claim. While in first acquisition reciprocity is reflected negatively and implicitly in the precondition of appropriation that requires the thing to be presently ownerless, the positive constitutive elements of first appropriation do not affirm the equal capacity for ownership of those who are excluded by its operation. There is no explicit and actual mutuality of recognition. But this is what the abstract equality of juridical persons requires.

To satisfy such equality, the necessary and sufficient requirements for appropriation must specify a bilateral relation in which each party acquires ownership (i.e., rightful exclusive control over something) just insofar as this involves mutual recognition by both of their rightful individual capacities for ownership. Now since, within the misfeasance framework, such recognition can only be with respect to what *already* belongs to another, mutual recognition must be as between two parties, each of whom counts and is recognized inter se as an actual owner of something. But, further, because we are seeking a principle of acquisition, the relation must be one, perhaps paradoxically, in which each party acquires from the other only on the condition that both sides remain and are recognized throughout as owners. This is what is conceptually required if there is to be a form of acquisition that is truly distinct from first acquisition by being fully reciprocal and bilateral. Acquisition must become transactional and be realized as a transfer of ownership.

The central feature of this new relation is that, as a condition of transactional acquisition, each party must recognize the other as an actual owner even as she obtains or yields rightful control, respectively, from or to the other. Consistently with the present framework of juridical personality, this requirement does not mean that parties must subjectively and conscientiously view each other in this way or that they are under any duty to adopt recognition of the other as their obligatory end—for as juridical persons, they do not have any such ends. The standpoint being external and transactional, it suffices if parties have interacted in such a way that each can reasonably be held to have recognized the other's actual ownership.

Now, for the condition of reciprocal acquisition to be satisfied, it is essential that the thing acquired must be appropriated or alienated as already under the other's rightful exclusive control or ownership. In other words, I appropriate it from you *as* something that you own, and it becomes mine *in* that condition. There cannot be conceptually even an instant when it ceases to be yours before I appropriate it. For if this happens, I can only acquire the thing in the condition of being unowned, not as something alienated by you to me. Accordingly, the acts of alienation and appropriation must be at the same time in the sense that they are represented as being simultaneous and copresent.[14] Moreover, since there cannot be a gap with respect to what is transferred, the parties must have rightful control over the same thing at the same time. Being owners of the same thing at the same time, the parties count—and objectively recognize each other—as abstractly *identical* persons with a capacity for ownership. If, then, the parties' mutual recognition as owners is to be objectively reflected in their transaction, it must be possible to construe their transaction in this way. It is this relationship of mutual recognition that is now the determinate element in which the parties' freedom and equality as juridical persons with the two moral powers exists.

Beginning with the normative conception of the person with a higher-order interest in asserting sheer independence, this is how ownership must be established and expressed if it is to fill out and complete the normative advance that original acquisition represents vis-à-vis bodily integrity. This goes beyond a merely interpretative claim that the transactional conception of contract fits with contract law and even the further argument, developed in Chapter 10, that to view it as a transfer of ownership is consistent with an underlying notion of ownership. My contention here is that this conception of contract—not less than property ownership—is an essential mode of recognizing and respecting the normative view of ourselves as free and equal juridical persons.

From this standpoint, how, more specifically, does contract law embody the juridical conception of the person? First, by entirely detaching the normatively determinative dimension from the physical conditions of holding and delivery and by placing it squarely with the relation between wills, contract represents a mode of acquisition that is fully consistent with the independence of personality. As participants in this relation, each side counts vis-à-vis the other as an exclusive and independent juridical self. But precisely because the relation of will to will is, in Hegel's words, "the true and proper ground in which freedom is existent," it is intrinsically necessary, because expressive of the power of independence, that this relation be the sole and exhaustive source of right so far as the parties' voluntary interaction goes, and hence that there be a clear normative separation between this ideal utterance consisting of their agreement and the physical execution of its terms.[15] The former is definitively regulative of the latter's juridical meaning and consequences. Further, because this relation of will to will exists in the medium of representational acts that are objectively viewed as communications of meanings, the inherent tendency is that this relation be expressed explicitly in the intellectual form of a unified declaration that embodies the parties' joint decision. The moment of agreement has a purely ideal determinate existence, which most suitably is embodied in language or other symbolic form; and, being a medium of communication that has a determinate content and context, the agreement consists not just in express stipulations, but also in implied terms. The existence of this implied dimension must be presupposed as an internal and organic feature of every contract.

If, as I am suggesting, the contractual agreement embodies the independence of juridical personality, it should represent the parties, acts, and objects as abstractly identical on both sides. This means, negatively, that their particularity and their differences are not per se contractually relevant and, positively, that the parties count throughout as abstractly equal (identical) owners exercising acts of ownership with respect to things that figure simply as determinate objects of ownership. This is the case.

At contract formation, the legal characterization of the elements of the contractual relation treats the two sides as absolutely identical in these very ways. Contract formation (i.e., the moment when an offer and its acceptance meet) is constituted by mutual and identical assents to identical terms that represent the parties at the same time as identically and reciprocally giving up and taking exclusive control of objects that count abstractly as a determinate something of value in the eye of the law. Because, at this instant, each side acquires something only insofar as he or she gives in return and both aspects are necessarily interconnected without reference to temporal succession, each side remains identically in rightful control of something of value irrespective of the particular features of what is promised. This is possible because their relation is viewed as a single unified transaction in accordance with the objective test and independent of any aspect of physical holding. But it is the conceptualization of the substance of the considerations as exchange value that brings out with full clarity contract's abstraction from particularity and its being an expression of the parties' abstract equality.

Exchange value is how the particular and qualitatively different things figure when given a determinate form that is purely relational and that abstracts from their qualitative differences, specifying them in purely quantitative terms. Therefore, value represents the determinate existence of objects viewed, not in their particularity, but simply and abstractly as usable things that can be appropriated and transferred as between free and equal juridical persons. What it makes determinate is their abstract normative significance (viz., that they are things identically and permissibly usable) and not their differing particular features. Represented in this way, objects refer to those who exercise exclusive control over them: the presence of the wills of mutually independent persons. They represent objectified free activity.[16] The substantive content of the transfer is now specified in accordance with its essential normative meaning, supposing that the relevant standpoint is that of juridical personality. In this way, contract fully completes first appropriation as a mode of expressing the freedom and equality of juridical persons in the medium of conduct and interaction.

Moreover, once the objects are analyzed in terms of exchange value, it becomes clear why equivalence is a supreme regulative principle of justice in transactions. By alienating and appropriating different things of the quantitatively same value, the parties acquire on condition of each having the very same abstract property throughout the transaction and they objectively recognize each other as being actual owners of the very same thing at the same time. This, I suggested above, is essential to the conceptual possibility of a transfer of ownership (in contrast to first acquisition) and to the transfer enshrining (and respecting) the parties' absolute identity and equality as owners. Value is the dimension of abstract equality of the objects of a transfer paralleling the abstract equality of the parties who do the transfer. It is the universal dimension in which the subjects of the contract participate.[17] Moreover, it is this abstract identity between objects as value coupled with the parallel abstract identity between parties as owners of such value—all effectuated in and through the medium of the parties' mutual recognition—that explains not only the possibility of the continuity of the same protected interest on both sides of the transaction but also the very possibility of a transfer of ownership prior to delivery in the first place.[18]

There is a related point about value to be made here. Value reflects the alienability of whatever one owns. If, as I have argued, contract can be viewed as a form of ownership acquisition, there should be the possibility of treating the contractual asset acquired at formation as itself alienable or, in other words, as a chose in action. This possibility must be a potential intrinsic to every contract. Of course, arising from transactional acquisition, the parameters of this asset are specified by the contract terms. But still, it must be possible within these limits to view what a person acquires contractually as itself a valuable asset that is potentially alienable and is always protected. A party's title in his or her contract right has as its object the asset so viewed. This, I suggest, is the rational basis of the possibility of assignment and more broadly of the different kinds of third-party quasi-proprietary effects of contracts discussed earlier.

In the interpretative discussion of the principle of unconscionability, I suggested that it must be understood as resting on a baseline presumption reasonably imputed to all parties that they intend to transact for equal value.[19] We can now see why this is morally necessary. For in this way, the parties necessarily express their equal juridical personality, and therefore this may be reasonably imputed to them as such persons. The principle of equivalence and the idea of bilateral relation that this presupposes are thus inherent to contract when it is viewed as a transfer of ownership and as embodying the juridical conception of the person. At the same time, in light of the parties' power to assert their independence, it cannot be either obligatory or required for persons to transact only for equal value. Just as one may freely choose to abandon or destroy one's thing under the principles of original acquisition, so here one may freely decide to give one's thing to another for something of lesser value or even approaching nothing at all in return: a gift rather than an exchange. The baseline assumption reasonably imputed to parties is that they intend to transfer for equal value and this is not violated, but is in fact honored, if departures from this must be justified on the basis of a party's donative intent or assumption of risk, reasonably and positively manifested in their transaction. Such a justified unequal exchange is fully consistent with the parties' abstract equality and their power to obtain equal value in return. We see here that the division of transactions into the two categories of gift and exchange is not only an ultimate classification of transaction-types but one that is wholly intrinsic to the concept of contract.[20]

This requirement of equivalence is normative and more exactly juridical, not economic. Precisely because it reflects the abstract equality of the parties, the relation is expressed in purely quantitative terms. Equivalence or the equality between thing and thing is thus the transactional sign of the equality of persons as owners. At the highest, this requirement stipulates only that individuals respect each other's equal power or entitlement to receive the value of what is *already* his or her own. It does not aim to redress differences in bargaining power per se or unfair and unequal starting points, nor does it ensure the satisfaction of needs, however urgent. This is consistent with the limits of the standpoint of juridical personality, which involves independence from needs altogether. The principle of equal value in contract is purely transactional and nondistributive in character.

The principle of equivalence is carried forward in the law's coercive redress of wrongs under compensatory justice. In the discussion of remedies for breach, I emphasized that compensatory justice requires that there be an underlying identity between injury and remedy, but because these two events are viewed in legal contemplation as qualitatively different things, this identity must be expressed as equivalence: to annul the wrong, the coercive response must represent and measure its value as a wrong, upholding the plaintiff's right and immunity as far as possible in the circumstances of breach. Further, compensatory justice for breach reflects and continues the same transactional-external normative analysis expressing the same juridical notion of respect that underpins contract formation. Because parties' purposes are not per se morally salient when they are viewed as juridical persons with the moral power for independence and a capacity for ownership, the remedial response can only operate as an external annulment of the wrong coercively enforced against the defendant; its justification need not depend on the defendant conscientiously adopting the response as his or her end.

A final point. In the whole account of rights, the principle of equal value first appears as a requirement of contract formation which, I have argued, embodies the private law idea of transaction in its pure and complete form. Because this principle stipulates equality between thing and thing in transactions, it explicitly and fully expresses the idea of corrective or commutative justice: a requirement of arithmetic equality in and for transactions.[21] Now within the framework of misfeasance, the establishment and existence of rights is normatively and conceptually presupposed by—and hence prior to—the analysis of wrongs. If so, the meaning and the role of transactional equality in the different kinds of involuntary transactions as well as in remedial justice should be understood in light of its meaning and operation in contract formation, as the pure form of voluntary transaction. Justice in contract is the paradigm of justice in transactions.

11.3. Concluding Remarks

In this chapter, I have tried to show that reasonable terms of interaction, which constrain individuals to act consistently with respect for others as free and equal persons, can include a requirement to recognize everyone's identical capacity for private ownership and whatever this entails by way of its exercise and embodiment. The more specific conception of the person on which this rests takes individuals as having a higher-order interest in a moral power of asserting their sheer independence vis-à-vis everything particular and given. Being specified for juridical relations only, this conception of the person and of our autonomy is not generally appropriate for moral relations in general. At the same time, because this conception views persons as having simply this negative power to distinguish themselves from what is given, it represents an utterly minimal notion of freedom without which it seems impossible to understand ourselves as unconditionally (i.e., truly) free and accountable sources of activity, worthy of respect. And in keeping with the nature of a public basis of justification, it is presented as implicit in and accessible to our ordinary reflective experience when we view ourselves as responsible agents in relations with others.

My core contention is that the right of ownership expresses respect for, and so is based upon, this specific conception of ourselves as free and equal persons: juridical persons with the power to assert our independence from everything given. My argument has been that there are three basic modes of embodying this minimal but nevertheless essential conception of freedom—namely, bodily integrity, property (original acquisition), and contract (derivative acquisition)—and that it is in contract, conceived as a transfer of ownership, that this conception is most fully realized. Without these three ways of expressing freedom, the meaning of freedom as sheer independence would not be recognized or respected in the actions of purposive and responsible beings, resulting in an unbridgeable gap in the coherent and complete articulation of the world of freedom. Similarly, acceptance of bodily integrity but rejection of property or contract would be arbitrary and incomplete from a moral point of view based on this juridical conception of freedom.

I wish to emphasize the very limited nature of the moral powers ascribed to individuals as juridical persons. In this juridical conception of the person, the fact that parties have and pursue determinate purposes and notions of their good does not have positive moral significance in itself, nor is it a basis for making any claims against others. The moral power that they assert is merely the negative ability to distance themselves *from* everything given to them, including any determinate end that they may happen to want to fulfill. Strictly speaking, therefore, this power, though it may be presupposed by, is not the same as a capacity to have and to pursue a conception of one's good.[22] It also follows that this conception of the juridical person provides no basis for specifying any notion of substantive goods that parties may be presumed to want and need as such persons.[23] Things do not count as owned by being goods or even means that one needs in order to pursue one's purposes but simply because, through the connection of control between persons and things, there is something to recognize and respect as a determinate expression of the existence of juridical personality in the here and now. Unless the account of ownership preserves but at the same time does not incorporate anything beyond this limited formal interest in parties' asserting their independence *from,* it is not based on and so does not express this conception of the person. Nor can it fit with the framework of liability for misfeasance only. For once purpose and need have any genuinely positive moral significance, the difference, so fundamental for misfeasance, between *already* and *not yet* having something cannot be per se decisive. To the contrary, justice would require that individuals have their fair share of what is needed by them to develop and pursue their conceptions of their good.

It is important to be clear about the role of contingencies and endowments in this account of acquisition. Certainly, contingencies do affect the course of acquisition—think of how pure luck and speed enabled the "saucy intruder" in *Pierson* to take the fox when the plaintiff, after hours of laborious pursuit, was just on the verge of capturing it.[24] For this reason, it may also seem that the principles of acquisition reward the successful claimant as deserving on the basis of these factors, however arbitrary these may be from a moral point of view.

This is not so. These principles do not reward anything at all, nor do they express a norm of moral desert in this sense. The only morally salient factor is this: someone has recognizably exercised control over something (either ownerless or transferred) for his or her own purposes. While this condition is always determined by contingent factors, it is not in virtue of any of these factors that the claimant's right of ownership is respected. To the contrary, as I have tried to emphasize, when we count as juridical persons, all these factors are devoid of any inherent moral significance and are viewed as such. Hence persons as owners do not count in their particularity, nor are they respected in these terms. Instead, a claimant's act is respected only because it manifests in the here and now the independence of juridical personality from all such factors and what this entails, namely, the normative difference between persons and things. Respect for a given claimant's ownership is necessary because in this way—and only in this way—is it possible to respect anyone as a juridical person with the power, identical in all, to assert one's independence from everything given. Necessarily, it is a given person as representative of everyone who is and must be the recipient of such respect.

Moreover, reflecting this limited standpoint of independence from particularities and liability for misfeasance, the requirement to respect ownership does not aim to maintain or to ensure some minimum of actual ownership for everyone, nor does it require individuals to appropriate at all. Rather, it simply affirms each person's inherent capacity for ownership—*as a capacity*—and it applies if and when individuals have actually appropriated something consistently with the principles of acquisition. Whether individuals choose to do so and the patterns of holdings (however unequal) that result are matters of indifference from this completely nondistributive juridical standpoint. These factors cannot affect the equal capacity for ownership or respect for it. The other side of this coin, which I take up and develop in Chapter 12, is that respect for this capacity for ownership does not positively require that there is ownership of anything in particular, including productive assets, or perhaps more surprisingly, that there is even a sphere of things available for private appropriation at all.[25] The right of ownership does not necessarily mandate, we will see, a libertarian theory of ownership claims or a capitalist system of production and distribution. What it enjoins is only this: supposing that there are things available for individual appropriation, no one may be arbitrarily barred from exercising his or her capacity for ownership or be injured in what he or she has acquired by exercising it in the requisite ways.

To conclude this discussion of the moral basis of contract, I would like briefly to return to the fundamental question of why contracts bind. Throughout, I have argued against the interpretative validity of approaches to contract law that invoke or depend on either the moral duty to keep one's promises or the idea that one is bound just because one intends or undertakes that obligation. The proposed account of the moral basis of contract in juridical personality reinforces this rejection. Clearly, the moral duty to keep one's promises rests on and brings into play normative factors that go well beyond the limited nature of respect for juridical personality in external relations. I shall discuss this further in Chapter 12. As for the view of contract as a form of robustly self-imposed obligation, this treats individual purposes as in themselves morally salient, indeed as duty-imposing—something that also goes beyond the conception of juridical persons, whose moral powers just consist negatively in the capacity to stand back from all substantive purposes and interests whatsoever. This precludes any such purpose-based justifications.

Instead, the approach that I have proposed takes a very different route that starts with the following idea: in light of each party's reciprocal decision to engage the other in an unambiguously and equally active two-sided relation, each can hold the other to the reasonable juridical meaning and implications of their voluntary interaction viewed as a relation or transactionally. It is the law that specifies this juridical meaning, and in doing so it expresses nothing but the reasonable in transactions. In legal contemplation, the parties' mutually related promises function as representations, which, insofar as they can be reasonably viewed as manifesting present complete decisions to move something of value from the exclusive control of one party into that of the other party, are attributed a juridical meaning in terms of ownership and a transfer of ownership. Intention is just a constitutive element of the requisite acts and has no independent role.

There is the following parallel between first possession and contract. In both, parties do certain definite voluntary acts that have operative juridical significance. In first possession, by taking physical possession of some thing, one is deemed to exercise ownership such that others can no longer make it their own and must not affect it without one's consent. In contract, a party also exercises her capacity for ownership, only here by giving up her thing in a way that yields it to another's rightful exclusive control and thereby enables the latter to take ownership of it via transactional acquisition. Both taking possession and alienation are definitive expressions of ownership, and a party can no more abjure the juridical meaning and effect of the exercise of her power of alienation as part of transactional acquisition than others can deny the juridical meaning of the exercise of her power of taking possession as the basis of original acquisition. In this way, juridical reason requires that it be morally possible to treat a promisor's contractual assent as an act of irrevocable alienation that vests ownership with the promisee at formation. This simply expresses the basic premise that persons are under a duty of right to conduct themselves in relation to others such that their interaction can, where applicable, be construed in terms of ownership.[26] Holding both parties to the juridical meaning of their interaction recognizes and respects them as free and equal persons with the moral power to be unconditionally independent in the face of everything given. The basis of parties being bound is thus the moral possibility of the realization of this fundamental and minimal juridical notion of freedom and responsibility. In this way, we express the moral fact of our juridical autonomy.

This completes my account of contract as a transfer of ownership. I have tried to show not only that this way of viewing contract is plausible as an interpretative matter, and in fact allows for a unified understanding of the different contract doctrines, but also that it reflects a notion of reasonableness and justice properly owed to individuals who can see themselves and others as free and equal juridical persons. There is still, however, a further final step in working out a public basis of justification for contract. It is not about the suitability of the proposed conception of contract as an interpretation of the law or about the moral basis of this conception taken by itself, but rather about the relations between this conception and other moral and social domains with which it may harmonize or not. Drawing here again on Rawls's approach, this final step concerns the normative stability and legitimacy of this conception of contract when it is assessed within this wider context. Chapter 12, the next and last chapter, is devoted to these questions.

Chapter 12

The Stability of Contract as Transfer

The public basis of justification for contract law as developed here comprises three steps. First, a conception of contract is worked up from the main contract doctrines and principles as a plausible interpretation of the law that aims to bring out contract law's unity and coherence in this complexity. This conception, I have argued, is contract as a form of transactional acquisition. Second, contract so understood must be shown to be reasonable in its own terms, consistent with fundamental and pervasive private law ideas such as ownership, and expressive of a suitably specified standpoint of justice that embodies a view of persons as free and equal. As part of this second step, contract as a form of transactional acquisition is explained as a transfer of ownership reflecting what I have called a juridical conception of person and relation. The third step, which I now take up in this chapter, addresses the question of the stability of this juridical conception of contract. What does this entail?

The question of stability is particularly important to vindicating legal and political conceptions that purport to be liberal and founded in public reason. As Rawls emphasizes in his discussion of the stability of his political conception of justice, the point of stability is not that a conception of justice should merely avoid futility.[1] Rather, according to Rawls, stability means that this conception should, when realized under favorable circumstances and in accordance with its aims, generate the right kind of support: on due reflection, citizens, as free and equal as well as reasonable and rational persons, must be able to endorse the conception not only as fair but also as congruent with their individual and social good. At the same time, I would add that the account of stability should reflect the specific kind of normative conception that is at stake—here, a juridical private law conception of contract as a transfer of ownership.

To see what stability might mean for this juridical conception of contract, we must therefore keep in mind its core distinctive features, such as its moral basis in the juridical conception of the person and the kind of social relationship that embodies this conception, reflecting the limited idea of liability for misfeasance. We have seen that the higher-order moral interest that parties have as juridical persons is in asserting their sheer independence from everything given or particular, with the consequence that their particular interests, needs, purposes, preferences, and subjective understandings are per se irrelevant to the contractual analysis of their relation. Given that the goal of this higher-order interest is merely negative independence from all these factors, the conception of justice that reflects it is similarly indifferent to the satisfaction of substantive needs and purposes and does not rely on an account of primary goods. The parties' equality consists just in their being abstractly equal or identical in such a way that, while this requires equivalence in exchange as a regulative transactional principle, it is per se indifferent to considerations coming under distributive justice. As I have presented it, the normative conception animating the principles of contract is categorically distinct from promissory morality, independent of economic norms, and nondistributive in character.

Yet contracts always involve promises, are the stuff of market relations, and are part of a greater system that embodies norms of distributive justice. Unless the specific conception of contract that I have argued for does not conflict but indeed is compatible with these other domains, this would seem to challenge its stability. It could not be fully accepted by citizens from these other standpoints. Accordingly, the particular question of stability posed here is this: given its distinct normative character, is the proposed conception of contract in tension with the point of view of conscientious promisors who also take seriously their moral duty to keep their promises, with the requirements of a market system, or with the fulfillment of reasonable distributive principles? As I now hope to show, not only is there no incompatibility between contract and these other imperatives, but they mutually support each other as distinct but integrated aspects of a more complete scheme of morality and justice. I begin with the relation between contract and promissory morality.

12.1. Between Contractual Obligation and Promissory Duty

Contracts are enforceable promises, and prima facie the moral duty to keep one's promises should apply to these no less than to other promissory commitments. At the same time, not only does the proposed conception of contract as transfer not invoke the moral duty to keep one's promise. We have also seen in earlier chapters that the key features which the transactional conception identifies as indispensable to the kind of bilateral relation that constitutes contract are precisely those that sharply differentiate it from a binding gratuitous promise, as the latter is viewed in everyday morality. Think of the objective test for contract formation and interpretation, the requirement of consideration, the idea of strict contractual liability within the framework of misfeasance, the exclusion of all considerations of purpose, regret and mistake, changed circumstances, save those that come within the limited and objective parameters of the doctrines of impossibility, frustration or mistake, the definition of breach, the role of mitigation, the analysis of coercive compensatory remedies, and so forth. Does this divergence give rise to an internal tension from the standpoint and motivations of morally conscientious persons who take seriously their duty to keep their promises, including importantly their gratuitous promises?[2] Is there anything in the juridical conception of contract that stands in the way of or, even worse, that directly or indirectly undermines the possibility of their wholehearted commitment to their fulfillment of promissory duty and therefore of their being able morally to endorse the juridical conception itself as an appropriate ordering principle even for strictly contractual relations?

The way to an answer, I suggest, lies in recognizing that the qualitative differences between contractual obligation and morally binding promissory duty specify two distinct kinds of normative relations, neither of which excludes the other as an intrinsically reasonable conception that is fully applicable and binding within its own proper framework. Let me elaborate.

To begin, unlike purely moral promissory duty, contractual obligation is specified in terms of a coercible external relation of rights. As I explained in detail, the main doctrines and features of contract law carve out a kind of two-sided strictly bilateral relation that fits with the principle of liability for misfeasance only. The objective test and the conception of liability being strict apply only because the parties' relation is established by their coequal participation, which vests exclusive rightful control in each from and as against the other. These features are part and parcel of a purely transactional analysis in which neither the parties' actual intentions nor their purposes are as such the source of their obligations or even per se contractually relevant. As noted earlier, given the way they have voluntarily interacted with each other, parties can recognize the reasonableness of their being held to this relational standpoint; and, supposing that something like the proposed account of contract is correct, they should also accept these doctrines and features as reasonable once this relational standpoint is applied. On this view, contract law is clearly understood as embodying a genuine normative conception of obligation, which binds parties as a matter of rights and reasonableness and which is vindicated by remedies that, in legal contemplation, treat breach as a civil wrong and hence as subject to coercive redress in accordance with the idea of compensatory justice. At no point does the proposed conception regard the promisor as having a legally recognized liberty to perform or pay damages or view remedies as being a "license fee" for permitted or even tolerated nonperformance. To the contrary, it categorically and consistently affirms the promisee's immunity from any and all acts or omissions that are inconsistent with his or her acquired contractual rights.

Now I take it to be a widely accepted ethical idea that we are under a general moral duty to act not only in accordance with but also from respect for others' rights.[3] In other words, ethics enjoins as a formal general moral duty that we should adopt respect for others' rights as one of our own obligatory ends. From a legal point of view, it is true, such conscientious respect is not required by the juridical conception of coercible obligation within its own framework of misfeasance. Thus contract law is indifferent to parties' actual motivations and inward intentions; it cares only that they do not act inconsistently with the contract terms. But this does not preclude such intention being morally relevant from a different standpoint. And so the law's indifference to motivation can be compatible with ethics commanding that parties act from respect for each other's rights as contractually established. This ethical standpoint can apply to the legal duty to perform under a contract precisely because the parties' contractual rights and duties can be justified as genuine and reasonable normative requirements of mutual respect (and not as mere markers of efficient activity) that express what they owe each other as free and equal juridical persons on the basis of their jointly voluntary relational point of view. And inasmuch as the legal obligation to perform engages a promisor's commitment as to future conduct, his or her conscientious execution of this commitment can also be required as a matter of ethical duty.

This ethical duty applies to the legal contractual obligation, the content of which it takes as given. In terms of its *form*, the ethical duty remains distinct from the latter merely juridical obligation. At the same time, because this ethical duty applies to an already existing juridical obligation as its substantive substratum, it does not as such require parties to act for the sake of anything more than what is established, or what they must reasonably recognize, as their actual obligations correlative to the other party's legal rights. Thus, the duty is compatible with self-seeking, even at the expense of others, as long as this does not injure what is recognizably under the latters' rights. If, for example, there is a bona fide dispute over the existence or interpretation of contractual terms, neither party—even as a matter of such ethical duty—is obliged to yield to the other's point of view or accede to the other's demands. In fulfilling this duty of ethics, one can certainly stand on one's own rights even as one must act from respect for the rights of others. This is only plausible because the underlying substantive duty is juridical, as distinct from moral, and is therefore specified in terms of mutually exclusive rights of control as between independent persons.

By specifying a morally appropriate (indeed obligatory) end for contracting parties, this ethical duty goes beyond merely juridical obligations that abstract from all such determinate purposes. The possibility of this ethical orientation shows that parties can conscientiously commit to complying with their contractual terms as a way of acting from requirements of mutual respect and that, to this extent, there need be no conflict between the transactional juridical conception and the standpoint of individual morality. A morally motivated person can conscientiously and fully endorse the juridical conception from within his or her moral viewpoint. Indeed, he or she can and will do so from duty, even apart from the threat of a legal sanction for failing to perform. In contrast with a purely economic analysis, there is nothing in the transactional analysis as proposed here that might preclude it being understood and adopted in this way.[4]

But clearly the concern about the impact of contract on moral promissory duty includes more than the relation between law and the kind of formal ethical duty just referred to. After all, an ethical duty to fulfill one's contractual commitments or to respect another's contractual rights would not require a promisor to keep his or her nonformal purely gratuitous promise (in the absence of detrimental reliance). And more generally, this second-order ethical duty would not directly depend upon or take into consideration what promisors actually intend or how they sincerely view their words because, ex hypothesi, the existence and content of the underlying substantive contractual obligation is decided in accordance with the objective test. Yet there must surely be a moral duty to keep one's merely gratuitous promises, and such a duty, it seems clear, should at least take into account a promisor's subjective understandings and circumstances. This moral duty would have to be distinct from and independent of the second-order formal ethical duty to fulfill one's promises as contractually binding and owed to others. It would not necessarily presuppose a contractual substratum. The more pressing issue of stability concerns the relation between this purely moral promissory duty and the juridical conception of contract.

To show this stability, it is not necessary, however, to argue that the juridical conception of contract in its own terms directly encourages or supports the sorts of moral sensibilities and considerations that are specific to the promissory duty. This is something that the juridical conception, which by its very nature is always coercive, need not do. Instead, we must specify a moral duty to keep promises that arises in connection with a kind of interaction or relation that moral agents would recognize as genuinely distinct from and as not presupposing contract. In this way, we can make sense of the binding nature of purely gratuitous promises. It is also on this basis that we may be able to show that the juridical conception does not exclude—precisely because it does not have any authority to pronounce upon—the moral responsibilities and expectations that we share as such promisors and promisees.

To this end, I shall now try to show that in addition to the kind of promissory relation that is contractual, there is a second that is normatively distinct from and irreducible to it. The central case of this second kind of promissory relation is the gratuitous promise, and in sharp contrast with contractual promises, the promissory duty that it gives rise to is, and must be, purely moral and noncoercible. Precisely because each of the two kinds of promising enshrines a different though acceptable normative character that is self-sufficient and self-limiting in its own terms, they both can make room for and cohere with the other. Reasonable agents can understand and appreciate their different prerequisites and can fully accept and comply with their divergent implications for their interactions with others. By contrast, theories that try to explain the legal obligation of contract as an instance of a general moral duty to keep one's promises or those that, conversely, construe the latter in terms that characterize the former (such as the idea that every promise involves a transfer of right between the parties) inevitably denature both and make it impossible for the two to coexist as inherently legitimate but distinct dimensions of our moral and legal public culture.[5]

If, then, there is to be a distinct moral promissory duty applicable to gratuitous promises, it cannot have the very features of the conception of contract that, I have suggested, make the latter a form of transactional acquisition that necessarily excludes gratuitous promises. For example, as already mentioned, it cannot construe the promissory relation in terms of a transfer of exclusive control over the promised subject matter from one party to the other at the moment of promising. The normative framework must not be limited to liability for misfeasance only, with its essential indifference to substantive ends and well-being and its exclusive concern with wrongful injury to ownership interests. The moral duty should not view the contents of the promissory relation in these terms. Nor can it simply invoke the objective test as the basis for determining the existence and contents of the promise. It may possibly take directly into account the self-understandings and subjective views of both promisor and promisee. At the same time, this noncontractual conception of promising does involve its own kind of relation between promisor and promisee and its own requirement of interpersonal respect. Supposing that this requirement cannot be accounted for merely on the basis of a promisor's intention to assume it, we need to identify some interpersonal moral principle or set of principles, expressing ideas of the reasonable and of respect, in light of which this obligation can be justified. What, in positive terms, might this be?

A good place to begin is to recall Charles Fried's account of the moral basis of promissory duty as rooted in the twin moral notions of trust and respect between promisor and promisee.[6] Although, for reasons discussed earlier, this cannot, in my view, illuminate the contractual relation, it does seem prima facie to provide a plausible moral conception that can underpin promising conceived independently of the juridical conception.[7]

Fried's discussion of trust and respect is highly compressed, taking up but a few pages of his book.[8] The core idea is that the promisor, having intentionally invited the promisee to trust the promisor—to make herself vulnerable in this way—cannot renege without wrongly using the promisee and abusing her trust. This holds whether or not the promisee has conferred any benefits on the promisor or has relied to her detriment on his promise. Fried supposes that the promisor invites trust by invoking a convention of promising whose function is to provide moral grounds for the promisee to expect the promised performance. But the proposed ground for the obligation to keep promises is, according to Fried, deeper than, and distinct from, the social utility of the practice of promising. To respect the promisee, the promisor is bound to perform simply because he has chosen to invite and has received the promisee's trust. This is the promise principle.

What about the case where a promisor regrets promising because, at the time when performance is due, he now values his performance differently than when the promise was originally made? The promise principle holds unequivocally that the promisor must perform. Otherwise, the promisor abuses the promisee's trust. The fact that the promisor may now regret the value judgment that led him to commit to certain terms is, Fried argues, the promisor's responsibility, not the promisee's.[9] The prior value judgment represents the promisor's free exercise of choice. By holding the promisor to his promise, the promisee respects the promisor as a free and rational person with a capacity to determine his own values, and such respect means allowing the promisor to take responsibility for the good he has chosen. And because the choosing self is not an instantaneous self, but one that persists over time, and the good chosen can be one to be conferred in the future, respect for the promisor entails taking seriously his choice to commit to do something in the future and thus to maintain a constancy of will over time. By contrast, allowing the promisor to shirk responsibility for this choice and thereby to shift it onto others would be to infantilize him.[10]

By grounding the promise principle in this way, Fried suggests a moral basis that seems to be both indispensable to gratuitous promises and genuinely different from and independent of the juridical conception of contract: the placing of trust by one in the integrity and fidelity of another does not depend upon the first party having control, to the exclusion of the second, over either the outcome or the process of bringing it about. To the contrary, trust is most fully evident where there is utter dependency by one merely on the other's integrity and conscientiousness. The idea of a transfer of rightful exclusive control, let alone one of ownership, seems to be foreign or at least unessential to understanding this relation of invited trust and required respect. As already mentioned, Fried's discussion of trust and respect as the moral basis of promissory duty is quite compressed. To bring out more fully how the juridical conception of contract and moral promissory duty are distinct yet mutually compatible, I think it will be helpful to consider a little more closely the roles of trust and respect in promissory relations. In the spirit of Fried's own Kantian approach, I shall do so by explaining this purely moral promissory duty as a Kantian duty of virtue.

In contrast with his relatively detailed account of the juridical obligation to perform one's contractual promises, Kant himself provides little discussion of promissory duty as a distinct duty of virtue. Nevertheless, one can try to develop a Kantian view of this duty that draws upon his more general analysis (as well as specific illustrations) of duties of virtue.[11] Both his account of rights and that of duties of virtue express the idea of persons as free and equal, though they do so in different ways. I should add that, even though I think that the following analysis is consistent with Kant's framework and basic premises, I present it not as an interpretation of Kant's work or, for that matter, as the only—or best—account of moral promissory duty, but rather as illustrating what I hope is a plausible view that enables us to see more clearly how contractual and noncontractual promissory obligations might be at once genuinely distinct and mutually compatible. For the purposes of a public basis of justification, the most important thing is that the proposed analysis sufficiently reflects and clarifies widely shared commonsense moral ideas concerning the basis of such promissory duty and the nature of the corresponding promissory relation.

On this Kantian view, we begin with the following basic contrast that frames the whole analysis: whereas juridical duties of right have to do with the permissibility of one's actions in relation to others, duties of virtue concern the ends that one ought to have and pursue.[12] Inasmuch as the moral point of view governs action and action is inherently directed toward some end, a complete morality must incorporate moral principles that specify and regulate the choice of ends: a doctrine of possibly obligatory ends. Now since, to constitute an end, something must be chosen *as an end,* it cannot be coerced. Thus if duties of virtue were coercible, they would not constitute a doctrine of obligatory ends: the possibility of coercion would, from an ethical standpoint, immediately turn the pursuit of these ends into means that are performed to avoid the coercive response.

According to Kant, noncoercible obligatory ends are themselves divided into two kinds: those that aim at the realization of one's own perfection (natural and moral) and those that are directed toward the happiness of others.[13] The former involve duties of virtue to oneself; the latter, duties of virtue to others. I shall assume that even though there may be aspects of promise-keeping that engage duties to oneself, the main moral significance of promising involves duties to others, centrally to the promisee.

Following Kant, duties to others in turn comprise two aspects that, while they can be represented as distinct kinds of duty, are in fact always united in any given duty of virtue to others: first, what Kant calls an aspect of *love,* which shapes the duties of beneficence and gratitude and which, not being owed to particular individuals, puts those for whom love is shown under a resulting obligation of virtue toward the benefactor; and, second, what he calls an aspect of *respect,* which *is* owed to everyone and to which everyone has a legitimate claim, so that being accorded respect does not give rise to a further obligation on the part of the one who receives it.[14] Conceived as a noncoercible duty of virtue to others, promissory duty should in principle be amenable to an analysis in terms of both these aspects.

As part of our shared moral understanding and agreeing with Kant, I shall suppose that everyone is under a general noncoercible duty of beneficence. Under the aspect of love, one must adopt and seek to realize as one's end the inner principle of contributing to the happiness of others. Now, ab initio, this requirement must be fitted with one's other obligatory ends, including those owed to oneself. Thus, what is required is not that one ought to do this or that act that promotes the happiness of others but only that one makes this principle one's end and that one strives to fulfill it in ways that are compatible with one's also having and striving to fulfill one's other obligatory ends.[15] While the fulfillment of this end may sometimes require the sacrifice of certain of one's own immediate interests in favor of others'—perhaps even without hope of return—there are no fixed or necessary parameters of the extent of such self-sacrifice. Not only is it permissible for individuals to ensure the fulfillment of their own happiness and true needs, but they must be left to decide for themselves what those needs are in light of their own sensibilities. This is part of the moral context, as it were, within which the duty of beneficence is understood and fulfilled.

In this way, the duty of beneficence—in sharp contrast with requirements of rights—does not specify or require any given determinate actions. At the same time, as a duty to promote the happiness of others, one does good to others, not primarily on the basis of one's own notions of happiness, but by appropriately taking into account *their* own.[16] One must have a reasonable basis for thinking that they view what one will do as conducive to their happiness and good. Stated in other terms, the duty of beneficence entails making the interests and ends of others the substance of one's own ends. Finally, the duty of beneficence does not require that one view all human beings on any given occasion as equally and identically subjects of one's concern and love. The duty of beneficence, which is manifested not in mere wishes but in a practical, active promotion of the good of others, is not violated if one is concerned more closely with the well-being of some compared with that of others. One's fulfillment of the duty can reflect these differences.

An obvious illustration of conduct that might, in principle, fulfill this duty is the actual conferring of some benefit on another. So long as the receiver wants the object—or at least does not reject it—the giver is entitled to see himself as striving to fulfill the duty of beneficence. Now the main difference between this and promising is that in the latter the conferral of benefit is intended to take place in the future and is therefore dependent on the constancy of the promisor's will in carrying through. Let me consider this a little more closely.

The object of the promise must be something that the promisee wants or at least does not reject. If at any point prior to performance the promisee changes her mind about the object's desirableness, the fulfillment of the promise cannot count as an act of contributing to her happiness and therefore as fulfilling the duty of beneficence. Rejection by the promisee does not so much release the promisor from his promissory obligation as mean that the promised act cannot qualify as the promotion of the promisee's ends and so cannot count as an act of beneficence. So far as the basic duty to promote the happiness of others is concerned, the promisor, once notified, can no longer regard performance as fulfillment of this duty. To the contrary, following through, or even viewing himself as obliged to follow through, would demonstrate a certain fundamental failure to recognize the promisee as an independent person with her own chosen ends and her own particular conception of her good.

What about the future-oriented character of promising, in contrast to the fully executed giving of a gift? Promising clearly presupposes a moral capacity for constancy of will: unless individuals can be appropriately viewed as having this capacity, there cannot be a moral relation between promisor and promisee. Promisors could not view themselves or be viewed by promisees as having the capacity to commit to, and therefore be judged with respect to following through on, what they promise. The components of this moral capacity for constancy of will seem clear enough.

I assume that any person capable of setting and pursuing ends has the capacity to direct his or her present and future conduct by presently chosen ends and, merely as rational, has the capacity to persevere in the execution of these ends even in the face of contrary impulses and desires, whether now or in the future. A capacity for constancy of will, where this is essential to the ongoing effective prosecution of ends, must be presupposed of all persons qua rational.

Now, whereas the pure concept of rationality entails the possibility of subordinating one's present or future desires to the steady pursuit of chosen ends, the duty of beneficence involves the possibility of a sacrifice (at least to some extent) of one's present and future desires to the pursuit of an end that incorporates the goals and interests of *others*. I shall suppose that the capacity to do this marks the agent, not merely as rational, but also as reasonable, and that, in contrast to the rational, it is a moral capacity. Reflecting the idea of the reasonable, this moral capacity shows that one recognizes, and gives standing to, the significance of the ends of others just as one does with respect to one's own. Here, the ends of others do not function merely as a negative limit on one's choices but are integrated as a positive constituent element of one's own ends and actions: the ends of others specify the content of one's own. Now, action is always directed toward an end. Thus, this moral capacity shows that one's action can fully embody reasonableness, because it can positively—that is, as an end—incorporate a moral relation to others in which they have independent standing in their own right. Moral theories on all sides take this capacity, in some form, as basic and essential. It is also fundamental to a promisor being under a noncoercible duty of respect toward the promisee.

Since everyone can view himself or herself as having this moral capacity for constancy of will with respect to the realization of ends important to others, promisors can, morally speaking, credibly commit in the present to the pursuit of such particular ends at a future point in time. Accepting this, however, does not show yet that the promisor is subject to a promissory duty to follow through. The capacity for constancy is simply a necessary condition. Given the wide latitude intrinsic to the duty of beneficence, a change of mind may simply mean that the promisor no longer wants to fulfill this general duty in this particular way and manner—someone else, including the promisor himself, may have competing needs to be fulfilled, or it may just be that the promisor wishes to meet this duty at a different time and in different circumstances. Just as no particular individual can legitimately claim against another that she in particular should be the beneficiary of the latter's general and wide duty to help others, so a promisee seemingly should not complain when the promisor changes his mind, for whatever reason, and declines to confer a promised benefit. Something more is necessary to establish a promissory duty. But what?

The answer, I wish to suggest, must bring into play the aspect of *respect* obtaining in the relation between promisor and promisee, established by the transaction of promising.[17] Not only must the promisor take as his end the doing of something that is in some sense subjectively wanted by the promisee; the promisor must also make explicitly or implicitly clear to the promisee that this is what the promisor proposes to fulfill and must do so in such a way that the promisee can in turn incorporate the promisor's adoption of this end as an ingredient in *her*—the promisee's—own thoughts, feelings, or plans.[18] This double feature of promising is crucial to understanding the duty of fidelity.

To elaborate: First, the promisor adopts as his end something that fits with or furthers the subjective interests and ends of the promisee. But second, the promisor invites the promisee to make the promisor's adoption of the promisee's own interests part of the promisee's ends. Unless or until the promisee conveys, implicitly or explicitly, to the promisor that she will do so, a promising transaction does not exist. By doing this, a promisee also establishes that she wants the promise and so confirms that the promise is for the promisee's own good as understood by her and thus within the scope of the promisor's duty of beneficence. However, beyond this and just as importantly, the significance of the promisee's uptake is that the promisee has accepted the promisor's invitation to incorporate it in setting (and whatever this entails, including just thinking and imagining) the promisee's own ends. As I will now explain, the reason why a promisor is subject to an other-directed duty of virtue of any kind with respect to promising is on account of this invited relation. For the latter brings into play the second aspect of noncoercible duties to others, namely, respect, and it is on this basis, I now suggest, that there is a promissory duty.

On the Kantian view that I am proposing, respect, as an aspect of other-related duties of virtue, is something that individuals owe each other. Moreover, everyone has a legitimate, though noncoercible, claim to respect from others. Indeed, we will see that in the promissory relation the requirement of respect goes both ways as between promisor and promisee. Now whereas what Kant calls the aspect of love in other-directed duties may be expressed as a duty to make others' ends one's own, the aspect of respect translates into a negative requirement of not exalting oneself above others and is analogous to, without being the same as, juridical duty that forbids one from encroaching upon what belongs to others.[19] The principle of mutual love directs individuals to come closer to each other; by contrast, respect requires that they keep themselves at a distance from one another. Respect for others demands that I take as the principle of my ends the maxim, in Kant's words, to "keep myself within my own bounds so as not to detract anything from the worth that the other, as a human being, is authorized to put upon himself."[20]

In the case of an outright gift, my benevolence should be effectuated in a way that preserves the equal dignity of the recipient.[21] Because the relation of giver and receiver is inherently unequal and can convey the impression that the receiver's well-being—and so the receiver herself—is dependent upon the giver's unowed generosity, the transfer carries with it the risk of humbling the recipient. Therefore, Kant emphasizes that the duty of respect requires that the donor credibly acts in a way that shows his giving as something that he owes the receiver rather than as an expression of his benevolence or generosity, thereby avoiding humiliation to the recipient and enabling her to maintain self-respect. Only in this way can the donor bestow a true benefit.[22]

Now assume a situation of promising in which the promisee is engaged in the manner described above and suppose that, at the time the promise is supposed to be performed, the promisor gives effectively no special weight at all to his promise but, viewing the good that it might confer on the promisee as just one possible goal among his various ends that can be evaluated anew at every point, decides upon a different course of action, which he thinks is a more compelling way of exercising his benevolence. In short, he acts as if he had never promised at all. If any decision procedure is incompatible with promissory duty, this surely is. How does the promisor's choice show lack of respect for the other qua promisee?

The promisor invites the promisee to incorporate, and the promisee does incorporate, the promise as part of her ends. This moment of the promisee's uptake of the promise is, I have said, essential to the establishment of the promissory relation and the duty of respect that applies therein. To show the promisee respect, the promisor, when deciding how to act and thus which ends to pursue, must accord the promise the moral weight that reflects the fact that it is not just one among the promisor's own ends, but is now *already* an integral part of *another's* (the promisee's) ends. In doing so, the promisor recognizes the promisee's capacity for ends as having equal standing to his own; and, moreover, the promisor does what he can to support the possibility of the promisee having ends that are stable and constant over time. The promisor's decision recognizes and affirms the promisee's own status as an independent agent who as such is worthy of another's beneficence.[23] The moral (not psychological) correlative of promisor respect for the promisee is the latter's trust in the promisor.[24] The promisee internalizes the promisor's promise on the assumption of the promisor's moral integrity, which includes the promisor's capacity to take into appropriate account the fact of this internalization and all that it entails when determining his course of action. The promisee's trust is rooted in her assurance that the promisor will shape his conduct in such a way that the promisor will be constrained by reasons that are also acceptable to the promisee.[25]

Because of the promisee's internalization of the promisor's promise as her end, the promisor's failure to give his promise the appropriate kind of moral significance cannot be construed merely as a redirection of effort or a simple change of mind within the wide latitude of the duty of beneficence. Having drawn in the promisee in this way, the promisor's indifference to his promise does not leave the promisee alone and untouched in the pursuit of her chosen ends. To the contrary, it directly impugns and detracts from the promisee's status as an independent subject worthy as such of the promisor's benevolence, thereby striking at the promisee's own self-respect, that is, the worth that the promisee is entitled to place upon herself as a rational and reasonable moral agent with her own needs and ends.

In connection with the promisor's duty of respect toward the promisee, I have suggested that it rests on the promisor treating his promise—which, at his invitation, has been internalized by the promisee as part of her ends—as involving the agency of another and thus not of the same kind as his other ends, which reflect only his own ends and sole agency. At the same time, it must also be emphasized that the making and the execution of the promise remain the promisor's ultimate and individual responsibility. The locus of immediate control and responsibility is in the promisor alone. The promise is the promisor's doing. Moreover, he does this, not in abstraction from his many ends, but in connection with them. Therefore, the promisor's subjective understanding of what he intended in inviting the promisee's trust, his good faith assessment of his changed circumstances as well as legitimate needs, purposes, and other responsibilities, and so forth can and should morally shape the ways in which the promisor fulfills his obligation to the promisee.

Clearly, in many instances, respect requires the promisor simply to keep his promise. But where there are conflicting and weighty changed circumstances, for example, the promisor may in fact be under a moral duty to pursue a course of action that requires him not to perform as promised. And yet the promisor continues to be under a duty of respect toward the promisee and must show this, whether by choosing an alternative performance that, within reasonable parameters and without imposing unreasonable burdens upon him, meets the promisee's legitimate expectations, or by explaining and apologizing for the nonperformance in a way that demonstrates his appreciation of its significance to the promisee and that reassures the promisee of his respect and concern. The duty to keep one's promise is founded upon the moral requirement of respect and therefore is not reducible to a duty to perform some action, nothing more or less. Unlike juridical obligations, here the moral duty in promise-keeping is not simply to do (or to abstain from doing) a determinate act.[26]

Moreover, the moral requirements of love and respect do not go in just one direction from promisor to promisee. These are original and general duties that apply to all persons in their various relations with others. Only if this background of general duties of virtue and corresponding moral capacities is presupposed can promises even be made and received in good faith. In their mutual dealings, parties fulfill the requirement of respect by adopting measures that are tailored to each other's particular understandings, temperaments, choices, and circumstances. The standpoint is genuinely intersubjective and shaped by particulars. Thus, as part of their promissory relation, the promisee is under an other-related duty of virtue toward the promisor as well.[27]

More specifically, the promisee must recognize that the promise that she has internalized is also another's (the promisor's) end—indeed, that it is one among the promisor's many ends, responsibilities, and interests, which comprise the latter's separate and independent moral agency. The promisee should recognize and accept as legitimate the good reasons that move a responsible promisor to keep or to refrain from keeping his promise, showing trust in the promisor's capacity as a responsible agent and judging matters also from the latter's own particular standpoint. This may require the promisee to take into account and to understand appropriately, from the promisor's own standpoint, the promisor's changed circumstances, other responsibilities, and needs as well as the relative substantive importance of the promised performance to her (the promisee) compared with these other considerations that weigh upon the promisor. And if the promisee has changed her assessment of the importance or value of the promised performance to her, it may be incumbent upon her to bring this to the promisor's attention and even to insist that she no longer expects performance.

Here, then, very briefly sketched, is an account of the main features and grounding of a distinct noncontractual idea of promissory duty that is suited to apply to the gratuitous promise as a central paradigmatic case. Note that, as we have seen so far with the transactional theory of contract, the proposed understanding of promissory duty does not treat the promissory transaction as institutional or as explicable only on the assumption of there being some general background convention brought into existence to further cooperation among individuals.[28] In both accounts, a certain definite kind of interpersonal relationship is the basic unit of analysis, and the underlying moral presupposition is not a general convention of promising (or of contract) but rather a corresponding normative conception of free and equal persons who, as reasonable, show respect for each other in and through their interactions.

On the proposed account, the moral duty to keep one's promises is qualitatively different and independent from the juridical obligation in contract. First, the promising relation, though bilateral, is constituted by an interaction that has its source in the promisor's decision and the fact that this is taken up by the promisee as the promisor's decision and responsibility.[29] It is not a transaction constituted by the parties' identically coactive reciprocal participation. The promissory relation involves no transfer of rightful exclusive control from one party to the other. Although a promisor may have, relative to the promisee, exclusive control over what he, without any legal constraint, chooses to promise the promisee, the organizing juridical idea of private ownership plays no constitutive role. Because reference to ends is essential to the very characterization and basis of the promissory duty, it cannot be part of the normative framework of liability for misfeasance only. Instead of a transfer of exclusive control, there is a relation of trust and respect in which each side, particularly the promisee, is dependent upon (and must show appropriate recognition of) the moral integrity of the other. The wrongfulness of breach of promissory duty is not wrongful injury to another's rightful possessions or holdings, but the failure to carry through with a commitment to benefit-conferring conduct in such a way that shows disrespect (in the sense discussed) for the promisee as a moral agent. Holding the parties in this kind of promissory relation to an objective test, to the norm of strict contractual liability qualified only by impossibility and other excusing doctrines, or to contractual determinations of performance, breach, and enforcement would clearly be out of sync with their shared moral understanding of what their interaction entails. A promisee could not reasonably expect, nor in good faith claim, this of the promisor.[30]

Given these fundamental qualitative differences between the two kinds of relations, the many divergences between contract and promising—and most importantly whether or not their respective requirements are coercible—are not only reasonable and expected but also morally essential. Individuals can reasonably know which sort of interaction they are engaged in and so can also form reasonable expectations of the moral requirements and consequences of their chosen dealings with others. Reasonable persons can wholeheartedly endorse, as expressive of their free and equal moral natures, the justifications for the different normative prerequisites, features, and consequences of contract and promise. Conflating them would confound their legitimate expectations. It is difficult to see how this could encourage and support proper compliance with the moral demands of either. At the same time, the juridical conception of contract, consistently with the legal point of view, treats all aspects of contract law as anchored in a normatively rightful relation between persons with the consequence, we have seen, that there is no obstacle to the parties also formally viewing their legal contractual requirements as aspects of their ethical duty. Precisely because of the limited normative character of the juridical contractual relation and its divergence from gratuitous promising, it does not even bear on, let alone trespass on or oust, the distinct moral domain of pure promissory duty. To the contrary, the fact that contractual obligation—being both genuinely distinct and also grounded in norms of juridical respect—can itself be viewed as an obligatory ethical end by the contracting parties fills in and strengthens their moral orientation as conscientious agents seeking to fulfill the requirements of the manifold shapes of promissory duty.

12.2. Between Contract and Markets: From Contract as Relation to Contract as Institution

The second question of stability concerns the relation between the proposed transactional conception of contract law and markets. Clearly, bilateral exchange relations are a paradigmatic instance of the promise-for-consideration contractual relation. For the purposes of the following discussion, I shall take the market to be a social cooperative practice involving the systematically decentralized coordination of indefinitely many exchange transactions via competitively determined and publicly knowable prices. Markets and prices realize the transactional, purely bilateral conception of contract as *an existing self-maintaining system of exchange relations*. The problem of stability arises as follows.

From the standpoint of the individuals engaged in exchange, the point and purpose of their participation is to obtain particular substantive satisfactions, and they can achieve this only through interaction with others who identically seek their own particular satisfactions in turn. For them, exchanges are thus a means of meeting their particular, though complementary, needs and so are something that they want and pursue as part of their good under the idea of the rational. Moreover, the efficacy of exchanges as such a means is proportionate to their being part of a system of ongoing and indefinitely many exchanges: a market. In addition, market participants share an identical formal interest in being able to know *ex ante* their rights and powers so that they can plan in advance what they can permissibly or effectively do from a legal contractual point of view in order to pursue their ends. They need a contract law that performs a public institutional function.[31] In these ways, the idea of the rational is pivotal in market relations. By contrast, we have seen that, understood in terms of the transactional conception, contract doctrines and principles seem to be per se indifferent to parties' needs and their satisfaction, and the proposed theory has viewed contract law solely in terms of the kind of two-sided relation that it presupposes without attributing to it a systemic institutional form or function.

How, then, can such a conception of contract, while retaining its essential normative character, fit harmoniously with, and possibly provide direction and support for, market transactors as participants in this system of economic exchanges? Also, how can they find in contract's norms of reasonableness the means to fulfilling their own rational (economic) good? Unless this is possible, contract, though transactionally justified, cannot be expected to generate the informed and rational support of the participants in the very practice in which contract law is realized. At the core of the practice of contract, there would be a basic tension and instability, not congruence. I must now try to develop the proposed theory of contract law to show that this need not be the case.

In broad terms, this will first involve identifying the normative presuppositions and character of an ideal type of market relations in a liberal democratic society. For this purpose, I briefly sketch what I think is a plausible ethical conception of the market, which views it, in Hegel's terms, as a kind of "system of needs."[32] But second, it will also be necessary to show how, without compromising the transactional conception's internal standpoint and requirements, it can be suitably developed to account for contract not merely as an ensemble of principles and doctrines specifying a two-sided relation but also as a set of institutional norms that appropriately incorporates both bilateral and systemic aspects in a way that supports the legitimate needs of market participants. In a sense, then, this discussion of the stability of contract vis-à-vis the market is also a further development of the complete account of contract law itself: contract law not only as bilateral juridical relation but also as an institutional system of public norms. I should emphasize here at the outset that this theoretical development of the account of contract law from juridical relation to legal institution is analytical and normative, not historical, temporal, or empirical. The contract law that we have is always and everywhere an institutional practice. But we can understand its being such by unpacking and connecting its different normative dimensions—what I have referred to as the juridical or transactional conception and now characterize as the institutional realization of that conception.[33] This is what I shall try to do.

12.2.1. The Presuppositions and Features of the Market as a "System of Needs"

Impelled by the necessity of satisfying their needs, individuals participate in market relations through exchanges regulated by a system of prices. But since their needs are not coercively imposed upon them by others against their will, their decisions to transact or not in response to given prices appear to be free and voluntary choices of whether to avail themselves of the opportunities for transacting and thereby to satisfy those needs. Viewed in this way, the market consists of interactions that can be conceived as wholly uncoerced and voluntary.[34]

However, as a number of writers have emphasized, this apparent purely voluntary process of transacting rests, in modern liberal societies, on the fact that what one needs is already owned by others and therefore something from which one may be coercively excluded, with the consequence that one must procure their consent—and so exchange—to meet one's own needs.[35] This precondition of market relations is juridical, not economic. Its noneconomic character is evident in the fact that the right of exclusive individual ownership imposes coercively enforceable constraints on others that hold irrespective of how owners choose to use their assets (i.e., whether productively, wastefully, irrationally, inefficiently, etc.). Not only does the notion of rightful coercion play no intrinsic role in economic market analysis, which supposes purely voluntary action in response to prices, but the juridical analysis of ownership is also indifferent to the very factors and considerations that are crucial from an economic point of view. At the same time, it is only on the basis of this noneconomic juridical presupposition that the relatively autonomous voluntary working of the economic processes regulated by prices is both possible and necessary.

The fact that market exchanges are not instantaneous brings into play a related noneconomic presupposition of market relations. In every noninstantaneous transaction, there are necessarily (at least) two different points in time when transactors can respond to going prices: first, at the moment of crystallized agreement and, later, when performance is due. The problem stems from the fact that, as a rational actor who chooses solely in response to prices, either party may change his or her mind and decide to withdraw. A party's decision to withdraw may be simply a rational response to relevant prices in real time. Economically, party defection represents merely a failure to transact, no differently than if the parties had never decided to exchange in the first place. From an economic point of view, there is of course no a priori requirement to transact. It is all a matter of rationally meeting one's preferences in light of a set of prices. However, unless this possibility of withdrawal can be excluded *ex ante* as a matter of general principle, potential transactors cannot presume, and thus be confident in, the future behavior of each other, with obvious consequences for the kinds of assets and forms of value that can be objects of exchange. If market transactions are to include noninstantaneous exchanges in a price-driven system of exchanges, parties must have a reasonable basis for treating agreed-upon terms (in response to actual or expected prices at the first point in time) as regulative irrespective of subsequent price opportunities and costs.[36]

For this purpose, it is essential that transactors can be held to their initial choices, even though their later rational decisions might be otherwise, and despite the fact that they are not obliged to do anything in the first place. This constraint can only be required and explained by incorporating a conception of reasonableness, not purely on the basis of economic market processes, including the price system. While there may be different ways of trying to establish this, the basis that I have suggested as most directly reflected in the actual law and as appropriate for a public basis of justification is the juridical idea that the agreement embodies the representation of a present transfer of assets (including services) having present value—that is, the conception of contractual exchange as a transfer of ownership.[37]

At least within a modern liberal framework, market relationships presuppose a third conceptually prior normative determination, which, like the previous ones, is also noneconomic. Every system of market relations must reflect some determination of the distinction between subjects and objects of exchange as well as of the question of who can participate in these relations. To be legitimate within a liberal framework, however, an exchange system must do so consistently with a view of persons as free and equal. Not only must persons not be permissible objects of ownership or exchange, but they must also all have at least formally equal standing—and an equal moral power—to acquire property, enter into contractual transactions, and participate in exchange relations.[38] As part of a liberal conception of contract, I have elucidated this noneconomic premise of market relations and processes in terms of the juridical conception of the person and whatever this entails.

My point here is that the first step in explaining the relation between the transactional conception of contract and markets involves making clear that a market presupposes definite *noneconomic* norms and constraints, which, I have suggested, are elaborated and justified on the basis of the transactional conception of contract, independently from economic considerations. Thus whatever is inherently part of this transactional conception—whatever the latter comprises and includes when it is fully worked out—is, and must be, presupposed by the purely economic market processes and mechanisms of decentralized price-driven coordination.

In view of the discussions in Part One, this noneconomic precondition is made up, therefore, of all the contract principles and doctrines that have been explained as integrated aspects of the basic promise-for-consideration relation. The purely economic aspect of market exchange relations presupposes *the whole of this as it is understood and justified within its own transactional framework*. On this view, the juridical conception of contract doctrines and principles is not only independent from, but lexically prior to, the elucidation of market relations.[39] It cannot be emphasized too much that this presupposition of market relations expresses, and has been wholly elucidated with reference to, the noneconomic purely normative juridical conception of the person as free and equal in the sense discussed earlier.[40] If this is so, the first and most fundamental justification of contract doctrines and principles cannot be that they serve to reflect, support, strengthen, or extend well-functioning markets.[41] Conversely, applying economic analysis directly to explain these doctrines not only misconstrues them but is counterproductive because it obscures the noneconomic normative character of the premises that modern markets presuppose.

The next step in this discussion of stability is to identify and elaborate the normative conception that is characteristic of the market itself. While it presupposes the juridical dimension with its purely bilateral idea of relations, the normativity of the market takes this analysis further by reconfiguring it as inherently systemic, such that no single exchange relation can be explained except as part of a system of such relations. Moreover, new normative considerations are brought into play. The systematic interdependence of everyone on everyone else is the necessary framework through which each participant can satisfy his or her particular needs and interests consistently with the freedom and equality of all. So, in contrast with the juridical conception's indifference to all aspects of particularity, the market supposes that the rational pursuit and satisfaction of substantive particular needs and interests is an essential moral element. Viewing the market as a kind of system of needs, to use Hegel's term, helps bring out its distinctive normative character.[42]

What, then, are the central features and characteristics of a system of needs and of the persons who participate in it? To begin, it presupposes that persons, as separate and mutually independent, have morally permissible needs and purposes and that it is part of (intrinsic to) their freedom to pursue and satisfy them as they choose, so long as this is consistent with respect for the equal standing and right of others. Persons view themselves and others, not just as abstractly identical subjects whose essential interest is in asserting their sheer independence from everything particular, but also as having the power to form, to revise, and rationally to pursue a conception of their good consisting of determinate preferences, interests, and purposes and as having a right to make claims on this basis. They now have a higher-order moral interest in asserting their capacity to form and to pursue permissible determinate purposes in meeting their diverse individual needs. The system of needs thus gives a most extensive free rein to individuals' self-chosen pursuit of their particular interests and purposes under the idea of the rational. However, the kinds of needs and purposes that characterize persons as participants in the system of needs have a certain form and content. As I will now elaborate, they are needs and purposes that are formed and fulfilled through direct, reciprocal, and mutually voluntary interactions with others. This reference to others brings into play the idea of the reasonable. But the way in which the rational and reasonable are specified and related here differs from how this is done in the juridical conception.

In the system of needs, the objects and means of satisfaction come from another who owns them, and insofar as these can only be obtained in this way, they must be external objects (goods, services, etc.) given with the other's consent. As a result, each is able to meet his needs only by reciprocally providing others with something that they want. The paradigmatic relation is exchange between separate and independent persons, each seeking to realize his own interests. Acquisition in the system of needs is paradigmatically transactional, not original.[43] Now, in this relation, even though each individual has his own good as his end, he must also take the satisfaction of the needs and purposes of others as a necessary means to that end. The satisfaction of their needs and purposes becomes to this extent part of his own purposes. Impelled by needs and by the necessity of social relation to satisfy those needs, each therefore acquires, produces, and works not only for his own interests but also and—supposing the multiplication of needs—mainly for those of others who themselves do the same in turn. Thus each is moved by the thought of what others may need or provide. At the same time, it should be emphasized that they remain mutually separate and independent and they take an interest in what others need or provide only because this is necessary to meet their own.

Because this *social* process confronts each participant as the inescapable and constraining means to individual satisfaction, individuals need, and rationally want, to engage in it and to do so as an equal with everyone else. In the juridical conception, parties are simply constrained by the requirements and implications of the reasonable flowing from relation to others. There, we saw, the standpoint of the reasonable, expressed via the objective test, is purely external and transactional: purposes, motives, and substantive interests are not directly relevant. Here, by contrast, participants in the system of needs come to treat this standpoint of the reasonable *as part of their subjective pursuit of their own interests* and are now led to internalize the requirements of the reasonable as a means to achieving their ends. In a real sense we may say that participation in the social processes of the system of needs *educates* them to this standpoint: they learn to be and to want to be reasonable.

For instance, they come to view themselves and others identically as owners of external things who satisfy their needs through exchange, without regard to any personal or social features that are not essential to their being such. Both the impersonal character of relations in the system of needs and the claim that everyone should have formally equal access to participate reflect this. Moreover, in addition to wanting to know others' needs and choices so that they can be ascertained and met, individuals need, and come to want, ready and reliable knowledge of the requirements of the reasonable, including the existence and consequences of ownership or other rights, the different kinds and effects of legal arrangements and transactions, and so forth. An interest of this kind is one that all individuals share *identically* as members of the system of needs. As we will shortly see, this has important implications.

By its very nature, this system of needs is best understood as an actually existing, self-generating social process that becomes ever more established, strengthened, and indispensable as individuals participate in it: the more they seek satisfaction of their needs and interests in this way—as they must—the more complete their dependence on each other becomes and the more pervasive and necessary the system itself. It is truly a system of social cooperation in which each participant, in acting and producing on his own account, eo ipso acts and produces for the needs and interests of everyone else. It figures as their common resource or capital—a socially created wealth generated by systematic interdependence—which participants collectively maintain and enhance insofar as they draw individual advantage from it.[44] Its actual existence and well-functioning now figure as part of everyone's purposes, so that each participant has an identical formal interest in ensuring this.

The contrast with the legal analysis of first possession and contract is striking. In the juridical conception, parties do not have any reasonable basis for expecting that there is or will be anything to acquire: whether an unowned thing is available for appropriation or an offer of something is made is entirely a matter of happenstance. As I tried to emphasize in Chapter 10, the principles of acquisition establish at most the moral *possibility* (permissibility) of acquisition, not its necessity. Whereas the idiom of the juridical conception is merely the possible, in the case of the system of needs it is the actual. By its very nature, the system of needs must be conceived as an existing, self-generating social reality vis-à-vis its members. In Llewellyn's phrase, it must be "a going scheme, a working set-up," which objectively engenders actual existing opportunities for mutually beneficial transactions and subjectively gives rise to justified expectation and confidence on the part of participants that this is and will be the case.[45]

Moreover, because individuals avail themselves of these opportunities by producing and providing things and services that meet the needs of others, they must develop the skills and knowledge to gauge others' needs, to imagine and spy out new needs and to produce via work the means of satisfying them. By contrast, in the case of the forms of acquisition under the juridical conception, all that matters is that one recognizably exercises effective control over something unilaterally or transactionally without violating others' rights. The fact of doing so is the sole and decisive point, and whether this takes the form of working on or with the object of control is not per se relevant. That the objects acquired may be the product of skill and work is crucially important from both an economic and, we will see, a distributive point of view. But from a juridical standpoint, this whole dimension is extrinsic and plays no essential role.

Now, offhand, it seems clear that a market constitutes a kind of system of needs. Viewing the market in these terms helps to bring out the important differences between its specific normativity and the juridical standpoint that informs contract doctrines and principles. The next step in the argument for the stability of the transactional conception of contract vis-à-vis the market is to discuss more specifically certain key features of market relations themselves. This will identify more clearly the need for contract law to assume an institutional function, the immediate basis for its doing so, and what that function must look like.

12.2.2. Market Features, Its Conception of Social Action, and the Needs of Market Participants

Following Max Weber's account, I shall suppose that a market exists wherever there is competition for actual opportunities of exchange among a plurality of potential parties and that a central and indispensable feature of modern markets is that these opportunities are communicated through a system of prices with the all-pervasive use of monetary calculation.[46] Weber defines what he calls "the market situation" of any object of exchange as consisting in "all the opportunities of exchanging it for money which are known to the participants in exchange relationships and aid their orientation in the competitive price struggle."[47] It is via prices that actors determine the question of costs, and, according to Weber, it is this that makes their deliberation and conduct specifically economic rather than merely technical.[48] With the use of monetary calculation, goods can be systematically compared with all potential future opportunities for use or profit, including their possible utility to an indefinite number of other persons who are potential transactors with the present owner.[49]

Viewed separately and by themselves, the transactions that make up the network of market exchanges are each deliberate and planned bilateral acquisitions of powers of control and disposal. With respect to completed transactions, the analysis of the exchange act correctly focuses only on the immediate bilateral acts of the parties inter se. But this does not exhaust their meaning as acts of market exchange since the full account must incorporate the preparatory dickering and decision-making. Weber emphasizes that in this respect the act of exchange is always what he calls "social action" insofar as the potential transacting parties are guided in their offers by the potential actions of an indeterminately large group of real or imagined competitors and not just by their own actions alone.[50] A going market embeds and continuously generates these potentialities as real opportunities for action. The use of money, already referred to, reinforces this social character of the act of exchange because its acceptability is based entirely on the relation to the potential actions of others—the expectation and confidence that it can and will continue to be further used. The indefinitely many and distinct bilateral relations belong to this complete interlocking network of transactions, with the rational (economic) choices of individual actors being regulated by the system of prices and based on abstract, purely quantitative monetary calculation.

In conjunction with the social nature of economic market action, Weber stresses the impersonality of the market relationship. Individuals are related only through reciprocal exchanges embedded in the system of exchanges. Theirs is a relationship between owners mediated by things. In Weber's words, parties "look toward the commodity, not the person of others," making the market "the most impersonal relationship of practical life into which humans can enter with one another."[51] Moreover, they remain throughout as individual transactors who have and assert their own interests, separate and distinct from those of others. Each attends to the interests of others only insofar as this is necessary to realize his or her own interests. This is not a relationship of sharing or caring—not a form of "fraternal community or consociation."[52] Rather, it is one of impersonal, reciprocal, and mutually voluntary giving and taking that operates on the basis of respect for each side's separate holdings and undertakings.[53]

Finally, as Weber emphasizes, there is no tendency inherent in market relations toward the realization of distributive justice. Quite the contrary. Even though it is a system that generates and satisfies needs, a market oriented to money prices and profit does not respond to needs directly, nor does it assure their direct satisfaction. It is not need as such but effective purchasing power—and more specifically control over marketable goods and currency—that determines the kind and quantum of need that is to be met. The satisfaction of need depends on the contingent existing distribution of purchasing power and on the opportunities for profit that happen to exist at any given time without any inherent tendency toward ensuring that everyone can draw his fair share from participation in—let alone have fair (as distinct from formally equal) access to—this system of cooperation, even assuming perfect competition.[54]

As mentioned above, Weber, like other analysts of the market, treats the role of prices as central. In my view, the relation between value and price points to the relation between the juridical conception of transactions and the market. In the discussion of contract, I suggested that equal value in exchange is a regulative baseline for contractual obligation, though subject to the parties' agreement to determine otherwise. In that respect, value need not be actually systemic. Thus, in the basic promise-for-consideration relation, value may be expressed simply and immediately as between two qualitatively and quantitatively different sides, and if this is what the parties reasonably intend, reference to going market prices may be irrelevant. At the same time, I argued that value is the proper content of ownership when ownership is viewed as relational and in the form of representation. All this is part and parcel of the juridical analysis of bilateral ownership relations.

But value need not be limited to this immediate comparison between two things. When value is systematically and generally established such that indefinitely many different objects of exchange, both present and future, are simultaneously comparable in purely quantitative relational terms, value takes the form of price. So understood, price is therefore representation from a general and systemic standpoint. As representation, it signals the determinate measure of an opportunity for and the cost of acquisition via reciprocal exchange in an ongoing network of exchanges. Now in the discussion of the system of needs, we saw that self-seeking activity takes the form of other-directed interaction. To satisfy their own interests, participants need and want to know, so as to be able to respond to, what others may be willing to do with their things in potential exchanges. Prices provide this needed information in a form that is appropriate for systematically interdependent market actors. Thus regulation by market price is perhaps the most complete and unrestricted public economic expression of the other-related orientation characteristic of action in the system of needs. It is the generalization and systematization of the value relation that regulates every contractual relation.[55]

Precisely on account of the other-related orientation and self-maintaining systematic interdependency that regulation by prices makes possible, participation in market relations not only generates new needs and new kinds of work and production, but it also drives the creation of new forms of transactional and economic relations that serve to channel the satisfaction of those interests and purposes.[56] Within the legal framework of enforceable transactions, those engaged in business and trade devise and implement different kinds of transactions (ever more specialized and subdivided) with the result that the common capital of interdependent cooperation is enhanced, strengthened, and made ever more useful to all. They do this to further their interests in the competitive struggle and on the basis of their localized experience and knowledge of the specifics of their diverse market situations and activities. Despite—indeed as a result of—these ever-increasing differentiations and specializations, all transactors share the very same market-based *formal* interest in knowing in advance and internalizing the specific features, requirements, and uses of the possible kinds of transactions.[57] In order to be able to engage in deliberate and planned acquisitions of powers of control and disposal, market participants need and want to know in advance not only what can be exchanged and on what terms but also this transaction-related information.[58] Whereas the first is made publicly available via the price system, the second, we will see in more detail, is established by contract law in its institutional role.

My contention is that the immediate impetus for contract law being institutional and what it does as institutional arise from what individuals need and do qua market transactors. Market relations are the central, indeed perhaps the only, instance of an existing self-perpetuating system of social relations that embodies the juridical conception itself as it is fully expressed in the mutual and reciprocal transaction of exchange. As such, the market represents a pattern of relations that contract law is impelled to draw out and to specify as a system of public authoritative norms expressing the juridical in institutional form.

To avoid misunderstanding, it should be emphasized again that this view does not assume that the determination and enforcement of contractual rights and duties is anything other than institutional. It does not suppose that the juridical conception exists somehow and somewhere in a merely preinstitutional form. What I am trying to do is to distinguish and to account for the different normative dimensions or strands of the practice of contract law as a whole. This is done via a certain conceptual sequence and order that starts with the juridical conception and culminates with its institutional realization. The central difference between these two dimensions, we will see, is that what the juridical conception is and requires implicitly is realized explicitly and publicly as a system of norms that can and must be actually recognized as reasonable, valid, and authoritative by those subject to it. Crucially, this institutional dimension is explained in a way that develops and enriches the juridical conception while fully preserving and building upon its basic normative character. Since the juridical conception entails that all persons mutually and simultaneously owe and in turn are owed respect for each other's ownership rights within the misfeasance framework, it implies the idea of an actual system of such rights that holds for all at once. This idea must be realized explicitly and necessarily as an existing and ongoing actual system of rights. According to the view that I am proposing, the middle term that allows for this transition is the ongoing, self-developing actual system of market relations as a system of needs and in particular the purely formal interest that all market transactors identically share in knowing *ex ante* the applicable bilateral and systemic legal norms that reasonably govern their transactions. The next section explains.

12.2.3. The Institutional Role of Contract Law

Bilateral relations effectuating transactional acquisition comprise an existing system of such relations when they take the form of a market. And it is when they have this kind of existence that there also arises the formal active need on the part of transacting parties for a system of knowable and calculable public norms stipulating both bilateral and systemic requirements, which together can be applied to single cases of particular transactions between definite individuals. In its role as adjudicator of bilateral transactional claims, contract law must show itself equal to the system of economic relationships by providing the kind of public and authoritative point of view that meets the formal needs of market transactors. To this end, contract law must assume an institutional form and role. Before entering into a more detailed discussion, I wish briefly to lay out in broad terms how this next step of contract law functioning as an institutional practice should be understood.

In its institutional role, contract law continues to focus solely on the external relation between transacting parties as owners and exchangers of commodities and recognizes each transaction as a distinct unit of analysis that exists as a result of the nonobligatory (hence optional) joint decisions of the parties to contract with each other. The transactional analysis of contract doctrines and principles remains valid and applicable within its own framework. Indeed, because the transactional analysis explains and justifies the coercive enforcement of contract claims of any kind, it must be presupposed as a fundamental premise in any application of contract law. This includes the juridical conception of contract as involving a transfer of ownership within the parameters of strict contractual liability for misfeasance. Consistent with this premise, at no point does the institutional realization of contract treat parties' individual substantive purposes, intentions, or needs as per se a basis for, or even as relevant to, claims arising in contract law. This is so even though market activity necessarily involves self-seeking satisfaction of substantive needs and interests.

The *sole* aspect of economic market activity of which contract law takes normative cognizance and that allows for a convergence between these two domains is the *specific kind of other-related character* of economic action: the fact that market action—and it alone—involves systematic other-relatedness among indefinitely many persons who count as free and equal owners and exchangers of commodities and who, constrained by force of economic necessity, must learn to internalize and thus to will this other-related standpoint and whatever it entails by way of reasonable terms of interaction. What contract in its institutional role does is to make explicit and to establish in its proper form the norms that are identically and reciprocally willed by individuals as such transactors in this system of exchanges. While transactors in their market activity view the norms of their interaction instrumentally as part of what they must unavoidably do in order to satisfy their wants, contract law in its institutional role reconfigures this economic necessity as a system of authoritative norms, which market participants can know and accept as free and equal persons with their separate and individual interests. Moreover, it posits these norms as noninstrumental requirements of respect that are in themselves valid and binding. The function of contract law is to make both the bilateral and systemic aspects that are immanent in market transactions known and secure as legal rights, duties, powers, and so on in ways that are formally and identically needed by each and every transactor at the point of decision with respect to any given particular exchange.

To meet transactors' formal need for the establishment of the requisite norms, contract law must take notice of the fact that any transaction before a court is an existing, working setup that is embedded in an ongoing system of market relations. We will see that one consequence of contract law viewing transactions in this way is that it not only vindicates a party's contractual rights against the other but, in doing so, also and at the same time fulfills a further institutional role of providing *ex ante* guidance to transactors as market participants. However, as already emphasized, this further role must preserve—and not derogate from, displace, or replace—the normative character of the juridical conception of contract. For the latter is the moral sine qua non of the coercive enforceability of ownership claims.

Hence, I would suggest, there must be the following division of labor between contract law and the market: whereas the law's work is solely to specify the reasonable for market transactors, the modalities of pursuing and satisfying substantive economic needs and interests—which engage the rational—are determined by autonomous market dynamics. As a system of private law, contract law neither inserts itself into this substantive economic activity nor tries to encourage, improve upon, or guide it. Unlike current economic approaches to the law, there is no thought of applying economic analysis directly to the exchange relation as part of contract law. It is particularly important that this division of labor be adhered to when specifying the systemic dimension in contract law. In this way, I hope to show, the juridical conception and the claims of market transactors can both be appropriately and fully respected in one integrated account of the institutional role of contract law.

Now the central factor that enables contract law to perform its institutional function is that it specifies and applies reasonable transactional norms in accordance with the objective test for formation and interpretation, all in a way that satisfies publicity. Indeed, doing this is contract law's indispensable contribution as an institutional practice. This step is not only needed by market transactors, but is already prefigured in and prepared by the kind of social action predicated of them. In this way, market relations are the middle term of the transition between the juridical conception and its institutional realization. I will elaborate briefly.

We have seen that the objective test holds parties to the standpoint of relation to another, such that neither side can impose on the other undisclosed or unexpected nonordinary understandings, assumptions, or considerations. The objective test thus represents a standpoint of the transactionally (reasonably) expected and understandable, making it fully suited to the two-sidedness of contract as a transfer of ownership as understood in the juridical conception. For this reason, we may say that the juridical conception inherently or implicitly requires this standpoint. Now this is also the precise kind of other-related standpoint that market participants must adopt and, even more importantly, the standpoint that they actually do learn to adopt through their participation in the transacting opportunities that the market provides. Developing the insights, skills, and moral sensibilities that are required to do this effectively is an essential means for participants to achieve their economic ends and so becomes itself an objective that they instrumentally want to internalize and effectuate, part of their settled and habitual ends. Through their participation in market activity, they are educated to act from this standpoint, not merely in accordance with it. In this way, as Weber emphasizes, their desires to act in conformity with legality and to respect the formal inviolability of their promises once given are the special elements of market ethics.[59] Holding parties to the objective (i.e., transactional) import of their words and deeds is therefore something that is not only fair and reasonable as between them from a legal point of view. It is also how they themselves learn to view others and in turn expect to be viewed by them.

Now it is one thing for the objective test to be inherently required by the very nature of the juridical conception and to be needed by market transactors. Even though, as I discussed in Chapter 10, the direct and reciprocal relation of contract provides the indispensable basis for the unified standpoint needed to apply the objective test, there must be someone with standing to determine how it applies in any given transaction. But here is the problem. Being unavoidably just one side of a transaction with his or her own particular interests and judgment, no transactor can credibly claim to represent vis-à-vis others this relational standpoint—the standpoint of a transaction as a whole. This is so despite the fact that exchange entails the parties' fully mutual and reciprocal recognition of each other as owners—the most complete reciprocity that is available within the misfeasance framework. To solve this impasse, all transactors must necessarily will the establishment of an agency that stands above market activity, that is not enmeshed in its substantive self-seeking, and that can therefore have for its end the *disinterested* determination and implementation of the reasonable in relation to others. In other words, what is now necessary is that there be a publicly established agency that has for its purpose the fulfillment of the purely formal interest that every transactor identically shares—an interest that is distinct from the substantive dimension of self-seeking economic activity.

This market-needed agency is the office of the judge.[60] Vis-à-vis the parties to any given transaction, the judge always counts as a *third*, who, unlike them, is not a party to their transaction and is therefore disinterested because she is not acting in order to realize any of her own substantive economic interests relative to them. The judge is thus the institutionally competent organ to represent and to declare the relational objective standpoint that all market transactors are presumed to will as part of their ends and to which they may reasonably be held as a matter of justice.[61] Very importantly, if the establishment of this public point of view is to be consistent with their freedom and equality as transactors and so be validated as having legitimate authority over them, it is essential not only that it embody reasonable requirements expressive of their freedom and equality, but that this be publicly shown and established *for* them. Hence the judicial standpoint must be anchored in the particular transaction before the court and seek to determine its reasonable meaning as between the parties. Not only would this satisfy their formal interest in having these matters known and settled, but it would also do so in a way that enables the transactors to recognize themselves and their interests in the court's determination, thereby respecting them as the purposeful agents that they are and ensuring, as far as the court is able, a congruence between the reasonable and their good.

Our central question now is, how more specifically does contract law fulfill this public institutional role? We start with the fundamental point that market actors want and need to know two dimensions of their exchange activity: first, its character as a single enforceable transaction and, second, its systemic side. The first dimension refers to both basic contract principles that apply to any transaction and the more specific requirements, incidents, and effects of different types of transactions. By contrast, the second dimension considers factors that operate at a systemic level, that characterize transactions in their interconnectedness as parts of a system, and that pertain to the essential existence and completeness of the market system itself. Both dimensions are distinct from the substantive objects and contents of individuals' wants. They are formal and abstract means that all transactors identically need to take into account if they are to form and satisfy those substantive interests via a system of exchange relations. Thus, as participants in the market, all can be attributed the very same formal interest with respect to them. I begin with the bilateral dimension.

First, there are the *general* doctrines, principles, and features of contract law, which specify the most basic kind of relation that any and every contract must instantiate if it is to give rise to coercible contractual rights and duties. Since these principles are distinct yet mutually supporting aspects of this unified conception of relation, they constitute a coherent system of norms. Being general, these principles and features can be articulated and known in advance of any particular instance of transacting, and they apply directly to economic exchanges as to any other bilateral relation satisfying the requirements for contract formation.[62] And being content-neutral, they hold irrespective of parties' different purposes and substantive interests, leaving these to the parties to decide on the basis of their particular market interests, driven by the market's own distinct dynamic. Even standards of contractual fairness allow for this division of labor by taking as their presumed measure of reasonableness generally available going market prices or their equivalent. Moreover, these doctrines—involving both rules and standards—satisfy requirements of simplicity and practicality. Unlike complex economic or other functions, they refer to facts and considerations that are reasonably accessible and comprehensible to parties in their everyday transactional pursuits. These doctrines do not impose requirements of foresight or knowledge of matters that would be beyond parties' ready grasp, such as society-wide social and economic ramifications of their particular interactions.[63] Finally, the fact that the principles are consonant with the freedom and equality of transactors in their external exchange relations with each other means that there is no barrier to market participants accepting their authority.

I have emphasized that these general principles treat the promised consideration of any contract as a normatively certain, present asset whose full and fair value is fixed at formation, irrespective of such factors as the particular circumstances, difficulties of performance, changing costs, and alternative opportunities that the promisor may encounter after formation (falling short of mistake, impossibility, and so forth). In so viewing the consideration, the law treats it as a distinct and determinate commodity with its own value, something that itself can in principle be bought and sold on a market. This makes possible the full development and expansion of what Weber called the marketability of objects as well as the impersonality of the market, where parties "look toward the commodity, not the person of others."[64] Moreover, an impersonal system of exchange relations necessarily presupposes that transactors can have general expectations about the conduct of others. The expectation of performance as a present asset is the only such general expectation that is consistent with the possibility of a credit market economy. Just as all transactors as economic agents have an identical formal interest in the existence of a price system, so they also have such an interest in upholding the legal standpoint that treats the promise-of-consideration as a present (purely rightful) asset.[65]

As a further part of its institutional role with respect to this bilateral dimension, contract law also specifies and fixes *different transaction-types*, each with its more specific party roles, features, and contractual incidents. These represent a sort of juridically a priori table of more specific forms of enforceable contractual relations that further determine the basic promise-for-consideration relation.[66] Whereas if the promise principle is taken as the basis of contract (so that the content of any contractual relation is simply and indeterminately whatever a party has decided to promise) there is little if anything to structure an internal division into multiple and distinct contract-types, this is not true of the basic promise-for-consideration relation. The latter, we saw, presupposes the distinction between nonphysical acquisition at formation and physical possession via performance, and it can be analyzed substantively in terms of the contrasting fundamental categories of gift and exchange. Further, the consideration may consist of goods, services, opportunities, rights, liberties, or currency itself; it may be something generic or unique; and the kind of exclusive interest it involves may be anything from full and complete ownership to the most limited use or possession. These possibilities and distinctions yield diverse forms of transaction-types, each of which is *ex ante* knowably enforceable: a gift of a thing (whether specific, generic, or currency) or of a service (e.g., safe-keeping of another's property) either outright or for a limited use and time; an exchange of things (for another specific thing, as in barter, or for currency) or of services (as with a contract for wages) either outright (e.g., in sale) or for a limited use and time (contract for rent); and the giving of security or pledge (which involves the cleavage between ownership and mere physical possession) in connection with either a gift or an exchange transaction.[67]

An important role of contract law is to articulate these forms of enforceable transaction-types as intelligible categories of contractual relations. But the classification represents merely possible transaction-types logically latent in the basic promise-for-consideration relation. It is the countless interconnected market actions of transactors that breathe life into them and give them particular content. They provide the material for contractual enforcement. Accordingly, a further and equally important contribution of law in attending to the multiplicity of contracts is to recognize in these ever-evolving market practices the actualization of transaction-types and to articulate their contractual meaning in light of transactors' interactions. Insofar as these social facts can be analyzed in terms of the basic form and variants of the promise-for-consideration relation, they can count in law as different types of enforceable bilateral transactions. In doing so, the law aims to delineate rights and duties for "an actual, working situation which has some pre-existing structure," and it looks to existing social relations as points of reference for the elaboration of the legal relation.[68] It is from this standpoint that the interpretation and implication of terms are undertaken. Following Llewellyn, this judicial interpretative methodology may be called "situation-sense."[69]

The work of judicial common law reasoning, situation-sense sees in the particularities of interaction definite transaction-types comprised of paradigmatic facts that are specified and interconnected not in virtue of some logical necessity but because this is how the transactions function in and are shaped by social economic processes of market exchange. The different forms of transactions become routinized and culturally familiar to market participants.[70] When parties decide to transact, they choose, not a transaction-in-general, but a particular transaction-type with its corresponding purposes, subject matter, and roles. Thus, exchanges are between merchant and buyer, owner and hirer, master and servant, landlord and tenant, mortgagor and mortgagee, pledger and pledgee, carrier and customer, builder and owner, retailer and consumer, financial manager and client, and so on. And each of these categories may in turn be further specified and subdivided.[71] Each is characterized by distinct features, incidents, background assumptions, trade usages, shared understandings, and practices, which crystallize and change through market activities.[72]

Situation-sense discloses the richness of transactional normative meanings and implications present in a given single interaction by bringing out its qualitative and determinate character.[73] It is always a matter of structured particulars at different levels of generality. The analysis takes seriously the shared understandings of parties in their social and economic roles in different transaction-types as these have developed and are continuing to develop over time. Judges consider how a given situation works and whether the legal analysis fits with what is already there or, to the contrary, would unnecessarily impede its proper functioning: is an application of doctrine "more than commerce can bear?"[74]

Moreover, contract law supposes that immanent in any given type of transaction is a certain kind of required balance and transactional coherence, which takes the transaction as a working setup with an expected pattern of risks of gains and losses. The implication of terms and conditions, which I discussed in detail, is premised on this analysis. The principle of unconscionability that holds for all contracts in general is applied to any given transaction in accordance with the objective test and situation-sense. Thus, what are fair and reasonable contractual terms or incidents that parties are presumed to intend are worked out for the kind of exchange relation at issue. This provides a baseline for analysis. Although parties can choose their own terms, whether they have done so and what they have chosen is determined by seeing how this compares to the baseline. If, from the standpoint of the objective test, it clearly appears that parties transactionally intended a certain kind of transaction but chose terms that, if enforced as is, would completely eviscerate the minimum content characteristic of such a transaction or convert their agreement into an altogether different kind of transaction-type, those terms become problematic and subject to being struck out for unconscionability and unreasonableness.[75]

Situation-sense analysis always culminates with a determination of the contractual rights and duties as between two parties. By doing so on the basis of this interpretative approach, the law decides rights and duties not only in a way that the parties themselves can accept as reasonable as between them but that also answers their rational need to know the reasonable dimension of their economic interaction and to have it authoritatively established for their use when they plan their activities. For, as part of ideal theory, we suppose here that transactors, even if only for instrumental reasons, want to know and to act consistently with each other's rights and the requirements of enforceable relations when applied to single transactions—which are the localized context of individual decision-making. When courts adjudicate single cases *ex post,* this is not only coercively to correct violations of right. From the standpoint of ideal theory, courts adjudicating single cases also specify the determinate juridical meaning of the requirements of respect in relation to a single transaction. By doing this in accordance with the objective test, courts must and do satisfy the right of transactors to be held only to what they could reasonably have known in the circumstances of their particular interaction. Despite the *ex post* nature of adjudication, parties can reasonably view the imposition of liability as consistent with their status as equal market participants and as free from the taint of unfair surprise.[76] It can be legitimate from their own point of view, and they can be confident in the general approach and protection provided by the law. Moreover, we should also keep in mind here that the transaction-types modeled by law are specified *general* categories of interaction, which are embedded in actual market relations and which therefore refer to ongoing, existing opportunities for market participation. By framing the analysis in these terms, the law can also potentially provide transactors in general with knowledge that they can take into account before they act.[77] To this extent at least, the *ex post* adjudication of contractual claims fulfills the *ex ante* institutional function of articulating principles, standards, and rules for the guidance of conduct in other transactions yet to come.

Clearly, situation-sense looks to social and market activity for determinate content in its discernment and analysis of transaction-types, and it treats the fact that contracts are existing transactions embedded in ongoing market activities and processes as normatively significant in its own right. But as I noted above, in taking this view, contract law does not make the establishment of markets and their well-functioning its goal. Rather, it sees in existing market practices—brought about through the economic actions of market participants themselves—the actualization of the juridical conception of transactional acquisition as an ongoing system of practicable public principles, standards, and rules, and it seeks to establish this knowledge publicly and authoritatively for transactors.

Contract law's institutional role is thus to establish as publicly knowable and fully authoritative the conception of relation to another which transactors need and want to know as interdependent members of the system of needs. In this way, the law satisfies a purely formal interest that is identically the same for every transactor as a market participant. The idea of relation to others, which is immanent in market activity and which transactors need to know, is exactly the juridical conception of contract itself. Relative to the juridical conception, contract law in its institutional role does not incorporate any new normative elements except the establishment of this conception as an actual system of publicly known, practicable, and authoritative standards and rules, in this way paralleling the economic role of the system of prices for market activity. At no point does it make the determination and satisfaction of transactors' substantive interests and needs part of that institutional function, but leaves this, and whatever relates to it, completely to their self-seeking economic action.

So far my discussion of the congruence between contract and the market and of the institutional role of contract has focused on the purely bilateral dimension in any given transaction as expressed through the main doctrines and principles of contract when these are brought to bear in accordance with the method of situation-sense. What about the *systemic* dimension in market transactions? This is also something that transactors need and want to know as market participants. Here again, the work of contract law in its institutional role is to discern in market relations systemic aspects that it can appropriately make explicit and establish in the form of public and authoritative principles, standards, and rules applicable to single cases. In this way, it answers the needs of transacting market actors. On the view that I am proposing, it is crucial that this further step also be consistent with, and build on, the normative character of the bilateral juridical dimension. The latter remains conceptually first in the sequence of normative analysis.

Now for something to qualify as a *contractually* relevant systemic aspect of market relations, the following must be the case: a given matter must be such that it is necessarily and identically willed by all transactors as market participants. Looking at any given transaction, we must be able to say that parties joined in accordance with the requirements of bilaterality *also* share, qua rational market actors and thus simultaneously with all other market participants, a completely identical, because formal, interest in needing and furthering this or that systemic aspect of market relations. Formulated in terms of the objective test, it can and indeed must be reasonable to impute this interest to any market participant. Looking at this point from a different angle, it should be the case that the inclusion of a given systemic aspect will help to actualize the juridical conception as a system of public, practicable, and authoritative norms *for* transactors in their ordinary market activity. This is the sign that contract law is fulfilling an institutional role. Contract law's ability to incorporate systemic aspects in this way is essential to showing the congruence between contract and market relations.

To illustrate and clarify these preliminary points, I will now discuss three well-known instruments and rules of contract law that, I will suggest, may be viewed as instances of contract law institutionally serving this systemic dimension: the promise under seal, the now abolished doctrine of market overt, and the development of negotiable instruments and documents. All three, it should be underlined, were established by common law judges as rules (as distinct from principles or standards) in the exercise of their inherent jurisdiction for the purposes of adjudicating transactional disputes. At the same time, these purely judge-made rules enable parties to produce legal effects that go beyond what would ordinarily follow from applying just the transactional juridical conception framed in terms of bilaterality. An important caveat here as elsewhere is that this must be accomplished without undermining or displacing the bilateral analysis. I begin with the seal.[78]

The common law seal, which is the oldest of the three and even antedates the doctrine of consideration, enables promisors to make contractually enforceable what might otherwise be deemed a gratuitous promise, thereby dispensing with the requirement of consideration. It applies to each promise as a separate undertaking independently of any reciprocal promise coming from the other side.[79] As David J. Ibbetson has noted with respect to sealed documents in medieval English law, "[f]ormal contracts, in essence, took effect unilaterally. The debtor must have acted voluntarily; the debtor must have sealed the document; and the debtor must have delivered the document to the creditor."[80] Sealed promises are enforceable as a result of parties voluntarily using a certain form specified by the law rather than fulfilling "requisites relating to the essential nature of the transaction."[81] Judicial development of the seal drew on the existing social-legal fact that the use of this formality to produce legal effects was publicly and generally known as part of actual and persisting customary practice from "time immemorial."[82] Now, because the promissory relation under seal is not intrinsically bilateral in the way of a promise-for-consideration relation, it cannot be explained just in terms of the juridical conception.[83] With good reason, then, the seal is generally viewed as dispensing with rather than satisfying consideration. Yet it can produce the very same contractual effects. By understanding the seal as a legal device that belongs to the systemic institutional dimension of contract law, we can justify it in a way that is not in tension with consideration or the juridical conception.

Both the apparent problem with and the justification of the seal revolve around the status of the gratuitous promise in basic contract doctrine. From the standpoint of the juridical conception, there is no doubt about its status. Because the nonformal gratuitous promise is not two-sided in a way that can unambiguously manifest representationally the transfer of a subject matter from the promisor's exclusive rightful control into that of the promisee, it cannot on that basis produce coercively enforceable contractual effects. At the same time, however, there is nothing in the idea of transfer that requires it to consist of only a full-fledged exchange. Conceptually, we saw, gift, no less than exchange, is a coequal basic form of transfer. Both can involve the mutually related acts of two sides—namely, united acts of alienation and appropriation. Moreover, we have seen that in principle whether a promise counts as two-sided is determined on the basis of the parties' representations as reasonably willed by them. In arm's-length dealings, parties ordinarily presume that neither of them is trifling but in fact wants their interaction to have legal effects unless he or she clearly indicates otherwise. It is on this basis that they form market expectations and develop confidence in each other's market conduct. Indeed, there are familiar instances involving market exchange relations where, despite the fact that promises are properly viewed as purely gratuitous because they are unsupported by consideration, the *parties themselves* appear to understand and assume that the promises are given as part of a two-sided relation.

A familiar example is where, in return for better terms, a party promises or does something that he or she already owes the other party under their existing contract.[84] Except in clear cases of opportunistic advantage-taking, market transactors—"all men of business"—ordinarily may view such dealings as reasonable adjustments that are essential to the continuing viability and efficacy of what they see as an ongoing transaction.[85] On the basis of established business norms of honesty and good faith, they certainly expect that the adjustment will be honored.[86] But the doctrine of consideration may deem the promised adjustment to be purely gratuitous and so as unenforceable. The juridical and market transactors' points of view seem here to be out of sync with each other.

The juridical conception of contract formation, even though fully reasonable within its own framework, seems nevertheless to be a source of uncertainty for market participants, who, we suppose, act from respect for legality and need legality in the form of clear and comprehensive regulative rules that match their ordinarily intended and wanted market interactions. One response to this market need is to change basic contract doctrine itself in order to make it harmonize better with market expectations and understandings. For example, the meaning and scope of the doctrine of consideration are changed.[87]

In contrast with such an approach, the one that I am proposing leaves the doctrine completely intact and fully applicable in the sphere of *nonformal* interaction between parties. This point is crucial to my argument. To address formal interests that all transactors may identically share as participants in market relations, contract law need not change basic doctrine. Indeed, it cannot do so because, supposing as I have argued that these doctrines do express what is reasonable as between parties to a contractual relation, the parties must be presumed to have an interest in upholding them. What contract law can do is to develop formal legal devices or their analogues rooted in requirements of general knowability and practicability. Here, in contrast with the justification of basic contract doctrines, it is appropriate to view the court as fashioning, in the strict sense, power-conferring rules *for parties to use* to produce intended legal effects.[88] In this way, not only the court but also the parties themselves can take into account what is certain and externally available without running the risk that, despite their interaction, one of them might change his or her mind, relying on the fact that the law may view his or her promise as gratuitous.[89] The giving and receiving of what counts in basic doctrine as a contractually unenforceable gratuitous promise can now count publicly as acts that produce the effects of a contract. That a device such as the seal is generally familiar as a matter of custom from time immemorial makes it well suited to be appropriated by a court in declaring a legally effective formality.[90]

Viewing the seal in this way, it is reasonable as between (and for) the parties to hold that its use can produce enforceable contractual rights and duties, even starting, as we have done, from the baseline that a nonformal interaction must satisfy consideration to constitute an enforceable contractual relation. Parties are held to have produced contractual effects just because this is what they wanted to do, as evidenced and made possible by their use of the formality. As such a device, the seal—in contrast with the requirement of consideration—is designed to serve what Fuller called the parties' channeling interest and, irrespective of the historical fate of the traditional common law sealed document, this formal interest, as many have noted, remains basic for transactors.[91] It also follows that if, to the contrary, the formal requirements associated with the seal have become diluted or their significance is no longer generally understood in practice, the case for enforcement on the basis of this formality is challenged and the parties' interaction must be assessed in accordance with the baseline requirement of consideration, even if this differs from the parties' actual market purposes and intentions. At stake here is the possible coercive enforcement of claims on the basis of non-formal interaction, and the corresponding requirements of the reasonable must therefore always be satisfied consistently with the parties' freedom and equality within the framework of the juridical conception of contract.

The second example, the rule of market overt, was part of English common law for over five hundred years until its abolition in 1995.[92] Unlike the common law seal, it is not simply a legal formality and device to be used by transactors to produce legal effects. Rather, it stipulates strictly defined general conditions concerning the place, time, and manner of transacting on the basis of which bona fide purchasers can be certain that their acquisition of goods (as distinct from real property) by exchange is final and indefeasible, not only against vendors but also vis-à-vis third parties, including those with potentially better title. The focus of the rule is a type of uncertainty in exchange relations, which arises as follows.

Suppose a vendor has stolen goods that he sells to a good faith purchaser without notice. Although the purchaser has an in personam claim against the seller for any unexcused departure from the contract terms, and so a right to expectation remedies, her title against third parties is, as discussed earlier, ordinarily no better than the seller's. Since the goods were stolen, the true owner can claim them back from whoever happens to have them, including therefore even a bona fide purchaser without notice. This simply applies the *nemo dat* rule, which is itself a general and formal principle that is integral to the juridical conception of acquisition. More generally, no one who has bought goods in good faith can be sure that at some point up the chain of title, there has not been some opposing better claim that affects prior and thus subsequent derivative title. This uncertainty of title that is intrinsic to possessory rights means that despite all reasonable appearances, parties to a market transaction cannot rely on the market being a self-sufficient and complete system through which entitlements acquired in good faith can be certain and final. Yet all transactors, as market participants, have the same identical formal interest in the market being such a system. How is this need to be met?

In my view, it is crucial that any court-imposed (as distinct from legislative) solution *not* entail the systemic overriding or subordination of third-party claims or in rem interests in favor of bilateral in personam transactional entitlements or vice versa.[93] This would be inconsistent with the lexically prior juridical conception itself, which comprises both dimensions, each with its own claims within its own framework and operating in tandem with the other on the basis of the *nemo dat* rule. Ensuring that the market can function as a complete and final system of entitlements is not to be achieved by changing or displacing the juridical conception. The institutional establishment of the juridical conception as a system of principles, standards, and rules does *not* change the basic content of the juridical conception: it merely actualizes *this* conception and all that it comprises such that it can be known and used by any and every transactor. It is this actualization of the juridical conception as a system of rules that market participants are viewed as needing and willing.

We suppose, then, that each transactor has the same formal interest in there being a system of exchanges in which all can know with certainty that reasonably apparent good faith transactional acts of alienation and acquisition are in law indefeasibly final and valid if concluded by the participants in that system. In the absence of title formalities or registration, this formal interest can be met if there are judicially instituted, actual legally operative markets that are fully insulated from any entitlement-determinations other than the local exchange relations (in accordance with the objective test) that comprise them. It must be possible to ensure that all relevant title holders are included and share the same public standpoint that fixes the meaning and effects of their interrelated exchange acts in a way that commensurates, without collapsing, the in personam and in rem meanings of their exchange entitlements. Now the crucial prerequisite for this is that it must be reasonable to view not only the seller and buyer but, in the example of stolen goods, also any prior owner of those goods as all participants in that system and so governed by its public determinations. To the extent that this is the case, title determination via any given exchange can potentially be final. My suggestion is that the rigorous requirements of the market overt rule are one way of achieving this.

In more detail, these requirements stipulate: (1) A market overt refers to a specific and designated physical location where sales are conducted. (2) It must be a market that is open, public, legally constituted, and established by a long and continual user, unless created by statute or by charter. (3) The doctrine covers sales (not pledges or gifts) of goods. The sales must be conducted in conformity with the usage of the particular market; the goods must be of a description that is customary or usual to find on sale in that market, must be openly exposed for sale there, and must be sold on an ordinary market day during regular or customary hours (usually between sunrise and sunset). (4) From start to finish, the entire transaction, comprising the sale, delivery, and payment, must be conducted openly and in plain public view within the market and according to the foregoing stipulations. Thus, if any aspect (however minor) of the transaction is not conducted in this way, the sale simply does not come within the rule.[94] (5) The purchaser must have actual possession of the goods in accordance with the completed and performed terms of their sale. (6) The purchaser must have transacted entirely in good faith and reasonably without notice of any problems or circumstances raising even the slightest question as to title (e.g., if the sale was without evident reason for significantly less than the ordinary market price).[95]

Where a market meets these requirements, and particularly where commerce is slower and more limited in scale, an owner, wrongly dispossessed of his or her goods, can and would reasonably be expected to pursue the goods to the particular market where it is well known that they would be openly and publicly sold. Even if the original owner obtained his or her goods from a different market or by way of gift or other means, the requirements provide a reasonable basis for holding that those goods are of a kind regularly bought and sold in the particular market where the impugned transaction has taken place and that he or she has ready access to it.[96] Consequently, a good faith purchaser would have reasonable grounds to suppose that, in the often-quoted words of Lord Blackburn, "no person but the owner would dare to expose them for sale here, and, therefore, I have a right to assume that the shop-keeper has a right to sell them."⁹⁷ Vis-à-vis all those who know or reasonably could know of the particular market and have access to it—and this would include the original owner—any such sale is transparent and public. And because the sale is public and open to them, it also is valid and definitive as among them. There is one public standpoint for all who access the market, and, vis-à-vis them, this standpoint determines fully and definitively ownership rights acquired via participation in that market.

Only insofar as the doctrinally required (or functionally equivalent) conditions actually obtain can the law enforce sales in this manner consistently with respect for the ownership of all and without unfair surprise to anyone. Where a sale takes place in market overt, all the relevant parties can reasonably be viewed simply as actual or potential participants in the same system of exchanges. The fact that the original owner may have obtained the goods by gift and so forth can now be irrelevant. The doctrine of market overt functions to carve out a system of exchanges that is the sole and complete determinant of valid title. It embodies the idea of complete and certain knowability of the requisite acts and effects of transactional acquisition. This, it must be emphasized, is possible only in virtue of the character of the system of which the sale is a part. In performing this function, the rule of market overt takes a further step in meeting the channeling interest that each and every market participant identically shares, consistently with their freedom and equality as transactors.⁹⁸

My third and last example of the common law's recognition and enforcement of a systemic dimension in exchange relations is the judicial development of the law of negotiable instruments. As a matter of history, it was Lord Mansfield, widely considered the "father of commercial law," who in particular gave a robust direction and solid intellectual basis to its development.⁹⁹ Clearly, in economic terms, this legal contribution was and continues to be pivotally important. From the standpoint of the theory of contract law, it represents perhaps the paradigmatic instance of contract law's establishment of the systemic dimension in market exchange relations as part of a system of publicly knowable and authoritative conduct-guiding legal norms.

The most complete systemic expression of market relations is the price system itself, which supposes the circulation of commodities through the use of money currency as the means and measure of the exchange of things of value. Money as currency is an object of ownership that is used only by being alienated in exchange for goods, services, and the like. The law of negotiability is a key part of the legal construction and validation of objects of ownership as currency and thus as part of the "great wheel of circulation" (which is nothing other than the actualization of the price system).[100] This is accomplished by designating certain objects of ownership as acquirable through and usable in exchange in such a way that they are fully insulated from any and all nonapparent contingencies of title affecting transactional acquisition under the *nemo dat* rule. The systemic character and basis are evident in the fact that transactionally acquired title in these objects is not governed by the transactional principle of *nemo dat*.[101] Lord Mansfield's seminal decision in *Millar v. Race* provides a particularly good illustration.[102]

In *Millar*, the plaintiff innkeeper brought an action in trover to recover from the defendant bank a banknote for the payment of £21 10s. The plaintiff had received the note in the ordinary course of its business wholly in good faith and without notice of any defect or unfair dealing from a person who, although making the appearance of a gentleman (as the report put it), had in fact stolen the note. For his part, the original owner of the note, on becoming aware of the robbery, ordered the defendant bank, acting as his agent, to stop payment. As a consequence, when the plaintiff handed the note over to the bank in order to receive payment, the bank refused to pay the note or to redeliver it back to the plaintiff. Hence the plaintiff's action to recover it.

The fundamental issue is clearly set by the court: Is the banknote just like any other item of stolen goods where title remains unaffected with the original owner so that he can follow it into whosoever hands it may come? Or, to the contrary, is it money that must be capable of circulating and therefore of becoming the property of the person who bona fide takes possession of it (for value) in the course of currency? From the early fourteenth century, merchants had been using banks to exchange, remit, and deposit money, and by the sixteenth century, the adjustment of accounts was the most important function of the fairs of Lyons, Spain, and Genoa.[103] In Lord Mansfield's words, "[I]n the ordinary course and transaction of business, by the general consent of mankind[,] which gives [banknotes] the credit and currency of money, to all intents and purposes . . . [a] bank-note is constantly and universally, both at home and abroad, treated as money, as cash; and paid and received, as cash."[104] It is "necessary, for the purposes of commerce, that their currency should be established and secured."[105]

Defendant's counsel had argued that the determination of title universally turns on whether an item of property has distinguishing marks and numbers on it that make it ascertainable and specific and hence properly recoverable by the original owner if lost or stolen. Since the banknote in question had an "ear-mark" and was fully ascertainable, the plaintiff's action for trover must fail. Against this view, Lord Mansfield insists that the crucial criterion is whether the banknote "has passed in currency"—that is, whether it is given and accepted as money and thus as a means of payment that performs the generally recognized function of systemic circulation.[106] Once the original owner's banknote has been so received for value and without notice by someone in the course of currency, the property in the note changes and becomes vested in its actual holder even against the "true owner." A contrary determination, Lord Mansfield notes, would result in trade and commerce being "much incommoded."[107] Of course, as against a finder or thief of the note or money, the true owner can recover it—for here the note would not yet have passed without notice in currency.[108]

In effect, as plaintiff's counsel suggested, the analysis of ownership in the case of a banknote given and accepted as money should be the same as the bona fide purchase of goods in market overt.[109] In the latter case, the transfer is final as against the world of actual and potential market participants, thereby enabling, within these parameters, the indefeasible circulation of goods. In the former, the transfer is final on the sole basis and for the reason that the object is attributed a function that is expressly and abstractly for the purpose of circulation, unlimited by time or place. Its sole function is that it makes possible a general system of exchange. It is upheld not with respect to a specified market, but on the basis of its being the abstract condition of *any* market. Note also that, paralleling both the seal and market overt, the designation of negotiability takes cognizance of the public and known customs regarding the treatment of something as currency. This provides the systemic content that is established and secured by contract law performing its institutional role and thereby satisfying without taint of unfair surprise the formal interest that is identically shared by all transactors as market participants.

There is a further point worth noting here. In the discussion of first possession as a basic principle of acquisition, we saw that even if the right thereby acquired is "against the world" in the sense of being directly against indefinitely many (potential) others, the ownership that characterizes this right is always intrinsically relative and defeasible in the face of one who can establish prior rightful possession. This is true despite the absence of apparent conflicting title at the moment of acquisition. The right cannot therefore be thought of as truly and conclusively valid against everyone else. Here, however, with the transfer of assets having the function of currency or publicly recognized exchangeability, the ownership factor in possession can be absolutely, and not merely relatively, valid against the world. This possibility is an incident of the law's recognition and enforcement of the systemic dimension of the external relation in the system of needs, which, we have seen, is and must entail a system of exchanges. Thus possession is actualized in its character as absolutely valid against everyone when acquisition is no longer unilateral (as in first possession) but rather transactionally realized in and through a system of interconnected bilateral exchanges.

12.2.4. Summary

The proposed argument for the stability of the transactional conception of contract in relation to the market is, I believe, consistent with my main thesis of contract law's independence and autonomy. The argument postulates both a division of labor and congruence between them. The market and contract law represent two different (though connected) domains, each with its own special character and dynamic as well as its own immanent and distinct purposes. Still, both the market and contract law are so constituted that they each fit with and are supportive of the other.

The fundamental contrast between them is that whereas contract law specifies a system of reasonable principles and rules that can coercively apply to the immediate contractual transaction between two parties, the market represents a system of purely voluntary interactions through which individuals seek to obtain their substantive satisfactions from each other. Even though legal institutions fix and guarantee the market's normative, noneconomic presuppositions, these are just the market's necessary conditions, not its distinctive features. Nor, on the other side, does the fact that contract law takes up economic interactions as its appropriate content make it dependent upon or rooted in the latter. Even in fulfilling its institutional role, contract law is wholly animated by considerations of justice, and the only requirements it specifies are those of the reasonable—and, more specifically, the juridical conception of transactions—which it discerns in the relational dimensions of market activity and makes explicit as a system of public, practicable, and authoritative norms. In doing so, it actualizes the juridical conception as such a system without changing its fundamental elements or parameters. The law authoritatively determines and thereby secures the negative coercible rights and duties of parties before the court on a basis that assesses market participants by standards and understandings that are at once immanent in their economic activity and morally reasonable between them as free and equal persons. Contract law thereby establishes a publicly available signaling and information-communicating mechanism that complements and, as it were, corresponds to, the public character and role of market prices—with the major difference being that whereas the latter comes under the idea of the rational, the former expresses nothing but the reasonable.

It should be emphasized that this institutional role of contract law both preserves and builds on the transactional analysis of contract as a juridical relation that is embodied in the basic doctrines and principles of contract discussed in Part One. There we saw that the basic promise-for-consideration relation need not be, in material terms, only a market exchange and that its analysis need not entail the systemic dimension characteristic of the market. While the move from contract as juridical relation to contract as institution is a further enrichment of the initial transactional conception, it presupposes and preserves the latter as normatively prior. This priority stems from the fact that the promise-for-consideration relation represents the indispensable fundamental moral basis for the coercive enforcement of any contractual rights and duties. The institutional regime of contract law carries forward and implements on a fully public basis the standpoint of the objective test, thereby vindicating the standpoint from which every aspect of any contractual relation is specified and assessed.

At the same time, showing that the initial transactional conception can be developed to fulfill its own proper institutional role suggests that this conception can be stable in the right way. When exchanges are embedded in a market as a system of needs, individuals count as transactors who each have the same identical formal interest in the existence, knowledge, and assurance of certain bilateral and systemic aspects and features, without which they cannot transact as rational and reasonable free and equal persons. The institutional contribution of contract law ensures the application of the reasonable to transactions in a way that market participants can view not only as legitimately imposed on them, but also as part of their own rational good, even if from a standpoint that initially treats these requirements as instrumentally good. Crucially, this congruence between contract and market exchange—and hence the stability of contract from the standpoint of market actors—is possible because of the character of the social or relational dimension that is shared by both these domains and that is formal in comparison with the substantive nature of market transactors' particular needs and interests. In its institutional role, contract law specifies this social relation in both its bilateral and systemic dimensions as a matter of authoritative and public justice.

Now, reflecting the fact that contract and market are each relatively autonomous and distinct in their own right, contract law does not seek to produce, but to the contrary, it merely recognizes, the existence of a market dynamic as an independent, self-sustaining, and ongoing reality, which has its own internal functions and goal-orientation as a system of exchange relations.[110] The key regulative feature of this system is the price mechanism, which is a purely economic process of coordinating the separate economic actions of different people in the pursuit of their diverse substantive preferences and objects, where the relevant information about these needs and their alternative satisfactions is localized and dispersed throughout society, not given to or by one and the same single mind. Courts dealing with single cases in their adjudicative capacity cannot possibly substitute for the price mechanism because they cannot credibly purport to effectuate its systemic function with respect to substantive need satisfaction. The rights and duties (as well as powers) of contract law can no more fulfill the function of prices in the economic sense than prices can plausibly be viewed as communicating principled judgments of justice. There is a genuine institutional division of labor between law and economy and the failure to follow through on and to respect this necessarily distorts and undermines the inherent legitimacy of both. Thus it cannot be the aim of contract law to fashion, or even to influence, exchanges so that they enable parties jointly to obtain their substantive satisfactions (and welfare) more efficiently. For the same reason, and contrary to much current theoretical orthodoxy, it cannot be an intrinsic goal of contract law to "reduce transaction costs" for the parties. The direct application of economic considerations to contract law cannot be part of a public basis of justification for contract.

12.3. Contract Law and Distributive Justice

We now come to the third and final issue of stability. This completes the proposed public justification of contract law. Precisely because the transactional conception of contract, including the nature of contract law as an institution, is nondistributive in character, this raises the question of its relation to distributive justice and more particularly whether it allows for, and in fact can fit together with, plausible and robust liberal principles of distributive justice, such as Rawls's second principle of justice, in one complete system of justice.[111] Rawls refers to this second principle, which comprises a requirement of fair equality of opportunity and the difference principle, as distributive justice in a narrower sense.[112] In the following discussion of the relation between distributive justice and contract law, it is this notion of distributive justice that will be centrally at issue. If the proposed account of justice in transactions were to rule this out—for example, by conflicting with the full application of a principle of fair (not merely formal) equality of opportunity—that, in my view, would bring the moral acceptability of this conception of contract law into question. My aim in this section is to explain why this need not be the case.

I shall argue that in sharp contrast with libertarian theory, the transactional conception that I have proposed for private law principles of acquisition and transfer not only makes room for suitable principles of distributive justice, but, as envisaged by Rawls, it also enables the former principles to be part of the following division of labor: between distributive principles that regulate the basic structure of society over time and are designed to preserve background justice from one generation to the next and those that apply directly to the separate and free transactions between individuals that take place within this basic structure.[113] Rawls's idea of a division of labor supposes that both sets of principles can work together in tandem in a way that preserves the distinctive role and relative autonomy of each—including therefore what Rawls refers to as "the important values expressed by free and fair agreements reached by individuals" within the basic structure.[114] However, because, as Rawls himself underlines, the focus of his account of domestic justice is almost exclusively on distributive principles, he does not fully explain how such a fit is possible.[115] The challenge to show this becomes even more acute if we suppose, as I have argued, that the publicly recognized and justified principles for transactions are purely nondistributive in character. A central aim of this section is to contribute to the needed analysis. While Rawls argues for the idea of a division of labor between these two kinds of principles from the standpoint of background distributive justice, it is also important to show that this is possible and necessary from the other side, the principles for transactions. This is the path that I now propose to take.[116]

For this purpose, it might be thought sufficient to refer simply to the juridical conception of contract law, as this is understood apart from its institutional role. But while this juridical conception, when taken by itself, does not rule out background distributive justice—or so I will argue—neither does it explain how there can be, or why morally there *should* be, a system of relations governed by both kinds of principles applied in tandem as two sides of a division of labor between them. To show this, I will maintain that we must refer once more to the idea of a system of needs, discussed in the previous section on the relation between contract law and the market. Fully elaborated, this idea of a system of needs is the pivotal unifying normative conception—the middle term—that explains not only the distinct institutional roles of principles for transactions and those for background distributive justice (such as Rawls's second principle) but also the fit between these two sets of principles as two sides of a division of labor between them, preserving thereby both the fundamental significance of the juridical conception and the regulative primacy of distributive principles. Rawls's conception of the division of labor is between these principles as they are realized in their appropriately different institutional forms. This emphasis on institutional form can also be justified when the two sets of principles are understood with reference to the system of needs.

12.3.1. A Moral Basis for the Institutional Division of Labor between Principles

Starting, then, from the standpoint of the juridical conception of principles for transactions, how might we arrive at a more comprehensive system in which both these principles and those for background distributive justice (specifically Rawls's second principle of justice) can fit together as two sides of a division of labor between them? Now the first thing to note is that, taken by itself, this juridical conception does not rule out the possibility of the regulative primacy of distributive principles. In this respect, the juridical conception should be contrasted with libertarian theory.[117]

Libertarian theory, I shall suppose, assumes an ideal initial situation in which there is a relative abundance for all and the configuration of individual holdings raises no questions of justice, and it then holds that any departures from this initial situation must be in accordance with principles of acquisition and transfer. If individuals act consistently with these principles, then, as a matter of pure procedural justice, all subsequent configurations of holdings must be fully just, irrespective of the cumulative effects of transactions on the opportunities for market participation and on the structure as well as background conditions of market relations. At least in ideal theory, the libertarian conception holds that there is no need or room for other distinctive distributive principles and so no basis for a division of labor between such principles and those for transactions.

According to this account, libertarian theory seems at one and the same time to assume that needs and their satisfaction via participation in transactions can be morally salient (at least with respect to the initial situation) but that principles, which ignore whether the necessary opportunities and background conditions for fair participation continue to exist on an ongoing basis, can be nevertheless acceptable and complete from the standpoint of justice. This is so even though the inevitable cumulative effects of the correct operation of principles of acquisition and transfer need not preserve but can in fact erode these requisite initial fair opportunities and background circumstances.

The approach taken by the juridical conception of transactions is fundamentally different. I have argued that principles of acquisition and transfer are distinct and independent from those of distributive justice precisely insofar as they express a juridical conception that views individuals' needs and their satisfaction as per se normatively irrelevant. Taken by themselves, these principles express *just* the freedom and equality of juridical persons with the moral power to assert their sheer independence. There is therefore no basis for supposing, even ideally, the kind of initial situation envisaged by the libertarian theory. The juridical conception, taken by itself, does not posit an initial situation that aims to satisfy needs or that, with respect to the pursuit of their satisfaction, establishes opportunities on a fair and equal basis. Thus, because of this moral irrelevance of needs, even as a matter of ideal theory, the operation of these principles can result in the most extreme inequalities of holdings and opportunities.[118]

Instead, the juridical conception, in accordance with the framework of misfeasance, can only suppose an initial situation in which (apart from the innate right of bodily integrity) everything is potentially available for appropriation by anyone, but no one needs to own anything.[119] This is in keeping with their sheer independence as juridical persons. As I discussed in the preceding chapter, the only thing that the juridical conception requires is that everyone's legal *capacity* for ownership be respected by others and that, if and when someone exercises his or her capacity in the requisite way, others must not interfere with the rightful control thereby established. But note that, crucially, this does not require or assure that there must be things—let alone things of a certain kind or amount—to acquire, or that there must be a domain in which people can exercise their capacity for ownership, or finally that individuals actually acquire anything at all. What it guarantees is merely the *possibility*, not the actuality, of acquisition and transfer. There is nothing in this view that inherently requires that there be actual appropriation or transfer. To the contrary.

From this it follows that when taken by itself, the juridical conception does not establish a baseline of actual acquired rights that is prior to, and that must be respected by, the operation of principles of distributive justice. At the extreme, the juridical conception is not necessarily violated by, but instead can be fully consistent with, the nonarbitrary withdrawal of everything from the reach of private appropriation, so that there is literally nothing available for such appropriation. Neither the independence of juridical persons nor their capacity for ownership is thereby infringed or compromised in the least. Thus in contrast with libertarian theory, the juridical conception does not exclude the operation of distributive principles in shaping and regulating the whole domain within which transactional principles might otherwise apply. I wish to emphasize that this conclusion follows precisely from the juridical conception's complete indifference to needs and its limited inherent aim of guaranteeing only the capacity for, not the actuality of, ownership. This goes to its core meaning.

There is a further point. The fact that the juridical conception of transactions does not preclude the operation of distributive principles is not sufficient to show, however, that and, if so how, there can be a fit between principles for transactions and those of background distributive justice as two sides of a division of labor between them. To establish this, it is necessary to suppose at a minimum that on the nondistributive side there is at least *some* domain in which transactions regulated by contract law actually do, and morally must, take place. There must be an ongoing set—or, better still, a system—of actual transactions: not merely the moral possibility but the actual necessity of such. Otherwise, why speak of a division of labor consisting of two sets of principles working in tandem? It will be this system of actual exchanges, governed by principles applicable to separate individual transactions, that background principles must take and respect as in some way already given, even while these background principles ensure distributive justice in accordance with their own proper nature and role. To establish a division of labor between contract law and distributive background principles, we therefore need some kind of underlying normative conception that comprises both these two sides in relation to such an ongoing system of transactions. What might that be? The needed normative conception, I shall now argue, is the already discussed idea of a system of needs. Let me elaborate.

In the preceding section, I tried to show that contract law assumes an institutional role in responding to the formal needs of market transactors as participants in the self-developing, ongoing system of exchange relations that represents a system of needs. We saw that the normative idea of the system of needs goes beyond the juridical conception by making morally salient the pursuit and satisfaction of permissible individual needs through a cooperative system of legally enforceable voluntary transactions. More specifically, with respect to things and services that can be individually owned and transferred, a market of some kind ensures a domain in which individuals can satisfy their own particular interests as independent and separate persons, consistently with the freedom and equality of everyone. Via market participation, individuals have the possibility of meeting their needs in furtherance of their particular conceptions of their good and consistently with the important liberties of free choice of movement and occupation. Without a market of some kind, there is no domain for this decentralized individual pursuit of particular interest and preferences on the basis of freedom of choice and association.[120] Therefore, a just society that embodies a liberal conception of the freedom and equality of persons must make room for *some* system of competitive market relations in which individuals transact with each other as owners on this basis.[121] Given the idea of a system of needs, there is now a moral and social necessity in there being a definite and actual sphere for such transactions and all that they presuppose. As I will now explain, it is via a full working through of two different aspects or parts of this idea of a system of needs that we can arrive at a division of labor between transactional and distributive principles.

The first aspect of the system of needs is the focus of the institutional role of contract law (and of private law more widely) as discussed in the previous section. Under this aspect of the system of needs, transactors are treated merely as juridical persons with the moral power to assert their sheer independence in relation to others. This standpoint abstracts from the substantive aspect of participants' efforts to meet their needs through this system of relations. The regime of contract law focuses rather on the *formal* needs for knowledge and security that all transactors identically share as participants in this system. These needs relate to both bilateral and systemic dimensions of their transacting. Contract law's response applies *directly* to each voluntary transaction taken by itself and has the normative resources to determine *completely* any and all issues of private contractual rights arising therefrom. It must be emphasized that in performing an institutional role, contract law addresses a certain kind of deficiency in market relations that only the law can remedy. It provides the kind of readily knowable and practicable rules that all transactors need to be able to apply in their individual transactions if they are to be able freely and effectively to realize their particular interests and good via market participation. And the way that contract law does this enables transactors themselves to recognize these rules as authoritative and legitimate law that upholds their freedom and equality as juridical persons and that expresses a conception of the reasonable which they want and need as part of their rational good.

In addition, there is a second aspect of the system of needs that, though already noted, has not yet been made the focus of a set of principles. Under this second aspect, the system of needs is viewed as a permanent shared capital resource—a system of social cooperation—to which individuals must have access in order to satisfy their *substantive* interests. The fact that transactors have and pursue determinate purposes and interests is now in itself a basis for legitimate claims. They are not viewed simply as having the moral power to be independent, but in addition are recognized as having a moral power to have and to pursue a determinate conception of their good. For this purpose, they need substantive means and goods, and it is through participation in the system of needs that these are obtained. As free and equal, individuals have the equal right to means, circumstances, and opportunities to participate in this system of cooperation and to share in the advantages made possible by it on a fair basis consistent with their freedom and equality.

Thus, under this second aspect, participants in the system of relations count as more than just mutually independent owners. What is now morally salient is their interdependence as free and equal persons who can rightly make interpersonal claims in light of their legitimate need to access and to find satisfaction via participation in the system of needs. The intuitive idea is this: since everyone's well-being depends upon this scheme of cooperation, the distribution of benefits and burdens should be such as to elicit the willing cooperation of all participants. But this can be expected as among equals only if there are reasonable principles for background justice.[122]

Such claims, it should be emphasized, are rooted in the very nature and significance of the system of needs as a system of fair and productive social cooperation between free and equal persons. Now insofar as a regime of contract law—and of private law more generally—arises in response to the needs of individuals as participants in this very system and so presupposes this system, it cannot deny the legitimacy of whatever this system entails, including therefore claims under this second aspect.

The problem is that contract law does not address, let alone meet, these claims. Indeed, not only is contract law wholly indifferent to individuals' substantive needs as such. Even more, via its coercively enforced protection of exclusive entitlements within the parameters of misfeasance, private law ensures their nonsatisfaction by barring propertyless free and equal persons from accessing the material they need because it consists in external things that are already owned by others and also from participating in market relations if they do not already have something of their own to exchange in return.[123] Just as the acquisition that contract law protects can be the outcome of factors that are morally contingent and arbitrary from the standpoint of need and opportunity, so can the resulting exclusion.[124] This is so even if, as I am supposing, contract law adequately embodies and fully lives up to its own norms of contractual fairness.

Moreover, market processes themselves do not fairly ensure against this influence of morally arbitrary contingencies.[125] To the contrary, unless set within a framework of appropriate background institutions that adjust the ongoing trends of economic forces to ensure that over time the structure of the system of markets and the antecedent distribution of income are fair, market dynamics need not and predictably will not preserve conditions essential for fair equality of opportunity.[126] As Rawls correctly emphasizes, the cumulative tendency of separate and independent transactions over time, even if fully free and fair as a matter of transactional justice and performed in good faith, is "away from and not toward background justice."[127] Consequently, a second and distinct set of principles is needed to ensure such background distributive justice over time.

However, given the nature and role of principles aiming to ensure fair background conditions over time, the systemic, unavoidably complex, and long-term nature of the factors that must be considered for this purpose cannot be feasibly known and readily followed by individual transactors in their circumscribed local situations or ascertained and assessed by courts in their adjudicative role. All this must be reasonably viewed as beyond their respective competences.[128] Far from meeting the market-generated demand for knowable rules and standards, imposing upon individuals or courts the burden of ensuring background justice would thus completely undermine that imperative and make the realization of background justice illusory. Therefore, to prevent the erosion of background justice, the requisite principles must have an institutional form that is distinct from the contract law that directly governs separate transactions.

There must be a division of labor between two kinds of principles—those that ensure transactional justice and others that preserve background justice—as these are realized in their appropriate institutional forms. With this division of labor, individuals are free to pursue their needs via legally enforceable voluntary transactions governed by knowable and practicable transactional principles, "secure," as Rawls writes, "in the knowledge that elsewhere in the social system the necessary corrections to preserve background justice are being made."[129] In this way, the demands of publicity and knowability, which market activity generates but cannot itself satisfy, can be met. The other side of the coin is that with this division, the principles for background justice need not be concerned with the complexities of the countless transactions of everyday life or keep track of the changing relative positions of particular individuals.[130] Not only does this further the requirements of simplicity and publicity in applying distributive justice, but it enables distributive justice to be a case of what Rawls calls "pure background procedural justice" that applies to the basic structure as a system of cooperation, now and going forward without any specified end in time.[131]

It is important to emphasize that in both this and the prior sections, I presuppose that only insofar as the market fulfills the ethical ideal of a system of needs for free and equal persons can it be justified within a framework of liberal justice. Both kinds of principles—for transactions and for background justice—are required to correct the inherent deficiencies of the market in fully meeting the requirements of a system of needs for such persons. Whereas the institution of contract law is needed to meet the formal needs of transactors as participants in the system of exchanges, distributive justice is essential to establish fair background conditions over time so that all individuals, present and future, can access this system on a fair basis to fulfill their substantive needs and purposes. If either set of principles is lacking or defective, the normative meaning and internal requirements of the system of needs as a whole cannot be fully realized.[132] On the view that I am proposing, since each set of principles functions as part of this unifying normative idea, the full moral acceptability of either depends therefore on the possibility of its fitting with the other in an institutional division of labor between them.

While I have discussed in detail the nature and basis of the transactional principles—the main subject of this book—it is important to consider, even if briefly, what my view of the priority of the juridical conception suggests about the possible content of distributive principles for background justice and how such background principles, when systemically regulative and taking the basic structure as the primary subject of political justice, might in turn bear on the operation of the principles for transactions within the proposed division of labor between them. Doing this will further elucidate the nature of this division of labor as well as the relation between contract law and distributive justice.

12.3.2. Between Contract Law and Distributive Principles

Even if distributive principles are systemically regulative in ensuring background justice, they are always to be applied in tandem with transactional principles in such a way that is consistent with the latter's autonomy and special character. More exactly, I would like to suggest, agreeing with Rawls, that distributive principles apply *directly* to the institutions and processes that determine background justice but only *indirectly* constrain individual transactions that take place within this basic structure, without displacing or derogating from their own internal norms and important transactional values.[133] My own route to this conclusion is based on the view that I take of the nature and role of these two sets of principles as distinct parts of the system of needs and in particular on my conception of the lexical priority of the juridical conception within that framework. Given this understanding of the nature and role of the juridical conception, what might principles of background distributive justice look like if they are to accommodate fully the other side of the division of labor comprising the principles for transactions? At the same time, how does contract law, within its own sphere and consistent with its own nature, adjust to the indirect application of distributive principles? In addressing these and related questions, I will frequently draw on aspects of Rawls's seminal account of justice to develop and illustrate my analysis.

To start, in order to sustain the view that distributive principles are to apply only indirectly but not directly to contract law, it seems necessary to suppose that contract law must be self-sufficient in its own terms and self-limiting in the right way. For if, to the contrary, the internal transactional norms of contract law were somehow incomplete or inherently conflicting with distributive principles and values, it might arguably be necessary for distributive principles directly to fill in, limit, or even oust contract principles in order to complete the transactional analysis or to ensure the goals of background justice.[134]

However, I have tried to show in detail that contract law—from its principles of formation to those governing fairness and remedies—is complete within its own framework and that, with its own purely nondistributive and transactional values, it can answer the main contractual issues that are essential to establishing, interpreting, and enforcing contractual relations. There is no point of entry and no need for supplementation by distributive or other kinds of principles and values. Moreover, I have argued that because of their *limited* nature and scope, contract law norms, embodying the juridical conception alone, cannot per se directly trespass on, let alone undermine, the regulation of the basic structure by rules of background justice. Thus far, there seems to be no reason for the latter principles to replace or displace the former by applying directly to transactions viewed separately and internally.

In fact, even from their own standpoint and consistent with their own nature and aims, the principles of background distributive justice—at least in Rawls's account—cannot apply directly to transactions or conflict with the requirements of transactional justice. First, to be morally legitimate and reasonable, these principles must themselves meet requirements of public reason and general knowability.[135] Therefore, such distributive principles cannot be applied directly to transactions because, as discussed above, the considerations and factors that must be ascertained and weighed in order to apply them are not accessible to those persons and agencies that would have to follow or implement them. Beyond this, in Rawls's overall political conception of justice, the principles of background justice expressly embed and uphold within their own framework the core normative requirements of the juridical conception itself in such a way that, in effect, precludes direct application of distributive principles to contract law and that ensures that there cannot be a fundamental conflict between the two sets of principles. Let me explain.

According to Rawls, under the first principle of justice free and equal citizens have among other equal basic liberties the inalienable right to hold and to have the exclusive use of some personal property (which includes forms of real property but not the means of production or natural resources) as well as the fundamental supporting liberties of freedom of movement and free choice of occupation.[136] Indeed, Rawls views the right to personal property as a universal human right that any well-ordered society, liberal or not, must recognize and enforce.[137] I assume that these rights would include the right to acquire and exchange whatever alienable subject matter these liberties involve. In Rawls's political conception of justice, the right to hold personal property and the free choice of occupation are justified because they help to establish a sufficient material basis for personal independence and a sense of self-respect, both of which are essential for the adequate development and exercise of the moral powers of free and equal citizens.[138] These liberties answer to citizens' fundamental interests as such persons within his political conception.[139]

As is well known, within Rawls's overall conception, such rights and their exercise are protected as part of the scheme of equal basic liberties that is accorded lexical priority relative to the requirements of distributive justice in a narrow sense (comprising Rawls's second principle).[140] What Rawls's view of the lexical priority of the first principle means is that the second principle, and specifically the fair equality of opportunity and difference principles, are always to be applied within a setting of background institutions that fully satisfy the requirements of the first principle. The latter provide the background framework against which principles of distributive justice in a narrower sense are meant to apply and operate in tandem.

It follows that, within this overall political conception, the free exercise of the right to acquire, hold, and exchange personal property and of the supporting liberties of free movement and occupation must, as basic liberties, also be taken as lexically prior when applying fair equality of opportunity and the difference principle. This has the following important implication: the latter principles—distributive justice in a narrow sense—cannot directly apply to or determine the internal nature and essential exercise of these liberties that can only be adjusted and worked out in conjunction with the other basic liberties in the scheme of equal basic liberties as a whole. While these distributive principles apply in tandem, they do so only against a background of the *results of the actual exercise* of these (and the other) basic liberties within their own framework.

This view of the lexical priority of basic liberties in Rawls's overall account of political background justice also has important implications for the relation between distributive justice (under the second principle) and contract law. This is because the right of property and the formal freedom of occupation that background political justice embeds and validates from its own standpoint as basic liberties are the very same in content as that which the institution of contract law works out from within its own framework—the only difference being that contract law specifies and justifies these rights as part of its juridical conception, whereas background justice upholds these same rights as part of its own normative political conception of what free and equal citizens need. Background justice seems to endorse from within its own standpoint exactly what contract law works out in its own different context of individual transactions. As I now explain, this congruence between the two sides is made possible because of the limited nature of what contract law requires as well as the manner in which contract law determines it. And once explained, this congruence may be seen to rule out the direct application of distributive justice to contract law.

Take the first point of the limited nature of contract law. We have seen that, as understood in terms of the juridical conception, contract law does not exhaustively and antecedently specify the particular subject matter or scope of the transactions that come within its purview. Contract law also leaves open and does not decide what and how much should be market-determined. This can vary across just liberal societies (both property-owning and democratic socialist) without undermining the normative role of the system of needs or that of the institution of contract in meeting transactors' formal interests arising therefrom. I have suggested that what the institutional role of contract does suppose and accommodate is only this: an existing system of needs comprising *some* domain of market relations through which individuals can enter legally enforceable voluntary bilateral transactions and in this way exercise their capacities for ownership and exchange in the pursuit (under the idea of the rational) of their particular interests and conceptions of good. In short, there must be at least the opportunity of acquiring and exchanging some forms of property, both assets and services. This criterion is fully satisfied even if limited to the narrow conception of personal property and the free choice of occupation that are enshrined in Rawls's first principle. More than this, contract law does not require.

For example, neither the juridical conception nor the institutional role of contract requires that—or even decides whether—natural resources or the means of production should be subject to private ownership and exchange. This normative basis of contract law is therefore perfectly consistent with Rawls's view that these questions should be decided at the legislative stage by assessing which kind of system of property better satisfies the principles of justice, taking into account a given society's history, traditions, and experiences.[141] The same is true of agreements that aim to concentrate market power, to limit the availability of relevant and accurate information regarding prices or product features, to maintain excessive working hours or unsafe working conditions, or other objectives that may clearly conflict with the requirements of background justice. Even if agreements of this kind may be formally consistent with the requirements of contract formation, the possibility of entering into such contracts is not required by or intrinsic to the limited core meaning of the juridical conception. The conception of freedom of contract required by contract law is not the doctrine of laissez-faire.[142]

It is crucial to keep in mind here that while contract law, and private law more generally, specifies the different forms of acquisition and the nature and kinds of objects—they must be alienable things or services, for example—that can be acquired or exchanged, it does not determine the particular contents of the modes and objects of acquisition or of the scope of the domain for private appropriation. Such particular content and scope are decided by the market actions of transactors themselves, as regulated by appropriate principles of distributive justice. Thus, because Rawls's two principles of justice contemplate a competitive and fair system of markets that ensures free choice of occupation and the active pursuit of one's conception of good against a background of diverse opportunities, his conception of background justice authorizes, and indeed normally requires, a system of exchanges that covers more than the acquisition and transfer of merely personal property.[143] In fact, these principles allow for the possibility of a property-owning democratic society with extensive and dispersed private ownership of a wide range of subject matter, including the means of production.[144] And since this more extensive market activity can be directly regulated by contract law on the basis of its transactional juridical norms, distributive justice itself allows for a wider domain for the operation of this second set of principles.

There is a further point going to the congruence between the kinds of entitlements in contract law and Rawls's first principle: the very manner in which contract law determines transactional entitlements within its own domain fits with what is necessary for entitlements, such as those pertaining to personal property, to be included as a basic liberty under the first principle. Here the argument that contract law can meet the formal needs of market participants is pivotal. This shows that contract law can determine entitlements in a way that can be wanted by and acceptable to individuals who interact not only as mutually independent owners but also as free and equal persons who have determinate conceptions of their good that they seek to satisfy via free market relations. This is exactly how citizens are viewed when attributed the limited but fundamental rights of ownership and freedom of occupation under Rawls's first principle. Moreover, contract law determines entitlements in a manner that satisfies requirements of publicity and simplicity for the purposes of transactional justice and that can count as a case of pure transactional procedural justice. Each transaction is separately and completely assessed in its own right without the need to refer to other transactions, let alone to the cumulative results of indefinitely many transactions over time. At no point does the transactional analysis need to refer to considerations of efficiency or to any nontransactional substantive value or good. Thus the determination of transactional entitlements takes place in accordance with what Rawls characterizes as legitimate claims and earned entitlements: "[w]hat individuals do depends on what the rules . . . say they would be entitled to; what individuals are entitled to depends on what they do."[145]

What emerges from this analysis is the following picture. The domain that is proper to the core meaning and operation of contract law (and to private law more generally) is consistent with what remains when distributive justice is applied directly to the basic structure as a whole to ensure just background conditions over time but not to individual and separate transactions.[146] From the standpoint of Rawls's political conception itself, this limit is required by the priority of the scheme of basic liberties vis-à-vis distributive justice in the narrow sense. Thus, his two principles of justice respect legitimate expectations based on the publicly recognized rules that govern transactions and the resulting transactional entitlements gained by individuals.[147] This limit is also consistent with and required by the juridical conception, taking the latter from its own standpoint and as an autonomous part in the whole system of coercible law (both juridical and political). At the same time, the juridical conception requires no more than this. And within its autonomous nondistributive domain, contract law directly and completely determines all matters of right essential to free and fair transactions viewed separately. Further, because the rules of background distributive justice apply directly only to the basic structure as a whole, not to transactions, individuals can know the incidence and effects of distributive rules *before* they decide to transact. Transactors can foresee these requirements and take them into account when they plan and execute their decisions.[148] Not only does the division of labor between the two kinds of principles satisfy the essential requirement of publicity. In this way, as Rawls notes, individuals are left free to pursue their ends as they deem most fit, secure in the knowledge that elsewhere in the social system the regulations needed to preserve background justice are in place.[149]

So far, I have tried to explain why principles necessary to secure background justice (in particular, Rawls's second principle of justice) need not—and indeed, from the standpoint of both sides of the division of labor between background and transactional justice, cannot—apply directly to the justice of particular transactions. But what does it mean to say that principles of background distributive justice can apply *indirectly* to transactions? And reflecting this possibility of indirect application, how, if at all, does contract law take into account these distributive justice principles within its own nondistributive domain? This further set of questions connects up with an important and challenging issue—one now being debated in many jurisdictions, particularly European—concerning the proper relation between contract law and fundamental rights. Commentators divide over whether fundamental rights should have what they call a "direct vertical" or an "indirect horizontal" effect on private law.[150] I would like to suggest very briefly and in broad strokes how the view proposed here would approach this controversy.

To begin with, and elaborating on earlier remarks, it seems that a *direct* vertical effect of fundamental rights or distributive principles on private contractual relations would be incompatible with the proposed idea of a division of labor between principles. As explained by Olha Cherednychenko, direct effect presupposes that fundamental rights or distributive principles are *general* moral values that apply (in principle) to any subject, including private law.[151] Basic rights are taken as expressions of general and fundamental values, such as dignity or equality, the meaning and role of which are fixed before we consider the internal normative character of the contractual relation to which they are applied. So conceived, these values flow into the contractual analysis and can directly determine the contractual rights and duties of contract law. Contract principles are taken—at least in part—to be purely formal and even empty placeholders to be filled by these paramount values.[152] On this view, for example, the doctrine of unconscionability might be a vehicle for directly incorporating Rawls's difference principle.[153]

But as Cherednychenko emphasizes, such direct effect of fundamental rights and distributive principles fails to recognize the possibility, for which I have argued in detail, that contract doctrines specify a distinct and complete code of publicly justifiable fair and reasonable principles for all matters having to do with the parties' coercible rights and duties arising from their bilateral voluntary interaction and holding as between them. These transactional principles treat the parties as free and equal juridical (as distinct from political) persons with appropriate moral and legal powers in a way that distinguishes this domain from others. Direct effect ignores the intrinsic differences between distinct kinds of relations.

If the direct effect view of fundamental rights and distributive norms is rejected, what would a model of indirect horizontal effect consist in? Given the central thesis of my account concerning the independence and completeness of contract law, we should look to its basic doctrines and principles themselves for models of embedding fundamental rights and distributive values.[154] Within this purely contractual framework, I suggest that contract law can appropriately take the latter values into account, not as directly determining its form or content, but rather when it specifies *contractually recognized presuppositions and limits* internal to the operation of its principles, as long as the following condition of justiciability is satisfied: whether such values are respected or violated must be clearly and definitely determinable by a court within the parameters of its institutional competence. We can form a preliminary idea of what this embedding of fundamental rights consists in by recalling what we can now see are some well-recognized limits discussed in earlier chapters.

For example, we saw in the discussion of the restraint of trade and other doctrines that contract law presupposes as a policy of the common law that there is an inalienable core of individual self-determination that cannot itself be the content of the promise-for-consideration relation.[155] This is the essential condition of parties being mutually independent sources of claims and units of responsibility in their contractual relations. As such, they stand in relation to each other as free and equal distinct transactors. Contract law characterizes as "oppressive" any term that impairs or denies some aspect intrinsic to this core of self-determination. A term that does so must be void ab initio.

Now based on the juridical conception alone, this inalienable core clearly includes the legal capacity to own and exchange property. But it need not stop there. Under this rubric of the policy of the law, it can incorporate everything that constitutes the inalienable moral identity of individuals in virtue of which they are free and equal participants in the different forms of fair social cooperation.[156] Also included, therefore, are the freedom to take part effectively in market relations and thereby to earn one's livelihood as well as the right to have the necessary means and opportunities to meet one's basic needs in a condition of nondependence upon the wills of others. Ultimately, this inalienable core comprises whatever can count as (or be presupposed by) a basic liberty in Rawls's sense, for example, freedom of religion and conscience, the political liberties and their fair value, freedom of association, and even a substantive claim (not to be confused with the difference principle) to have one's basic needs met.[157]

With respect to whatever is thus included, contract law holds that its denial cannot be an enforceable and legitimate contractual interest. So, for example, this can never form part of the needed justification in a case of restraint of trade. A term that, upon analysis, must be reasonably construed, not as necessary for the protection of a party's own assets, but as only for the purpose of limiting the other party's access to other market relations and opportunities or of effectively sterilizing his or her productive activity will be deemed per se unreasonable and void. The same is true of so-called "shackling" or "servile" contracts that give one party general or excessive control over the other's ability to maintain his or her own material and psychological independence. And we saw a similar concern at work when courts not only decline to order specific performance of a positive covenant of personal service but also, and perhaps especially, refuse to enforce a negative prohibition against a party working for others, if to do so would compel him or her to choose between idleness and continuing to work for the other contracting party.[158] More generally, we should expect that no term that threatens substantially the core of any of a party's basic liberties can pass the test of justification in any of these doctrines. Note that this analysis is distinct from, and in fact is conceptually more basic than, a determination of unconscionability. Unconscionability assesses the transactional fairness of terms on the assumption that these involve assets and services that do not belong to persons' inalienable core but, to the contrary, are distinct from it, so that they can all be properly the subject matter of exchange.

In short, we see in the above examples that the salience and role of these values is explained solely in and through the nature of the contractual relation itself. The values are not viewed as wholly flowing from outside and into contract law. It is contract law that, by its own internal requirements, must take them into account, bring out their salience, and fix their role. This is not direct vertical effect by another means.[159] In this way, the basic liberties are ensured indirect application and continue to hold throughout the domain of private law, just as in other associations and institutions within the basic structure of society. Transactors count always as citizens whose equal status and equal claims with respect to basic liberties are inalienable and protected wherever they are.[160]

What about contractual respect for other aspects of background justice, such as the requirements of formal and fair equality of opportunity or the difference principle? In other words, can these also apply indirectly to contract law? To begin with fair equality of opportunity and the difference principle, not only would these have to be applied in a way that is consistent with the priority of the basic liberties, but there is the further difficulty that these principles are general and systemic norms that cannot be readily and effectively applied by courts in their adjudicative function. It is exceedingly difficult, even though not necessarily impossible, for a court to conclude with the requisite confidence that in any given single case before it, a contractual term has clearly violated a party's claims under either of these principles. In fact, Rawls emphasizes that even at the constitutional level, the application of these norms is ordinarily not justiciable. These matters usually are best regulated via legislative action.[161] We should keep in mind that contract doctrines provide a complete and independent code for the kind of fairness that is properly within a court's competence, such that the systemic and complex considerations required to apply fair equality of opportunity or the difference principle should not play a role in the determination of contractual enforceability or the parties' contractual rights and duties.[162]

The analysis of the more limited requirement of *formal* equality of opportunity—"careers open to talents"—must be more nuanced. Application of this norm would seem to be more readily practicable and justiciable before a court. The difficulty here is different. On their face, the principles of contract formation give parties an unfettered liberty to offer to transact with whomever they wish. No one is obliged to make an offer to anyone in particular. As a result, the doctrine of offer and acceptance seems to permit one to decline to engage with someone else on whatever basis, including his or her race, gender, religious affiliation, and the like, in apparent direct conflict with the basic requirement of formal equality of opportunity. How can the latter norm be given indirect effect as part of contract law and from within its own framework without conflicting with this seemingly core feature of contract formation? For we are supposing that any such application must be consistent with the constituent norms of contract law.

By way of answer, I would suggest that, for the norm of formal equality of opportunity to apply indirectly and thus consistently with the internal makeup of contract law, a court must be able to find that an offer, when reasonably construed, cannot be viewed as made with the intent to solicit offerees as this or that individual, according to one's wishes. Rather, the offer must reasonably be held to be directed, not to chosen particular individuals, but instead to a kind of universal offeree, that is, to members of the public in general.[163] If the offer can reasonably be so construed, it cannot at the same time expressly or by necessary implication make distinctions on a basis that is not justified by a legitimate performance interest. One cannot make an offer to all that excludes some on an arbitrary basis. Contract law would be justified in viewing—and refusing to validate—such an offer as treating those whom it excludes as not forming part of the public, thereby denying them formally equal standing to participate in contractual relations. Whether an offer should be so viewed can clearly depend on the offeror's particular intent (always reasonably construed). In addition, this construction may arguably be imputed to the offeror as a fixed contractual incident (similarly to implication in law) when the offeror has legal exclusive control over a resource or facility sufficient to affect a legitimate interest of access that all members of the public are deemed to share (e.g., access to transportation, employment, education, and housing).[164] Here also, contract law accepts or, better, takes into account the norms of distributive justice when it specifies, under the rubric of presumed intent, the particular contents and incidents of the subject matter that can be acquired and transferred in accordance with contract principles. In determining whether the conditions for imputing this public-oriented character exist, courts may draw on legislative enactments (grants of monopoly, provisions regulating housing, education, etc.) as well as purely common law notions (such as necessity).[165] In this way and based on its own normative makeup, contract law can appropriately integrate the requirement of formal equality of opportunity within its own framework—thereby confirming the indirect application of principles of distributive justice to contract law.

This completes my account of the nature and genesis of a division of labor between background justice and contract law that is consistent with the lexical priority of the juridical conception, and therefore of transactional justice, as one part of the system of needs. This understanding of the division of labor is consonant, I believe, with what Rawls proposes and upholds as his view of the regulative primacy of background distributive justice with respect to the basic structure of society as a whole. I have reached this conclusion through an ordered sequence of moral conceptions and subjects, beginning with the juridical conception, followed by the system of needs, and culminating with its twofold division into, first, the institutional role of contract law and, second, institutional principles for background distributive justice. The system of needs is thus the pivotal middle term that postulates a self-reproducing actual scheme of productive social cooperation among free and equal persons, which is itself fulfilled by the dual aspects of juridical transactional justice and distributive background justice working in tandem as two sides of a division of labor between them. If this approach is sound, Rawls's idea of the primacy of background justice (and of the basic structure of society as the first subject of justice) would seem to be compatible with—and explicable as part of—an account that treats the nondistributive juridical conception as utterly basic and distinct in a liberal normative analysis of coercively enforceable rights and duties. This may not be something that might have been thought plausible before working through the steps of the proposed analysis.[166]

12.3.3. Concluding Remarks: A Liberalism of Freedom

To complete this discussion of the relation between contract law and distributive justice as well as my theory of contract as a whole, I want to return to the following central themes: first, the two sets of principles are qualitatively different because they regulate different kinds of social relations; but second, there is at the same time an underlying unity and fit between them of the kind required for a public basis of justification within a liberal framework of justice.

Contract law, I have argued, may be understood as articulating reasonable principles for external promissory relations between parties, in accordance with which these relations are juridically construed as constituting a mode of transactional acquisition that is fully established and complete at formation prior to and independent of actual performance. This acquisition is as between the parties and is effectuated in and through the purely representational medium of their mutual assents. Consistently with wider ideas of acquisition and ownership, this transactional acquisition may reasonably be characterized as a transfer of ownership between the parties.

Not only do these principles—and the doctrines that embody them—express a transactional conception of justice. As embodied in the main contract doctrines, this transactional conception reflects a definite view of persons which I have called juridical (in contrast to political or otherwise), and it presupposes particular notions of freedom and equality specified in terms of the innate mutual independence of all persons in relation to others. The juridical conception of the person with these corresponding notions of freedom and equality is specific to contractual relations in particular and, I would argue, to private law relations in general. These notions of freedom and equality are utterly minimal. They do nothing more than recognize the basic and immediate moral difference between persons (nonusable subjects) and things (usable objects), so far as this difference operates in relations with others. And, without relying on any extrinsic considerations economic or otherwise, this moral difference is further specified through the idea that persons can reasonably assert vis-à-vis each other a legal capacity for ownership, which, both as a capacity and when exercised, must be respected by others. This is fully brought out in contract, through its being constituted by mutually related acts that represent each party's reciprocal recognition of the other as exercising this capacity for ownership. Within this framework, each can assert coercively enforceable claims against the other, which both sides can reasonably expect the other to recognize in his or her capacity as free and equal, not as subordinated or as subject to another's will. In this way, justice in transactions enshrines a definite criterion of reciprocity.

Now even though contracts are voluntary transactions and so suppose that parties enter them in order to satisfy their various needs and purposes, contractual analysis expresses primarily an idea of the reasonable in transactions that does not depend on parties having this or that particular purpose or their positively intending to produce contractual effects. The only thing requisite is that they interact in a way that can reasonably—that is, objectively—be construed as a promise-for-consideration relation or some strictly bilateral analogue. Nor does it impute to parties or hold them to any substantive ends, including the promotion of their joint welfare or the fulfillment of the moral duty of promise-keeping. Reflecting the parameters of misfeasance, parties' purposes, needs, and well-being are not per se part of this analysis: these are not in themselves grounds for establishing contractual rights and duties. As juridical persons, parties are viewed as having a higher-order interest in their capacity to assert their sheer independence from everything given, not in forming and rationally pursuing a conception of their substantive good. For this reason, contract law does not presuppose an account of means necessary to satisfy individuals' legitimate substantive needs as free and equal persons—there are no contractually specified primary goods that parallel the social primary goods in Rawls's political conception.[167]

Here as elsewhere, it is important to take seriously the fact that the ordinary operation of contract law can involve the imposition of coercively enforceable rights and duties as an *ex post* reasonable interpretation of the parties' interaction, whether or not the parties consciously intended this interpretation or knew in advance the doctrine upon which this is based. At the same time, to be legitimate, this interpretation must be a fair implication of the parties' voluntary interaction. Each party must be able to say: if I had reasonably considered what my interaction with the other entailed as a matter of justice and reasonableness between us, I could have recognized the appropriateness of something like the interpretation—and its underlying principle or rule—by which our interaction has been judged. To be legitimate and morally acceptable to the parties, all of basic contract doctrine must approach this standard. The aim of a public basis of justification for contract is to show that actual contract law can in fact be so viewed.

I have also argued that this juridical transactional conception of contract can be institutionally realized to meet the bilateral and systemic interests of transactors in their contractual relations. To understand contract's specifically institutional role, I have suggested that parties are to be viewed as equal participants in a system of needs, that is, a system of social interdependence and cooperation that makes ethically salient the satisfaction of their substantive needs and purposes through productive activities and exchange relations with others. My crucial claim is that even when assuming this institutional function, contract law does not derogate from or displace the juridical conception. Instead, the institution of contract preserves and builds upon it.

Thus, we have seen that even in performing its institutional function, contract law does not specify the parties' rights and duties so as to ensure the satisfaction of their substantive needs and purposes. Nor does it treat contractual relations as cooperative arrangements in the robust sense of a shared resource or joint undertaking. Rather, contracts still count as external relations between separate and independent owners who engage in reciprocal exchange, whereby what belongs to one passes to the other in return for something else moving from the latter to the former.

As discussed previously, the only interests that contract law recognizes are those that can be identically willed by each and every market participant in virtue of his or her strictly formal interests *ex ante* in the determination of the legal incidents and effects of transaction-types, in having a publicly certain and knowable system of market relations, and so on. To be formally the same for all participants, it must be something that can be imputed to them as parties to a bilateral transaction who exchange in accordance with the principles for transactions. So parties can have such a formal interest in the designation of objects as currency and therefore in the negotiability of contracts; but an interest, say, against oligopolistic tendencies would not seem to be imputable to them in this way. Economic relations marked by oligopoly or even monopoly still constitute a market system and can result from market activity via separate transactions following transactional principles of justice, including those of contractual fairness. Moreover, reliable diagnosis and correction of these tendencies is ordinarily beyond the institutional competence of courts. Accordingly, it would not be the task of contract law—in contrast to that of economic and social policy under distributive justice—to regulate market concentration and to correct such tendencies.

For contract law, the fact that the system of needs is a system of social cooperation that is always *productive* is not salient per se.[168] The juridical conception views objects of ownership rights as subject to exclusive control, not as produced or made possible by—and so arising from—productive social cooperation. Whether an object is taken as is from nature or is a product of human labor does not affect the basis and operation of the principles of acquisition and transfer. This dimension simply does not enter the picture, even when contract law assumes its institutional role. The only question is whether persons represent to others that they have done something with or to a thing that reasonably manifests the requisite exclusive acquisition or transfer of control or interference with that control. It is for this reason that the bilateral relation can be the fundamental subject at all conceptual stages (from contract as relation to contract as institution) of the contractual analysis.

In sharp contrast with the principles for transactions, we have seen that distributive principles, such as Rawls's, regulate background justice by taking as central those very aspects of the system of needs that are irrelevant to the juridical conception. Thus principles for background distributive justice reflect the fact that free and equal persons have a higher-order interest in forming, pursuing, and realizing their permissible substantive ends and also expect to be able, on fair terms, to access and to benefit from participation in society viewed as a shared productive system of social cooperation, now and going forward in time across generations. At the same time, seeing that the two sets of principles refer to two distinct aspects or parts of one and the same normative idea of a system of needs, we should be able to show continuity, fit, and ultimately a kind of unity between them. This should be true with respect to their underlying conceptions of the person and their character as liberal principles. The kind of continuity and fit between these conceptions should be consistent with the fact that the juridical conception sets out in the most elementary way the moral terms of a relation to another involving interpersonal coercible claims and duties. Being conceptually basic, this should be presupposed by all other instances of such relations, however developed and complex these may be—and thus even where, as in Rawls's theory, the relation is political and between individuals and institutions representing citizens as a collective body. That this is the case is suggested, for example, by the way persons and objects are conceived in Rawls's political conception of justice.

According to Rawls, as part of the political conception, citizens have the moral power for a conception of the good. Having this power as free persons, citizens view themselves in a certain way: not as inevitably tied to the pursuit of any particular conception of good but rather as claiming the right to view their persons as "independent from and not identified with any particular conception of the good, or scheme of final ends."[169] On this basis, citizens are conceived as having the capacity to adjust their wants and to take responsibility for their ends in light of their expected fair share of goods made possible through social cooperation.[170] Citizens are not viewed as mere passive carriers of desires. To the contrary, they are reasonably taken to understand and accept that the basis of their claims concerning their good cannot be simply that they want or desire something, however intensely.

Thus individuals' claims must be only for things that can count *relationally* as the objects of their legitimate needs and interests qua free and equal citizens. These are goods specified in light of the particular normative conception of persons in democratic political relations. Such are the so-called social primary goods that include the basic rights and liberties, income and wealth understood as all-purpose means, and the social bases of self-respect.[171] Rawls emphasizes that these goods are publicly and externally ascertainable: they are "given by reference to objective features of citizens' social circumstances, features open to public view."[172] It is only on this or some similar basis that there can be a public interpersonal standard that all may reasonably be expected to accept. And such a standard is required when it is a matter of justifying rules that are coercively enforceable, as is the case with political association and state power.[173] Having these goods specifies the advantageous or beneficial for the purposes of political justice. Citizens accept that the individual satisfaction or utility (and different levels thereof) that may or may not result from using these goods for their different ends is a distinct matter that is not per se normatively relevant from the standpoint of justice. Consequently, the primary social goods are not to be viewed as a measure of citizens' well-being or of how well they succeed in advancing their various ends.[174]

We saw that the essential and sole moral power of juridical persons is the capacity to affirm themselves as independent from and as not identified with anything given to them, and this entails that the mere fact that one may want or need something (whatever its content) cannot itself be a basis of claims against others. This purely negative moral power of independence is conceptually more basic than—because it is presupposed by—the moral power to have and to pursue a determinate conception of the good. Consequently, the juridical conception establishes, and would seem to be the indispensable minimal basis for establishing, what the political conception quite reasonably maintains: that for purposes of justice there can and must be a distinction between mere desires or preferences and *permissible* interests or ends, and further that free and equal persons are reasonably expected to take responsibility for their ends. With the juridical conception in place, the rational can now begin to be specified within the framework of the reasonable and constrained by its requirements. Both the juridical and political conceptions express the priority of the reasonable. But it is the juridical that establishes this priority in the very first way in which it can be thought and shown. In the order of intelligibility, it would seem to be the indispensable first step.

In the discussion of the relation between Rawls's principles and the requirements of the juridical conception, I suggested that whatever directly expresses juridical personality—for instance, being a subject who can own but never be owned—is also incorporated and preserved within his overall view as part of the scheme of basic liberties. Supposing that the juridical conception is utterly basic in the whole system of justice, it seems, in virtue of its nondistributive and noninstrumental character, to provide the conceptually *initial* paradigm of the kind of fundamental freedoms and their priority vis-à-vis distributive justice in the narrow sense that we find in Rawls's first principle. This point also holds good for the specification and role of the social primary goods in Rawls's theory as well. Thus the juridical conception's wide definition of possible objects of contractual acquisition as things (including incorporeal rights) having exchange value provides once again the conceptually first and most general instance of something that can count as an external and publicly ascertainable usable means to persons' ends: something substantive that they can rightly claim as a matter of coercible justice in relation to others. Being mere usable objects and thus not directly expressive of personality as such, their regulation can belong to distributive justice in a narrow sense, always operating in tandem within a setting of background institutions that fully realize the principle of equal basic liberties and their priority. And as I have emphasized throughout, in the juridical conception, entitlement to the objects of acquisition and transfer is publicly ascertainable and conceived in abstraction from the satisfaction or well-being that may result from their possession and use. Note importantly that the moral relevance of these objects is specified in the juridical conception, not in light of empirical facts, but as what is essential to embody juridical personality as a normative external reality worthy of respect in relation to others. All these features of the rudimentary conceptions of persons and objects at the stage of the juridical conception are preserved as well as further developed in the richer and more complex standpoint of Rawls's political conception.

It is important to recall here and to emphasize once more that the fact that the juridical conception of ownership is indifferent to the role of physical and other contingencies (which I suppose to be undeserved from any reasonable standpoint) in affecting who acquires what and how much is not incompatible with the way these contingencies are treated in Rawls's political conception, including the difference principle. There would be serious incompatibility if the juridical conception's indifference had to be construed as allowing for contingencies to be intrinsically part of its view of the freedom and equality of persons or of its justification of the right of ownership. This, emphatically, is not the case.[175]

What juridical personality and the right of ownership that expresses it represent are rather the complete independence from all such factors, which are therefore treated as not in any way part of its view of persons or ownership. The one who can rightfully claim ownership—whether by first possession or transfer—can and must do so only as representing the juridical personality that all persons share in abstraction from their particular differences. What the juridical conception of ownership upholds in the medium of human action is simply and solely this moral fact that everyone is first a juridical person with the moral power to abstract from everything given. Only on this basis can we understand and show that ownership enshrines a conception of reciprocity via merely negative requirements of respect within the parameters of misfeasance.

When in connection with the system of needs and more specifically market relations, particular interests come to have intrinsic moral significance, this is only as already framed by the reasonable constraints entailed by this juridical conception. And I have also tried to show that contract law does not and cannot deny the authority of distributive principles directly to regulate further the role of social, economic, or other contingencies to ensure the background justice of the basic structure over time. Paralleling the transactional analysis with its negative injunction but now suitably reconfigured as part of distributive justice, the difference principle, on Rawls's view, embeds its own specific conception of reciprocity that "expresses the idea that, starting from equal division, the more advantaged are not to be better off at any point *to the detriment* of the less well off."[176]

I wish to end by underlining the deep affinity between the juridical and political conceptions as specific kinds of public basis of justification.[177] Rawls develops and presents his account of background justice as a public basis of justification specifically framed for the basic structure of a modern liberal democratic society when viewed as a fair system of social cooperation among free and equal citizens across generations. Rawls notes that besides this political conception, what is the appropriate conception of justice for other kinds of relationships among individuals "is a separate and additional question, to be considered anew in any particular instance, given the nature and role of the . . . relation at hand."[178] A central aim of this book has been to take seriously this core insight of Rawls and to try to work out a justification that is suitable for principles of contract law.

Being specifically framed for the contractual relation, the proposed justification is certainly distinct from the political public basis of justification. Still, it has fundamental features that mark it as juridically liberal, in a way that parallels Rawls's conception of what is politically liberal. Justice in transactions, as I have presented it, embraces principles that are not conditioned upon persons endorsing any particular comprehensive doctrine or a particular conception of their good—something that would be incompatible with the crucial fact of reasonable pluralism and the kind of neutrality of aim that are the hallmark of liberal conceptions of justice.[179] Thus, I have tried to ensure that the proposed conception of contract as transfer is drawn solely from, and is truly latent in, the principles and values of contract law. I have presented and explained these principles and values as intuitive ideas that form part of the public legal culture accessible to the educated common sense of transactors and citizens. The proposed view does not rely on philosophical premises or notions as articulated in any particular philosophical framework. The conception of contract as transfer is worked out and presented wholly as implicit in the promise-for-consideration relation and whatever this relation entails. And, like Rawls's political conception, the resulting juridical conception would seem to be a case of pure procedural justice: when individuals follow the publicly recognized rules of transactional justice and honor the claims that these rules specify, the resulting entitlements are acceptable as just within this framework, whatever the entitlements turn out to be. Even though the juridical conception of entitlement with its corresponding idea of persons as free and equal must seem problematic and unsatisfactory when taken as a complete and general theory of justice, it—no differently than the political conception—should not be so taken. Emphatically, it is framed specially for a distinct set of relations and therefore cannot be the whole but only a part of justice. But it is precisely when the theory of contract is properly viewed as such that the nondistributive principles of contract law can be understood as intrinsically reasonable and mutually supportive in their own terms and also shown to embody a plausible specific conception of justice that fits within a wider liberal framework. No less than political liberalism, justice in transactions represents, in Rawls's words, a liberalism of freedom.

NOTES

TABLE OF CASES

ACKNOWLEDGMENTS

INDEX

Notes

Preface

1. Samuel Williston, "Consideration in Bilateral Contracts," *Harvard Law Review* 27 no.6 (1914): 512.

Introduction

1. The most influential, and still the most important, exemplar of this approach is Charles Fried, *Contract as Promise: A Theory of Contractual Obligation*, 2nd ed. (New York: Oxford University Press, 2015).

2. Lon L. Fuller and William F. Perdue Jr., "The Reliance Interest in Contract Damages: 1," *Yale Law Journal* 46, no. 1 (1936): 52–96, and "The Reliance Interest in Contract Damages: 2," *Yale Law Journal* 46, no. 3 (1937): 373–420. Although the Fuller and Perdue article is most often cited for its discussion of the three interests (and particularly the reliance interest) protected by contract damages, its enduring significance for contract theory, I suggest below, lies in the challenge the authors raise against the widely assumed compensatory character of expectation remedies. I have discussed this in earlier papers, starting with Peter Benson, "Toward a Pure Theory of Contract Law" (LL.M. thesis, Harvard Law School, 1983). See also Peter Benson, "Contract," in *The Companion to the Philosophy of Law and Legal Theory*, ed. Dennis Patterson (New York: Blackwell Publishing, 1996), 24–29; and Peter Benson, "The Expectation and Reliance Interests in Contract Theory: A Reply to Fuller and Perdue," *Issues in Legal Scholarship* (online ed.) 1, no. 1 (2001), https://doi.org/10.2202/1539-8323.1004. It is worth noting that, centuries earlier, a similar challenge impelled theorizing in the civilian tradition, producing a continuous line of perhaps the most important theoretical discussions of contractual

obligation anywhere or at any time. On this parallel, see James Gordley, "A Perennial Misstep: From Cajetan to Fuller and Perdue to 'Efficient Breach,'" *Issues in Legal Scholarship* (online ed.) 1, no. 1 (2001), https://doi.org/10.2202/1539-8323.1003.

3. Fuller and Perdue, "The Reliance Interest: 1," 52.

4. Here and in the rest of the paragraph, I draw on the long and important footnote 7 in Fuller and Perdue, "The Reliance Interest: 1," 56.

5. Pierre de Tourtoulon, *Philosophy in the Development of Law,* trans. Martha McC. Read (New York: Macmillan, 1922), quoted in Fuller and Perdue, "The Reliance Interest: 1," 56n7.

6. Fuller and Perdue, "The Reliance Interest: 1," 56–57.

7. Fuller and Perdue, "The Reliance Interest: 1," 57.

8. Instructive judicial references to this distinction include Cardozo's judgment in H. R. Moch Co. v. Rensselaer Water Co., 159 N.E. 896 (N.Y., 1928) and Lord Diplock's speech in Home Office v. Dorset Yacht Co. Ltd., [1970] AC 1004, 1060 (Eng. H.L.). I discuss the meaning and parameters of misfeasance more fully in Chapters 7 and 11. See also Peter Benson, "Misfeasance as an Organizing Normative Idea in Private Law," *University of Toronto Law Journal* 60, no. 3 (2010): 731–798.

9. I have argued elsewhere that this is why courts traditionally deny liability for negligence in certain situations of so-called pure economic loss. See Peter Benson, "The Basis for Excluding Liability for Pure Economic Loss in Tort Law," in *The Philosophical Foundations of Tort Law,* ed. David G. Owen (New York: Oxford University Press, 1995), 427–458.

10. For a clear and instructive discussion of this point by a leading economic theorist of contract law, see Richard Craswell, "Instrumental Theories of Compensation: A Survey," *San Diego Law Review* 40, no. 4 (2003): 1135–1180.

11. This, in my view, is the difficulty with Fried's justification for the expectation measure, which he presents thus: "If I make a promise to you, I should do as I promise; and if I fail to keep my promise, it is fair that I should be made to hand over the equivalent of the promised performance. In contract doctrine this proposition appears as the expectation measure of damages for breach." Fried, *Contract as Promise,* 17. Within the parameters of the morality of promise-keeping, it is by no means evident why it is *fair* to the promisee or even reasonably to be expected by her that the promise-breaker should be *made* to hand over the value of the performance as equivalence or compensation. This is precisely what Fuller and Perdue challenge.

12. See, for example, Hugo Grotius, *The Rights of War and Peace* (1625), ed. Jean Barbeyrac and Richard Tuck (Indianapolis: Liberty Fund, 2005), book 2, chapter 11, sections 2–4; and Samuel Pufendorf, *On the Law of Nature and Nations* (1688), trans. Charles Henry Oldfather and William Abbott Oldfather (Oxford: Clarendon Press, 1934), book 3, chapter 5, sections 5–7. For detailed instructive discussion, see James Gordley, *The Philosophical Origins of Modern Contract Doctrine* (Oxford: Clarendon Press, 1991), 69–112. A similar distinction is developed by Hobbes, in *Leviathan,* part 1, chapter 14 (66–68), and underpins the accounts of Kant and Hegel.

13. For Rawls's discussion of this idea, see, for example, John Rawls, *Justice as Fairness: A Restatement,* ed. Erin Kelly (Cambridge, MA: Belknap Press of Harvard University Press, 2001), 26–29.

14. John Rawls, *A Theory of Justice* (Cambridge, MA: Belknap Press of Harvard University Press, 1971), 29.

15. See Rawls's clear statement of this point—from which I draw—in *Justice as Fairness,* 89–90 and elsewhere.

16. See Richard A. Posner's admonitions against the judicial use of economic analysis in "Some Uses and Abuses of Economics in Law," *University of Chicago Law Review* 46, no. 2 (1974): 298–301. Rawls himself gives "elaborate economic theories of general equilibrium" as an example of such nonpublic forms of reasoning. Rawls, *Justice as Fairness,* 90. See also Rawls's discussion of whether the difference principle should be treated as a constitutional provision that courts should interpret and apply, in *Justice as Fairness,* 48–49, 162.

17. Rawls, *Justice as Fairness,* 31–32.

18. Here, again, it is Rawls who makes and elucidates this distinction most satisfactorily, and it is clearly appropriate to draw on his account as I do here. See John Rawls, *Political Liberalism* (New York: Columbia University Press, 1996), 48–54, and Rawls, *Justice as Fairness,* 6–8.

19. See, for example, Louis Kaplow and Steven Shavell, *Fairness versus Welfare* (Cambridge, MA: Harvard University Press, 2002), chapters 1, 2, and 4. Note that, strictly speaking, their account purports to be teleological in that it views the aim of contract enforcement as that of maximizing the individual well-being of both parties. Note also that the conception of well-being is both comprehensive and content-neutral and certainly need not be materialistic or selfish in the ordinary sense.

20. Contrary to the sharp separation Kaplow and Shavell wish and need to draw between welfare and fairness for their argument to go through, the requirement that *each* party's individual well-being must be advanced (as distinct from the sum or average of their well-being) seems implicitly to rest on an egalitarian criterion expressing the reasonable. I ignore this point for the purposes of this illustration.

21. Michael J. Trebilcock has made this point, calling it the "Paretian dilemma," in *The Limits of Freedom of Contract* (Cambridge, MA: Harvard University Press, 1993), 244 and elsewhere.

22. Arguably, Rawls's account of the principle of fidelity does not connect parties in this direct way. See Rawls, *A Theory of Justice,* 342–350.

23. The most important and influential example of this approach is of course Charles Fried's promise principle as set out in *Contract as Promise,* chapter 2.

24. This would be the case, for example, if the conception of contract—and more particularly that of contractual freedom—requires the view taken in Lochner v. New York, 198 U.S. 45 (1905).

25. Aristotle, *Nicomachean Ethics,* book 5, 1131a–1132b.

26. Aristotle, *Nicomachean Ethics,* book 5, 1132b–1133b.

A. Formation

1. See David J. Ibbetson, *A Historical Introduction to the Law of Obligations* (Oxford: Oxford University Press, 1999), 71–76. For the role of consent in continental medieval thought, see James Gordley, *The Philosophical Origins of Modern Contract Doctrine* (Oxford: Clarendon Press, 1991), 40–61.

2. It is worth mentioning here that these two kinds of promising might be compared to the imperfect and perfect promises of the seventeenth-century natural rights theorists. As I noted in the Introduction, they viewed only perfect promises as coercively enforceable and as the moral basis of contract. The second kind of promising is similar to perfect promises in their normative character and legal effect. For the distinction between imperfect and perfect promises, see Hugo Grotius, *The Rights of War and Peace* (1625), ed. Jean Barbeyrac and Richard Tuck (Indianapolis: Liberty Fund, 2005), book 2, chapter 11, sections 2–4; and Samuel Pufendorf, *On the Law of Nature and Nations* (1688), trans. Charles Henry Oldfather and William Abbott Oldfather (Oxford: Clarendon Press, 1934), book 3, chapter 5, sections 5–7.

3. "Promises—and therefore contracts—are fundamentally relational; one person must make the promise to another, and the second person must accept it." Charles Fried, *Contract as Promise: A Theory of Contractual Obligation*, 2nd ed. (New York: Oxford University Press, 2015), 45.

4. Once again, this is the view taken by Fried.

5. On the common law's reception of the doctrine of offer and acceptance, see A. W. B. Simpson, "Innovation in Nineteenth Century Contract Law," *Law Quarterly Review* 91 (1975): 247.

6. This is the view Fried takes in *Contract as Promise*, chapters 3 and 4. In this respect, his account harkens back to the nineteenth- and early twentieth-century will theorists, both common law and civilian, for whom offer and acceptance was also the organizing idea, in contrast to consideration or *causa*, which they found more problematic and less essential within their frameworks.

7. I suppose here that a promise that the promisee does not want in any way but still, for some inexplicable reason, wishes to hold the promisor to would not illustrate promising—or a promissory relation giving rise to a duty to perform—in its central case. In Chapter 12, I present a more detailed analysis of the morality of promissory duty.

8. Unlike the view that I take in the text, Fried seems to regard this change of mind and dependence as an act—"the act of acquiescing in the promissory benefit that . . . is necessary to complete a binding promise." *Contract as Promise,* 45. But there is nothing in the promisee's reaction that can be likened to the promisor's communicated expression of fixed intent and decision: there is only an internal decision, which need not always be communicated and which is com-

pletely alterable, to trust the promisor and to form expectations of future performance. If it is an "act," it certainly does not rise to the level of the same kind as the promise.

1. Consideration

1. For helpful historical accounts, see David J. Ibbetson, *A Historical Introduction to the Law of Obligations* (Oxford: Oxford University Press, 1999); David J. Ibbetson, "Consideration and the Theory of Contract in the Sixteenth Century Common Law," in *Towards a General Law of Contract,* ed. John Barton (Berlin: Duncker & Humblot, 1990), 67–124; John H. Baker, "Origins of the 'Doctrine' of Consideration, 1535–1585," in *On the Laws and Customs of England,* ed. Morris S. Arnold, Thomas A. Green, Sally A. Scully, and Stephen D. White (Chapel Hill: University of North Carolina Press, 1981), 336–358; John H. Baker, ed., *The Reports of Sir John Spelman* (London: Selden Society, 1977), chapter 9; and Warren Swain, "The Changing Nature of the Doctrine of Consideration, 1750–1850," *Journal of Legal History* 26, no. 1 (2005): 55–72.

2. In Arthur T. von Mehren's words, "Consideration stands, doctrinally speaking, at the very center of the common law's approach to contract law. It represents an ambitious and sustained effort to construct a general doctrine." "Civil-Law Analogues to Consideration," *Harvard Law Review* 72, no. 6 (1959): 1009.

3. For representative statements, see John P. Dawson, *Gifts and Promises* (New Haven, CT: Yale University Press, 1980), 197, and Stephen A. Smith, *Contract Theory* (Oxford: Oxford University Press, 2004), 215–216.

4. Charles Fried, *Contract as Promise: A Theory of Contractual Obligation,* 2nd ed. (New York: Oxford University Press, 2015), 29, 35. My discussion is in Section 1.2 below.

5. Andrew Burrows, *Understanding the Law of Obligations* (Oxford: Hart Publishing, 1998), 197.

6. Lon L. Fuller, "Consideration and Form," *Columbia Law Review* 41, no. 5 (1941): 799–824.

7. Fuller, "Consideration and Form," 806. Fuller states, "The future of consideration is tied up to a considerable extent with the future of the principle of private autonomy" (823).

8. Fuller discusses these alternative bases of contract liability in "Consideration and Form," 810–813.

9. Fuller, "Consideration and Form," 800–806, 813–814.

10. Fuller, "Consideration and Form," 805.

11. Fuller, "Consideration and Form," 805, 815–816.

12. Fuller, "Consideration and Form," 813–815.

13. Fuller, "Consideration and Form," 815 ("[A] gift is, in [Claude] Bufnoir's words, a 'sterile transmission'").

14. Thorp v. Thorp, (1702) 12 Mod. 445, 449 (K.B. 1702), quoted in Fuller, "Consideration and Form," 816.

15. See Andrew Kull's critical discussion of this aspect in "Reconsidering Gratuitous Promises," *Journal of Legal Studies* 21, no. 1 (1992): 39.

16. Kull emphasizes this point in "Reconsidering Gratuitous Promises," 49–55, 59. See the instructive discussion in Richard A. Posner, "Gratuitous Promises in Economics and Law," *Journal of Legal Studies* 6, no. 2 (1977): 412–414. The point has also been made by Fried, *Contract as Promise*, 37, and Robert Cooter and Thomas Ulen, *Law and Economics*, 5th ed. (Boston: Pearson Education, 2008), 201–202.

17. This conclusion is widely shared. See Kull, "Reconsidering Gratuitous Promises," 47, and, more recently, Randy Barnett, *Contracts* (Oxford: Oxford University Press, 2010), 147–187.

18. "If words of obligation are used in the writing, then the writing itself is the cause of the obligation." Ibbetson, *A Historical Introduction*, 21.

19. Similarly, the objective test, which, I argue, takes up a transactional-bilateral standpoint, does not apply. See Robert Stevens, "Objectivity, Mistake, and the Parol Evidence Rule," in *Contract Terms*, ed. Andrew Burrows and Edwin Peel (Oxford: Oxford University Press, 2007), 102–103.

20. Lon L. Fuller, *Basic Contract Law* (St. Paul, MN: West Publishing, 1947), 313–319.

21. Fuller, *Basic Contract Law*, 316.

22. Fuller, *Basic Contract Law*, 316.

23. Fuller, *Basic Contract Law*, 317. See also Alan Brudner, *The Unity of the Common Law*, 2nd ed. (Oxford: Oxford University Press, 2013), 198–200.

24. Early on, the common law recognized the parallelism and exhaustive quality of these two categories. See Lord Holt's statement in Thorp v. Thorp. In developing my account of contract, the discussion will often focus explicitly on the bilateral contract even though the basic analysis holds for both categories. This is because the bilateral contract presents theory with its single most fundamental challenge of explaining the contractual enforceability of a purely executory agreement formed in and through the purely representational medium of the parties' mutual promises alone.

25. As stated by Justice Patteson in Thomas v. Thomas, (1842) 2 Q.B. 851, 859.

26. For a historical discussion of these cases, see Ibbetson, "Consideration and the Theory of Contract," 79–81.

27. This point is brought out by Williston's famous example of a benevolent person telling a tramp, "If you go around the corner to the clothing shop there, you may purchase an overcoat on my credit." See Samuel Williston, *A Treatise on the Law of Contracts* (New York: Baker, Voorhis, 1922), section 112.

28. Wisconsin & Michigan Railway Co. v. Powers, (1903) 191 U.S. 379, 386 (per Holmes, J.).

29. As noted earlier, this is not true of promises under seal.

30. Wisconsin v. Powers, 386. See also Oliver Wendell Holmes, *The Common Law*, ed. Mark DeWolfe Howe (Cambridge, MA: Belknap Press of Harvard University Press, 1963), 230 ("[I]t is the essence of a consideration that, *by the terms of the agreement*, it is given and accepted as the motive or inducement of the promise" [emphasis added]).

31. A representative early statement is in Nichols v. Raynbred, (1615) Hob. 88 ("The promises must be at one instant, for else they will be both *nuda pacta*").

32. This requirement, I think, underpins the common law analysis of so-called "past consideration" cases, where the alleged consideration is completed before the promise is given. Unless the consideration can be objectively viewed as expressly or impliedly requested by the promisor in return for compensation and as done in response to her request, it does not qualify as valid. But if there is such request, though the promise follows after, the two elements are viewed as joined in one unified transaction of promise-for-consideration. This is the explicit formulation in the early seminal case of Lampleigh v. Braithwait, (1615) Hob. 105. See also Ibbetson's discussion in "Consideration and the Theory of Contract," 88–96.

33. "A valuable consideration, in the sense of the law, may consist either in some right, interest, profit, or benefit accruing to the one party, or some forbearance, detriment, loss, or responsibility given, suffered, or undertaken by the other." Currie v. Misa, (1875) L.R. 10 Exch. 153, 162.

34. See, for example, Allegheny College v. National Chautauqua County Bank, 159 N.E. 173 (N.Y. 1927); De Cicco v. Schweizer, 117 N.E. 807 (N.Y. 1917); and Hamer v. Sidway, 27 N.E. 256 (N.Y. 1891).

35. Wiseman v. Cole, (1585) 2 Co. Rep. 15a, 15b; Co. Litt. 47, as cited in Ibbetson, *A Historical Introduction*, 141.

36. The term "invented" is from G. H. Treitel, "Consideration: A Critical Analysis of Professor Atiyah's Fundamental Restatement," *Australian Law Journal* 50 (1976): 440.

37. Philpot v. Gruninger, 81 U.S. 570 (1871), quoted with approval by Judge Cardozo in McGovern v. City of New York, 234 N.Y. 377, 138 N.E. 26 (1923), 31, who adds that "[t]he fortuitous presence in a transaction of some possibility of detriment, latent but unthought of, is not enough."

38. Where there is a preexisting contractual duty on the part of one party toward the other to do x because the first has already promised this to the second, the first party is not, in legal contemplation, at liberty with respect to doing x and so cannot promise it again or do it as fresh consideration for any new promise coming from the second. This is the basis of the so-called preexisting duty rule first stated in Stilk v. Myrick, (1809) 2 Camp. 317. In my view, this rule is a necessary corollary—in fact, simply the application—of the requirement of consideration and cannot be rejected without rejecting the requirement itself. What a party has already moved

to the other as consideration is no longer on her side to move again. Further, if a promise is to have value in the eye of the law, it must already include at formation the value of the performance itself. Actual performance of the same promise cannot convey a contractually cognizable distinct and additional value. Thus, in my view, the analysis proposed in the well-known English decision Williams v. Roffey Bros. & Nicholls (Contractors) Ltd., [1991] 1 Q.B.1 (Eng. C.A.), is incompatible with the settled understanding of consideration. By contrast, US decisions such as King v. Duluth, M. & N. Railway Co., 63 N.W. 1105 (S.C. Minn. 1895), and Linz v. Schuck, 67 A. 286 (C.A. Md. 1907), as well as *Restatement of the Law of Contracts* (1932), section 76, illustration 8, and *Restatement (Second) of Contracts* (1981), section 89, are arguably not inconsistent in the same way. These decisions hold that for the new promise to be enforceable, it must be given in fundamentally changed circumstances, not contemplated by their agreement, that impose on the promisee serious additional burdens of performance. In such circumstances, it is reasonable to infer that by modifying the original terms, the parties have implicitly treated each other as at liberty to exit their contract and have entered a new arrangement. Whether this is explained as an implicit rescission of the first agreement, the parties can reasonably be held jointly to have treated their relation as consisting of two distinct transactions, with the second supplanting the first. See King v. Duluth, 1107. A similar approach is suggested by C. F. Hamson, "The Reform of Consideration," *Law Quarterly Review* 54 (1938): 237–240, and briefly proposed in G. H. Treitel and F. M. B. Reynolds, "Consideration for the Modification of Contracts," *Malaysian Law Review* 7, no. 1 (1965): 20–23. For an illuminating economic analysis that aligns with this approach, see Varouj A. Aivazian, Michael J. Trebilcock, and Michael Penny, "The Law of Contract Modifications: The Uncertain Quest for a Bench Mark of Enforceability," *Osgoode Hall Law Journal* 22 (1984): 173–212.

39. As in Hamer v. Sidway. Here Nephew's self-restraint was, as a forbearance, a detriment to him but at the same time, as a negative service moved to Uncle at his request, a benefit to the latter.

40. See, for example, A. W. B. Simpson, *A History of the Common Law of Contract: The Rise of the Action of Assumpsit* (Oxford: Oxford University Press, 1975), 72–74.

41. Contra Fuller's explanation. See Fuller, "Consideration and Form," 820.

42. As part of his historical survey of the case law, James Gordley makes this point in "Equality in Exchange," *California Law Review* 69, no. 6 (1981): 1652–1654.

43. It is not, for example, $100 for a $1 bill signed by Paul McCartney.

44. See, for example, Schnell v. Nell, 17 Ind. 29 (1861).

45. This point is expressly noted by Cardozo in McGovern, 32. See also von Mehren, "Civil-Law Analogues to Consideration," 1031, 1033.

46. Fried, *Contract as Promise*, 29, 35.

47. The two propositions that form the basis of Fried's refutation of consideration are really just different formulations of Fuller's amalgam of substance (first prop-

osition) and form (second proposition). Whereas the latter expresses an unrestricted conception of private autonomy, the former limits its application to economic exchanges. Fuller seeks to defend the doctrine on the basis of this amalgam, whereas Fried's argument does the exact contrary. Both arguments fail, I believe, because they misunderstand the nature and role of the basic bilateral relation that consideration requires.

48. In Rann v. Hughes, (1778) 7 T.R. 350n (Eng. H.L.).

49. For helpful accounts of gifts, see R. A. Brown, *The Law of Personal Property*, 2nd ed. (Chicago: Callaghan, 1955), chapter 7 (US law), and Michael G. Bridge, *Personal Property Law*, 3rd ed. (Oxford: Oxford University Press, 2002), 93–100 (English law). For a comprehensive comparative law treatment, see Richard Hyland, *Gifts: A Study in Comparative Law* (Oxford: Oxford University Press, 2009).

50. See Brown, *Personal Property*, section 7.3. For a brief discussion of symbolic and constructive delivery in relation to this standard case, see below.

51. See Standing v. Bowring, (1883) L.R. 31 Ch.D. 282, 288, as discussed in Brown, *Personal Property*, 128.

52. On this analysis, delivery is not treated as a needed natural legal formality evidencing a gift (as per Fuller) but is taken as a constitutive element of the gift. This is in keeping with Lord Esher's view stated in the leading case of Cochrane v. Moore, (1890) L.R. 25 Q.B.D. 57: "[A]ctual delivery in the case of a 'gift' is more than evidence of the proposition of law which constitutes a gift ... it is a part of the proposition itself. It is one of the facts which constitute the proposition that a gift has been made." Similarly, see Brown, *Personal Property*, section 7.1, note 7, and sections 7.5–7.6.

53. On this view, therefore, "constructive" delivery and merely "symbolic" delivery are distinct. As Brown explains in *Personal Property* (sections 7.5–7.6), the central case of the former operates in circumstances where manual delivery of the whole object is very inconvenient, if not impossible (e.g., because of its bulk or distance from the parties), and the donor gives the donee the exclusive means of obtaining control and possession of the object or in some other manner relinquishes control over it in favor of the donee. By contrast, in the central case of symbolic delivery, the donor gives the donee some object that is meant merely to represent the actual subject matter of the gift and does not in any way enable the donee to obtain physical control over it. As a case approaches the extreme of a symbolic delivery, it becomes more problematic as a gift. This difficulty parallels the one noted earlier with respect to the operation of nominal consideration, which the law distinguishes from a purely symbolic consideration.

54. This premise, which is central to my proposed account of consideration and of contract itself, is emphasized by Hobbes in his analysis of contracts (enforceable in principle) as distinguished from unenforceable promises. See Hobbes, *Leviathan*, part 1, chapter 14, 66–68.

55. Jeffrey Gilbert, "Of Contracts" (written about 1710), British Library (Hargrave MS 265, folio 39), quoted in Stephen M. Waddams, *Principle and Policy in Contract Law: Competing or Complementary Concepts?* (Cambridge: Cambridge University Press, 2011), 59.

56. Even in the law of gifts, there can be a valid transfer of ownership over something (i.e., a completed gift) in which the donee obtains "a present gift of the *right* to the subject matter, with the *enjoyment* [and physical possession] only postponed to a later date." Brown, *Personal Property,* 116 (emphasis in original).

57. See the discerning analysis in Gregory Klass, "Three Pictures of Contract: Duty, Power, and Compound Rule," *New York University Law Review* 83, no. 6 (2008): 1726, 1744. For a recent theoretical account that expressly adopts this approach, see Hanoch Dagan and Michael Heller, *The Choice Theory of Contracts* (New York: Cambridge University Press, 2017).

58. I discuss the second model of promising and the natural law distinction between perfect and imperfect promises in Section A, Introduction, and elsewhere.

59. For an overview of US law, see E. Allan Farnsworth, *Contracts,* 4th ed. (New York: Aspen Publishers, 2004), section 2.19. For discussions of Anglo-Commonwealth law, see Mindy Chen-Wishart, *Contract Law,* 2nd ed. (New York: Oxford University Press, 2008), 162–179; Ben McFarlane, "The Protection of Pre-contractual Reliance: A Way Forward?," *Oxford University Commonwealth Law Journal* 10, no. 1 (2010): 95–122; Ben McFarlane, "Understanding Equitable Estoppel: From Metaphors to Better Laws," *Current Legal Problems* 66, no. 1 (2013): 267–305; and Andrew Robertson, "The Reliance Basis of Proprietary Estoppel Remedies," *Conveyancer and Property Lawyer* 72, no. 4 (2008): 295–321.

60. This is the view taken, for example, by Edward Yorio and Steve Thel, "The Promissory Basis of Section 90," *Yale Law Journal* 101, no. 1 (1991): 111–167.

61. See Lon L. Fuller and William R. Perdue Jr., "The Reliance Interest in Contract Damages: 2," *Yale Law Journal* 46, no. 3 (1937): 396, 419, and elsewhere.

62. Important judicial statements of this view include Imperator Realty Co. v. Tull, 228 N.Y. 447, 127 N.E. 263 (C.A. N.Y. 1920); Hoffman v. Red Owl Stores Inc., 133 N.W.2d 267 (S.C. Wisc. 1965); Skycom Corp. v. Telstar Corp., 813 F.2d 810 (7th Cir. 1987); Miller v. Taylor Insulation Co., 39 F.3d 755 (7th Cir. 1994); Cyberchron Corp. v. Calldata Systems Development, 47 F.3d 39 (2d Cir. 1995); and Cosgrove v. Bartolotta, 150 F.3d 729 (7th Cir. 1998) (US cases). English and Commonwealth cases include Grundt v. Great Boulder Pty. Gold Mines Ltd., (1937) 59 C.L.R. 641 (H.C. Australia); Walton Stores (Interstate) Ltd. v. Maher, 164 C.L.R. 387 (H.C. Australia); Crabb v. Arun District Council, [1976] Ch. 179 (Eng. C.A.); and Thorner v. Major, [2009] 1 W.L.R. 776 (Eng. H.L.). And there is of course *Restatement (Second) of Contracts,* section 90. The classic scholarly statement of this view is Warren A. Seavey, "Reliance upon Gratuitous Promises or Other Conduct," *Harvard Law Review* 64, no. 6 (1951): 913–928.

63. As Seavey put it, "The wrong is not primarily in depriving the plaintiff of the promised reward but causing the plaintiff to change position to his detriment." "Reliance upon Gratuitous Promises," 926. This is the view expressly adopted by all of the representative US and Anglo-Commonwealth cases cited above.

64. For a lucid formulation and discussion of this factor, see Stephen M. Perry, "Protected Interests and Undertakings in the Law of Negligence," *University of Toronto Law Journal* 42, no. 3 (1992): 247–317.

65. In Thorner v. Major, 779, Lord Hoffmann rightly emphasizes the objective character of this determination.

66. Thus, the idea of reliance-based promissory liability is at bottom the very same as the principle of liability for negligent representations enunciated in cases such as Glanzer v. Shepard, 135 N.E. 275 (C.A. N.Y. 1922), where the plaintiff detrimentally relied on the accuracy of the defendants' certificate (and by implication the care with which the defendants performed a service that was recorded in that certificate) by making a payment to a third party on its basis, or Hedley Byrne & Co. v. Heller & Partners Ltd., [1964] A.C. 465 (Eng. H.L.), where the plaintiff relied on the bank's statement that a third party was creditworthy. I have discussed the tort of negligent misrepresentation in Peter Benson, "The Basis for Excluding Liability for Economic Loss in Tort Law," in *The Philosophical Foundations of Tort Law*, ed. David G. Owen (New York: Oxford University Press, 1995), 450–455.

67. See Justice Cardozo's judgment in Imperator Realty v. Tull, 456–457, which I have paraphrased in the above text. For representative statements in leading Anglo-Commonwealth decisions, see the classic discussion of the principle by Dixon J. (as he then was) in Grundt v. Great Boulder, 674, and the equally lucid treatment by Brennan J. in Walton Stores v. Maher, 420–430; see, more recently, Steria v. Ronald Hutchison, [2006] EWCA Civ 1551 (Eng. C.A.), paragraphs 125–129 (per Neuberger, L.J.).

68. This is the view expressly adopted by all of the representative US and Anglo-Commonwealth cases cited above.

69. See Imperator Realty v. Tull. For Anglo-Commonwealth case law, see the judgment of Justice Brennan in Walton Stores v. Maher, 423–429, and Ajayi v. R. T. Briscoe (Nigeria) Ltd., [1964] 3 All E.R. 556, 559 (P.C.) ("[T]he promisor can resile from his promise on giving reasonable notice . . . giving the promisee a reasonable opportunity of resuming his position").

70. For an excellent discussion of Anglo-Commonwealth law, see Robertson, "The Reliance Basis." For a detailed analysis and discussion of US cases that emphasizes the flexibility of remedial responses, see Robert A. Hillman, "Questioning the 'New Consensus' on Promissory Estoppel: An Empirical and Theoretical Study," *Columbia Law Review* 98, no. 3 (1998): 601–602, 609–610, 615–618.

71. As put by Chief Justice Mason in Commonwealth v. Verwayen, [1990] 170 C.L.R. 394, 413 (H.C. Australia). This concern is also reflected in the *Restatement (Second) of Contracts,* section 90.

72. See the observation of Learned Hand, C. J., to this effect in James Baird Co. v. Gimbel Bros., Inc., 64 F.2d 344 (1933, 2d Cir. C.A.), 343.

73. Recalling the two models of promising discussed earlier, the kind of promissory relation involved in reliance-based liability is the first kind. By contrast, the promise-for-consideration relation, I have suggested, involves promising of the second kind.

74. This was Seavey's view as well in "Reliance upon Gratuitous Promises," 926. For a different classification, see Andrew Robertson, "Estoppels and Rights-Creating Events: Beyond Wrongs and Promises," in *Exploring Contract Law,* ed. Jason W. Neyers, Richard Bronaugh, and Stephen G. A. Pitel (Oxford: Hart Publishing, 2009), 199, 207–224.

75. This seems to be, for example, Randy Barnett's view. See Barnett, *Contracts,* 186–187. For a recent detailed critical discussion of this approach, see Mindy Chen-Wishart, "Consideration and Serious Intention," *Singapore Journal of Legal Studies,* 2009, 434–456.

76. To a similar effect, see McFarlane, "Pre-contractual Reliance," 108 (Anglo-Commonwealth law), and Hillman, "Questioning the 'New Consensus,'" 581 (US law).

77. For a helpful overview, see David J. Ibbetson and Eltjo J. H. Schrage, "*Ius quaesitum tertio:* A Comparative and Historical Introduction to the Concept of Third Party Contracts," in *Ius Quaesitum Tertio,* ed. Eltjo J. H. Schrage (Berlin: Duncker & Humblot, 2008), 1–34.

78. Fried rightly raises these and other questions and problems in connection with the law's treatment of third-party claims and notes that the "law has long been in confusion" about them. *Contract as Promise,* 44.

79. See David J. Ibbetson and Warren Swain, "Third Party Beneficiaries in English Law: From *Dutton v. Poole* to *Tweddle v. Atkinson,*" in *Ius Quaesitum Tertio,* ed. Eltjo J. H. Schrage (Berlin: Duncker & Humblot, 2008), 205–206, and Vernon V. Palmer, *The Paths to Privity: The History of Third Party Beneficiary Contracts at English Law* (San Francisco: Austin & Winfield, 1992).

80. Thus in Roman law: *alteri stipulari nemo potest.* For discussion, see Ibbetson and Schrage, "A Comparative and Historical Introduction," 2–7, and Reinhard Zimmermann, *The Law of Obligations: Roman Foundations of the Civilian Tradition* (New York: Oxford University Press, 1996), 34–40.

81. American contract law took a different turn in the nineteenth century, recognizing within certain limits third-party beneficiary claims. For historical accounts of the American position, see S. P. de Cruz, "Privity in America: A Study in Judicial and Statutory Innovation," *Anglo-American Law Review* 14, no. 3 (1985): 265–281.

82. Coulls v. Bagot's Executor & Trustee Co. Ltd., (1966–1967) 119 C.L.R. 460, 498 (H.C. Australia) (per Windeyer, J.).

83. This necessity of being a promisee who gives consideration underpins Tweddle v. Atkinson, (1861) 121 E.R. 762.

84. Holmes makes this point in *The Common Law*, 265–266.

85. See, for example, Samuel Williston, "Contracts for the Benefit of a Third Person," *Harvard Law Review* 15, no. 10 (1902): 767–809, and Williston, *Law of Contracts*, section 354.

86. See, for example, Robert Flannigan, "Privity—the End of an Era (Error)," *Law Quarterly Review* 103 (1987): 564–577.

87. By contrast, Fried considers "acceptance" by a third party to be "acceptance in its purest form, untinctured by any element of counterpromise or exchange." *Contract as Promise*, 45.

88. For the parallel requirement in tort law, see Cardozo's judgment in Palsgraf v. Long Island Railroad Co., 162 N.E. 99 (N.Y. C.A. 1928) ("The plaintiff sues in her own right for a wrong personal to her, and not as the vicarious beneficiary of a breach of duty to another").

89. Tweddle v. Atkinson, 399.

90. This whole discussion presupposes, for obvious reasons, that the third party's claim is not based on any invited detrimental reliance—which would establish a direct relation between the third party and the party or parties inviting reliance. Where a third party satisfies the doctrinal requirements for reliance-based liability, she can certainly recover (reliance) damages in her own right as recognized in, for example, section 90 of *Restatement (Second) of Contracts*.

91. Melvin A. Eisenberg, "Third-Party Beneficiaries," *Columbia Law Review* 92, no. 6 (1992): 1358–1430.

92. See *Restatement (Second) of Contracts*, section 302.

93. This remedial analysis was clearly recognized by Williston ("Contracts for the Benefit of a Third Person," 773), among other writers. As for judicial recognition, Beswick v. Beswick, [1968] A.C. 58 (Eng. H.L.), and Coulls v. Bagot's Executor, 499–504 (per Windeyer, J.), are clear and important modern examples. I discuss the concept of *remedial* adequacy in Chapter 8.

94. Neil Jones, for example, notes these features in "Aspects of Privity in England: Equity to 1680," in *Ius Quaesitum Tertio*, ed. Eltjo J. H. Schrage (Berlin: Duncker & Humblot, 2008), 146. Consider, for example, the facts in the famous old English case of Dutton v. Poole, 2 Lev. 210 (1677), discussed at length in Palmer, *The Paths to Privity*, 75–78, 172–173.

95. Prime instances where third parties are donee-beneficiaries include life-insurance contracts, testamentary dispositions, family settlements, and so forth where the promise is to be performed after the promisee's death. See Seaver v. Ransom et al., 120 N.E. 639, 641 (1918 N.Y. C.A.). For discussion of creditor-beneficiaries, see Clarke B. Whittier, "Contract Beneficiaries," *Yale Law Journal* 32, no. 8 (1923): 790–807. Eisenberg discusses both categories in "Third-Party Beneficiaries," 1389–1392.

96. "A recognized third-party beneficiary has a power, not a right, and the power is derivative, not direct; that is, the power of the beneficiary to bring suit derives from the desirability of allowing the beneficiary to enforce the contract so as to

effectuate the performance objectives of the contracting parties." Eisenberg, "Third-Party Beneficiaries," 1426.

97. The question of whether the appropriate circumstances for according the third party standing to sue exist can, but need not always, be readily determinable by a court in its adjudicative role. I believe that this is why English courts, prior to the legislative response of the Contracts (Rights of Third Parties) Act 1999, called for a legislative solution but at the same time indicated that the courts would address the issue if no such solution was forthcoming within a reasonable time. See, for example, Beswick v. Beswick, 72 (per Lord Reid).

98. This view is also taken by Eisenberg, who argues that it "has been largely accepted by *Restatement Second*," although "it is still burdened with some doctrinal baggage ... as are the courts." "Third-Party Beneficiaries," 1414.

99. Eisenberg emphasizes this in "Third-Party Beneficiaries," 1420–1421.

100. Contra the *Restatement (Second) of Contracts*, section 309 (3), comment c.

101. In his careful examination of English legislative recognition of third-party beneficiary rights, Robert Stevens also brings out this difficulty if third-party standing to sue is understood (incorrectly in his view) as a direct right. See Robert Stevens, "The Contracts (Rights of Third Parties) Act 1999," *Law Quarterly Review* 120 (2004): 320.

102. There are many historical accounts of assignment. For a helpful summary, see Greg Tolhurst, *The Assignment of Contractual Rights*, 2nd ed. (Oxford: Hart Publishing, 2018), chapter 2. For the early history of assignment first in equity and then at common law, see Palmer, *The Paths to Privity*, 138–158.

103. See William Searle Holdsworth, "The History of the Treatment of *Choses* in Action by the Common Law," *Harvard Law Review* 33, no. 8 (1920): 997, 1030.

104. For the purposes of the following discussion, I have drawn on many sources, only some of which are expressly noted here and below. In addition to Tolhurst, *The Assignment of Contractual Rights*, which focuses on Anglo-Australian law, there is Farnsworth, *Contracts*, chapter 11 for a detailed and lucid account of US law. There are also a number of important judicial formulations. For a particularly helpful and learned recent summary statement of the basic propositions of assignment, see Pacific Brands Sport & Leisure Pty. Ltd. v. Underworks Pty. Ltd., [2006] FCAFC 40, paragraph 32 (per Finn and Sundberg, JJ.).

105. Norman v. Federal Commissioner of Taxation, (1963) 109 C.L.R. 9, 26 (per Windeyer, J.).

106. The locus of obligation can be changed only with the obligee's consent (in effect via novation of the original contract), whereby a new contractual relation—with a different obligor—comes into existence. On the difference between assignment and novation, see Tolhurst, *The Assignment of Contractual Rights*, section 3.06. On novation in Roman and civil law, see Zimmermann, *The Law of Obligations*, 60–67.

107. A leading case on this question is Tolhurst v. Associated Portland Cement Manufacturers, [1903] A.C. 414.

108. This is widely presupposed in the case law. See, for example, Pacific Brands Sport & Leisure Pty. Ltd. v. Underworks Pty. Ltd., paragraph 34, and McGowan v. Commissioner of Stamp Duties, [2001] Q.C.A. 236, paragraph 14 (Queensland C.A.). See also Tolhurst, *The Assignment of Contractual Rights,* section 6.71.

109. There are many judicial statements of this point. A particularly clear example is Fitzroy v. Cave, [1905] 2 K.B. 364, 372–373. (Eng. C.A).

110. See Torkington v. Magee, [1902] 2 K.B. 427, 432.

111. See Tolhurst's discussion of transfer in *The Assignment of Contractual Rights,* sections 3.01–3.27. He contrasts this transfer model with an alternative "contractual" model that analyzes "assignment" in terms of two (not three) direct (contractual) relations, namely, one between obligor and assignor and another between assignor and assignee (sections 4.05–4.08). The only duty that the obligor owes in these circumstances is a direct contractual duty to the assignor. She has no direct duty of any kind to the assignee. At most (as part of an older equitable analysis), the assignor's conscience may be bound by her promise to the assignee to take the necessary measures to ensure that the assignee receives the benefit of the performance that she, the assignor, has promised. According to Tolhurst, this analysis does not even require that there be a distinct category of legal relations called "assignment." For a defense of this approach, see Chee Ho Tham, "The Nature of Equitable Assignment and Anti-Assignment Clauses," in *Exploring Contract Law,* ed. Jason W. Neyers, Richard Bronaugh, and Stephen G. A. Pitel (Oxford: Hart Publishing, 2009), 283–318.

112. Tolhurst, *The Assignment of Contractual Rights,* sections 1.02–1.03, 3.12, and elsewhere. The *"nemo dat* rule" refers to the principle *Nemo dat quod non habet* (no one gives what one does not have).

113. Tolhurst, *The Assignment of Contractual Rights,* sections 3.10 and 3.27.

114. There are countless discussions of the nature and scope of rights counting as choses in action. For helpful overviews, see Tolhurst, *The Assignment of Contractual Rights,* sections 2.02–2.06, and T. Cyprian Williams, "Property, Things in Action and Copyright," *Law Quarterly Review* 11 (1895): 223. For a recent judicial definition, see Investors Compensation Scheme Ltd. v. West Bromwich Building Society, [1998] 1 W.L.R. 896 at 915 (Eng. H.L.) (per Lord Hoffmann) ("[C]hose in action is property, something capable of being turned into money").

115. On this point, see Pacific Brands Sport & Leisure Pty. Ltd. v. Underworks Pty. Ltd., paragraphs 38–42. See also Walter Wheeler Cook's instructive discussion in "The Alienability of Choses in Action," *Harvard Law Review* 29 (1916): 816, 819–820.

116. This is emphasized by Tolhurst. See, for example, *The Assignment of Contractual Rights,* section 8.61.

117. For example, contract modifications made within the rule of King v. Duluth or *Restatement (Second) of Contracts* (1981), section 89.

118. Tolhurst expressly underlines this point. See *The Assignment of Contractual Rights*, section 3.10.

119. There are differences in the precise role notice plays in equitable and legal assignments. Equitable assignments are complete between assignor and assignee and are binding on the obligor even prior to notice to the obligor. At the same time, it is only with receipt of notice that the obligor must take into account the assignee's position and perform to the assignee, not the assignor. For detailed discussion of these and other aspects of the notice requirement, see Tolhurst, *The Assignment of Contractual Rights*, sections 4.10–4.20, 7.18, 7.38, 8.06. By contrast, my brief reference to notice is only intended to explain its normative role in the underlying juridical analysis of assignment.

120. De Mattos v. Gibson, (1859) 4 De G. & J. 276. The term "equitable servitudes on chattels" is taken from Zechariah Chafee Jr., "Equitable Servitudes on Chattels," *Harvard Law Review* 41, no. 8 (1928): 945–1013, and is used in cases such as Waring v. WDAS Broadcasting Station Inc., 194 A. 631, 637–638 (1937, S.C. Pa.).

121. Lumley v. Gye, (1853) 2 El. & Bl. 114. For the historical context and the theoretical issues raised in this case and in Lumley v. Wagner, (1852) 1 De Ge. M. & G. 604 (Ch.D.), see Stephen M. Waddams, "Johanna Wagner and the Rival Opera Houses," *Law Review Quarterly* 117 (2001): 431–458. For general treatment of the tort, see Dan B. Dobbs, "Tortious Interference with Contractual Relationships," *Arkansas Law Review* 34, no. 3 (1980): 335, and William L. Prosser, W. Page Keeton, Dan B. Dobbs, Robert E. Keeton, and David G. Owen, eds., *Prosser and Keeton on the Law of Torts*, 5th ed. (St. Paul, MN: West Group, 1984), 978–1013 (US tort law). For instructive in-depth analysis, see Francis Sayre, "Inducing Breach of Contract," *Harvard Law Review* 36, no. 6 (1923): 633–703, and Richard Epstein, "Inducement of Breach of Contract as a Problem of Ostensible Ownership," *Journal of Legal Studies* 16, no. 1 (1987): 1–41.

122. See, for example, Sayre, "Inducing Breach," 685–686, and Waddams, "Johanna Wagner," 453–454. This concern is a main theme in Dobbs, "Tortious Interference." The fairly recent important decision of the House of Lords in OBG Ltd. v. Allan, [2008] 1 A.C. 1, tries to clarify the meaning and scope of the tort of inducement in relation to the main economic torts, characterizing it as a tort of accessory liability.

123. This was one of the main points of objection made by Justice Coleridge in his powerful dissent in Lumley v. Gye, 246.

124. For judicial statements of this, see Beekman v. Marsters, 80 N.E. 817, 819 (Mass. 1907), and Citizens' Light, Heat and Power Co. v. Montgomery Light and Water Power Co., 171 Fed. 553, 560–561 (M.D. Ala. 1908).

125. The distinction draws on the explanation of malice by Lord Justice Brett in the leading English case of Bowen v. Hall, (1881) 6 Q.B.D. 333, 338 (C.A. Q.B.D.).

126. As commentators have noted, to be tortious, the defendant's receipt must be connected to the contracting party's breach, and this in turn presupposes that the latter's in personam duty to the plaintiff must be to provide a thing or service that is not generic and so is normally protected by specific performance. See, for example, Waddams, "Johanna Wagner," 453–454. Within the proposed framework of analysis, it is only via a breach that the plaintiff's ownership in her performance interest can be affected by anyone. Therefore, if the defendant's receipt is to qualify as an interference with that title, the content of the duty breached and what the defendant misappropriates must be the very same.

127. See Sayre, "Inducing Breach," 679–686.

128. This analysis seems to be in tension with viewing the tort as one of accessory liability (as does *OBG v. Allan*) if the latter view treats the defendant as a co-participant with the breaching party in the violation of the plaintiff's in personam right to performance.

129. For a representative case, see Raymond v. Yarrington et al., 96 Tex. 443, 451 (Tex. 1903). More recently, see OBG v. Allan, 32, per Lord Hoffmann. See also Prosser and Keeton et al., *Law of Torts,* 981.

130. While I cannot discuss it here in detail, Justice Pitney's famous majority opinion in International News Service v. The Associated Press, (1918) 248 U.S. 215, 235–242, illustrates the same underlying analysis in a particularly clear and instructive way. Justice Pitney holds that even though the plaintiff publisher (INS) does not have, as against the public, any property in the uncopyrighted news after its first publication, the plaintiff does have, as against the defendant competitor (AP), an equitable ownership right in the news treated as "stock in trade" and "mere material" for its business of gathering and transmitting news to the public for profit. The opinion emphasizes that the defendant competitor, simply by taking and using the plaintiff's news for the same business purpose, also treats it as having "exchange value" and that for this reason and as between the parties the news "must be regarded as *quasi* property, irrespective of the rights of either as against the public" and "has all the attributes of property necessary for determining that a misappropriation of it by a competitor is unfair competition because contrary to good conscience" (236–240). A key point is that in so characterizing the plaintiff's protected interest, the opinion views it as proprietary *transactionally* as between the parties, though not resting on any contractual relation between them and being potentially applicable to indeterminately anyone who interacts with the plaintiff's business interest in this way. Does this amount to according the plaintiff title in its business activity as a chose in action?

131. This was noted already in 1879 by William Anson, though with misgivings: "[I]t is important to bear in mind that a considered judgment of the Court of Queen's Bench has laid it down that a contract confers rights *in rem* as well as *in personam;* that it not only binds together the parties by an obligation, but that it imposes upon all the world a duty to respect the contractual tie." William Reynell

Anson, *Principles of the English Law of Contract,* 1st ed. (Oxford: Clarendon Press, 1879), 199.

132. For example, according to Epstein's approach in terms of "ostensible ownership," "[T]he gist of the tort [of inducement] is the third party's *receipt* of the property [or labor] with knowledge that someone else is the true owner." "Inducement of Breach," 27–28 (emphasis in original). This rationale clearly applies to the first scenario but prima facie not to the second.

133. See Bowen v. Hall.

134. Sayre discusses a number of instances where such justification applies and, in general, views it as negating the existence of malice, rather than as requiring a balancing between policies and rights. "Inducing Breach," 685, 686n69.

135. Epstein reaches the same conclusion in "Inducement of Breach," 27.

136. "Although the *existence* of this exception [in *De Mattos*] to the rule against imposing restrictions on a third party's use of property acquired is established, the *basis of the exception* remains clouded." Mindy Chen-Wishart, *Contract Law,* 5th ed. (New York: Oxford University Press, 2015), 199 (emphasis in original). Instructive judicial discussions of the *De Mattos* principle include Lord Strathcona Steamship Co. Ltd. v. Dominion Coal Co. Ltd., [1926] A.C. 448 (P.C.) (Lord Shaw); Waring v. WDAS Broadcasting Station; Nadell & Co. v. Grasso, (1959) 346 P.2d 505 (Dist. Ct. App., Cal.); Swiss Bank Corp. v. Lloyds Bank Ltd., [1979] Ch. 548 (per Browne-Wilkinson, J.); and Law Debenture Trust Corp. v. Ural Caspian Oil Corp. Ltd., [1993] 1 W.L.R. 138 (Ch.D.) (per Hoffmann, J., as he then was). Scholarly discussions include Chafee, "Equitable Servitudes on Chattels"; E. C. S. Wade, "Notes," *Law Quarterly Review* 42, no. 2 (1926): 139–141; G. H. Treitel, "Limited Interests in Chattels," *Modern Law Review* 21, no. 4 (1958): 433–438; Simon Gardner, "The Proprietary Effect of Contractual Obligations under *Tulk v. Moxhay* and *De Mattos v. Gibson,*" *Law Quarterly Review* 98 (1982): 279–323; and Andrew Tettenborn, "Covenants, Privity of Contract, and the Purchaser of Personal Property," *Cambridge Law Journal* 41, no. 1 (1982): 58–86. All these commentators contend that, properly understood, the *De Mattos* principle is based on reasonable considerations in its own right, not inconsistent with other parts of the law, especially equity. It should also be noted that the same analysis is already evident in the earlier case of Tulk v. Moxhay, 2 Ph. 774 (1848). Gardner's careful and detailed analysis of the relation between the two decisions is particularly instructive. He argues persuasively that the general principle in *De Mattos* is identical with the fundamental reasoning in *Tulk.* See Gardner, "The Proprietary Effect," 316–317.

137. De Mattos v. Gibson, 282.

138. De Mattos v. Gibson, 282–283.

139. De Mattos v. Gibson, 283.

140. De Mattos v. Gibson, 288–301.

141. De Mattos v. Gibson, 299–301.

142. As will become clear below, I depart from Lord Justice Knight Bruce's apparent view that the defendant's liability for resulting loss can be determined *solely* on the basis that he used the boat "in a manner not allowable to [Curry]." De Mattos v. Gibson, 282. This formulation would seem, incorrectly in my view, to ignore the defendant's own rights as mortgagee and possessor.

143. So the way the defendant's wrong transpires here seems to be different from the circumstances involved in the tort of procuring breach. The same is true with regard to the circumstances of wrong for which the third-party injunction was ordered in the famous case of Lumley v. Wagner. This decision, it is worth noting, was cited before the lower court in *De Mattos* and was expressly followed by Lord Chelmsford on appeal. In *Wagner,* the Court of Chancery issued an injunction prohibiting the third party, Gye, from receiving the services of Johanna Wagner in a manner that conflicted with her performing her contractual obligation to Lumley. While there is little in the decision by way of underlying reasons, its correctness has never been judicially doubted. Courts and commentators have noted the quasi-proprietary dimension that this presupposes, paralleling the transactional proprietary analysis in the other instances that I have discussed. See Waddams, "Johanna Wagner," 450–454. For judicial discussion, see Waring v. WDAS Broadcasting Station, 637–641, and Nadell v. Grasso, 510, which also point out the parallels between *De Mattos* and *International News Service v. The Associated Press*. Despite their differences, these instances of third-party effects seem to share the same underlying analysis.

144. The decisions that approve or discuss the *De Mattos* principle emphasize this. See the earlier statement of this point by Lord Shaw in Lord Strathcona Steamship v. Dominion Coal, 117–120, 125, and the more recent statement by Justice Hoffmann (as he then was) in Law Debenture v. Ural Caspian, 151–152.

145. Lord Chelmsford gives this hypothetical example and says that an injunction might have been issued in such circumstances. See De Mattos v. Gibson, 299.

146. See my comments in note 143 above.

147. Of course, in the assignment scenario, the obligor always has notice of the contract right owed the promisee. Notice is relevant to the question of whether the obligor can be liable to the assignee for not performing to the latter, who, via assignment, is now owner of the chose.

2. Offer and Acceptance, the Objective Test, and Contractual Intent

1. See, for example, E. Allan Farnsworth, *Contracts,* 4th ed. (New York: Aspen Publishers, 2004), 108, 110–111 ("[Offer and acceptance are] the outward appearance of the agreement process by which the parties satisfy the requirement of bargain

imposed by the doctrine of consideration"). Similarly, *Restatement (Second) of Contracts* (1981) begins its presentation of offer and acceptance (chapter 3) with "Requirement of a Bargain" (section 17).

2. I draw on Arthur Linton Corbin, "Offer and Acceptance and Some of the Resulting Legal Relations," *Yale Law Journal* 26, no. 3 (1917): 169–206.

3. In addition to legislative requirements, the common law public or common calling cases that involve inns, ferries, carriers and the like have been exceptions that regulate the mode of offer and acceptance as well as the terms of these transactions.

4. For discussion, see A. W. B. Simpson, "Innovation in Nineteenth Century Contract Law," *Law Quarterly Review* 91 (1975): 257–262 and David J. Ibbetson, *A Historical Introduction to the Law of Obligations* (Oxford: Oxford University Press, 1999), 222. See also Reinhard Zimmermann, *The Law of Obligations: Roman Foundations of the Civilian Tradition* (New York: Oxford University Press, 1996), 571.

5. As famously stated by Solicitor General Egerton in *Golding's Case*, "In every action upon the case upon a promise, there are three things considerable, consideration, promise, and breach of promise." Golding's Case, 2 Leonard 72, 74 Eng. Rep. 367, 367 (1586).

6. In my view, the famous case of Cooke v. Oxley, 3 T.R. 653 (K.B. 1790), decided just prior to the reception of the doctrine of offer and acceptance, reflects this analysis. On this point, see Joseph Perillo's discussion of *Cooke* in "The Origins of the Objective Theory of Contract Formation and Interpretation," *Fordham Law Review* 69, no. 2 (2000): 436. To a similar effect, see Simpson, "Innovation," 261.

7. Corbin, for one, emphasized this point in "Offer and Acceptance."

8. Hohfeld, and, following him, Corbin in "Offer and Acceptance," emphasized the importance and role of this feature of offer and acceptance. See Wesley Newcomb Hohfeld, "Some Fundamental Legal Conceptions as Applied to Judicial Reasoning," *Yale Law Journal* 23, no. 1 (1913): 16, 49. It is worth noting that in *Cooke*, the court did not even consider the possibility that the plaintiff had a power of acceptance. On the facts, had the court done so, this would arguably have led it to the opposite conclusion.

9. The issue of whether an offer has to state a promise has been the focus of serious discussion. See, for example, See Samuel Williston, "Is an Offer a Promise?" *Illinois Law Review* 22 (1927): 788–789, and "An Offer Is a Promise," *Illinois Law Review* 23 (1928): 100–104. See also the *Restatement of the Law of Contracts* (1932), section 24, "Special Note" ("An offer necessarily looks to the future").

10. The offer cannot refer to an already completed act, for the latter would amount to an unrequested past consideration and, in that case, could not possibly satisfy the requirement of consideration.

11. Both Restatements suggest that while the usual course is for one party to make a proposal that is then taken up or declined by the other, it is "theoretically

possible for a third person to state a suggested contract to the parties and for them to say simultaneously that they assent to the suggested bargain." *Restatement of the Law of Contracts,* section 22, comment A. See also *Restatement (Second) of Contracts,* section 22, comment A. For this possibility, however, neither Restatement gives illustrations. Similarly, while both Williston and Corbin suggest that a non-sequenced process of formation may be exceptionally possible and valid, they acknowledge that they do not know of any decision or case on point. Interestingly, Kant suggests to the contrary that, when viewed as taking place in time and space, the parties' mutual assents effectuating contract formation must be temporally sequenced. See Immanuel Kant, *The Metaphysics of Morals,* ed. Mary Gregor (Cambridge: Cambridge University Press, 1996), 6:272–3.

12. Note that this basic interaction must be satisfied in every situation of contracting, even in circumstances governed by the so-called "mailbox rule" or in other situations where the parties are not physically in the presence of each other. These latter situations raise a different issue: what counts as acceptance (or retraction) of an offer in such circumstances? More specifically, the problem is whether, to count as an effective acceptance, actual notice of the acceptance must be received by the offeror, *not* whether the offeree must respond to an offer that comes first. See the instructive analysis of this issue, namely, of notice in the famous case of Carlill v. Carbolic Smoke Ball Co. [1893] 1 Q.B. 256 (Eng. C.A.).

13. See Arthur Linton Corbin, *Corbin on Contracts: One Volume Edition* (St. Paul, MN: West Publishing, 1952), section 12.

14. See Tinn v. Hoffman & Co., (1873) 29 L.T. 271 (Ex.).

15. This solution is adumbrated in the analysis of past consideration cases where courts, as early as the late sixteenth century, held that "when the payment is laid to be at his [the promisor's] request, the consideration doth continue." Beaucamp v. Neggin, 78 Eng. Rep. 536, 536 (K.B. 1591). See also Barker v. Halifax, 78 Eng. Rep. 974 (1598), and the famous statement in Adams v. Lindsell, 106 Eng. Rep. 250, 251 (K.B. 1818).

16. Kennedy v. Lee, 36 Eng. Rep. 170, 173 (Ch. 1817) (emphasis added).

17. In his account of offer and acceptance, Charles Fried expressly emphasizes the relational character of promising. On this basis, he argues for the necessity of acceptance. However, the relation that he envisages is one of promising for or to another, not robustly with another who must coactively and reciprocally contribute to the promissory relation. Thus, Fried "admits unease ... about insisting on acceptance in the case where ... it would be captious to doubt that the promisee is delighted by the promise." Charles Fried, *Contract as Promise: A Theory of Contractual Obligation,* 2nd ed. (New York: Oxford University Press, 2015), 43. The undoubted necessity for acceptance is explicable once offer and acceptance are viewed as applying fully in tandem with consideration, with both requirements embodying the same robustly bilateral structure and relation.

18. Emmanuel Gounot makes this same point with respect to the civil law. See his *Le principe de l'autonomie de la volonté en droit privé: Contribution à l'étude critique de l'individualisme juridique* (Paris: Arthur Rousseau, 1912), 150–156.

19. Kennedy v. Lee, 451.

20. The First Restatement distinguishes six different standpoints or standards of interpretation of which four are objective because not necessarily based on the actual intention of one or both parties. See *Restatement of the Law of Contracts*, section 227. What I refer to as the "detached" observer standard fits with the Restatement's standards of general and limited usage, whereas the proposed transactional approach would favor its standards of reasonable expectation and understanding. For helpful scholarly discussions of the different approaches, see E. Allan Farnsworth, "'Meaning' in the Law of Contracts," *Yale Law Journal* 76, no. 5 (1967): 939–965; William Howarth, "The Meaning of Objectivity in Contract," *Law Quarterly Review* 100 (1984): 265–281; J. P. Vorster, "A Comment on the Meaning of Objectivity in Contract," *Law Quarterly Review* 103 (1987): 274–283; Timothy Endicott, "Objectivity, Subjectivity, and Incomplete Agreements," in *Oxford Essays in Jurisprudence*, 4th series, ed. Jeremy Horder (New York: Oxford University Press, 2000), 251–271; and Mindy Chen-Wishart, *Contract Law*, 5th ed. (New York: Oxford University Press, 2015), section 2.1.

21. For an example, see M. P. Furmston, *Cheshire, Fifoot, and Furmston's Law of Contract*, 15th ed. (Oxford: Oxford University Press, 2007), 306 ("[T]he question is not what the parties had in their minds, but what reasonable third parties would infer from their words or conduct").

22. Perillo provides examples of this approach in "The Origins of the Objective Theory," 443–452.

23. Noteworthy recent judicial statements include The Hannah Blumenthal, [1983] 1 A.C. 854, 914 (Eng. H.L.) (per Lord Diplock) ("To create a contract by exchange of promises between two parties where the promise of each constitutes the consideration for the promise of the other, what is necessary is that the intention of each *as it has been communicated to and understood by the other* (even though that which has been communicated does not represent the actual state of mind of the communicator) should coincide. That is what English lawyers mean when they resort to the Latin phrase consensus ad idem and the words that I have italicized are essential to the concept of consensus ad idem, the lack of which prevents the formation of a binding contract in English law"). See also the very important speeches of Lord Hoffmann in Investors Compensation Scheme Ltd. v. West Bromwich Building Society, 912–913 (Eng. H.L.), and Mannai Investment Co. v. Eagle Star Life Insurance Co., [1997] A.C. 749, 774–775 (Eng. H.L.). For a thoughtful scholarly account, see Adam Kramer, "Common Sense Principles of Contract Interpretation," *Oxford Journal of Legal Studies* 23, no. 2 (2003): 173–196.

24. See, for example, Smith v. Hughes, (1870–1871) L.R. 6 Q.B. 597 at 607 (Eng. C.A.) (per Lord Blackburn), and Embry v. Hargadine, McKittrick Dry Goods Co., 105 S.W. 777, 779 (Mo. App. 1907).

25. This need not involve any detrimental reliance on the offeree's part, as Williston and others have rightly noted. See Samuel Williston, "Mutual Assent in the Formation of Contracts," *Illinois Law Review* 14, no. 2 (1919): 85, 88, and, more recently, Vorster, "A Comment on the Meaning," 285.

26. This is emphasized by Lord Hoffmann in BCCI v. Ali, [2001] 2 W.L.R. 735, 749 (Eng. H.L.). See discussion in Kramer, "Common Sense Principles." See also Berke Moore Co. v. Phoenix Bridge Co., 98 A.2d 150, 156 (1953) (S. Ct. N.H.).

27. This is how Judge Easterbrook characterizes the parties' expressions in Skycom Corp. v. Telstar Corp., 813 F.2d 810, 814–815 (7th Cir. 1987).

28. This formulation draws on Lord Hoffmann's extrajudicial formulation in "The Intolerable Wrestle with Words and Meanings," *South African Law Journal* 114 (1997): 656, 658.

29. See the excellent discussion of this point in Kramer, "Common Sense Principles," 175.

30. This addressor standpoint is the fifth standard of interpretation in the *Restatement of the Law of Contracts*, section 227, and it coincides with Lord Blackburn's canonical statement of the test in *Smith v. Hughes*. In my view, properly understood the addressor-oriented and the addressee-oriented approaches coincide.

31. Fried views the court's recourse to the objective standard of reasonableness as "palpably . . . imposing an external standard on the parties." Fried, *Contract as Promise*, 61 and elsewhere.

32. Randy Barnett thinks so and refers to this as a "subjective twist" to the objective theory. See Randy Barnett, *Contracts* (Oxford: Oxford University Press, 2010), 68–75.

33. As in Smith v. Hughes, 607 (per Lord Blackburn).

34. Depending on the kind of transaction, it may be perfectly reasonable merely to presume that a party acted on a particular understanding where she gave no thought to the matter (see Farnsworth, *Contracts*, section 3.6, note 10). This is the scenario in Raffles v. Wichelhaus ["The Peerless"], 154 Eng. Rep. 375 (Ex. 1864), as the case is standardly viewed.

35. "Surely if one party shows that the other attached the same meaning that the first party did, the other party should not be able to avoid that meaning by showing that a reasonable person would have attached a different one." Farnsworth, *Contracts*, 446.

36. Or in the vivid words of Judge Easterbrook, "'[I]ntent' does not invite a tour through [the plaintiff's] cranium, with [the plaintiff] as guide." Skycom Corp. v. Telstar Corp., 814.

37. In accord, see Corbin, *Corbin on Contracts*, section 539; George E. Palmer, "The Effect of Misunderstanding on Contract Formation and Reformation under

the Restatement of Contracts Second," *Michigan Law Review* 65, no. 1 (1966): 40–42; Melvin A. Eisenberg, "The Responsive Model of Contract Law," *Stanford Law Review* 36 (1984): 1122–1123; Farnsworth, "'Meaning' in the Law of Contracts," 949–951; David W. McLauchlan, "Objectivity in Contract," *University of Queensland Law Journal* 24 (2005): 479, 485; and David W. McLauchlan, "The Contract That Neither Party Intends," *Journal of Contract Law* 29 (2012): 26, 36.

38. Similarly, imagine a scenario where parties A and B agreed to a sale of an item, x, for $100 with the proviso that all questions of interpretation would be decided by A's actual understanding at formation (established by sufficient evidence). If interpreted on this basis, this would still be in accordance with the objective test because it would be transactionally intended.

39. As Fried argues with respect to all promises, whether gratuitous or not. See note 29 above.

40. For insightful treatment of this point, see A.I. Melden, *Rights and Persons* (Berkeley: University of California Press, 1977), chapter 2.

41. See, for example, M. P. Furmston, *Cheshire, Fifoot, and Furmston's Law of Contract,* 14th ed. (Oxford: Oxford University Press, 2001), 121. Helpful historical accounts of English law include Ibbetson, *A Historical Introduction,* 233–234, and Simpson, "Innovation," 263–265. For an excellent comparative discussion of US and English approaches, see Gregory Klass, "Intent to Contract," *Virginia Law Review* 95, no. 6 (2009): 1437–1503.

42. This is consistent with the *Restatement (Second) of Contracts,* section 21. See also C. F. Hamson, "The Reform of Consideration," *Law Quarterly Review* 54 (1938): 241–257.

43. Samuel Williston, *A Treatise on the Law of Contracts* (New York: Baker, Voorhis, 1922), section 21.

44. Drawing on Williston, *Law of Contracts,* and *Restatement (Second) of Contracts,* section 19 ("A 'manifestation' of assent is not a mere appearance; the party must be in some way responsible for the appearance").

45. By contrast, where a party assents as a result of duress, fraud, or wrongful imposition, the agreement is voidable and may be set aside if that party so wishes. The basic and very limited conception of voluntariness that is necessary for there to be a legally operative manifestation of assent in the first place is, however, satisfied. See, for example, Davis v. Gifford, 182 App. Div. 99 (1918, N.Y.S.C. App. Div.).

46. For a representative judicial statement of this point, see Sulzbach v. Town of Jefferson, 155 N.W.2d 921, 923 (S.D. 1968).

47. The classic statement is Balfour v. Balfour, [1919] 2 K.B. 571, 578–579 (Eng. C.A.) (per Atkin, L.J., as he then was).

48. See Edwards v. Skyways Ltd., [1964] 1 W.L.R. 349, 355 (Q.B.). For detailed discussion, see Klass, "Intent to Contract," 1453–1460.

49. Lord Atkin's formulation in Balfour v. Balfour.

50. See McGovern v. City of New York, 234 N.Y. 377, 138 N.E. 26 (1923), 31 (per Cardozo, J.). This is the view taken by Williston, *Law of Contracts*, section 21, and later by Hamson, "The Reform of Consideration," 254–255; as well as by J. Unger, "Intent to Create Legal Relations, Mutuality and Consideration," *Modern Law Review* 19, no. 1 (1956): 98–99, and B. A. Hepple, "Intention to Create Legal Relations," *Cambridge Law Journal* 28, no. 1 (1970): 128.

51. At opposite poles from everything contractual: "My bounty is boundless as the sea, / My love as deep: the more I give to thee, / The more I have, for both are infinite." William Shakespeare, *Romeo and Juliet* (Oxford: Oxford University Press, 1994), act 2, scene 2.

52. Rose and Frank Co. v. J. R. Crompton & Bros. Ltd., [1923] 2 K.B. 261 (Eng. C.A.), 293 (per Atkin, L.J.); Balfour v. Balfour, 580 (per Atkin, L.J.).

53. As pointed out in Rose and Frank v. Crompton & Bros., 293 (per Atkin, L.J.) and 288 (per Scrutton, L.J.).

54. Judicial references to "rebuttable presumptions" of fact here are usually—and should only be—the way courts express prima facie assumptions about the ordinary (but always evolving) sociological interpretations of given relations, nothing more. In the end, each particular interaction must be assessed on its own facts. There is no legal inference one way or another that a party must rebut. For an excellent example, see Jones v. Padavatton, [1969] 1 WLR 328 (Eng. C.A.) (per Salmon, L.J.).

55. See Hamson's thoughtful discussion of these points in "The Reform of Consideration."

56. I completely agree with Williston that "an expression of mutual assent, and not the assent itself, is the essential element of contractual liability.... [I]ntention is sought here not because it is primarily important but in order to show the true nature of the external act." "Mutual Assent," 87, 91.

57. An agreement that is not void ab initio may still be unenforceable against a party who establishes that she entered it as a result of fraud, duress, misrepresentation, and so forth. At the same time, this party can enforce the agreement as is precisely because it meets the necessary conditions of voluntary interaction required for contract formation. See note 45 above.

58. This is Williston's formulation: "[T]hough both parties may think they have made a contract, they may not have done so. The[ir] views ... as to what are the requirements of a contract, as to what mutual assent means, or consideration ... are wholly immaterial. They are as immaterial as the views of an individual as to what constitutes a tort. In regard to both torts and contracts, the law, not the parties, fixes the requirement of legal obligation." *Law of Contracts*, section 21.

3. Implication

1. Sometimes a further distinction is drawn between interpretation and construction. See, for example, Edwin W. Patterson, "The Interpretation and Construction of Contracts," *Columbia Law Review* 64, no. 5 (1964): 833–836. The following discussion does not invoke or depend upon the distinction.

2. I take this distinction between primary or independent and secondary or dependent from Adam Kramer, "Implication in Fact as an Instance of Contractual Interpretation," *Cambridge Law Journal* 63, no. 2 (2004): 391.

3. An example is Wood v. Lucy, Lady Duff-Gordon, 118 N.E. 214 (N.Y. 1917), where Cardozo held that, reasonably construed as a whole, the express terms of an agreement implicitly required supplementation by an implied promise that constituted the consideration necessary to make the other party's promise enforceable and not gratuitous.

4. For a remarkable decision that recognizes this point, see Readhead v. Midland Railway Co., (1868–1869) L.R. 4 Q.B. 379, 392–393 (Ex. Chamber) (per Montague Smith, J.).

5. By way of examples, see Charles Fried's discussion in *Contract as Promise: A Theory of Contractual Obligation,* 2nd ed. (New York: Oxford University Press, 2015), chapter 5 ("Gaps"), and Robert Cooter and Thomas Ulen, *Law and Economics,* 5th ed. (Boston: Pearson Education, 2008), 197–207. Notable recent exceptions include Andrew Morris, "Practical Reasoning and Contract as Promise: Extending Contract-Based Criteria to Decide Excuse Cases," *Cambridge Law Journal* 56, no. 1 (1997): 147–174; Kramer, "Implication in Fact"; and Robert Stevens, "Objectivity, Mistake, and the Parol Evidence Rule," in *Contract Terms,* ed. Andrew Burrows and Edwin Peel (Oxford: Oxford University Press, 2007), 101–122.

6. For a systematic account taking this view and arguing for a welfarist approach, see Louis Kaplow and Steven Shavell, *Fairness versus Welfare* (Cambridge, MA: Harvard University Press, 2002), chapter 4.

7. This observation is commonplace in the literature, particularly economic. For general discussion, see E. Allan Farnsworth, "Disputes over Omission in Contracts," *Columbia Law Review* 68, no. 5 (1968): 868–873, and Kramer, "Implication in Fact," 387–388.

8. See George Triantis, "Contractual Allocation of Unknown Risks: A Critique of the Doctrine of Commercial Impracticability," *University of Toronto Law Journal* 42, no. 4 (1992): 450–483.

9. If, as some propose, a contractual undertaking should ordinarily be viewed as comprising an option to perform x or to transfer its equivalent in value (as measured by expectation damages), this alternative would be always available. See, for example, Richard A. Posner, "Let Us Never Blame a Contract Breaker," in *Fault in American Contract Law,* ed. Omri Ben-Shahar and Ariel Porat (New York: Cam-

bridge University Press, 2010), 3–19 (particularly 4–5). For more detailed discussion of this view, which is not generally followed in Anglo-American cases, see Chapter 9.

10. Paradine v. Jane, (1647) Aleyn 26, 82 E.R. 897.

11. See the discussion of this possibility in Alan Schwartz and Robert E. Scott, "Contract Theory and the Limits of Contract Law," *Yale Law Journal* 113, no. 3 (2003): 609.

12. See David Charny, "Hypothetical Bargains: The Normative Structure of Contract Interpretation," *Michigan Law Review* 89, no. 7 (1991): 1815–1879.

13. For helpful overviews and detailed discussions of the different approaches, in addition to Charny, "Hypothetical Bargains," see Dennis Patterson, "The Pseudo-Debate over Default Rules in Contract Law," *Southern California Interdisciplinary Law Journal* 3, no. 1 (1993): 252–264, and C. A. Riley, "Designing Default Rules in Contract Law," *Oxford Journal of Legal Studies* 20, no. 3 (2000): 367–390. Jules L. Coleman, Douglas D. Heckathorn, and Steven M. Maser bring out clearly the great intrinsic complexity and indeterminacy of the hypothetical bargain procedure—a feature that, I argue, makes it unsuited to be part of a public basis of justification—in "A Bargaining Theory Approach to Default Provisions and Disclosure Rules in Contract Law," *Harvard Journal of Law and Public Policy* 12, no. 3 (1989): 639–709.

14. See Schwartz and Scott, where they state, "The somewhat surprising answer we derive from contract theory is that most state-created defaults will be useless or inefficient." "Limits of Contract Law," 594. See also Robert E. Scott, "A Relational Theory of Default Rules for Commercial Contracts," *Journal of Legal Studies* 19, no. 2 (1990): 597–616, and Robert E. Scott, "Rethinking the Default Rule Project," *Virginia Journal* 6 (2003): 84–96.

15. This difficulty is recognized and thoughtfully discussed in Coleman, Heckathorn, and Maser, "A Bargaining Theory Approach," 641–650.

16. John P. Dawson, "Judicial Revision of Frustrated Contracts: The United States," *Boston University Law Review* 64, no. 1 (1984): 1–38. Dawson's answer was, "I do not propose to spend time looking for the source of the power. I am convinced that it does not exist" (38).

17. Richard Craswell, "Contract Law, Default Rules, and the Philosophy of Promising," *Michigan Law Review* 88, no. 3 (1989): 489–529. See also his still unpublished piece, Richard Craswell, "Expectation Damages and Contract Theory Revisited" (Stanford Law and Economics Olin Working Paper No. 325, August 2006), https://ssrn.com/abstract=925980.

18. See in particular Craswell, "Default Rules," 514–516.

19. Recall here that under the idea of the rational, a party forms and seeks effectively to pursue his or her own interests and purposes (e.g., when deciding whether or not to contract and on which terms). By contrast, the reasonable is always a term of respectful relation between the parties, according to which they must treat each other fairly as equals with independent standing.

20. A point rightly emphasized in the leading accounts of mistake and impossibility. See, for example, George E. Palmer, *Mistake and Unjust Enrichment* (Columbus: Ohio State University Press, 1962), chapter 2 ("Avoidance of Transactions for Mistake").

21. This point is made clearly by Lord Hoffmann in Attorney-General of Belize v. Belize Telecom Ltd., [2009] UKPC 10, paragraph 17.

22. As Farnsworth puts it, "A court, having determined that there is a contract, cannot refuse to decide a case on the ground that the parties failed to provide for the situation." "Disputes over Omission," 860n2.

23. Utica City National Bank v. Gunn, 118 N.E. 607 (N.Y. 1918). The issue in *Gunn* was one of interpretation: "to fix the sense in which the words were used in the contract now before us" (608). If taken literally or in a legal technical sense, their meaning would "make the whole transaction futile" (608). Thus a contextualized application of the objective test was dispositive. Similarly, in his other well-known decisions, Moran v. Standard Oil Co. of New York, 105 N.E. 217 (N.Y. 1914), and Wood v. Lucy, Cardozo implies primary terms via presumed intention to include them on the basis that, among other factors, this was essential to avoid making their promises valueless and illusory or placing "one party . . . at the mercy of the other" and to give their transactions "such business 'efficacy, as both parties must have intended that at all events it should have.'" Wood v. Lucy, 214, 215, quoting from The Moorcock, (1889) 14 P.D. 64 (Eng. C.A.), 64, 68. What is more, Cardozo employs a similarly contextualized understanding of transactions to imply primary terms or other features of the relation that are needed to make sense and to ensure the efficacy of nonbusiness agreements that include significant altruistic or donative components. Thus in Allegheny College v. National Chautauqua County Bank, 159 N.E. 173, 175 (N.Y. 1927), Cardozo brings out the "implications inherent in subscription and acceptance" in the particular circumstances of a promise to make a gift to a college coupled with a request that the money be used to establish a scholarship named after the promisor. For an excellent discussion, see Curtis Bridgeman, "*Allegheny College* Revisited: Cardozo, Consideration, and Formalism in Context," *U.C. Davis Law Review* 39, no. 1 (2005): 149–186.

24. As suggested by Randy Barnett, "The Sounds of Silence: Default Rules and Contractual Consent," *Virginia Law Review* 78, no. 4 (1992): 821, 875, and by Fried, *Contract as Promise*, 60–61.

25. For centuries, this wider sense of the term has been used regularly in decisions. An influential example is Lord Mansfield's judgment in Moses v. Mcferlan, (1760) 2 Burr. 1005. Williston explains and defends this use of the term in Samuel Williston, *A Treatise on the Law of Contracts* (New York: Baker, Voorhis, 1922), section 814. For further discussion, see Stephen M. Waddams, *Principle and Policy in Contract Law: Competing or Complementary Concepts?* (Cambridge: Cambridge University Press, 2011), 89–91.

26. Kingston v. Preston, 99 Eng. Rep. 437 (K.B. 1773), and quoted in the argument of counsel in Jones v. Barkley, 2 Douglas 684, 99 E.R. 434 (K.B. 1781). The court implied what have since been called "constructive conditions of exchange." See E. Allan Farnsworth, *Contracts,* 4th ed. (New York: Aspen Publishers, 2004), section 8.9.

27. Kingston v. Preston, 438.

28. I draw here on Waddams, *Principle and Policy,* 2–3.

29. Williston, *Law of Contracts,* section 813.

30. Jones v. Barkley, 685, 694 (per Lord Mansfield). This concern is made explicit in Goodisson v. Nunn, (1792) 4 T.R. 761, in which Lord Kenyon, upholding Lord Mansfield's new view against the "old cases," refers to the risks of bankruptcy and of insolvency (764–765). See Waddams's discussion in *Principle and Policy,* 1–7.

31. In addition to well-known early English cases that state this explicitly, such as Duke of St. Albans v. Shore, (1789) 1 H. Bl. 270; Phillips v. Fielding, 2 H. Bl. 123; Goodisson v. Nunn (1792); and Morton v. Lamb, (1797) 7 T.R. 125. See representative US cases such as Bank of Columbia v. Hagner, (1828) 26 U.S. 455, 464, which Williston quotes in *Law of Contracts,* section 825.

32. See *Restatement (Second) of Contracts* (1981), section 232, which states that in a bilateral contract the parties' performances "taken collectively are treated as performances to be exchanged under an exchange of promises unless a contrary intention is clearly manifested."

33. For more detailed discussion, see Farnsworth, *Contracts,* section 8.11.

34. See also Williston, *Law of Contracts,* section 827 and section 814. Williston's approach to these matters has too often been mischaracterized even by influential contemporary commentators who do not appreciate sufficiently that it is centrally animated by transactional and concrete considerations of justice and reasonableness between the parties. See, for example, Fried, *Contract as Promise,* 64 (on "gaps" and impossibility); Schwartz and Scott, "Limits of Contract Law," 569 (on interpretative approaches); and Hanoch Dagan and Michael Heller, *The Choice Theory of Contracts* (New York: Cambridge University Press, 2017), 7–9, 136–137. A notable exception is Melvin A. Eisenberg's discussion in *Foundational Principles of Contract Law* (New York: Oxford University Press, 2018), 388–390.

35. Williston, *Law of Contracts,* section 825.

36. Boone v. Eyre, (1777) 1 H. Bl. 273.

37. "Root" or "foundation" are the terms used by Lord Blackburn in The Mersey Steel and Iron Co. v. Naylor, Benzon and Co., (1884) 9 App. Cas. 434, 443.

38. See also the statement in Duke of St. Albans v. Shore, 279 ("[B]ut where [nonperformance] did not go to the whole, but only to a part, there it is not a condition precedent, and each party must resort to his separate remedy; and for this plain and obvious reason, because the damages might be unequal") (per Lord Loughborough).

39. Williston, *Law of Contracts,* section 827.

40. Jacob & Youngs Inc. v. Kent, 230 N.Y. 239 (1921). My understanding of this case has benefited much from Todd Rakoff's superb essay "The Implied Terms of Contracts: Of 'Default Rules' and 'Situation-Sense,'" in *Good Faith and Fault in Contract Law,* ed. Jack Beatson and Daniel Friedmann (Oxford: Clarendon Press, 1995), especially 205–215.

41. Jacob & Youngs v. Kent, 891.

42. Jacob & Youngs v. Kent, 891.

43. "Nowhere will change be tolerated . . . if it is so dominant or pervasive as in any real or substantial measure to frustrate the purpose of the contract." Jacob & Youngs v. Kent, 891.

44. In Williston's words: "In the nature of the case precise boundaries are impossible. The question which must be decided is whether on the whole it is fairer to allow the plaintiff to recover, requiring the defendant to bring a cross action . . . , or whether it is fairer to deny the plaintiff a right of recovery on account of his breach, even at the expense of compelling him to forfeit any compensation for such part performance as he has rendered. The decision of this question must vary with the special circumstances of each case." *Law of Contracts,* section 841. In Jacob & Youngs v. Kent, 891, Cardozo quotes the first line of this passage.

45. In this paragraph, all quotes are from Cardozo's judgment in Jacob & Youngs v. Kent, 891. See also Rakoff's presentation in "The Implied Terms of Contracts," starting at 209.

46. In reaching this conclusion, Cardozo notes, without further discussion, that had the builder's breach been "willful" rather than careless, the court might not have given the builder relief despite the risk of forfeiture. Jacob & Youngs v. Kent, 891. What amounts to willfulness and why it should be a relevant factor here are difficult issues, and the proper analysis is far from self-evident. Supposing that bad faith breach can be suitably distinguished as something fundamentally different from what parties reasonably contemplate, breach might no longer be deemed trivial and the harshness of resulting forfeiture no longer viewed as salient. Arguably, a party should not reasonably be presumed to intend to perform in the face of the other's opportunistic and willful breach so defined. The doctrine of part performance might not apply. Williston's discussion of this point is nuanced and tentative. See *Law of Contracts,* section 842, note 52.

47. Jacob & Youngs v. Kent, 891.

48. For example, a purchaser's bad faith rejection of the plaintiff's performance in order to resile from their agreement in circumstances of declining prices. Rakoff integrates this concern consistently with a transactional analysis. "The Implied Terms of Contracts," 214.

49. The Moorcock, 68, following the earlier important formulation of Justice Montague Smith in Readhead v. Midland Railway, 392.

50. The Moorcock, 70. More recently, Lord Hoffmann makes this point in A-G of Belize v. Belize Telecom, paragraph 30.

51. The Moorcock, 68 (my emphasis).

52. The Moorcock, 68.

53. The Moorcock, 69.

54. The Moorcock, 70, quoting Lord Holt in Coggs v. Bernard, (1703) Ld. Raym. 909, 918.

55. The transactional analysis that animates *The Moorcock* where the obligation is sometimes characterized as "implied-in-fact" also applies, mutatis mutandis, to cases of obligations implied-in-law. In the latter, the particular transaction is treated as an instance of a larger, generic transaction-type. A leading English illustration is Liverpool City Council v. Irwin, [1977] A.C. 239, where the House of Lords held that in a rental agreement between the defendant city council landlord and the plaintiff tenants, there is an implied obligation on the defendant to take reasonable care to maintain and repair the common areas of the building that remained under its immediate control. A comparable US case is Javins v. First National Realty Corp., 428 F.2d 1071 (1970). In *Irwin*, Lord Wilberforce makes clear that the basis of the implied obligation is transactional: the obligation is necessary if the plaintiffs are to obtain the beneficial use of the facilities that they have been promised as consideration for their own counterpromise of rent and so forth. The absence of this obligation would thus be "inconsistent totally with the nature of this relationship." Liverpool City Council v. Irwin, 255. The difference between such implication-in-law for generic types of transactions and implication-in-fact that arises in particular situations is, as Lord Wilberforce notes in his discussion of *The Moorcock*, a difference in "shade[s] on a continuous spectrum." Liverpool City Council v. Irwin, 255.

56. This formulation is from Trollope & Colls Ltd. v. North West Metropolitan Regional Hospital Board, [1973] 1 W.L.R. 601, 609 (Eng. H.L.) (per Lord Pearce), and quoted in A-G of Belize v. Belize Telecom, paragraph 19 (per Lord Hoffmann).

57. A-G of Belize v. Belize Telecom, paragraph 22 (per Lord Hoffmann). See also the clear explicit statements in representative cases such as Re an Arbitration between Comptoir Commercial Anversois and Power, Son & Co., [1920] 1 K.B. 868, 899–900 (C.A.) (per Scrutton, L.J.); Denny, Mott & Dickson Ltd. v. James B. Fraser & Co. Ltd., [1944] A.C. 265, 275 (Eng. H.L.) (per Lord Wright); and Davis Contractors Ltd. v. Fareham Urban District Council, [1956] A.C. 696, 719–721 (Eng. H.L.) (per Lord Reid).

58. Moreover, despite the fact that a normative economic theory may view joint welfare maximization as the goal of contract enforcement, it should not be forgotten that this is not itself a legal prerequisite for contract formation and that there can be offer and acceptance, consideration and so full unqualified enforceability, irrespective of whether it is satisfied on any occasion.

59. Jacob & Youngs v. Kent, 891.

60. Robert Scott proposes a somewhat different division of labor when he writes: "Rather than framing the default rule project as replicating the terms that most parties would probably have chosen had they bargained in advance, I propose to re-frame the question: The project of the law should be to replicate those terms (and only those terms) that individual parties would choose not to bargain over if they knew that the state would provide them." "Rethinking the Default Rule Project," 90. The fundamental difference between his division of labor and the one that I have proposed here is that his is elaborated solely under the idea of the rational, whereas my own aligns with the distinction between the rational and the reasonable.

61. For reasons of space, I discuss these excusing doctrines but not mistake in fundamental assumptions. However, in legal practice and in theory, the same basic analysis underpins both, the only difference being the fact that in the latter, the excusing fact already exists at formation, whereas in impossibility and frustration it arises only after formation.

62. Paradine v. Jane, (1647) Aleyn 26.

63. Paradine v. Jane, 27. How exactly the decision in *Paradine* and the early common law on this issue should be understood are matters of some historical dispute. See David J. Ibbetson, "Absolute Liability in Contract: The Antecedents of *Paradine v. Jayne*," in *Consensus ad Idem: Essays on the Law of Contract in Honour of Guenter Treitel*, ed. F. D. Rose (London: Sweet & Maxwell, 1996), 3–37.

64. Denny, Mott & Dickson v. James B. Fraser, 272.

65. As Justice Holmes put it: "One who makes a contract never can be absolutely certain that he will be able to perform it when the time comes, and the very essence of it is that he takes the risk within the limits of his undertaking." Day v. United States, 245 U.S. 159, 161 (1917). For a representative English judicial statement, see Larrinaga & Co. v. Société Franco-Américaine des Phosphates de Medulla, (1923) 92 L.J.K.B. 455, 464–465 (per Lord Sumner). This point is emphasized in Lee B. McTurnan, "An Approach to Common Mistake in English Law," *Canadian Bar Review* 41, no. 1 (1963): 3–4.

66. This point is persuasively and carefully elaborated by George Triantis in "Contractual Allocation of Unknown Risks." This same point applies to the analysis of liability for consequential loss under Hadley v. Baxendale, (1854), 9 Exch. 341, 156 E.R. 145. See discussion in Chapter 8.

67. For discussion of these instances, see Farnsworth, *Contracts*, section 9.5, 620–621.

68. Taylor v. Caldwell, (1863) 3 B. & S. 826; Krell v. Henry (1903), [1903] 2 K.B. 740. Impossibility is sometimes termed "commercial impracticability," especially in US contract law. See Uniform Commercial Code, section 2-615, and *Restatement (Second) of Contracts*, section 261.

69. Taylor v. Caldwell, 833.

70. A good statement of this point is P. S. Atiyah, *An Introduction to the Law of Contract,* 5th ed. (Oxford: Clarendon Press, 1995), 232–236, 240–241. Virtually all judicial decisions, both US and English, share this view. See *Restatement (Second) of Contracts,* section 261, comments b and d. For a fairly recent US decision, see Karl Wendt Farm Equipment Co., Inc. v. International Harvester Co., 931 F.2d 1112 (6th Cir. 1991). Leading English judicial statements include Davis Contractors v. Fareham, 724 (per Lord Reid) and 730 (per Lord Radcliffe). See also Blackburn Bobbin Co. v. T. W. Allen & Sons Ltd., [1918] 2 K.B. 467, 469 (Eng. C.A.) (per Pickford, L.J.).

71. Taylor v. Caldwell, 833–834 (emphasis added).

72. As a later influential judgment put it: "[A] contractual obligation has become incapable of being performed because the circumstances in which performance is called for would render it a thing radically different from that which was undertaken by the contract." Davis Contractors v. Fareham, 729 (per Lord Radcliffe).

73. Davis Contractors v. Fareham, 729 (per Lord Radcliffe).

74. Note that, implicitly, the court does not consider the payment of damages as a genuine alternative performance that, being possible, might therefore prevent excuse. For general discussion, see Farnsworth, *Contracts,* section 9.6, and Williston, *Law of Contracts,* section 1961. The impossibility analysis presupposes a conception of performance that does not generally or inherently entail what some commentators have called a "dual performance" view involving "alternative performances" of trading or giving money value. See further discussion in Chapter 9.

75. See Davis Contractors v. Fareham, 729 (per Lord Radcliffe): "[I]t is not hardship or inconvenience or material loss itself which calls the principle of frustration into play. There must be as well such a change in the significance of the obligation that the thing undertaken would, if performed, be a different thing from that contracted for." Among the very few scholarly defenses of the view that a sufficiently drastic quantitative change in costs or prices alone might result in impracticability or frustration, see, for example, Eisenberg, *Foundational Principles of Contract Law,* 643–653, and Jack Beatson, "Increased Expense and Frustration," in *Consensus ad Idem: Essays on the Law of Contract in Honour of Guenter Treitel,* ed. F. D. Rose (London: Sweet & Maxwell, 1996), 121–140. For a judicial decision that treats a dramatic change in costs as per se decisive, see Aluminum Co. of America v. Essex Group Inc., 499 F. Supp. 53 (W.D. Pa. 1980). This opinion, which in my view provides very little by way of concrete contractual or transactional analysis to support its conclusion, has not generally been approved by courts or scholars. See the incisive critical discussion in Dawson, "Judicial Revision," 26.

76. See the clear statements of this point in Davis Contractors v. Fareham, 730–731 (per Lord Radcliffe) and 733–734 (per Lord Somervell).

77. This formulation draws on George E. Palmer's brilliant account of mistake in assumptions in *Mistake and Unjust Enrichment,* 50–51, 88.

78. Canadian Industrial Alcohol Co., Ltd. v. Dunbar Molasses Co., 178 N.E. 383 (1932 N.Y. C.A.). In the 1938 revised edition of Williston's *Law of Contracts, Canadian Industrial Alcohol* is the most cited decision in the chapter on impossibility (eight times), and a crucial passage from it is quoted in full. See Samuel Williston, *A Treatise on the Law of Contracts*, rev. ed. (New York: Baker, Voorhis, 1938), section 1952. Interestingly, this very same transactional analysis was proposed much earlier by the seventeenth-century natural law jurists (in the civilian tradition), such as Hugo Grotius, *The Rights of War and Peace* (1625), ed. Jean Barbeyrac and Richard Tuck (Indianapolis: Liberty Fund, 2005), book 2, chapter 11, section 6 ("Of Promises").

79. Canadian Industrial Alcohol v. Dunbar Molasses, 384.

80. Canadian Industrial Alcohol v. Dunbar Molasses, 384.

81. The leading opinion is by Lord Justice Vaughan Williams.

82. Krell v. Henry, 745.

83. Krell v. Henry, 743–744.

84. This possibility troubled Lord Justice Romer, but did not prevent him from concurring in the result. Krell v. Henry, 755.

85. Krell v. Henry, 752–753.

86. Williston explicitly makes this point in *Law of Contracts* (1922 ed.), section 1953.

87. In this regard, see *Restatement (Second) of Contracts*, section 265, comment a: "The object must be so completely the basis of the contract that, as both parties understand, without it the transaction would make little sense."

88. Krell v. Henry, 752. For a carefully reasoned and almost contemporaneous US decision that adopts a similar approach to determining frustration, see The Stratford Inc. v. Seattle Brewing & Malting Co., 162 P. 31 (1916) (agreement to lease premises as a saloon frustrated by the prohibition law). In this case also, the foreseeability or unforeseeability of the frustrating event is not treated as a threshold, independent factor. In fact, given the inherent powers of the legislature and the particular subject matter of the lease (i.e., a saloon exclusively selling liquor), the court seems to assume that the event was *not* unforeseeable. The Stratford v. Seattle Brewing, 33.

89. US decisions also make this point explicitly. See, for example, Transatlantic Financing Corp. v. United States, 363 F.2d 312, 318 (1966 U.S.C.A.); Washington State Hop Producers Inc., Liquidation Trust v. Goschie Farms, 773 P.2d 70, 76 (Wash., 1989); and The Opera Company of Boston Inc. v. The Wolf Trap Foundation for the Performing Arts, 817 F.2d 1094, 1100–1103 (4th Cir. 1987). By contrast, in Lloyd v. Murphy, (1944) 153 P.2d 47, 50 (Cal. S.C.), Judge Traynor seems to treat nonforeseeability as a threshold requirement for impossibility or frustration.

90. See the formulation of this point in the Uniform Commercial Code, section 2-615, comment 8.

91. The same analysis applies, mutatis mutandis, to the role of the price term. Thus an agreement at an enhanced price may be a factor that is relevant, though not per se decisive, in assessing whether a party has taken on a risk of performance, can be held to the other's purpose, and so forth. In *Krell,* the enhanced price, combined with other factors, suggests that the plaintiff can be held to the defendant's purpose of viewing the procession. Where, by contrast, the higher price is the only such factor and simply reflects the going market price because of, for example, temporarily increased demand—as in the famous Epson taxi hypothetical discussed in *Krell*—it does not provide a solid basis for holding the receiving party to the other's purposes. Finally, if the parties advert to certain risks of performance in virtue of which they agree to a lower price—imagine that the parties in *Krell* discussed the chance that the procession would be canceled and the plaintiff did not charge the very high going rate—the reasonable inference would ordinarily be that the promisee has accepted the risk (e.g., of cancellation) and must therefore pay when that risk materializes.

92. Representative illustrations include Berg v. Erikson, (1916) 234 Fed. Rep. 817, 823–825; Bank Line v. Arthur Capel & Co., [1919] A.C. 435, 458–459 (per Lord Sumner); and (the subtle analysis in) Northern Pacific Railway Co. v. American Trading Co., 195 U.S. 439, 465–469; (1904) 25 Sup. Ct. Rep. 84, 92–94.

93. For explicit recognition of this point, see W. J. Tatem Ltd. v. Gamboa, [1939] 1 K.B. 132, 138–140. See also *Restatement (Second) of Contracts,* chapter 11, introductory note, section 261, comments b and c; section 265, comment a.

94. The same is not true of approaches that aim to influence what parties decide or prefer as part of their rational pursuit of their advantage. Since the whole rationale of these approaches is to affect parties' calculations in a definite way and toward a definite end, there needs to be a correct answer that measures accurately how this should be done. Otherwise, there is no assurance that the intervention will not make individuals worse off or at least not as well-off as they might have been via a different solution. But the unavoidable indeterminacies that beset these approaches prevent them from meeting this internal demand. For example, in their important economic account of impossibility, Richard Posner and Andrew Rosenfield acknowledge the difficulties and indeterminacies in applying the relevant economic criteria in a variety of situations, including even those decided by leading cases considered above, as a result of the needed empirical information being too complex or speculative for judges to access and the relevant factors pointing in different, sometimes contrary, directions. See Richard Posner and Andrew Rosenfield, "Impossibility and Related Doctrines in Contract Law: An Economic Analysis," *Journal of Legal Studies* 6, no. 1 (1979): 102, 108, 110, and elsewhere. See also the excellent discussion of this problem in Michael J. Trebilcock, "The Role of Insurance Considerations in the Choice of Efficient Civil Liability Rules," *Journal of Law, Economics, and Organization* 4, no. 2 (1988): 249–255.

95. Posner and Rosenfield, "Impossibility and Related Doctrines," 86.

96. From the standpoint of a public basis of justification of contract, the Posner-Rosenfield analysis is problematic because, though purporting to be "severely positive" and "implicit in the judicial decisions," it directly applies economic criteria that single out factors that play no role in judicial reasoning and it also rejects out of hand as "meaningless semantics" or irrelevant those very factors and distinctions that the law treats as crucial and pertinent. "Impossibility and Related Doctrines," 89, 97, and 106. Notable also is the complete absence of any consideration of the idea that a contract may be entered into on the basis of implied or tacit presuppositions, despite the fact that this underpins, sometimes explicitly, the analysis of impossibility in the decisions discussed in the article and is also a key aspect of section 2-165 of the Uniform Commercial Code, which the authors refer to (108–110). If, as Posner and Rosenfield think, a contract's express terms are controlling and preclude judicial intervention on an economic basis, why is the same not true of its implied dimension, which in legal contemplation makes up a contract no less than the express terms? The article does not explain why this should not be so. For further discussion, critical but instructive, of the article, see Eisenberg, *Foundational Principles of Contract Law*, 655–659.

97. What this contrast suggests is that an economic analysis is unsuited to provide a public basis of justification capable of *directly* explaining and justifying contract law. This does not, however, preclude economic theories from endorsing the transactional analysis, whether its principles or its outcomes, as something that may itself make economic sense. Doing this would connect economic analysis *to contract law*. For example, Posner, in discussing contract interpretation, argues that enforcing the meaning of actual or even hypothetical choice is economically superior to the direct determination of efficiency, if this can be done at a reasonable cost. See Richard Posner, "The Law and Economics of Contract Interpretation," *Texas Law Review* 83, no. 6 (2005): 1590–1591. Further, he underlines the cost-effectiveness of "common sense" presumptions making up what he calls the "best guess" rule—such as that parties do not ordinarily intend a wildly unequal exchange or an interpretation that does not make commercial sense or one that would produce transactionally absurd results (1603–1607). Finally, he notes that "most businessmen are literalists [but] want judges to resolve interpretative issues in the way that a reasonable businessman would" (1606). By holding fast to the actual agreement and implying only where necessary to make reasonable sense of its express terms and root purpose as well as to avoid rendering the consideration illusory or absurd, the judicially practicable transactional approach that I have laid out may arguably satisfy the first-best method of ensuring efficiency at a reasonable cost. That, of course, would have to be shown.

98. See also Uniform Commercial Code, sections 1-304 and 1-201(b) (20) (2008). For helpful succinct overviews of American good faith doctrine, see Robert S. Summers, "The Conceptualization of Good Faith in American Contract Law: A Gen-

eral Account," in *Good Faith in European Contract Law,* ed. Reinhard Zimmermann and Simon Whittaker (Cambridge: Cambridge University Press, 2000), 118–144, and Robert S. Summers, "Good Faith Revisited: Some Brief Remarks Dedicated to the Late Richard E. Speidel—Friend, Co-author, and U.C.C. Specialist," *San Diego Law Review* 46, no. 3 (2009) 723–732. See also E. Allan Farnsworth, "Good Faith in Contract Performance," in *Good Faith and Fault in Contract Law,* ed. Jack Beatson and Daniel Friedmann (Oxford: Clarendon Press, 1995), 153–170.

99. *Restatement (Second) of Contracts,* section 205, comment a; Uniform Commercial Code, section 1-304.

100. The most notable exception being English contract law. But see recent English judicial statements arguing for recognition, such as the thoughtful discussion in Yam Seng Pte Ltd. v. International Trade Corp. Ltd., [2013] EWHC 111 (Q.B.), paragraphs 121–132 (per Leggatt, J.). There is also the decision of the Supreme Court of Canada in Bhasin v. Hrynew, [2014] 11 W.W.R. 641 (S.C.C.) that for the first time recognizes the duty of good faith in performance as a general organizing principle of Canadian contract law. For discussion of Australian law, see John W. Carter and Elisabeth Peden, "Good Faith in Australian Contract Law," *Journal of Contract Law* 19 (2003): 155–172. A requirement of good faith in performance, enforcement, and even negotiations is standardly recognized in civil law systems. See Reinhard Zimmermann and Simon Whittaker, eds., *Good Faith in European Contract Law* (Cambridge: Cambridge University Press, 2000).

101. Since good faith in performance is the central and most discussed instance in both the case law and contract scholarship, I will focus on it rather than on good faith in enforcement, let alone the much more disputed issue of a possible precontractual good faith requirement. For discussion of good faith in enforcement in US law, see Eric G. Andersen, "Good Faith in the Enforcement of Contracts," *Iowa Law Review* 73, no. 2 (1988): 299–349.

102. See, for example, the official comment to Uniform Commercial Code section 1-304 (comment 1) and representative decisions such as Metropolitan Life Insurance Co. v. RJR Nabisco Inc., 716 F. Supp. 1504 (S.D. N.Y. 1989), 1517, and Kham & Nate's Shoes No. 2 v. First Bank, 908 F.2d 1351, 1357–1358 (7th Cir. 1990).

103. Daniel Markovits properly emphasizes this in "Good Faith as Contract's Core Value," in *Philosophical Foundations of Contract Law,* ed. Gregory Klass, George Letsas, and Prince Saprai (Oxford: Oxford University Press, 2014), particularly 276–284.

104. For a representative judicial statement, see Kham v. First Bank, 1357. This is a central theme in Markovits's instructive account in "Contract's Core Value."

105. See, for example, the influential statement in Rio Algom Corp. v. Jimco Ltd., 618 P.2d 497, 505 (Utah 1980), and Market St. Assocs. Ltd. P'ship v. Frey 41 F.2d 588, 593–595 (7th Cir. 1991). This is specifically highlighted in the recent English case of Yam Seng v. International Trade, paragraphs 134–135.

106. Transamerica Life Canada Inc. & Aegon Canada Inc. v. ING Canada Inc., (2004) 234 D.L.R. (4th) 367, paragraph 53.

107. As stated in Kirke La Shelle Co. v. Paul Armstrong Co., 188 N.E. 163, 167 (N.Y. 1933) ("[I]n every contract there is an implied covenant that neither party shall do anything which will have the effect of destroying or injuring the right of the other party to receive the fruits of the contract").

108. Transamerica Life v. ING, paragraph 53.

109. This is how Whittaker and Zimmermann describe the requirement of good faith in German civil law. See Simon Whittaker and Reinhard Zimmermann, "Good Faith in European Contract Law: Surveying the Legal Landscape," in *Good Faith in European Contract Law*, ed. Reinhard Zimmermann and Simon Whittaker (Cambridge: Cambridge University Press, 2000), 30–32.

110. See Summers, "Good Faith in American Contract Law," 136.

111. Carter v. Boehm, (1766) 3 Burr. 1905, 1910–1911.

112. The phrases are from, respectively, Summers, "Good Faith in American Contract Law," 136; Carter and Peden, "Good Faith in Australian Contract Law," 158; and Markovits, "Contract's Core Value," 272, 291–293. Markovits suggests that good faith *"constitutes* the distinct form of legal obligation that contracts establish." Markovits, "Contract's Core Value," 272 (emphasis in original).

113. For helpful discussion, see J. F. Burrows, "Contractual Co-operation and the Implied Term," *Modern Law Review* 31, no. 4 (1968): 390, and also Williston's treatment in the 1938 revised edition of the *Law of Contracts* at sections 677, 1293, and 1293A.

114. See, for example, Barque Quilpue Ltd. v. Brown, [1904] 2 K.B. 264, 271–272 (1903, C.A.) (per Vaughan Williams, L.J.). Whereas American law associates it with good faith, English law has described the underlying principle as one of "common honesty." See, for example, Harmer v. Jumbil (Nigeria) Tin Areas Ltd., [1921] 1 Ch. 200, 225 (per Younger, L.J.).

115. For example, Colley v. Overseas Exporters, [1921] 3 K.B. 302.

116. Mackay v. Dick, (1881) 6 App. Cas. 251 (Eng. H.L.).

117. Patterson v. Meyerhofer, 204 N.Y. 96; 97 N.E. 472 (N.Y. 1912).

118. Bhasin v. Hrynew, paragraph 70, explicitly makes this point.

119. Steven Burton makes this point in "Breach of Contract and the Common Law Duty to Perform in Good Faith," *Harvard Law Review* 94, no. 2 (1980): 384–385. See also Williston, *Law of Contracts* (1938 rev. ed.), sections 677 and 1293A.

120. Consonantly with Summers's well-known "excluder" analysis, adopted by the *Restatement (Second) of Contracts,* section 205, comment a. See Robert S. Summers, "The General Duty of Good Faith—Its Recognition and Conceptualization," *Cornell Law Review* 67 (1982): 810–820.

121. See the formulation in Patterson v. Meyerhofer, 100.

122. In Mackay v. Dick, for example, a transactional analysis is presented at 263–265 (per Lord Blackburn).

123. See Food Fair Stores Inc. v. Blumberg, 200 A.2d 166 (C.A. Md. 1964), and Goldberg 168-05 Corp. v. Levy, 9 N.Y.S.2d 304 (1938).

124. See City of Dublin Steam Packet Co. v. The Ring, (1908) 24 T.L.R. 798 (Eng. C.A.).

125. As emphasized by Lord Wright in Luxor (Eastbourne) Ltd. v. Cooper, [1941] A.C. 108, 138 (Eng. H.L.). For this point about expanding, upgrading, or reorganizing, see Food Fair Stores v. Blumberg, 174, and Southwest Natural Gas Co. v. Oklahoma Portland Cement Co., 102 F.2d 630, 633 (10th Cir. C.A., 1939).

126. "[T]he cases recognize what surely must be a universal truth: a party is not likely to bargain away his right to run his business according to his best judgment." John C. Weistart, "Requirements and Output Contracts: Quantity Variations under the UCC," *Duke Law Journal*, no. 3 (1973): 629.

127. See Goldberg v. Levy, 306.

128. For representative English cases, see City of Dublin Steam Packet Co. v. The Ring (transactional analysis at 799–801); Dare v. The Bognor Urban District Council, (1912) 28 T.L.R. 489 (Eng. C.A.) (transactional analysis at 489, per Vaughan Williams, L.J.); Peech v. Best, [1931] 1 K.B. 1 (transactional analysis at 9–15, per Scrutton, L.J.); and Luxor v. Cooper (transactional analysis at 137–142, per Lord Wright). For US cases, see Food Fair Stores v. Blumberg (transactional analysis at 174–175); HML Corp. v. General Foods Corp., 365 F.2d 77 (1966, 3d Cir. C.A.) (transactional analysis at 81–82); and Van Valkenburgh, Nooger & Neville Inc. v. Hayden Publishing Co., 281 N.E.2d 142 (1972, N.Y. C.A.) (transactional analysis at 144–145).

129. As one court put it: "The requirement of good faith is the means by which ... self-interest in its undistorted form is maintained as the standard." HML v. General Foods, 81.

130. See Carpenter v. Virginia-Carolina Chemical Co., 35 S.E. 358 (1900). For well-known cases involving express discretion that provide instructive transactional analysis of the good faith issue, see Boone v. Kerr-McGee Oil Industries, 217 F.2d 63, 65 (10th Cir. 1954); Loudenback Fertilizer Co. v. Tennessee Phosphate Co., 121 Fed. Rep. 298, 302–303 (6th Cir. C.A., 1903); and Southwest Natural Gas v. Oklahoma Portland Cement, 633.

131. As in Tymshare v. Covell, 727 F.2d 1145, 1153 (D.C. Cir. 1984).

132. In "Breach of Contract," Steven Burton, in my view correctly, highlights the discretion-conferring aspects of agreements in connection with the good faith requirement. More specifically, he characterizes bad faith as the exercise of discretion for the purpose of recapturing opportunities that the promisor necessarily gave up by undertaking to perform. I would want to emphasize, however, that the ultimate determining (and determinate) criterion is always the contract itself, including its tacit assumptions and objectives as reasonably construed, without which one cannot say in the first place whether or not the opportunity that the party "recaptured" is one that he or she should be deemed to have forgone by entering the contract.

133. Tymshare v. Covell, 1153 (per Scalia, J.).

134. Socimer International Bank Ltd. (in liquidation) v. Standard Bank London Ltd., [2008] EWCA Civ 116 (Eng. C.A.), paragraph 66 (per Rix, L.J.). See also Dalton v. Educational Testing Service, 663 N.E.2d 289, 293 (N.Y. 1995), which emphasizes this point with respect to the kind of discretion at issue in that case.

135. ASB Allegiance Real Estate Fund v. Scion Breckenridge, 50 A.3d 434, 440 (Del. Ch. 2012); Kirke La Shelle v. Paul Armstrong, 168; Williston, *Law of Contracts* (1938 rev. ed.), section 1293A.

136. Loudenback Fertilizer v. Tennessee Phosphate, 302.

137. Loudenback Fertilizer v. Tennessee Phosphate, 303. The same analysis applies to so-called "output" contracts. See, in general, Weistart, "Requirements and Output Contracts."

138. The example is from Tymshare v. Covell, 1153.

139. See MacDougald Construction Co. v. State Highway Department, 188 S.E. 2d 405, 407 (1972) ("What the intent of the parties was in making the contract must control; it is possible to so draw a contract as to leave decisions absolutely to the uncontrolled discretion of one of the parties and in such a case the issue of good faith is irrelevant" [quoted in Tymshare v. Covell, 1153]). Fraud is excluded as bad faith not as a consequence of policy but rather because it cannot reasonably be presumed that a party assumes the risk that the other will decide to lie to or defraud her: "Absent explicit anti-reliance language pursuant to which a sophisticated party knowingly assumes risk . . . a court can presume that the question 'Can I lie to you?' would have been met with a resounding 'No.' Proof of fraud therefore violates the implied covenant . . . because 'no fraud' is an implied contractual term." ASB Allegiance v. Scion Breckenridge, 443.

140. See the particularly instructive discussion in Tymshare v. Covell, 1154.

141. For example, see Boone v. Kerr-McGee Oil, 65.

142. Tymshare v. Covell, 1154. See, for example, Fortune v. National Cash Register, 364 N.E.2d 1251 (Mass. 1977).

143. The Uniform Commercial Code, section 1-201, official comment 20, specifies that "both . . . subjective and objective elements are part of the standard of 'good faith.'"

144. I draw here on the clear and careful discussion in ASB Allegiance v. Scion Breckenridge, 442–444. See also the instructive analysis in Yam Seng v. International Trade, paragraph 144.

145. Uniform Commercial Code, section 1-302.

146. As expressly noted in the Uniform Commercial Code, section 1-304, official comment 1. For a recent judicial statement to this effect, see Bhasin v. Hrynew, paragraphs 74–77.

147. On this point, see Tymshare v. Covell, 1154 ("Where what is at issue is the retroactive reduction or elimination of a central compensatory element of the contract—a large part of the *quid pro quo* that induced one party's assent—it is simply

not likely that the parties had in mind a power quite [so] absolute.... In the present case, agreeing to such a provision would require a degree of folly ... we are not inclined to posit where another plausible interpretation of the language is available").

148. Jacob & Youngs v. Kent, 891.

149. In Tymshare v. Covell, 1152, 1152n6, Judge Scalia, correctly in my view, makes this connection between the implied good faith requirement and what he calls the "Cardozan" approach to contract construction and interpretation.

B. Fairness

1. For a helpful overview (with primary materials) of contractual fairness in the common law and civil law systems, see James Gordley and Arthur T. von Mehren, *An Introduction to the Comparative Study of Private Law: Readings, Cases, Materials* (Cambridge: Cambridge University Press, 2006), 461–494.

2. Gordley and von Mehren, *Comparative Study of Private Law*, 468.

3. Gordley and von Mehren, *Comparative Study of Private Law*, 494.

4. For thoughtful discussion, see Stephen M. Waddams, *Principle and Policy in Contract Law: Competing or Complementary Concepts?* (Cambridge: Cambridge University Press, 2011), 117.

4. The Paradigm of Contractual Fairness

1. Arthur Allen Leff, "Unconscionability and the Code—the Emperor's New Clause," *University of Pennsylvania Law Review* 115, no. 4 (1967): 485–559. In my view, the most compelling and instructive response to Leff's article remains M. P. Ellinghaus, "In Defense of Unconscionability," *Yale Law Journal* 78, no. 5 (1969): 757–815.

2. This is a major theme of James Gordley's seminal article "Equality in Exchange," *California Law Review* 69, no. 6 (1981): 1587–1656, and in Stephen M. Waddams's extensive writing on all aspects of contractual fairness, beginning with his pathbreaking piece "Unconscionability in Contracts," *Modern Law Review* 39 (1976): 369–393.

3. For an example of a liberal view, see Charles Fried, *Contract as Promise: A Theory of Contractual Obligation,* 2nd ed. (New York: Oxford University Press, 2015), 103–111. At page 150, note 1, Fried refers to "the important distinction between procedural and substantive unconscionability." For examples of libertarian views, see Richard Epstein, "Unconscionability: A Critical Reappraisal," *Journal of Law and Economics* 18, no. 2 (1975): 293–298, and Randy Barnett, *Contracts* (Oxford: Oxford University Press, 2010), 230–232.

4. See Epstein, "Unconscionability: A Critical Reappraisal," 297.

5. Fried, *Contract as Promise*, 106.

6. See, for example, the famous United States Supreme Court decision in Post v. Jones, 19 How. (60 U.S.) 150 (1856), and the often-cited English case Akerblom v. Price, Potter, Walker & Co., (1881) 7 Q.B.D. 129 (C.A.). Salvage agreements are one of the settled categories of contractual unfairness discussed by Lord Denning, M.R., in Lloyds Bank v. Bundy, [1975] 1 Q.B. 326, 338–339 (C.A.), and by Melvin A. Eisenberg in his "The Bargain Principle and Its Limits," *Harvard Law Review* 95, no. 4 (1982): 754–763. For an overview, see Grant Gilmore and Charles Black, *The Law of Admiralty*, 2nd ed. (Mineola, NY: Foundation Press, 1975), 559.

7. Fried, *Contract as Promise*, 109–111.

8. Fried, *Contract as Promise*, 111.

9. Fried, *Contract as Promise*, 110–111.

10. Here I am drawing on Michael J. Trebilcock's superb "An Economic Approach to the Doctrine of Unconscionability," in *Studies in Contract Law*, ed. Barry Reiter and John Swan (Toronto: Butterworths, 1980), 381–421.

11. See Trebilcock, "An Economic Approach," 395–396.

12. It is worth noting that Leff himself justifies his account of unconscionability by drawing, not on settled applications of unconscionability, but instead on doctrines such as illegality that are process-independent and other doctrines such as fraud and duress that are term-independent. Leff, "Unconscionability and the Code," 488. No wonder he ends up with two separate kinds of unconscionability and an account that cannot make sense of the actual case law!

13. This is presently the majority view among US courts. See Samuel Williston, *A Treatise on the Law of Contracts*, 4th ed., ed. Richard A. Lord (Rochester, NY: Lawyers Cooperative Publishing, 2001), volume 8, section 18, 9–10 ("Elements of Unconscionability"). Scholars who have emphasized this same point include, among others, Eisenberg, "The Bargain Principle," 800; Gordley, "Equality in Exchange," 1633–1637; P. S. Atiyah, "Contract and Fair Exchange," in *Essays on Contract* (Oxford: Oxford University Press, 1986), 334; Waddams, "Unconscionability in Contracts"; and John P. Dawson, "Economic Duress—an Essay in Perspective," *Michigan Law Review* 45, no. 3 (1947): 253–290.

14. A similar but more detailed argument is made by Mindy Chen-Wishart, *Unconscionable Bargains* (Wellington: Butterworths, 1989), 102–103, 108–109 ("Limits of Procedural Rationales"). See also Gordley, "Equality in Exchange," 1625–1637 ("[a]ttempts to explain relief without the principle of equality").

15. For examples, see Rotheram v. Browne, (1747) 8 Bro. P.C. 297; 3 E.R. 594, 598, and cases referred to in Gordley, "Equality in Exchange," 1652–1654.

16. Chen-Wishart, *Unconscionable Bargains*, 108.

17. Lloyds Bank v. Bundy, 336–339.

18. It is important to note that this conception of contractual fairness is not parochial to common law systems or equity but was first discussed and elaborated in depth and detail by the mainly continental philosophers and legal theorists from Thomas Aquinas and John Duns Scotus in the thirteenth century to Grotius and Pufendorf in the seventeenth, culminating with Hegel. For discussion of these and other such writers, see James Gordley, *The Philosophical Origins of Modern Contract Doctrine* (Oxford: Clarendon Press, 1991). I have presented Hegel's account in Peter Benson, "Abstract Right and the Possibility of a Nondistributive Conception of Contract: Hegel and Contemporary Contract Theory," *Cardozo Law Review* 10, nos. 5–6 (1989): 1077–1198.

19. Contract terms that are unfair may sensibly be said to import either unfair surprise (where, for example, there is price ignorance) or oppression (in circumstances of necessity, as in the salvage scenarios). This characterization is found throughout the case law and is enshrined in Uniform Commercial Code, section 2-302, comment 1.

20. See, for example, Frederick Pollock, *Principles of Contract,* 1st ed. (London: Stevens and Sons, 1876), 154, and William Reynell Anson, *Principles of the English Law of Contract,* 1st ed. (Oxford: Clarendon Press, 1879), 63. Both are discussed in Stephen M. Waddams, *Principle and Policy in Contract Law: Competing or Complementary Concepts?* (Cambridge: Cambridge University Press, 2011), 99–101.

21. On this point, see A. W. B. Simpson, *A History of the Common Law of Contract: The Rise of the Action of Assumpsit* (Oxford: Oxford University Press, 1975), 447; Dawson, "Economic Duress," 276–277; Gordley, "Equality in Exchange," 1594–1598; and Waddams, *Principle and Policy,* 88–89.

22. See Waddams, *Principle and Policy,* 101–109; Gordley, "Equality in Exchange," 1598; and Dawson, "Economic Duress," 277.

23. The distinction between use value and exchange value has a long intellectual history going back at least to Aristotle's works in politics and ethics. Marx provides a particularly lucid account. See, for example, Karl Marx, *Capital: A Critique of Political Economy,* volume 1, trans. Ben Fowkes (New York: Vintage Books, 1977), part 1, and Karl Marx, *Grundrisse: Foundations of the Critique of Political Economy,* trans. Martin Nicolaus (New York: Vintage Books, 1973), 113–238, 881–883.

24. This last point is emphasized by Marx, *Capital,* volume 1, part 1, chapter 2 ("Exchange").

25. This basic point was already emphasized by Aristotle. See Aristotle, *Nicomachean Ethics,* trans. Robert Crisp (Cambridge: Cambridge University Press, 2012), book 5, page 1138a. See also Hegel's formulation in his *Philosophy of Right,* trans. T. M. Knox (Oxford: Oxford University Press, 1952), paragraph 63, addition ("[In property and contract] the quantitative character which emerges from the qualitative is value. Here the qualitative . . . is as much preserved in the quantity as superseded by it").

26. For a parallel, although differently framed, analysis of these two kinds of judgment, see Gordley's important discussion of what he refers to as two different types of autonomy in "Equality in Exchange," 1617–1622.

27. I draw on Gordley's use of purchasing power in his account of equality and the market price. "Equality in Exchange," 1609–1617.

28. P. S. Atiyah, referring to William Paley's work, also frames the analysis in terms of this basic presumed intention. Atiyah, "Contract and Fair Exchange," 351. See also William Paley, *The Principles of Moral and Political Philosophy* (New York: B. & S. Collins, 1835), 81–82. To the same effect, see Eisenberg, "The Bargain Principle," 779–781.

29. For an argument expressly along these lines, see Emmanuel Gounot, *Le principe de l'autonomie de la volonté en droit privé: Contribution à l'étude critique de l'individualisme juridique* (Paris: Arthur Rousseau, 1912), 163–164. This still untranslated work—a doctoral dissertation—makes a major contribution to contract theory.

30. On this point, see Grotius's influential formulation: "But in all permutatory Contracts, this Equality is to be punctually observed; nor must any one pretend, that what is promised more than is due by either Party, is to be looked on [necessarily] as a Present: For this is seldom the Design of those that make such Contracts; nor is it to be presumed, unless it appear so." Hugo Grotius, *The Rights of War and Peace* (1625), ed. Jean Barbeyrac and Richard Tuck (Indianapolis: Liberty Fund, 2005), book 2, chapter 12, section 11, paragraph 1.

31. For discussion, see Gordley, "Equality in Exchange," 1604–1609.

32. I draw on the discussions of the competitive market price in Eisenberg, "The Bargain Principle," 746–747; Trebilcock, "An Economic Approach"; and Gordley, "Equality in Exchange," 1604–1617. The "common estimation or judgment" is the so-called *communis aestimatio* of the earlier writers, discussed by Gordley in "Equality in Exchange."

33. For discussion of the difference between the allocative and distributive functions of prices, see John Rawls, *A Theory of Justice* (Cambridge, MA: Belknap Press of Harvard University Press, 1971), 273–274.

34. Many of Epstein's examples of transactions that, in his view, should not be set aside for "substantive unconscionability" would come under this aspect of the proposed analysis. See Epstein, "Unconscionability: A Critical Reappraisal," 305–315.

35. This formulation is from Thomas Aquinas, *Summa Theologica*, trans. Fathers of the English Dominican Province (New York: Benziger Bros., 1948), part 2-2, question 77, article 1.

36. This is Epstein's objection in "Unconscionability: A Critical Reappraisal," which I noted but did not address earlier.

37. This seems to be also true in civil law jurisdictions. See the discussions in John P. Dawson, "Economic Duress and Fair Exchange in French and German Law," parts 1 and 2, *Tulane Law Review* 11, no. 3 (1937): 345–376; 12, no. 1 (1937):

42–73; John P. Dawson, "Unconscionable Coercion: The German Version," *Harvard Law Review* 89, no. 6 (1976): 1041–1126; and Gordley, "Equality in Exchange," 1625–1633.

38. Grotius notes and addresses this point in *The Rights of War and Peace,* book 2, chapter 12, section 12, paragraph 2.

39. In an early anonymous work, *Treatise on Equity* (1737), attributed to Henry Ballow, the author writes that "a small damage, even in the law of nature, is not sufficient to break off a bargain, for the benefit of traffic and the ease of the magistrate." Book 1, chapter 2, section 9, cited in J. L. Barton, "The Enforcement of Hard Bargains," *Law Quarterly Review* 103 (1987): 123. I discuss more fully the institutional role of contract law in Chapter 12.

40. Insofar as a court is unable to do this, an institutional limit has been reached and there is no credible basis for the court declaring a transaction to be unconscionable (as distinct from procured by fraud, duress and so on.) Contract law has nothing more to say or do with respect to the market failure. This of course does not preclude other legal or institutional responses.

41. See Trebilcock, "An Economic Approach." See also Gordley's discussion of this point in "Equality in Exchange," 1620–1621.

42. Lloyds Bank v. Bundy, 336 (per Lord Denning, M.R.).

43. On this point, see Waddams's excellent discussion in *Principle and Policy,* 112–113.

44. Lloyds Bank v. Bundy, 339.

45. Earl of Aylesford v. Morris, (1872–1873) L.R. 8 Ch. App. 484, 490 (per Lord Selborne). In his discussion of German civil law, Gordley reaches the same conclusion about whether it is necessary to show morally reprehensible conduct or exploitation as a distinct requirement for a violation of article 138 of the German Civil Code (Bürgerliches Gesetzbuch). Gordley, "Equality in Exchange," 1631–1633, 1647–1648.

46. This view is taken by several recent English and Commonwealth decisions. See, for example, Hart v. O'Connor, [1985] A.C. 1000 (P.C.), and Boustany v. Pigott, (1993) 69 P. & C.R. 298 (P.C.). See also the detailed discussions in Nicholas Bamforth, "Unconscionability as a Vitiating Factor," *Lloyd's Maritime and Commercial Law Quarterly,* no. 4 (1995): 538–560.

47. This, in my view, is the proper interpretation of Uniform Commercial Code, section 2-302, comment 1, which clarifies that the purpose of unconscionability is "the prevention of oppression and unfair surprise . . . not . . . the disturbance of allocation of risks because of superior bargaining power." See the excellent discussion in Ellinghaus, "In Defense of Unconscionability," 766–767. Contra Epstein's view, which seems to ascribe this function to unconscionability. Epstein, "Unconscionability: A Critical Reappraisal," 303.

48. See discussion of US cases in Ellinghaus, "In Defense of Unconscionability," 767–768. A number of the unconscionability decisions cited in Uniform Commer-

cial Code, section 2-302, comment 1, as illustrations of the underlying basis of unconscionability include agreements between businesses. Within certain parameters, such agreements can also be set aside for contractual unfairness under English legislation, such as the Unfair Contract Terms Act 1977. See Elizabeth Macdonald, "Unfair Contract Terms Act—Thirty Years On," in *Contract Terms*, ed. Andrew Burrows and Edwin Peel (Oxford: Oxford University Press, 2007), 153–172.

49. "Commutative justice" is the term Thomas Aquinas uses in place of Aristotle's "corrective" or "rectificatory" justice. I adopt it because, by giving it a name that parallels that of distributive justice, it brings out clearly that the two kinds of justice are, as Aristotle himself emphasized, justice in transactions and justice in distributions. Note also that almost without exception, the natural law exponents from Thomas Aquinas onward (culminating with Hegel's account in *Philosophy of Right*, paragraph 77) conceived of equivalence in exchange as a nondistributive requirement of justice. The modern French civilian theorist Emmanuel Gounot argues that in matters of contract, the supreme rule of justice is summed up in the principle of commutative justice, which he takes to be a principle of equivalence rather than one of social distributive justice. See Gounot, *Le principe de l'autonomie de la volonté en droit privé*, 210–211. For an excellent economic analysis of why unconscionability need not and should not incorporate distributive considerations, see Trebilcock, "An Economic Approach," 407–409, 419–421.

5. Three Other Doctrines about Fair Terms

1. For the purposes of this discussion, I draw mainly on English law for the doctrine of undue influence. Leading cases include Huguenin v. Baseley, (1807) 14 Ves. Jun. 273; Tate v. Williamson, (1866) L.R. 2 Ch. App. 55; Allcard v. Skinner, (1888) 36 Ch.D. 145 (C.A.); Wright v. Carter, [1903] 1 Ch. 27 (C.A.); Tufton v. Sperni, [1952] 2 T.L.R. 516 (C.A.); In Re Brocklehurst's Estate, [1978] 1 Ch. 14 (C.A.); Barclays Bank plc v. O' Brien, [1994] 1 A.C. 180 (H.L.); Royal Bank of Scotland plc v. Etridge (No. 2), [2001] UKHL 44 (H.L.); and R v. A-G for England and Wales, [2003] UKPC 22 (P.C.). Although this longstanding traditional division into two categories has not been favored since *Etridge*, I don't believe that my discussion turns on which approach is chosen. Even post-*Etridge*, these traditional categories remain substantially intact and the notion of presumed undue influence, which is my focus, remains fully operative. The major difference between the older and current approaches concerns the way presumed undue influence is proved. See the excellent survey and discussion in Mindy Chen-Wishart, *Contract Law*, 5th ed. (New York: Oxford University Press, 2015), 342–357. For an overview of US contract law, see E. Allan Farnsworth, *Contracts*, 4th ed. (New York: Aspen Publishers, 2004), section 4.20. It is the topic of *Restatement (Second) of Contracts* (1981), section 177. In

addition, see John P. Dawson, "Economic Duress—an Essay in Perspective," *Michigan Law Review* 45, no. 3 (1947): 262–267, and, more recently, Mindy Chen-Wishart, "Undue Influence: Vindicating Relationships of Influence," *Current Legal Problems* 59, no. 1 (2006): 231–266.

2. I take this formulation from Royal Bank of Scotland v. Etridge, paragraph 24. For discussion, see Chen-Wishart, *Contract Law,* 352–354.

3. In Lloyds Bank v. Bundy, [1975] 1 Q.B. 326, 338 (C.A.), Lord Denning, M.R. includes undue influence as the third of the five categories of cases that he brings under his general statement of contractual unfairness.

4. Allcard v. Skinner, 178–180, 184 (per Lindley, L.J.); 189–190 (per Bowen, L.J.).

5. Lord Justice Lindley's often-cited formulation in *Allcard* is "if the gift is so large as not to be reasonably accounted for on the ground of friendship, relationship, charity, or other ordinary motives on which ordinary men act." Allcard v. Skinner, 185.

6. Bank of Credit and Commerce International SA v. Aboody [1990] 1 QB 923, 965. For examples and discussion, see Chen-Wishart, *Contract Law,* 352–354.

7. That wrongdoing is not necessary is recognized in most though not all decisions. In the leading case of *Allcard*, the court noted that the defendant had acted selflessly throughout: "I acquit her most entirely of all selfish feeling in the matter. I can see no sort of wrongful desire to appropriate to herself any worldly benefit from the gift." Allcard v. Skinner, 190–191 (per Bowen, L.J.). For a more recent representative decision, see Pesticcio v. Huet, [2004] EWCA Civ 372, paragraph 20.

8. This formulation combines Lord Justice Bowen's words in Allcard v. Skinner, 190 ("This is not a limitation placed on the action of the donor; it is a fetter placed upon the conscience of the recipient of the gift, and one which arises out of public policy and fair play"), and Lord Nicholl's in Royal Bank of Scotland v. Etridge, 7 ("The means used is regarded as an exercise of improper or 'undue' influence, and hence unacceptable, whenever the consent thus procured ought not fairly to be treated as the expression of a person's free will").

9. This is emphasized by leading commentators such as Chen-Wishart, *Contract Law,* 343-345 and Dawson, "Economic Duress," 264.

10. Dawson, "Economic Duress," 264. To the same effect, see the often-cited submission of Sir Samuel Romilly (for the complainant) in the old case of Huguenin v. Baseley, 287.

11. Recent cases that uphold challenged transactions on this basis include R v. A-G for England and Wales; Dailey v. Dailey, [2003] UKPC 65 (P.C.); National Commercial Bank (Jamaica) Ltd. v. Hew, [2003] UKPC 51; and Turkey v. Awadh, [2005] EWCA Civ 382.

12. Campbell Soup Co. v. Wentz, 172 F.2d 80 (3d Cir. 1948); Uniform Commercial Code, section 2-302, official comment 1.

13. See John P. Dawson, "Unconscionable Coercion: The German Version," *Harvard Law Review* 89, no. 6 (1976): 1103n154 (emphasis in original). *Campbell*

Soup v. Wentz is also the basis of *Restatement (Second) of Contracts* (1981), section 208, illustration 1, and is noted in comment b.

14. This is Dawson's translation of *Knebelung,* the term of art in German contract law.

15. Dawson, "Unconscionable Coercion," 1071–1103.

16. The former is a violation of the German Civil Code (Bürgerliches Gesetzbuch), article 138 (2), while the latter is a violation of article 138 (1).

17. Dawson, "Unconscionable Coercion," 1078, 1095.

18. I borrow Dawson's apt description of the provision in "Unconscionable Coercion," 1103; Campbell Soup v. Wentz, 83.

19. Campbell Soup v. Wentz, 83 ("Nor are we suggesting any excuse for the grower in this case").

20. Interestingly, subsequent to the *Wentz* decision, Campbell Soup changed its standard form agreement by, among other things, eliminating this provision and the one-sided liquidated damages clause. The reformed terms were upheld as fair and balanced and equally for the benefit of both Campbell Soup and farmers in Campbell Soup Co. v. Diehm 111 F. Supp. 211, 215 (E.D. Pa. 1952).

21. Campbell Soup v. Wentz, 83.

22. Young v. Timmins, 1 C. & J. 332 (1831).

23. On the facts, it appeared that the manufacturer had no realistic prospect of doing serious business outside of Birmingham.

24. Young v. Timmins, 344.

25. Esso Petroleum Co. v. Harper's Garage (Stourport) Ltd., [1968] A.C. 269, 294 (per Lord Reid); 328–329 (per Lord Pearce).

26. For the standard comprehensive source on this doctrine in Anglo-Commonwealth law see, John Dyson Heydon, *The Restraint of Trade Doctrine* 3d ed. (Chatswood, N.S.W.: LexisNexis Butterworths, 2008). For US law, see Farnsworth, Contracts, section 5.3 and *Restatement (Second) of Contracts,* Ch.8, topic 2, sections 186-188. For a particularly thoughtful and detailed discussion of underlying issues, see Stephen A. Smith, "Reconstructing Restraint of Trade," Oxford Journal of Legal Studies 15, no.4 (1995): 565–595.

27. Mitchel v. Reynolds, (1711) 1 P. Wms. 181 (Ch.D.).

28. There have been different judicial formulations of the test. These standardly involve a two or three stage analysis. See, Smith, "Reconstructing Restraint of Trade," 566–567.

29. This is the term used by Lord Pearce in Esso Petroleum v. Harper's Garage, 328–329.

30. See the excellent discussion of this point by Lord Reid in A. Schroeder Music Publishing Ltd. v. Macaulay, [1974] 1 W.L.R. 1308, 1313–1314 [Eng. H.L.].

31. "[A] man may, by his own consent, for a valuable consideration, part with his liberty; as in the case of a covenant not to erect a mill on his own lands." Mitchel v. Reynolds, 189.

32. This point is made in the Scottish case of Stewart v. Stewart, (1899) 1 F. 1158, 1171 (per Lord Trayner).

33. This is clearly stated in Mitchel v. Reynolds, 190. In keeping with this policy, Lord Macclesfield distinguishes the case of an old man who, wishing to retire from business and to live off his savings, agrees to sell his business and to refrain from engaging in it in the future. Mitchel v. Reynolds, 191. Such terms would not come within the restraint of trade doctrine.

34. Thus, it is the policy of the law that "determines what is an interest of the private party concerned which he has a right to have protected." Petrofina (Great Britain) Ltd. v. Martin, [1966] 1 Ch. 146, 182 (C.A.) (per Diplock, L.J.).

35. For the first point, see Vancouver Malt and Sake Brewing Co. Ltd. v. Vancouver Breweries Ltd., [1934] A.C. 181, 192 (P.C.) (per Lord Macmillan). See also *Restatement of the Law of Contracts* (1932), section 513, comment a. The second point is emphasized by all leading decisions. See the representative statement by Lord Pearce in Esso Petroleum v. Harper's Garage, 324.

36. The present writer is not aware of any decision in which a contract in restraint of trade, clearly shown to be reasonable as between the parties, has nevertheless been voided for being challenged under and not satisfying the second prong of reasonableness vis-à-vis the public. Indeed, supposing that first prong of reasonableness is construed as I will suggest—the restraint being shown to be essential to protecting the restraining party's legitimate interests arising in connection with their contract and as against the other party—there would seem offhand to be no further judicially ascertainable and applicable norm that could justify voiding a contract. The second prong becomes superfluous. Smith reaches the same conclusion. See Smith, "Reconstructing Restraint of Trade," 591–595.Why does this second prong persist in judicial formulations? I conjecture that it is the historical residue of the original pre-*Mitchel* prohibition of all restraints of trade as per se illegal and against public policy. For judicial discussion of this issue, see Stephens v. Gulf Oil Canada Ltd., 49 D.L.R. (3d) 533 (1975) (Ont. C.A.), paragraphs 46–55.

37. "[F]or a restraint to be reasonable in the interests of the parties it must afford no more than adequate protection to the party in whose favour it is imposed." Herbert Morris Ltd. v. Saxelby, [1916] A.C. 688, 707 (Eng. H.L.) (per Lord Parker). Smith also uses the term "investment" to refer to the restraining party's legitimate interest. See Smith, "Reconstructing Restraint of Trade," 574, 576–577. I agree with Smith's analysis of this crucial point.

38. For a discussion of clauses protecting trade secrets, see the *Herbert Morris* case. Examples of restraints to ensure sellers do not derogate from the full value of the goodwill of a business include Mitchel v. Reynolds and the leading case of Nordenfelt v. Maxim Nordenfelt Guns & Ammunition Co. Ltd., [1894] A.C. 535 (H.L.). Well-known English and Commonwealth cases that involve the abovementioned interest in maintaining systems of distribution include, in addition to Esso Petroleum v. Harper's Garage and Petrofina v. Martin, McEllistrim v. Bally-

macelligott Co-operative Agricultural and Dairy Society, [1919] A.C. 549 (P.C.), and English Hop Growers Ltd. v. Dering, [1928] 2 K.B. 174.

39. For example, an employer ordinarily has no legitimate transactional interest in controlling a former employee's post-employment use of skills that the employee developed as a practically inevitable by-product of her work-related efforts. The employer is entitled to their use during the period of employment, but not after. Nor does a party have a reasonable transactional interest in per se preventing the possibility of competing transactions. For a representative judicial statement of this last point, see McEllistrim v. Ballymacelligott Co-operative Society, 563 (per Lord Atkinson).

40. Mitchel v. Reynolds, 190. Thus, where the restraint is "in gross" or not ancillary to other terms—for example, a simple promise to refrain from productive or economic activity in general in return for compensation—the constraint is normally conclusively void. This is assumed by the *Restatement (Second) of Contracts,* section 187. See also Farnsworth, *Contracts,* section 5.3.

41. Horner v. Graves, 7 Bing. 735 (1831) (per Tindal, C.J.) (emphasis added). In Mitchel v. Reynolds, 183, Lord Macclesfield refers to an unjustified restraint as "merely injurious and oppressive." We are assuming that the restraint cannot be justified on the second prong as reasonable in relation to the public interest. But see my remarks about this second prong in note 36 above.

42. In Chapter 11, where I discuss the underlying moral basis of the transactional conception of contract, this inalienable dimension is explained as expressing the inviolability of the idea of the person—juridical personality—that underpins contract and indeed private law as a whole. The content of what is included in this inalienable basis of personality can comprise ultimately any normative feature or power that constitutes the juridical, political, or even constitutional autonomy of moral agents. In Chapter 12, I develop the latter point in connection with the important question of the relation between fundamental rights and contract law.

43. This is explicitly recognized in, for example, Esso Petroleum v. Harper's Garage, 300 (per Lord Reid), and Vancouver Malt v. Vancouver Breweries, 190 (per Lord MacMillan) ["[t]he receipt of a sum of money can generally be shown to be advantageous to a businessman, but his liberty to trade is not an asset which the law will permit him to barter for money except in special circumstances."] A possible such special circumstance might be the retirement scenario mentioned in Mitchel v. Reynolds, 191 and referred to above in note 33.

44. Thus, as noted earlier, there cannot be a justified restraint "in gross."

45. This is in keeping with judicial rationales. See, for example, Esso Petroleum v. Harper's Garage, 23 ("Where there are no circumstances of oppression, the court should tread warily in substituting its own views for those of current commerce generally and the contracting parties in particular.") (per Lord Pearce).

46. I reach the same conclusion as Smith who rightly stresses this point.

47. The fact that parties to a contract in restraint of trade are sophisticated and knowledgeable may provide an *evidentiary* basis for a court inferring that, in the absence of cognitive errors, the restraint was properly proportioned to protect a legitimate interest. This may play a role particularly where it is difficult for a court readily to assess the relevant factors. See Smith's discussion in "Reconstructing Restraint of Trade," 585–587.

48. This is presupposed in all the leading cases and Smith rightly emphasizes this point. See "Reconstructing Restraint of Trade," 594-595.

49. See Smith's discussion of this point at 578-80.

50. Ellinghaus's characterization of these scenarios as instances of "overall imbalance" that involve substantive unconscionability is thus to the point. See M. P. Ellinghaus, "In Defense of Unconscionability," *Yale Law Journal* 78, no. 5 (1969): 777–786. There is nothing in this analysis of unfairness that precludes its application to transactions between businesses, and indeed this is done in both German and common law systems. For example, see Dawson's discussion of the US case In Re Elkins-Dell Manufacturing Co. 253 F. Supp. 864 (E.D. Pa. 1966), cited in "Unconscionable Coercion," 1088. Dawson concludes: "But for myself, I see no reason why an American court should hesitate in concluding that [the agreement in Re Elkins-Dell] is well-beyond the boundaries, a plain case of full-scale shackling—of unconscionability if a more familiar word is preferred." See also the excellent discussion of this case in Ellinghaus, "In Defense of Unconscionability," 782–784.

51. In Horwood v Millar's Timber and Trading Co. Ltd., [1917] 1 K.B. 305 (Eng. C.A.), the court similarly refused to sever oppressive provisions or to enforce the contract, which, for the purpose of securing a loan, vested near total control in the plaintiff moneylender over the defendant's productive powers, assets both personal and financial, and economic opportunities. If ever there was a shackling contract, this was it. The court held the contract void as being unduly in restraint of trade. The discussion of whether to sever is detailed and instructive. Horwood v Millar's Timber and Trading, 312–319.

52. Dunlop Pneumatic Tyre Co. Ltd. v. New Garage and Motor Co. Ltd., [1915] A.C. 79 (H.L.(E)). An earlier leading US case is Jaquith v. Hudson, 5 Mich. 123. For comparative treatments of penalty clauses in the civil law jurisdictions, see G. H. Treitel, *Remedies for Breach of Contract: A Comparative Account* (Oxford: Clarendon Press, 1988), chapter 7, and, more recently, Lucinda Miller, "Penalty Clauses in England and France: A Comparative Study," *International and Comparative Law Quarterly* 53, no. 1 (2004): 79–106.

53. See, for example, *Restatement (Second) of Contracts*, section 356 (1) and comment a.

54. This point is rightly emphasized by Seana Valentine Shiffrin in "Remedial Clauses: The Overprivatization of Private Law," *Hastings Law Journal* 67, no. 2 (2016): 407–442.

55. Elsey v. J. G. Collins Insurance Agencies Ltd., (1979) 83 D.L.R. (3d) 1, 15 (S.C.C.). See also AMEV-UDC Finance Ltd. v. Austin, (1986) 162 C.L.R. 170, 193 (H.C. Australia).

56. See, in particular, Stephen M. Waddams, "Unconscionability in Contracts," *Modern Law Review* 39 (1976): 369–393, and Stephen M. Waddams, *Principle and Policy in Contract Law: Competing or Complementary Concepts?* (Cambridge: Cambridge University Press, 2011), chapter 4. For other recent essays arguing for this approach, see Mindy Chen-Wishart, "Controlling the Power to Agree Damages," in *Wrongs and Remedies in the Twenty-First Century,* ed. Peter Birks (Oxford: Clarendon Press, 1996), 271–299, and John W. Carter and Elisabeth Peden, "A Good Faith Perspective on Liquidated Damages," *Journal of Contract Law* 23, no. 3 (2007): 165.

57. Cavendish Square Holding BV v. Talal El Makdessi and ParkingEye Ltd. v. Beavis, [2015] UKSC 67 (Eng. H.L.).

58. "[T]he issue [whether a sum is excessive] has to be determined objectively, judged at the date the contract was made." Philips Hong Kong Ltd. v. A-G of Hong Kong, (1993) 61 B.L.R. 41, 59 (per Lord Woolf).

59. Samuel Williston, *A Treatise on the Law of Contracts* (New York: Baker, Voorhis, 1922), section 777. For this reason as well, I think it is appropriate to place the principal discussion of this issue here rather than in Chapter 8, which dealt with remedies.

60. A representative leading US decision is Banta v. Stamford Motor Co., 92 A. 665, 667 (Conn. 1914), discussed in Farnsworth, *Contracts,* sections. 813–814, 817.

61. Williston, *Law of Contracts,* section 778.

62. This was inherited from equity and already settled in the leading English case of Kemble v. Farren, 6 Bing. 141 (1829), 147–148, and forcefully defended in the leading early US case of Jaquith v. Hudson. For a more recent and equally forceful judicial statement of this point, see Campbell Discount Co. Ltd. v. Bridge, [1962] A.C. 600, 622 (P.C.) (per Lord Radcliffe).

63. Here I draw upon Lord Elphinstone v. Monkland Iron & Coal Co., (1886) 11 App. Cas. 332, 346 (per Lord FitzGerald) ("In determining the character of these stipulations, we endeavor to ascertain what the parties must reasonably be presumed to have intended, having regard to the subject matter, and certain rules have been laid down as judicial aids"), as well as William F. Fritz, "'Underliquidated' Damages as Limitation of Liability," *Texas Law Review* 33, no. 2 (1954): 198.

64. This point is widely recognized, even if sometimes difficult to apply in particular circumstances. See Farnsworth, *Contracts,* section 12.18, 817. I should emphasize that even though a genuine alternative performance provision cannot count as a penalty clause, it is still subject—like all other terms—to the principle of unconscionability.

65. This view, sometimes referred to as the "look-forward rule," is widely accepted by the great majority of decisions in American, English, and Common-

wealth contract law. For a representative and emphatic judicial statement of the point that parties cannot invent new heads of damages, see Jaquith v. Hudson.

66. Philips v. Hong Kong, 59 (per Lord Woolf). See the excellent discussion of this point by Carter and Peden, "A Good Faith Perspective," 164–165. Here I should mention the contested question of whether stipulated damages that are fixed reasonably at formation should still be enforced where there is no resulting loss whatsoever. Interestingly, the *Restatement (Second) of Contracts,* section 356, comment b and illustration 4, answers that they should not. One commentator concludes that "when directly faced with the question, most American courts will not *knowingly* enforce a liquidated damages clause when there is no actual damage." Justin Sweet, "Liquidated Damages in California," *California Law Review* 60, no. 1 (1972): 139. In support of this conclusion, I suggest that unless parties, viewed objectively, specifically intend the provision to apply even in these circumstances—in other words, unless they assume this particular risk—they must reasonably but implicitly intend the stipulated damages clause to apply only if there is *some* resulting loss or injury, even if impossible to measure or establish before a court. On this analysis, in circumstances of no loss, the clause would not be per se unenforceable as a penalty but rather simply not be enforced, by reason of this tacit condition. A clause characterized as reasonable at formation and thus enforceable would not be deemed penal at a later stage.

67. The interdependence of terms is a recurrent theme in the cases. See, for example, Cavendish Square v. Talal El Makdessi, paragraph 75 (per Lord Neuberger and Lord Sumption).

68. This formulation draws on Lord Robertson's statement of the issue in Clydebank Engineering & Shipbuilding Co. Ltd. v. Don Jose Ramos Yzquierdo y Castaneda, [1905] A.C. 6 (H.L.), 20 ("The questions remains, Had the respondents no interest to protect by that clause, or was that interest palpably incommensurate with the sums agreed on?"), and on the formulations of Lords Neuberger and Sumption in Cavendish Square v. Talal El Makdessi, paragraph 23. In the latter case, the law lords correctly show in detail that this is how the issue is framed in leading decisions both past and present.

69. Dunlop Tyre v. New Garage, 86 (per Lord Dunedin). At the time of *Dunlop,* for such a breach the common law would only give the exact sum as damages—sometimes with interest, but no more. See the speech of Lord Parmoor, Dunlop Tyre v. New Garage, 101.

70. Dunlop Tyre v. New Garage, 86.

71. By contrast, on an economic approach, this preference and therefore the benefits and costs of its satisfaction, must be taken into account in any complete analysis. See, for example, Charles J. Goetz and Robert E. Scott, "Liquidated Damages, Penalties and the Just Compensation Principle: Some Notes on an Enforcement Model and a Theory of Efficient Breach," *Columbia Law Review* 77, no. 4 (1977): 562.

72. As all the leading decisions emphasize. For representative statements, see Philips v. Hong Kong, 54–55; AMEV-UDC Finance v. Austin, 193–194 (per Mason, J., and Wilson, J.); and Jaquith v. Hudson, 8. See also the excellent discussions in Fritz, "'Underliquidated' Damages," 197–200, and in "Limitations on Freedom to Modify Contract Remedies," Notes and Comments, *Yale Law Journal* 72, no. 4 (1963): 752–777.

73. Robophone Facilities Ltd. v. Blank, [1966] 1 W.L.R. 1428, 1447 (Eng. C.A.) (per Diplock, J., as he then was).

74. Uncertainty of foreseeable loss is not a necessary threshold requirement for a provision qualifying as a valid liquidated damages clause but is rather a factor to be weighed along with others in determining the provision's reasonableness. See Farnsworth, *Contracts*, section 12.18, 817.

75. Robophone v. Blank, 1447.

76. For a case involving a noncompete covenant, see Jaquith v. Hudson. For oil exploration, see the leading California case of Escondido Oil Co. v. Glaser, (1904) 144 Cal. 494, 77 Pac. 1040, and discussion in John Ballem, "Some Second Thoughts on Damages for Breach of a Drilling Commitment," *Canadian Bar Review* 48, no. 4 (1970): 698–714. For an agreement in relation to marketing or trade associations, see Dunlop Tyre v. New Garage. For undertakings affecting goodwill, see the discussion of illustrative cases in Sweet, "Liquidated Damages," 124–125, 131. Finally, for contracts with public and governmental entities, see the discussions in the leading English case of Clydebank Engineering v. Castaneda, 11–13 (per Earl of Halsbury, L.C.), and, more recently, in Philips v. Hong Kong, 60 (per Lord Woolf).

77. Dunlop Tyre v. New Garage, 92, 97 (per Lord Atkinson).

78. Hadley v. Baxendale, 9 Ex. 341 (1854). I discuss this case and its principle in detail in Chapter 8. This same approach can and should be taken with respect to intangible, and even idiosyncratic, interests in performance. This addresses one of the concerns raised by Goetz and Scott against the current penalty doctrine in "Liquidated Damages," 572 and elsewhere. I suppose here that recovery for nonpecuniary losses is in principle legally recognized and reasonable, and further that such losses are subject, like other forms of indirect loss, to the sort of analysis set out in *Hadley*.

79. Hadley v. Baxendale, 354.

80. See the instructive analysis of this point in Robophone v. Blank, 1447–1448 (per Diplock, L.J.).

81. Hadley v. Baxendale, 354.

82. For example, agreed damages for delays in building or repair contracts where both parties know in advance that timely performance is ordinarily subject to a range of risks, often beyond the control of either party, and that this can seriously affect the parties' interests. See Philips v. Hong Kong, 54. An excellent example is Hanlon Drydock & Shipbuilding Co. Inc. v. McNear Inc., 232 P. 1002 (1925) (Dist.

Ct. App. Cal.) For more illustrations, see the detailed discussion in Sweet, "Liquidated Damages," 116–123 ("Construction Contracts").

83. A clear example is Callanan Road Improvements Co. v. Colonial Sand & Stone Co. Inc., 72 N.Y.2d 194 (1947), 198–199 ("Plaintiff and defendant . . . knew the subject matter . . . [and] were dealing with a specialized field. . . . They were free to accept the future market, which they could not exactly foresee, or fix their own standard of damage").

84. Robophone v. Blank, 1447. Thus, as *Philips* makes clear, in these scenarios, courts will not mechanically apply the well-known tests to assist construction set out by Lord Dunedin in Dunlop Tyre v. New Garage, 86. This is in contrast with the approach to damages provisions where foreseeable loss is direct and involves a fixed amount—cases at the other end of the continuum.

85. On this point, see Philips v. Hong Kong, 58–59.

86. That enforceable damages must not be *in terrorem* means simply that they *must* be justified within the framework of compensation. It does not refer to a non-breaching party's motives or conduct. See, for example, Cavendish Square v. Talal El Makdessi, paragraph 31; also Williston, *Law of Contracts,* section 778.

87. This is now more widely recognized in leading decisions. See, for example, Philips v. Hong Kong, 58–59 (per Lord Woolf).

88. As argued by Melvin A. Eisenberg in "The Limits of Cognition and the Limits of Contract," *Stanford Law Review* 47, no. 2 (1995): 225–236.

89. See Cavendish Square v. Talal El Makdessi, paragraph 34.

90. I discuss compensatory justice in Chapters 7 and 8.

91. Indeed, arguably this would violate good faith. See Carter and Peden, "A Good Faith Perspective," 160–161, and Williston, *Law of Contracts,* section 777.

6. Fairness and Assent in Standard Form Contracts

1. Karl N. Llewellyn, *The Common Law Tradition: Deciding Appeals* (Boston: Little, Brown, 1960), 362–371. See also Karl N. Llewellyn, review of *The Standardization of Commercial Contracts in English and Continental Law,* by Otto Prausnitz, *Harvard Law Review* 52, no. 4 (1939): 700–705. Llewellyn also discussed this question in "The Effect of Legal Institutions on Economics," *American Economic Review* 15, no. 4 (1925): 673–675; "What Price Contract? An Essay in Perspective," *Yale Law Journal* 40, no. 5 (1931): 731–734; and "On Warranty of Quality and Society: II," *Columbia Law Review* 37, no. 3 (1937): 394–404. Perhaps Llewellyn's most important statement is the 1941 "First Draft of Revision to the Uniform Sales Act" (section on form contracts), which was an early version of the later much-changed provision on unconscionability in the Uniform Commercial Code, section 2-302. This draft is fully reproduced in Michael Meyerson, "The Reunification of Contract

Law: The Objective Theory of Consumer Form Contracts," *University of Miami Law Review* 47, no. 5 (1992): 1327–1333 (appendix).

2. For a historical account, see Otto Prausnitz, *The Standardization of Commercial Contracts in English and Continental Law* (London: Sweet & Maxwell, 1937), 8–20.

3. This is why the French jurist Raymond Saleilles coined the special term "contract of adhesion" in 1911. For Saleilles's statement in translation, see Edwin W. Patterson, "The Interpretation and Construction of Contracts," *Columbia Law Review* 64, no. 5 (1964): 856.

4. See, for example, Margaret Radin, *Boilerplate: The Fine Print, Vanishing Rights, and the Rule of Law* (Princeton, NJ: Princeton University Press, 2012), prologue and chapter 1.

5. This is emphasized particularly by writers who adopt an economic approach. See Alan Schwartz, "Seller Unequal Bargaining Power and the Judicial Process," *Indiana Law Journal* 49 (1974): 367; Lewis Kornhauser, "Unconscionability in Standard Forms," *California Law Review* 64, no. 5 (1976): 1179–1182 ; Michael J. Trebilcock, "An Economic Approach to the Doctrine of Unconscionability," in *Studies in Contract Law,* ed. Barry Reiter and John Swan (Toronto: Butterworths, 1980), 412–419; Russell Korobkin, "Bounded Rationality, Standard Form Contracts, and Unconscionability," *University of Chicago Law Review* 70, no. 4 (2003): 1253; and, more recently, Douglas G. Baird, *Reconstructing Contracts* (Cambridge, MA: Harvard University Press, 2013), chapter 8.

6. See, for example, Jason Johnston, "The Return of Bargain: An Economic Theory of How Standard-Form Contracts Enable Cooperative Negotiation between Businesses and Consumers," *Michigan Law Review* 104, no. 5 (2006): 857–889, and David Gilo and Ariel Porat, "The Hidden Roles of Boilerplate and Standard-Form Contracts: Strategic Imposition of Transaction Costs, Segmentation of Consumers, and Anticompetitive Effects," *Michigan Law Review* 104, no. 5 (2006): 983–1032.

7. See the comments on the paucity of empirical studies in Florencia Marotta-Wurgler, "What's in a Standard Form Contract? An Empirical Analysis of Software License Agreements," *Journal of Empirical Legal Studies* 4, no. 4 (2007): 677–713.

8. For discussion of legislative issues and responses, see, on English law, Hugh Beale, "Legislative Control of Fairness: The Directive on Unfair Terms in Consumer Contracts," in *Good Faith and Fault in Contract Law,* ed. Jack Beatson and Daniel Friedmann (Oxford: Clarendon Press, 1995), 231–261; see also Varda Lusthaus, "Standard Contracts in Israel: New Developments," *Rabel Journal of Comparative and International Private Law* 54, no. 3 (1990): 551–578.

9. Similarly, with respect to section 211 of the *Restatement (Second) of Contracts* (1981). See, for example, Korobkin's critical assessment, "Bounded Rationality," 1270.

10. As well, the proposed approach is found in the remarkable "Limitations on Freedom to Modify Contract Remedies," Notes and Comments, *Yale Law Journal* 72, no. 4 (1963): 735–746; M. P. Ellinghaus, "In Defense of Unconscionability," *Yale Law Journal* 78, no. 5 (1969): 795–803; John P. Dawson, "Unconscionable Coercion: The German Version," *Harvard Law Review* 89, no. 6 (1976): 1041–1126; and Meyerson, "The Reunification of Contract Law."

11. For an instructive and somewhat different account, see Todd Rakoff, "Contracts of Adhesion: An Essay in Reconstruction," *Harvard Law Review* 96, no. 6 (1983): 1176–1180. For judicial discussion, see Rudbart v. Water Supply Commission, 605 A.2d 681, 685–689 (N.J. 1992).

12. A representative statement is *Restatement (Second) of Contracts,* section 211, comment a. Llewellyn emphasized this point in all his discussions. See, for example, Llewellyn, review of *The Standardization of Commercial Contracts,* 701, and Llewellyn, *The Common Law Tradition,* 362.

13. As Llewellyn and others have pointed out, in a variety of trades and lines of business, standard terms, though not individually negotiated, are developed through mutual consultation and input from groups or associations representing both sides. Such terms tend, therefore, to be more balanced. See Llewellyn, "First Draft of Revision," 1(e), 2(c), comment A (1) and (5), and, for example, Prausnitz, *The Standardization of Commercial Contracts,* 22–24. For explicit judicial recognition of this difference, see A. Schroder Music Publishing Co. Ltd. v. Macaulay, [1974] 1 W.L.R. 1308, 1316 (H.L.) (per Lord Diplock).

14. These are Eisenberg's terms. See Melvin A. Eisenberg, "The Limits of Cognition and the Limits of Contract," *Stanford Law Review* 47, no. 2 (1995): 241.

15. See *Restatement (Second) of Contracts,* section 211 (1).

16. See *Restatement (Second) of Contracts,* section 211 (2) and comment e ("Equality of Treatment"). This aspect was emphasized by Saleilles—see Patterson, "The Interpretation"—and also in German contract law cases. See Dawson, "Unconscionable Coercion," 1110.

17. See Llewellyn, *The Common Law Tradition,* 371. To the same effect, *Restatement (Second) of Contracts,* section 211 (1) and comment b ("Assent to Unknown Terms").

18. See Llewellyn, *The Common Law Tradition,* 370. Llewellyn himself recognized that even though such terms might not be actively negotiated, at least that they would be discussed and thought about by the parties. See his "First Draft of Revision," comment A (3).

19. See Korobkin, "Bounded Rationality," 1225.

20. As expressly recognized by Llewellyn. See, for example, "First Draft of Revision," (c) and elsewhere.

21. See Rakoff's discussion of such other factors in "Contracts of Adhesion," section 3, part A.

22. See, for example, the discussion in *Restatement (Second) of Contracts,* comments a and b.

23. I agree with Barnett's analysis of this issue. See Randy Barnett, *Contracts* (Oxford: Oxford University Press, 2010), 112–114. Where I differ is with respect to Barnett's account of the limits of enforceability, discussed in *Contracts,* 114–122.

24. On this point, see the influential English "ticket" case, Parker v. South Eastern Railway Co., (1876–1877) L.R. 2 C.P.D. 416 (C.A.), to be discussed shortly.

25. On this point, see also *Restatement (Second) of Contracts,* section 211 (1), comments b and c.

26. For a discussion of the relevant case law, see John Calamari, "Duty to Read—a Changing Concept," *Fordham Law Review* 43, no. 3 (1974): 341–362.

27. See, for example, Llewellyn, "First Draft of Revision," section 1-C, (2) (a) (ii), 1328.

28. In *Restatement (Second) of Contracts,* section 211, comment b makes this point explicitly.

29. This term appears in *Restatement (Second) of Contracts,* section 211, comment b. See also comment f ("Terms Excluded").

30. Parker v. South Eastern Railway, 428 (per Bramwell, L.J.).

31. Llewellyn, *The Common Law Tradition,* 370–371. See also the explicit judicial statement in Campbell Discount Co. Ltd. v. Bridge, [1962] A.C. 600, 629 (P.C.) (per Lord Denning).

32. This analysis is found in the judicial decisions and scholarly writings of German contract law; see Dawson, "Unconscionable Coercion," 1108. It is also found in the work of French scholars; for example, Emmanuel Gounot, *Le principe de l'autonomie de la volonté en droit privé: Contribution à l'étude critique de l'individualisme juridique* (Paris: Arthur Rousseau, 1912), 227–231.

33. See *Restatement (Second) of Contracts,* section 211 (3) and comment f.

34. Tilden Rent-A-Car Co. v. Clendenning, (1978) 83 D.L.R. (3d) 400 (Ont. C.A.). For parallel US cases, see Syme v. Marks Rentals Inc., 520 A.2d 1110 (Md. Ct. Spec. App. 1987) and others cited in Meyerson, "The Reunification of Contract Law," 1302–1303.

35. Tilden Rent-A-Car Co. v. Clendenning, 402.

36. Tilden Rent-A-Car Co. v. Clendenning, 402.

37. L'Estrange v. F. Graucob Ltd., [1934] 2 K.B. 394. For US cases taking a similar view, see Meyerson, "The Reunification of Contract Law," 1271–1274.

38. See Tilden Rent-A-Car v. Clendenning, 408.

39. For helpful detailed discussions of this point, see Elizabeth Macdonald, "The Duty to Give Notice of Unusual Contract Terms," *Journal of Business Law,* 1988, 375–385, and Edwin Peel, "Whither *Contra Proferentem?,*" in *Contract Terms,* ed. Andrew Burrows and Edwin Peel (Oxford: Oxford University Press, 2007), 53–75, particularly 66–74.

40. Tilden Rent-A-Car v. Clendenning, 408.

41. As stated in Neuchatel Asphalte Co. Ltd. v. Barnett, [1957] 1 W.L.R. 356, 360 (Eng. C.A.).

42. Uniform Commercial Code, section 2-302 ("Unconscionable Contract or Clause"), official comment 1. As Leff correctly notes, in the unconscionable merchant-to-merchant transactions referred to in the Uniform Commercial Code comment to section 2-302, there is little or no evidence of unequal bargaining power, and the standard terms are relatively transparent and accessible to the complaining party. See Arthur Allen Leff, "Unconscionability and the Code—the Emperor's New Clause," *University of Pennsylvania Law Review* 115, no. 4 (1967): 502.

43. See Andrews Bros. v. Singer & Co., [1934] 1 K.B. 17 (Eng. C.A.) (business-to-business sale of new car); Meyer v. Packard Cleveland Motor Co., 140 N.E. 118 (1922) (sale of refurbished used truck advertised as equivalent to a new one); F. C. Austin Co. v. J. H. Tillman Co., 209 P. 131 (1922) (business-to-business sale of asphalt mixing plant of a given type).

44. The same analysis can apply to scenarios where a form contract includes a printed provision that directly undercuts the reasonable interpretation of a purely oral express representation. Notwithstanding the parole evidence rule, the printed terms may not be enforced in such circumstances. See the carefully reasoned leading Canadian decision on the parole evidence rule, Gallen v. Allstate Grain Co. Ltd., (1984) 9 D.L.R. (4th) 496 (B.C.C.A.).

45. The same view is taken by German civil law. See Dawson, "Unconscionable Coercion," 1103–1121, and Erike von Hippel, "The Control of Exemption Clauses: A Comparative Study," *International and Comparative Law Quarterly* 16, no. 3 (1967): 591–612.

46. Llewellyn, *The Common Law Tradition*, 370.

47. "[T]he boiler-plate is assented to en bloc, 'unsight, unseen,' on the implicit assumption and to the full extent that . . . it does not alter the fair meaning of the dickered terms when read alone." Llewellyn, *The Common Law Tradition*, 371.

48. Thus law and economics approaches generally view standardized nonsalient terms as just one more product attribute bundled with other attributes such as physical features, price, and so forth. For a noneconomic theoretical approach along these lines, see Brian Coote, *Contract as Assumption: Essays on a Theme*, ed. Rick Bigwood (Oxford: Hart Publishing, 2010), chapter 6 ("The Function of Exception Clauses").

49. Edwin Peel makes this point in relation to Coote's approach. See Peel, "Whither *Contra Proferentem?*," 69–70.

50. See Schwartz, "Seller Unequal Bargaining Power," 378.

51. Ellinghaus, "In Defense of Unconscionability," 799. See also Note, "Freedom to Modify Contract Remedies," 742.

52. Llewellyn, *The Common Law Tradition*, 370–371. See also *Restatement (Second) of Contracts*, section 211, comment e.

53. In my view, the analysis of the mandatory arbitration agreement and terms in Armendariz v. Foundation Health Psychcare, Inc., 6 P.3d 669 (Cal. 2000), especially 691–694, reflects the kind of transactional approach developed here. See also Douez v. Facebook Inc. 2017 S.C.C. 33, paragraphs 78–118 (per Abella, J.).

54. Henningsen v. Bloomfield Motors Inc., (1960) 161 A.2d 69 (S.C.N.J.).

55. For example, Fried supposes that the *Henningsen* court views the market concentration and cartelization of the auto industry as the core problem. See Charles Fried, *Contract as Promise: A Theory of Contractual Obligation*, 2nd ed. (New York: Oxford University Press, 2015), 105–108.

56. Friedrich Kessler, "Contracts of Adhesion—Some Thoughts about Freedom of Contract," *Columbia Law Review* 43, no. 5 (1943): 632, quoted in Henningsen v. Bloomfield Motors, 86.

57. Ellinghaus is in accord: "[I]nsofar as [the decision in *Henningsen*] rests on public policy, [this] must surely also be understood as something of an affirmation of the notion of transactional essence." "In Defense of Unconscionability," 798–799n193.

58. Henningsen v. Bloomfield Motors, 85.

59. Henningsen v. Bloomfield Motors, 79. For helpful accounts of the nature and history of the warranty of merchantability, see the classic article by William L. Prosser, "The Implied Warranty of Merchantable Quality," *Minnesota Law Review* 27 (1943): 117–168, and the more recent overview in Michael Phillips, "Unconscionability and Article 2 Implied Warranty Disclaimers," *Chicago-Kent Law Review* 62, no. 2 (1986): 199–267. By developing the implied warranty of merchantability, the courts ensure that parties receive not only what they contract for (under the warranty of description) but, further, its fair value (consisting of ordinary usage and exchange value). The analysis is transactional and is framed in terms of presumed intent. As famously (and bluntly) stated in Gardiner v. Gray, (1815) 4 Camp. 144, 145 (per Lord Ellenborough): "[T]he intention of both parties must be taken to be, that [the thing bought] shall be saleable in the market under the denomination mentioned in the contract between them. The purchaser cannot be supposed to buy goods to lay them on a dunghill."

60. In connection with this point, it is worth noting here that a comparable warranty limitation (with regard to auto defects) was deleted as unconscionable in Eckstein v. Cummins, (1974) 321 N.E.2d 897 (C.A. Ohio) without any reliance on or even reference to such systemic market factors. The court expressly relied upon a purely transactional analysis (e.g., "It cannot be presumed that a buyer will voluntarily and knowingly agree to pay a full and adequate consideration for a pseudo-obligation"), while citing *Henningsen* along with cases referred to in the Uniform Commercial Code, comment to 2-302. Eckstein v. Cummins, 904.

61. See Henningsen v. Bloomfield Motors, 88–93. The cases discussed or referred to include some of those cited by the Uniform Commercial Code, section 2-302, official comment 1, as reflecting the basis of its provision on unconscionability.

62. As contemplated under the Uniform Commercial Code, section 2-302 (2). See the full discussion in Zuckerman v. Transamerica Insurance Co., 650 P.2d 441, 445–448 (Ariz. 1982), and the excellent, albeit brief, discussion in Ellinghaus, "In Defense of Unconscionability," 783–785.

63. Henningsen v. Bloomfield Motors, 18. See also Henningsen v. Bloomfield Motors, 20: "But does the doctrine that a person is bound by his signed agreement, in the absence of fraud, stand in the way of any relief?"

64. I have noted at several points the *Henningsen* court's concern with the printed express warranty's effect of deleting the plaintiff's remedial rights. I propose the same basic analysis here as with the deletion of the plaintiff's implied warranty—the only difference being that in this instance the printed term affects a remedy that the law provides rather than a term that the law implies. As I elaborate more fully in Chapter 7, I suppose that all contractual rights are, as such, protected by appropriate remedies as a matter of compensatory justice. These remedies secure the transactionally contemplated fair and full value of those rights. Otherwise, the rights are illusory. Hence, standard form stipulations that, for example, limit damages or preclude ordinary modes of remedial redress (by requiring mandatory arbitration) must also be tested against the basic criterion: do these departures from what would otherwise be potentially available damages or modes of redress reflect the demonstrable particular risks and needs of the form-giver's business and such other terms as the price charged but at the same time still ensure the form-taker's reasonable remedial protection commensurate with the circumstances of the kind of transaction? In answering this question, and particularly the latter point about reasonable remedial protection, the starting baseline is always what parties are entitled to or can reasonably expect in the absence of the printed term. For a fairly recent decision that exemplifies this analysis, see Armendariz v. Foundation Health Psychcare Services, Inc.

65. Paralleling the analysis in other areas of contractual fairness such as the penalty clause and restraint of trade doctrines discussed above in Chapter 5.

66. This formulation is from the Uniform Commercial Code, section 2-313, comment 4. See also Eckstein v. Cummins, 904. Prosser makes a similar point in "The Implied Warranty," 159. There are powerful English and Commonwealth judicial statements to the same effect. See, for example, Suisse Atlantique Société d'Armement Maritime S.A. v. N.V. Rotterdamsche Kolen Centrale, [1967] 1 A.C. 361, 432 (Eng. H.L.) (per Lord Wilberforce), and B. G. Linton Construction Ltd. v. Canadian National Railway Co., [1975] 2 S.C.R. 678 (S.C.C.) (per Laskin, C.J.C.).

67. Although the *Henningsen* court does not discuss this form of embedding explicitly, it quotes a passage from a case, French v. Bekins Moving & Storage Co., 195 P.2d 970, 971–972 (1948), that does. *French* holds that where the standard form provides the form-taker with a reasonable choice between two different levels of protection at appropriately different, not "arbitrary," corresponding prices, a limitation of warranty may be upheld as a fair and reasonable departure from what

the law would otherwise have required. Quoted in Henningsen v. Bloomfield Motors, 91. For equivalent English decisions, see Smith v. Eric S. Bush, [1989] 2 All E.R. 514 (Eng. H.L.), and the earlier but particularly instructive discussion in Peek v. North Staffordshire Railway Co., [1862–1863] 10 H.L.C. 473, 513 and 530 (per Blackburn, J., and Cropton, J.). For a civil law perspective, see von Hippel, "The Control of Exemption Clauses," 611.

68. Leff, "Unconscionability and the Code," 504.

69. On the need for notice, see Hugh Beale's discussion in "Unfair Contracts in Britain and Europe," *Current Legal Problems* 42, no. 1 (1989): 205–207, and also Macdonald, "The Duty to Give Notice."

70. Llewellyn, *The Common Law Tradition*, 370.

71. Llewellyn, *The Common Law Tradition*, 368.

72. For valuable discussions, see Ellinghaus, "In Defense of Unconscionability," 796–803; Dawson, "Unconscionable Coercion," 1112–1120; and Todd Rakoff, "The Implied Terms of Contracts: Of 'Default Rules' and 'Situation-Sense,'" in *Good Faith and Fault in Contract Law,* ed. Jack Beatson and Daniel Friedmann (Oxford: Clarendon Press, 1995), 195–197. For judicial discussion, see Shell UK Ltd. v. Lostock Garage Ltd., [1976] 1 W.L.R. 1187, 1196–1197 (Eng. C.A.), and Liverpool City Council v. Irwin, [1977] A.C. 239 (Eng. H.L.). I further discuss the basis and role of transaction-types in Chapter 12.

73. See John Wightman, "Beyond Custom: Contract, Contexts, and the Recognition of Implicit Understandings," in *Implicit Dimensions of Contract: Discrete, Relational and Network Contracts,* ed. David Campbell, Hugh Collins, and John Wightman (Oxford: Hart Publishing, 2003), 143–186.

74. On this difference, see Stephen M. Waddams, *Principle and Policy in Contract Law: Competing or Complementary Concepts?* (Cambridge: Cambridge University Press, 2011), 102–106, 120–121.

75. As put by Waddams: "The substance of the transaction was that the conveyance is as a security. Therefore it was unjust that the mortgagee should get the land on default, even though this consequence was expressly agreed, when adequate compensation could be made by payment of principal, interests, and costs." Stephen M. Waddams, *The Law of Contracts,* 5th ed. (Toronto: Canada Law Book, 2005), paragraph 444.

76. From Lord Northington's statement in the often-cited equity case of Vernon v. Bethell, (1762) 2 Eden. 110,113: "This court, as a court of conscience, is very jealous of persons taking securities for a loan, and converting such securities into purchases."

77. Dawson's term, in "Unconscionable Coercion," 1112–1113 (with respect to German contract law).

78. Heffron v. Imperial Parking Co., (1974) 46 D.L.R. (3d) 642 (Ont. C.A.) (per Estey, J.).

79. Heffron v. Imperial Parking, paragraph 22.

80. Williams v. Walker-Thomas Furniture Co., 350 F.2d 445 (D.C. Cir. 1965).

81. Williams v. Walker-Thomas Furniture, 447. See Eisenberg's explanation of the provision's effect in Melvin A. Eisenberg, *Foundational Principles of Contract Law* (New York: Oxford University Press, 2018), 70, notes 7 and 524.

82. Also referred to as a "dragnet" clause. See Pride Hyundai Inc. v. Chrysler Financial Co., 369 F.3d 603, 612 (1st Cir. 2004). See also E. Allan Farnsworth, *Contracts*, 4th ed. (New York: Aspen Publishers, 2004), section 4.28.

83. Williams v. Walker-Thomas Furniture, 450. The court further suggested that in some circumstances the one-sidedness of an agreement may itself be evidence of procedural defects, as recognized in the common law doctrine of intrinsic fraud where fraud was "presumed from the grossly unfair nature of the terms of the contract" (450).

84. Williams v. Walker-Thomas Furniture, 450.

85. Williams v. Walker-Thomas Furniture, 450, quoting Uniform Commercial Code, section 2-307 (2). The court did not seem to view the procedural features of standard form contracting as per se unconscionable.

86. For an interesting law and economics analysis of the case, see Russell Korobkin, "A 'Traditional' and 'Behavioral' Law-and-Economics Analysis of *Williams v. Walker-Thomas Furniture Company*," *University of Hawaii Law Review* 26, no. 2 (2003): 441–468. More recently, Douglas G. Baird has focused on the fact that the clause gave the store access to assets that would otherwise be out of bounds and ordinarily exempt: "The cross-collateralization clause served this purpose and no other." Baird, *Reconstructing Contracts*, 138. Baird suggests that, in contrast to ordinary warranty disclaimers, such clauses should be deleted, perhaps even banned, on the basis of paternalist and societal concerns to protect the consumer and to regulate the use of state force that may compromise process or privacy values. *Reconstructing Contracts*, 140.

87. At trial, the defendant testified that this was what she in fact understood the agreements to mean. See Williams v. Walker-Thomas Furniture Co., 198 A.2d 914, 915 (D.C.C.A. 1964).

88. See, for example, Penney v. First National Bank of Boston, 433 N.E.2d 901, 905–906 (S.C. Mass. 1982).

89. Here, the impact on the purchaser was even more severe because, to the actual knowledge of the company, she was in an extremely precarious financial situation with no savings to use to feed, clothe, and support herself and her seven children. All the sales took place at purchaser's home.

90. See discussion in Korobkin, "Analysis of *Williams v. Walker-Thomas*," 467.

91. My discussion in this chapter has focused on standard form clauses in mass consumer transactions and in those between businesses that are characterized by similar one-sidedness. Without elaborating in detail, I want to indicate that the kind of transactional approach that I am proposing can also be extended to contracts between sophisticated market transactors. In keeping with the nature of this

approach, the extension takes into account the specific features and circumstances of these transactions. Thus prima facie, the appropriate analysis should be different in certain respects from that in mass consumer contracts. For instance, in contracts between sophisticated transactors with relatively equal bargaining power, the inclusion of standardized provisions ordinarily reflects an allocation, not a unilateral shifting, of risks as between two parties who can understand and appreciate their significance and consequences. Since businesspeople will ordinarily be more interested in and better informed about the consequences of nonperformance, it is more likely that the central terms (such as price) will be considered and discussed in conjunction with the terms bearing on these other matters. See the excellent judicial discussion of this point in Watford Electronics Ltd. v. Sanderson CFL Ltd., [2001] EWCA Civ 317, paragraphs 48 and 54 (per Chadwick, L.J.). But even as between such sophisticated parties, the requirements of good faith, in the sense of reasonable commercial standards of fair dealing, apply. See Pride Hyundai v. Chrysler Financial, 615–618. Moreover, even here, issues of transactional unfairness may arise where the actual literal operation of facially clear provisions—limiting warranties, remedies, and so forth—may in circumstances of a particular breach unexpectedly result in one party losing substantially the whole benefit of what was reasonably contemplated by their contract, hence subjecting the party to unfair surprise (see, e.g., Motours Ltd. v. Euroball (West Kent) Ltd., [2003] EWHC 614 (Q.B.)) even though the facially wide limitation or disclaimer is conspicuous and transparent. See also A & M Produce Co. v. FMC Corp., 135 Cal. App. 3d 473, 484–485 (C.A. Cal. 1982). This need not depend on any finding of inequality of bargaining power. See, for example, Majors v. Kalo Laboratories Inc., 407 F. Supp. 20, 23 (1975).

92. Jacob & Youngs Inc. v. Kent, 230 N.Y. 239 (1921), 891.

93. Suisse Atlantique Société d'Armement Maritime S.A. v. N.V. Rotterdamsche Kolen Centrale [1967] 1 A.C. 361, 435 (Eng. H.L.) (per Lord Wilberforce).

94. In accord with the *Restatement (Second) of Contracts* view, see section 211, comment f.

95. Llewellyn, "On Warranty of Quality," 403.

7. Fundamental Ideas

1. *Restatement (Second) of Contracts* (1981), chapter 11, introductory note.

2. For illustrations of these different views, see the collection of essays in Omri Ben-Shahar and Ariel Porat, eds., *Fault in American Contract Law* (New York: Cambridge University Press, 2010).

3. As reflected in the title of Stephen A. Smith's interesting discussion of strict liability in contract law. See Stephen A. Smith, *Contract Theory* (Oxford: Oxford

University Press, 2004), chapter 10 ("Breach of Contract: The Puzzle of Strict Liability").

4. For helpful discussion of this point, see Barry Nicholas, "Fault and Breach of Contract," in *Good Faith and Fault in Contract Law,* ed. Jack Beatson and Daniel Friedmann (Oxford: Clarendon Press, 1995), 337–355.

5. A representative judicial statement is Samuels v. Davis, [1943] 1 K.B. 526, 230 (per du Parcq, L.J.). For a comparative law treatment, see G. H. Treitel, *Remedies for Breach of Contract: A Comparative Account* (Oxford: Clarendon Press, 1988).

6. Treitel, *Remedies for Breach,* 13–20.

7. "[T]he agreement to sell and supply goods for a price which may be assumed to represent their value is a contract of a different nature from a contract to carry, and has essentially different incidents attaching to it." Readhead v. Midland Railway Co., (1868–1869) L.R. 4 Q.B. 379, 386 (per Montague Smith, J.). The whole discussion in the *Readhead* case, particularly at pages 392–393, is very instructive. For a modern and similarly transactional analysis, see Liverpool City Council v. Irwin, [1977] A.C. 239 (Eng. H.L.).

8. It follows that the meaning of contractual liability being strict should not be assumed to be the same as that in so-called strict liability accidental torts, as in Rylands v. Fletcher, (1868) L.R. 3 H.L. 330 (Eng. H.L.). In the latter, "strict liability" refers to the level or intensity of obligation owed and parallels the question in contract of what level of obligation a particular contractual transaction imports.

9. This same point also applies to the role of reasonable foreseeability in determining liability for consequential loss under the principle in Hadley v. Baxendale, 9 Ex. 341 (1854). Discussed in Chapter 8.

10. Chapter 11, introductory note.

11. As Lord Edmund Davies states in Rainieri v. Miles [1981] AC 1050, 1086: "It is axiomatic that, in relation to a claim for damages for breach of contract, it is, in general, immaterial why the defendant failed to fulfill his obligations, and certainly no defence to plead that he has done his best."

12. As I explain in Chapter 8, the same point applies to the contractual requirement of reasonable foreseeability for recovery of consequential loss: it is always part and parcel of a determination of what the defendant owes the other party as part of the latter's protected interest in performance.

13. Fuller and Perdue note this parallel but, for their own reasons, do not pursue it. See Lon L. Fuller and William F. Perdue Jr., "The Reliance Interest in Contract Damages: 1," *Yale Law Journal* 46, no. 1 (1936): 59.

14. Kuwait Airways Corp. v. Iraqi Airways Co. and others (Nos. 4 and 5), [2002] 2 A.C. 883, 1092 (per Lord Nicholls). For helpful discussions of conversion, see Michael G. Bridge, *Personal Property Law,* 3rd ed. (Oxford: Oxford University Press, 2002), 52–79 (English law); Ben McFarlane, *The Structure of Property Law* (Oxford: Hart Publishing, 2008), 142–143, 194–204 (English law); and William L. Prosser,

"The Nature of Conversion," *Cornell Law Quarterly* 42, no. 2 (1957): 168–184 (US law). Leading judicial formulations include Fouldes v. Willoughby, 8 M. & W. 540 (1841); Francis Hollins v. George Fowler, (1875) L.R. 7 H.L. 757; Lancashire and Yorkshire Railway Co. v. MacNicoll, [1918–1919] All E.R. Rep. 537; and Kuwait Airways v. Iraqi Airways.

15. Caxton Publishing Co. Ltd. v. Sutherland Publishing Co., [1939] A.C. 178, 201 (H.L.) (per Lord Porter).

16. Cooper v. Chitty, (1756) 1 Burr. 20, 33.

17. This is the term used by Lord Nicholls in Kuwait Airways v. Iraqi Airways, 1090. Such basic loss may include the costs of retrieving or repairing the converted item.

18. If prior to judgment the defendant tenders the goods to the plaintiff and the latter accepts them, nominal damages can still be awarded for the conversion even where there is no further loss. See Bridge, *Personal Property Law*, 73.

19. See Prosser, "The Nature of Conversion," 170–171.

20. Kuwait Airways v. Iraqi Airways, 1106 (per Lord Hoffmann).

21. Even though the wrong of negligence consists not in an interference with possession but just with use or value, it is a legal injury only if it impairs the use or value of something in which the plaintiff has a possessory or proprietary right—and one that is superior to the defendant's. The requirement that the plaintiff has superior title to the damaged item is a prerequisite of the defendant owing the plaintiff a duty of care with respect to the item in the first place and has nothing to do with the determination of whether the defendant has acted negligently. Rather, it is necessary if the failure to use reasonable care is to count as a wrong sounding in misfeasance. Thus the fact that the defendant mistakenly but reasonably may have thought the thing belongs to himself is irrelevant. McFarlane makes this point in *The Structure of Property Law*, 196n263.

22. See Marzetti v. Williams, (1830) 1 B. & Ad. 415, 426 (per Taunton, J.), which expressly notes the parallel availability of nominal damages for both trespass and breach of contract.

23. I briefly addressed the possible meaning and relevance of willful breach in Chapter 3, note 46.

24. See my earlier discussion in Chapter 1.

25. For thorough discussion of the doctrine in US law and scholarship, see Keith A. Rowley, "A Brief History of Anticipatory Repudiation in American Contract Law," *University of Cincinnati Law Review* 69, no. 2 (2001): 565–639. For Anglo-Commonwealth law, see J. C. Smith, "Anticipatory Breach of Contract," in *Contemporary Issues in Commercial Law: Essays in Honour of Professor A. G. Guest*, ed. Eva Z. Lomnicka and Christopher George John Morse (London: Sweet & Maxwell, 1997), 175–193, and Francis Dawson, "Metaphors and Anticipatory Breach of Contract," *Cambridge Law Journal* 40, no. 1 (1981): 83–107.

26. Hochster v. De La Tour, (1853) 2 El. & Bl. 678, 689. A similar conception of the contractual relation underlies civil law. See James C. Gulotta, "Anticipatory Breach—a Comparative Analysis," *Tulane Law Review* 50, no. 4 (1976): 941.

27. Frost v. Knight, (1872) L.R. 7 Ex. 111, 114 (per Cockburn, C.J.).

28. "[U]ntil the moment when a refusal to perform is a wrong, the promisee has a right to expect that when the time comes a wrong will not be done." P. P. Emory Manufacturing v. Columbia Smelting & Refining Works, 60 N.E. 377 (Mass. 1901), 378 (per Holmes, J.).

29. See Uniform Commercial Code, section 2-609, official comment 1. A particularly lucid formulation is in Equitable Trust Co. of New York v. Western Pacific Railway Co., (1917) 244 Fed. Rep. 485, 502 (per Learned Hand, J.): "[The] basis in principle is that a promise to perform in the future by implication includes an engagement not deliberately to compromise the probability of performance. A promise is a verbal act designed as a reliance to the promisee, and so as a means to the forecast of his own conduct. Abstention from any deliberate act before the time of performance which makes impossible that reliance and forecast ought surely to be included by implication. Such intermediate uncertainties as arise from the vicissitudes of the promisor's affairs are, of course, a part of the risk, but it is hard to see how, except by mere verbalism, it can be supposed that the promisor may within the terms of his undertaking gratuitously add to these uncertainties by announcing his purpose to default." A similar analysis is found in civil law. See Gulotta, "Anticipatory Breach," 941–943.

30. That the promisee must be given an option either to sue immediately or to await the date of performance ensures that the promisor's unilateral action cannot compel the promisee to do anything that she would not otherwise have had to do absent the repudiation, even if choosing to await the performance date instead of suing immediately results in greater actionable losses recoverable against the promisor. If the promisee exercises this option to ignore the repudiation, the mitigation principle cannot apply during the preperformance period. US law is divided on this analysis, but the majority view seems to be in support of the promisee's option. See Robert E. Scott, "In (Partial) Defense of Strict Liability in Contract," in *Fault in American Contract Law*, ed. Omri Ben-Shahar and Ariel Porat (New York: Cambridge University Press, 2010), 27. English law solidly upholds the promisee's choice. See G. H. Treitel, *The Law of Contract*, 14th ed., ed. Edwin Peel (London: Sweet & Maxwell, 2015), 20-068. For a vigorous defense, see Tredegar Iron and Coal Co. v. Hawthorn Bros. and Co., (1902) 18 T.L.R. 716 (Eng. C.A.).

31. Against the doctrine in *Hochster*, Williston argued that the only consequence of anticipatory repudiation should be the innocent party's excused nonperformance, not a power to sue for breach. See Samuel Williston, "Repudiation of Contracts," *Harvard Law Review* 14, no. 6 (1901): 432.

32. "Axiomatic" is the language used by Lord Nicholls in A-G v. Blake, [2000] 3 W.L.R. 625, 635 (H.L.). I discuss the nature of specific performance and its relation to damages in Chapter 8.

33. For helpful leading judicial statements, see Livingstone v. Rawyards Coal Co., (1880) 5 App. Cas. 25 (Eng. H.L.), 34–37 (per Lord Hatherley) and 39–43 (per Lord Blackburn); Watson, Laidlaw & Co. v. Pott, Cassels & Williamson, 1914 S.C. (H.L.) 18, 29–32 (per Lord Shaw); Radford v. De Froberville, [1977] 1 W.L.R. 1262 (Ch.D.) at 1268 (per Oliver, J., as he then was); A-G v. Blake, 632–640 (per Lord Nicholls); and Alfred McAlpine Construction Ltd. v. Panatown Ltd., [2001] 1 A.C. 518 (Eng. H.L.). Thomas Aquinas's account of this matter, though simply stated and centuries old, remains exceptionally clear and illuminating. See Thomas Aquinas, *Summa Theologica*, trans. Fathers of the English Dominican Province (New York: Benziger Bros., 1948), part 2-2, question 62 ("Of Restitution"). See also Ernest Weinrib's very instructive treatment in Ernest J. Weinrib, *Corrective Justice* (Oxford: Oxford University Press, 2012), chapter 3. On this topic in German civil law, see the valuable comments by Reinhard Zimmermann, *The Law of Obligations: Roman Foundations of the Civilian Tradition* (New York: Oxford University Press, 1996), 824–825.

34. See The Argentino, (1888) 13 P.D. 191, 200 (Eng. C.A.), where Lord Justice Bowen states, "Speaking generally as to all wrongful acts whatever arising out of tort or breach of contract, the English law only adopts the principle of restitutio in integrum." The term "asset" is widely adopted in the case law. See, for example, McAlpine Construction v. Panatown, 534 (per Lord Clyde). For purposes of this discussion, "asset" includes not only physical objects but also one's body, services and anything from which one can exclude others as being under one's own exclusive rightful control.

35. I discuss this idea in detail and try to show how it animates different parts of private law, in Peter Benson, "Misfeasance as an Organizing Normative Idea in Private Law," *University of Toronto Law Journal* 60, no. 3 (2010): 731–798.

36. For a representative judicial statement, see Watson v. Pott, 32 (per Lord Shaw) ("[T]he cardinal question which always remains to be answered . . . : 'What would have been the condition of the plaintiff if the defendants had acted properly instead of improperly. That condition if it can be ascertained will . . . be the proper measure of the plaintiff's *loss*'" [emphasis added]).

37. On this point about the relation between remedy and pre-wrong position, see Thomas Aquinas, *Summa Theologica*, question 62, article 1, answer and reply, objection 2.

38. See the clear analysis of Justice Windeyer in Coulls v. Bagot's Executor & Trustee Co. Ltd., (1966–1967) 119 C.L.R. 460, 504 (H.C. Australia).

39. As the Supreme Court of Canada correctly emphasized in Fidler v. Sun Life Assurance Co. of Canada, [2006] 2 S.C.R. 3, paragraph 44: "[In assessing compen-

satory damages for breach of contract] the court should ask 'what did the contract promise?' and provide compensation for those promises."

40. Williams Bros. v. Ed. T. Agius Ltd., [1914] A.C. 510, 531 (Eng. H.L.) (per Lord Moulton).

41. "A breach of contract may cause a loss, but is not in itself a loss in any meaningful sense. When one refers to a loss in the context of a breach of contract, one is in my view referring to the incidence of some personal or patrimonial damage." McAlpine Construction v. Panatown, 534 (per Lord Clyde).

42. McAlpine Construction v. Panatown, 534 (per Lord Clyde). This understanding of the relation between right, injury and remedy is what Weinrib refers to as the "continuity thesis", which he presents and defends in *Corrective Justice*, 92–93.

43. See Marzetti v. Williams, 846 (per Taunton, J.) There can also be loss without injury (*damnum sine injuria*), in which case the "loss" is not the materialization of any injury to the plaintiff's rights (e.g., in all instances of nonfeasance). This distinction between injury and loss largely aligns with that between normative and material conceptions of gain and loss drawn by Weinrib in Ernest J. Weinrib, "The Gains and Losses in Corrective Justice," *Duke Law Journal* 44 (1994): 277, 282–284.

44. Nonstandard situations include threatened wrongs possibly subject to injunctions *quia timet*. Even here, legal intervention should be viewed as a coercive response to a (threatened) violation of rights, hence to a civil wrong consisting in unexcused nonperformance.

45. See Coulls v. Bagot's Executor, 504 (per Windeyer, J.). Stephen A. Smith makes a similar point in his "Remedies for Breach of Contract: One Principle or Two?," in *Philosophical Foundations of Contract Law*, ed. Gregory Klass, George Letsas, and Prince Saprai (Oxford: Oxford University Press, 2014), chapter 17, 348–354, and in "Duties, Liabilities, Damages," *Harvard Law Review* 125, no. 7 (2012): 174–179.

46. Craswell sets out clearly the most important differences between economic theory and compensatory approaches, including the complete irrelevance to economic analysis of the ideas of compensation and ownership that are so central in the legal point of view and the transactional conception elaborated here. See Richard Craswell, "Instrumental Theories of Compensation: A Survey," *San Diego Law Review* 40, no. 4 (2003): 1135–1180.

47. As is necessarily done by the different versions of efficient breach. See the valuable discussions of efficient breach in Richard Craswell, "Two Economic Theories of Enforcing Promises," in *The Theory of Contract Law: New Essays*, ed. Peter Benson (New York: Cambridge University Press, 2001), 19–44, and Craswell, "Instrumental Theories of Compensation."

48. "Decoupling" is Craswell's term in "Instrumental Theories of Compensation."

49. This is a standard assumption of economic theories. See, for example, Richard Craswell, "Contract Remedies, Renegotiation, and the Theory of Efficient Breach," *Southern California Law Review* 61, no. 3 (1988): 636. For noneconomic or pluralist approaches that take this view, see Charlie Webb, "Justifying Damages," in *Exploring Contract Law,* ed. Jason W. Neyers, Richard Bronaugh, and Stephen G. A. Pitel (Oxford: Hart Publishing, 2009), 157–165, and Melvin A. Eisenberg and Robert Cooter, "Damages for Breach of Contract," *California Law Review* 73, no. 5 (1985): 1435–1438.

50. For examples, see Hawkins v. McGee, 146 A. 641 (1929) (medical procedure); Fidler v. Sun Life Assurance (insurance contract); and Jarvis v. Swan Tours Ltd., [1973] Q.B. 233 (C.A.) (vacation package).

51. As I explain in Chapter 8, ordinarily such emotional loss is best understood as consequential loss recoverable under the principle in *Hadley v. Baxendale*.

52. Guido Calabresi and A. Douglas Melamed, "Property Rules, Liability Rules, and Inalienability: One View of the Cathedral," *Harvard Law Review* 85, no. 6 (1972): 1089–1128. For an excellent, though critical, discussion of this view, see Weinrib, *Corrective Justice*, 98–107.

53. For discussion of this issue, see Melvin A. Eisenberg and Brett H. McDonnell, "Expectation Damages and the Theory of Overreliance," *Hastings Law Journal* 54, no. 5 (2003): 1335–1374. Keep in mind that throughout we are supposing a framework of contract-based liability, not reliance. I am also assuming here that the defendant has not done anything that constitutes a breach of contract or an anticipatory repudiation that the innocent party "accepts." As I discuss in Chapter 8, in the latter circumstances, the principle of mitigation requires the innocent party to treat nonperformance as certain (not merely probable) and to act reasonably in light of this.

54. As, for example, Craswell expressly argues. See my discussion in Chapter 9.

55. See, for example, Alan Schwartz, "The Case for Specific Performance," *Yale Law Journal* 89, no. 2 (1979): 271–306, and, more recently, Gregory Klass, "Efficient Breach," in *Philosophical Foundations of Contract Law,* ed. Gregory Klass, George Letsas, and Prince Saprai (Oxford: Oxford University Press, 2014), 383–386. I discuss the choice between specific performance and damages in Chapter 8, where I argue that both fit within the legally mandatory framework of compensatory justice and reflect the fundamental ideas discussed here.

8. Unity and Diversity in the Law of Contract Remedies

1. See Lon L. Fuller and William F. Perdue Jr., "The Reliance Interest in Contract Damages: 1," *Yale Law Journal* 46, no. 1 (1936): 52–96, and "The Reliance Interest in Contract Damages: 2," *Yale Law Journal* 46, no. 3 (1937): 373–420. See *Restatement (Second) of Contracts* (1981), chapter 16.

2. Fuller and Perdue, "The Reliance Interest: 2," 396.
3. Fuller and Perdue, "The Reliance Interest: 1," 53–54.
4. Fuller and Perdue, "The Reliance Interest: 1," 56.
5. Hence, as Craswell argues, there is nothing in the Fuller and Perdue account that singles out, privileges, or requires just these three interests. It all depends on the postulated purpose or set of purposes that the law (according to the theorist) ought to adopt. For further discussion, see Richard Craswell, "Against Fuller and Perdue," *University of Chicago Law Review* 67, no. 1 (2000): 99.
6. See E. Allan Farnsworth, "Legal Remedies for Breach of Contract," *Columbia Law Review* 70, no. 7 (1970): 1145–1216.
7. See G. H. Treitel, *Remedies for Breach of Contract: A Comparative Account* (Oxford: Clarendon Press, 1988), chapter 3, 47–74. Zimmermann contrasts modern legal systems with classical Roman law, which restricted remedies to monetary awards. See Reinhard Zimmermann, *The Law of Obligations: Roman Foundations of the Civilian Tradition* (New York: Oxford University Press, 1996), 825. In the following discussion, I suppose the standard meaning of specific performance that refers to the enforcement in specie of a contractual obligation, where there has been an actual breach or at least a threatened breach. Specific performance thus represents a remedial response to threatened or actual wrong. See Andrew Burrows, *Remedies for Torts and Breach of Contract*, 3rd ed. (New York: Oxford University Press, 2004), 544–545, and *Restatement (Second) of Contracts*, section 357. Specific performance also has a more narrow meaning that refers not to a remedy for breach but to the equitable jurisdiction to compel "execution in specie of a contract that requires some definite thing to be done in order that the legal rights of the parties be settled and defined in the manner intended." I. C. F. Spry, *The Principles of Equitable Remedies: Specific Performance, Injunctions, Rectification and Equitable Damages*, 6th ed. (Pyrmont, NSW: Lawbook Company, 2001), 51. This does not come within the scope of the present chapter.
8. See Anthony Kronman, "Specific Performance," *University of Chicago Law Review* 45, no. 2 (1978): 354.
9. "Equity will grant specific performance when damages are inadequate to meet the justice of the case." Beswick v. Beswick, [1968] A.C. 58, 102 (per Lord Upjohn). See also *Restatement of the Law of Contracts* (1932), section 358, and *Restatement (Second) of Contracts*, section 359. Also see Edward Yorio, *Contract Enforcement: Specific Performance and Injunctions* (Boston: Little, Brown, 1989), chapter 2, 27 ("[T]he adequacy doctrine remains the linchpin of the rules governing specific performance in American law").
10. For representative English cases, see Harnett v. Yielding, (1805) 2 Sch. & Lef. 549, 553; Alley v. Deschamps, 13 Ves. Jun. 226, 228 (1806); Adderley v. Dixon, 1 Sim. & St. 606, 610 (1824); and Falcke v. Gray, (1859) 4 Drewry 651, 657–658. For US cases, see Fleischer v. James Drug Stores Inc., 62 A.2d 383, 387–388 (1948) and Laclede Gas Co. v. Amoco Oil Co., 522 F.2d 33, 39–40 (1975) (8th Cir. U.S. C.A.).

Both Restatements presuppose this analysis: *Restatement of the Law of Contracts*, section 361, comments f and g; *Restatement (Second) of Contracts*, section 360, comment c.

11. See Williams Bros. v. Ed. T. Agius Ltd., [1914] A.C. 510, 531 (Eng. H.L.).

12. A classic example of something inherently unique is the two china vases—"articles of unusual beauty, rarity and distinction"—in Falcke v. Gray, 658. For goods that become circumstantially unique, see the long-term supply contracts in Sky Petroleum Ltd. v. V.I.P. Petroleum Ltd., [1974] 1 All E.R. 954 (Ch.) (English), and in Laclede Gas v. Amoco Oil, 40, and Eastern Airlines Inc. v. Gulf Oil Corp., 415 F. Supp. 429, 442–443 (1975) (S.D. Fla.).

13. Some examples include the choice between cost of completion versus diminution in value damages, promisee damages for a performance intended to benefit a third party, and gain-based damages. Apart from the gain-based damages that I briefly consider in the endnotes, I cannot explore the other issues within the limits of the present work.

14. Both Charlie Webb and Stephen Smith acknowledge this point, although they reject the implications that I draw from it. See Charlie Webb, "Justifying Damages," in *Exploring Contract Law,* ed. Jason W. Neyers, Richard Bronaugh, and Stephen G. A. Pitel (Oxford: Hart Publishing, 2009), 143n10, and Stephen A. Smith, "Substitutionary Damages," in *Justifying Private Law Remedies,* ed. Charles Rickett (Oxford: Hart Publishing, 2008), 107.

15. This possibility of assigning a pecuniary value to almost anything is noted in Falcke v. Gray, 658–659, 664–665. Difficulties in assigning value may be mitigated by the court employing certain presumptions either in favor of the plaintiff or against the defendant, depending upon the particulars of a contract or its breach. For an economic perspective on this issue, see Kronman, "Specific Performance," 358–359.

16. See the Uniform Commercial Code, section 1-305 (a). Both the First and Second Restatements take this to be axiomatic.

17. Harnett v. Yielding, 553. See the US case Laclede Gas v. Amoco Oil, 40 ("And a remedy at law adequate to defeat the grant of specific performance 'must be as certain, prompt, complete, and efficient to attain the ends of justice as a decree of specific performance'" [citation omitted]). This is a major theme in Ralph Cunnington, "The Inadequacy of Damages as a Remedy for Breach of Contract," in *Justifying Private Law Remedies,* ed. Charles Rickett (Oxford: Hart Publishing, 2008), 115–145.

18. This "liberalized" tendency is noted and affirmed by the Uniform Commercial Code, section 2-716, comment 1, and by *Restatement (Second) of Contracts,* chapter 16, topic 3, introductory note, and section 359, comment a.

19. "So a Court of Equity will not, generally, decree performance of a contract for the sale of stock or goods because . . . damages at law, calculated upon the market price of the stock or goods, are as complete a remedy as the delivery of the stock or

goods contracted for; inasmuch as, with the damages, he may purchase the same quantity of the like stock or goods." Adderley v. Dixon, 610. Similarly stated in Falcke v. Gray, 658.

20. As standardly assumed by economic theories. For a noneconomic theory taking this view, see Melvin A. Eisenberg, "Actual and Virtual Specific Performance, the Theory of Efficient Breach, and the Indifference Principle in Contract Law," *California Law Review* 93, no. 4 (2005): 975–1050.

21. Treitel, *Remedies for Breach,* 43–46. Note also that the *Restatement (Second) of Contracts* classifies remedies into the two basic categories as "enforcement by award of damages" and "enforcement by specific performance and injunction" (chapter 16, topics 2 and 3).

22. Alley v. Deschamps, 228.

23. As suggested by Richard Brooks in his thoughtful piece "The Efficient Performance Hypothesis," *Yale Law Journal* 116, no. 3 (2006): 568–596; see in particular 587–596.

24. Specific performance may be against public policy where, for instance, the contract stipulates a positive covenant of personal service.

25. See, for example, Caspar Rose and Henrik Lando, "On the Enforcement of Specific Performance in Civil Law Countries," *International Review of Law and Economics* 24, no. 4 (2004): 473–487, and, more generally, Solene Rowan, *Remedies for Breach of Contract: A Comparative Analysis of the Protection of Performance* (Oxford: Oxford University Press, 2012).

26. Epstein v. Gluckin, (1922) 135 N.E. 861, 862.

27. Dori Kimel argues along similar lines in *From Promise to Contract: Towards a Liberal Theory of Contract* (Oxford: Hart Publishing, 2003), 100–109. Note that the proposed analysis does not depend on the institutional fact that in common law jurisdictions, specific performance is backed by the more severe sanction of contempt of court for noncompliance. Of course, this fact only reinforces the argument.

28. For an example of a possible exception, see Walgreen Co. v. Sara Creek Property Co., B.V., 966 F.2d 273 (7th Cir. 1992).

29. Great Lakes & St. Lawrence Transportation Co. et al. v. Scranton Coal Co., (1917) 239 Fed. Rep. 603 (7th Cir. C.A.).

30. Representative and particularly instructive English cases on hardship include City of London v. Nash, (1747) 1 Ves. Sen. 13; Wedgwood v. Adams, (1843) 6 Beav. 600, 605; Webb v. Direct London and Portsmouth Railway Co., (1852) 1 De G. M. & G. 521, 528–530; Patel v. Ali, [1984] 1 Ch. 283, 286–289; and Jaggard v. Sawyer, (1995) 1 W.L.R. 269, 283 and 288–289. For scholarly discussions, see Spry, *The Principles,* 185–201, and Yorio, *Contract Enforcement,* 105–112.

31. See, for example, Patel v. Ali, 288 ("[The defendant] in a sense ... can say she is being asked to do what she never bargained for.... [S]he can fairly assert that specific performance would inflict upon her 'a hardship amounting to injustice.' ...

Equitable relief may . . . be refused because of an unforeseen change of circumstances not amounting to legal frustration"). In *Patel,* the court declined to order specific performance because it would have seriously affected the defendant's health, among other basic interests.

32. An excellent statement of this view in the context of nuisance law is Shelfer v. City of London Electric Lighting Co., [1895] 1 Ch. 287, 322–323 (Eng. C.A.) (per A. L. Smith, L.J.).

33. See Jaggard v. Sawyer, 283 ("It is important to bear in mind that the test is one of oppression, and the court should not slide into application of a general balance of convenience test").

34. In Anglo-Commonwealth law, this is done under a jurisdiction that originated with the Chancery Amendment Act 1858 ("Lord Cairns's Act") to award damages in substitution for or in addition to orders in specie, whether injunctions or specific performance. See further J. A. Jolowicz, "Damages in Equity—a Study of Lord Cairns's Act," *Cambridge Law Journal* 34, no. 2 (1975): 224–252.

35. This distinction between the two kinds of damages is reflected in judicial analysis. See, for example, Watson, Laidlaw & Co. v. Pott, Cassels & Williamson, 1914 S.C. 18, 30–31 (H.L.) (distinction between restoration "to the status quo ante in fact" and restoration by "compensation," where the first is difficult or impossible). It seems to parallel the distinction between forms of compensation drawn by German civil law in Bürgerliches Gesetzbuch, sections 249 and 250 (1). See Zimmermann, *The Law of Obligations,* 825–826. Finally, Hegel clearly draws this contrast. See G. W. F. Hegel, *Philosophy of Right,* trans. T. M. Knox (Oxford: Oxford University Press, 1952), paragraph 94.

36. In the following sections, I will suggest that both gain-based and reliance damages may be justified as legitimate contractual measures of recovery insofar as they effectuate compensation for lost performance value. Almost always, damages for consequential loss, including intangible loss, do so as well. Examples of measures based on conjecture and estimate include the awards in the well-known English cases of Chaplin v. Hicks, [1911] 2 K.B. 493 (C.A.); Anglia Television v. Reed, [1972] 1 Q.B. 60 (C.A.); and Jarvis v. Swan Tours Ltd., [1973] Q.B. 233 (C.A.).

37. See, for example, Fuller and Perdue, "The Reliance Interest: 1," 84–88, and Melvin A. Eisenberg, "The Principle of *Hadley v. Baxendale,*" *California Law Review* 80, no. 3 (1992): 568.

38. As in the leading English case of Jarvis v. Swan Tours.

39. See, for example, Parsons (H.) (Livestock) Ltd. v. Uttley Ingham & Co. Ltd., [1978] 1 All E.R. 525 (C.A.) (plaintiff farmer's valuable pig herd decimated by disease from ingesting nuts made moldy by food hopper improperly installed by defendant manufacturer-vendor).

40. See, for example, Mindy Chen-Wishart, "A Bird in the Hand: Consideration and Contract Modifications," in *Contract Formation and Parties,* ed. Andrew Burrows and Edwin Peel (New York: Oxford University Press, 2010), 94.

41. Robert Pothier, *A Treatise on the Law of Obligations, or Contracts,* volume 1, trans. William David Evans (Philadelphia: Robert H. Small, 1839), number 161, 71.

42. Hadley v. Baxendale, (1854) 9 Exch. 341, 354.

43. Treitel, *Remedies for Breach,* 84. Treitel argues that this is true of both common law and civilian systems.

44. Adam Kramer, "An Agreement-Centred Approach to Remoteness and Contract Damages," in *Comparative Remedies for Breach of Contract,* ed. Nili Cohen and Ewan McKendrick (Oxford: Hart Publishing, 2005), 249–286 and in particular 259–262.

45. For a recent and exceptionally illuminating judicial statement of this view, see the speech of Lord Hoffmann in Transfield Shipping Inc. v. Mercator Shipping Inc. ("The Achilleas"), [2009] 1 A.C. 61, 69 (Eng. H.L.): "It must be in principle wrong to hold someone liable for risks for which the people entering into such a contract in their particular market would not reasonably be considered to have undertaken." This same view is clearly supposed by Cardozo's brilliant analysis of remoteness in Kerr Steamship Co. v. RCA, (1927) 157 N.E. 140 (C.A. N.Y.).

46. Kramer also emphasizes this point. See Kramer, "An Agreement-Centred Approach," 256–258. See also Farnsworth, "Legal Remedies," 1209.

47. Hadley v. Baxendale, 356.

48. Samuel Williston, *A Treatise on the Law of Contracts* (New York: Baker, Voorhis, 1922), section 1357 ("Basis of the Rule in *Hadley v. Baxendale*").

49. This crucial point is explicitly underlined by Lord Hoffmann in The Achilleas, paragraphs 14–15.

50. Hadley v. Baxendale, 356.

51. Hadley v. Baxendale, 356.

52. Hadley v. Baxendale, 356.

53. As does the court in the well-known case of Victoria Laundry (Windsor) Ltd. v. Newman Industries Ltd., [1949] 2 K.B. 528 (Eng. C.A.).

54. This problem has been recognized and noted in a number of judicial opinions. See Kerr v. RCA; Banque Bruxelles Lambert S.A. v. Eagle Star Insurance Co. Ltd. [1997] A.C. 191, 211; South Australia Asset Management Corp. v. York Montague Ltd., [1997] A.C. 191, 211; and Jackson v. Royal Bank of Scotland plc, [2005] UKHL 3, paragraph 46.

55. Lord Hoffmann, "The *Achilleas:* Custom and Practice or Foreseeability," *Edinburgh Law Review* 14, no. 1 (2010): 53.

56. The Achilleas, paragraphs 15, 16 (per Lord Hoffmann).

57. This is the approach taken in The Achilleas, paragraphs 22–26. Lord Hoffmann's analysis is outstandingly clear and cogent and is surely among the most compelling—if not *the* most compelling—of contemporary judgments in any common law jurisdiction.

58. South Australia Asset Management v. York Montague, 212 (per Lord Hoffmann).

59. Another example is the transaction in Kerr v. RCA.

60. For examples, see Victoria Laundry v. Newman and Parsons v. Uttley Ingham.

61. This point is emphasized by Chief Judge Cardozo in Kerr v. RCA, 141–142. Cardozo concludes, correctly in my view, that in these circumstances—where a general description would entail an assumption of responsibility for indeterminate interests and an unquantifiable, open-ended liability—the notion of "ordinary," "natural," or "general" loss has no meaning or application ("There is a contradictio in adjecto when we speak of the general damage appropriate to an indeterminate transaction" [Kerr v. RCA, 142]). This focus on the specter of indeterminate liability is also crucial to Cardozo's treatment of the duty of care in negligent misrepresentation cases. See Ultramares v. Touche, 174 N.E. 441, 444 (C.A. N.Y. 1931). But note that in both instances, Cardozo's reasoning is not policy-driven but reflects his view about the kind of presumed intent that can reasonably be imputed to parties in the circumstances of their interaction. It is a completely transactional analysis.

62. The Achilleas, 68 (per Lord Hoffman). See also Lord Hoffmann, "The *Achilleas*: Custom and Practice," 57–58, and Andrew Robertson, "The Basis of the Remoteness Rule in Contract," *Legal Studies* 28, no. 2 (2008): 183.

63. Hadley v. Baxendale, 355.

64. Victoria Laundry v. Newman, 541.

65. For an even more striking example, see the analysis of liability in Parsons v. Uttley Ingham, 111–113, holding that the consequential loss was ordinary and recoverable under the rule in *Hadley*. There the loss consisted in the destruction of the plaintiff's pig herd from bacterial disease caused by moldy food nuts that resulted from the defendant's faulty installation of a feed hopper. The majority found that neither party could have foreseen this particular sequence of events. Nevertheless, it described the relevant type of loss in very general terms ("physical injury" of some kind) that abstracted entirely from the admittedly unforeseeable more specific circumstances. The transaction was a highly individualized contract of sale.

66. See, for example, Eisenberg, "The Principle of *Hadley v. Baxendale*," 567, 577.

67. As emphasized by Lord Hoffman, "The *Achilleas*: Custom and Practice," 57–58: "The distinction lies not in the degree of probability of damage occurring but in the difference in the commercial relationship between the parties. It is this which determines the nature of the duty to compensate which each would reasonably be regarded as having undertaken."

68. A striking illustration is the determination of liability in *The Achilleas*, at least as analyzed by Lords Hoffmann and Hope.

69. I draw on Lord Reid's remarks in Koufos v. C. Czarnikow Ltd. [Heron II], [1969] A.C. 350, 385–386 (Eng. H.L.), and on those of Lord Hope in The Achilleas, 73.

70. Where, as in situations of invited reliance on representations or other conduct, the relation in tort is established through a mutually voluntary (though noncontractual) interaction, analysis of liability in terms of assumption of responsibility may certainly apply and there can be other parallels with the account of remoteness in contract. For further discussion, see John Cartwright, "Remoteness of Damage in Contract and Tort: A Reconsideration," *Cambridge Law Journal* 55, no. 3 (1996): 488–514.

71. As suggested, for example, in Robert Cooter and Thomas Ulen, *Law and Economics*, 6th ed. (Boston: Addison-Wesley / Pearson Education, 2012), 216, 274–275. For detailed discussion of whether the principle in *Hadley* can be justified on this and other economic grounds, see Eisenberg, "The Principle of *Hadley v. Baxendale*," 581–598.

72. As stated explicitly in the important Supreme Court of Canada case of Fidler v. Sun Life Assurance Co. of Canada, [2006] 2 S.C.R. 3.

73. This point is noted by Lord Nicholls in the important case of A-G v. Blake, [2000] 3 W.L.R. 625, 640 (Eng. H.L.).

74. For a representative statement, see Tito v. Waddell (No. 2), [1977] Ch. 106, 332.

75. See the brief but instructive comment by Peter Birks, "Profits of Breach of Contract," *Law Quarterly Review* 109, no. 4 (1993): 521. For a good illustration, see A-G v. Blake, and in particular Lord Nicholls's majority opinion at 628–642. A comparable US decision (though not as carefully reasoned) is Snepp v. United States, (1980) 444 U.S. 507. For helpful discussion, see Cunnington, "The Inadequacy of Damages." In *Blake*, the Crown, which was the plaintiff, was found to have a legitimate and indeed a paramount performance interest in preventing members of its Secret Intelligence Service from divulging, and having financial incentives to divulge, any information (whether classified and not) gained through their employment. When the defendant breached by publishing without the Crown's prior approval an autobiography containing prohibited information and was to receive royalties from its sale, the House of Lords awarded damages measured by this profit. The effectiveness of the S.I.S. depended crucially on the mutual confidence, morale, and trust among members. To ensure this, an "absolute rule against disclosure, visible to all" was contractually justified. A-G v. Blake, 641. This interest was clearly of a kind the breach of which could give rise to consequential loss that comes under *Hadley*; and, on the facts, damages were inadequate, an injunction was no longer available and the loss, though real, was indirect, nonfinancial, and impossible to measure. In these circumstances, taking the defendant's royalties as the measure of lost performance value damages not only matched, but also was rationally connected to the promotion of, the plaintiff's performance interest.

76. A further important and controverted issue in law and legal scholarship that seems to challenge the primacy of compensatory justice itself is whether punitive damages should ever be given for breach of contract. Very briefly, I think that the key here is in fact not to view or to try to justify such supracompensatory damages as

punishment. This would go beyond a court's ordinary function in civil suits and raise serious concerns about institutional legitimacy. Instead, I suggest that such damages be viewed as genuinely ancillary to the realization of compensatory justice because needed, paradoxically it might seem, to vindicate the integrity of the compensatory character of ordinary damages at least in certain circumstances. This may be so where a defendant's breach is not limited to mere nonperformance—what might be called a non-malicious breach—but involves conduct that specifically demonstrates a manifest malicious intent (evidenced often by fraud or conscious recklessness) that in effect denies the plaintiff's very capacity to have and to enjoy any contractual rights at all. Here the defendant does not merely leave the plaintiff to prove and claim under their contract, but instead acts in a way that says to the plaintiff: "I will do what I can to make sure that you are disqualified from making or having any contractual claims at all under our contract, however valid they might be. Your contract rights shall mean and come to nothing." In my view, a clear example of such a breach, is in Whiten v. Pilot Insurance Co., [2002] 1 S.C.R. 595 (S.C.C.) where the defendant insurance company fraudulently and publicly insisted that the plaintiffs had acted not only illegally but in a manner that, if true, would have barred them from claiming any insurance proceeds under their contract for the total accidental destruction by fire of their insured house. We suppose that a plaintiff has been fully compensated for all physical, financial, and intangible loss resulting from the breach. Within the framework of compensatory justice, this is the limit of legal redress. A court cannot directly respond to the further aspect of the breach being malicious. Still, the court, as the guardian of rights, has an institutional interest in ensuring that the defendant does not—and cannot appear to—rely, even implicitly, on this limit when he decides to breach in this way. The court must not allow itself or its act of compensation to appear to be part of and a motivating factor in—and thus to be indifferent toward—the defendant's malicious wrong. Otherwise, its purely compensatory response risks not having the clear public significance of being purely and wholly a coercive nullification of wrong. Where the circumstances of breach warrant, supracompensatory damages may be given therefore, not for the purpose of punishing the defendant but rather to vindicate—hence the traditional term "vindictive damages"—the integrity of compensatory damages as being and, importantly, signaling purely a coercive response to wrongs. So understood, supracompensatory damages manifest the settled judicial practice of shaping remedies to ensure that a wrongdoer "must not qualify his own wrong" and that the court is not a "tribunal for legalizing wrongful acts," per Livingstone v. Rawyards Coal Co., (1880) 5 App. Cas. 25, 39 (Eng. H.L.), and Shelfer v. City of London Electric Lighting, 315. And because punitive damages aim to vindicate the transactional integrity of a particular award of compensatory damages so that it does not appear to license the denial of the plaintiff's capacity for rights, it is perfectly reasonable that the plaintiff, not someone else, receives them. Certainly, no one has a better claim.

77. See discussion in Fuller and Perdue, "The Reliance Interest: 1," 78–79.

78. "[T]here being no other element of certainty by which the damages can be *accurately* measured, resort must be had to such principle or basis of calculation applicable to the circumstances of the case (if any be discoverable) as will be most likely to *approximate* certainty . . . and though it may be less certain as a scale of measurement, yet if the principle be just in itself, and more likely to approximate the *actual damages*, it is better than any rule, however certain, which must certainly produce injustice, by excluding a large portion of the damages actually sustained." Gilbert v. Kennedy, (1871) 22 Mich. 117, 135–136 (italics in original), quoted in Security Stove & Manufacturing Co. v. American Railway Express Co., 51 S.W. (2d) 572, 577 (Mo. 1932).

79. As emphasized in several of the judgments in Commonwealth of Australia v. Amann Aviation Pty. Ltd., (1991) 174 C.L.R. 64 (H.C. Australia); see, for example, 127–128 (per Deane, J.) and 155 (per Gaudron, J.). In easier and more straightforward cases, the benefits will be pecuniary, but this need not be so, and the analysis may still apply where the benefits of performance are not directly financial.

80. See the clear judicial statement of this point in Bowlay Logging Ltd. v. Domtar Ltd., 135 D.L.R. (3d) 179 (B.C.C.A 1978).

81. This reasoning underpins Lord Denning's well-known judgment in Anglia Television v. Reed.

82. See the recent and clear judicial statement of this point in Yam Seng Pte Ltd. v. International Trade Corp. Ltd., [2013] EWHC 111 (Q.B.), paragraphs 188–190.

83. See, for example, Security Stove v. American Railway Express (US); L. Albert & Son v. Armstrong Rubber Co., 178 F.2d 182 (2d Cir. 1949) (US); Bowlay Logging v. Domtar (Canadian); McCrae v. Commonwealth Disposals Commission, (1951) 84 C.L.R. 377, 412–415 (per Dixon, J., and Fullagar, J.) (Australian); Commonwealth of Australia v. Amann Aviation (Australian); Omak Maritime Ltd. v. Mamola Challenger Shipping Co., [2011] 2 All E.R. 155 (Q.B.D.) (English); and Yam Seng v. International Trade (English).

84. An award of reliance damages "is not an exception to the fundamental principle . . . that the aim of an award of damages for breach of contract is to put the injured party, so far as money can do it, in the same position as if the contract had been performed but [rather] is a method of giving effect to that fundamental principle." Yam Seng v. International Trade, paragraph 186. There are many statements to this effect in the leading cases.

85. There appears to be a tension between the general formulation of the "reliance interest" in *Restatement (Second) of Contracts*, section 344 (b), including comment a (which states the purpose of reliance damages in terms of precontractual position), and its more particular discussion of "damages based on reliance interest," section 349 and comment a (which reflects the approach taken in the text).

86. As in Anglia Television v. Reed and Security Stove v. American Railway Express.

87. See the analysis in *Restatement of the Law of Contracts*, section 333, and in the recent case of Yam Seng v. International Trade, paragraph 186 (titled "Claim for Wasted Expenditure").

88. See, for example, P. S. Atiyah, *An Introduction to the Law of Contract*, 5th ed. (Oxford: Clarendon Press, 1995), 458; Rowan, *Remedies for Breach of Contract*, 142, 151–152; and Michael G. Bridge, "Mitigation of Damages in Contract and the Meaning of Avoidable Loss," *Law Quarterly Review* 105 (1989): 406–408.

89. To simplify matters, I consider mitigation only in relation to actual breach, not anticipatory repudiation.

90. McClelland v. Climax Hosiery Mills, (1930) 169 N.E. 605, 609–610 (C.A. N.Y.). For a leading English statement of the rule, see British Westinghouse Co. v. Underground Electric Railway Co., [1912] A.C. 673 (Eng. H.L.), and for a comparative law account, see Treitel, *Remedies for Breach*, 179–192. As has been pointed out on innumerable occasions, mitigation is not a duty because there is no corresponding claim-right in the promisor and no liability for failing to mitigate. Hence Cardozo's use of quotation marks in the judgment above.

91. An instructive example is Asamera Oil Corp. Ltd. v. Sea Oil & General Corp., (1978) 89 D.L.R. (3d) 1 (S.C.C.), both for its facts and for the court's careful application of the mitigation principle to those facts.

92. Seana Valentine Shiffrin has forcefully made this objection in "The Divergence of Contract and Promise," *Harvard Law Review* 120, no. 3 (2007): 708–753.

93. Charles Fried, *Contract as Promise: A Theory of Contractual Obligation*, 2nd ed. (New York: Oxford University Press, 2015), 131; Charles Fried, "The Convergence of Contract and Promise," *Harvard Law Review Forum* 120, no. 1 (2007): 7–8. See also Melvin A. Eisenberg, "The Duty to Rescue in Contract Law," *Fordham Law Review* 71, no. 3 (2002): 654.

94. George Letsas and Prince Saprai refer to fairness in "Mitigation, Fairness, and Contract Law," in *Philosophical Foundations of Contract Law*, ed. Gregory Klass, George Letsas, and Prince Saprai (Oxford: Oxford University Press, 2014), 318–340. Charles J. Goetz and Robert E. Scott invoke efficiency in "The Mitigation Principle: Toward a General Theory of Contractual Obligation," *Virginia Law Review* 69, no. 6 (1983): 967–1024. More recently, Fried also suggests that "the mitigation rule is quite well supported . . . on efficiency grounds." Fried, *Contract as Promise*, 146.

95. The approach proposed here is most consistent with Dori Kimel's account in *From Promise to Contract*, 109–112.

96. I discuss the morality of promising more fully in Chapter 12.

97. The argument assumes that obtaining an appropriate damage award (when a substitute performance is readily available—the ideal case) is ordinarily not a significantly more uncertain, more unlikely, or longer process than the process for obtaining an order of specific performance.

9. Expectation Damages and Contract Theory

1. Richard Craswell, "Expectation Damages and Contract Theory Revisited" (Stanford Law and Economics Olin Working Paper No. 325, August 2006), 20, https://ssrn.com/abstract=925980.

2. In Lon L. Fuller and William F. Perdue Jr., "The Reliance Interest in Contract Damages: 1," *Yale Law Journal* 46, no. 1 (1936): 52–96, and "The Reliance Interest in Contract Damages: 2," *Yale Law Journal* 46, no. 3 (1937): 373–420.

3. Their account begins, "It is convenient to distinguish three principal purposes which may be pursued in awarding contract damages." Fuller and Perdue, "The Reliance Interest: 1," 53.

4. Richard Craswell develops this point convincingly in "Against Fuller and Perdue," *University of Chicago Law Review* 67, no. 1 (2000): 99–161.

5. Letter from Lon L. Fuller to Karl N. Llewellyn (December 8, 1938), excerpted in Robert S. Summers and Robert A. Hillman, *Contract and Related Obligation: Theory, Doctrine and Practice*, 3rd ed. (St. Paul, MN: West Group, 1997), 41.

6. Fuller and Perdue, "The Reliance Interest: 1," 56. The authors characterize this purpose of justice as that of Aristotelian corrective justice.

7. Fuller and Perdue, "The Reliance Interest: 1," 56.

8. Fuller and Perdue, "The Reliance Interest: 1," 56–57.

9. Fuller and Perdue, "The Reliance Interest: 1," 54.

10. Fuller and Perdue, "The Reliance Interest: 1," 56.

11. Fuller and Perdue, "The Reliance Interest: 1," 61.

12. Fuller and Perdue, "The Reliance Interest: 2," 419.

13. Fuller and Perdue, "The Reliance Interest: 2," 419.

14. Fuller and Perdue, "The Reliance Interest: 1," 70 and elsewhere.

15. Fuller and Perdue, "The Reliance Interest: 2," 419.

16. Fuller and Perdue, "The Reliance Interest: 1," 58.

17. Fuller and Perdue, "The Reliance Interest: 1," 58.

18. Most recently in Craswell, "Expectation Damages"; earlier in Richard Craswell, "Contract Law, Default Rules, and the Philosophy of Promising," *Michigan Law Review* 88, no. 3 (1989): 489–529.

19. See section 3.1 in Chapter 3.

20. Craswell, "Expectation Damages," 11.

21. See Craswell, "Against Fuller and Perdue," 157 ("[C]ontract law still treats expectation damages as the standard remedy"); also Richard Craswell, "Instrumental Theories of Compensation: A Survey," *San Diego Law Review* 40, no. 4 (2003): 1135–1180.

22. The authors expressly acknowledge that they are building on and carrying forward Craswell's basic insight. See Daniel Markovits and Alan Schwartz, "The Myth of Efficient Breach: New Defenses of the Expectation Interest," *Virginia Law Review* 97, no. 8 (2011): 1948n22.

23. While the authors frame their argument in terms of the Calabresi-Melamed distinction between liability and property rules, I do not think that their argument depends on the validity of this schema.

24. See the succinct and helpful summary of the authors' argument in Daniel Markovits and Alan Schwartz, "The Expectation Remedy and the Promissory Basis of Contract," *Suffolk University Law Review* 45, no. 3 (2012): 812–813.

25. While Oliver Wendell Holmes is often associated with this view, as Markovits and Schwartz correctly point out, he did not exactly share it. See Markovits and Schwartz, "The Myth of Efficient Breach," 1981–1982. For detailed discussion, see Joseph Perillo, "Misreading Oliver Wendell Holmes on Efficient Breach and Tortious Interference," *Fordham Law Review* 68, no. 4 (2000): 1085–1106.

26. Markovits and Schwartz, "The Myth of Efficient Breach," 1954.

27. Markovits and Schwartz claim that the dual performance hypothesis provides, better than alternative theories, a "reconstruction" of contract law that makes coherent the "immanent structure of actual legal rules" and of the "doctrinal edifice" that underpins them. "The Expectation Remedy," 814, 824.

28. Markovits and Schwartz, "The Myth of Efficient Breach," 1978, 1990.

29. Markovits and Schwartz, "The Myth of Efficient Breach," 1985n79.

30. Markovits and Schwartz, "The Myth of Efficient Breach," 1987.

31. Markovits and Schwartz, "The Myth of Efficient Breach," 1978; see also Markovits and Schwartz, "The Expectation Remedy," 813.

32. Markovits and Schwartz, "The Expectation Remedy," 811.

33. Markovits and Schwartz, "The Expectation Remedy," 814. Markovits also emphasizes this point in his very thoughtful discussion of good faith. See Daniel Markovits, "Good Faith as Contract's Core Value," in *Philosophical Foundations of Contract Law,* ed. Gregory Klass, George Letsas, and Prince Saprai (Oxford: Oxford University Press, 2014), 285–291.

34. As in Wood v. Lucy, Lady Duff-Gordon, 118 N.E. 214 (N.Y. 1917), discussed in Chapter 3. For a case illustrating this possibility in connection with alternative performances, see Davis v. Isenstein 100 N.E. 940, 942 (S. Ct. Ill. 1913).

35. For representative and helpful US cases on alternative performances, see Pearson v. Williams' Administrators, 24 Wend. 244 (S. Ct. N.Y. 1840); Burgoon v. Johnston, 46 A. Rep. 65 (S. Ct. Pa. 1899); Manchester Dairy System Inc. v. Hayward, 132 A. Rep. 12 (S. Ct. N.H. 1926); Rubenstein v. Rubenstein, 244 N.E.2d 49 (C.A. N.Y. 1968); and, more recently, Edge Group Waiccs LLC v. Sapir Group LLC, 705 F. Supp. 2d 304 (S.D. N.Y. 2010). See also E. Allan Farnsworth, *Contracts,* 4th ed. (New York: Aspen Publishers, 2004), section 12.18, 817–818.

36. In such a case, the sum can count at most as a valid liquidated damages provision upheld as reasonable under the penalty doctrine. Note that even where a provision is so upheld, this does not automatically preclude specific performance

where damages would be inadequate in the particular circumstances of the breach. See Bauer v. Sawyer, 134 N.E.2d 329, 332–334 (S. Ct. Ill. 1956), and Karpinski v. Ingrasci, 268 N.E. 751 (C.A. N.Y. 1971). Markovits and Schwartz seem to assume the contrary. See Markovits and Schwartz, "The Expectation Remedy," 821.

37. Other elements supposed by the dual performance theory such as post-formation negotiation, promisor opportunity costs that do not excuse under the doctrines of impossibility or frustration, changes in promisee preferences for the promised performance, and so forth cannot be relevant factors for the purposes of implication because they are not directly taken into account by the principles of contract formation in establishing the parties' rights and duties or in determining whether there is impossibility or frustration.

38. Markovits and Schwartz, "The Myth of Efficient Breach," 1953, 1948. See also Markovits and Schwartz, "The Expectation Remedy," 808.

39. For a different and interesting discussion of this difficulty with the argument, see Seana Valentine Shiffrin, "Must I Mean What You Think I Should Have Said?," *Virginia Law Review* 98, no. 1 (2012): 159–176.

40. Because an estimate of value can in principle be assigned to any asset or service, the dual performance approach should view any promise of goods or service, even if unique and thus warranting specific performance, as impliedly accompanied with a transfer term, thereby precluding specific performance of the trade term. This would be a further inconsistency with the law, in effect ensuring that damages could never be inadequate and abolishing the remedy of specific performance in its usual role.

41. To avoid this conclusion, one would have to argue that the transfer prong should be conditioned on the nonoccurrence of excusing circumstances. But this would merely pile a further layer of implausible and unnecessary implication on the existing ones.

42. Smith makes a similar point, though not with reference to implication. See Stephen A. Smith, "Duties, Liabilities, Damages," *Harvard Law Review* 125, no. 7 (2012): 174–179.

43. Markovits and Schwartz, "The Myth of Efficient Breach," 1978. See also Markovits, "Contract's Core Value," 285–291.

44. Markovits and Schwartz emphasize the limits of a liberal conception of contract throughout their defense of the dual performance hypothesis. See Markovits and Schwartz, "The Expectation Remedy," 811, and "The Myth of Efficient Breach," 2003. See also Markovits, "Contract's Core Value."

45. As discussed in Craswell, "Instrumental Theories of Compensation."

46. See also the discussion of Craswell in Chapter 3, Section 3.1.

47. Fuller and Perdue, "The Reliance Interest: 1," 56n7.

48. Fuller and Perdue, "The Reliance Interest: 1," 60.

10. Contract as a Transfer of Ownership

1. I take this formulation from the early natural law theorist Lessius (1554–1623), quoted and discussed in Helge Dedek, "A Particle of Freedom: Natural Law Thought and the Kantian Theory of Transfer by Contract," *Canadian Journal of Law and Jurisprudence* 25, no. 2 (2012): 324.

2. Keep in mind here that by donative intent, I do not mean an altruistic intent—which would confuse consideration with motive—but rather the manifest intent to give something in return for something else of lesser value.

3. Compare this to Kant's view that the object of a contractual transfer is the promisor's act of choice or promise. See Immanuel Kant, *The Metaphysics of Morals*, ed. Mary Gregor (Cambridge: Cambridge University Press, 1996), 6:274 and elsewhere. Depending on how Kant's formulation is interpreted, it may or may not be consistent with the analysis presented here.

4. Lon L. Fuller, "Consideration and Form," *Columbia Law Review* 41, no. 5 (1941): 806.

5. See, for example, the representative discussion in Stephen A. Smith, *Contract Theory* (Oxford: Oxford University Press, 2004), 97–103.

6. See Kant's statement of this point in "Part I: Metaphysical First Principles of the Doctrine of Right," in *The Metaphysics of Morals*, 6:249.

7. This point is emphasized by Helge Dedek in his historical presentation of the natural law conception of contractual transfer. See Dedek, "A Particle of Freedom," 328–329. See also G. W. F. Hegel, *Lectures on Natural Right and Political Science: The First Philosophy of Right; Heidelberg,1817–1818, with Additions from the Lectures of 1818–1819*, trans. J. Michael Stewart and Peter C. Hodgson (Oxford: Oxford University Press, 2012), paragraph 35: "Performance is necessary for the simple reason that [otherwise] what the other owns would incur injury.... Performance is therefore ... a consequence as a pure matter of right, that I should not injure what I have recognized as owned by the other."

8. This is the conception of breach presented in Chapter 7. It should be recalled that, according to this conception, even if performance refers—as it usually does—to the promisor's acts or omissions that factually enable the promisee to take possession of or to receive the actual consideration as promised, the promisor's acts or omissions count within the framework of misfeasance merely as the contractually specified *physical mode or manner* in which the *promisee* is to exercise her right to have or take possession of what she has acquired at formation. The promisor's contribution via performance has no distinct rights-producing significance whatsoever.

9. See, for example, Smith, *Contract Theory*, 101–102.

10. Thus, if the promisor can no longer do something simply because it would be inconsistent with the promised terms, this restriction on his liberty or self-determination of choice is, once again, not the object but rather the normative

consequence of the transfer. Indeed, it can also be the moral consequence of a merely gratuitous promise.

11. This is Hegel's term. See G. W. F. Hegel, *Philosophy of Mind: Part Three of the Encyclopaedia of the Philosophical Sciences (1830)*, trans. William Wallace and A. V. Miller (Oxford: Clarendon Press, 1971), paragraph 493.

12. Frederick Pollock, *A First Book of Jurisprudence for Students of the Common Law*, 4th ed. (London: Macmillan, 1918), 172. See also J. W. Harris, *Property and Justice* (Oxford: Oxford University Press, 1996), 68.

13. Another difference, implied by the first, is that one cannot effectively alienate one's body to another, whether gratuitously or via an exchange.

14. See, for example, Thomas W. Merrill and Henry E. Smith, *Property: Principles and Policies* (New York: Foundation Press, 2007), chapter 2 ("Original Acquisition"), 81–243. For comparative law discussion, see James Gordley and Arthur T. von Mehren, *An Introduction to the Comparative Study of Private Law: Readings, Cases, Materials* (Cambridge: Cambridge University Press, 2006), 141–157, and Peter Birks, "The Roman Law Concept of Dominium and the Idea of Absolute Ownership," *Acta Juridica*, 1985, 1–38.

15. Carol Rose notes this point at the beginning of her influential piece "Possession as the Origin of Property," *University of Chicago Law Review* 52, no. 1 (1985): 73–88.

16. Pierson v. Post, 3 Cai. R. 175, 2 Am. Dec. 264 (N.Y. Sup. Ct. 1805). For a recent detailed account of this famous decision in its historical and social context, see Angela Fernandez, *Pierson v. Post: The Hunt for the Fox; Law and Professionalization in American Legal Culture* (Cambridge: Cambridge University Press, 2018).

17. Later, in Chapter 12, I consider the role and basis of legal formalities.

18. Our mental or physical powers can become external to us and therefore can be "things" only when we exercise those powers—and so give them particularized expression—whether this involves changing external objects (e.g., creating a sculpture) or not (e.g., singing a melody). However, such particular expressions of our activity, whether or not embodied in products, cannot be appropriated by others without our consent and so do not come within the purview of original acquisition. They can only be the objects of derivative acquisition. Of course, every act of appropriation involves the exercise of our powers on something external. But in that case it is the thing, not our activity, that is the object of acquisition and as long as we do so with respect to something that is presently unowned, we can make it ours by right of first possession. Hegel's discussion of these points is instructive. See G. W. F. Hegel, *The Philosophy of Right*, trans. T. M. Knox (Oxford: Clarendon Press, 1952) paragraphs 43, 67.

19. In Chapter 11, I discuss the important further question of whether such acquisition is fully consistent with the equality of all, as it must be if it is to be morally legitimate within a liberal framework of justice.

20. Hegel, *The Philosophy of Right,* addition to paragraph 50.

21. For instructive analysis, see Frederick Pollock and Robert S. Wright, *An Essay on Possession in the Common Law* (Oxford: Clarendon Press, 1888); Oliver Wendell Holmes, *The Common Law,* ed. Mark DeWolfe Howe (Cambridge, MA: Belknap Press of Harvard University Press, Brown, 1963), lecture 6 ("Possession"); Michael G. Bridge, *Personal Property Law,* 3rd ed. (Oxford: Oxford University Press, 2002), chapter 2; and James Gordley, *Foundations of Private Law* (Oxford: Oxford University Press, 2006), part 2, chapter 3 ("Possession and Ownership"), 49–65.

22. On this point about exclusion, see Holmes's remarks in *The Common Law,* 185.

23. Thus, unless parts of air, water, sunlight, and so forth are separated and "captured" for individual use, these elements do not qualify as objects of original acquisition. However, what is included in a unit held or marked for use will often be subject to dispute. When I touch the end of this piece of wood lying on the ground, I reasonably may be viewed as taking the whole stick into my possession. But what else is included, since everything is connected to something else? These kinds of questions are unavoidable but cannot be determinately answered by the concept of original acquisition. Such inherent indeterminacy distinguishes original acquisition from contract, as I discuss further in this section and in Section 10.3. This difficulty with original acquisition is brought out clearly and emphasized by Hegel, *Lectures on Natural Right,* paragraph 20, and *The Philosophy of Right,* paragraphs 55–58. See also note 47 below.

24. On the idea of an ownership spectrum, see Harris, *Property and Justice,* 5–6, 66–68, and elsewhere.

25. "[W]hen we speak of a power to exclude others, we mean no more than a power which so appears in its manifestation." Holmes, *The Common Law,* 185.

26. "The act of bringing something within his control is the taking of the object. Thus possession can also be represented as continuous taking." Immanuel Kant, *Lectures and Drafts on Political Philosophy,* ed. Frederick Rauscher (Cambridge: Cambridge University Press, 2016), 23:213.

27. I draw here on Kant's analysis in *The Metaphysics of Morals,* 6:245–255.

28. "Everyone agrees that it is not necessary to have always a present power over the thing, otherwise one could only possess what was under his hand.... When certain facts have once been made manifest which confer a right, there is no general ground on which the law need hold the right at an end except the manifestation of some fact inconsistent with its continuance." Holmes, *The Common Law,* 186.

29. In Chapter 11, I suggest that this possibility of nonphysical but rightful holding should be recognized on the basis of our freedom as juridical persons.

30. See, for example, the accounts in David J. Ibbetson, "Sale of Goods in the Fourteenth Century," *Law Quarterly Review* 107, no. 3 (1991): 480–499, and "From

Property to Contract: The Transformation of Sale in the Middle Ages," *Journal of Legal History* 13, no. 1 (1992): 1–22. According to Ibbetson, this model is reflected in Germanic legal systems of the early Middle Ages and in the treatment of sale in the common law as described by the twelfth and thirteenth-century jurists Glanvill and Bracton. By contrast, already in the thirteenth century, the Law Merchant across Europe and the practice of the English borough courts had gone quite a way toward recognizing the binding force of contracts even prior to delivery or payment of the price.

31. I draw here on Hegel's early discussion of exchange in his "System of Ethical Life." G. W. F. Hegel, *"System of Ethical Life" (1802/3) and "First Philosophy of Spirit" (Part III of the System of Speculative Philosophy 1803/4)*, trans. H. S. Harris and T. M. Knox (New York: State University of New York Press, 1988), 121–123.

32. Hegel put it best when he wrote: "The inwardness of the will which surrenders and the will which accepts the property is in the realm of ideation, and in that realm the word is deed and thing—the full and complete deed, since here the conscientiousness of the will does not come under consideration . . . and the will refers only to the external thing." *Philosophy of Mind*, paragraph 493.

33. What about the kinds of objects in immediate exchange? They must also be physically existing separate entities, since immediate exchange also exists only through immediate physical acts of giving and taking. Arguably, its objects can include currency, which emerges from indefinitely many barter transactions.

34. See, for example, Stephen Martin Leake, *An Elementary Digest of the Law of Property in Land*, 1st ed. (London: Stevens, 1874), 1–2, quoted in full in Wesley Newcomb Hohfeld, *Fundamental Legal Conceptions as Applied in Judicial Reasoning, and Other Legal Essays*, ed. Walter Wheeler Cook (New Haven, CT: Yale University Press, 1919), 77–78, 100.

35. According to Hohfeld, the analysis applies to privileges, powers, immunities, and so forth, but I refer to rights only for the sake of simplicity. Hohfeld limits most of his own discussion to the analysis of rights. *Fundamental Legal Conceptions*, 71.

36. Hohfeld, *Fundamental Legal Conceptions*, 77.

37. Hohfeld, *Fundamental Legal Conceptions*, 77.

38. As contended, for example, by John Austin. See John Austin, *Lectures on Jurisprudence, or, The Philosophy of Positive Law*, 5th ed., ed. Robert Campbell (London: J. Murray, 1885), 369–370, quoted and discussed in Hohfeld, *Fundamental Legal Conceptions*, 81–82.

39. Hohfeld points to another difference between them: in contrast to paucital rights, multital rights are "always constructive rather than consensual [insofar as] they and their correlating duties arise independently of even an approximate expression of intention on the part of those concerned." *Fundamental Legal Conceptions*, 74n23. This suggests that they differ with respect to the kinds of interactions that give rise to them. But Hohfeld does not seem to pursue or develop this

point, which, I shall argue, is fundamental to a proper understanding of the in rem / in personam distinction.

40. Of the many different treatments of this topic, I find important parallels between the proposed approach and that of Albert Kocourek in "Rights in Rem," *University of Pennsylvania Law Review* 68 (1920): 322–336. See also Walter Wheeler Cook, "The Alienability of Choses in Action," *Harvard Law Review* 29, no. 8 (1916): 816–837, and Walter Wheeler Cook, "The Alienability of Choses in Action: A Reply to Professor Williston," *Harvard Law Review* 30, no. 5 (1917): 449–485.

41. Kocourek also makes this point and treats it as crucial to understanding in rem rights. See "Rights in Rem," 335.

42. In his discussions of the alienability of choses in action (cited note 40 above), Cook in particular makes use of a distinction between potential and actual rights, powers, and the like.

43. Prior to doing something, persons are, in Kant's phrase, juridically beyond reproach. See Kant, *The Metaphysics of Morals*, 6:238 ("Division of the Doctrine of Right," section B).

44. Hohfeld, *Fundamental Legal Conceptions*, 91–96.

45. See the clear statement (quoted in Hohfeld, *Fundamental Legal Conceptions*, 94–95) in McGhee v. R. Co., (1908) 147 N.C. 142, 146 (per Connor, J.): "It is elementary that plaintiff had no cause of action against defendants for placing the dynamite in the shanty. He must establish some relation between *defendants* and *himself* from which a *duty to him* is imposed upon *defendants*. 'The expression "duty" properly imports a *determinate person to whom* the obligation is owing, *as well as the one who owes* the obligation. There must be *two determinate parties* before the relationship of obligor and obligee of a duty can exist'" (emphasis in original). Perhaps the greatest judicial statement and exploration of this point is Cardozo's judgment in Palsgraf v. Long Island Railroad Co., (1928) 162 N.E. 99 (N.Y.C.A.).

46. See discussions in Rose, "Possession as the Origin," 82–88, and in Richard Epstein, "Possession as the Root of Title," *Georgia Law Review* 13, no. 4 (1979): 1230. See also Holmes, *The Common Law*, 168–172.

47. Kant writes that this indeterminacy "with respect to the quantity as well as quality . . . of the external object that can be acquired makes this problem (of the sole, original external acquisition) the hardest of all to solve." Kant, *The Metaphysics of Morals*, 6:266. See, for example, the whaling cases such as Ghen v. Rich, (1881) 8 F. 159 (U.S.D.C. Mass.) or cases involving indigenous land claims discussed in Rose, "Possession as the Origin." Hegel helpfully addresses this issue in *Lectures on Natural Right*, paragraph 21. See also note 23 above.

48. Thus, whereas the objective test in contract is applied determinately and specifically to the particular transaction between the contracting parties—it aims to construe *their* transaction in light of the particular (sometimes even idiosyncratic)

expectations, understandings, standards, and so forth to which they can reasonably be held in light of their interaction—the application of the test in negligence and nuisance, for example, must unavoidably refer to more general, not immediately contextualized, and therefore indeterminate standards such as a reasonable person, ordinary community expectations and norms, and so on, which even though often the same as "the average" are never reducible to this as their measure.

49. In characterizing the difference between the right in things and so-called personal right, Kant contrasts them as involving, respectively, "the possibility of the unification of the powers of choice regarding an object" and the "actuality of this unification." See Kant, *Lectures and Drafts*, 23:218.

50. As Leake, among others, suggested. See Leake, *An Elementary Digest*.

51. See Kant's formulation in his *Lectures and Drafts*, 23:219 ("*Through my acquisition* others receive an obligation to perform or to refrain from something which prior to my action they did not have" [emphasis added]).

52. See Chapter 1, Section 1.5.

53. Recall the analysis of quasi-property in the tort of inducement. Also worth mentioning in this connection is International News Service v. The Associated Press, (1918) 248 U.S. 215, briefly referred to in Chapter 1, Section 1.5. I suggested that courts designate protected interests as "quasi-property" when they are recognizing what is in fact a form of transactional ownership interest specified and valid as between plaintiff and defendant.

54. "Delivery would, of course, automatically pass full ownership, if the seller was owner." F. H. Lawson, "The Passing of Property and Risk in Sale of Goods—a Comparative Study," *Law Quarterly Review* 65 (1949): 865. Holmes explains this possibility under the rubric of what he calls "privity of title" in connection with succession after death and inter vivos. See Holmes, *The Common Law*, lectures 10 and 11; also Oliver Wendell Holmes, "The Arrangement of the Law—Privity," *American Law Review* 7 (1872–1873): 46–66.

55. Holmes emphasizes this point. See *The Common Law*, lecture 10, 286, and "The Arrangement of the Law," 54–55.

56. This seems to be the view taken by Kant in *The Metaphysics of Morals*, 6:275–276. It also may underpin the conception of sale in German law. See Reinhard Zimmermann, *The Law of Obligations: Roman Foundations of the Civilian Tradition* (New York: Oxford University Press, 1996), 240, 290–292, regarding the German principles of "separation" and "abstraction," which hold respectively that there must be two transactions and that the validity of the second (which effectuates the transfer of in rem ownership rights) can be independent of the first. See also Lawson, "The Passing of Property," 853–854, 861–866.

57. See Zimmermann, *The Law of Obligations*, 240. According to Zimmermann, Roman law took the contract of sale to have a double function: to establish and contain not only an obligatory act but also *iusta causa traditionis* "in the sense that

it implicitly contained the will of the parties to transfer ownership on the basis of [the] sale . . . [and] thus contained everything that was necessary to transfer ownership except *traditio* . . . that was postponed for the time being" (240, 291). This also seems to be the view underlying French law.

58. However, it does not necessarily follow from this that the German model of two transactions is therefore defective. The German model, it seems, supposes that the use of legal formalities is required for the purposes of ensuring publicity and certainty of title. If so, the German principles of "separation" and "abstraction" seem justifiable. This need not challenge my proposed analysis, which—as in the prior chapters dealing with the main doctrines of contract law—is here framed in terms of fundamental juridical relations as they can be understood independently of legal formalities and allows for regimes of positive contract law that differ as to when "property passes." My discussion of the need for and the role of legal formalities in contract law is in Chapter 12.

59. Compare this analysis with the idea of "opposabilité" in French doctrine. See, for example, Jacques Ghestin, Christophe Jamin, and Marc Billiau, eds., *Les effets du contrat,* 3rd ed. (Paris: Librairie générale de droit et de jurisprudence, 2001), paragraphe 678. By contrast, Kant seems to equate the role of the act of taking possession via delivery with that of the possessory act needed for original acquisition. See Kant, *The Metaphysics of Morals,* 6:276 ("The Doctrine of Right").

60. Paralleling the promisee's proprietary interest at the point of delivery, we saw that the assignee's proprietary interest is tied to the vulnerabilities of the assignor's chose in action insofar as it presupposes and refers to the in personam contractual relation between assignor and obligor. And in different ways, this is also true of the analysis of liability for tortious interference and the principle in *De Mattos.*

61. Kant, *Lectures and Drafts,* 23:232, 278.

62. To avoid misunderstanding, I should briefly discuss here the English law of sale, which holds that "property" can pass on the basis of the parties' intentions alone. Despite some similarities with the proposed view of contract as transfer of ownership, I do not view it as directly illustrating or corroborating the theory, although the two are mutually consistent. The specific requirements in English law for the passing of property by sale must be emphasized. Party intentions are effective to pass property prior to delivery or payment of the price only if they are part of a completed "bargain and sale." Not only must there be terms that stipulate an exchange of ascertained particular goods for a money price, but the seller must also have physically done everything necessary to put the goods in a deliverable state so as to be immediately available to be taken by the purchaser for his or her contractually contemplated uses. Even contracts that would be specifically enforceable need not always meet these criteria. A bargain and sale that does satisfy these requirements is as close as possible to an immediate cash sale between parties *inter praesentes.* From a practical commercial perspective, parties would view it as such with the usual accompanying shift in extrinsic risks. See, for example, Michael G. Bridge, *The Sale of*

Goods, 3rd ed. (Oxford: Oxford University Press, 2014), section 3.06. Also Zimmermann, *The Law of Obligations* (237–238), emphasizes this point in connection with the Roman law of sale. At the same time, as several authors have underlined, English law distinguishes between a bargain and sale's immediate legal effects for the contracting parties alone and its further effects for third parties, which generally turn on the location of possession. It is certainly not the case that the complete bargain and sale immediately vests with the purchaser in rem rights against third parties unqualifiedly of the same kind and with the same effects as property acquisition does. See, for example, Lawson, "The Passing of Property"; Zimmermann, *The Law of Obligations;* and, more recently, Ho Hock Lai, "Some Reflections on 'Property' and 'Title' in the Sale of Goods Act," *Cambridge Law Journal* 56, no. 3 (1997): 571–598. The legal analysis of sale would seem to be the historical outcome of expressing and transposing the immediate executed exchange transaction, which transfers property and which necessarily affects third parties, in the form of a contractual relation involving rights and duties prior to actual delivery. For historical discussion, see Ibbetson, "Sale of Goods" and "From Property to Contract." On account of this historical process—and the customary expectations and practices associated with the executed sale—the law of sale should not be taken as exemplifying a pure contractual analysis. Unlike the promise-for-consideration relation, it cannot represent a general conception of contract. Nor is it merely a more specific instance of that relation.

63. Kant's presentation of this relation: "I acquire an object of another's power of choice that is also an object of my power of choice from him through the actual unification of the powers of choice through accepting, i.e. by taking into possession while the other withdraws from possession (to my advantage): hence *through bilateral action* (giving and accepting)." *Lectures and Drafts,* 23:221 (emphasis in original). A better abstract model of the promise-for-consideration relation could not be wished for!

64. Even Hohfeld, despite his valuable and still important criticisms of the standard view of in rem/in personam rights, invokes this distinction without justifying or exploring it. See *Fundamental Legal Conceptions,* 73.

65. See Chapter 1.

11. A Moral Basis for Contract as Transfer

1. Hegel also emphasizes this difference. G. W. F. Hegel, *Philosophy of Right,* trans. T. M. Knox (Oxford: Oxford University Press, 1952), paragraph 75. Interestingly, whereas earlier, public law was mistakenly equated with the private contractual relation, now the converse mistake is too often made.

2. Chapter 7, Section 7.3.

3. In connection with his presentation of the political conception of the person, Rawls stresses that it is part of, and specific to, his account of social and political

justice for the basic structure of society. See John Rawls, *Justice as Fairness: A Restatement,* ed. Erin Kelly (Cambridge, MA: Belknap Press of Harvard University Press, 2001), 19.

4. This is Rawls's phrase. See John Rawls, "Social Unity and Primary Goods," in *Collected Papers,* ed. Samuel Freeman (Cambridge, MA: Harvard University Press, 1999), 369.

5. As Hegel puts it, each is "a unit of freedom aware of its sheer independence." *Philosophy of Right,* addition to paragraph 35. For Rawls's lucid and accurate discussion of Hegel's thought on this point, see John Rawls, *Lectures on the History of Moral Philosophy,* ed. Barbara Herman (Cambridge, MA: Harvard University Press 2000), 340–344. Not only is this view of ourselves familiar in everyday experience, but it is also not dependent on accepting a particular philosophical account. For a compelling non-Kantian presentation of this power, see Henry Sidgwick, *The Methods of Ethics,* 7th ed. (London: Macmillan, 1907), 65–70.

6. Rawls, *Justice as Fairness,* 23–24.

7. Thus paralleling the account in John Rawls, *Political Liberalism* (New York: Columbia University Press, 1996), 33–34.

8. Hegel captures this point well when he writes, "Hence the imperative of right is: 'Be a person and respect others as persons.'" *Philosophy of Right,* paragraph 36.

9. While the following discussion often draws on insights and arguments from various philosophical accounts, my aim is to present them (and everything else) as part of an analysis that can stand on its own as part of a public basis of justification for contract.

10. The person/thing contrast is a categorical normative distinction that, I believe, is clear and valid in its own terms. The further, and sometimes difficult, question of assigning any particular entity to one or the other of the two categories is a different matter. I assume here as settled that anyone who is biologically a human being must always be treated as a person and that items of inorganic nature or artifacts are examples of things. For an instructive discussion of the question of who comes under the protection of rights, see Alexandre Kojève, *Outline of a Phenomenology of Right,* trans. Bryan-Paul Frost and Robert Howse (Lanham, MD: Rowman and Littlefield, 2000), 42–66.

11. Ernest Weinrib emphasizes and explores this central feature of private law in his many writings. See, for example, Ernest Weinrib, *The Idea of Private Law,* 2nd ed. (Oxford: Oxford University Press, 2012), chapter 5.

12. See Hegel's remarks on this point. *Philosophy of Right,* paragraph 155; and *Philosophy of Mind: Part Three of the Encyclopaedia of the Philosophical Sciences* (1830), trans. William Wallace and A.V. Miller (Oxford: Clarendon Press, 1971), paragraph 486.

13. See Chapter 10, Section 10.2.

14. Kant emphasizes that transfer by contract must take place in accordance with this idea, which he called the "law of continuity" (*lex continui*). See Immanuel Kant, *The Metaphysics of Morals,* ed. Mary Gregor (Cambridge: Cambridge University

Press, 1996), 6:274. The same idea is found in Hegel's account, *Philosophy of Right*, paragraphs 72–73.

15. Hegel, *Philosophy of Right*, paragraph 71.

16. See Marx's striking formulation: "[Objects] exist as equals as long as they exist as activity." Karl Marx, *Grundrisse: Foundations of the Critique of Political Economy*, trans. Martin Nicolaus (New York: Vintage Books, 1973), 613.

17. This is Hegel's phrase. See *Philosophy of Right*, paragraph 77.

18. In Chapter 10, Section 10.3.2., I discussed the automatic transfer of the promisor's protected interest to the promisee, whether at formation or at delivery, as a crucial feature of transactional acquisition. I would suggest here that the possibility of such automatic transfer rests on this abstract identity between subjects and the parallel identity between objects of the contractual transfer. Compare this explanation of identity between persons, which is transactional and based on an idea of juridical persons as free and equal owners, with Holmes's suggestion that the identity necessary for automatic transfer should be understood via a fiction of the transferee assuming the very "persona" of the transferor (who loses it)—an idea that, according to Holmes, first appears in the historically earlier legal doctrines of family succession. See Oliver Wendell Holmes, *The Common Law*, ed. Mark DeWolfe Howe (Cambridge, MA: Belknap Press of Harvard University Press, 1963), lectures 10 and 11, and Holmes, "The Arrangement of the Law—Privity," *American Law Review* 7 (1872–1873): 46–66. Holmes notes that once sale is so understood, "a sale without delivery becomes conceivable." "The Arrangement of the Law," 55.

19. See Chapter 4.

20. The classifications of contract-types proposed by Kant and Hegel reflect this division. See Kant, *The Metaphysics of Morals*, 6:284–286, and Hegel, *Philosophy of Right*, paragraph 80. Note that the fact that consideration requires quid pro quo need not be viewed as inconsistent with this division. As I tried to explain, the role of quid pro quo is simply to establish an unambiguously two-sided relation in the medium of promises. Within this two-sided framework, there can be transactions for both equal and unequal value. In Chapter 12, I discuss the basis and role of transaction-types more fully. See Section 2.3.

21. On arithmetic equality and corrective justice, see Aristotle, *Nicomachean Ethics*, book 5, 1131a–1132b, and particularly Thomas Aquinas, *Summa Theologica*, trans. Fathers of the English Dominican Province (New York: Benziger Bros., 1948), part 2-2, question 61.

22. I have in mind here anything like Rawls's second moral power, consisting of a capacity for a conception of the good. See Rawls, *Justice as Fairness*, 19.

23. Unlike Rawls's account of distributive justice. See Rawls, *Justice as Fairness*, 57–61.

24. Pierson v. Post, 3 Cai. R. 175 (N.Y. Sup. Ct. 1805) (per Livingston, J.).

25. In Chapter 12, Section 2.3.

26. Compare with Kant's view that everyone is under "a duty of right to act towards others so that what is external (usable) could also become someone's." Kant, *The Metaphysics of Morals*, 6:252. Similarly, see Hegel, *Philosophy of Mind: Part Three of the Encyclopaedia of the Philosophical Sciences (1830)*, paragraph 486.

12. The Stability of Contract as Transfer

1. For example, in John Rawls, *Justice as Fairness: A Restatement*, ed. Erin Kelly (Cambridge, MA: Belknap Press of Harvard University Press, 2001), part 5.

2. See the discussion in Seana Valentine Shiffrin, "The Divergence of Contract and Promise," *Harvard Law Review* 120, no. 3 (2007): 709.

3. See the discussion of this general ethical duty in Immanuel Kant, *The Metaphysics of Morals*, ed. Mary Gregor (Cambridge: Cambridge University Press, 1996), 16:218–221.

4. Much of Shiffrin's critique is aimed at the economic justification of contract. See, for example, "The Divergence," 729.

5. For recent examples of accounts of promissory morality as transfer, see Seana Valentine Shiffrin, "Promising, Intimate Relationships, and Consequentialism," *Philosophical Review* 117 (2008): 481, and David Owens, "A Simple Theory of Promising," *Philosophical Review* 115 (2006): 51.

6. Charles Fried, *Contract as Promise: A Theory of Contractual Obligation*, 2nd ed. (New York: Oxford University Press, 2015).

7. I discussed these reasons in the Introduction as well as at various points in Chapter 1.

8. Fried, *Contract as Promise*, 16–17.

9. Fried, *Contract as Promise*, 20–21.

10. Fried, *Contract as Promise*, 20–21.

11. The discussion that follows draws on Kant, *The Metaphysics of Morals*, part 2 (*Metaphysical First Principles of the Doctrine of Virtue*).

12. Kant, *The Metaphysics of Morals*, 6:382–386.

13. Kant, *The Metaphysics of Morals*, 6:386–389.

14. Kant, *The Metaphysics of Morals*, 6:448–450.

15. See, for example, Kant, *The Metaphysics of Morals*, 6:390–391, 6:451–452.

16. Kant, *The Metaphysics of Morals*, 6:388 and elsewhere.

17. Here and in what follows, I draw on A. I. Melden's acute and subtle analysis of promissory relations in *Rights and Persons* (Berkeley: University of California Press, 1977), particularly chapters 2, 4, and 5.

18. This may, but need not, involve detrimental reliance (in the legal sense) on the part of the promisee.

19. Kant, *The Metaphysics of Morals*, 6:450.

20. Kant, *The Metaphysics of Morals*, 6:450.

21. Kant, *The Metaphysics of Morals*, 6:453.

22. Kant, *The Metaphysics of Morals*, 6:453.

23. In Melden's words, "The promisor, for his part, however it is that he goes about his own affairs, must now see the promised action as one that he performs if and only if he is to respect the other as an agent." *Rights and Persons*, 48.

24. See Melden's discussion of the moral versus psychological distinction in *Rights and Persons*, 36.

25. Melden, *Rights and Persons*, 134.

26. Indeed, as Melden notes, even the fact that the promisee no longer wants the promised act done may not always absolve the promisor from any further responsibility in the matter. See Melden, *Rights and Persons*, 33.

27. On this point, see Melden, *Rights and Persons*, 43, 116.

28. This point is emphasized by Melden, for example, in *Rights and Persons*, 44, 116. In Section 12.2, I explain how the transactional conception of contract is institutionalized in form and function.

29. "I promise—this is what I do—and what I achieve in a central or nuclear case of promising is my doing too." Melden, *Rights and Persons*, 45.

30. C. J. Hamson emphasizes this point in "The Reform of Consideration," *Law Quarterly Review* 54 (1938): 244–247, 253–257.

31. I follow Rawls's definition of institution as "a public system of rules which defines offices and positions with their rights and duties, powers and immunities, and the like. These rules specify certain forms of action as permissible, others as forbidden; and they provide for certain penalties and defenses, and so on, when violations occur. As examples of institutions . . . we may think of . . . markets and systems of property. . . . In saying that an institution . . . is a public system of rules, I mean that everyone . . . taking part in an institution knows what the rules demand of him and of the others. He also knows that the others know this and that they know that he knows this, and so on. . . . The publicity of the rules of an institution insures that those engaged in it know what limitations on conduct to expect of one another and what kinds of actions are permissible." John Rawls, *A Theory of Justice* (Cambridge, MA: Belknap Press of Harvard University Press, 1971), 55–56.

32. G. W. F. Hegel, *Philosophy of Right*, trans. T. M. Knox (Oxford: Oxford University Press, 1952), paragraphs 189–208, and G. W. F. Hegel, *Lectures on Natural Right and Political Science: The First Philosophy of Right*, trans. J. Michael Stewart and Peter C. Hodgson (Oxford: Oxford University Press, 2012), paragraphs 93–108. For helpful discussion, see Lisa Herzog, *Inventing the Market: Smith, Hegel, and Political Theory* (Oxford: Oxford University Press, 2013). This same notion is found in Marx. See, for example, Karl Marx, *Grundrisse: Foundations of the Critique of Political Economy*, trans. Martin Nicolaus (New York: Vintage Books, 1973), 239–250.

33. This distinction parallels (without being exactly the same as) the difference between the state of nature and the civil state in natural rights theories. It more

closely corresponds to the distinction between private right and public right in Kant and that between abstract right and civil society in Hegel.

34. Max Weber viewed market exchange as the paradigmatically and "specifically peaceful form of acquiring economic power.... The appropriation of goods through free, purely economically rational exchange ... is the conceptual opposite of appropriation of goods by coercion of any kind, but especially physical coercion." Max Weber, "The Market: Its Impersonality and Ethic (Fragment)," in his *Economy and Society: An Outline of Interpretive Sociology,* ed. Guenther Roth and Claus Wittich (New York: Bedminster Press, 1968), volume 1, part 2, chapter 7, 640.

35. Well-known representative writers who emphasize this point include Robert Hale, John R. Commons, and Karl N. Llewellyn. Commons provides a systematic theoretical account in his *Legal Foundations of Capitalism* (New Brunswick, NJ: Transaction Publishers, 2007).

36. Indeed, the same point applies to the possibility of party regret even after an executed instantaneous exchange.

37. Keep in mind that a utilitarian justification also specifies a norm that goes beyond the rational as defined here: the obligatory end of maximizing utility in some form. I have rejected it, not because it is untenable, but because it does not directly and perspicuously fit with a public basis of justification for contract.

38. A liberal theory of the justice of market relations also requires that there be fair, and not merely formal, equality of opportunity to participate in these relations. This further requirement goes beyond the purely juridical conception of justice and belongs to distributive justice, as I discuss in Section 12.3.

39. In Rawls's sense of "lexically prior." See, for example, Rawls, *A Theory of Justice,* 42–44 and elsewhere. According to Rawls, principle A is lexically prior to B if B is explained and applied only on the condition of and within a setting that fully satisfies A in accordance with A's own terms and requirements.

40. If, as I have argued, the juridical conception of transactions—including the right of ownership, the principles and forms of acquisition, the kind of objects of acquisition, and so forth—can be justified on this basis of respect for juridical personality, Marx must be mistaken in viewing the juridical dimension as a mere inert form that is not at all able to shape its own content but that can only express a content wholly determined by a historically given mode of production. This point is also reflected in my argument that, as an expression of freedom, the juridical conception is lexically prior to the system of needs and therefore to the economic system understood in these terms. For Marx's view, see, for example, Karl Marx, *Capital,* volume 3, ed. Friedrich Engels (New York: International Publishers, 1967), chapter 21. See also Rawls's instructive discussion of Marx in John Rawls, *Lectures on the History of Political Philosophy,* ed. Samuel Freeman (Cambridge, MA: Belknap Press of Harvard University Press, 2007), 337–342.

41. This is the view that Nathan Oman seems to take in his interesting book *The Dignity of Commerce: Markets and the Moral Foundations of Contract Law* (Chicago: University of Chicago Press, 2016), chapter 2.

42. See Hegel, *Philosophy of Right,* paragraphs 189–208.

43. As Hegel notes in *Philosophy of Right,* paragraph 217, and in *Lectures on Natural Right,* paragraph 89.

44. As Hegel emphasizes and explains with great clarity. See Hegel, *Philosophy of Right,* paragraph 199, and *Lectures on Natural Right,* paragraph 98.

45. Karl N. Llewellyn, *The Common Law Tradition: Deciding Appeals* (Boston: Little Brown, 1960), 261. Commons also emphasizes this. See Commons, *Legal Foundations of Capitalism,* 19–25, 245.

46. Weber, *Economy and Society,* volume 1, part 2, chapter 7, 635.

47. Weber, *Economy and Society,* volume 1, part 1, chapter 2, section 8, 82.

48. "In a market economy every form of rational calculation . . . is oriented to expectations of prices and their changes as they are determined by the conflicts of interests in bargaining and competition and the resolution of these conflicts." Weber, *Economy and Society,* volume 1, part 1, chapter 2, section 8, 92. Weber puts the question of costs this way: "[W]hat would be the effect on the satisfaction of other wants if this particular means were not used for satisfaction of one given want. The 'other wants' may be qualitatively different present wants or qualitatively identical future wants" (66).

49. Weber, *Economy and Society,* volume 1, part 1, chapter 2, section 8, 81.

50. Weber, *Economy and Society,* volume 1, part 1, chapter 7, 635–640.

51. Weber, *Economy and Society,* volume 1, part 1, chapter 7, 639.

52. Weber's term in *Economy and Society,* volume 1, part 1, chapter 7, 637.

53. Weber refers to the economically undeveloped "silent trade" as a dramatic illustration of this ethical character of the market: "The silent trade is a form of exchange which avoids all face-to-face contact and in which the supply takes the form of a deposit of the commodity at a customary place; the counter-offer takes the same form, and dickering is effected through the increase in the number of objects being offered from both sides until one party either withdraws dissatisfied or, satisfied, takes the goods left by the other party and departs." *Economy and Society,* volume 1, part 1, chapter 7, 637. See also Oman, *The Dignity of Commerce,* 34–35, and Hegel, *Philosophy of Right,* addition to paragraph 80.

54. This point is emphasized by Weber, *Economy and Society,* volume 1, part 2, chapter 2, as well as by philosophers with very different theoretical standpoints such as Hegel, *Philosophy of Right,* paragraphs 195, 200, 230–245, and Henry Sidgwick, *The Methods of Ethics,* 7th ed. (Indianapolis: Hackett Publishing, 1981), book 3, chapter 5 ("Justice"), 286–289.

55. On this role of prices, see the seminal discussion of Friedrich Hayek, "The Use of Knowledge in Society," *American Economic Review* 35, no. 4 (1945): 519–530. See also Rawls's discussion of the role of prices in *A Theory of Justice,* 272–274.

56. Hegel notes this creative aspect of market participation and views it as the characteristic of what he calls the "business class." *Philosophy of Right,* paragraph 204. See also the excellent discussion of this point in James M. Buchanan and Viktor J. Vanberg, "The Market as a Creative Process," in *The Philosophy of*

Economics: An Anthology, 3rd ed., ed Daniel M. Hausman (Cambridge: Cambridge University Press, 2008), 378–398.

57. This shared formal interest is emphasized by many theorists of the market. For Hegel, it is a central feature. See *Philosophy of Right,* paragraphs 183, 208, 217. It is presupposed by Weber in his very definition of "market situation." *Economy and Society,* volume 1, part 1, chapter 2, section 8.

58. Weber, *Economy and Society,* volume 1, part 2, chapter 2, section 1, note 6.

59. Weber, *Economy and Society,* volume 1, part 2, chapter 7 ("The Market: Its Impersonality and Ethic"), 636. Following Rawls, such desires may be characterized as a "conception-dependent" insofar as the object of desire cannot be described without referring to rational or reasonable principles that form part of an ideal conception of self, which transactors want to be and to realize in their conduct. See John Rawls, *Political Liberalism* (New York: Columbia University Press, 1996), 83–84.

60. This point is emphasized by Alexandre Kojève in his brilliant account of the specificity and autonomy of (juridical) right or justice (*droit*). See his *Outline of a Phenomenology of Right,* trans. Bryan-Paul Frost and Robert Howse (Lanham, MD: Rowman & Littlefield, 2000), 178 ("When a merchant works out an exchange that he is about to make, he must not only take into account his own interest but also that of his partner . . . he must look at things from the point of view of an 'impartial and disinterested third.' . . . The merchant is naturally inclined to regulate his commercial activity by Judges or Arbiters—that is, by juridical legislation ultimately"). Kojève's entire discussion of the relation between the market and adjudication, from which I draw on here, is highly instructive.

61. "[T]he spokesman of the fair and reasonable [person], who represents after all no more than the anthropomorphic conception of justice, is and must be the court itself." Davis Contractors Ltd. v. Fareham Urban District Council, [1956] A.C. 696, 729 (Eng. H.L.) (per Lord Radcliffe).

62. One way of framing general principles *ex ante* is through codification. Although this is not characteristic of common law systems, these must have their appropriate analogues.

63. I draw on Rawls's discussion of this point in *Political Liberalism,* 267–269.

64. Weber, *Economy and Society,* volume 1, part 2, chapter 7, 636.

65. Commons emphasizes the centrality of viewing the promised consideration as a normatively certain, present asset in his account of the relation between law and capitalism. See *Legal Foundations of Capitalism,* chapter 7 and elsewhere.

66. Though presented as part of the common law, the approach proposed here draws on the long and highly developed intellectual tradition of contract classification beginning with Thomas Aquinas, continuing with the natural law writers such as Domingo de Soto and Hugo Grotius, and culminating with the accounts by Kant and Hegel. By being conceptually continuous with the general conception of contractual relation, the proposed account of this pluralism of particular contract-types differs from current theoretical discussions of contractual multi-

plicity. See, for example, Hanoch Dagan and Michael Heller, *The Choice Theory of Contracts* (New York: Cambridge University Press, 2017).

67. See the tables in Kant, *The Metaphysics of Morals*, 6:285–286, and Hegel, *Philosophy of Right*, paragraph 80.

68. Todd Rakoff, "The Implied Terms of Contracts: Of 'Default Rules' and 'Situation-Sense,'" in *Good Faith and Fault in Contract Law*, ed. Jack Beatson and Daniel Friedmann (Oxford: Clarendon Press, 1995), 222, 228.

69. See Llewellyn, *The Common Law Tradition*, 121–157 ("Situation-Sense and Reason") and elsewhere. My brief discussion of situation-sense draws heavily on Rakoff's important account in "The Implied Terms of Contracts." A similar notion is also in Hegel's account of the administration of justice, *Philosophy of Right*, paragraph 213.

70. For helpful discussion, see John Wightman, "Beyond Custom: Contract, Contexts, and the Recognition of Implicit Understandings," in *Implicit Dimensions of Contract: Discrete, Relational and Network Contracts*, ed. David Campbell, Hugh Collins, and John Wightman (Oxford: Hart Publishing, 2003), in particular 143–149. On this same point, see Rakoff, "The Implied Terms of Contracts," 220–221.

71. See Wightman, "Beyond Custom," 149–167.

72. See, for example, Rakoff's discussion of the changing character of the modern lease and how, in decisions such as Javins v. First National Realty Corp., 428 F.2d 1071 (1970) (per Wright, J.), the analysis was modeled on situation-sense. Rakoff, "The Implied Terms of Contracts," 217.

73. An excellent judicial illustration is still Cardozo's majority judgment in Jacob & Youngs Inc. v. Kent, 230 N.Y. 239 (1921), which I have discussed in Chapter 3. Rakoff's detailed discussion of this case in "The Implied Terms of Contracts" (205–215) sets the standard for contract scholarship.

74. Rakoff, "The Implied Terms of Contracts," 218.

75. See discussion of unfairness and transaction-types in Chapter 6. This requirement of balance in transaction-types is a pervasive theme and concern in Llewellyn's writings.

76. One can only agree with Rakoff that by enforcing contracts in accordance with situation-sense, courts contribute to justice by ensuring that transactors are "judged by the standards that fairly inhere in one's society . . . not a goal so easy to attain that its fulfillment can be assumed." "The Implied Terms of Contracts," 228.

77. This function is rightly emphasized by Karl N. Llewellyn, "The Effect of Legal Institutions upon Economics," *American Economic Review* 15, no. 4 (1925): 671.

78. The following discussion addresses issues similar to those analyzed by Kant with respect to the "four cases" in *The Metaphysics of Morals*, 6:297–306, and more recently by Ernest Weinrib in his important piece on this part of Kant's account, "Private Law and Public Right," *University of Toronto Law Journal* 61, no. 2 (2011): 191–211. Given limits of space, I cannot discuss the differences as well as the similarities between these and my own approach.

79. See, for example, Samuel Williston, *A Treatise on the Law of Contracts,* rev. ed. (New York: Baker, Voorhis, 1938), section 214.

80. David J. Ibbetson, *A Historical Introduction to the Law of Obligations* (Oxford: Oxford University Press, 1999), 73.

81. Williston, *Law of Contracts,* section 4.

82. See, for example, R. C. Backus, "The Origin and Use of Private Seals under the Common Law," *American Law Review* 51, no. 3 (1917): 369–380, and Lon L. Fuller, *Basic Contract Law* (St. Paul, MN: West Publishing, 1947), 313–319.

83. Indeed, in my view, the seal, being and functioning as a legal formality, should not be understood on the model of *any* juridical relation, including a gift transaction. The fact that both the seal and the gift require delivery does not efface this difference.

84. I choose this illustration because it relates to market transactions, not because it is statistically or socially the most important way in which a seal or its analogue may be used. I briefly discuss the traditional common law approach to this issue in Chapter 1, note 38.

85. Foakes v. Beer, (1884) 9 H.L. & P.C. 605, 622 (Eng. H.L.) (per Lord Blackburn).

86. This concern is raised both judicially and in scholarly writing. Representative examples include Lord Blackburn's speech in Foakes v. Beer, as well as John P. Dawson, *Gifts and Promises* (New Haven, CT: Yale University Press, 1980), 197, 210.

87. For a fairly recent judicial example, see Williams v. Roffey Bros. & Nicholls (Contractors) Ltd., [1991] 1 Q.B. 1 (Eng. C.A.).

88. I follow here Gregory Klass's analysis of power-conferring rules in "Three Pictures of Contract: Duty, Power, and Compound Rule," *New York University Law Review* 83, no. 6 (2008).

89. Compare with Kant, *The Metaphysics of Morals,* 6:298.

90. The use of the seal approaches the ideal of what civilians refer to as an "abstract" promise or obligation the enforceability of which is independent of "the shifting sands of fact on which it was built, with a view to rendering its legal effect certain and predictable." Fuller, *Basic Contract Law,* 329. See also Lon L. Fuller, "Consideration and Form," *Columbia Law Review* 41, no. 5 (1941): 802.

91. Fuller, "Consideration and Form," 823–824. For a more recent expression of this view, see Eric M. Holmes, "Stature and Status of a Promise under Seal as a Legal Formality," *Willamette Law Review* 29, no. 4 (1993): 665. See also Williston's unequivocal statement in *Law of Contracts,* section 219.

92. Sale of Goods (Amendment) Act 1994, chapter 32. My discussion of market overt draws mainly upon the informative and detailed account in Peter M. Smith, "Valediction to Market Overt," *American Journal of Legal History* 41, no. 2 (1997): 225–249.

93. For a recent case that does not appear to respect this limit and proposes a version of market overt going well beyond the traditional rule, see Caterpillar Far

East Ltd. v. CEL Tractors Pte Ltd., [1994] 2 S.L.R. 702 (H.C. Singapore), critically discussed in Ho Hock Lai, "Can a Thief Pass Title to Stolen Goods?," *Singapore Academy of Law Journal* 6, no. 2 (1994): 439–450.

94. On this fourth requirement, see The Case of Market-Overt, (1596) 5 Co. Rep. 83b.

95. A helpful brief overview of the preceding requirements is found in Ho Hock Lai, "Title to Stolen Goods," 440–441.

96. Historically, where the subject matter of a sale, for example, horses, could readily be resold in a market to which the owner might not have easy access (the mobility of horses enabling a thief to remove a stolen horse quickly to another part of the country where it could be resold in the open market), special statutory measures were taken to protect the owner, including recording sales by the market's bookkeeper, requiring the horse to be on public view for at least an hour in the usual part of the market for such sales, and so forth. Moreover, the original owner's claim was not barred if the sale had taken place and the claim was brought within six months of the theft. See Smith, "Valediction to Market Overt," 242.

97. Crane v. London Dock Co., (1864) 5 B. & S. 313, 320 (Eng. H.L.).

98. Abolition of the market overt rule does not mean that the formal interest that it met has also disappeared or that this interest does not continue to be worthy of legal recognition and protection. On this last point, see Smith, "Valediction to Market Overt," 248–249.

99. S. Todd Lowry, "Lord Mansfield and the Law Merchant: Law and Economics in the Eighteenth Century," *Journal of Economic Issues* 7, no. 4 (1973): 606. For further background historical discussion, see John H. Baker, "The Law Merchant and the Common Law before 1700," *Cambridge Law Journal* 38, no. 2 (1979): 295–322, and C. H. S. Fifoot, *Lord Mansfield* (Oxford: Clarendon Press, 1936), 104.

100. Adam Smith's famous phrase in *An Inquiry into the Nature and Causes of the Wealth of Nations* (London: W. Strahan and T. Cadell, 1776), book 2, chapter 2. On the systemic role and significance of circulation, see Hegel's remarks in *Lectures on Natural Right*, paragraph 104. Hegel was a close and deep reader of Smith.

101. Commons emphasizes this point. *Legal Foundations of Capitalism*, 251.

102. Millar v. Race, (1758) 1 Burr. 452 (K.B.).

103. See Lowry, "Lord Mansfield and the Law Merchant."

104. Millar v. Race, 457–459.

105. Millar v. Race, 459.

106. Millar v. Race, 457. As plaintiff's counsel put it: "Our right is not by assignment, but by the law, by the usage and custom of trade. I do not contend that the robber, or even the finder of a note, has a right to the note; but after circulation, the holder upon a valuable consideration has a right." Millar v. Race, 455.

107. Millar v. Race, 457.

108. Millar v. Race, 457–458.

109. Millar v. Race, 455.

110. Consistent with Commons's view: "Thereafter it became possible for the courts to build up the law of business in proportion as business itself developed." *Legal Foundations of Capitalism,* 235.

111. Rawls's second principle of justice reads: "Social and economic inequalities are to satisfy two conditions: first, they are to be attached to offices and positions open to all under conditions of fair equality of opportunity; and second, they are to be to the greatest benefit of the least-advantaged members of society (the difference principle)." *Justice as Fairness,* 42–43.

112. See Rawls, *Justice as Fairness,* 43, 61.

113. Rawls sets out this idea of a division of labor between principles in *Justice as Fairness,* 53–55, and in *Political Liberalism,* 265–269. Briefly stated, "background justice" for Rawls refers to the principles that directly regulate the justice of the "basic structure of society." The basic structure of society consists in how the main social, economic, and political institutions (including the political constitution, forms of property, the market, and the family in some form) fit together as one system of social cooperation and the way they assign basic rights and duties and shape the division of advantages arising from this cooperation over time from one generation to the next. Rawls views his theory as taking the basic structure as the primary subject of justice insofar as it requires that there be distinctive principles that apply directly to the basic structure for the purpose of ensuring background justice over time. Within this framework of the basic structure, individual transactions, voluntary associations, and the like take place. Internally, these different kinds of transactions (including contracts) and associations are governed by their own special principles, depending on their distinctive aims and requirements. Principles of background justice apply only indirectly to them. See Rawls, *Justice as Fairness,* 10–14. In what sense, then, is contract law (like the market, forms of property, the family, etc.) to be viewed as an institution *of* the basic structure? Briefly stated: insofar as the regime of contract law, as one part of the system of productive and fair social cooperation, performs an important ongoing societal function relating to the production and division of advantages made possible by that social cooperation. The principles of distributive justice are applied directly to the social background circumstances, the scope, and the cumulative effects of contracting viewed in this way, to ensure background justice over time.

114. Rawls, *Justice as Fairness,* 53.

115. See Rawls, *Justice as Fairness,* 10. Previous discussions of this question regarding Rawls's account include Arthur Ripstein, "The Division of Responsibility and the Law of Tort," *Fordham Law Review* 72 (2004): 1811; Samuel Scheffler, "Distributive Justice, the Basic Structure and the Place of Private Law," *Oxford Journal of Legal Studies* 32, no. 2 (2015): 213–235; and Samuel Freeman, *Liberalism and Distributive Justice* (New York: Oxford University Press, 2018), chapter 5.

116. In "Distributive Justice, the Basic Structure and the Place of Private Law," Scheffler concludes by suggesting the need to identify specifically nondistributive norms of justice for transactions and to consider how they should be integrated with distributional norms such as Rawls's. This is what I hope to do.

117. For example, Robert Nozick, *Anarchy, State, and Utopia* (New York: Basic Books, 1974). My brief discussion follows Rawls's summary in *Political Liberalism*, 262–265.

118. For the same reason, the juridical conception need not include or require within its own framework the further corrective of something like the Lockean proviso to ensure that throughout the subsequent process "as much and as good" remains available to others to appropriate.

119. Keep in mind that this "initial situation" is not to be understood as a historically existing reality, even possibly so. It represents simply the normative baseline that is entailed by the juridical conception within the parameters of liability for misfeasance only.

120. On this point, see Rawls, *A Theory of Justice*, 272–274, 310.

121. As Rawls emphasizes, this holds true for both liberal property-owning societies in which there is private ownership of the means of production and liberal socialist societies in which there is not. *A Theory of Justice*, 273–274.

122. As presented by Rawls in *A Theory of Justice*, 15.

123. As noted by Hegel, *Philosophy of Right*, paragraph 195.

124. It is crucial to keep in mind here that this arbitrariness from the standpoint of need and opportunity does not contradict the point, made earlier in Chapter 11, that the juridical conception of ownership is itself inherently nonarbitrary in virtue of its expressing the freedom and equality of juridical persons with the moral power to assert their sheer independence from everything given.

125. Rawls emphasizes this point in *A Theory of Justice* (277) and in his other writings.

126. In contrast with formal equality of opportunity, which requires that positions be formally open to all ("careers open to talents"), Rawls views fair equality of opportunity as requiring that all have a fair chance of attaining them. Among other things, this requires institutions that ensure similar roughly the same chances of education and achievement for persons similarly motivated and endowed. See Rawls, *Justice as Fairness*, 43–44.

127. Rawls, *Political Liberalism*, 267.

128. Once again, see Rawls's clear and instructive discussion of this point. *Political Liberalism*, 267–268.

129. Rawls, *Political Liberalism*, 269.

130. Rawls, *Justice as Fairness*, 54.

131. According to Rawls, the idea of pure background procedural justice requires that "the basic structure is arranged so that when everyone follows the publicly

recognized rules of cooperation, and honors the claims the rules specify, the particular distributions of goods that result are acceptable as just ... whatever these distributions turn out to be." *Justice as Fairness*, 50, 54. Note that the principles of transactional justice, though different from those of background justice, are also a case of pure (transactional) procedural justice understood in this sense.

132. "Defects in either kind of principle can result in a serious failure of the conception of justice as a whole." Rawls, *Justice as Fairness*, 54.

133. See Rawls, *Justice as Fairness* (162–166), where Rawls illustrates this point with respect to the family. See his statement regarding the fit between rules of background justice and the "important values expressed by free and fair agreements reached by individuals ... within the basic structure" (53).

134. See the classic article by Anthony Kronman, "Contract Law and Distributive Justice," *Yale Law Journal* 89, no. 3 (1980): 472–511. Kronman argues that a nondistributive normative basis for contract law must be incomplete, necessitating recourse to distributive justice to explain even the most basic feature of voluntariness in contract law. I have discussed Kronman's view in detail in Peter Benson, "Abstract Right and the Possibility of a Nondistributive Conception of Contract: Hegel and Contemporary Contract Theory," *Cardozo Law Review* 10, nos. 5–6 (1989): 1119–1145.

135. See Rawls, *Justice as Fairness*, 91–92.

136. The first principle reads: "Each person has the same indefeasible claim to a fully adequate scheme of equal basic liberties, which scheme is compatible with the same scheme of liberties for all." Rawls, *Justice as Fairness*, 42. For discussion of the basic liberties, including the right to personal property, see *Justice as Fairness*, 42–43, 104–106, 113–114.

137. See John Rawls, *The Law of Peoples* (Cambridge, MA: Harvard University Press, 1999), 65.

138. These powers include a capacity for a conception of the good, paralleling the moral power that is attributed to transactors as participants in the system of needs.

139. Rawls, *Justice as Fairness*, 114.

140. Rawls's first principle of justice includes constitutional and other fundamental political rights and freedoms. These express a political dimension that, in contrast to the second principle, goes beyond the idea of the system of needs as set out in this chapter. (Interestingly, Hegel characterizes the system of needs as a *pre*political domain of freedom.) The reason that I have brought the first principle into the discussion at this point is to show how Rawls's overall political conception and his view of the role of distributive justice (the second principle) within it support my proposed analysis of the relation between distributive justice and contract law as two sides of a division of labor between them.

141. Rawls, *Justice as Fairness*, 114, 178–179.

142. As reflected in Lochner v. New York, 198 U.S. 45 (1905). Rawls expressly rejects this doctrine. See *Political Liberalism*, 362.

143. See Rawls's discussion of market relations in *A Theory of Justice*, 272–274.
144. Rawls, *Justice as Fairness*, 135–140.
145. Rawls, *Justice as Fairness*, 72.
146. This is how Rawls describes the relation between the domains of background and local justice. See *Justice as Fairness*, 167.
147. As Rawls himself notes in *Justice as Fairness*, 52 and 52n18.
148. Rawls, *Justice as Fairness*, 51–52.
149. Rawls, *Justice as Fairness*, 54.
150. For valuable discussion, see Olha Cherednychenko, *Fundamental Rights, Contract Law and the Protection of the Weaker Party: A Comparative Analysis of the Constitutionalisation of Contract Law, with Emphasis on Risky Financial Transactions* (Munich: Sellier, European Law Publishers, 2007). See also the essays collected in Daniel Friedmann and Daphne Barak-Erez, eds., *Human Rights in Private Law* (Oxford: Hart Publishing, 2003).
151. Cherednychenko herself argues convincingly in *Fundamental Rights* for a "weak indirect horizontal effect" of fundamental rights, as discussed below.
152. This kind of view, we saw, is the basis of Craswell's critique of so-called autonomy theories of contract. See earlier discussions in Chapters 3 and 9.
153. This suggestion is no different from a view that, contrary to Rawls's own clear statements, would apply the difference principle directly to the internal life of a family or to some voluntary association. See Rawls, *Justice as Fairness*, 164–165.
154. The view that I am proposing is, I believe, consistent with what Cherednychenko refers to as the "weak indirect horizontal effect" of fundamental rights in contract law. *Fundamental Rights*, 564–569. Through her detailed treatment of different jurisdictions, Cherednychenko argues persuasively for the theoretical and practical superiority of this approach.
155. As discussed in Chapter 5.
156. This view is clearly Rawls's as well. See *Political Liberalism*, 261–262. It is also Hegel's. See his *Philosophy of Right*, paragraph 66.
157. Rawls presupposes as lexically prior even to his first principle of justice a substantive requirement that every citizen's basic needs (physical, cognitive, and social) be met, ensuring that they have the means or conditions (sustenance, housing, etc.) and opportunities (educational) not only to exist but also to understand and fruitfully exercise their basic liberties and rights guaranteed under the first principle. See Rawls, *Political Liberalism*, 7, and *Justice as Fairness*, 44n7, 47–48.
158. For further examples, see Prince Saprai, "The Principle against Self-Enslavement in Contract Law," *Journal of Contract Law* 26, no. 1 (2009): 25.
159. I agree with Cherednychenko, *Fundamental Rights*, 545.
160. Rawls, *Justice as Fairness*, 166.
161. See Rawls, *Justice as Fairness*, 48–49.
162. This does not preclude the possibility that there may be contractual arrangements that clearly and blatantly violate these distributive norms and so are justi-

ciable before a court. Normally, such arrangements would also be caught by the contract doctrines discussed above. The very idea of a division of labor between rules for background justice and those for transactions requires nonenforcement. On this point, see Rawls, *Justice as Fairness*, 162.

163. An example of such an offer was that made in the well-known case of Carlill v. Carbolic Smoke Ball Co., [1893] 1 Q.B. 256 (Eng. C.A.).

164. Samuel Freeman makes a similar point in his thoughtful discussion of the relation between private law and Rawls's principles of justice. See Freeman, *Liberalism and Distributive Justice*, 167 and in particular 177–179.

165. Historically, the so-called common calling cases—involving common inns, shops, carriers, ferries, and the like—are clear examples at common law of offers construed as having fixed contractual incidents on the basis of legal grants of monopoly, the claims of necessity, and so forth. For further discussion, see Peter Benson, "Equality of Opportunity and Private Law," in *Human Rights in Private Law*, ed. Daniel Friedmann and Daphne Barak-Erez (Oxford: Hart Publishing, 2003), 227–243. For a rightly influential example that draws on the equal opportunity norms embedded in legislation, see Shelley v. Kramer, 334 U.S. 1 (1948). For other cases and further discussion, see Thomas W. Merrill and Henry E. Smith, *Property: Principles and Policies* (New York: Foundation Press, 2007), 445–480.

166. Interestingly, at one point Rawls presents the order of analysis in the sequence proposed here: "Altogether then we have three levels of justice, moving from inside outward: first, local justice (principles applying directly to . . . associations [and transactions]); second, domestic justice (principles applying to the basic structure of society); and finally, global justice (principles applying to international law)." *Justice as Fairness*, 11.

167. See Rawls's discussion of primary goods in *Justice as Fairness*, 57–61.

168. Rawls emphasizes that social cooperation is "always productive, and without cooperation there would be nothing produced and so nothing to distribute." *Justice as Fairness*, 61.

169. Rawls, *Justice as Fairness*, 21.

170. See, for example, in John Rawls, *Collected Papers*, ed. Samuel Freeman (Cambridge, MA: Harvard University Press, 1999), "Reply to Alexander and Musgrave," 241–242, and "Social Unity and Primary Goods," 368–371. According to Rawls, this capacity is the basis of a "social division of responsibility" between society (which is responsible for providing a fair share of primary goods) and citizens (who accept responsibility for adjusting their needs and purposes in view of their expected fair share). See "Social Unity," 371–374. Note that this division of responsibility, being part of the conception of distributive justice itself, is different from, and is not itself the basis of, the division of labor between transactional and distributive principles of justice.

171. Rawls, *Justice as Fairness*, 58–59.

172. Rawls, *Justice as Fairness*, 59.

173. "[P]olitical power is, of course, always coercive power backed by the state's machinery for enforcing its laws." Rawls, *Justice as Fairness*, 182.

174. Rawls, "Social Unity," 370.

175. Thus the juridical conception as I have presented it is neither a "right" nor "left" libertarian view as defined by G. A. Cohen and Keith Graham, "Self-Ownership, Communism and Equality," *Proceedings of the Aristotelian Society, Supplementary Volumes*, 64 (1990): 25–61. This allows it to be compatible with Rawls's difference principle. See Rawls, *Lectures on the History of Political Philosophy*, 367–370.

176. Rawls, *Justice as Fairness*, 124 (emphasis added). Rawls notes that this is the most reasonable reciprocity condition that he can think of, given the freedom and equality of citizens represented in the original position. As mentioned in the text, on this view of the difference principle there is no need to construe it as imposing genuinely positive duties to benefit others—which would be equivalent to imposing liability for nonfeasance in private law.

177. In light of these comparisons, a further question is whether the principles for transactions might be aptly presented as chosen by parties in an initial situation, analogously to the choice of principles for background justice in Rawls's original position. Since the juridical conception views individuals as strictly equal, it should be possible to represent them as parties symmetrically situated in some kind of initial situation. But we should not assume that the latter would necessarily be the same as the original position setup in Rawls's account. An initial situation for private law principles would have to model the particular conception of the person, the notions of reasonableness and rationality, and the sort of relation at issue (transactions in abstraction from productive social cooperation) that characterize the juridical conception. Because there would be no primary or other such goods, it is not clear how the parties should be presented as choosing principles in light of any rational preferences. Further, the fundamental distinction between physical and purely representational possession would have to be incorporated. Perhaps something like the original position reasoning that Rawls uses in *The Law of Peoples*—where parties simply consider the merits of different formulations or interpretations of principles of equality and independence among peoples—could also be appropriate for the selection of principles of transactional justice. See Rawls, *The Law of Peoples*, 30–34, 39–42, 68–70. But I cannot pursue these interesting questions further here.

178. Rawls, *Justice as Fairness*, 164.

179. On the fact of reasonable pluralism and the idea of neutrality of aim, see Rawls, *Justice as Fairness*, 33–34, 153n27.

Table of Cases

The following references are to sections and endnotes. A section in boldface type indicates that the case is discussed or mentioned in that section.

A & M Produce Co. v. FMC Corp., 6.3n91
A-G v. Blake, 7.3nn32–33, 8.2nn73, 75
Adams v. Lindsell, 2.1n15
Adderley v. Dixon, 8.1nn10, 19
Ajayi v. R. T. Briscoe (Nigeria) Ltd., 1.4n69
Akerblom v. Price, Potter, Walker & Co., 4.1n6
Alfred McAlpine Construction Ltd. v. Panatown Ltd., 7.3nn33–34, 41–42
Allcard v. Skinner, **5.1**, 5.1nn1, 4–5, 7–8
Allegheny College v. National Chautauqua County Bank, 1.2n34, 3.2n23
Alley v. Deschamps, 8.1nn10, 22
Aluminum Co. of America v. Essex Group Inc., 3.3n75
AMEV-UDC Finance Ltd. v. Austin, 5.3nn55, 72
Andrews Bros. v. Singer & Co., 6.2n43
Anglia Television Ltd. v. Reed, 8.1n36, 8.3nn81, 86
Armendariz v. Foundation Health Psychcare Services, Inc., 6.2n53, 6.3n64
Asamera Oil Corp. Ltd. v. Sea Oil & General Corp., 8.4n91
ASB Allegiance Real Estate Fund v. Scion Breckenridge, 3.4nn135, 139, 144
Attorney-General of Belize v. Belize Telecom Ltd., 3.2nn21, 50, 56–57

B. G. Linton Construction Ltd. v. Canadian National Railway Co., 6.3n66
Balfour v. Balfour, 2.3nn47, 49, 52
Bank Line Ltd. v. Arthur Capel & Co., 3.3n92

Bank of Columbia v. Hagner, 3.2n31
Bank of Credit and Commerce International S.A. v. Aboody, 5.1n6
Banque Bruxelles Lambert S.A. v. Eagle Star Insurance Co. Ltd., 8.2n54
Banta v. Stamford Motor Co., 5.3n60
Barclays Bank plc v. O'Brien, 5.1n1
Barker v. Halifax, 2.1n15
Barque Quilpue Ltd. v. Brown, 3.4n114
Bauer v. Sawyer, 9n36
BCCI v. Ali, 2.2n26
Beaucamp v. Neggin, 2.1n15
Beekman v. Marsters, 1.5.2n124
Berg v. Erikson, 3.3n92
Berke Moore Co. v. Phoenix Bridge Co., 2.2n26
Beswick v. Beswick, 1.5.1nn93, 97, 8.1n9
Bhasin v. Hrynew, 3.4nn100, 118, 146
Blackburn Bobbin Co. v. T. W. Allen & Sons Ltd., 3.3n70
Boone v. Eyre, **3.2**, 3.2n36
Boone v. Kerr-McGee Oil Industries, Inc., 3.4nn130, 141
Boustany v. Pigott, 4.3n46
Bowen v. Hall, 1.5.2nn125, 133
Bowlay Logging Ltd. v. Domtar Ltd., 8.3nn80, 83
British Westinghouse Co. v. Underground Electric Railway Co., 8.4n90
Burgoon v. Johnston, 9n35

Callanan Road Improvements Co. v. Colonial Sand & Stone Co. Inc., 5.3n83

Campbell Discount Co. Ltd. v. Bridge, 5.3n62, 6.1n31
Campbell Soup Co. v. Diehm, 5.2n20
Campbell Soup Co. v. Wentz, **5.2**, 5.2nn12–13, 18–21
Canadian Industrial Alcohol Co., Ltd. v. Dunbar Molasses Co., **3.3**, 3.3nn78–80
Carlill v. Carbolic Smoke Ball Co., 2.1n12, 12.3.2n163
Carpenter v. Virginia-Carolina Chemical Co., 3.4n130
Carter v. Boehm, 3.4n111
Caterpillar Far East Ltd. v. CEL Tractors Pte Ltd., 12.2.3n93
Cavendish Square Holding BV v. Talal El Makdessi, **5.3**, 5.3nn57, 67–68, 86, 89
Caxton Publishing Co. Ltd. v. Sutherland Publishing Co., 7.1n15
Chaplin v. Hicks, 8.1n36
Citizens' Light, Heat and Power Co. v. Montgomery Light and Water Power Co., 1.5.2n124
City of Dublin Steam Packet Co. v. The Ring, 3.4nn124, 128
City of London v. Nash, 8.1n30
Clydebank Engineering & Shipbuilding Co. Ltd. v. Don Jose Ramos Yzquierdo y Castaneda, **5.3**, 5.3nn68, 76
Cochrane v. Moore, 1.3n52
Coggs v. Bernard, 3.2n54
Colley v. Overseas Exporters, 3.4n115
Commonwealth v. Verwayen, 1.4n71
Commonwealth of Australia v. Amann Aviation Pty. Ltd., 8.3nn79, 83
Cooke v. Oxley, 2.1nn6, 8
Cooper v. Chitty, 7.1n16
Cosgrove v. Bartolotta, 1.4n62
Coulls v. Bagot's Executor & Trustee Co. Ltd., 1.5.1nn82, 93, 7.3nn38, 45
Crabb v. Arun District Council, 1.4n62
Crane v. London Dock Co., 12.2.3n97
Currie v. Misa, 1.2n33
Cyberchron Corp. v. Calldata Systems Development, 1.4n62

Dailey v. Dailey, 5.1n11
Dalton v. Educational Testing Service, 3.4n134
Dare v. The Bognor Urban District Council, 3.4n128

Davis v. Gifford, 2.3n45
Davis v. Isenstein, 9n34
Davis Contractors Ltd. v. Fareham Urban District Council, 3.2n57, 3.3nn70, 72–73, 75–76, 12.2.3n61
Day v. United States, 3.3n65
De Cicco v. Schweizer, 1.2n34
De Mattos v. Gibson, **1.5.2**, 1.5.2nn120, 136–145, **10.3.2**, 10.3.2n60
Denny, Mott & Dickson Ltd. v. James B. Fraser & Co. Ltd., 3.2n57, 3.3n64
Douez v. Facebook Inc., 6.2n53
Duke of St. Albans v. Shore, 3.2nn31, 38
Dunlop Pneumatic Tyre Co. Ltd. v. New Garage and Motor Co. Ltd., **5.3**, 5.3nn52, 69–70, 76–77, 84
Dutton v. Poole, 1.5.1n94

Earl of Aylesford v. Morris, 4.3n45
Eastern Airlines Inc. v. Gulf Oil Corp., 8.1n12
Eckstein v. Cummins, 6.3nn60, 66
Edge Group Waiccs LLC v. Sapir Group LLC, 9n35
Edwards v. Skyways Ltd., 2.3n48
Elsey v. J. G. Collins Insurance Agencies Ltd., 5.3n55
Embry v. Hargadine, McKittrick Dry Goods Co., 2.2n24
English Hop Growers Ltd. v. Dering, 5.2n38
Epstein v. Gluckin, 8.1n26
Equitable Trust Co. of New York v. Western Pacific Railway Co., 7.2n29
Escondido Oil Co. v. Glaser, 5.3n76
Esso Petroleum Co. v. Harper's Garage (Stourport) Ltd., **5.2**, 5.2nn25, 29, 35, 38, 43, 45

F. C. Austin Co. v. J. H. Tillman Co., 6.2n43
Falcke v. Gray, 8.1nn10, 12, 15, 19
Fidler v. Sun Life Assurance Co. of Canada, 7.3nn39, 50, 8.2n72
Fitzroy v. Cave, 1.5.2n109
Fleischer v. James Drug Stores Inc., 8.1n10
Foakes v. Beer, 12.2.3nn85–86
Food Fair Stores Inc. v. Blumberg, 3.4nn123, 125, 128
Fortune v. National Cash Register, 3.4n142
Fouldes v. Willoughby, 7.1n14
Francis Hollins v. George Fowler, 7.1n14

TABLE OF CASES

French v. Bekins Moving & Storage Co., 6.3n67
Frost v. Knight, **7.2**, 7.2n27

Gallen v. Allstate Grain Co. Ltd., 6.2n44
Gardiner v. Gray, 6.3n59
Ghen v. Rich, 10.3.1n47
Gilbert v. Kennedy, 8.3n78
Glanzer v. Shepard, 1.4n66
Goldberg 168-05 Corp. v. Levy, 3.4nn123, 127
Golding's Case, 2.1n5
Goodisson v. Nunn, 3.2nn30–31
Great Lakes & St. Lawrence Transportation Co. et al. v. Scranton Coal Co., 8.1n29
Grundt v. Great Boulder Pty. Gold Mines Ltd., 1.4nn62, 67

Hadley v. Baxendale, 3.3n66, **5.3**, 5.3nn78–79, 81, **7.1**, 7.1n9, 7.3n51, **8.2**, 8.2nn42, 47, 50–52, 63, 65, 71, 75, **9**
Hamer v. Sidway, 1.2nn34, 39
Hanlon Drydock & Shipbuilding Co. Inc. v. McNear Inc., 5.3n82
Harmer v. Jumbil (Nigeria) Tin Areas Ltd., 3.4n114
Harnett v. Yielding, **8.1**, 8.1nn10, 17
Hart v. O'Connor, 4.3n46
Hawkins v. McGee, 7.3n50
Hedley Byrne & Co. Ltd. v. Heller & Partners Ltd., 1.4n66
Heffron v. Imperial Parking Co., 6.3nn78–79
Henningsen v. Bloomfield Motors Inc., **6.3**, 6.3nn54–61, 63–64, 67
Herbert Morris Ltd. v. Saxelby, 5.2nn37–38
HML Corp. v. General Foods Corp., 3.4nn128–129
Hochster v. De La Tour, 7.2nn26, 31
Hoffman v. Red Owl Stores Inc., 1.4n62
Home Office v. Dorset Yacht Co. Ltd., Introduction n7
Horner v. Graves, 5.2n41
Horwood v Millar's Timber and Trading Co. Ltd., 5.2n51
H.R. Moch Co. v. Rensselaer Water Co., Introduction n7
Huguenin v. Baseley, 5.1nn1, 10

Imperator Realty Co. v. Tull, 1.4nn62, 67, 69
In Re Brocklehurst's Estate, 5.1n1
In Re Elkins-Dell Manufacturing Co., 5.2n50

International News Service v. The Associated Press, 1.5.2nn130, 143, 10.3.2n53
Investors Compensation Scheme Ltd. v. West Bromwich Building Society, 1.5.2n114, 2.2n23

Jackson v. Royal Bank of Scotland plc, 8.2n54
Jacob & Youngs Inc. v. Kent, **3.2**, 3.2nn40–47, 59, 3.4n148, 6.4n92, 12.2.3n73
Jaggard v. Sawyer, 8.1nn30, 33
James Baird Co. v. Gimbel Bros., Inc., 1.4n72
Jaquith v. Hudson, **5.3**, 5.3nn52, 62, 65, 72, 76
Jarvis v. Swan Tours Ltd., 7.3n50, 8.1n36, 8.2n38
Javins v. First National Realty Corp., 3.2n55, 12.2.3n72
Jones v. Barkley, 3.2nn26, 30
Jones v. Padavatton, 2.3n54

Karl Wendt Farm Equipment Co., Inc. v. International Harvester Co., 3.3n70
Karpinski v. Ingrasci, 9n36
Kemble v. Farren, 5.3n62
Kennedy v. Lee, 2.1n16, 2.2n19
Kerr Steamship Co. v. RCA, 8.2nn45, 54, 59, 61
Kham & Nate's Shoes No. 2, Inc. v. First Bank of Whiting, 3.4nn102, 104
King v. Duluth, M. & N. Railway Co., 1.2n38, 1.5.2n117
Kingston v. Preston, **3.2**, 3.2nn26–27
Kirke La Shelle Co. v. Paul Armstrong Co., 3.4nn107, 135
Koufos v. C. Czarnikow Ltd. [Heron II], 8.2n69
Krell v. Henry, **3.3**, 3.3nn68, 82–85, 88, 91
Kuwait Airways Corp. v. Iraqi Airways Co. and others (Nos. 4 and 5), 7.1nn14, 17, 20

L. Albert & Son v. Armstrong Rubber Co., 8.3n83
Laclede Gas Co. v. Amoco Oil Co., 8.1nn10, 12, 17
Lampleigh v. Braithwait, 1.2n32
Lancashire and Yorkshire Railway Co. v. MacNicoll, 7.1n14
Larrinaga & Co. v. Société Franco-Américaine des Phosphates de Medulla, 3.3n65
Law Debenture Trust Corp. v. Ural Caspian Oil Corp. Ltd., 1.5.2nn136, 144

L'Estrange v. F. Graucob Ltd., **6.2**, 6.2n37
Linz v. Schuck, 1.2n38
Liverpool City Council v. Irwin, 3.2n55, 6.3n72, 7.1n7
Livingstone v. Rawyards Coal Co., 7.3n33, 8.2n76
Lloyd v. Murphy, 3.3n89
Lloyds Bank v. Bundy, **4.1**, 4.1nn6, 17, 4.3nn42, 44, **5.1**, 5.1n3
Lochner v. New York, I.4n24, 12.3.2n142
Lord Elphinstone v. Monkland Iron & Coal Co., 5.3n63
Lord Strathcona Steamship Co. Ltd. v. Dominion Coal Co. Ltd., 1.5.2nn136, 144
Loudenback Fertilizer Co. v. Tennessee Phosphate Co., 3.4nn130, 136–137
Lumley v. Gye, **1.5.2**, 1.5.2nn121, 123
Lumley v. Wagner, **1.5.2**, 1.5.2nn121, 143
Luxor (Eastbourne) Ltd. v. Cooper, 3.4nn125, 128

MacDougald Construction Co. v. State Highway Department, 3.4n139
Mackay v. Dick, **3.4**, 3.4nn116, 122
Majors v. Kalo Laboratories Inc., 6.3n91
Manchester Dairy System Inc. v. Hayward, 9n35
Mannai Investment Co. v. Eagle Star Life Insurance Co., 2.2n23
Market St. Assocs. Ltd. P'ship v. Frey, 3.4n105
Marzetti v. Williams, 7.1n22, 7.3n43
McClelland v. Climax Hosiery Mills, **8.4**, 8.4n90
McCrae v. Commonwealth Disposals Commission, 8.3n83
McEllistrim v. Ballymacelligott Co-operative Agricultural and Dairy Society, 5.2nn38–39
McGhee v. R. Co., 10.3.1n45
McGovern v. City of New York, 1.2nn37, 45, 2.3n50
McGowan v. Commissioner of Stamp Duties, 1.5.2n108
Metropolitan Life Insurance Co. v. RJR Nabisco Inc., 3.4n102
Meyer v. Packard Cleveland Motor Co., 6.2n43
Millar v. Race, **12.2.3**, 12.2.3nn102, 104–109
Miller v. Taylor Insulation Co., 1.4n62

Mitchel v. Reynolds, **5.2**, 5.2nn27, 31, 33, 36, 38, 40–41, 43
Moran v. Standard Oil Co. of New York, 3.2n23
Morton v. Lamb, 3.2n31
Moses v. Mcferlan, 3.2n25
Motours Ltd. v. Euroball (West Kent) Ltd., 6.3n91

Nadell & Co. v. Grasso, 1.5.2nn136, 143
National Commercial Bank (Jamaica) Ltd. v. Hew, 5.1n11
Neuchatel Asphalte Co. Ltd. v. Barnett, 6.2n41
Nichols v. Raynbred, 1.2n31
Nordenfelt v. Maxim Nordenfelt Guns & Ammunition Co. Ltd., 5.2n38
Norman v. Federal Commissioner of Taxation, 1.5.2n105
Northern Pacific Railway Co. v. American Trading Co., 3.3n92

OBG Ltd. v. Allan, 1.5.2nn122, 128–129
Omak Maritime Ltd. v. Mamola Challenger Shipping Co., 8.3n83

P. P. Emory Manufacturing v. Columbia Smelting & Refining Works, 7.2n28
Pacific Brands Sport & Leisure Pty. Ltd. v. Underworks Pty. Ltd., 1.5.2nn104, 108, 115
Palsgraf v. Long Island Railroad Co., 1.5.1n88, 10.3.1n45
Paradine v. Jane, **3.1**, 3.1n10, **3.3**, 3.3nn62–63
Parker v. South Eastern Railway Co., **6.1**, 6.1nn24, 30
ParkingEye Ltd. v. Beavis, **5.3**, 5.3n57
Parsons (H.) (Livestock) Ltd. v. Uttley Ingham & Co. Ltd., 8.2nn39, 60, 65
Patel v. Ali, 8.1nn30–31
Patterson v. Meyerhofer, **3.4**, 3.4nn117, 121
Pearson v. Williams' Administrators, 9n35
Peech v. Best, 3.4n128
Peek v. North Staffordshire Railway Co., 6.3n67
Penney v. First National Bank of Boston, 6.3n88
Pesticcio v. Huet, 5.1n7
Petrofina (Great Britain) Ltd. v. Martin, 5.2nn34, 38
Philips Hong Kong Ltd. v. A-G of Hong Kong, **5.3**, 5.3nn58, 66, 72, 76, 82, 84–85, 87

Phillips v. Fielding, 3.2n31
Philpot v. Gruninger, 1.2n37
Pierson v. Post, **10.2**, 10.2n16, **11.3**, 11.3n24
Post v. Jones, 4.1n6
Pride Hyundai Inc. v. Chrysler Financial Co., 6.3nn82, 91

R v. A-G for England and Wales, 5.1nn1, 11
Radford v. De Froberville, 7.3n33
Raffles v. Wichelhaus ["The Peerless"], 2.2n34
Rainieri v. Miles, 7.1n11
Rann v. Hughes, 1.2n48
Raymond v. Yarrington et al., 1.5.2n129
Re an Arbitration between Comptoir Commercial Anversois and Power, Son & Co., 3.2n57
Readhead v. Midland Railway Co., 3.1n4, 3.2n49, 7.1n7
Rio Algom Corp. v. Jimco Ltd., 3.4n105
Robophone Facilities Ltd. v. Blank, 5.3nn73, 75, 80, 84
Rose and Frank Co. v. J. R. Crompton & Bros. Ltd., 2.3nn52-53
Rotheram v. Browne, 4.1n15
Royal Bank of Scotland plc v. Etridge (No. 2), 5.1nn1-2, 8
Rubenstein v. Rubenstein, 9n35
Rudbart v. Water Supply Commission, 6.1n11
Rylands v. Fletcher, 7.1n8

Samuels v. Davis, 7.1n5
Schnell v. Nell, 1.2n44
Schroeder (A.) Music Publishing Co. Ltd. v. Macaulay, 5.2n30, 6.1n13
Seaver v. Ransom et al., 1.5.1n95
Security Stove & Manufacturing Co. v. American Railway Express Co., 8.3nn78, 83, 86
Shelfer v. City of London Electric Lighting Co., 8.1n32, 8.2n76
Shell UK Ltd. v. Lostock Garage Ltd., 6.3n72
Shelley v. Kramer, 12.3.2n165
Sky Petroleum Ltd. v. V.I.P. Petroleum Ltd., 8.1n12
Skycom Corp. v. Telstar Corp., 1.4n62, 2.2nn27, 36
Smith v. Eric S. Bush, 6.3n67

Smith v. Hughes, 2.2nn24, 30, 33
Snepp v. United States, 8.2n75
Socimer International Bank Ltd. (in liquidation) v. Standard Bank London Ltd., 3.4n134
South Australia Asset Management Corp. v. York Montague Ltd., 8.2nn54, 58
Southwest Natural Gas Co. v. Oklahoma Portland Cement Co., 3.4nn125, 130
Standing v. Bowring, 1.3n51
Stephens v. Gulf Oil Canada Ltd., 5.2n36
Steria v. Ronald Hutchison, 1.4n67
Stewart v. Stewart, 5.2n32
Stilk v. Myrick, 1.2n38
Suisse Atlantique Société d'Armement Maritime S.A. v. Rotterdamsche Kolen Centrale N.V., 6.3n66, 6.4n93
Sulzbach v. Town of Jefferson, 2.3n46
Swiss Bank Corp. v. Lloyds Bank Ltd., 1.5.2n136
Syme v. Marks Rentals Inc., 6.2n34

Tate v. Williamson, 5.1n1
Taylor v. Caldwell, **3.3**, 3.3nn68-69, 71
The Argentino, 7.3n34
The Case of Market-Overt, 12.2.3n94
The Hannah Blumenthal, 2.2n23
The Mersey Steel and Iron Co. v. Naylor, Benzon and Co., 3.2n37
The Moorcock, **3.2**, 3.2nn23, 49-55
The Opera Company of Boston Inc. v. The Wolf Trap Foundation for the Performing Arts, 3.3n89
The Stratford Inc. v. Seattle Brewing & Malting Co., 3.3n88
Thomas v. Thomas, 1.2n25
Thorner v. Major, 1.4nn62, 65
Thorp v. Thorp, 1.1n14, 1.2n24
Tilden Rent-A-Car Co. v. Clendenning, **6.2**, 6.2nn34-36, 38, 40, **6.3**
Tinn v. Hoffman & Co., 2.1n14
Tito v. Waddell (No. 2), 8.2n74
Tolhurst v. Associated Portland Cement Manufacturers (1900) Ltd., 1.5.2n107
Torkington v. Magee, 1.5.2n110
Transamerica Life Canada Inc. & Aegon Canada Inc. v. ING Canada Inc., 3.4nn106, 108
Transatlantic Financing Corp. v. United States, 3.3n89

Transfield Shipping Inc. v. Mercator Shipping Inc. ("The Achilleas"), 8.2nn45, 49, 56–57, 62, 68–69
Tredegar Iron and Coal Co. v. Hawthorn Bros. and Co., 7.2n30
Trollope & Colls Ltd. v. North West Metropolitan Regional Hospital Board, 3.2n56
Tufton v. Sperni, 5.1n1
Tulk v. Moxhay, 1.5.2n136
Turkey v. Awadh, 5.1n11
Tweddle v. Atkinson, **1.5.1**, 1.5.1nn83, 89
Tymshare v. Covell, 3.4nn131, 133, 138–140, 142, 147, 149

Ultramares v. Touche, 8.2n61
Utica City National Bank v. Gunn, 3.2n23

Van Valkenburgh, Nooger & Neville Inc. v. Hayden Publishing Co., 3.4n128
Vancouver Malt and Sake Brewing Co. Ltd v. Vancouver Breweries Ltd., 5.2nn35, 43
Vernon v. Bethell, 6.3n76
Victoria Laundry (Windsor) Ltd. v. Newman Industries Ltd., **8.2**, 8.2nn53, 60, 64

W. J. Tatem Ltd. v. Gamboa, 3.3n93
Walgreen Co. v. Sara Creek Property Co., 8.1n28
Walton Stores (Interstate) Ltd. v. Maher, 1.4nn62, 67, 69

Waring v. WDAS Broadcasting Station Inc., 1.5.2nn120, 136, 143
Washington State Hop Producers Inc., Liquidation Trust v. Goschie Farms, 3.3n89
Watford Electronics Ltd. v. Sanderson CFL Ltd., 6.3n91
Watson, Laidlaw, & Co. v. Pott, Cassels, & Williamson, 7.3nn33, 36, 8.1n35
Webb v. Direct London and Portsmouth Railway Co., 8.1n30
Wedgwood v. Adams, 8.1n30
Whiten v. Pilot Insurance Co., 8.2n76
Williams v. Roffey Bros. & Nicholls (Contractors) Ltd., 1.2n38, 12.2.3n87
Williams v. Walker-Thomas Furniture Co., **6.3**, 6.3nn80–81, 83–85, 87
Williams Bros. v. Ed. T. Agius Ltd., 7.3n40, 8.1n11
Wisconsin & Michigan Railway Co. v. Powers, 1.2nn28, 30
Wiseman v. Cole, 1.2n35
Wood v. Lucy, Lady Duff-Gordon, 3.1n3, 3.2n23, 9n34
Wright v. Carter, 5.1n1

Yam Seng Pte Ltd. v. International Trade Corp. Ltd., 3.4nn100, 105, 144, 8.3nn82–84, 87
Young v. Timmins, **5.2**, 5.2nn22, 24

Zuckerman v. Transamerica Insurance Co., 6.3n62

Acknowledgments

The core argument of this book first occurred to me as a third-year law student when writing a paper on contract theory at the University of Toronto Faculty of Law. I further developed and expanded it in my LLM thesis, "Toward a Pure Theory of Contract," written under the supervision of Charles Fried at the Harvard Law School. But the complete argument as presented here has taken shape over more than three decades of teaching and writing about contract law and private law theory, starting at McGill, and then at the University of Toronto law schools. My first debt of gratitude is therefore to the many students who over the years found these matters sufficiently interesting to share with me their ideas, challenges, and questions. I have tried to present as much of the argument as possible in a way that motivated students, who are taking first-year private law courses, should be able to find accessible and helpful. My hope is that the book conveys even a little of how truly interesting and deep contract law can be when we let it speak to us for itself.

I wish to acknowledge my special intellectual debts to Charles Fried and Ernest Weinrib. Fried's elegantly written and carefully argued *Contract as Promise* is, in my view, still the most important and most interesting modern work in contract theory, consistently setting out a compelling view of the underlying moral unity of the many doctrines of contract law as a whole. Any effort to provide yet another theory must engage his arguments and has the burden of showing not only that the proposed alternative is needed but also that it is better able to make sense of the law and its moral basis. That is the standard that I have set for myself and if I have failed, it is not for want of trying. In our times, Weinrib's *The Idea of Private Law* has singlehandedly renewed systematic theoretical inquiry into the nature and foundations of private law. I am fortunate to have had Ernie first as my teacher and now as my colleague. Through his writings, he has shown what theorizing about private law requires and also what it can be; and in many discussions with him over the years, he helped me understand better what needs to be said and what I was trying to say. I will always be grateful to him for this.

In the text and endnotes, I have tried to acknowledge other important debts, of which there are many. But in addition I would like particularly to thank the following friends and colleagues for their much appreciated encouragement, instructive discussions, and important suggestions over the long period of preparing the book: Gregory Bordan, Alan Brudner, Bruce Chapman, Hanoch Dagan, Abraham Drassinower, Martin Friedland, Brian Heller, Jennifer Nadler, Jason Neyers, Benjamin Porat, Peggy Radin, Arthur Ripstein, Nicholas Sage, Lionel Smith, Stephen Smith, Robert Stevens, Michael Trebilcock, Stephen Waddams, and Arnold Weinrib. I also wish to thank Fredrick Schumann, Kathryn Hart, and Yona Gal, who, as my research assistants at the University of Toronto, not only read and commented on earlier iterations and drafts of the book but also helped me clarify fundamental aspects of the argument. Thanks to Emma Ryan of the class of 2020 for editing and proofreading the next-to-final version of the whole draft. To Sooin Kim and Sufei Xu, both of the Bora Laskin Law Library, thanks for their indispensable help over more than ten years in cheerfully providing me with the seemingly endless number of cases, articles, and materials that I needed to prepare and write the book. To Thomas LeBien, executive editor-at-large at the Harvard University Press, my gratitude for his guidance and encouragement throughout, for his belief in the manuscript's worthiness to be published, and for shepherding it so smoothly through the different stages. Thanks also to Kathleen Drummy, assistant to the editor, for her much appreciated help and to the external readers whose important suggestions enabled me to improve the draft. I also wish to express my special appreciation to Yara Wilcox, class of 2021, for her painstaking work of reviewing and correcting the proofs, her helpful suggestions, and for compiling the table of cases. Finally, my sincere thanks to Sherry Gerstein, production editor at Westchester Publishing Services, for "going beyond duty" by graciously accepting—and doing the hard work of inputting—my endless final corrections, managing the complex publication process with cheerfulness, encouragement, and great expertise. A more helpful and supportive editor I could not have hoped for.

My deepest gratitude is to my family. First and foremost, I wish to remember with love my dear parents, Robert and Norma Betty Benson, who both passed away while I was writing the book. My gratitude for everything they gave me is endless and my respect for all they were is without bounds. But for the certain knowledge that they would have wanted me to complete this book, I do not think that I could have done so. To my sons, David, Joseph, and Noah, who, to my surprise and delight, are all studying law, my appreciation for their encouragement over the years but even more for our many discussions. I hope that they find the end product interesting. Finally, to my wife, Marina. No words can properly express the depth of my gratitude. Because of her—her constant patience, love, and insight gently reminding me what is most important and what I am trying to do—I have been able to write the book. For this and so much more, I dedicate it to her.

Index

Note: For each of the main topics discussed in the book, I have provided index entries that follow the analytical development of ideas in order of their appearance in the text, in addition to standard alphabetical entries. Page numbers followed by an n or nn indicate notes.

Alderson, Baron, 279–280
Allcard v. Skinner, 193–194, 525n5, 525nn7–8
Alternative performances: consideration and, 308–309, 560nn34–35; impossibility and, 311, 511n74; unconscionability and, 530n64; dual performance hypothesis and, 304–313
Anticipatory repudiation, 241, 253–255, 545nn30–31. *See also* Breach of contract, nature of
Aquinas, Thomas, 30, 521n18, 522n35, 524n49, 546n33, 546n37, 571n21, 576n66
Aristotle, 30–31, 524n49
Assignment, of contractual rights, 84–91, 354–355; main features of, 84–86; judicial statement of, 492nn104–105, 493nn107–109; assigned right is distinct from but presupposes *in personam* contractual right to performance, 86–88; as a transfer of ownership of chose in action from assignor to assignee, 86–88; chose in action defined, 493n114; relation between consideration and contract right as chose in action, 87; every contract right a chose in action but not always assignable, 87–88; transfer model *vs.* "contractual" approach, 493n111; contract-based limits on assignability, 88–89; vulnerability of assigned right in relation to assignor's contractual right, 89–90; nature of obligor's duty toward assignee, 90–91; and *in rem* dimension of contract, 354–355. *See also* Third-party effects and contract

"Bargain and sale" in English law: contrasted with conception of contract as transfer of ownership, 568n62. See also *In rem* rights

Barnett, Randy E., 484n17, 490n75, 501n32, 506n24, 519n3 (chap. 4), 536n23
Blackburn, Lord, 146–147, 441
Bodily integrity, right of, 326, 328, 332–333, 340, 375, 379–381, 390, 563n18. *See also* Moral basis of ownership and contract
Boone v. Eyre, 137
Bowen, Lord Justice, 140–141
Bramwell, Lord Justice, 222–223
Breach of contract, as strict liability, 243–250; what it is not, 244–245; what it is, 245–247; involves a *per se* basic injury, 245–247; liability for consequential loss presupposes but distinct from basic injury, 250; consistent with voluntary basis of contract, 246–247; compared with negligence and conversion, 247–250; *per se* injury of conversion involves direct interference with plaintiff's possessory right, 248; parallel with conversion sheds light on nature of breach, 250–255. *See also* Breach of contract, nature of
Breach of contract, nature of, 8, 24, 66, 250–255; and conversion, 251; breach always imports a negative injury, 251–252; juridical significance of delivery, 251–252, 257; the doctrine of anticipatory repudiation presented and explained, 253–255, 545nn29–30; juridical significance of anticipatory repudiation, 254–255. *See also* Breach of contract as strict liability
Breach of contract and compensatory justice, 255–262; compensatory justice in general, 255–256; judicial statements of, 546n33; within framework of liability for misfeasance, 255; requires coercive response to wrongful interference with plaintiff's exclusive control over asset and aims to put her in position equivalent to pre-wrong,

Breach of contract and compensatory justice (*continued*)
256; analysis applies to contract law, with rightful asset promised as part of promise-for-consideration relation, 256, 546n34; party's performance interest defined, 257; plaintiff has immunity with respect to performance interest, 256–257; all contract remedies aim to do compensatory justice by redressing injury to performance interest, 257; remedies represent defendant's liability to plaintiff, not fulfillment of duty to perform, 258–259; specify kinds and measures of losses resulting from injury to performance interest, 257–258; distinction between injury (*injuria*) and loss (*damnum*), 257–258, 547n41, 547n43; analysis applies transactionally to particular contract between particular parties for particular injury and loss, 259; not an indifference principle concerned with well-being, 260; no basis for "liability" and "property" rules classification, 261; categorical distinction between enforceable express or implied terms and remedies, 261–262; remedies not product of parties' choices, 262; punitive damages and, 555n76. *See also* Expectation damages and contract theory; Remedies for breach of contract: unity and diversity

Brown, R.A., 487n49, 487nn50–53, 488n56

Brudner, Alan, 484n23

Calabresi, Guido, 261

Campbell Soup Co. v. Wentz, 197–199, 204

Canadian Industrial Alcohol Co., Ltd., v. Dunbar Molasses Co., 149–150, 512n78

Cardozo, Justice Benjamin, 133, 137–138, 139–140, 143, 149–150, 239, 271, 291–292, 480n8, 485n37, 486n45, 489n67, 491n88, 503n50, 506n23, 508nn40–47, 553n45, 554n61, 558n90, 566n45, 577n73

Cavendish Square Holding BV v. Talal el Makdessi, 205–206

Chelmsford, Lord, 97, 98

Chen-Wishart, Mindy, 173, 490n75, 496n136, 520n14, 524–525nn1–2, 530n56, 552n40

Cherednychenko, Olha, 463, 583nn150–151, 583n154

Chose in action. *See* Assignment, of contractual rights

Commons, John R., 574n35, 575n45, 576n65, 579n101, 580n110

Commutative (or corrective) justice, 6, 30–31, 190, 300, 301, 389, 524n49, 571n21. *See also* Distributive justice and contract law

Compensatory Justice. *See* Breach of contract and compensatory justice

Consequential loss. *See* Conversion, tort of; Remedies II, damages for consequential loss under *Hadley v. Baxendale*

Consideration: doctrine of, 40–69; contractual liability necessarily based on, 22, 41–42, 69, 73–75, 79; doctrine directly constitutes promise-for-consideration as fundamental contractual relation, not a control device or evidence of something else such as promissory intent, 22, 38, 41–42, 58; contemporary contract theories and, 41–47; Fuller's qualified defense of, 43–47; contrast between bilateral nature of promise-for-consideration relation and the seal, 46–47; the main features of, 47–56; requirements of structure of, 47–52; substantive requirements of, 52–56; meaning and role of benefit, detriment and value in, 52–55; idea of reciprocity in, 51–53, 63; "past consideration" and "pre-existing duty" discussed, 485n32, 485n38; requires promissory relations constituted by two qualitatively distinct and reciprocally related sides that include both substantive exchanges and also transactions involving donative intent, 56; the doctrine's indifference to comparative value discussed, 54–56; nominal consideration a logical possibility, 55 (*see also* Unconscionability, the principle of); transaction-types and, 22, 55–56, 235–236, 339; reply to Charles Fried's critique of, 56–58; comparison between executed gifts and, 58–65; promise-for-consideration relation as transactional acquisition and transfer in the element of representation, 61–66; distinction between agreement and performance, 62; right to performance the legal consequence, not object, of contractual transfer, 65–66; consideration-based contractual liability contrasted with reliance-based promissory liability, 69–75;

INDEX

objective test applies to all elements of, 50, 110–117. *See also* Contract as a transfer of ownership; Contract as transactional acquisition; Contracts under seal; Contractual intent; Donative intent; Gratuitous promises; Nominal consideration; Objective test for contract formation and interpretation; Reliance as substantive basis of liability; Unconscionability, the principle of

"Consideration and Form" (Fuller), 40, 43–47, 323

Contract as a transfer of ownership, 319–365; overview, 319–320; a theoretical formulation of contract as transactional acquisition, 25–27, 319–320; second part of public justification of contract law, 319–320; promise-for-consideration relation can be construed as, 320–325, 338–342, 349–364; idea of ownership in private law, 325–326; right of bodily integrity distinguished from ownership of things, 326, 328; ownership of things must always be acquired, 326; respect for ownership entails respect for persons' acts of acquisition, 326; two kinds of acquisition: original (based on unilateral acts) *vs.* derivative (based on bilateral acts), 326–327 (*see also* Derivative (transactional) acquisition; Original Acquisition); relation of property and contract to two forms of acquisition, 328; nature, elements and limits of original acquisition, 328–333, 336; conceptual transition to derivative acquisition as more complete expression of private law idea of ownership, 333–334; immediate executed exchange as first form of derivative acquisition, 334–338; limits of immediate exchange, 337–338; contractual transfer of ownership resolves tensions in original acquisition and immediate exchange, 338–340, 341; the acts constituting contractual transfer fully transactional and independent of physical holding: hence "representational", 338–339, 341; two fundamental categories of acts of contractual transfer: gift and exchange, 339; the wide nature and kinds of objects of contractual transfer, 340–341; contract formation as most complete and unqualified mode of ownership acquisition in private law, 341–2; compatibility between contract rights being *in personam* and, 352–353; relation between *in rem* dimension of contract and, 355–360; concluding remarks about, 360–365. *See also* Contract as transactional acquisition; *In personam* rights; *In rem* and *in personam* rights, distinction between; *In rem* rights

Contract as Promise (Fried), 56–57, 479n1, 482n6

Contract as transactional acquisition: organizing idea implicit in main contract doctrines, 8; direct answer to Fuller and Perdue challenge, 8–9; answer to similar challenge in civilian tradition, 479n2, 480n12, 482n2; as working hypothesis for Justice in Transactions, 9; embodies specific conception of the reasonable, 19; in the element of representation (promissory), 63–65; promise-for-consideration as a form of, 60–68. *See also* Contract as a transfer of ownership; Derivative (transactional) acquisition; Moral basis of ownership and contract

Contract formation: overview, 22–23; introduction to contract formation, 35–39. *See also* Implication; Offer and acceptance. *See also under* Consideration

Contracts under seal: promise-for-consideration relations and, 46–47; objective test and, 484n19; as legal formality, 436–439, 484n18

Contract theories. *See* Economic theories of contract law; Justice in Transactions, a theory of contract law; Promissory theories of contract law

Contractual intent, 23, 110–112, 113–114, 116, 117–121, 467, 503n54; nature of, 117–118; relation between intent and promise-for-consideration relation, 120–121; not a separate requirement for contract formation, 121; actual intent to create legal relations neither necessary nor sufficient for contractual effects, 120–121. *See also* Objective test for contract formation and interpretation; Voluntariness. *See also under* Power-conferring conception of contract law

Contractual obligation: explained on basis of the reasonable, 67–68, 120–121, 363–364, 392–394, 397–398; not based on power-conferring conception of duty, 67, 121, 364, 392; contrasted with moral duty to keep promises, 401–413

Conversion, tort of: defined, 247–248; strict liability and, 247–249; consequential loss and, 247, 249–250; compared with breach of contract and negligence, 247–255. *See also* Breach of contract, as strict liability

Corbin, Arthur, 108, 498n2, 498n7, 498n11

Craswell, Richard, 129, 130, 303–304, 308, 312–314, 480n10, 547nn46–48, 548n54

Dagan, Hanoch, 488n57, 507n34, 576–577n66

Damages for breach of contract. *See* Enforcement; Gain-measured damages for breach of contract; Lost performance value damages; Nominal damages; Punitive damages for breach of contract; Remedies I, expectation (or performance) damages *vs.* specific performance; Remedies II, damages for consequential loss under *Hadley v. Baxendale*; Remedies III, reliance damages

Dawson, John P., 128, 195, 197, 505n16, 511n75, 520n13, 522n37, 524n1, 525nn9–10, 529n50, 535n10, 535n16, 536n32, 540n77, 578n86

Default rule paradigm, 125–130. *See also* Implication

De Mattos, principle of, 95–98, 354–355, 496n136; nature and limits of principle, 96–98; relation between contract and third-party effects, 99; and *in rem* dimension of contracts, 354–355; *Lumley v. Wagner* compared with, 497n143. *See also* Equitable servitudes on chattels

De Mattos v. Gibson, 95–98, 355, 496n136

Denning, Lord, 173–174, 188, 194, 225

Dependent covenants, doctrine of, 136–137. *See also* Implication

Derivative (transactional) acquisition: defined, 326–328; discussed, 327, 329, 333–339, 341–343, 349–360, 361–363, 384, 390, 419; *in rem/in personam* dimensions in, 349–360. *See also* Contract as a transfer of ownership; Contract as transactional acquisition; *In personam* rights; *In rem* rights

Distributive justice. *See* Distributive justice and contract law

Distributive justice and contract law, 448–468; overview, 448–449; stability of contract law with respect to distributive justice satisfied if both can be part of division of labor proposed by Rawls, 448–449, 580n113; focus on distributive justice "in a narrower sense", 580nn111–112; Justice in Transactions contrasts sharply with libertarian theory, 449–452; idea of system of needs with two parts as basis of division of labor between transactional (contractual) and background distributive principles, even supposing the lexical priority of the juridical conception of contract, 452–456; division of labor is consistent with both Rawls's political conception and contract law, 457–462, 582n136; special role of the basic liberties in, 457–462; how contract law effectuates indirect application of fundamental rights within its own transactional framework, 462–467; summary of argument, 467–468. *See also* Institution, contract law as; Justice in transactions, a theory of contract law; Rawls, John

Distributive justice "in narrower sense", 448, 580n112

Donative intent: defined, 173, 562n2; contract as transfer and, 388, 562n2; unconscionability and, 173, 182–183; undue influence and, 194, 195–196

Dual performance hypothesis, 304–313, 511n74, 561n37, 561n40, 561n44

Dubin, Chief Justice Charles, 225

Dunedin, Lord, 209

Dunlop Pneumatic Tyre Co. v. New Garage and Motor Co., 205, 210

Duty to mitigate. *See* Remedies IV: mitigation

Economic theories of contract law: tenets of, 1; at odds with main doctrines and norms of contract law, 3–4; cannot provide a public basis of justification for contract law, 3–4, 9–10, 13–14, 514nn96–97; and power-conferring conception of rules, 3–4; do not answer Fuller and Perdue challenge, 9; and idea of the reasonable, 16–18; does not include idea of compensatory justice, 547n46; cannot apply directly to contract law without denaturing it, 447; development of default rule paradigm for non-express terms, 125–128; contrasted with transactional analysis of implication, 155–156, 513n94, 514nn96–97; remedies in, 270–272, 303–313, 315, 549n5, 551n23; unconscionability in, 168–171, 187; standard form contracts in, 216, 537n48; welfare in, 1, 17, 72, 170, 216, 509–510n58; and issue of congruence between contract law and market relations, 447

Eisenberg, Melvin A., 80, 491n91, 491n96, 492nn98–99, 507n34, 511n75, 514n96, 520n6, 520n13, 533n88, 535n14, 541n81, 548n53, 551n20, 555n71, 558n93

Eldon, Lord, 109

Ellinghaus, M.P., 228, 519n1 (chap. 4), 523n47, 529n50, 537n51, 538n57, 539n62

Enforcement, overview, 241–242. *See also* Expectation damages and contract theory; Remedies for breach of contract, fundamental ideas in; Remedies for breach of contract: unity and diversity

Epstein, Richard, 496n132, 496n135, 519n3 (chap. 4), 520n4, 522n34, 522n36, 523n47, 566n46

Equality in exchange. *See* Moral basis of ownership and contract; Unconscionability, the principle of

Equitable servitudes on chattels. See *De Mattos,* principle of

Essential reliance, 287–288, 290

Esso Petroleum Co. v. Harper's Garage (Stourport) Ltd., 199

Expectation damages and contract theory, 298–316; restatement of central claim concerning performance entitlement and its protection via compensatory justice, 298–299; three theories that challenge this claim, 300–315; Fuller and Perdue, 300–302, 314–315; Craswell's critique of noninstrumental theories of remedies, 303–304, 313–314; Markovits and Schwartz "dual performance" view, 304–312. *See also* Dual performance hypothesis; Economic theories of contract law; Fuller and Perdue challenge

Fairness in contractual relations: the relation between liberty and fairness in contract law a central issue in modern contract theory and practice, 2, 23. *See* Moral basis of ownership and contract; Penalty doctrine; Restraint of trade; Standard form contracts; Unconscionability, the principle of; Undue influence

Farnsworth, E. Allan, 265, 497n1, 501nn34–35, 506n22, 541n82, 549n6

Foreseeability: of consequential losses, 283–285, 290, 543n9, 543n12, 554n65; implication and, 152–153, 512nn88–89; strict liability and, 243, 246, 248–250. *See also* Conversion, tort of; Implication; Negligence, liability for; Remedies II, damages for consequential loss under *Hadley v. Baxendale*

Francis, Justice John J., 230

Fried, Charles, 42, 56–57, 58, 169–170, 401–403, 479n1 (intro.), 480n11, 481n23, 482n3, 482n4, 482n6, 482n8, 483n4, 484n16, 486n47, 490n78, 491n87, 499n17, 501n31, 502n39, 504n5, 506n24, 507n34, 519n3 (chap. 4), 538n55, 558nn93–94

Frost v. Knight, 253

Fuller, Lon L., 5–10, 25, 40, 43–47, 264–265, 287–288, 299–304, 314–316, 323, 361–362, 439, 443, 479n1 (intro.),, 486n41, 486n47, 487n52, 552n37, 557n77, 559n3, 559n6, 578n82, 578n90

Fuller and Perdue challenge, 5–12, 300–302, 314–316; raises fundamental question for modern contract theory, 5; similar challenge in the civilian tradition, 479n2; aim of Justice in Transactions to answer it, 9, 362

Fundamental rights, and contract law, 463–467

Gain-measured damages for breach of contract, 286–287, 552n36, 555n75

Gifts (executed): requirements for at common law, 58–60; role of delivery in, 59–60; contrasted with promise-for-consideration relation, 45, 58–65; transfer of ownership with, 488n56; contrasted with gratuitous promises, 62; undue influence and, 195–196

Gilbert, Jeffrey, 62

Good faith in performance, 156–164; implied covenant of, 156; trend toward recognition across common law jurisdictions, 156; what it is not, 156–157; as general norm of reasonableness in contract, 157; its more specific role, 158–164; the duty of cooperation cases, 158–159; a transactional

Good faith in performance (*continued*)
analysis of, 159–164; exercise of powers, liberties, discretion and, 159–163; judicial statements of transactional analysis, 517nn128–131, 518n147, 519n149; how mandatory, 163–164. *See also* Implication

Gordley, James, 479n2 480n12, 482n1, 486nn41–42, 486n47, 519n1 (Part B), 519n2 (chap. 4), 520nn13–15, 521n18, 521nn21–22, 522nn26–27, 522nn31–32, 523n41, 523n45

Gounot, Emmanuel, 500n18, 522n29, 524n49, 536n32

Gratuitous promises: contrast with promise-for-consideration relation fundamental to contract law, 10; as first kind of promissory relation, 37; in contrast to promise-for-consideration, 57–58, 62–63, 397–398, 411–413; in contrast to gifts, 62–63; morality of, 401–411; reliance and, 70. *See also* Consideration; Gifts (executed)

Grotius, Hugo, 10, 480n12, 482n2, 512n78, 521n18, 522n30, 523n38, 576n66

Hadley v. Baxendale, 210, 274–287, 310
Harnett v. Yielding, 267
Hegel, G. W. F., 329, 385, 414, 418, 480n12, 521n18, 521n25, 524n49, 552n35, 562n7, 563n11, 563n18, 565nn31–32, 566n47, 569n1, 570n5, 570n8, 570n12, 570n14, 571n17, 571n20, 572n26, 573n33, 575nn43–,44, 575n54, 575n56, 576n57, 576n66, 577n67, 577n69, 579n100, 581n123, 582n140

Heller, Michael, 488n57, 507n34, 576–577n66
Henningsen v. Bloomfield Motors Inc., 229–232

Hobbes, Thomas, 480n12, 487–488n54
Hoffmann, Lord, 281, 493n114, 497n144, 500n23, 501n28, 506n21, 509n56, 553n57
Hohfeld, Wesley Newcomb, 343, 347–348, 498n8, 565n35, 565–566n39, 569n64
Holmes, Justice Oliver Wendell, 485n30, 491n84, 510n65, 545n28, 560n25, 564n22, 564n25, 564n28, 567nn54–55, 571n18

Ibbetson, David J., 436, 482n1, 483n1, 484n18, 485n32, 510n63
Immediate barter and exchange, 334–335, 336–339, 565n33
Implication, 122–164; overview, 23, 122–123; distinction between primary or independent express terms and secondary or dependent terms, 123–124; puzzles at basis of, 124–125; issue of legitimacy raised by, 125; prevailing economic and promissory theories employ default rule paradigm, 125–128; presuppositions of default rule paradigm, 125–128; Richard Craswell on the necessity of default rule paradigms, 129–130; alternative transactional analysis of implication based on the reasonable in contract law and wholly anchored in the actual transaction, 129–164; transactional analysis brings out objective meaning of primary terms, ensuring their fair value without changing or improving on them, 131–133, 141–144; division of labor between the reasonable and the rational in contract law, 131–132; judicial statements of transactional view, 506n23, 509nn56–57; contracts are complete and have no gaps, 131–132; transactional analysis uses notions of presumed intent, transactional necessity and failure of consideration, 132–144; transactional approach applied to constructive conditions of exchange and implied obligations-in-fact, 132–144; impossibility and frustration, 144–155; judicial statements of impossibility analysis, 149–150; role of foreseeability in impossibility and frustration, 152–153; role of price term, 513n91; strict liability and frustration, 245; transactional analysis contrasted with economic approach, 155–156, 513n94, 514n96; economic analysis cannot be applied directly to contract law but may endorse a transactional analysis from its own economic standpoint, 514n97; implied covenant of good faith in performance, 156–164. *See also* Good faith in performance

Implied Obligations. *See* Implication
Impossibility and Frustration, 144–155. *See also* Implication
Incidental reliance, 287–288, 290
Inducement of breach of contract: tort of, 91–95, 354–355; main features of, 91–92; concerns raised by recognition of, 92, 94–95; two scenarios distinguished, 93; nature and role of malice requirement in each scenario, 93–94; defendant interferes with plaintiff's right as chose in action,

93–95; specific notice requirement, 94–95; summary statement, 95; and *in rem* dimension of contracts, 354–355. *See also* Third-party effects and contract; *In rem* rights

Injury *vs.* loss, 257–258, 286, 547n43. *See also* Breach of contract and compensatory justice

In personam rights: distinct dimension that combines with *in rem* dimension for both original and derivative acquisition, though differently, 26, 343–344; in original acquisition, 346–349; in derivative acquisition and contract, 77–80, 349–352; comparison between original and derivative acquisition with regard to, 352; compatible with contract formation being a transfer of ownership, 352–353; compatible with *in rem* dimensions operative at formation and upon delivery, 354–360, 362; summary, 360. See also *In rem* rights

In rem and *in personam* rights, distinction between: standard view of, 342–343; Hohfeld's view of, 343, 347, 565n39; Justice in Transactions does not view *in rem/in personam* distinction as ultimate but as anchored in distinctive features of the two modes of acquisition, original and derivative, 26, 344. See also *In personam* rights; *In rem* rights

In rem rights: distinct dimension that combines with *in personam* dimension for both original and derivative acquisition, though in different ways, 26, 343–344; in original acquisition, 344–346, 348–349; in derivative acquisition and contract, 83–100, 354–360; at formation and prior to performance, 353–354; role of notice in, 355; upon performance, 355–359; automatic passing of promisor's proprietary claim discussed and explained, 356–358; rejection of two transaction model, 356–358, 567n56, 568n58; contract as *iusta causa traditionis*, 358, 567n57; promisee's proprietary interest via delivery distinct from entitlement based on original acquisition, 359, 568n59; Holmes's view of "succession" compared, 567n54, 571n18; "bargain and sale" in English law contrasted with *in rem* contractual analysis, 568n62; summary, 360–361. See also *In personam* rights

Institution, contract law as: overview, 28, 395–397, 424–427; idea of institution defined, 573n31; distinction between contract as juridical relation ("the juridical conception of contract") and contract as institution is normative-conceptual, not empirical or historical, 28, 415, 425; does not derogate from, displace, or compromise but fully preserves juridical conception of contract, 28, 427; lexical priority of juridical conception and, 427; Marx's view of the juridical, 574n40; part of argument for stability vis-à-vis the market and distributive justice, 28, 395–397. *See also* Distributive justice and contract law; Market relations and contract law

Jacob & Youngs v. Kent, 137–139, 143

"Juridical conception of contract." *See* Institution, contract law as; Moral basis of ownership and contract

Juridical conception of persons, 26–27, 367–374, 472–474; fits with contract as transfer of ownership and with normative framework of liability for misfeasance, 367–368, 374; part of public justification for contract, 26–27, 369; accessible to everyday moral experience and draws on public legal culture, 26–27, 369; distinct from political conception of citizens, 26–27, 368–369, 569n3; juridical persons have two moral powers and are free and equal, 369; first moral power: capacity for sheer independence, 369–371, 570n5; second moral power expresses capacity for reasonableness: to recognize and respect the moral implications of the independence of persons, 371; juridical persons respected as self-relating ends in themselves, 371; juridical persons as free and equal, 371–373; in what sense free, 371–372; in what sense equal, 372–373; the role of contingencies, 474; relation between juridical conception of persons and ownership norms, 373–389 (*see also* Moral basis of ownership and contract); contrasts with the political conception of the person in political liberalism, 472–474

Justice in Transactions, a theory of contract law: main aims of ix–xii, 3; first task of, 1–3; relation to modern contract law, 3–4; central goal to develop a public justification for contract law, 3; seeks to answer Fuller and Perdue challenge, 9, 362; overview of the argument as a whole, 19–29; outline of chapters, 22–29; scope of theory, 29–31; and Aristotle, 30–31; public justification developed in two main parts, 20–21; first part, "Principles," (chapters 1–9) not to provide treatise on the law but to draw out unifying conception of contractual relation implicit in main contract doctrines: this is contract formation as transactional acquisition, 2, 11, 20–21, 25, 315–316 (*see also* Principles, of contract law); second part, "Theory," (chapters 10–12) takes conception of contract as transactional acquisition to higher level of abstraction, theorizing it in two steps: (a) as morally defensible and reasonable in its own framework (chapters 10 and 11) and (b) as stable with respect to other domains of a liberal democratic society (chapter 12), 21, 25–29, 393–397, 319–476; political liberalism and, 468–476; as liberalism of freedom, 476. *See also* Contract as a transfer of ownership; Moral basis of ownership and contract; Stability of contract as transfer

Kant, Immanuel / Kantian view, 360, 403–408, 480n12, 498n11, 562n3, 562n6, 564nn26–27, 566n43, 566n47, 567n49, 567n51, 567n56, 568n59, 569n63, 570n14, 571n20, 572n26, 572n3, 573–574n33, 576n66, 577n67, 577n78, 578n89
Kaplow, Louis, 481n19, 481n20, 504n6
Kessler, Friedrich, 230
Kingston v. Preston, 134–136
Klass, Gregory, 488n57, 502n41, 548n55
"Knebelung" ("Shackling"), 197, 202
Knight Bruce, Lord Justice, 96–97
Kojève, Alexandre, 570n10, 576n60
Kokourek, Albert, 566n40
Korobkin, Russell, 218, 534n9, 541n86
Kramer, Adam, 278, 500n23, 504n2, 553n44
Krell v. Henry, 146, 150–152, 513n91
Kronman, Anthony T., 549n8, 582n134

Laissez-faire, doctrine of, 460
Leff, Arthur Allen, 167, 169, 233, 520n12, 537n42
L'Estrange v. F. Graucob Ltd., 225
Libertarian theory, 29, 392, 448, 450, 451, 519n3 (chap. 4), 585n175
Liquidated damages. *See* Penalty Clauses
Llewellyn, Karl N., 213, 215, 217, 218, 221, 223, 227–228, 234–235, 237, 240, 420, 432, 533n1, 535nn12–13, 535nn17–18, 535n20, 537nn46–47, 537n52, 540nn70–71, 542n95, 559n5, 574n35, 575n45, 577n69, 577n75, 577n77
Lloyds Bank v. Bundy, 173–174, 194
Loan, contracts of, 235–236
Look-forward rule, 530n65
Lost performance value damages: meaning and role of "lost performance value" damages *vs.* "enforced performance" remedies, 273–274; examples of lost performance value damages: damages for consequential loss, 274–286; gain-measured damages, 286–287, 555n75; and reliance damages, 287–291
Lumley v. Gye, 91, 93
Lumley v. Wagner, 497n143

Mackay v. Dick, 158
Macmillan, Lord, 145
Mansfield, Lord, 134, 137, 139, 141, 157, 248, 442–444
Market relations, the nature of, 415–425; market as price-regulated economic system of purely voluntary interactions, 415, 421–422; presupposes noneconomic juridical premises embodying coercible reasonable norms referred to as the "juridical conception of contract", 415–417; juridical presuppositions established by operation of contract law within its own framework, 417; the idea of a "system of needs" as distinctive normative conception characteristic of market relations, 418–421; main features of system of needs, 418–420; contrast between system of needs and juridical conception of contract, 420–421; main features of market as self-maintaining actual system of social cooperation, its conception of social action and the needs of market participants, 421–425; Max Weber's account of impersonal, rational

INDEX   603

and nondistributive nature of market relations, 421–425; market action is socially determined and always other-related, both in formal and in substantive terms, 422–425; idea of formal interests identically shared by individuals qua market transactors, 424–425; identical formal interest in knowing and securing the reasonable in transactions determined in accordance with the objective test, 426–429; formal interest with respect to bilateral and systemic aspects of market relations, 426–429; institutional role of contract law meets these formal interests, thereby showing the stability of contract with respect to market relations, 425–445 (*see also* Institution, contract law as; Market relations and contract law); summary of argument, 445–447

Market relations and contract law, 413–447; overview of stability with respect to, 395–397, 413–415; contract law as institution fully consistent with juridical conception of contract, 28, 427 (*see also* Institution, contract law as); correspondence between other-related orientation of contract law and that of market transactors' formal interests, 426–427; both contract law and market transactors endorse the objective test, 427–428; transactors need knowable and authoritative determinations of transactionally reasonable terms of exchange covering both bilateral and systemic aspects of market relations, 427–429; contract law as institution, via court, establishes this, 428–429, 576n60; division of labor between court and market, 427, 434–435, 445–447; contract law and bilateral aspects of market relations, 429–435; includes situation sense applied to transaction-types, 431–435; contract law and systemic aspects of market relation, 435–446; three illustrations: contracts under seal, 436–439 (*see also* Contracts under seal); market overt, 439–442; negotiable instruments, 442–445; contract as institution providing power-conferring rules, 438, 578n88; combines the reasonable and the rational in contract law, 412–413, 433–435,

437–439, 445–447; summary comments about congruence between contract law and market relations, 445–447; contrast with economic theories on relation between contract law and market, 447. *See also* Market relations, the nature of; Moral basis of ownership and contract

Markovits, Daniel, 304–313, 515n103, 516n112

Marx, Karl, 521nn23–24, 571n16, 573n32, 574n40

McClelland v. Climax Hosiery Mills, 291

Melamed, A. Douglas, 261

Melden, A.I., 561n40, 572n17, 573nn23–29, 578n88

Millar v. Race, 443

Misfeasance: defined, 7; nonfeasance *vs.*, 7; judicial statements of, 480n8; fundamental framework of responsibility and liability in private law, 255; breach of contract as, 7, 24, 241, 257, 562n8; compensation and, 255, 257; nondelivery as, 66; ownership and liability for, 325, 329, 331, 351, 354, 363, 364, 367–369, 373, 377, 383–384, 387, 451, 562n8; personhood conception and, 373, 377, 383–384, 387, 391; reliance-based liability claim and, 74; stability of contract as transfer in framework of, 398, 426, 451

Mistake in fundamental assumptions, 149, 245, 510n61; unconscionability and, 168, 171, 172

Mitchel v. Reynolds, 200

Mitigation, doctrine of. *See* Remedies IV: mitigation

Moorcock, The, 140–141, 509n55

Moral basis of ownership and contract, 21, 26–27, 366–394; expresses respect for free and equal juridical persons in medium of action, 373–374 (*see also* Juridical conception of persons); involves negative and other-directed duty not to injure the external embodiment of another's capacity for independence, 374–375, 379; based on categorical distinction between nonusable persons and usable things, 376–377, 570n10; main features of private ownership reflect person/thing distinction and what it implies, 377–378; detailed elucidation of right of bodily integrity and of ownership entitlements on this basis, 380–389; bodily integrity respects the external *existence* of

Moral basis of ownership and contrac (*continued*)
juridical persons, 380–381; ownership entitlement in original acquisition respects external *actions* of free and equal juridical persons, without reference to their particularities, 381–384, 391; in original acquisition respect not yet mutual because requisite act unilateral and nonreciprocal, 383–384; transition to contract where acts are fully reciprocal and mutual within misfeasance framework, 384; contract fulfills equality and freedom of persons within this framework, 384–385; contract express fully normative meaning and basis of private law ownership, 385–386; role and normative significance of equivalence in exchange, 386–389; basis for imputing presumed intent to receive equal value, 387–388; normative analysis continues at remedial stage as compensatory justice, 388–389; nondistributive character of equivalence requirement as paradigm of commutative justice, 388–389, 392–393; summary of view, 389–394; comparison with distributive justice, 450–456, 470–472

Negligence, liability for: pure economic loss and, 480n9; contrasted with contract liability, 247–250, 284–285, 566n48; contrasted with intentional tort liability, 247–250, 544n21; objective test for, 567n48; reliance-based liability and, 73–74, 489n66; injury to use or value and, 544n21

Nemo dat rule: assignment subject to, 86, 88, 89 (*see also* Assignment of contractual rights); market exchanges under, 439–440, 443; ownership under, 335

Nominal consideration, 55

Nominal damages, 26, 55, 248, 249–250, 258

Objective test for contract formation and interpretation, 4, 22–23, 110–117; difference between subjective and objective tests, 110–111; the impossibility of a subjective test, 111; not a detached observer or external standard test but transactional, 112, 500n20, 501n31; reasonably apparent manifestations of assent as ultimate elements of contractual analysis, 102, 110, 117; applications and flexibility of the objective test geared to particular transactions, 111–116, 501nn34–36; embodies the reasonable as between particular parties, 120–121; provides unified standpoint for transactional analysis of all questions of rights and duties arising in contractual framework, 23; suited for contractual promises but not for gratuitous promises, 117; objective test and original acquisition, 340; objective test and derivative acquisition (contract), 341–342; market transactors have formal interest in, 426–428; objective test and standpoint of court, 429, 576n61; central role of contract law in performing institutional function, 427–428. *See also* Contractual intent; Contractual obligation; Institution, contract law as; Market relations and contract law

Occupancy, and ownership, 329–330, 336, 349

Offer and acceptance: doctrine of, 101–121; overview, 22–23, 39, 101–102; main features of, 102–103; in tandem with consideration, 36–39, 50, 101–105, 109–110, 177, 482nn6–8, 498n10, 499n15, 499n17, 569n63; ambiguities of, if specified prior to consideration, 36–38; specifies dynamic process of interaction necessary for promise-for-consideration relation, 22, 104; gratuitous promises *vs*., 102, 116–117; bilateral and transactional nature of, 102, 103–105, 106–107, 109–110, 113–114, 116, 177, 499–500n17, 569n63; offer must always state a promise, 105–106; each side must state whole reciprocal and bilateral interaction, 106–107; offer must precede acceptance in time, 107–109; must be "at one instant" at formation, 109–110; withdrawal of offer, 103, 105, 106; meaning of *consensus ad idem*, 103, 109, 111, 114, 177, 500n23; judicial statement of view of, 500n23; objective test applies to all elements, 110–117; contractual intent and voluntariness, 102, 107, 117–121, 502n45, 503n57; third-party and, 79, 82, 108, 491n87; in standard form contracts, 215, 220–222; indirect horizontal effect of distributive justice and, 466–467. *See also* Contractual intent; Objective test for contract formation and interpretation

"On Contracts" (Gilbert), 62

INDEX

Original Acquisition: defined, 326–328; discussed, 327–334, 336–338, 340–342, 344–349, 359–360, 361–362, 381–383, 385, 387, 390, 393, 420–421; *in rem/in personam* dimensions in, 344–349. *See also* Contract as a transfer of ownership; *In personam* rights; *In rem* rights; Moral basis of ownership and contract

Ownership, in private law, 325–328. *See also* Contract as a transfer of ownership; Derivative (transactional) acquisition; Moral basis of ownership and contract; Original Acquisition

Pacta sunt servanda, 66, 157, 245, 368
Palmer, George E., 506n20, 511n72
Palmer, Vernon V., 490n79, 491n94, 492n102
Paradine v. Jane, 126, 144–145
Parker v. South Eastern Railway Co., 222–223
ParkingEye Ltd. v. Beavis, 206
Patterson v. Meyerhofer, 158
Penalty doctrine, 205–214; brief statement of, 205; apparent tensions with freedom of contract and legal determination of remedies for breach, 205–206; meaning and role of intention in, 206–208; nature of the requisite presumed intent, 207–208; not a direct determination of damages, 207–208; application of proposed analysis to main scenarios, 208–211; compared with unconscionability, 211–212; how a policy of the common law, 205, 213; embodies the reasonable not in tension with freedom of contract or the legal determination of remedies, 212–214

Perdue, William F., Jr., 5–10, 25, 264–265, 287–288, 299–304, 314–316, 361–362, 479n2

Performance, right to: explained, 65–66; not object transferred but requirement of respect arising from transfer, 66. *See also* Contract as a transfer of ownership; *In personam* rights; Third-party effects and contract

Performance interest: "in possession", 267–269 (*see also* Remedies I: expectation (or performance) damages *vs.* specific performance); "in use", 275–277 (*see also* Remedies II: damages for consequential loss)

Pierson v. Post, 328, 391
Pitney, Justice Mahlon R., 495n130
Posner, Richard A., 481n16, 484n16, 504n9, 513n94, 514nn96–97
Pothier, Robert, 277–278
Power-conferring conception of contract law: defined, 3–4; incompatible with promise-for-consideration, 66–67; contract as transfer of ownership alternative to, 363–364; incompatible with juridical conception of the person, 392–393; and contract law's institutional role, 438, 578n88

Principles, of contract law, Part One, 35–316. *See also* Contract formation; Enforcement; Fairness in contractual relations

Privity of contract. *See* Third-party effects and contract

Promise-for-consideration relation: the basic contractual relation, 22; as second kind of promissory relation, 38–39; compared with perfect promises of civilian theorists, 68; reciprocal nature of, 51–52; as a kind of transactional acquisition, 60–68, 320–325; as a transfer of ownership, 337–342; compared with gift (*see* Gifts); compared with gratuitous promises (*see* Gratuitous promises). *See also* Consideration; Contract as a transfer of ownership; Contract as transactional acquisition; Moral basis of ownership and contract; Offer and acceptance

Promises, imperfect and perfect (in natural law theory), defined, 10, 482n2

Promissory morality: consideration and, 324; constancy capacity and, 406–407; as noncoercible duty of virtue, 403–411; future oriented character of, 406–407; gratuitous promises and, 397, 400–401, 403, 411; intent and, 398, 401; doctrine of mitigation not part of, 295; contractual obligation *vs.*, 397–413; the reasonable governing, 18–19, 398, 406; respect and trust in, 18–19, 398–399, 401–403, 404, 407–413. *See also* Promissory morality and contract

Promissory morality and contract: as issue of stability, 397–413; overview, 395–397; distinguishing normative features and incidents of contractual *vs.* noncontractual promissory relations, 397–398; general

Promissory morality and contract (*continued*)
ethical (nonjuridical) duty to respect contractual rights and to perform contractual duties even apart from threat of sanction, 398–400; compatibility of contract with promissory morality must also include noncontractual purely gratuitous promises, 400; an account of moral duty to keep (gratuitous) promises, 401–411; compatibility between contract as a transfer of ownership and promissory morality so understood, 411–413

Promissory relations, two kinds of: "promises to another" *vs.* "promises to and with another", 35–36; distinction pivotal to understanding contract law, 36, 397–398, 411–413; natural law distinction between imperfect and perfect promises compared with, 482n2. *See also* Gratuitous promises; Promise-for-consideration relation; Promises, imperfect and perfect (in natural law theory)

Promissory theories of contract law: defined, 1; *Contract as Promise* (Fried) most important example of, 479n1 (intro.); at odds with main doctrines and norms of contract law, 3; and power-conferring conception of rules, 3–4; cannot answer Fuller and Perdue challenge, 9; assume single conception of promissory relation, 9–10; contract as transfer distinguished from, 9–10, 12, 19; critique of consideration in, 56–58; default rule paradigm and implication in, 125–128; Richard Craswell, on the necessary incompleteness of promissory theories, 129; remedies in, 303–304, 313–314, 480n11

Public basis of justification, idea of: in general, 12–15; Rawls on, 3, 11, 12–13, 367, 394, 448, 475–476; distinct from interpretative and normative theories, 12; need for and main features of, 12–15; draws on normative ideas latent in public legal and political culture without relying on philosophical doctrines, 13–14; for contract law: the aim of Justice in Transactions, 3; specifically worked out for distinctive nature of contractual relations, 13; Justice in Transactions and, 11, 15, 26–27, 30, 475–476; scope of application of, in Justice as Transactions, 29–30; economic analysis unsuited for, 514nn96–97; principles of contract law and, 20; for implication, 132, 133; for fairness, 170, 179; for enforcement and remedies, 12–15, 264, 312, 316; moral basis for contract as transfer and, 11–15, 19–20, 25, 26–27, 29–30, 366–367, 369, 390, 394, 570n9; free and equal parties and, 12–14, 26, 316, 366–367, 369, 390, 394; ownership and, 316, 319–320, 390, 394; stability of contract as transfer and, 395, 447, 448–449, 468, 470, 475–476, 574n37; contract law as a liberalism of freedom and, 468–476

Pufendorf, Samuel, 10, 521n18

Punitive damages for breach of contract, 555n76

Quasi-property interests, 94, 387, 495n129, 497n143, 567n53

Rakoff, Todd, 72–73, 76, 508n40, 535n11, 535n21, 577nn68–69

Rawls, John: on public basis of justification, 3, 11, 12–13, 367, 394, 448, 475–476; the reasonable and the rational and other features of political liberalism in, 15–16, 471–476, 569n3; on the division of labor between principles for transactions and principles for background political justice, 27, 29, 448–449, 454–455, 456, 467, 580n113; on stability, 395; the basic structure of society and of background justice in, 580n113; pure procedural background justice in, 581n131; the political conception of citizens as free and equal and of social primary goods in, 472, 583n157, 584n170; idea of the original position in, 585n177; the first principle of justice stated, 582n136; the second principle of justice stated, 580n111; the role of the basic liberties including the right to hold personal property, 458; the difference principle, 448, 463, 585n176; the principle of fair equality of opportunity, 581n126; the duty to perform promises in, 481n22; *See also* Distributive justice and contract law

Reasonable, the idea of: a moral idea *vs.* the rational, 15–17, 142–143, 473, 505n19; in Rawls's work, 15–17, 481n18; specified

INDEX   607

according to nature of particular relation and different for contractual, moral and political relations, 15–16; contract theories without the reasonable, 16–18; contract theories with a conception of the reasonable not suited to distinct nature of contractual relations, 18–19; promissory morality governed by distinctive conception of, 18–19, 398, 406; promise-for-consideration relation and, 51–52, 60–62, 67–68, 75, 178; expressed in contract as transfer, 11, 15–19, 25, 371, 374, 389–390, 398, 406, 416, 418–420, 425, 427, 433–434, 469–470, 473; enforcement and remedies based on, 15–19, 271, 281, 284–286, 294, 297, 313; fairness representing, 15–16, 67–68, 166, 171–172, 178, 200–204, 207–213, 216, 222–223, 226–228, 233–234, 527n36, 532n74, 537n44; free and equal parties' capacity for, 371, 374, 469–470, 473; good faith enshrining, 156–164; implication expressing, 131–139, 141–144, 151–164, 507n34, 510n60; presumed intent reflecting, 18–19, 117–118, 133–139, 141–143; justified reliance as matter of, 72, 75; market exchanges presuppose, 416, 418–420, 425, 427, 433–434, 576n59; mitigation and, 294, 297; moral basis for contract as transfer and, 11, 15–19, 25, 371, 374, 389–390; objective test and, 112–116, 244; contractual obligation based on, 67–68, 120–121, 363–364, 392–394, 397–398; offer and acceptance based on, 107–110, 112–116, 501nn35–36; penalty doctrine and, 207–213, 532n74; restraint of trade and, 200–204, 527n36; standard form contracts expressing, 216, 222–223, 226–228, 233–234, 537n44; stability of contract as transfer in relation to, 398, 406, 416, 418–420, 425, 427, 433–434, 469–470, 473; division of labor between rational and reasonable in contract law, 313, 412–413, 433–435, 437–439, 445–447

Reciprocity: consideration and, 47–48, 53, 57, 60–64, 102, 139, 175, 177, 315–316, 321–322, 324–325; Rawls's difference principle and, 585n176; of market exchanges, 419, 422, 423–424; in offer and acceptance, 106; in ownership transfer, 335–337, 341, 350–353, 356, 383–384, 474–475; presumed intent and, 134; the reasonable embodying, 15

Reliance as substantive basis of liability, 69–75; distinguished from reliance as measure of contract damages, 287; main features of, 70–73; judicial statements of, 488n62, 489n67; does not challenge necessity of consideration for contractual obligation, 73; a kind of tort liability, 73–74, 489n66; does not imply underlying unitary conception of promissory liability, 74–75. *See also* Consideration; Remedies III: reliance damages

"The Reliance Interest in Contract Damages" (Fuller & Perdue), 5–10, 287–288, 479n2

Remedies for breach of contract: unity and diversity, 263–297; overview of basis of unity and diversity, 263–265; proposed transactional approach departs from Fuller and Perdue analysis of contract remedies and protected interests, 264–265. *See also* damages for consequential loss under *Hadley v. Baxendale*; Gain-measured damages for breach of contract; Lost performance value damages; Mitigation; Nominal damages; Punitive damages for breach of contract; Remedies III, reliance damages; Remedies I, expectation (or performance) damages *vs.* specific performance

Remedies for breach of contract, fundamental ideas in: contractual liability as strict liability, its meaning and implications, 243–250; the nature of breach, including anticipatory repudiation, 250–255; compensatory justice, 255–262. *See also* Breach of contract and compensatory justice; Breach of contract as strict liability; Breach of contract, nature of; Expectation damages and contract theory; Remedies II, damages for consequential loss under *Hadley v.* Baxendale

Remedies I, expectation (or performance) damages *vs.* specific performance, 265–274; specific performance defined, 549n7; the relation between specific performance and damages, 266–272; judicial statement of relation, 267; the meaning and role of

Remedies I (*continued*)
adequacy of damages, 266; specific performance and expectation damages (where adequate) share single aim of compensating for injury to plaintiff's performance interest in possessing what has been promised: the "enforced performance" of contract terms, 266–269; contrasted with "lost performance value" damages, 273–274; anything not part of this performance interest irrelevant to transactional remedial analysis, 270; comparison with efficient breach and efficient performance theories, 270; neither specific performance nor expectation damages default or exceptional remedy, 270–271; unreasonable to privilege specific performance over (adequate) expectation damages, 271–272; hardship as reason for declining specific performance, 272–273; no balancing costs and benefits of performance, 272–274. *See also* Lost performance value damages

Remedies II, damages for consequential loss under *Hadley v. Baxendale*, 274–286; standard view of *Hadley* as limit on full compensation, 274–275; *Hadley* as principle of inclusion fully consistent with compensatory justice protecting plaintiff's performance interest in use, 275–277; protected interest in use transactionally determined at contract formation within framework of particular contract, objectively interpreted, 275–277; judicial statements of this view, 553nn56–57; liability anchored in voluntary basis of contract via normative ideas of assumption of responsibility and presumed intent, 278–286; nature of assumption of responsibility, 278–279; the unstated normative premise underlying analysis in *Hadley*, 279–281, 553n54; as applied in different paradigmatic scenarios, 281–283; the role of foreseeability in this transactional analysis, 283–285, 554n67; *Hadley* expresses the transactionally reasonable and is complete and self-sufficient as such, 285–286; *Hadley* as general principle for contractually recoverable loss, 286, 555n72; gain-measured damages for breach of contract, 286–287, 555n75

Remedies III, reliance damages, 287–291; contrast with reliance as noncontractual substantive basis of liability, 287; "essential" and "incidental" reliance, 287–288; as measure of lost performance value damages via wasted expenditures, 288–291; given to protect performance interest and cannot oust claim to expectation damages when proved and adequate, 290; judicial statements of this view, 557nn82–84; substantive reliance not essential to recovery of reliance damages, 290–291

Remedies IV: mitigation, 291–297; defined, 291-2; judicial statement of, 291; reflects requirements of the reasonable at remedial stage, 292–293; and three stages of (1) pre-contractual mutual independence, (2) contractual mutual dependence, and (3) post-performance mutual independence, 292–295; provides basis for distinguishing reasonably unavoidable from avoidable loss, 293–295; implements the reasonable consistent with compensatory justice, 296–297; not applicable to breach of noncoercible moral promissory duties, 295. *See also* Gratuitous promises

Restraint of trade: doctrine of, 199–204; *Campbell Soup Co. v. Wentz* and, 197–199, 204; "shackling" contracts and, 197, 202; kind of contracts coming within scope of, 200–201; how a policy of the common law, 201; requirements of reasonableness for, 201–202; nature of unfairness in, 202–203; compared with unconscionability, 203–204; indirect horizontal effect of fundamental rights and, 464–465

Scalia, Justice Antonin, 519n149
Schwartz, Alan, 304–313, 505n11, 505n14, 534n5, 548n55
Scott, Robert E., 505n11, 505n14, 510n60, 532n78, 545n30
Scotus, John Duns, 30, 521n18
Shavell, Steven, 481n19, 481n20, 504n6
Shiffrin, Seana Valentine, 529n54, 558n92, 561n39, 572n2, 572nn4–5
Sidgwick, Henry, 570n5, 575n54
Situation-sense, 432–434, 577n76. *See also* Transaction-types

Smith, Stephen A., 483n3, 526n26, 526n28, 527nn36–37, 528–529nn46–48, 542n3, 547n45, 550n14, 561n42, 562n5
Specific Performance. *See* Enforcement; Remedies I: expectation (or performance) damages vs. specific performance
Stability of contract as transfer: overview and questions of, 21, 27–29, 395–397; in Rawls, 395; as last step in public justification for contract law, 395; with respect to promissory morality, the market, and principles of distributive justice, 319–476. *See also* Distributive justice and contract law; Institution, contract law as; Market relations and contract law; Promissory morality and contract
Standard form contracts: fairness and assent in, 215–240; overview, 215–217; proposed transactional analysis draws on Llewellyn's work, 217, 223, 226–229, 234–236, 240; limits of present discussion, 216; distinctive features of standard form contracts, 217–220; rational functions of standard form contracts, 219–220; mass consumer contracts as central case, 220; assent to standard form contracts, 220–221; salience of terms defined, 218; role of confidence and trust in relation to nonsalient standardized terms, 222–223; how standard form contracts may be transactionally unreasonable, 223, 226–229, 232–233; contrast with prevailing theoretical approaches, 227–228; the idea of *"intra-transactional"* conflict between nonsalient standardized term *vs.* salient express terms, implied terms or transaction-types, 227–229; conflict between standardized terms and express primary terms, 224–227; conflict with implied terms, 229–234; role of procedural factors, assumption of risk and market features in transactional approach, 231–234; idea of embedding of reasonable terms, 233–234; conflict between standardized terms and transaction-types, 234–239; transaction-types and relation to consideration, 22, 55–56, 235–236, 339, 431–435; conflict between standardized terms and legally available remedies, 539n64; distinctive nature of the disproportion in unfair standardized terms

compared with that in unconscionability, 232–233, 239–240; transactional analysis applied to standard form contracts between businesses, 231, 541n91. *See also* Offer and acceptance; Transaction-types; Unconscionability, the principle of
Stevens, Robert, 492n101, 484n19, 504n5
System of needs. *See* Distributive justice and contract; Market relations and contract; Market relations, the nature of

Taylor v. Caldwell, 146–148, 151
Third-party effects and contract: contractual privity and doctrine of consideration, 76–83; rational core meaning of privity, 79–80; breach not an injustice to third party, 80–82; third-party beneficiary does not have *in personam* contractual right, 80–82; third-party beneficiary has power to sue in limited circumstances, 80–82; contrasted with reliance-based claims, 82–83; third party "proprietary" effects prior to performance, 83–100; why proprietary, 98–100; comparison with *International News Service v. Associated Press,* 495n130; role of notice, 99–100; "proprietary" effects resulting from performance, 355–360. *See also* Assignment, of contractual rights; *De Mattos,* principle of; Inducement of breach of contract; *In personam* rights; *In rem* rights
Tilden Rent-A-Car Co. v. Clendenning, 224–226, 231–232
Tolhurst, Greg, 86, 492n102, 492n104, 492n106, 493nn111–114,116, 494nn118–119
Tourtoulon, Pierre de, 6, 7
Transaction-types, 22, 55–56, 235–236, 339, 431–435; situation-sense and, 432–434, 576n66, 577n69, 577n73, 577n76
Transfer of ownership: by gift, 58–60; by immediate executed exchange, 334–338; by contract formation, 337–341; by contractual delivery or performance, 355–360, 571n18; by "bargain and sale", 568n62. *See also* Contract as a transfer of ownership; Derivative (transactional) acquisition; *In rem* rights; Moral basis of ownership and contract
Trebilcock, Michael J., 481n21, 485n38, 513n94, 520n10

Treitel, Guenter. H., 269, 278, 485n36, 496n136, 529n52, 543nn5–6, 549n7, 553n43, 558n90
Triantis, George, 504n8, 510n66
Trust: promissory morality and, 18, 401–403, 409–412; the reasonable in relation to, 18; relation of influence based on, 194, 196; in relation to standard form contract terms, 222–223
Tweddle v. Atkinson, 79

Unconscionability, the principle of: paradigm of contractual fairness, 166, 190; in contract theories, 23, 165, 168–171; the prevailing theoretical model: the procedural and substantive unconscionability dichotomy, 168–173; alternative transactional analysis of unconscionability proposed, 171–175; judicial statement of, 173–174; unconscionability distinct from traditional defences of duress, fraud, misrepresentation, 171; libertarian objection to, 186; to be unconscionable, terms must involve striking value disproportion not explicable via assumption of risk or donative intent, 172–173; donative intent defined, 173; role of impaired bargaining power in the analysis of, 172; the relation between doctrine of consideration and, 175–184; consideration's indifference to comparative value does not preclude distinct principle of fairness, 175–177; ideas of use value and exchange value defined and contrasted, 177–178; exchange value and the reasonable, 178; presumed intent to transact for equal exchange value is juridical, 181; equality and purchasing power, 181–182, 423; confirms exchange and gift as the two ultimate categories of promise-for-consideration relation, 183; a division of labor between consideration and, 183–184; role and significance of market price in, 184–185; flexibility of the standard of equivalence in, 185–186; why the disproportion between values must be large and striking, 187–188; legal fault or wrongdoing not essential to, 188–189; not a principle of redress and completely nondistributive in character, 189–190; unconscionability as paradigm of transactional or commutative justice, 190–191. *See also* Contract as a transfer of ownership; Contract as transactional acquisition; Moral basis of ownership and contract
Undue influence: doctrine of, 192–197; overview, 192–193; requirements and main features of "presumed undue influence", 193–195; transactional analysis of unfair terms in exchanges and gifts, 194–196; compared with unconscionability, 195–197
Unfair surprise: implication and, 140, 144; market exchanges should be free from, 434; in standard form contracts, 223, 228, 233–234, 239; unconscionability doctrine preventing, 197, 239, 521n19, 523n47
Uniform Commercial Code, 197, 226, 239, 514n96, 523n47, 537n42

Vaughan Williams, Lord Justice, 151
Victoria Laundry (Windsor) Ltd. v. Newman Industries Ltd., 283
Voluntariness: of market exchanges, 415, 460; of offer and acceptance, 102, 107, 120–121, 502n45, 503n57; remedies reflecting, 284–286; strict liability and, 244, 248

Waddams, Stephen M., 488n55, 494nn121–122, 495n126, 497n143, 506n25, 507n28, 507n30, 519n2 (chap. 4), 520n4, 521n20, 521n22, 523n43, 530n56, 540nn74–75
Warranties: express, 230–232, 234, 539n64; implied, 124, 140, 142, 147, 219–221, 227, 229–232, 282, 538nn59–60, 539n64
Weber, Max, 421–423, 428, 430–431, 574n34, 575n48, 575nn53–54, 576nn57–59
Weinrib, Ernest J., 546n33, 547nn42–43, 548n52, 570n11, 577n78
Williams v. Walker-Thomas Furniture Co., 236–239
Williston, Samuel, x, 117, 136–137, 206, 279, 484n27, 498n11, 501n25, 502n44, 503n56, 503n58, 506n25, 507n34, 508n44, 512n78, 512n86, 545n31
Wright, J. Skelly, 237

Young v. Timmins, 199, 201

Zimmermann, Reinhard, 490n80, 492n106, 516n109, 546n33, 549n7, 552n35, 567nn56–57, 568n62